U.S.A. 20/21

STUDIES IN RECENT AMERICAN HISTORY

NUMBER ONE

RESHAPING AMERICA

RESHAPING AMERICA

Society and Institutions
1945–1960

WITHDRAWN

Edited by Robert H. Bremner
and Gary W. Reichard

OHIO STATE UNIVERSITY PRESS : COLUMBUS

Library of Congress Cataloging in Publication Data
Main entry under title:

Reshaping America.

(Studies in recent American history; no. 1)
Includes index.
1. United States—Social conditions—1945–1960.
I. Bremner, Robert Hamlett, 1917–   . II. Reichard, Gary W.,
1943–   . III. Series.
HN58.R44   306'.0973   82-3409
ISBN 0-8142-0308-6   AACR2

Contents

Introduction

Between the end of World War II and the beginning of the sixties, a great many changes occurred in the ways Americans lived. Statistical measures revealed dramatic growth and important shifts in the population as well as in social, political, and economic matters. New developments in almost every aspect of American life strained and tested institutional arrangements and relationships.

Demographic changes were perhaps the most important developments in the decade and a half after the war. The population grew rapidly, rising from an estimated 139.9 million in 1945 to 180.6 million in 1960—an increase of almost 30 percent. These figures reflected the baby boom of the postwar years; in 1945 there were an estimated 33.5 million children aged 14 or younger (24 percent of the population), whereas in 1960 there were 56 million in that age group (31 percent of the total). Accordingly, issues such as the family, child-rearing, juvenile delinquency, education, and community services gave increasing concern to American society, and a highly visible "youth culture" dominated the latter part of the period. The nonwhite population grew even more quickly than the total, rising from 14.6 million in 1945 to 20.6 million fifteen years later, a 41 percent increase. This growth, plus the migration of hundreds of thousands of blacks from the rural South to cities of the Northeast, Midwest, and Far West, combined to nationalize the problems of racial discrimination, which had long been treated as a "southern problem." Another demographic shift brought additional challenges: the number of Americans aged 65 and over increased by more than 50 percent in the period 1945–60 (going from 10.4 million to 16.6 million). Ways had to be found, in a society wherein the concept of extended family was not well developed, to provide for these elder citizens. The floor of security provided by the New Deal, as well as the public commitment to providing that security, were put to severe test by these developments.

Much of the expansion in numbers was taking place in urban settings, particularly in the newly labeled Standard Metropolitan Statistical Areas, 168 of which were identified for the first time in the 1950 census. By 1960 the census listed 212 such areas, with a total population of more than 112 million—or over 60 percent of all Americans. This metropolitan population included the burgeoning suburbs in addition to central cities. Racial polarization was a notable feature of the postwar growth pattern, which saw whites flee to the new suburban neighborhoods, leaving blacks and other minority groups behind in the inner cities. Again, broad social forces raised grave political challenges. The other half of this story was the continuing decline of rural America, more precipitous than ever after the close of World War II. The nation's rural population, estimated at 24.4 million (17.5 percent of the population) in 1945, declined to 15.6 million (8.7 percent) by 1960. Despite this shrinkage and a corresponding decrease of 30 percent in the number of farms in the United States, the amount of land in cultivation and value of farm property increased during the period—a clear reflection of the trend toward large-scale business operations in postwar American agriculture.

The economy as a whole underwent sweeping transformations. Overall, the postwar era was very prosperous, with output per worker increasing almost 50 percent and average annual earnings for all workers more than doubling. Moreover, inflation—except for the months immediately after World War II—was not a serious problem, perhaps because of the steadily increasing output of the economy. In such circumstances workers could and did compete successfully for a larger share of the economic pie, even while corporations piled up high profits; corporate receipts, which stood at $255 billion in 1945, rose to $849 billion by 1960. Encouraged by such trends, more and more Americans went into business: the number of American business enterprises nearly doubled in the fifteen-year period. Much of this business expansion occurred at great long-range cost (though it was unremarked at the time); natural resources were gobbled up at a fearsome rate, and American dependence on imported energy sources—particularly petroleum—increased significantly. Crude petroleum imports, which stood at 74.3 million barrels in 1945, totaled 371.5 million barrels fifteen years later—even while domestic crude oil production increased by nearly half. By 1960 Americans were not yet ready to confront the problems this misuse of resources would bring on, though the day of reckoning was bound to come.

The same was true in other areas of American life. Despite the generally upbeat spirit in the country and an image of an ever-widening, comfortable middle class, certain inequalities deepened. While the percentage of families earning under $3,000 per year declined from 49.4 percent after the war (1947) to only 21.7 percent in 1960, the figures for non-whites were starkly worse: 81.1 percent and 46.5 percent, respectively. Women, entering and remaining in the work force in greater numbers, continued to experience job frustrations and extensive discrimination by employers. Yet civil rights activism and feminist agitation remained relatively undeveloped, and much of the American public seemed oblivious to the impending problems.

The decade and a half after World War II was important not only for what happened but for what did not. Demographic changes such as the baby boom, increased longevity for Americans, higher levels of education and literacy, increasing wealth, greater women's employment, widespread migration of blacks, and the "metropolitanization" of the population received a great deal of attention. But there was also much continuity in American life. Some potential explosions did not occur, and a number of needed changes did not come about—particularly in the shape and scope of American institutions. The years 1945 to 1960, after all, were dominated by the cold war, a state of perpetual nervousness about war with the Soviet Union. That war, of course, did not break out in the period. Nor did American politics change much in these years. In general, political developments failed to keep pace with social change; social reform measures spawned by the New Deal in the 1930s were generally maintained and a few were even slightly strengthened (Social Security, for instance), but no new programs were developed to meet emerging new realities. Certainly it can be said that political and institutional changes in the period were greatly overshadowed by demographic changes.

The essays in this volume are intended to illuminate both the changes and the continuities marking American life in this important decade and a half. Together they expand upon four basic themes of the postwar period: the pervasiveness of the cold war, the accelerating struggle of minorities to achieve equality, problems of dealing with affluence, and the spread of a new kind of urbanization. The impact of the cold war is a major theme in the essays on education (by Ronald Lora), government-science relations (Kenneth M. Jones), congressional-executive relations (Gary W. Reichard), party politics (Bernard Sternsher), and popular culture (Roland Marchand). The second theme underlies essays in the collection on civil rights (William H. Chafe) and feminism and the status of women (Leila J. Rupp). Several of the essays, including those treating poverty and welfare (James T. Patterson), the family (Robert H. Bremner), workers and unionization (John Barnard), and developments in American business (Arthur M. Johnson) deal with the problems of affluence. Finally, the essays on cities and suburbs (Mark I. Gelfand), crime and law enforcement (Eugene J. Watts), and rural America (Thomas E. Williams) relate to the spread of a new kind of urbanization—rapid growth of suburbs directly contiguous to city cores becoming increasingly nonwhite, together with urbanization of the whole country through the rise of a mass culture fostered by television and other social and technological developments.

The essays in this volume, although presenting a broad panorama of American life and institutions in the period 1945–60, do not cover every subject. For various reasons plans to include separate studies on constitutional developments, ethnicity, and religion did not materialize. And since a future volume in this series will focus exclusively on cultural developments in the United States during the twentieth century, the essays do not deal with American art and literature in the postwar era.

But if the present volume does not cover all possible topics, we hope it effectively describes much of what was going on in postwar American life. In any event, we believe that the fourteen essays which follow support the argument implicit in the title of this volume: that, even though certain anticipated changes failed to occur and much continued to be in flux after 1960, the fifteen-year period beginning in 1945 truly witnessed a reshaping of American life and institutions, giving to the United States a character that differed significantly from that which it possessed at the close of World War II.

ROBERT H. BREMNER
GARY W. REICHARD

PART ONE
SOCIAL AND CULTURAL CHANGE

Families, Children, and the State

Robert H. Bremner

"It was an exciting period for a demographer to live through," Paul C. Glick said of the years 1939 to 1974, "because it was marked by sharp changes which called for careful measurement and perceptive interpretation." Glick, whose service in the Bureau of the Census spanned the thirty-five years he was reviewing, pointed out that the 1950s differed from both the start and finish of the period in marriage, birth, fertility, and divorce rates, median age at first marriage, and proportion of single women in the 20–24-year age bracket. In the 1950s Americans married at earlier ages, produced more babies, and divorced less frequently than during and just after World War II or in the 1960s and 1970s. Glick used the word "familistic" to describe the mid-century years and to characterize the style of life then in favor among Americans. As he read the statistics, the cold war era, compared to what came before and after, was an age of "relatively stable marriage and a generally high regard for family life."[1]

At the end of World War II, the most distinctive feature of American family life was diversity. "Never before in human history," declared Ernest W. Burgess in 1948, "has any society been composed of so many divergent types of families."[2] Families differed by social and economic classes, by ethnic and religious groups, by sections of the country, even by communities within a given city; they varied according to life cycle, style of life, number and role of members, and locus of authority within the group. Although authorities recognized the variety of family forms, they agreed that the modal American family was semipatriarchal:

the husband supported the family, and the wife kept house and raised the children. In 1947 Reuben Hill, a leading student of the family, acknowledged that such a division of responsibility was constantly being challenged "by insurgent mothers who rebel against the confining role of wife-and-mother and by a few fathers who feel strongly that it takes two to make a home," but concluded that for the time being the semipatriarchal family seemed to be accepted as the norm.[3]

Margaret Mead saw the American family following an urban, middle-class pattern. "Upper-class patterns occur, and lower-class practice deviates sharply from middle-class standards, and rural family life still retains the stamp of an earlier historical period," she wrote in 1948, but "films, comic strips, radio, and magazines presuppose a middle-class family."[4] Like Hill, Mead noted the general acceptance of the delegation of earning to the husband, "management of consumption" to the wife. In a paper presented at the 1947 National Conference of Social Work, she observed, "I do not at all think that most married women do not want to stay at home, but I do think that most married women would like not to have it taken quite so for granted that they should stay home." Speaking as an anthropologist, however, Mead maintained that in the few instances in which society had done away with the family, "all that was done was to substitute the mother's brother and the mother's father [for the husband] as the men that looked after the children. . . . One of the really human things about our humanity is the universality with which men have looked after women and children."[5]

Diagnosis of the state of American families in the late 1940s ranged from Carle Zimmerman's contention that the modern family was in decay and tending rapidly toward a climactic break up, to Ruth Cavan's characterization of the Middle Western family as "independent, conservative, and self-satisfied."[6] Although Reuben Hill was willing to raise the question of whether the American family had become more frequently a source of problems than of solutions to them, a conference on family life sponsored by 124 national organizations in Washington, D.C., in 1948 took as its theme "The Family—America's Greatest Asset."[7] Mead, although confident of the family's ability to survive enormous strains, described the postwar American family as "fragile" because of the heavy demands placed on inexperienced, unsupported, isolated couples, the meager assistance provided them, and acceptance of the idea that marriage was terminable. "There is no security even for the mother of young children," Mead said in 1947. "She too is faced every day, according to the advertisements, with the possibility that if she lets herself go, if she gains two more pounds, if she does not keep her stocking seams straight, she will lose her husband."[8]

Nearly all observers in the postwar era agreed with the point made by William F. Ogburn in *Recent Social Trends* (1933) that because of major social changes such as urbanism, industrialism, and mobility the institutional functions of the family had declined, the personality functions become more important. Institutional functions had included production of food and clothing, education, and introduction of children to the world of work and adult responsibilities. Personality functions, as defined by Ogburn, were "those which provide for the mutual adjustments among husbands, wives, parents and children and adaptation of each member of the family to the outside world."[9] *The Family*, a highly praised and widely used college textbook by Ernest W. Burgess and Harvey J. Locke first published in 1945, retained *From Institution to Companionship* as its subtitle in its 1950, 1953, and 1960 editions. In the 1971 edition, the word "Traditional" was substituted for "Institution," but the central thesis remained constant through the four editions: the family's principal function is to provide "intimate, affectional association"; it is held together not by external pressure or internal authority but by "mutual affection, sympathetic understanding, and comradeship."[10]

Despite the shift in functions, the family continued to bear heavy responsibilities. Lawrence K. Frank, who had written the essay on childhood and youth for *Recent Social Trends*, spelled out family obligations in a 1948 article, "What Families Do for the Nation":

> The family is the only socially recognized relation for childbearing and the essential agency for child rearing, socialization, and introducing the child to the culture of the society, thereby shaping the basic character structure of our culture and forming the child's personality. The family is the primary agency for protecting physical and mental health. Moreover, the family must provide what adult men and women need for their fulfillment as personalities.[11]

Most of the young people who, wittingly or unwittingly, assumed the awesome responsibilities of raising families in the postwar years were themselves born in the 1920s, grew up in the thirties, and were adolescents or young adults during World War II. They had all been affected, although in different ways, by how their families fared in the Great Depression and whether, in their own cases, the war brought hardship, opportunity, or something of both. Their parents had been born a few years before or shortly after 1900, their children would live well into the twenty-first century. As a group they had had more years in school and college than earlier generations and the advantage of lifelong familiarity with movies, radios, automobiles, airplanes, electrical appliances, and inside plumbing.

In 1950 men and women entering marriage for the first time were, on the average, more than a year younger than in 1940 and several years younger than in 1890.[12] One reason why earlier marriages were feasible was that, contrary to postwar assumptions, it was not uncommon for women to continue working after marriage. Between 1948 and 1958 the number of employed women with children under eighteen rose from 4.1 million in 1948 to 7.5 million, an increase of 80 percent, a decade later. "The working mother, even the one who has young children, is here to stay," declared a speaker at the 1955 National Conference of Social Work. "So much of the way we live today invites women to seek employment outside the home," observed Mrs. Randolph Guggenheimer at a day-care conference held in 1960. The item to which she called particular attention was "the stress on prestige and status related to material possession." She might also have cited preference and opportunity for employment as an alternative to full-time homemaking and motherhood, and economic necessity in cases where the husband's earnings alone could not support the family. Some wives worked to help put the husband, and later the children, through college.[13]

For women, holding a job and contributing to family income was not a new phenomenon but a revival, in modern dress, of women's traditional function of helping produce food, clothing, and other household needs. Looked at from another perspective, increasing employment of mothers—including those with young children—outside the home meant acceptance by broader segments of the population of a practice familiar both to poor women and to those wealthy enough to hire nursemaids and housekeepers.

In the 1930s and 1940s critics noted and often deplored the American tendency to make women responsible for nearly all aspects of home life and parenthood while men concentrated on work and matters outside the home. Taking a job in store, factory, or office did not automatically release wives from housekeeping and child-rearing tasks or guarantee that husbands would assume a greater share of in-home responsibilities—but it was a good reason for, and a strong argument in favor of, their doing so. In the postwar years, whether or not their wives worked, husbands were constantly admonished to devote more time to home and family. In 1947 Margaret Mead, who regarded Americans' heavy demands on wives as unfair to women and hard on children, offered a

suggestion—more practical before than after the advent of television—
for getting fathers involved with their children:

> As we move into the five-day week, free Saturday mornings are appearing
> all over the country, unpre-empted by church or state or golf club. Here is a
> situation that should interest every person who is concerned with changing
> the tone or pattern of our culture. Nobody knows what a man ought to do on
> Saturday morning. Saturday morning is one fourteenth of the week; if every
> American father spent one fourteenth of the week with his children, the
> American family would present a very different picture from what we have
> now. We have the opportunity before a pattern freezes, before some com-
> mercialized interest gets hold of Saturday morning, to set Saturday morning
> up as father's morning.[14]

Ed Richtscheidt, *McCall's* idea of "a modern American husband and
father," devoted much more than Saturday morning to helping his wife
Carol make a home for their three children. "He and Carol have centered their lives almost completely around their children and home,"
McCall's reported approvingly in 1954. The Richtscheidts' domesticity,
according to the magazine, was typical of that of millions of other American couples in the 1950s. *McCall's* rejoiced that the old fashioned father, "disciplinarian and bogeyman," had been "pretty well replaced by
the father who's pal and participator." But even that was not enough.
Fathers, according to *McCall's*, "should wield more authority in their
families than they are currently doing. They are just as responsible as
their wives for the way children are going to turn out. For the sake of
every member of the family, the family needs a head. This means Father,
not Mother."[15]

Some notion of how mothers and fathers viewed parenthood and
judged their performance as parents may be obtained from an interview
survey conducted in 1957 by The Survey Research Center of the University of Michigan for the Joint Commission on Mental Illness and
Health. The survey team selected interviewees to represent the total
population of the United States in age, sex, education, income, occupa-
tion, and place of residence. Those interviewed, therefore, presumably
expressed the point of view of "the 'normal', stable, adult population of
the United States." Children ranked with money (defined as "material
comforts, adequacy of living, and the security it can buy") as considerations most often cited by interviewees as central to their happiness. On
the other hand, while interviewees identified lack of money as a major
cause of unhappiness, few spontaneously mentioned family relationships as a source of distress. "All in all," the survey stated, "it is clear that

well over half the population finds its greatest happiness in the home, a state that is conditioned strongly by feelings of economic security." A higher percentage of women (78 percent) than of men (70 percent) reported having encountered problems in raising children and more women (51 percent) than men (41 percent) acknowledged having sometimes felt inadequate as parents. Men were more inclined than women to worry about failing to make adequate material provision for children, and both men and women—but for different reasons—were concerned about "the parent-child affiliative relationship":

> Women, spending a lot of time with children, get concerned and guilty not over lack of an affiliative relationship but over their exasperation and loss of temper from too much interaction. Men, not spending much time with their children, are guilty over the lack of a warm relationship ("I don't spend enough time with them").[16]

The survey team, like *McCall's*, interpreted fathers' guilt feelings over emotional neglect of children as a reflection of "an important cultural change, now in process, where affiliation is becoming a central part of the fathers' role."[17] This change was part of the general upgrading of American social and economic conditions in the first half of the twentieth century that allowed ordinary people to adopt attitudes and feel concerns once the prerogatives of the well-to-do.

Anthropologist Ruth Benedict's contribution to the anthology *The Family: Its Function and Destiny* (1949), emphasized the extraordinary freedom of choice that characterized American, as opposed to other countries', family life. She viewed the lack of authoritarianism in American families as a source of strength and stability rather than as cause for alarm:

> No strong father image is compatible with our politics or our economics. We seek the opportunity to prove that we are as good as the next person, and we do not find comfort in following an authoritarian voice—in the state or in the home . . . which will issue a command from on high. We learn as children to measure ourselves against Johnny next door, or against Mildred whose mother our mother knows in church, and this prepares us for living in a society with strongly egalitarian ideals. We do not learn the necessity of submitting to unquestioned commands as the children of many countries do. The family in the United States has become democratic.

In Benedict's opinion the free choice and nonauthoritarian aspects of the American family were consistent with, and appropriate to, the major emphases of national life.[18]

In at least one important family matter—birth control—freedom of choice, although probably more widely exercised than ever before, was still limited by authoritarian religious and legal constraints. In 1948 Pope Pius XII advised the International College of Surgeons that sterilization, birth control, and childbirth operations in which the mother's life was saved at the expense of the child's were not permissible for Roman Catholics; organizations such as Catholic War Veterans took a leading part in defeating efforts to lift Connecticut's ban on contraceptive materials and information; and church authorities, even where the practice was legal, opposed provision of birth control devices in public hospitals.[19] At the end of the 1950s thirty states, including Connecticut and Massachusetts where the prohibitions were most complete, had legislation of varying stringency restricting the sale, advertisement, or dispensation of information about contraceptives. Federal laws imposing penalties for importing, mailing, or transporting contraceptives or disseminating information about their use remained on the statute books but after 1930 had been greatly modified by a series of Supreme Court decisions. By 1960, as a result of judicial interpretation, federal laws allowed contraceptives intended for medical use, for treatment or prevention of disease, and contraceptive literature not written in obscene language to be freely imported, transported, and mailed. "In practice," commented a legal scholar in 1960, "this means that contraceptives must be going to or coming from doctors or other professional persons, or anyone acting at their direction or under their supervision. . . . Private persons, importing, mailing, or transporting contraceptives purely for the purpose of preventing conception, with no medical indication for their employment, would still, at least theoretically, be caught by the statutes."[20]

Despite religious objections and legislative curbs, contraceptives—sometimes labeled and sold "for prevention of disease" or "for feminine hygiene"—were obtainable even in states like Connecticut and Massachusetts. In 1938 *Fortune* called the traffic in contraceptives "a $250,000,000 business, slightly bigger than the barbershop business and very slightly smaller than the jewelry business." Users complained not so much of unavailability as unreliability of the products. Margaret Sanger and Katharine Dexter McCormick's search for a " 'foolproof' female birth control method" led in the 1950s to McCormick's subsidizing Gregory Pincus's work on the birth control pill, first put on sale in 1960. Meanwhile, numerous surveys in the late 1940s showed overwhelming support among women polled for making birth control information readily available to all married women; 83 percent of the fecund couples interviewed in 1955 in a national sample reported they had adopted some means of birth control, and 7 percent said they planned to do so after they had had the one or more children they wanted. In 1960 as in 1945, the chief sufferers from restrictive legislation were women too poor to be able to afford private consultation with a doctor, and those who because of poverty, inexperience, lack or denial of information, neglected precautions against pregnancy or relied on the less efficient methods of contraception.[21]

"Trust yourself" was the advice Benjamin Spock, M.D., gave readers at the start of *The Common Sense Book of Baby and Child Care* (1945). "Don't take too seriously all that the neighbors say. Don't be afraid to trust your own common sense. Bringing up your child won't be a complicated job if you take it easy, trust your own instincts, and follow the directions that your doctor gives you." Of his own book Spock said "It's not infallible." All the book attempted to do was offer "sensible present-day ideas of the care of a child, taking into account his physical and emotional needs."[22]

The basis of Spock's easy-going nonauthoritarianism was confidence both in the natural ability of parents ("the more people have studied different methods of bringing up children the more they have come to the conclusion that what good mothers and fathers instinctively feel like doing for their babies is usually best after all") and in the equally natural willingness of infants to adjust and adapt in due time and in accordance with individual development patterns to socially acceptable behavior. Instead of compiling what David Reisman called "tricks of the child-rearing trade: feeding and toilet training schedules," Spock advised that babies did not have to be sternly trained: "In the first place, you can't get a baby regulated beyond a certain point, no matter how hard you try. In the second place you are more apt, in the long run, to make him balky and disagreeable when you go at his training too hard."

> . . . You don't have to be grimly determined [Spock continued], in order to bring up a healthy, agreeable, successful child. It's the parents who have a natural self-confidence in themselves and a comfortable, affectionate attitude toward their children who get the best results—and with the least effort.

Whether parents trusted themselves or not, a great many of them trusted Doctor Spock. Looking back from the vantage point of 1960, a writer in *Ladies Home Journal* recalled the warm reception accorded Spock's book: ". . . There has probably never been such overwhelming trust placed in an author. The postwar baby boom was on, and young parents were ready for a new, non-rigid technique of bringing up baby."[23]

Young parents of the baby-boom era may themselves have been

brought up under a more rigorous regimen. The government publication *Infant Care*, used as a guide by many mothers since its original publication in 1914, advocated a no-nonsense approach to baby care with strict adherence to tight schedules for feeding, sleeping, and toilet training. A revised edition issued in 1929, prepared under the direction of Martha M. Eliot, M.D., warned at the outset:

> Parents must remember that the character building of their child is closely tied up with the way his physical needs are met. His future mental health, as well as physical health, will depend largely on the habits he builds during the first year of life, especially the early months. Some of these habits can be started as soon as the baby is born.

Dr. Eliot maintained that the new baby received his first lessons in character-building through training in regularity of feeding, sleeping, and elimination:

> He should learn that hunger will be satisfied only so often, that when he is put into his bed he must go to sleep, that crying will not result in his being picked up or played with whenever he likes. He will begin to learn that he is part of a world bigger than that of his own desires.[24]

The 1945 edition of *Infant Care*, much revised since 1929, continued to emphasize the desirability of establishing regular habits but in a much milder tone than in earlier editions and with more concern for physical and mental well-being than for character-building: "Most babies can get used at an early age to eating and sleeping at regular times, and they are usually happier and eat and sleep better if habits of regularity are established. . . . Babies thrive on doing the same thing at the same time, day after day." The 1951 and 1955 editions took a middle course between baby's gratification and mother's convenience. *Infant Care* (1951) acknowledged "a newborn baby can't immediately fit into our ways, so at first we have to adjust to him." Letting a baby have a chance to establish a feeding rhythm of his own admittedly required more judgment on the part of a parent than feeding him at set intervals, "but it's much easier than having an unhappy baby." The 1950s versions of *Infant Care*, however, saw no harm in modifying the baby's schedule to help the mother meet her other obligations. "To let him dictate exactly when he must be fed leaves your needs completely out of account. A baby's needs won't be met if his mother's needs are forgotten."[25]

Geoffrey Gorer, an English anthropologist residing in the United States, was amused by the notion of a government bureau issuing "pamphlets distributed by the million to tell young mothers how to bring up their offspring." Noting periodic revisions in *Infant Care*, Gorer commented that a comparison of the different editions provided "an interesting synopsis of the vagaries of the most accepted theories of child rearing." The "vagaries," however, represented not the whim of bureaucrats but change in professional knowledge in areas such as child development, nutrition, and mental health. Each edition of *Infant Care*, although compiled in the U.S. Children's Bureau, was reviewed by specialists in many fields before publication. The 1951 edition, for example, utilized the advice of seventy persons outside the bureau, including general practitioners, pediatricians, psychiatrists, psychologists, and social workers as well as parents and expectant parents.[26]

One of the pediatricians who advised both Spock and the Children's Bureau was C. Andrews Aldrich, professor of pediatrics of the University of Minnesota and recipient of the 1948 Lasker Award in mental hygiene. His works, especially *Babies Are Human Beings: An Interpretation of Growth* (1938), written in collaboration with his wife, Mary M. Aldrich, exercised a strong influence on mid-century thought about the nature and needs of children. The quality of his influence is best illustrated by Aldrich's dissent from the advice often given parents (as, for example, by Martha Eliot in the 1929 edition of *Infant Care*) that they must exert firmness and discipline so that the baby would learn that he could not have whatever he wanted. "This process of parental thwarting can never lead to a happy family relationship," wrote Aldrich. "Furthermore, such an attitude is superfluous since the world does not lack for opportunities in which he can learn to adjust to antagonistic and unpleasant requirements." On the subject of "spoiled children," Aldrich observed:

> Every doctor has the opportunity of knowing many such youngsters, but I have never seen one who was spoiled because his parents consistently planned his life to meet his basic needs. In my experience most spoiled children are those who, as babies, have been denied essential gratifications in a mistaken attempt to fit them into a rigid regime. Warmth, cuddling, freedom of action and pleasant associations with food and sleep have been pushed out of the way to make room for a technique. The lack of these things is so keenly felt that by the time babyhood is past, such children have learned their own efficient technique of whining and tantrums as a means of getting their desires. In this way is fostered the belligerent, fussy, unpleasant personality of the typical "spoiled child," who insists on undue attention because he has missed this fundamental experience. A satisfied baby does not need to develop these methods of wresting his comforts from an unresponsive world. It is axiomatic that satisfied people never start a revolution.[27]

Children born in the postwar era were bound to leave their mark on American history when they reached maturity in the last three decades of the twentieth century. Because of their extraordinary number, however, the sixty million children born between 1945 and 1961 made their presence felt almost from birth. "There are so many of them and they are so dictatorical in effect that a term like *filiarchy* would not be entirely facetious," wrote William H. Whyte in *The Organization Man* (1956). By 1960, when the oldest were still in their teens and words and phrases like "counterculture" and "me generation" had not yet been invented, the needs and tastes of the baby-boom children had already exerted a significant influence on the nation's economic and social life. "They forced our economy to feed, clothe, educate, and house them," asserted Landon Y. Jones (b. 1943), viewing the impact of the baby-boomers from the standpoint of 1980. "Their collective buying power made fads overnight and built entire industries."[28]

Even before the advent of the baby-boom generation, students like Margaret Mead recognized the importance of age-grouping and the extent to which peer pressure superseded family standards at adolescence. Prior to the 1950s, however, younger children were thought to receive the vast majority of their experience in their homes and neighborhoods and to carry the behavior patterns and conceptions of right and wrong learned there into school and community life. Thus August B. Hollingshead, in *Elmtown's Youth*, a work published in 1949 but based on research conducted in 1941 and 1942, maintained that upper-, middle-, and lower-middle-class parents in the study were remarkably successful in guiding their children into conformity with, and along lines approved by, their respective class cultures.[29] Later commentators on children and families, although not indifferent to the influence on children of social class, home, and neighborhood—whether suburb or ghetto—tended to place more emphasis than Hollingshead on character-forming agents other than parents and outside the home. Peer group and mass media, particularly television, were recognized as factors of critical significance in shaping values and behavior even in young children. Mead, in 1970, believed that as early as 1920 the media had begun to set styles "in the name of each successive adolescent group"; by the 1960s parents, whether willingly or not, "expected to accede to the urgent demands their children were taught to make, not by the school or by other, more acculturated children, but by the mass media."[30]

In the 1950s, as before and since, conservatives deplored diminution or relaxation of parental influence as bad for children and society. The trend toward autonomy, however, was seemingly irreversible. "Our society is changing at an ever increasing rate," wrote James S. Coleman in *The Adolescent Society* (1961); "adults cannot afford to shape their children in their own image." In similar vein Talcott Parsons and Winston White argued that greater permissiveness toward children and treatment of them as persons were not an abdication of parental responsibility but a way of preparing children for adulthood. " . . . As a socializing agent the family cannot do its job unless it emancipates its children from dependence on the parents, an emancipation that precludes parents from being too definite role-models for the child's own life course."[31] At the start of a decade that would be greatly concerned with the achievement of equality, Coleman recognized that "weakening of family power" promoted equality of opportunity. What worried Coleman (b. 1926) and many of his contemporaries was the waning of *any* adult influence on young people who, from nursery school through college, were set apart from the rest of society and allowed to associate mainly with each other. "To put it simply," said Coleman, "these young people speak a different language."[32]

Generalizations about American families based on an urban middle-class model—or any other model—are subject to numerous qualifications. So, too, to call the post–World War II generation "the biggest, richest, best-educated generation America has ever produced" and to say that "the boom babies were born to be the best and brightest" may be valid, as generalizations go, but leave out of consideration many persons whose life experience has been different from that of the more fortunate members of the group.[33] One way to get them back into the picture is to examine the family, not as a private institution, but as a subject of public concern.

What the state should do to help families was a question with as many answers as there were different kinds of families. In 1945 middle-aged and elderly Americans could remember what had happened to families in the not-too-distant past when there was no public relief for the poor in their own homes, no workmen's compensation when the father was injured or killed at work, no unemployment or old age insurance, and when asylums and poorhouses were the best society could offer orphans and needy old people. As far as families were concerned, "the results were disastrous," recalled Bailey B. Burritt of the Community Service Society of New York. The social awakening, social legislation, and social changes that had transformed America since 1900 had completely altered the situation. "No longer do we see family life in any significant amount broken up through the disaster of death, sickness, accident, unemployment, and other misfortunes to the stability of family life," Burritt exulted in 1948. The problem of the postwar era, he said was "how far and how rapidly is it wise to go in extending present welfare services. . . . How far can the State go in extending welfare work and the so-called security to all families without weakening human efforts to better themselves?"[34]

President Harry Truman championed his administration's Fair Deal Policies on the grounds that the nation should go farther than it had yet ventured in the direction of extending security to all families. "Governments are formed for the purpose of being of service to the family," he told the delegates to the 1948 Conference on Family Life. "The welfare and security of the family is vital to every government in the world." Truman devoted most of his welcoming address to a plea for passage of the Taft-Ellender-Wagner housing bill then pending in Congress. One of the cases he cited to illustrate the need for public housing involved a young man and his wife, their baby and dog, who had been ejected from a campsite on a parking lot in Washington, D.C.

> And they had no place to go [he said]. They couldn't find a place in this great city of Washington that would let a baby and a dog come and live.
> How are you going to raise a family under that condition?
> Children and dogs are as necessary to the welfare of this country as Wall Street and the railroads—or any part of the country!

Truman advised the delegates to tell their congressmen to pass the housing bill. "They will probably listen to you better than they will to me," he said. "Some of them are running for reelection next fall."[35]

A year later, after the Democrats had regained control of Congress but when it appeared that members of the House might still be more ready to listen to "the real estate lobby" opposing the housing bill than to veterans, municipal, labor, church, and social welfare organizations supporting it, Truman issued another strong appeal for its adoption. "The real issue," he declared on 17 June 1949, "is whether the Federal Government should provide practical, workable and carefully limited assistance in improving the standard of housing of the American people and relieving the conditions of slum housing in which too many of our families are now forced to live." He scoffed at the charge that providing public housing for low-income families would have an adverse affect on their morale:

> The plain fact is that thrift, industry, and initiative are encouraged, not discouraged, by clean and decent housing. It is among people who are forced to live in firetraps, in crowded tenements, in alley dwellings, that are found the highest rates of poor health, poor education, juvenile delinquency and the other disabilities that sap energy and initiative, and result in heavy costs to the community. The provision of adequate housing for the people to be aided by this bill will be a long step forward toward a happier, more thrifty and industrious people in our Nation.[36]

The president's vigorous support was an important factor in the passage, on 15 July 1949, of the long-delayed Housing Act of 1949. The act went beyond earlier federal legislation to declare "the general welfare and security of the Nation and the health and living standards of its people" demanded housing production to overcome the existing shortage, eliminating of substandard housing, and achievement as soon as feasible of "the goal of a decent home and a suitable living environment for every American family." Its most controversial provision authorized completion of 810,000 low-rent public housing units within six years.[37]

The "prospect of decent homes in wholesome surroundings for low-income families now living in the squalor of the slums" President Truman envisaged when he signed the Housing Act of 1949 was not to be realized. Scarcely a year later, at the outbreak of the Korean War, Truman asked agency heads to restrict credit for residential building and to limit construction of public housing in order to reduce demand for material required for national defense purposes. Besides cutting the number of public housing units to be built in the last half of 1950 from 67,500 to 30,000, Truman directed reexamination of the public housing program "in terms of the developing international situation."[38] For the rest of the 1950s, determined and skillful lobbying by private housing organizations, hostility to the program on the part of many congressmen, opposition to the establishment of public housing projects in a number of cities, and lack of support from the White House kept public housing construction on a modest scale. Only 200,000 of the 810,000 public housing units projected in 1949 had been built by 1956 and fewer than 300,000 by 1960.[39]

In contrast to public housing's indifferent record, private residential construction, fostered by various governmental programs, made enormous progress in the 1950s. The sixteen million new units (including mobile homes) built between 1950 and 1959 ended the housing shortage for most American families. No longer was it necessary, as immediately after the war, for married couples to share living quarters with others. Both public and private financing plans made it possible for a larger number of Americans than ever before to achieve the dream of owning their homes. Increasingly the homes were in the suburbs, and, wherever located, the number of dwelling units equipped with hot and cold running water, a private bathroom, and classified as "not dilapidated" increased from 63 percent of the total in 1950 to 76 percent toward the end of the decade. Critics, using the same figures, might exclaim, "As late as 1960 one out of four housing units in the United States was dilapidated, deteriorated, and/or lacking in complete plumbing!" In 1940, however, the figure had been close to 50 percent. At least some of the change could be attributed to billions of dollars made available by federal loans and grants for home improvement, remodeling, and rehabilitation.[40]

The quantity and quality of housing available is bound to have an impact, for good or ill or both, on the circumstances and quality of family life. In the United States rapid expansion of urban and suburban housing in the 1950s meant that millions of new families were able to raise children in more commodious and healthful surroundings than the parents had known in their childhood. "This relatively favorable environment for family life," declares Anthony Downs, "was one of the factors that generated record levels of new babies in the late fifties and early sixties, when the number of births exceeded 4 million per year." Easing the housing shortage, the prime target of government housing policy, allowed Americans to indulge their preference for living in nuclear as opposed to extended families. In 1948 Margaret Mead contrasted "a three-generation family with many collateral lines" with "the tiny biological family of the modern three-room apartment dwellers." A decade later the more fortunate of the apartment dwellers might live—still without relatives nearby—but, like *McCall's* Ed and Carol Richtscheidt, "in a gray shingle split-level house with three bedrooms, one bath and an unfinished basement room that will one day be the game room." Less fortunate families whose mobility was restricted by income or race might still obtain better living quarters by moving from slums to surrounding lower-density and better-quality housing areas. The least fortunate, confined to the slums by race and poverty, continued to occupy districts that were deemed worst in physical condition of housing and that became worse in every other way because of the concentration of misery and helplessness within them.[41]

INFANT AND MATERNAL MORTALITY RATES, 1940–60[42]

Year	Number of Infant Deaths under One Year (Exclusive of Fetal Deaths) per 1,000 Live Births			Number of Maternal Deaths from Deliveries and Complications of Pregnancy, Childbirth, and the Puerperium per 10,000 Live Births		
	Total	White	Nonwhite	Total	White	Nonwhite
1940	47.0	43.2	73.8	37.6	32.0	77.4
1945	38.3	35.6	57.0	20.7	17.2	45.5
1950	29.2	26.8	44.5	8.3	6.1	22.2
1955	26.4	23.6	42.8	4.7	3.3	13.0
1960	26.0	22.9	43.2	3.7	2.6	9.8

Rates of infant and maternal mortality are among the basic indices of family health and welfare. As indicated in the table below, both infant and maternal death rates dropped sharply in the 1940s, less markedly in the 1950s. Reduction in the rates in the forties is attributable to progress in the control of infectious diseases, improved care for prematurely born infants, and expanded child and maternal health programs at the state and local levels made possible by federal grants in aid under Title V of the Social Security Act. Between 1943 and 1949 the Emergency Maternal and Infant Care (EMIC) program operated by state health departments with funds supplied through the U.S. Children's Bureau gave free medical, nursing, and hospital, maternity and infant care to wives and babies (up to one year of age) of enlisted men in the four lowest pay grades—about three-fourths of the armed forces. EMIC, the largest public medical care program the United States had yet attempted, served a total of approximately one and a half million maternity and infant cases. At its peak it covered one out of seven of all births in the country. Although EMIC's justification was improvement in servicemen's morale, its result was to improve standards and raise levels of maternal and child care. In evaluating the program in 1949, the *American Journal of Public Health* stated: "Many mothers whose husbands were not in service learned from EMIC patients what to expect in the way of good medical care throughout pregnancy, at delivery, and after the baby's birth. They learned for the first time what good health supervision and medical care for an infant really is.[43]

In a message to Congress in November 1945 recommending adoption of the Wagner-Murray-Dingell national health bill, President Truman cited EMIC along with wartime programs for industrial hygiene and control of venereal disease, malaria, and tuberculosis as precedents for continued and expanded cooperation between federal and state governments in public health services and maternal and child health care. "The health of American children, like their education," declared the president, "should be recognized as a definite public responsibility. . . . We should . . . see to it that our health programs are pushed most vigorously with the youngest section of the population."[44]

Both the president's message and a study conducted by the American Academy of Pediatrics in 1946 and 1947 noted recent gains in protecting children's health. The death rate for preschool children (ages one to five) had dropped from 10 deaths per 1,000 population in 1920 to 1 per 1,000 in 1945; for preschool children the death rate from all causes was lower in 1945 than from pneumonia, influenza, and other communicable diseases in 1935. While giving due attention to progress achieved in health services for children, the Academy study noted disparities in care between rural and urban areas. Thus, within a single state (Virginia) infant mortality rates ranged from 25 per 1,000 live births in a metropolitan county to 59 per 1,000 in isolated rural counties. Infant mortality tables also made clear the inferior status of children of racial minorities in terms of medical care: in 1946 in the nation as a whole, the infant mortality rate was 32 per 1,000 live births for whites, 50 for nonwhites; among Indians in New Mexico it was 152. Children of migrant families, whether black or white, faced special problems. "They belong to the low-income group," the report said of migrant children, "thus often being excluded from private practice," but "the hospitals and clinics to which they would be eligible on the basis of their economic status are frequently closed to them because of admission policies based on residence or race."[45]

The Wagner-Murray-Dingell bill, first introduced in 1943 and resubmitted with Truman's endorsement in 1945 and 1947, proposed to deal with the high cost of medical care—which Truman identified as the principal reason people failed to receive the care they needed—by a compulsory health insurance program financed by a Social Security–type payroll tax. The bill also authorized (without specifying a dollar figure) an expansion of federal grants to the states for maternal and child health and crippled children's services. Another measure introduced in 1945, the maternal and child welfare bill sponsored by Senator Claude Pepper with strong backing by the U.S. Children's Bureau, authorized grants of approximately $100 million a year to states to provide maternity care, medical care for children, services for crippled children, and child welfare services. A significant provision in the Pepper bill required states to make services and facilities available to all mothers and children who elected to participate in the programs without discrimination "because of race, creed, color, or national origin," and without a means test or residence requirement.[46]

Neither the Wagner-Murray-Dingell nor Pepper bills won congressional approval, but through the efforts of Senators Pepper and Robert Taft, the Social Security Amendments of 1946 nearly doubled authorizations and appropriations for the three Title V programs (maternal and child health, crippled children, and child welfare services). Congress raised the authorizations again in 1950, 1958, and 1960, but during the 1950s appropriations seldom matched authorization. In the decade 1951–61 there was only one year—1958—in which appropriations for maternal and child health equaled the modest amount ($16.5 million) authorized to be spent. Very little progress was made in the 1950s in reducing infant mortality rates; for nonwhites the rate was slightly higher in 1960 than in 1955. This stagnation, in the words of William M. Schmidt, M.D., of the Harvard School of Public Health, "reflected both inadequacy of city and state response to deteriorating urban situations and lack of essential federal help."[47]

Child welfare services, the smallest of the Title V programs in 1945, underwent the most extensive changes in the 1950s. The Social Security Act authorized the Children's Bureau to make grants to states for "establishing, extending, and strengthening, especially in predominantly rural areas," child welfare services for the protection and care of "homeless, dependent, and neglected children and children in danger of becoming delinquent." Before 1960 the federal grants did not have to be matched by state funds, and they were necessarily small because annual appropriations for the program—$3.5 million in the late 1940s, $7.2 million in the mid-50s, and $13 million in 1960—were even lower than for maternal and child health or crippled children's services. Small though the grants were, they allowed states to finance professional training of child welfare workers and encouraged state and local agencies to establish adoption, foster care, licensing, and counseling services in areas previously without them. The Social Security Amendments of 1950 authorized use of federal funds for the return of runaway children across state lines to their own communities and provided for the utilization of the facilities and services of voluntary agencies in development of state programs; the amendments of 1958 removed the "predominantly rural areas" restriction; and those of 1962 required each state to make provisions for extending child welfare services to all areas of the state by 1 July 1975. In 1960 Katherine B. Oettinger, chief of the Children's Bureau, observed that in the twenty-five years since passage of the Social Security Act the focus of child welfare services had shifted from concern about care of children in institutions for the dependent, neglected, and delinquent to efforts to preserve and strengthen families and to prevent break-up of homes. No one—least of all officers of the Children's Bureau—pretended that the services were adequate or available to all children and families in need of them; but by 1960 the foundations had been laid in every state for assistance to troubled children and children in incapacitated, neglectful, and abusive families. Where the services were available, they were for the most part free of the means and residence tests imposed in other state welfare programs.[48]

"Every effort should be made to preserve for the young child his right to have care from his mother, since the normal development of the young child depends upon an affectional relationship with her." This statement, published in 1945, reaffirmed the Children's Bureau's traditional view that the first duty of a mother, especially one with young children, was in the home. The conviction had been sorely tried during World War II but never entirely abandoned. Between 1942 and 1946 federal grants under the Lanham Act helped finance day-care centers serving an estimated 600,000 children in communities with concentrations of war-production activities. By the last year of the war, the Children's Bureau recognized that "pressures of personal problems and the burden of full responsibility for their children" caused many mothers who might wish to care for their babies to go to work. Citing the findings of authorities in psychiatry, child welfare, child health, and child development, the Bureau concluded negatively, "Group care is not a satisfactory method of caring for children under 2 years of age," and positively, "Decisions as to the care of young children should be made in the light of the child's needs, which should be given primary emphasis."[49]

The end of the war did not result in the expected or hoped-for exodus of mothers from employment. As already noted, the era of the baby boom was a time of continued and widening involvement of women in the work force. Increased employment of women in the late 1940s and 1950s occurred without any significant public expenditure for, or investment in, day-care services. Early in the 1950s a publication of the Women's Bureau of the Department of Labor credited the federally assisted child-care programs of World War II with having won general understanding of "the working mothers' problems and the community's responsibilities in assisting with them." In fact, when federal grants under the Lanham Act ceased in 1946, most state and local support for day care also ended. By 1953 only a few cities and three states— Massachusetts, California, and New York (the last only for children of migrant workers)—provided financial aid for day care. The Defense Housing and Community Facilities and Services Act of 1951, a Korean War measure, authorized federal grants for day-care centers, but Congress appropriated no funds for that purpose.[50] A 1958 Census Bureau survey of child-care arrangements of mothers who had children under 12 disclosed that 80 percent of the 5 million children under review received care at home by fathers, other relatives, including brothers and sisters, neighbors, or other nonrelatives. Relatives or neighbors also looked after most of the children receiving care away from home. Only about 121,000 of the 5 million children went to day nurseries, day-care centers, nursery schools, or after-school centers. About 1 in 13 of the children was without supervision from the end of school until a parent returned from work. Whether more use would have been made of group-care facilities if they had been more numerous and less expensive is not known. "Many parents cannot pay the full cost of good care," asserted Judith Cauman, a day-care advocate. "Good care is not even available to those who can pay."[51]

Dr. Spock, who included a section on "The Working Mother" in his guide to baby and child care, said, "It would save money in the end if the government paid comfortable allowance to all mothers (of young children) who would otherwise be compelled to work.

> You can think of it this way [he continued]: Useful, well-adjusted citizens are the most valuable possessions a country has, and good mothers' care during early childhood is the surest way to produce them. It doesn't make sense to let mothers go to work . . . and have them pay other people to do a poorer job of bringing up their children.[52]

In 1945 the Aid to Dependent Children program established under Title IV of the Social Security Act was nearly ten years old. It offered grants-in-aid to states to enable them to assist needy dependent children under sixteen who were deprived of parental support because of the "death, continued absence from the home, or physical or mental incapacity" of a parent and who lived with a mother or some other close relative. The act laid down general guidelines that had to be complied with by all states participating in the program, but the rules were not stringent and left major decisions regarding implementation and administration to the states. From the beginning, quality of administration, eligibility standards, and benefit levels varied from state to state. ADC thus exemplified the states' rights philosophy that Gilbert Steiner asserts dominated American welfare policy prior to 1962, "a policy tailored to the interests of the individual states with an absolute minimum of insistence upon uniformity."[53]

In the 1940s the staff of the Bureau of Public Assistance, the federal agency charged with administering ADC, although unable to establish uniformity between states, sought to obtain more equitable administration within states and to promote aceptance of definitions of "continued absence" and "incapacity" that would permit more children to be brought under the program. The number of children receiving ADC declined during the war (944,000 in 1941, 639,000 in 1944) but began to rise in 1945 and by 1950 reached a postwar peak of 1,661,000, more than twice as many as at the end of the war. Congress, alarmed by the increase, which some members attributed to mounting desertion rates, considered the pros and cons of making abandonment of dependents a federal crime. Instead, the NOLEO provision of the Social Security Amendments of 1950 required public assistance workers to give prompt "notice to appropriate law enforcement officers" when ADC was furnished to children deserted or abandoned by a parent. NOLEO, which went into effect 1 July 1952, left determination of the amount of effort and expense to be devoted to pursuing and prosecuting deserting fathers to local authorities, but subjected mothers who failed to cooperate with them to harassment and possible loss of eligibility.[54]

The Social Security Amendments of 1950 corrected one of the oversights of the original act by permitting payments not only to dependent children but also (as in military pensions) to their mothers or other adult caretakers. ADC was further liberalized in 1956 by allowing assistance to children living with cousins and even nieces and nephews. Although the 1956 amendments declared the goal of ADC was "to help maintain and strengthen family life," children fortunate or unfortunate enough to have able-bodied fathers at home continued to be excluded from the program. The conviction that fathers *should* support their children was so deeply ingrained in the American consciousness that even after Congress, in 1961, authorized extension of ADC to families in which the father was present and able-bodied but unemployed, only half the states took advantage of the option.[55]

In the 1950s, while the federal government relaxed restrictions on who might receive ADC, states maintained or tightened eligibility standards and administrative procedures intended to enforce paternal responsibility and to avoid countenancing illicit sexual relationships. "Man in the house" rules, midnight searches, and "suitable home" provisions adopted by numerous states, often attributed to official penury and officious bureaucracy, reflected deeply held and widely shared popular convictions about proper—or improper—family conduct.

From 1951 to 1955 the number of families, children, and caretakers aided by ADC was lower than in 1950. The same was true of recipients of Old Age Assistance (OAA), but whereas the latter continued to decline through the decade, ADC caseloads began to increase about the mid-fifties; and by 1957, in terms of numbers of persons aided, ADC had replaced OAA as the country's largest public assistance program. In 1960 a total of 3,080,000 people—850,000 more than in 1950—received ADC; but the number of children receiving ADC per 1,000 of population under eighteen was the same—35—as in 1950. Meanwhile, the number of children per 1,000 of population under eighteen receiving social security under Old Age, Survivors, and Disability Insurance (OASDI) had nearly doubled, rising from 14 per 1,000 in 1950 to 27 in 1960. Even more than in 1950, the ADC family was likely to be one in which the father had divorced, deserted, or never married the mother.[56]

A quarter of a century after adoption, ADC was both praised for its role in strengthening family life by preventing separation of children from their homes and criticized for encouraging unstable family relations and unmarried parenthood. Kathryn D. Goodwin, director of the Bureau of Public Assistance, acknowledged grave shortcomings—for example, average monthly payments to ADC recipients were less than half those received by beneficiaries of old age assistance, aid to the blind, and aid to the permanently and totally disabled—but defended ADC's contributions to both children and motherhood:

> The program of aid to dependent children has enabled the needy parent and child to remain together in their home, and has given the children an opportunity to grow up within their own family setting and to continue their schooling. The mother or other relative caring for the children has been enabled to continue the rearing of the children and in other ways to carry the usual parental role in the family and community.

The Advisory Council on Public Welfare, appointed by Secretary of Health, Education, and Welfare Arthur Flemming in accordance with a provision of the Social Security Amendments of 1958, took note of current criticisms of ADC but concentrated on its basic flaw: denial of assistance to children living with two able-bodied parents. "A hungry ill-clothed child is as hungry and ill-clothed in an unbroken home as if he were orphaned," the council declared, and recommended that ADC be expanded "so that all needy children outside foster homes and institutions, whether they be legitimate or illegitimate, orphaned or half-orphaned, victims of a deserting parent or members of a stable healthy family, qualify under the category."[57]

Neither the Advisory Council nor the Bureau of Public Assistance, in a study ordered by the Senate Appropriations Committee in 1959, found evidence to support the notion, prevalent in legislative chambers, that women bore illegitimate children in order to obtain the meager support (less than $20 per month in a generous state) offered by ADC. The problem of illegitimacy, declared the Bureau of Public Assistance study, "long preceded the establishment of public assistance programs, and its problems are deeper than merely the availability of financial aid." Illegitimate births, numbering slightly more than 200,000 in 1957, had increased from about 4 per 100 live births in the late 1930s to 5 per 100 in 1957. At the time of the report, 16 percent (around 380,000) of the 2.37 million children receiving ADC had been born out of wedlock, and their families comprised 20 percent (600,000) of the total ADC caseload. Their support consumed $600 million of the $2 billion appropriated for ADC in 1960. More important in the long run, as events in the 1960s demonstrated, was the fact that only a fraction (one-eighth) of all the children under eighteen born out of wedlock received ADC in 1960. Many of the rest were also poor, and potential clients of ADC, or AFDC (Aid for Families of Dependent Children), as the program was renamed in 1962.[58]

If law and public opinion had permitted, public officials might have dealt with illegitimacy by providing welfare recipients with birth control information and materials. In 1960 use of public funds for contraceptive purposes—especially for unmarried women—was as controversial as use of public funds for abortions twenty years later. In lieu of birth control, states particularly adverse to supporting illegitimate children relied on the time-honored methods of social pressure and intimidation.

In 1960 nearly half (twenty-four) of the states required as a condition of eligibility for ADC that the dependent child be living in a "suitable home." Most states having such a provision used it as a means of bringing about more wholesome living conditions, continued assistance to the family while efforts were made to improve the home, or made other arrangements (for instance, foster care) for the children if improvement was impossible. A few states used the suitable home provision as a way of denying assistance to unwed mothers and their children. In the latter case, as federal officials and other critics pointed out, states punished children for their parents' behavior and protected them by denying them subsistence. In the summer of 1960, the state of Louisiana cut off aid to 23,000 children, without making any other provision for them, on the grounds that their mothers' sexual promiscuity rendered their homes unsuitable. The Department of Health, Education, and Welfare might have withheld the federal share of ADC funds from the state, thus imperiling still more children. Instead, after long negotiation, the department obtained assurances that Louisiana would modify its program to comply with federal standards. In 1961, as a result of the controversy, Secretary Flemming issued a policy statement forbidding states to impose suitable home qualifications without making adequate provision for the support of children affected by the denial of aid. The "Flemming rule," incorporated in the Public Welfare Amendments of 1962, was the most significant advance since 1945 in the protection of children's rights in the ADC program.[59]

The adult categories of public assistance—state-administered but federally aided programs for the needy aged, blind, and disabled—were less controversial than ADC. Payments were larger than under ADC, involved fewer restrictions, and carried less of a stigma than welfare. For many old people who had never worked outside the home or in jobs covered by Social Security, old age assistance provided maintenance and a measure of dignity in their own homes, in proprietary rest homes, or (after 1950) in public institutions. People receiving aid to the blind could be contributing members of their families rather than financial burdens on parents or children. Average monthly payments under aid to the blind doubled in dollar amounts between 1946 and 1960, and those for old age assistance increased 94 percent in the period. Aid to workers who became disabled before reaching retirement age, and hence, prior to eligibility for Social Security, was inaugurated by the Social Security Amendments of 1950. It was the fastest-growing of the adult public assistance programs, the number of recipients increasing 500 percent between 1950 and 1960, with average monthly payments at about the same level as those in old age assistance.[60]

Eligibility for old age assistance (but not for Social Security or veterans' or servicemen's benefits) was complicated and adversely affected by filial responsibility laws, under which twenty-one states required adult children to contribute to a needy parent's support and fourteen others withheld or reduced old age assistance to parents with adult children on the theory that the children, regardless of the needs of their own families, could and should support parents. Such laws were hard to enforce, difficult to administer, resisted by parents, and resented by children. In a comprehensive study of the problem published in 1960, Alvin Schorr called the application of filial responsibility to old age assistance an example of the conflict between poor-law principles and American ethics, the latter treating an adult's responsibility for nuture of his/her children as a more pressing obligation than the care of parents. His study showed that in the 1950s money contributions were relatively unimportant in extended families. "Helping each other with chores, visiting, and showing concern, which cannot be compelled," was the dominant pattern.[61]

Old Age and Survivors Insurance—after 1956 Old Age, Survivors, and Disability Insurance—was not only the broadest and most important of the social security programs but the one most consistent with the values of self-help and responsibility of the head of the family for support of legal dependents. Beginning in 1939 a series of amendments extended coverage to more and more workers and improved benefits to insured workers and their dependents. Despite liberalization of the retirement test (the amount of money a beneficiary could earn and still be considered to have retired) and reduction in the retirement age from 65 to 62 for widows and (with reduced benefits) for wives and working women, the basic principles of the program remained constant. Social

Security was not a general annuity system or pension program but a form of insurance intended to protect workers and their families against loss of earning caused by retirement in old age, death, or disability. It was based on work, financed by contributions of workers (including the self-employed) and employers, and benefits were determined not by need but by the individual worker's earnings and contributions. As a result of amendments adopted in 1939 and during the 1950s, OASDI was strongly family-oriented, that is, directed toward protecting those members of the family—children, wives or husbands, widows or widowers, and in a few instances parents—dependent on the workers.[62]

Even before 1960, largely because of amendments adopted in the 1950s, coverage under OASDI was nearly universal. Nine out of ten persons working in 1958 were earning credits for retirement, and nine out of ten mothers and young children had survivorship protection in the event the husband/father died. The number of children receiving survivors' benefits increased from 163,000 in the 1940s to 1,160,000 in the late 1950s. In 1959 OASDI supported approximately two-thirds of the nation's fatherless children.

In 1959 OASDI provided income for 10 million (64 percent) of the 15.7 million Americans aged 65 or older; another 1 million aged workers were fully insured under the program and could receive benefits when they retired. The total number of OASDI recipients rose from less than 1 million in 1944 to almost 14 million in 1959 and, because of increases approved in 1950, 1952, and 1954, average monthly benefit payments were substantially larger in 1960 than in 1945. Economic conditions in the 1950s made it possible for the majority of all old people to maintain independent living arrangements, but the rate of increase in independent living was larger for OASDI recipients than for the aged population as a whole.

In spite of improvements in benefits and extensions of coverage during the 1950s—the latter for the first time bringing significant numbers of blacks into the social security system—2.8 million old people (18 percent of the total aged population) were without income from earnings or social insurance in 1959, dependent on public assistance or relatives, and living with children, other relatives, or in public institutions. Even this situation represented a considerable change over conditions twenty-five years earlier when half the aged population was estimated to be dependent on friends and relatives.[64]

Expansion and liberalization of the social insurance and public assistance programs inaugurated by the Social Security Act, particularly extension of the protction and benefits of OASDI to the great majority of American workers, was about as far as postwar America was prepared to go in public action to promote family welfare and security. The period was characterized not by the development of new approaches to those problems but by realization of the prewar goal of preventing family breakup resulting from the death, retirement, disability, unemployment, or absence from the home of the primary breadwinner, ordinarily the father. Americans continued to assume that the normal family consisted of a working father and home-making mother, and neither voters nor legislators were disposed to interfere in family life, even under the guise of providing needed assistance. Even recommendations (by the Midcentury White House Conference on Children and Youth and a Senate Resolution in 1955) proposing simply *study* of the system of family allowance in effect in Canada and most Western industrialized nations went unheeded.[65]

The social consequences of family instability compounded by poverty began to be noted before the end of the 1950s.[66] The failure of Americans to deal more effectively with the problem during a familistic decade was not entirely the result of indifference or complacency. In the 1950s, as before and since, reverence for the ideal family and concern for its autonomy limited the scope of public efforts to help real families meet their responsibilities.

1. Paul C. Glick, *Some Recent Changes in American Families* (Washington, D.C., 1975), pp. 1–2; Paul C. Glick and Arthur J. Norton, "Perspectives on the Recent Upturn in Divorce and Remarriage," *Demography* 10 (1973): 301. In analyzing statistics relating to marriage and family life for the years 1939–74, Glick noted that the high or low inflection points (depending on the variable) came near the middle of the period. Live births, occurring at the rate of 19.4 per 1,000 of population in 1940, reached 26.6 per 1,000 in 1947 and remained about 24 per 1,000 during the 1950s; in 1957, at the peak of the "baby boom," 4.3 million children were born in the United States. The birth rate declined in the 1960s, and by 1973 had fallen to 15 per 1,000, even lower than in 1933. Median age at first marriage moved downward from 24.3 for men and 21.5 for women in 1940 to a record low in 1956, 22.5 years for men, 20.1 for women. In 1960 only 28 percent of American women 20–24 years of age were unmarried; a decade and a half later (1974), when the median age of first marriage for women was approximately one year older than in the mid-1950s, 40 percent of the women aged 20–24 were single. The divorce rate, relatively low in the 1930s (about 10 divorces per 1,000 married women under 44 years of age), rose steeply to 24 per 1,000 in 1946, fell to 15 per 1,000 in the mid-1950s, and climbed to 26 per 1,000 in the early 1970s.

2. Ernest W. Burgess, "The Family in a Changing Society," *American Journal of Sociology* 53 (1947–48): 417.

3. Reuben Hill, "The American Family: Problem or Solution," *American Journal of Sociology* 53:129.

4. Margaret Mead, "The Contemporary American Family as an Anthropologist Sees It," *American Journal of Sociology* 53:454.

5. Margaret Mead, "What Is Happening to the American Family?", *Journal of Social Casework* 28 (1947): 324, 328.

6. Carle Zimmerman, *Family and Civilization* (New York, 1947), p. 805; Ruth Schonle Cavan, "Regional Family Patterns: The Middle Western Family," *American Journal of Sociology* 53:431.

7. Hill, "The American Family," p. 125; Ernest Osborne, "The National Conference on Family Life," *American Journal of Sociology* 53:494; conference discussions and reports are summarized in *Survey Midmonthly* 84 (1948): 199–207.

8. "What Is Happening to the American Family," pp. 325–27.

9. William F. Ogburn, with the Assistance of Clark Tibbitts, "The Family and Its Functions," in President's Research Committee on Recent Social Trends, *Recent Social Trends in the United States*, 2 vols. (New York, 1933), 1:661; M. F. Nimkoff, *Marriage and the Family* (Boston, 1947), chap. 3, restates Ogburn's view. For a sampling of scholars' opinions on the American family at the end of World War II, see the May 1948 issue of the *American Journal of Sociology*.

10. Ernest W. Burgess and Harvey J. Locke, *The Family: From Institution to Companionship* (New York, 1945), p. vii, and Burgess, Locke, and Mary Margaret Thomas, *The Family: From Traditional to Companionship* (New York, 1971), p. v.

11. Lawrence K. Frank, "What Families Do for the Nation," *American Journal of Sociology* 53:471.

12. Paul C. Glick, "The Life Cycle of the Family," *Marriage and Family Living* 17 (1955): 3.

13. Henry C. Lajewski, *Child Care of Full-Time Working Mothers* (Washington, D.C., 1959), quoted in Robert H. Bremner et al., eds., *Children and Youth in America: A Documentary History*, 3 vols. (Cambridge, Mass., 1970–74), 3:701–2, hereafter cited as *Children and Youth*; Judith Cauman, "What Is Happening in Day Care: New Concepts, Current Practice, and Trends," *Child Welfare* 35 (1956), quoted in *Children and Youth*, 3:697; and Gertrude L. Hoffman, comp., *Day Care Services: Form and Substance. A Report of a Conference, November 17–18, 1960* (Washington, D.C., 1960), quoted in *Children and Youth*, 3:705. Guggenheimer was president of the National Committee for the Day Care of Children.

14. "What Is Happening to the American Family," p. 329; for attitudes on "woman's place" and distribution of tasks and responsibilities within the family, see William H. Chafe, *The American Woman: Her Changing Social, Economic, and Political Role, 1920–1970* (London, 1972), pp. 199–225.

15. "Live the Life of McCall's," *McCall's*, May 1954, pp. 29, 35.

16. Gerald Gurin, Joseph Veroff, and Sheila Feld, *Americans View Their Mental Health* (New York, 1960), pp. xi–xiii, 130. The Joint Commission on Mental Illness and Health was a nongovernmental, nonprofit, multidisciplinary organization composed of thirty-six national agencies concerned with mental health.

17. Ibid., pp. 132–33; Gurin, Veroff, and Feld state (pp. 141–42): "We would expect this concern over the relationship with the child is a more prominent aspect of the father's role today than it was a generation or two ago, and that in their expression of this concern, the fathers in our sample are reflecting what are recent cultural emphases in this area"; cf. David Riesman, *The Lonely Crowd: A Study of the Changing American Culture* (New Haven, Conn., 1950), p. 53: "The other-directed parent . . . has to win not only his child's good behavior but also his child's good will."

18. Ruth Benedict, "The Family: Genus Americanum," in Ruth Nanda Anshen, ed., *The Family: Its Function and Destiny* (New York, 1949), p. 165. For another view of

American family relationships, see Erik H. Erikson, *Childhood and Society* (New York, 1950), pp. 254–55.

19. Thomas H. Leonard, *Day By Day: The Forties* (New York, 1977), p. 793; *New Republic* 116 (1947): 8; *Time*, 25 August 1958, p. 51, *Newsweek*, 4 August 1958, p. 48, and 29 September 1958, p. 81.

20. Norman St. John-Stevas, *Birth Control and Public Policy* (Santa Barbara, Calif., 1960), pp. 16–22; St. John-Stevas was also author of *Life, Death, and the Law: Christian Morals in England and the United States* (Bloomington, Ind., 1961).

21. St. John-Stevas, *Birth Control and Public Policy*, pp. 26–28; "The Accident of Birth," *Fortune*, February 1938, pp. 83–84; James Reed, "Katharine Dexter McCormick" and "Margaret Sanger," in *Notable American Women: The Modern Period*, ed. Barbara Sicherman and Carol Hurd Green (Cambridge, Mass., 1980), pp. 441–42, 623–27; "What Do You Think of Birth Control?", *Woman's Home Companion*, July 1948, pp. 7–8. On the 1955 survey see Ronald Freedman, Pascal K. Wheepton, and Arthur A. Campbell, *Family Planning, Sterility, and Population Growth* (New York, 1959), pp. 57–62.

22. Benjamin Spock, M.D., *The Common Sense Book of Baby and Child Care* (New York, 1945), pp. 2–3. Spock explained that he referred to the baby as "he" or "him" in order to reserve use of "she" and "her" for the mother.

23. Reisman, *The Lonely Crowd*, pp. 38–39; Spock, *Baby and Child Care*, pp. 4, 20–21; Hildegarde Dolson, "Who Is Doctor Spock?", *Ladies Home Journal*, March 1960, pp. 135–36.

24. U.S., Children's Bureau, *Infant Care* (Washington, D.C., 1929), pp. 1, 3. Eliot was successively director of the child-hygiene division of the Children's Bureau, assistant chief, and from 1951 to 1956, chief.

25. U.S., Children's Bureau, *Infant Care* (Washington, D.C., 1945), p. 1; U.S., Children's Bureau, *Infant Care* (Washington, D.C., 1951), pp. 8–9; U.S., Children's Bureau, *The Story of Infant Care* (Washington, D.C., 1963), p. 18.

26. Geoffrey Gorer, *The American People: A Study in National Character* (New York, 1948), p. 73; *The Story of Infant Care*, p. 18.

27. C. Anderson Aldrich and Mary M. Aldrich, *Babies Are Human Beings: An Interpretation of Growth* (New York: 1947), pp. 113–14 (first published 1938). On Aldrich see "Presentation of the Lasker Award in Mental Hygiene," *Mental Hygiene* 33 (1949): 123–24, and an obituary by George F. Munns, *Child Development* 20 (1949): 169–71.

28. William H. Whyte, *The Organization Man* (New York, 1956), p. 378. Landon Y. Jones, *Great Expectations: America and the Baby Boom Generation* (New York, 1980), p. 1.

29. August B. Hollingshead, *Elmtown's Youth: The Impact of Social Classes in Adolescence* (New York, 1949), pp. 439–43.

30. Riesman, *The Lonely Crowd*, pp. 36–55; Mead, "The American Family as an Anthropologist Sees It," p. 458.

31. James S. Coleman, *The Adolescent Society: The Social Life of the Teenager and Its Impact on Education* (New York, 1961), pp. 1–3; 311–13; Talcott Parsons and Winston White, "The Link Between Character and Society," in Seymour Martin Lipset and Leo Lowenthal, eds., *Culture and Social Character: The Work of David Riesman Reviewed* (New York, 1961), pp. 117–19.

32. Coleman, *Adolescent Society*, p. 3.

33. Jones, *Great Expectations*, p. 1.

34. Bailey B. Burritt, "Welfare Measures and Their Effect upon the Family," *American Journal of Public Health and the Nation's Health* 39 (1949): 214–15. Burritt's comments were part of a round-table discussion at the Twenty-Fifth Annual Conference of the Milbank Memorial Fund, 17–18 November 1948.

35. "Remarks at the National Conference on Family Life, May 6, 1948," *Public Papers of the Presidents of the United States: Harry S. Truman, 1948* (Washington, D.C., 1964), pp. 246–47.

36. "Letter to the Speaker on the Housing Bill, June 17, 1949," ibid., *1949* (Washington, D.C., 1964), pp. 301, 305.

37. Public Law 171, 63 Stat. 413 (1949).

38. *Public Papers of the Presidents of the United States: Harry S. Truman, 1949*, p. 381, ibid. *1950* (Washington, D.C., 1965), pp. 525–26.

39. Leonard Freedman, *Public Housing: The Politics of Poverty* (New York, 1969), pp. 2, 6.

40. Anthony Downs, "The Impact of Housing Policies on Family Life in the United States since World War II," *Daedalus* 106 (Spring 1977): 168; U.S., Interdepartmental Committee on Children and Youth, *Children in a Changing World: A Book of Charts* (Washington, D.C., 1960), pp. 8–9, 47; Congressional Quarterly Service, *Congress and the Nation*, 4 vols. to date (Washington, D.C., 1965–77), 1:459–62.

41. Downs, "The Impact of Housing Policies on Family Life," pp. 168–69, 171–74; Mead, "The Contemporary Family as an Anthropologist Sees It," p. 454; "Live the Life of McCall's," p. 29.

42. U.S., Bureau of the Census, *Historical Statistics of the United States, Colonial Times to 1970*, 2 vols. (Washington, D.C., 1975), 1:57.

43. "Close of the EMIC Program," *American Journal of Public Health* 29 (1949): 1579–81. The total amount appropriated for EMIC 1943–48 was $133.5 million (*Congress and the Nation*, 1:1286).

44. Harry S. Truman, "Special Message to the Congress Recommending a Comprehensive Health Program, November 19, 1945," *Public Papers of the Presidents of the United States: Harry S. Truman, 1945* (Washington, D.C., 1961), pp. 475–85.

45. American Academy of Pediatrics, Committee for the Study of Child Health Services and Pediatric Education, *Child Health Services and Pediatric Education* (New York, 1949), quoted in *Children and Youth*, 3:1283–91.

46. For the Wagner-Murray-Dingell and Pepper bills, see, *Children and Youth*, 3:1267–73.

47. Ibid., p. 1208; for authorization and appropriations for Title V programs, 1936–64, see *Congress and the Nation*, 1:1286.

48. Katherine B. Oettinger, "Title V of the Social Security Act: What It Has Meant to Children," *Social Security Bulletin*, August 1960, p. 49; Mildred Arnold, "The Growth of Child Welfare Services," *Children* 7 (1960): 131–35; for effect of federal policies on foster care, see Gilbert Y. Steiner, *The Futility of Family Policy* (Washington, D.C., 1980), pp. 135–37.

49. "Care of Infants Whose Mothers Are Employed: Policies Recommended by the Children's Bureau," *Child* 9 (1945): 132; on day care under the Lanham Act, see Mary-Elizabeth Pidgeon, *Employed Mothers and Child Care* (Washington, D.C., 1953), pp. 18–20.

50. Pidgeon, *Employed Mothers and Child Care*, p. 20; U.S., Interdepartmental Committee on Children and Youth, *Planning Services for Children of Employed Mothers* (Washington, D.C., 1953), pp. 10–14.

51. Lajewski, *Child Care of Full Time Working Mothers*, quoted in *Children and Youth*, 3:701–3; Cauman, "What Is Happening in Day Care," quoted in *Children and Youth*, 3:701.

52. Spock, *Baby and Child Care*, p. 484.

53. *Children and Youth*, 3:531–34; Gilbert Y. Steiner, *Social Insecurity: The Politics of Welfare* (Chicago, 1966), p. 46; cf. Charles I. Schottland, "Toward Greater Security in Childhood," *Social Security Bulletin*, April 1955, p. 3.

54. *Historical Statistics of the United States*, 1:356; Public Law 734, 64 Stat. 550 (1950); Joel F. Handler, *Reforming the Poor: Welfare Policy, Federalism, and Morality* (New York, 1972), pp. 30–32.

55. *Congress and the Nation*, 1:1276–77.

56. *Historical Statistics of the United States*, 1:356–57.

57. Kathryn D. Goodwin, "Twenty-five Years of Public Assistance," *Social Security Bulletin*, August 1960, p. 35; "Public Assistance: Report of the Advisory Council," *Social Security Bulletin*, February 1960, pp. 11–12.

58. U.S., Bureau of Public Assistance, *Illegitimacy and Its Impact on the Aid to Dependent Children Program* (Washington, D.C., 1960), pp. iii, 60.

59. Winifred Bell, *Aid to Dependent Children* (New York, 1965), pp. 57–59; Steiner, *Social Insecurity*, pp. 122–25; *Children and Youth*, 3:576–89.

60. *Historical Statistics of the United States*, 1:356–57; *Congress and the Nation*, 1:1276–77; W. Andrew Achenbaum, *Old Age in the New Land: The American Experience since 1790* (Baltimore, 1978), p. 151.

61. Alvin L. Schorr, *Filial Responsibility in the Modern American Family* (Washington, D.C., 1960), pp. 18–19, 22–24.

62. Charles I. Schottland, "Government Economic Programs and Family Life," *Journal of Marriage and the Family* 29 (1967): 95–97; Colin C. Blaydon and Carol B. Stack, "Income Support Policies and the Family," *Daedalus* 106 (1977): 149. Schorr, *Filial Responsibility*, p. 22, pointed out that in 1959 only 35,000 of the 10,000,000 persons receiving payment from OASDI were dependent parents; their number was expected to decline even further as more people became entitled to benefits based on their own or their spouses' earnings.

63. Neota Larson, "Family Security under Old-Age and Survivors Insurance," *Marriage and Family Living* 20 (1958): 224–25; Ida C. Merriam, "Social Security Status of the American People," *Social Security Bulletin*, August 1960, pp. 9, 13. The Social Security Amendments of 1956 provided for benefit payments to severely disabled children (if disabled before age eighteen) of deceased and retired workers; the amendments of 1958 made benefits availabel to dependents of disabled workers on the same basis as those for dependents of workers retired because of old age.

64. Merriam, "Social Security Status," pp. 8, 11; Schorr, *Filial Responsibility*, pp. 19–20; Larson, "Family Security," p. 229.

65. "Recommendations of the Midcentury White House Conference on Children and Youth," *Social Security Bulletin* 14 (1951): 13; James C. Vadakian, *Family Allowances: An Analysis of Their Development and Implications* (Coral Gables, Fla., 1958), p. 3.

66. See, for example, Harrison Salisbury, *The Shook-Up Generation* (New York, 1958).

The Survival of American Feminism:
The Women's Movement in the Postwar Period

Leila J. Rupp

Domesticity, motherhood, suburbia: the image we hold of American women's lives in the 1950s is a powerful one, little examined but widely accepted.* Betty Friedan's coining of the term "the feminine mystique" in 1963 catapulted her to fame and solidified the image of the 1950s as a period of super-domesticity for American women.[1] Feminism has no place in the image: in terms of women's movement activity, these are reputed to have been "the bleak and lonely years."[2] And yet out of these years of baby boom, flight to the suburbs, cold war, and McCarthyism emerged a new women's movement composed of groups and organizations stretching from the respectably liberal to the solidly radical, a social movement about whose origins we know very little. The radical feminist branch of the movement grew in the late 1960s from its roots in civil rights and the New Left, but the liberal feminist branch flowered first, and this has been little studied.[3]

The contemporary women's movement did not emerge in the 1960s out of barren ground, despite the traditional assumption that the movement died in 1920 with the winning of the vote. Although it is true

* The research for this essay was made possible by a 1978–79 research grant and a 1979–80 research leave from the Ohio State University, and a 1979–80 fellowship from the Radcliffe Research Scholars Program. I would like to thank the following individuals for reading and commenting on drafts of this paper: Ami Bar-On, Carl Brauer, George Cotkin, Cynthia Harrison, Susan Hartmann, Rebecca Klatch, Frances Kolb, Donna Lenhoff, Beth Litwak, Tahi Mottl, Gary Reichard, and Warren Van Tine. I am especially grateful to Verta Taylor for sharing her knowledge and interpretation of social movement theory with me and for commenting extensively on successive drafts of this paper.

that the large organized suffrage movement splintered after the suffrage victory, movement activity continued throughout the post-1920 decades. Historians have begun to explore feminism and the women's movement in the interwar period, but the assumption that the post-World War II period was devoid of feminist activity has held.[4] In fact, the women's movement continued to exist in the years after 1945, although not as a powerful mass movement, and an analysis of feminism and the women's movement in this period is essential to an understanding of the resurgence of the movement in the 1960s.

This essay explores some roots of the contemporary movement by examining, first, the societal context of middle-class women's lives, and, second, the characteristics of the women's movement in the postwar period. It briefly describes the heightened conflict between the traditional ideology of "woman's place" and the reality of the ever increasing employment outside the home of married middle-class women with children, as well as the conflict between work and family roles so familiar to poor women and women of color, but newly experienced by large numbers of white middle-class women in the postwar years. It then considers why discontent did not lead to mass feminist protest by exploring the antifeminist backlash and the nature of the women's movement, focusing especially on the feminist group culture created within the National Woman's Party, an elite organization that served as the core of the women's movement. Feminism in the 1950s remained primarily a white middle-class matter, so, although issues of class and race are crucial to an analysis of the women's movement, the focus here is on white middle-class women. Although this essay attempts neither an overview of American women's history nor a comprehensive explanation for the rise of the contemporary women's movement, its exploraiton of feminism and the women's movement suggests some new perspectives on women's history in the period 1945 to 1960.

THE PARADOX OF "WOMAN'S PLACE"

World War II brought millions of women into the labor force for the first time, moved millions from their old jobs into ones previously reserved for men, and opened up the military to women. The end of the war brought a concerted effort to push women out of their new jobs to make room for returning veterans.[5] One of the weapons—less direct than the immediate postwar layoffs of women in industry—in the battle to return to prewar ways was the intensification of propaganda designed to sell women their "place." The "Happy Housewife" of the 1950s is an image so familiar it can only be belabored: the smiling, pretty, suburban matron, devoted mother of three, loyal wife, good housekeeper, excellent cook.[6] Like all American social imagery, especially in the conformist 1950s, it is an image determinedly white and middle-class, in total disregard of the diversity of American women, and thus a typical product of the "snow blindness" and middle-class myopia of American society.[7]

Betty Friedan presented the feminine mystique as a new phenomenon created in the postwar period, when in fact it was simply the postwar version of the traditional ideal, a successor to nineteenth-century "True Womanhood."[8] The assumptions behind the traditional image of women are fairly simple: women and men differ in fundamental ways, since biological differences have profound social and psychological consequences; therefore, "woman's place" in society centers on the home and family and the complementary roles of wifehood and motherhood. Women's magazines, along with television, commercial films, and advertising, sold the ideology of "woman's place," and thus provide a clear picture of the cultural ideal set up for women.[9] A 1948 *Good Housekeeping* article, "Most Likely to Succeed," summed up the message in typical fashion: success for women meant marriage and family, not brilliance, so that the college woman with a C-average was in fact "more likely to succeed" than the extraordinarily intelligent woman so voted by her classmates.[10] Put another way in *Ladies Home Journal*, a woman loved and needed by a man would become "the fragile, feminine, dependent, but priceless creature every man wants his wife to be." Using revealing commercial metaphors, the author noted that there is "actual cash value" in being kind to women, since a happy wife is an "asset" and the proper actions will pay "immediate and lasting dividends."[11] Numerous articles lauded traditional domesticity in an attempt to glorify the housewife's role. From "I'd Hate to Be a Man" to "I'm Lucky! Lucky!," the magazines told women that, despite what their own experience might tell them about life in patriarchal society, it was better to be a woman.[12]

The concept of "woman's place" found legitimacy not only through its long tradition but also, in the 1950s, in the developing intellectual school of functionalism, which gave added and scholarly weight to the traditional division of labor. The functionalist perspective, which grew out of the attempt to apply the "objectivity" of the natural sciences to the social sciences, seeks to analyze social behavior or institutions in terms of the consequences or functions they have for maintaining the larger society or social system in which they exist. But functionalism rapidly developed into a conservative school of thought that scholars used to pronounce the status quo the best possible arrangement. For functionalists American society required the traditional division of labor between women and men; society functioned best with women in the home caring for the children while men brought home the bread.[13]

The feminine mystique, then, was simply the traditional ideal dressed up in 1950s garb. The irony was that conformance to the ideal, which had never been possible for women in the labor force, was out of the question for increasingly large numbers of middle-class women as the decade progressed.

The postwar period saw a continuation and acceleration of the long-term trend of increased employment of women outside the home. The labor force participation rate—the percentage of all women fourteen years and older in the labor force—grew from 25.4 percent in 1940 to 29.0 percent in 1950 to 34.5 percent in 1960.[14] But even more importantly, the composition of the female labor force changed in the postwar period from predominantly young and single to older and married. This too represented a long-term trend toward the employment of older married women, but the postwar period saw the firm establishment of the new pattern. What these changes meant, translated into the lives of individual women, was that more and more women returned to work after, or remained at work while, raising families. Even married middle-class women worked outside the home. In fact, the improved standard of living for the middle class depended on the employment of women, and many families attained middle-class status only through the earnings of the woman.[15] As employment outside the home increasingly became commonplace for middle-class women, as it had been for poorer women and women of color, the justification tended to be financial need—need not for bread alone but for a second car, a house in the suburbs, a college education for the children.

Just because more and more women went to work outside the home and contributed their earnings to the family income does not mean that public attitudes had changed. Although the public had rather readily accepted the need for women's labor during the war emergency, postwar opinion continued to disapprove of the employment of married women. In 1945 only 18 percent of a Gallup poll sample approved of a married woman working if she had a husband capable of supporting her. Attitudes did begin to change—by 1967, 44 percent approved when asked the same question—but it is clear that no wholesale reversal of traditional notions had occurred as a result of the war.[16]

The increased labor force participation of middle-class women came at a time when these women's reproductive roles also expanded. The postwar baby boom resulted from women marrying younger and bearing more children. Fewer married women remained childless—only 6.8 percent in the 1950s compared with 14 percent in the 1900s—and the number of women bearing second and third children increased enough to raise the birthrate from 86 offspring per 1,000 women of childbearing age in 1945 to 123 in 1957.[17] Women began their childbearing earlier and lived an increasing number of years after their children had grown. Many women returned to work after completing their child-rearing responsibilities, but even mothers of young children were moving into the labor force. In 1950 twelve percent of women with children under six years were employed, and this figure increased to nineteen percent by 1960. In 1955 thirty-five percent of women with children six years and older worked.[18] Employed mothers of young children still tended to come more frequently from lower-income families, but clearly the domestic ideal fit with the daily reality of ever fewer women. Although the traditional picture of middle-class women isolated in the home while their children were young is not wholly inaccurate, more and more women began to work during the years of their children's growth. No wonder that a *Ladies' Home Journal* survey showed that twice as many adults believed that women's lives were harder than men's than vice versa.[19]

Accompanying the baby boom was a renewed emphasis on family life. Suburbanization underscored the existence of the nuclear family as a discrete unit by eliminating old family and neighborhood ties, often leading to isolation for women who did not work outside the home.[20] Women's magazines pushed "togetherness" for the suburban family, and a "do-it-yourself" craze encouraged leisure-time pursuits within the four walls of home. Critics denounced suburbia as a "matriarchy," but despite a daytime world of women and children, the family, husband in command, remained the essential unit. Child care, ever the woman's responsibility, became more difficult for the employed woman with a large family. Women juggled their roles with little or no help from the government, which quickly scrapped the meager day care programs that had been set up during the war. In addition the 1950s brought a new emphasis on the quality of child-rearing, including the encouragement of breast feeding, a popularized Freudian notion of the crucial importance of a child's first years, and the emergence of a new corps of child-rearing experts, including Dr. Spock, who warned of the dire consequences of anything less than full time attention from a mother for her children's well-being.[21] All of this came at least partly in response to factors that limited the time spent in child care, such as the development of commercially prepared infant food, the increase in kindergarten attendance, and, despite the propaganda for breast-feeding, the massive shift to bottle-feeding (from 35 percent of mothers in 1946 to 63 percent in 1956).[22]

Even the sex object of the 1950s, the full-breasted Marilyn Monroe type, emphasized the physical attributes of motherhood. Although the Kinsey report on female sexuality that appeared in 1953 amid a flurry of publicity in the women's magazines dealt with women's sexual fulfillment, the sexual ideology of the 1950s continued to subordinate women's sexuality to reproduction.[23]

The contradictions between the ideal and reality for even white middle-class women, as well as the conflicts between work and family roles created by increasing labor force participation and the rising birthrate, gave rise to an atmosphere of dissatisfaction among American women. Marilyn French's contemporary novel *The Women's Room* explores the discontent of middle-class suburban women in the 1950s; judging by the popularity of the book and its rapid transformation into a television movie, it struck a responsive chord among American women.[24] Even at the time, the media assumed that American women had a problem. In 1947 *Life* defined the American woman's dilemma in terms of her decision whether or not to work, assuming that housewifery alone could not keep a woman abreast of her husband's interests, although admitting that full-time work combined with motherhood could prove exhausting.[25] In 1949 *Life* proclaimed that "suddenly and for no plain reason the women of the United States were seized with an eerie restlessness," and went on to picture women filing for divorce, beating their husbands, appearing in public in scanty clothing, and swimming the English Channel.[26] A special issue of *Life* in 1956 focused on the problems of American women. The introduction suggested that those problems might be the consequence of a preoccupation with rights, since women no longer seemed to cherish their "privileges," which *Life* defined as femininity, childbearing, and devotion to beauty. "Historians of the future may speak of the 20th Century as 'the era of the feminist revolution,' " *Life* proclaimed.[27]

The culmination of the scattered reports of dissatisfaction came when Betty Friedan discovered in 1956 and 1957 that her Smith College alumnae classmates were often discontented, troubled, perhaps even wretched. These highly educated women found housework and childrearing insufficient outlets for their energy. Fearing just such an outcome from higher education for women, Mills College president Lynn White, Jr., in his 1950 book *Educating Our Daughters*, had urged a college education for women that would prepare them for marriage and motherhood.[28] Advertisers—the "captains of consciousness" who sought to expand markets by manipulating consumers—urged women to find fulfillment through buying. Television, the powerful new medium of the 1950s, depended on advertising revenues, and thus the advertisers' attempt to sell products by capitalizing on personal discontent not only reached an unprecedented mass audience but also controlled the programming itself.[29] Not coincidentally, television images of women reinforced the traditional stereotypes. Consumerism assigned American women the weighty task of buying and eased the crisis of overproduction that beset the American economic system, but did not solve women's problems.[30]

Why, then, did women not rise up in the 1950s to demand changes that would ease their burdens? Heightened conflict between work and family roles, as well as the contradiction between social imagery and reality, made middle-class women likely prospects for discontent and rebellion. American women were not content and complacent in the 1950s, but discontent alone is not sufficient to generate a revolt.[31] We need to look at other factors that may have kept a mass women's movement from forming. One of these was a powerful and pervasive antifeminist backlash, the existence of which suggests that the potential for revolt was real and that feminism had survived the demise of the mass suffrage movement in the 1920s.

ANTIFEMINISM, FEMINISM, AND THE WOMEN'S MOVEMENT

Feminism is an ideology with a long history and broad scope. With roots in the eighteenth-century application of Enlightenment ideas to women and current development in the direction of socialist feminism, cultural feminism, and lesbian feminism, the ideology covers a vast territory. For the purposes of this essay, feminism can be defined as a world view that ranks gender as a primary, if not necessarily exclusive, explanatory factor and/or category of analysis for understanding the unequal distribution of power and resources in society; integral to this world view is a commitment to changing that unequal distribution. Feminists may hold differing views of the origins of inequality that lead to entirely different solutions, but their feminism provides them with elements of a common conceptual framework and a basic perception of women *as a group*.[32]

Feminism originated and developed in the Western world as a middle-class ideology that, in its early form, asserted the equality of middle-class women with middle-class men. That is, it originated as an extension of the ideology of liberalism and individualism to women, and historically its appeal was to middle-class women, although some upper-class and working-class women also embraced feminism and joined feminist movements. In the United States, feminism gained adherents in the mid-nineteenth century as a consequence of the tensions created by the growth of industrial capitalism. The suffrage movement, which espoused a feminist ideology in its early years, grew away from that ideology as it increased in size and effectiveness. The much-lamented "death of feminism" in the post-suffrage period was in reality the splintering of a mass women's movement that had already shed much of its feminist ideology by 1920.[33]

By 1945 the mass women's movement of the suffrage struggle had long since disintegrated because the goal so intently focused upon had finally been achieved and because the fundamental disagreement between feminists and reformers broke open over the Equal Rights Amendment.[34] The National Woman's Party, the militant suffragist group that demonstrated in front of the White House during World War I, first introduced the ERA in 1923. Throughout the first decades of its existence, the ERA provoked strong opposition from women and women's organizations, particularly those associated with labor, that believed in equality for women but did not agree that a constitutional amendment was the method by which it should be obtained. They believed that the ERA would hurt women by eliminating protective legislation, including the hard-won minimum wage and maximum hours laws, whereas the amendment's supporters believed that such laws discriminated against women. The conflict centered on the best way for women to win equal rights and involved a dispute over the fundamental meaning of equality.

World War II encouraged leaders of women's organizations and women prominent in government and public life to expect major improvements in women's status in American society. The ERA, for example, began to receive national publicity during the war, leading its backers to believe that it would pass Congress by 1944 and win ratification by 1948. But the cold war atmosphere of the postwar years did not create an environment hospitable to social protest in any form.

The end of the war brought, instead of gains for women, a vicious antifeminist backlash. Even before the fighting ended, a *Life* editorial attacked the wartime performance of American women and accused too many of being helpless and hopeless, lazy, apathetic, and ill-informed.[35] Returning GIs, in a manner reminiscent of the post–World War I period, lamented their return to American women after their experiences with the more "womanly" European women who sought to please their men.[36] In the tradition of Philip Wylie, author of the venomous attack on American mothers, *Generation of Vipers*, a psychiatric consultant to the secretary of war blamed women for the shockingly high number of men rejected for military service on psychological grounds.[37] Both feminists and antifeminists seized upon the poor mental health of American boys to prove their points. The feminists argued that women frustrated by the limitations of their traditional roles produced overprotected and neurotic sons, and the antifeminists countered that the problem lay precisely in women's rejection of traditional roles: if only women would renounce feminist goals and devote themselves to wifehood and motherhood, all would be well in American society.

The most influential attack on feminism came from Ferdinand Lundberg and Marynia Farnham, authors of *Modern Woman: The Lost Sex*.[38] From a Freudian perspective Lundberg and Farnham analyzed feminists as severe neurotics responsible for the problems of American society and urged federally subsidized psychoanalysis, cash subsidies for motherhood, and other measures to restore American women, and thus the American family, to health. The impact of *Modern Woman* was far-reaching. A 1950 study of the feminist movement described Marynia Farnham as "possibly the most frequently quoted writer on the modern woman."[39] A *Ladies' Home Journal* article noted the increasing attacks on women and cited Wylie's "Momism" and *Modern Woman*.[40] Feminists viewed the Farnham book with alarm. The National Woman's Party called a special meeting to decide on strategy for countering the threat, and one party member believes that the book set the movement back a decade.[41] Mary Beard, author of *Woman as Force in History*, wrote to the president of Radcliffe College out of concern for the impact of the book on Harvard men.[42]

Lundberg and Farnham were by no means alone in their denunciations of feminism. A "noted figure in criminal psychopathology," for example, explained in *Collier's* why women's progress toward emancipation was dangerous and why women did not want full equality under the law.[43] *This Week*, the magazine distributed nationwide in Sunday newspapers, carried an article by a Barnard College sociologist who argued the need for women to give up their jobs, bear children for the good of the race, and submit to the personal ascendancy of men.[44]

The antifeminist backlash had wide-ranging ramifications in the media. One woman, in a *Good Housekeeping* article, condemned women for treating each other so badly. In a classic blame-the-victim analysis, she attributed sex discrimination to "feminine malice and pettiness."[45]

Ladies' Home Journal carried an article entitled "Should Women Vote?," thereby questioning the only major advance women had made in the twentieth century.[46] An angry letter to the editor of the Washington Star complained about a feature on Anna Lord Strauss, president of the League of Women Voters: "Whenever I see these smug pictures of women who have abdicated their normal functions and entered the field of politics and the like I instinctively say failure and slacker. Such women have flunked at their own jobs and yet pretend to tell men what they should do in their normal field."[47] In the same vein a syndicated newspaper article attacked Sally Butler, president of the National Federation of Business and Professional Women's Clubs (BPW), as the "boss-lady of the National Federation," noting that "this rebellion has been growing since the war. . . . One of these days the ladies are going to have to decide between the kitchen or the council chamber."[48]

Even women who had once identified as feminists jumped on the antifeminist bandwagon. In a manner reminiscent of the confessions of former feminists that had appeared in the media after World War I and the suffrage victory, they declared that feminism was dead.[49] Dorothy Thompson, journalist and radio commentator, herself full of contradictions, proclaimed her belief in the superiority of men.[50] Writer Cornelia Otis Skinner lashed out at "those 'what-women-are-doing' enthusiasts who still go under the outdated term of feminists."[51] Doris Fleischman, a successful public relations counsel who had kept her own name while married for twenty-six years, explained in "Notes of a Retiring Feminist" why she decided to give it up.[52]

As a consequence of the antifeminist backlash, the label "feminist" took on a pejorative cast and was assiduously avoided by most women, even those working toward equality, with some significant exceptions. The negative connotations were by no means entirely new in the postwar period. Already in the 1920s feminism had come to evoke militance, prudishness in sexual matters, and a seriousness out of tune with the Roaring Twenties. During World War II prominent women believed that equality would be won without the agitation of "a militant sisterhood," or, as Margaret Hickey, president of the BPW put it, that "the days of the old, selfish, strident feminism are over."[53] In the public eye feminism had become "as quaint as linen dusters and high button shoes."[54]

It is not surprising, then, that few individuals or organizations openly identified as feminist. The League of Women Voters, for example, explicitly disavowed feminism and even denied any particular concern with women's issues. Anna Lord Strauss, president of the league from

1944 to 1950, complained to her office staff, for example, "If I hear much more about women's rights I am going to turn into a violent anti-feminist."[55] Throughout the 1950s the league asserted that it was a citizen's group rather than a women's organization, and even considered changing its name to the "League of Active Voters."[56] The league withdrew in 1951 from the International Alliance of Women, an organization with roots in the nineteenth-century women's movement, because it was too feminist; left the Women's Joint Congressional Committee, a coalition lobbying group that opposed the ERA, because it did not want to be affiliated solely with women's organizations; and even dropped opposition to the ERA from its program in 1954 because it did not seem important and the membership knew little about it. The league was a solidly liberal organization that, like the country's most prominent liberal woman, Eleanor Roosevelt, rejected a feminist identification while serving as an example of what women could do in leadership roles.

Although the backlash threatened feminism, it did not destroy it. A number of diverse groups and individuals working for feminist reforms continued to constitute a movement, although it was not a monolithic, unified, mass movement with a common ideology and leadership. Recent social movement theory suggests that movements are often comprised of a number of relatively independent movement organizations that differ in ideology, goals, and tactics; are characterized by a decentralized leadership; and are loosely connected by multiple and overlapping membership, friendship networks, and cooperation in working for a common goal.[57] The women's movement in the postwar period fits this pattern, with the National Woman's Party (NWP) serving as a kind of core of the movement. An analysis of the characteristics of the women's movement, and particularly of the NWP, helps to explain why the movement did not mobilize masses of women in the 1940s and 1950s.

Founded by Alice Paul as a militant suffrage organization, the NWP was a small elite organization with 4,000 to 5,500 members on paper in the period between 1945 and 1960, 600 to 800 of these listed as active (active membership meant that a woman paid yearly dues of ten dollars). By constitutional provision, only women could join. The membership was composed of a high proportion of professional women, especially lawyers, some leisured upper-class women, and a few workers. The party consisted almost entirely of white women, although Mary Church Terrell, founder of the National Association of Colored Women, did belong. The NWP was a single-issue organization on an unswerving course toward its goal of legal equality. Year after year, it worked to have the ERA introduced in Congress, questioned candidates on their position on the ERA, built the list of congressional sponsors, fought to keep the ERA in all major party platforms (the Republican platform first included it in 1940, the Democratic platform in 1944), lobbied senators and representatives, sought the endorsements of other organizations, pressured the appropriate subcommittees, pressured the full committees, lobbied again—always, until 1972, to no avail, but always without losing hope.

It was an elite group that dwindled over the years as the older members died. Some of the members were socially and politically conservative, as well as anti-Semitic and racist. While the League of Women Voters and the American Association of University Women struggled in the 1950s with the question of integration within local branches, the issue rarely arose for the NWP, and the party steadfastly refused to connect its struggle in any positive way with the burgeoning civil rights movement. Party members, some of whom applauded McCarthy's witch hunt, used the Communist Party's opposition to the ERA to try to win support for the amendment from anti-Communist groups and individuals.[58] Not all NWP members shared a racist and conservative attitude—the major fact about the party was that the only common bond was commitment to feminism and the ERA—but the party gained a reputation based on the most unsavory attitudes of its members.

The NWP was small, but it had an influence out of all proportion to its numbers. This was not because it was well liked; to the contrary, most of the other women's organizations detested the party (especially if they opposed the ERA) or at best mistrusted it, either because of the conservative politics of its members (and especially Alice Paul) or because they disliked its proprietary attitude toward the ERA and feared that it would rather see the amendment go down to defeat than relinquish leadership of the struggle. But no individual or group concerned with women's issues could ignore it because of its persistence and perseverance.

A variety of groups fought the party because they opposed the ERA. The American Association of University Women, for example, worked to win opportunities for women in education and employment and sought to win policy-making positions for women, but opposed the ERA and the NWP. The Women's Bureau of the Department of Labor spearheaded the opposition to the ERA and the National Woman's Party, but sought to improve the lives of working women through other means.

Some of the groups that supported the ERA attempted to cooperate with the National Woman's Party. The BPW worked actively, lobbying and trying to win the support of other organizations, throughout the postwar period.[59] It launched a special top-priority lobbying campaign in 1953–54, "Operation Buttonhole," aimed at getting the ERA through Congress. Representatives from the BPW and the NWP met occasionally to plan strategy, although party members who belonged to the BPW sometimes complained that the business and professional women were not devoted enough to the ERA, and BPW officials often blamed NWP jealousy and ineffectiveness for the lack of progress.[60] The General Federation of Women's Clubs, the largest women's organization in the country, also supported the ERA, if not as actively as the BPW. The party set up and dominated the Women's Joint Legislative Committee for Equal Rights (the counterpart of the anti-ERA Women's Joint Congressional Committee), supposedly a coalition of women's organizations that supported the ERA. Such tactics led to charges that the NWP jealously guarded its leadership of the ERA forces and refused to cooperate with other organizations—which was, to some extent, true, and is typical of exclusive and highly committed groups.[61]

Other backers of the ERA refused ties with the NWP, sometimes breaking off from the party, but found themselves relying on the party for information and even, at times, guidance. Florence L. C. Kitchelt, a liberal and League of Women Voters founder, converted in 1943 from opposition to support of the ERA and promptly joined the NWP. She rather quickly found herself embroiled in a major conflict within the group and soon resigned, devoting her efforts to her own organization, the Connecticut Committee for the Equal Rights Amendment. Although she consistently and publicly denied that the Connecticut Committee had any ties to the NWP, she kept in contact and relied on the party publications for information. She tried to encourage the formation of similar state committees throughout the country—successfully in the case of Massachusetts—as an alternative to the NWP; but, despite her distaste for the party, she occasionally considered rejoining and never broke off entirely. She kept in touch with former party members, forming a network of pro-ERA individuals who felt that they could not work within any of the existing organizations.[62]

A last category of groups and individuals in the women's movement was composed of those involved primarily in work for other feminist issues and only secondarily in work for the ERA. One network of individuals focused on winning recognition for the pioneers of the women's movement and kept in contact with a NWP committee set up for that purpose.[63] Other individuals—for example, historian Mary Beard—concentrated on writing and teaching women's history. Most of the women devoted to such issues supported the ERA and kept informed about NWP activity. It is significant, however, that the women involved in this women's movement network were *not* involved with issues such as birth control or even, to any great extent, equal pay. (The NWP supported equal pay, as did other middle-class women's organizations, but much of the work for an equal pay bill went on within the Women's Bureau. The NWP kept silent on the issue of birth control.)

The women's movement as described here, with the NWP as its core, did not take in all women's organizations, even all those working for social change. Black women, for example, organized in the National Council of Negro Women, which opposed the ERA but in any case did not identify as part of the women's movement. One black women's group did support the ERA and established some contact with the NWP. The National Association of Colored Women regularly sent representatives to the party-dominated Joint Legislative Committee for Equal Rights, and its founder, Mary Church Terrell, belonged to the NWP and worked with Alice Paul on occasion. But racism in the women's movement as well as in the larger society kept the movement predominantly white. In the 1950s black women played leading roles in civil rights movement organizations, and by the early 1960s began to speak out about the sexism they encountered within the movement.[64]

Working-class women organized within the union movement, sometimes in separate groups, as in the case of the Women's Bureau of the United Auto Workers, but union opposition to the ERA was so strong that there was little contact between union women and pro-ERA feminists until the resurgence of the liberal branch of the women's movement in the 1960s, when UAW women played a major role in the founding of the National Organization for Women.[65] The Communist Party, headed in this period by Elizabeth Gurley Flynn, expressed support for the goal of women's emancipation on occasion, but fiercely opposed the ERA and denounced the activities of bourgeois feminists, particularly Alice Paul and the NWP.[66]

Although organized black women, union women, and women in the Communist Party worked with and for other women, they would not for the most part have identified themselves as part of the women's movement. The movement consisted of a loose network of groups and individuals devoted to improving the status of women in society. The various movement organizations acted independently, but often cooperated to try to pass the ERA, the major feminist goal of the period. Many women belonged to more than one organization, and this helped create ties among the different groups.

The remainder of this essay will focus on the feminist group culture created within the NWP. An examination of this group culture helps explain both how feminists managed to survive and work in a period especially hostile to feminism and, returning to the question raised above, why the women's movement remained relatively small and weak, unable to mobilize the masses of women suffering from the intensified contradictions of the period.

THE FEMINIST GROUP CULTURE OF THE NATIONAL WOMAN'S PARTY

The Equal Rights Amendment was the raison d'être of the National Woman's Party, but the party also played a significant role for its members by creating a feminist group culture.[67] Four aspects of that group culture suggest its contours: the importance of suffrage history, explicit feminist identification, intense commitment to the feminist cause, and the centrality of friendship and intimacy among the members.

Suffrage history played a major role in the NWP, affecting the organization in a number of ways. Most obviously, many of the most active members, and especially the officers, had joined the party during the suffrage struggle and carried their memories and experiences into later party work. By the postwar period they were no longer young women, and they often reminisced about the good old days of the suffrage movement. " . . . I felt as I read your letter the warm glow that always comes when old suffrage ties are renewed," one member wrote in typical fashion.[68] Others commented on their vivid recollections of a first suffrage meeting or parade. Having been a suffragist, and especially having been jailed, gave one status within the NWP. One member wrote that people in her city flocked to see and hear a party speaker because she had been in prison: " . . . The work for suffrage is now far enough in the past to cast glamor and appeal on those who worked for it. . . . "[69] Women running for party office who had served a jail term for suffrage activities listed this proudly as a prized accomplishment. Members too young to have been in the suffrage movement adopted a humble attitude toward the pioneers; one wrote, for example, "I was too young to enter the brilliant and successful campaign . . . but you must admit I tried to make up for it after I became a member of the National Woman's Party."[70]

What publicity the party attracted inevitably mentioned the suffrage past. There is irony in the fact that the media tended to describe the NWP as militant, although the organization had employed militance for only a brief period in its history. The leadership apparently never considered engaging in militant actions on behalf of the ERA and even opposed them once the National Organization for Women, in the early 1970s, took over leadership of the ERA fight.[71] Party members often, however, applied lessons learned in the suffrage past to work for the ERA. The decision to draft and pass a constitutional amendment came naturally to women who had fought for the suffrage amendment. And in more minor ways as well as in this major one, the suffrage struggle influenced what feminists in later years did, and even how they did it.[72] The many similarities between the suffrage and the ERA fights—especially the nature of the opposition and the arguments raised against the amendments—were evident to NWP members. Although one can easily imagine the opposite effect, they took courage from the long years of the suffrage struggle, rarely losing hope over the years. Perhaps the experience of the suffragists with the victorious culmination of the seventy-two-year fight gave them a unique and optimistic perspective. In any case, they often hoped that they would not have to work as long for the passage of the ERA.[73]

The party used suffrage history quite consciously to further its current program. The Committee on Woman Pioneers kept contact with women throughout the country working to win recognition for suffrage leaders Susan B. Anthony, Elizabeth Cady Stanton, and Lucretia Mott. The NWP regularly celebrated birthdays of suffragists and anniversaries of historic events such as the Seneca Falls convention. Party members like Anita Pollitzer, who reported to a friend the wonderful experience of reading for two hours in her six-volume *History of Woman Suffrage*, believed that suffrage history had shaped their perceptions, could teach them useful lessons, and would inspire women all over the country to join the ERA fight.[74]

A second characteristic of the feminist group culture was the explicit feminist identification of most of the members. The NWP was the only national self-proclaimed feminist organization in this period. In the context of the antifeminist backlash and the ensuing labeling of feminists as neurotics suffering from penis envy, it required a great deal of courage to identify publicly as a feminist. Yet party members continued to wear the label proudly, and publicity on the party consistently identified it as a feminist organization. The party journal, *Equal Rights*, carried a column entitled "A Feminist Thinks It Over" and reported information as "Feminist Firsts" and "Feminist Milestones." Nora Stanton Barney, granddaughter of pioneer suffragist Elizabeth Cady Stanton and daughter of militant suffragist Harriot Stanton Blatch, sought to define feminism in a letter published in *Equal Rights* and submitted to *Collier's*. For her "a feminist is one who thinks that women are primarily human beings with the same minds, ambitions, ability and skill, consciences, and power for evil and good, as men."[75]

Over and over, in private correspondence, members complimented other members and friends by describing them as "good feminists," "active feminists," "staunch feminists," "strong articulate feminists," or proudly claimed the label for themselves.[76] Alice Paul, herself with a reputation as a "super-feminist," described women as "born feminists."[77] Party members were fully aware of society's hostility. One woman, in response to Barney's definition of feminism, noted that she avoided the term because it was so widely misunderstood.[78] Another, one of the party's rare working-class members, repeatedly condemned the term for its unfavorable effect, especially on men.[79] But these were the exceptions. Despite the prevailing societal conviction that feminists were "kooks," "freaks," or "eccentrics," party members remained true to their feminist identity.[80] It is significant, however, that two women active in feminist causes but only peripherally involved with the NWP remember total avoidance of the label "feminist" and even assert that Alice Paul would not have used the term.[81] One of these women discussed how carefully sympathetic women used the word "feminist" among themselves in the early 1960s—she described it as an in-house term—which suggests that this may have increasingly become a label used only within the group culture as the 1950s wore on.

Feminism, of course, meant different things to different members. NWP members often expressed the view that inequality pervaded American society—they believed, that is, that discrimination on the basis of sex influenced their lives in many ways. Sometimes they erupted in outbursts against male arrogance and destructiveness, blaming men for the calamitous world situation. Some women asserted the superiority of women and female values in the nineteenth-century tradition of belief in women's moral superiority. Members sometimes deplored the indifference of the majority of women, but usually cited structural, rather than biological or psychological, causes for this situation. One longtime member wrote to another complaining about women and lamented: "Oh dear—sometimes I run and hide to keep up my faith in them, but I'll never tell *one man* that—and you are the only woman."[82]

Although the general indifference of the large majority of women sometimes discouraged members, they seemed to maintain confidence that women united would attain equality. Although some women wanted to bring men into a more central role in the party's work, most members hoped to build strength for the amendment by working to get support from other women's organizations. Many party members belonged to other organizations—the National Federation of Business and Professional Women's Clubs, the American Association of University Women, the Women's Christian Temperance Union, the General Federation of Women's Clubs, even the arch-rival, the League of Women Voters—and worked from within those organizations to gain support for the ERA. Most of the NWP efforts aimed at winning endorsements from the League of Women Voters and the American Association of University Women (AAUW). One party member, for example, joined her local league in order to obtain the mailing list so she could send out pro-ERA material.[83] Others attended league meetings to talk about the ERA or participated in formal debates with league members on the issue.[84] The American Association of University Women seemed a more likely prospect so the NWP supported both formal and informal efforts to win its endorsement of the ERA, establishing a Committee on College Women in 1945 to educate college women on the amendment and obtain endorsements from local AAUW branches.[85] Party members also sought endorsements from a variety of other organizations including conservative women's organizations (the Women's Christian Temperance Union and the Daughters of the American Revolution), liberal organizations (the American Civil Liberties Union), and labor (the AFL-CIO). The party set up a pro-ERA organization of working-class women, the Industrial Women's League for Equality, in order to counter charges that ERA supporters were only rich women who did not care about the welfare of working-class women. Although the NWP made some attempt to win over the AFL-CIO, the most powerful opponent of the ERA by the postwar period, the focus remained on elite women's organizations, in part because the party believed that the male-dominated labor unions benefited from discrimination against women and therefore had no incentive to eliminate it; in part because party members' natural contacts and orientation led them to organizations such as the AAUW and the League of Women Voters; and in part because party members maintained the belief that one member attributed to Alice Paul in relation to the vote: that it was more dignified to ask it of other women than to beg it of men.[86]

Another great hope for building collective strength lay in winning young women to the party. The most active members, who tended to be women who had joined during the suffrage struggle, were no longer young by the postwar period. Yet the party's correspondence often rang with optimism, as in the case of one member who wrote: "But new blood—in the form of the younger women, many of whom are coming to the rescue of we older crusaders—makes me feel sure that eventually the men who hold the power will succumb."[87] Although the party's attempt to organize young women into special "junior" groups failed and members sometimes expressed disgust with the younger generation as a "hopeless" group "not interested in anything but cosmetics, T.V. and modern amusements," hope, as one member put it, sprung eternal: "If a thing is *right*, it is bound to come to pass eventually!"[88]

The NWP was unique in this period in its identification as feminist. For party members to express the views they did and embrace the label "feminist" suggests the strength of their convictions and the extent of their "deviance" in relation to the other larger and more socially acceptable women's groups of the time, such as the Business and Professional Women and the League of Women Voters. By the 1950s the NWP was an organization of predominantly older women, many with suffrage pasts, who fiercely defended a label and the ideology it represented in a hostile society that brushed them aside as fanatics and anachronisms.

A third important characteristic of the feminist group culture was the central role that commitment to the feminist cause played in the members' lives. In the NWP feminism could be one's life work. The model for intense commitment to what the members referred to as "the Cause" was Alice Paul, founder and leading light of the party. By 1945 Paul had already established a reputation, almost legendary, as a dedicated, iron-willed "super-feminist," a fanatic and a martyr.[89] She continued to devote herself to the ERA, sometimes seemingly running the campaign single-handedly, into the 1970s. Not all members dedicated their lives to the Cause in this way. Sometimes family responsibilities intervened and prevented members from attending meetings or doing party work, and often the elaborate apologies revealed guilt at having to put something else first.[90] One long-time member, for example, apologized to Paul for failing to get to Washington and remarked: "How you must dislike the interference of personal matters. . . . It is the price one pays for children, I guess."[91] For other women work responsibilities prevented greater commitment to the party. The advanced age of many members sometimes interfered, although many women remained active in their eighties and nineties—Emma Guffey Miller, for example, a powerful figure in the Democratic party, became national chairman at the age of eighty-six.

Other members approached the level of Paul's commitment. Fannie Ackley, a retired linotype operator in Spokane, Washington, and one of the few active working-class members, wrote and published booklets of pro-ERA doggerel that she sent to senators and representatives, once spending $350 of her own money—an enormous sum for a retired worker, if miniscule for a powerful lobby—on a single session of Congress. A "zealot," as one friend and coworker described her, she kept at it until her death. Her twin sister wrote to Alice Paul, commenting that "EQUAL RIGHTS was Fannie's life work."[92] Elsie Wood, who lived with party member Mabel Griswold, commented after a serious auto accident that eventually killed Griswold that Griswold "could bear the broken bones but the breaking up of her life's work was far harder to take."[93]

Party work periodically demanded that members come to Washington for extended visits of lobbying or office work, and many members responded to a summons to Washington despite the required sacrifices. Despite the pressure and the occasional collapse into inactivity, the dedication of members was evident to those without, as well as within, the party. One new member commented that the secret of the party's ability to do so much in the face of enormous odds lay in its ability to attract devotion and loyalty.[94] A woman who stayed briefly at the party's headquarters in Washington wrote: "It was something of a revelation to my friends and myself to meet women who are working with such dedication to achieve benefits for all women."[95]

People who devote themselves to a cause, as Alice Paul and other members did, generally receive personal rewards in return for their sacrifices, and this was undoubtedly true of many NWP members. One woman stated this explicitly in writing of Fannie Ackley: "It seems such a pity to take money from her, yet I firmly believe that in that giving she is benefitted beyond what we can realize."[96] The same was true of the giving of time and energy. This may seem odd, given the lack of concrete results from the party's work for the ERA, but the rewards of the work itself were great enough to lead to accusations from the outside that the members did not want the ERA to pass, since it constituted their life work.[97] Such charges no doubt stung party members, but it is clear that, without work for the amendment, many would have considered their lives empty.

The fulfillment that fighting for a cause brought to women in the NWP relates directly to the fourth aspect of the group culture, the centrality of friendship and intimacy among members. Women's historians have recently begun to explore female friendship and women's support networks, long overlooked or trivialized, as a key issue in women's past.[98] Within the NWP women's relationships grew out of, and in turn supported, the work for the ERA. Correspondence among members—

and there was little separation between "official" and personal concerns, a manifestation of the intensely personal nature of the party's political work—rang with expressions of friendship. A few examples provide an idea of the warmth that pervades the letters. One member wrote to Alice Paul: "You are so thoughtful and understanding. I cannot tell you how much it means to have a friend who is just that."[99] Another longtime member wrote of her cousin and coworker who had just died: "We were *'best friends'* for seventy-five years & her nobility of character & her love were a sustaining joy & influence through all the years."[100] On the death of another member, her sister-in-law wrote: "I know what a sense of loss you feel in your organization, just as we feel here in the family circle. You, personally, loved her too, I know, just as she loved you."[101]

Often these ties were of long duration, especially for women who had been active together in the NWP during the suffrage struggle. Nina Allender, the cartoonist of the suffrage movement, wrote an emotion-filled letter to Alice Paul in which she recalled the first time they had met and the impact that meeting had on her life.[102] Betty Gram Swing, also a suffragist, wrote to Paul: "My, what a long and wonderful association we have had. . . . "[103]

The intimacy of the NWP letters often seems to have grown out of the female world in which some party members lived. Many of the most active members lived in couple relationships with other women or seemed to function in a world populated primarily by women. Members, in their letters, accepted these relationships as primary commitments. For example, few letters to Jeannette Marks, chairman of the New York branch of the party in the 1940s and professor of English at Mount Holyoke College, failed to inquire about Mary Woolley, former president of Mount Holyoke and the woman with whom Marks lived, whose serious illness clouded Mark's life and work.[104] Alma Lutz, feminist biographer and author of the column "A Feminist Thinks It Over," shared a Boston apartment and a country home for forty-one years with her Vassar College roommate, Marguerite Smith. They lived together, worked together in the party, vacationed together, and when Smith died in 1959, Lutz struggled with her grief and pain while friends wrote sympathetic and consoling letters.[105] Agnes Wells, an Indiana University dean and chairman of the party in the 1950s, wrote of the death of her "friend of forty one years and house-companion for 28 years." "I cannot yet realize the finality of it all," she wrote, and she could not continue living in the house they had shared together.[106] The existence of such couple relationships between women, whatever their nature—and I think that it is important that we recognize both the common bonds and the real differences between women who lived together and loved each other as these women did and women who were part of the lesbian culture of the 1950s—had an impact on the party's culture. Party members saw the centrality of such relationships and affirmed the importance of women's relationships with other women.

Certainly not all NWP members lived in primary relationships with other women, but, even for the married women, the party created a female world on occasion. One important resource for this was the Alva Belmont House, party headquarters in Washington. The Belmont House, a historic mansion on Capitol Hill, served (and continues to serve) not only as an office but as a clubhouse and a feminist hotel for visitors coming to Washington. A number of women lived at Belmont House and in two other party-owned houses, and others stayed there for periods ranging from days to months while engaged in lobbying. Although some rooms were rented to non-party individuals, even men, Belmont House played an important role in maintaining the culture of the party. One member even wondered if being married would prevent one's acceptance there.[107] Another member who traveled to Washington to serve as house manager emphasized the importance of the house: "It seems so natural to again be a part of Headquarters—this house has so much [*sic*] as a basis for a big contribution to the national and world woman-movement."[108] Some of the members made their home there; one woman wrote that she was "looking forward with joy to my return home, and *Home* to me now, means the dear Alva Belmont House. . . . "[109]

Just as the Belmont House served as home for some members, the organization became for some the "Woman's Party family."[110] In fulfilling its function as a family, the NWP provided support of various kinds to its members. For example, Alice Paul, concerned about her old friend Nina Allender's loneliness, encouraged her to come to Washington to live: "I think we could make you comfortable. You would be surrounded by loving friends and by people who know and appreciate the very great gift that you have made to our movement."[111] The daughter of another recently deceased member wrote to thank the party members at headquarters whose kindness and consideration had made it possible for her mother to continue her work as long as she did.[112] Members sometimes tried to provide financial support for other members in need: one woman collected a fund to provide another with dentures.[113] Often members offered emotional support in times of stress, proffering sympathy, for example, on the illness or deaths of friends and family. Members worried about Paul's health in particular, urging her to rest, telling her what to eat, encouraging each other to take care of her.[114]

Although the Belmont House served as a center of the female world of the NWP, many members were married and some included their husbands in their party work. Members sometimes sent greetings from their husbands in their letters, and the party sent some much-appreciated messages of concern to husbands who were ill. Anita Pollitzer, during her term as national chairman, brought her husband Elie Edson (several members did not change their names when they married) to headquarters for weekends. One letter from a member whose husband had just died describes an easy relationship between one man and the party: "Byron and I have always felt so much a part of the Woman's Party family. . . . As you know Byron and I spent four happy years there, and I am sure he worked about as hard for our cause as I did, and certainly he was heart and soul in it."[115] For married women active participation was probably only possible with supportive husbands.[116]

The importance of women's relationships within the party did not mean that this was a conflict-free world. Bitter disputes almost tore the party apart on several occasions, most seriously in 1947 when one faction took the officers to court in a dispute over the name, property, and resources of the party. Like a similar but less serious split in the mid-1930s, the 1947 lawsuit revolved around the issues of Alice Paul's leadership and the structure of the party.[117] Although the personnel of the rebellion changed in the decade between these two conflicts—some of those supporting Paul in the 1930s led the insurgency in the 1940s—the charges against Paul and the party remained the same. Paul, the accusations ran, controlled the party in a dictatorial, even fascistic, manner, causing the organization to remain small and elite. The conflict grew to such proportions that the Paul faction locked the insurgents out of party headquarters and, suspecting sinister forces at work, alerted the House Committee on Un-American Activities to the doings of the rebels.[118] The party survived both the 1935 schism and the 1947 lawsuit, but the conflicts remained unresolved, erupting again in 1953 with the resignation of the national chairman over the issue of expansion of membership. Throughout the NWP papers is evidence of conflict, often but not always centered on Paul's leadership. The bitterness of the disputes was in part a result of the intermingling of personal and political ties for many NWP members. Even those directly involved in these crises sometimes returned to work with the party—and those who broke off entirely usually continued to work for the ERA individually or in other organizations, and they usually kept in contact with other former party members.

Personal ties both survived and helped fan the flames of the disputes that tore through the party, but they also provided inspiration for many of the members. The personal support that participation in the party offered seemed sometimes to be the key to the NWP's perseverance in the face of societal indifference or hostility. Members wrote to each other expressing the satisfaction derived from working together. Betty Gram Swing wrote that she hoped to be able to get to a party convention "if for no other reason [than] to see you all again. What a bond our crusade is!"[119] Another member described a speaking tour she had undertaken for the party as the happiest vacation trip she had ever spent.[120] Inez Haynes Irwin, author of the party history, wrote to Paul to thank her for her praise of the history and added: "I enjoyed writing it. How I enjoyed writing it! How I enjoyed every moment that I spent at Headquarters."[121] All of this supports the notion that the feminist group culture of the NWP gave women a great deal as they devoted their energy and time to the cause of the ERA.

The feminist group culture of the NWP helped make it possible for women in the postwar period to work for a feminist cause in a society either indifferent or hostile to feminist concepts and values. It provided a supportive environment anchored in the suffrage past that valued feminism, gave meaning to one's life through commitment to a cause, and facilitated and nurtured warm friendships. But some of the very strengths of that culture outlined here—suffrage bonds, the level of commitment, the intensity of relationships—worked to further the elitism and exclusivity of the party. Limited participation was difficult in this world, and this fact, combined with both the class and racial composition of the party and the unsavory social and political views of some of its members, ensured that the party would remain small and elite. Not surprisingly, as a more mass-based women's movement began to grow in the 1960s, the NWP faded into insignificance. Nevertheless, the party's persistence played a role in the establishment of the President's Commission on the Status of Women in 1961, which contributed to the growth of the women's movement, and in the fight to include the word "sex" in Title VII of the Civil Rights Act of 1964, which prohibited discrimination in employment and served as the focus for the early efforts of the National Organization for Women (NOW) after its founding in 1966.[122] The National Woman's Party remained aloof from NOW but pressed for support of the ERA, which came in 1967. By the late 1960s the program of the NWP had been swept up by a surging new movement. Although the party still works for ratification of the ERA, leadership of the fight has long since passed to NOW. Although NOW in its early days had little use for the party, it has come to revere Alice Paul and the NWP, if only as symbols of feminist survival.[123]

CONCLUSION

The late 1940s and 1950s saw middle-class women faced with increasing conflict between the cultural ideals of domesticity and femininity, on the one hand, and the realities of their lives, on the other, as well as between their expanding work and family roles. The paradox of "woman's place" in the 1950s provides the context for understanding the resurgence of the women's movement in the 1960s, but it does not explain why the movement grew in the 1960s rather than the 1950s. The postwar antifeminist backlash certainly played a role; although feminism has never been a part of the American societal ideal, the postwar period saw an especially vigorous denunciation of feminism. The avoidance of feminist identification by groups such as the Business and Professional Women and the American Association of University Women, and the antifeminism of the League of Women Voters—all groups with feminist origins or with some commitment to feminist goals—suggests the effectiveness of the antifeminist campaign. In the 1950s, with the threat of McCarthyism darkening the political skies, the danger of deviance was all too clear. Only a group as exclusive and committed as the National Woman's Party dared to call itself feminist, and the Woman's Party was hardly the sort of organization to attract large numbers of women. An exclusive single-issue group that demanded a high level of commitment, it did not offer the "average" middle- or working-class woman a solution to her problems, although it did provide essential support for women already committed to feminism. Dedicated women kept alive a women's movement working for an improvement of women's status in American society, but it was not the sort of movement to win large numbers of adherents. The central role of the National Woman's Party ensured that liberals and labor would not move to support the ERA, at least in part because of long-standing animosity.

In the 1960s, in the context of the flowering of social protest movements in the United States and throughout the world, a number of factors helped spark the formation of a more mass-based movement among dissatisfied women. These included the establishment of the president's commission, the publication of Friedan's *The Feminine Mystique*, and the inclusion of "sex" in Title VII. When the liberal branch of the women's movement began to coalesce, it brought together women newly interested in feminist issues with women from the women's movement of the postwar period. That link is important in understanding the history of the movement.

This study does not pretend to provide definitive answers to all the questions it raises. We need to know a great deal more about women in the postwar period before we will know why the 1960s witnessed the resurgence of the contemporary women's movement. The movement today differs in significant ways from the beleaguered movement of the 1950s, but the lessons of the past are important. Jo Freeman, a major scholar of the contemporary women's movement, has suggested that the American political system responds less to those who protest loudest than to those who protest longest.[124] If this is indeed the case, the modern movement cannot afford to overlook the history of feminist survivors.

1. Betty Friedan, *The Feminine Mystique* (New York, 1963). See also Betty Friedan, *It Changed My Life: Writings on the Women's Movement* (New York, 1976). Despite serious flaws in the analysis in *The Feminine Mystique* and a damaging lack of sensitivity to the problems of poor and minority women, it remains an important work.

2. "The Bleak and Lonely Years" is the title of the chapter on the 1940s and 1950s in June Sochen, *Movers and Shakers: American Women Thinkers and Activists 1900–1970* (New York, 1973).

3. Sara Evans, *Personal Politics: The Roots of Women's Liberation in the Civil Rights Movement and the New Left* (New York, 1979), is an excellent study of the emergence of the radical feminist branch of the movement. Ethel Klein, "A Social Learning Perspective on Political Mobilization: Why the Women's Liberation Movement Happened When It Did (Ph.D. diss., University of Michigan, 1979), explores the origins of the contemporary women's movement. I am grateful to Ethel Klein for sharing the results of her research with me. Several works touch on, but do not explore in depth, the origins of the liberal feminist branch: William H. Chafe, *The American Woman: Her Changing Social, Economic, and Political Role, 1920–1970* (New York, 1972); Barbara Sinclair Deckard, *The Women's Movement: Political, Socioeconomic, and Psychological Issues*, 2d ed. (New York, 1979); Jo Freeman, *The Politics of Women's Liberation* (New York, 1975); and Judith Hole and Ellen Levine, *Rebirth of Feminism* (New York, 1971).

4. J. Stanley Lemons, *The Woman Citizen: Social Feminism in the 1920's* (Urbana, Ill., 1972), argues that feminism died in 1930 rather than 1920. Lois Scharf, *To Work and to Wed: Female Employment, Feminism, and the Great Depression* (Westport, Conn., 1980) dates the demise of feminism in the Great Depression years. Estelle Freedman has written a provocative essay, "Separatism as Strategy: Female Institution Building and American Feminism, 1870–1930," *Feminist Studies* 5 (Fall 1979): 512–29, in which she attributes the death of feminism in the 1920s to the decline of women's culture. Susan D. Becker, "An Intellectual History of the National Woman's Party, 1920–1941" (Ph.D. diss., Case Western Reserve University, 1975), explores feminism in the National Woman's Party, and Susan M. Hartmann, "The Organized Woman," paper presented to the Organization of American Historians, New York, 1978, analyzes feminism during World War II. Nancy F. Cott is currently engaged in research on feminism in the 1920s and 1930s.

5. See Lyn Goldfarb, *Separated and Unequal: Discrimination against Women Workers after World War II* (Washington, D.C., n.d.); Karen Beck Skold, "The Job We Left Behind: American Women in the Shipyards during World War II," in Carol R. Berkin and Clara M. Lovett, eds., *Women, War, and Revolution* (New York, 1980), pp. 55–75; and Sheila Tobias and Lisa Anderson, "What Really Happened to Rosie the Riveter," MSS Modular Publications, Module 9 (1974).

6. The phrase "Happy Housewife" is Friedan's, in *Feminine Mystique*.

7. I am indebted for the term "snow-blindness" to describe the invisibility to white society of women of color to Adrienne Rich, " 'Disloyal to Civilization:' Feminism, Racism, and Gynephobia," *Chrysalis* 7 (1979): 9–27.

8. The classic description and analysis of the nineteenth-century image is Barbara Welter, "The Cult of True Womanhood, 1820–1860," *American Quarterly* 18 (1966): 151–74.

9. L. Ann Geise, "The Female Role in Middle Class Women's Magazines from 1955 to 1976: A Content Analysis of Nonfiction Selections," *Sex Roles* 5 (1979): 51–62; Kathryn Weibel, *Mirror, Mirror: Images of Women Reflected in Popular Culture* (Garden City, N.Y., 1977); Janice Welsch, "Actress Archetypes in the 1950's: Doris Day, Marilyn Monroe, Elizabeth Taylor, Audrey Hepburn," in Karyn Kay and Gerald Peary, eds., *Women and the Cinema* (New York, 1977), pp. 99–111; Stuart Ewen, *Captains of Consciousness: Advertising and the Social Roots of the Consumer Culture* (New York, 1976), pp. 159–84; and Douglas T. Miller and Marion Nowak, *The Fifties: The Way We Really Were* (Garden City, N.Y., 1977).

10. Judith Tarcher, "Most Likely to Succeed," *Good Housekeeping (GH)* 126 (June 1948): 33. Other articles echoed the idea that a brilliant woman was not a successful woman: for example, Dorothy Thompson, "The Century of Women's Progress," *Ladies' Home Journal (LHJ)* 65 (August 1948): 11–12; and Waverly Root, "Women Are Intellectually Inferior," *American Mercury* 69 (October 1949): 407–14.

11. Bea Carroll, "How to Get Along with Women," *LHJ* 67 (January 1950): 73. For another example of commercial terminology, see Louise Paine Benjamin, "Femininity Begins at Home," *LHJ* 64 (January 1947): 136–37, which advised the reader to be "equipped with enough femininity to hold your own in any market, including the matrimonial."

12. Elaine Whitehall, "I'd Hate to Be a Man," *Coronet* 37 (January 1955): 27–30; "I'm Lucky! Lucky!," *LHJ* 77 (February 1960): 63. See also Poppy Cannon, "It's a Man's World . . . Maybe," *Woman's Home Companion* (WHC) 74 (January 1947): 40; Fredda Dudley Balling, "The Meeker Sex," *GH* 132 (March 1951): 64; "The New (?) Woman," *LHJ* 69 (April 1952): 54–55; Benjamin Spock, "What's She Got That I Haven't," *LHJ* 69 (October 1952): 56–57; Michael Drury, "The Women in My Life," *GH* 114 (January 1957): 55.

13. See Friedan, *Feminine Mystique*, pp. 117–41; and Miller and Nowak, *Fifties*, pp. 150–51.

14. Valerie Kincade Oppenheimer, *The Female Labor Force in the United States* (Berkeley, Calif., 1970), p. 3.

15. Chafe, *American Woman*, pp. 183, 192.

16. See Hazel Erskine, "The Polls: Women's Role," *Public Opinion Quarterly* 35 (Summer 1971): 282–87; and Barbara McGowan, "Postwar Attitudes toward Women and Work," in Dorothy McGuigan, ed., *New Research on Women and Sex Roles* (Ann Arbor, Mich., 1976).

17. See Klein, "Social Learning Perspective," pp. 72–77; and D'Ann Campbell, "Wives, Workers, and Womanhood: America during World War II" (Ph.D. diss., University of North Carolina, 1979). I am grateful to Campbell for sending me a copy of her dissertation.

18. Klein, "Social Learning Perspective," p. 37.

19. Barbara Benson, "Do Men or Women Lead the Harder Life?" *LHJ* 64 (May 1947): 44–45.

20. See Herbert J. Gans, *The Levittowners* (New York, 1967).

21. See Miller and Nowak, *Fifties*, p. 155.

22. Klein, "Social Learning Perspective," pp. 83–96.

23. Alfred C. Kinsey et al, *Sexual Behavior in the Human Female* (Philadelphia, 1953). See Miller and Nowak, *Fifties*, p. 157.

24. Marilyn French, *The Women's Room* (New York, 1977).

25. "American Woman's Dilemma," *Life*, 16 June 1947, pp. 101–11.

26. "The Girls," *Life*, 15 August 1949, pp. 39–40.

27. "An Introduction by Mrs. Peter Marshall," *Life*, 24 December 1956, pp. 2–3.

28. Lynn White, Jr., *Educating Our Daughters* (New York, 1950); see Miller and Nowak, *Fifties*, pp. 160–62.

29. See Miller and Nowak, *Fifties*, chap. 13.

30. For a discussion of the relationship between images of women and business, see Friedan, *Feminine Mystique*, pp. 197–223; Weibel, *Mirror, Mirror*, pp. 135–73; and especially Ewen, *Captains of Consciousness*, pp. 159–84.

31. Herbert Blumer, "Social Movements," in A. M. Lee, ed., *New Outline of Principles of Sociology* (New York, 1951), pp. 165–222. Recent development in social movement theory emphasizes the need to consider the internal dynamics and resources as well as the societal support and constraint that affect the growth of social movements. See Jo Freeman, "Resource Mobilization and Strategy: A Model for Analyzing Social Movement Organization Actions," in Mayer N. Zald and John D. McCarthy, eds., *The Dynamics of Social Movements* (Cambridge, Mass., 1979), pp. 167–89; John D. McCarthy and Mayer N. Zald, *The Trend of Social Movements in America: Professionalization and Resource Mobilization* (Morristown, N.J., 1973); and Charles Tilly, *From Mobilization to Revolution* (Reading, Mass., 1978).

32. See Joan Cassell, *A Group Called Women* (New York, 1977).

33. Ellen Carol DuBois, *Feminism and Suffrage: The Emergence of an Independent Women's Movement in America, 1848–1869* (Ithaca, N.Y., 1978), deals with the issues discussed here. For the later movement see Aileen S. Kraditor, *The Ideas of the Woman Suffrage Movement, 1890–1920* (New York, 1965).

34. I use the terms "feminists" and "reformers" in place of the customary "hard-core feminists" and "social feminists," terms introduced by William L. O'Neill, *Everyone Was Brave: A History of Feminism in America* (Chicago, 1971).

35. "American Women," *Life*, 29 January 1945, p. 28. See Leila J. Rupp, *Mobilizing Women for War: German and American Propaganda, 1939–1945* (Princeton, N.J., 1978), pp. 160–61.

36. See, for example, John P. Dolch, "American Girls Are Swell, But . . . ," *American Magazine* 141 (January 1946): 45; and Agnes E. Meyer, "A Challenge to American Women," *Collier's*, 11 May 1946, p. 15.

37. Philip Wylie, *Generation of Vipers* (New York, 1942); Chafe, *American Woman*, p. 201.

38. Ferdinand Lundberg and Marynia F. Farnham, *Modern Woman: The Lost Sex* (New York, 1947). See Miller and Nowak, *Fifties*, pp. 153–55.

39. Arnold W. Green and Eleanor Melnick, "What Has Happened to the Feminist Movement?", in *Studies in Leadership: Leadership and Democratic Action* (New York, 1950), p. 283.

40. Struthers Burt, "Women, Dog Dab 'Em!" *LHJ* 64 (November 1947): 11.

41. Interview No. 1, 28 September 1979; interview No. 2, 5 October 1979; conducted by Verta Taylor and Leila Rupp. This and all other interviews cited in this essay were conducted under a 1979–80 Ohio State University research grant awarded to Verta Taylor.

42. Mary Beard to W. K. Jordan, 4 April 1947, Mary Beard papers, Box 2(29), Schlesinger Library, Cambridge, Massachusetts.

43. Ralph S. Banay, "The Trouble with Women," *Collier's*, 7 December 1946, p. 21.

44. Willard Waller, "The Coming War on Women," *This Week*, n.d.; clipping in Florence L. C. Kitchelt papers, Box 3(36), Schlesinger Library.

45. Florence Howitt, "Women Don't Give Women a Chance," *GH* 129 (October 1949): 33.

46. Ann MacLeod, "Should Women Vote?" *LHJ* 75 (February 1958): 6.

47. Letter to the editor of the *Star*, 3 November 1946.

48. Robert C. Ruark, quoted in Marguerite Rawalt, *History of the NFBPWC*, vol. 2 (Washington, D.C., 1969), pp. 46–47.

49. See Rupp, *Mobilizing Women*, pp. 68–71.

50. Dorothy Thompson, "Are Women Different?," *WHC* 68 (November 1951): 11. On Thompson, see Rupp, *Mobilizing Women*, pp. 70–71.

51. Cornelia Otis Skinner, "Women Are Misguided," *Life*, 24 December 1956, p. 73. See also Robert Coughlan, "Changing Roles in Modern Marriage," *Life*, 24 December 1956, 108–18; and Edith M. Stern, "Every Woman Has Five Lives," *WHC* 81 (September 1954): 38–39.

52. Doris E. Fleischman (Bernays), "Notes of a Retiring Feminist," *American Mercury* 68 (February 1949): 161–68.

53. Margaret Barnard Pickel, "There's Still a Lot for Women to Learn," *New York Times*, 11 November 1945, VI, p. 14; Margaret Hickey, quoted in *New York Times*, 26 February 1945, p. 9.

54. Robert Coughlan, "Changing Roles in Modern Marriage," *Life*, 24 December 1956.

55. Anna Lord Strauss to office, n.d. (recd. 19 August 1946), League of Women Voters Papers, Box 751, Library of Congress, Washington, D.C.

56. Anna Lord Strauss, "Arguments for and against changeing (*sic*) name of League of Women Voters to League of Active Voters (or some such)," 21 April 1953, LWV Papers, Box 1198, Library of Congress.

57. Luther P. Gerlach and Virginia H. Hine, *People, Power, Change* (Indianapolis, 1970). Cassell, *Group Called Women*, applies this multigroup model to the contemporary women's movement.

58. Interview No. 2, 5 October 1979.

59. See Rawalt, *History of the NFBPWC*, vol. 2.

60. Margaret Hickey to Alice Paul, 15 January 1945, NWP Papers, reel 84; Mary C. Kennedy to Alice Paul, 25 March 1945, NWP Papers, reel 85; Caroline Babcock to Lucy Rice Winkler, 25 June 1945, NWP Papers, reel 86; Geneva F. McQuatters to Anita Pollitzer, 10 February 1949, NWP Papers, reel 94; Dorothy Spinks to Nina Horton Avery, 22 May 1949, NWP Papers, reel 95; Mrs. Earl Hunsinger to Agnes Wells, 26 September 1949, NWP Papers, reel 96; Mary C. Kennedy to Agnes Wells, 14 November 1950, NWP Papers, reel 97; Elizabeth Forbes to Ernestine Powell, 10 September 1953, NWP Papers, reel 99; Helen G. Irwin to Nina Horton Avery, 21 June 1954, NWP Papers, reel 100; Mary C. Kennedy to (Mildred Palmer), 21 August 1954, NWP Papers, reel 100; Priscilla Wagoner to NWP, 25 August 1954, NWP Papers, reel 100; Mary C. Kennedy to Alice Paul, 7 September 1954, NWP Papers, reel 100; Alice Paul to Mabel Griswold, 18 October 1954, NWP Papers, reel 100; Alice Paul to Mary C. Kennedy, 5 March 1955, NWP Papers, reel 101; Mary C. Kennedy to Alice Paul, 28 March 1955, NWP Papers, reel 101; Lucy Rice Winkler to Emma Newton, 7 August 1960, NWP Papers, reel 106. The National Woman's Party Papers have been microfilmed and are distributed by the Microfilming Corporation of America.

61. Dorothy Spinks to Nina Horton Avery, 22 May 1949, NWP Papers, reel 95; Helen G. Irwin to Nina Horton Avery, 21 June 1954, NWP Papers, reel 100; Priscilla Wagoner to NWP, 25 August 1954, NWP Papers, reel 100; Florence Kitchelt to Alice Paul, 29 August 1954, NWP Papers, reel 100.

62. The relationship between the Connecticut Committee and the NWP is documented in the papers of Florence L. C. Kitchelt, Schlesinger Library.

63. This network is documented in the papers of Rose Arnold Powell, Schlesinger Library.

64. See Evans, *Personal Politics*, on black women in the civil rights movement. The newly opened National Archives for Black Women's History, in Washington, D.C., contains the papers of the National Council of Negro Women.

65. See Nancy Gabin, "Women Workers and the UAW in the Post-World War II Period: 1945–1954," *Labor History* 21 (1970–80): 5–30.

66. See, for example, Communist Party leader Elizabeth Gurley Flynn's autobiography, *The Rebel Girl* (New York, 1955). Flynn spoke on "the woman question" in her first public speech, but she never described herself as a feminist. She, like other Communist women, believed that women's emancipation would follow the overthrow of capitalism. See also Peggy Dennis, *The Autobiography of an American Communist* (Berkeley, Calif., 1977); and Ellen Kay Trimberger, "Women in the Old and New Left: The Evolution of a Politics of Personal Life," *Feminist Studies* 5 (1979): 451–61.

67. I am using the term "group culture" to describe a set of values, understandings, and behaviors shared by the members of the NWP. See Gary Alan Fine and Sherryl Kleinman, "Rethinking Subculture: An Interactionist Analysis," *American Journal of Sociology* 85 (1979): 1–20, for a new conceptualization of subculture and its relationship to group culture and subsociety.

68. Caroline Babcock to Grace Cook Kurz, 8 July 1946, NWP Papers, reel 89.

69. Mabel Griswold to Agnes Wells, 4 August 1950, NWP Papers, reel 97.

70. Mabel Van Dyke Baer to Anna Kelton Wiley, 12 August 1947, NWP Papers, reel 91; also Mabel Griswold to L.J.D. Daniels, 24 May 1948, NWP Papers, reel 93; and Mabel Griswold to Mrs. G. M. Fuller, 24 May 1948, NWP Papers, reel 93.

71. Communication from Frances Kolb, winter 1980. Kolb is currently writing a history of the first ten years of the National Organization for Women.

72. Caroline Babcock to Florence L. C. Kitchelt, 10 January 1945, NWP Papers, reel 84; Elsie Hill to Ethel Ernest Murrell, n.d. (October 1951), NWP Papers, reel 98; Emma E. Newton to Marie Forrest, 2 April 1956, NWP Papers, reel 102; Mildred Taylor to Alice Paul, 15 April 1945, NWP Papers, reel 85; Caroline Katzenstein to Mamie Sydney Mizen, 30 October 1948, NWP Papers, reel 94.

73. Mabel Griswold to M. E. Owens, 19 August 1947, NWP Papers, reel 91; Lillian H. Kerr to Alice Paul, 9 September 1958, NWP Papers, reel 105.

74. Anita Pollitzer to Mrs. Betts, 20 November 1957, NWP Papers, reel 104.

75. Nora Stanton Barney to Bella Dodd, 17 January 1945, NWP Papers, reel 84.

76. Dora Ogle to Mrs. Charles Metcalf, 1 May 1945, NWP Papers, reel 86; Alice Park to Martha Souder, 26 May 1949, NWP Papers, reel 95; Catherine R. Dobbs to Agnes Wells, 13 February 1950, NWP Papers, reel 96; Jane Norman Smith to Ethel Ernest Murrell, 11 June 1951, NWP Papers, reel 98; (Mildred Palmer) to Lucy Rice Winkler, 5 September 1951, NWP Papers, reel 98; Anne (Carter) to Norma (Wheaton), 1 August 1954, NWP Papers, reel 100; Dora Ogle to Marjorie Longwell, 16 September 1957, NWP Papers, reel 104; Anita Pollitzer to Emma Guffey Miller, 10 November 1962, NWP Papers, reel 108.

77. Alice Paul, "Conversations with Alice Paul: Woman Suffrage and the Equal Rights Amendment," an oral history conducted in 1972 and 1973 by Amelia R. Fry, Regional Oral History Office, University of California, 1976, pp. 551–91.

78. Florence L. C. Kitchelt to Nora Stanton Barney, 5 February 1945, NWP Papers, reel 84.

79. Fannie Ackley to Caroline Babcock, 6 November 1946, NWP Papers, reel 90; Fan-

nie Ackley to Olive Beale, 18 May 1948, NWP Papers, reel 93; Fannie Ackley to Alice Paul, 5 August 1948, NWP Papers, reel 94.

80. Interview No. 1, 28 September 1979; Interview No. 5, 10 December 1979.

81. Interview No. 3, 15 October 1979; Interview No. 4, 15 October 1979.

82. Mary C. Kennedy to Florence Armstrong, 23 March 1945, NWP Papers, reel 85.

83. Lucy Rice Winkler to Alice Paul, 5 January 1945, NWP Papers, reel 84.

84. Marjorie Rea to Caroline Babcock, 29 January 1945, NWP Papers, reel 84; Nora Stanton Barney to Alice Paul, 9 February 1945, NWP Papers, reel 84; Marjorie Rea to Caroline Babcock, 18 May 1945, NWP Papers, reel 86; Nora Stanton Barney to Alice Paul, 21 May 1945, NWP Papers, reel 86; Memo from Alma Lutz, 19 April 1946, NWP Papers, reel 89; Louise S. Earle to Caroline Babcock, 28 April 1946, NWP Papers, reel 89; Caroline Babcock to Florence Kitchelt, 22 May 1945, NWP Papers, reel 89; Report of Part of an Interview by a Member of the League of Women Voters, R. Gussie Vickers, n.d. (14 January 1949), NWP Papers, reel 94.

85. Clara Snell Wolfe to Alice Paul, 12 January 1945, NWP Papers, reel 84; Aurelle Burnside to Alice Paul, 21 January 1945, NWP Papers, reel 84; Caroline Babcock to Alice Morgan Wright, 25 January 1945, NWP Papers, reel 84; Caroline Babcock to Alice Morgan Wright, 3 February 1945, NWP Papers, reel 84; Florence Armstrong to Mary C. Kennedy, 25 February 1945, NWP Papers, reel 84; Mary C. Kennedy to Alice Paul, 26 April 1945, NWP Papers, reel 85; Alice Morgan Wright to Sarah Hughes, 5 May 1945, NWP Papers, reel 86; Caroline Babcock to Mrs. Percil Stephenson, 5 May 1945, NWP Papers, reel 86; Elizabeth M. Hine to Agnes Wells, 8 May 1945, NWP Papers, reel 86; Agnes Wells to Caroline Babcock, 10 May 1945, NWP Papers, reel 86; Caroline Babcock to Jeannette Marks, 1 June 1945, NWP Papers, reel 86; Margaret W. Corson to Nora Stanton Barney, 20 June 1945, NWP Papers, reel 86; Charlotte Johnson Opheim to Anita Pollitzer, 14 April 1949, NWP Papers, reel 95; Agnes Wells to Mabel Griswold, 6 July 1949, NWP Papers, reel 95.

86. Inez Haynes Irwin, *The Story of Alice Paul and the National Woman's Party* (1921; rpt. Fairfax, Va., 1977), p. 12.

87. Freda M. Klauden to Dora Ogle, 10 September 1946, NWP Papers, reel 89. Also May G. Schaeffer to Caroline Babcock, 14 March 1945, NWP Papers, reel 85; Nora Stanton Barney to Alice Paul, 7 May 1945, NWP Papers, reel 86; Dorothy Granger to Caroline Babcock, 19 March 1946, NWP Papers, reel 88; Caroline Katzenstein to Mamie Sydney Mizen, 30 October 1948, NWP Papers, reel 94; Agnes Wells to Amelia Himes Walker, 20 December 1950, NWP Papers, reel 97; Lucy Rice Winkler to Ethel Ernest Murrell, 3 March 1952, NWP Papers, reel 98.

88. Lillian H. Kerr to Alice Paul, 12 April 1956, NWP Papers, reel 102. Also Mary E. Owens to Caroline Babcock, 11 September 1945, NWP Papers, reel 87; and Mrs. Robbins Gilman to Norma Olson, 12 February 1946, NWP Papers, reel 88. On the attempts to organize young women: Neenah Hastings Lessemann to Alice Paul, 16 May 1945, NWP Papers, reel 86; Barbara Westebbe to Miss Hiatt, 25 August 1949, NWP Papers, reel 95; Ernestine Bellamy to Elizabeth Forbes, 14 April 1950, NWP Papers, reel 96; Ernestine Bellamy to Ethel Ernest Murrell, 8 August 1951, NWP Papers, reel 98; Marjorie Barstow Greenbie to Emma Guffey Miller, 10 July 1961, NWP Papers, reel 107. These efforts continued into the late 1960s, to no avail.

89. On Alice Paul, see Irwin, *Story of Alice Paul*; Doris Stevens, *Jailed for Freedom* (1920; rpt. New York, 1976); and Becker, "Intellectual History of the NWP." Amelia R. Fry, who interviewed Alice Paul, is currently working on a biography of Paul. See Paul, "Conversations with Alice Paul."

90. Susan Pringle Frost to Alice Paul, 7 May 1945, NWP Papers, reel 86; Clara Snell Wolfe to Mabel Griswold, 8 May 1947, NWP Papers, reel 91; Anita Pollitzer to Agnes Wells, 14 January 1951, NWP Papers, reel 97; Anita Pollitzer to Ethel Ernest Murrell, 9

October 1951, NWP Papers, reel 98; Anita Pollitzer to NWP Friends, 6 October 1953, NWP Papers, reel 99; Anita Pollitzer to Alice Paul, 22 February 1956, NWP Papers, reel 102.

91. Betty Gram Swing to Alice Paul, 25 April 1948, NWP Papers, reel 93.

92. Fannie Ackley to Mabel Griswold, 20 June 1948, NWP Papers, reel 93; Mary Elizabeth Nye to Agnes Wells, 1 March 1950, NWP Papers, reel 96; Mary Elizabeth Nye to Amelia Himes Walker, 20 October 1955, NWP Papers, reel 101; Mrs. Margaret Davis to Alice Paul, 5 February 1956, NWP Papers, reel 102.

93. Elsie M. Wood to Alice Paul, 1 February 1955, NWP Papers, reel 101.

94. Mamie Sydney Mizen to Florence Armstrong, 25 October 1948, NWP Papers, reel 94.

95. Lorraine Bentley to Alice Paul, 21 April 1956, NWP Papers, reel 102.

96. (Mildred Palmer) to Amelia Himes Walker, 21 August 1950, NWP Papers, reel 97.

97. Ethel Ernest Murrell to Alice Paul, 8 December 1952, NWP Papers, reel 99; Ernestine Powell to Florence Armstrong, n.d. (recd. 8 October 1953), NWP Papers, reel 99; Ernestine Powell to Alice Paul, 12 October 1953, NWP Papers, reel 99.

98. Carroll Smith-Rosenberg, "The Female World of Love and Ritual: Relations between Women in Nineteenth-Century America," *Signs* 1 (1975): 1–29, is a groundbreaking article on female friendship. See also Nancy F. Cott, *The Bonds of Womanhood: "Woman's Sphere" in New England, 1780–1835* (New Haven, Conn., 1977), chap. 5; Blanche Wiesen Cook, "Female Support Networks and Political Activism: Lillian Wald, Crystal Eastman, and Emma Goldman," *Chrysalis* 3 (1977): 43–61; Nancy Sahli, "Smashing: Women's Relationships before the Fall," *Chrysalis* 8 (1979): 17–27; the lesbian history issue of *Frontiers: A Journal of Women Studies* 4 (Fall 1979); Lillian Faderman, *Surpassing the Love of Men* (New York, 1981); and Leila J. Rupp, " 'Imagine My Surprise': Women's Relationships in Historical Perspective," *Frontiers* 5 (Fall 1980): 61–70.

99. Helen Hunt West to Alice Paul, 24 May 1945, NWP Papers, reel 86.

100. Elizabeth Kent to Agnes Wells, 31 December 1950, NWP Papers, reel 97.

101. Janet H. Griswold to Alice Paul, 2 February 1955, NWP Papers, reel 101.

102. Nina Allender to Alice Paul, 5 January 1947, NWP Papers, reel 90.

103. Betty Gram Swing to Alice Paul, 3 February 1948, NWP Papers, reel 92.

104. The relationship of Mary Woolley and Jeannette Marks is the subject of a recent book by Anna Mary Wells, *Miss Marks and Miss Woolley* (Boston, 1978). Wells set out to write a biography of Mary Woolley and almost abandoned the plan when she discovered the love letters of Woolley and Marks. Ultimately Wells went ahead with the book, but only after she decided, as she explains in the preface, that there was no physical relationship between the two women, that they were loving and intimate but not lovers. This book is a perfect example of the ways in which heterosexism can distort the writing of history. See Blanche Cook, "The Historical Denial of Lesbianism," *Radical History Review* 20 (1979): 60–65.

105. Telegram from Alice Paul to Alma Lutz, 5 July 1959, NWP Papers, reel 105; Alma Lutz to Florence L. C. Kitchelt, 29 July 1959, Florence L. Kitchelt Papers, Box 7 (178), SL.

106. Agnes Wells to Anita Pollitzer, 24 August 1946, NWP Papers, reel 89.

107. Elizabeth Osgood to Caroline Babcock, 4 September 1945, NWP Papers, reel 87.

108. Martha Souder to Ethel Adamson, 8 April 1948, NWP Papers, reel 93.

109. Mary Alice Matthews to Alice Paul, 24 March 1945, NWP Papers, reel 85.

110. See, for example, Martha Souder to Perle Mesta, 15 August 1949, NWP Papers, reel 95; Ernestine Bellamy to Alice Paul, 23 March 1958, NWP Papers, reel 104.

111. Alice Paul to Nina Allender, 20 November 1954, NWP Papers, reel 100; Kay Boyle to Alice Paul, 5 December 1954, NWP Papers, reel 100; Alice Paul to Nina Allender, 6 December 1954, NWP Papers, reel 100.

112. Dorothy Ogle Graham to Marion Sayward, 14 July 1960, NWP Papers, reel 106.

113. Edith Goode to Alice Paul, 27 February 1959, NWP Papers, reel 105.

114. Elsie Hill to Alice Paul, 10 February 1945, NWP Papers, reel 84; Anita Pollitzer to Alice Paul, 14 February 1945, NWP Papers, reel 84; Elsie Hill to Florence Armstrong, 28 February 1945, NWP Papers, reel 84; Marion May to Alice Paul, n.d. (May 1947), NWP Papers, reel 91; Dora Ogle to Florence Bayard Hilles, 29 December 1947, NWP Papers, reel 92; Mary Burt Messer to Alice Paul, 3 January 1948, NWP Papers, reel 92.

115. Helen Hunt West to Dora Ogle, n.d. (April 1952), NWP papers, reel 98.

116. Interview No. 3, 5 October 1979; Interview No. 4, 15 October 1979.

117. On the 1930s schism, see Becker, "Intellectual History of the NWP," pp. 56–95.

118. Lavinia Dock to NWP, 30 May 1947, NWP Papers, reel 91; Frances Green to Agnes Wells, 20 August 1947, NWP Papers, reel 91; Alice Paul to Caroline Katzenstein, 7 October 1948, NWP Papers, reel 94.

119. Betty Gram Swing to Cecil Norton Broy, 9 May 1951, NWP Papers, reel 98.

120. Amelia Himes Walker to Agnes Wells, 10 August 1950, NWP Papers, reel 97.

121. Inez Haynes Irwin to Alice Paul, 4 July 1956, NWP Papers, reel 102.

122. The papers of the PCSW, in the John F. Kennedy Library, Boston, Massachusetts, document the history of the establishment of the commission. Cynthia E. Harrison is currently working on a dissertation, "Federal Policy Concerning Women, 1945–1966," that includes a section on the PCSW. I am grateful to Harrison for sending me a draft of her essay, " 'A New Frontier' for Women: The Public Policy of the Kennedy Administration," now published in *Journal of American History* 67 (December 1980): 630–46. I would also like to thank Carl M. Brauer for sharing with me a draft of his paper, "Title VII of the Civil Rights Act of 1964," which analyzes the process by which "sex" was added to Title VII.

123. Communication from Cynthia Harrison, winter 1980.

124. Jo Freeman, "Crisis and Conflicts in Social Movement Organizations," *Chrysalis* 5 (1977): 43–51.

The Civil Rights Revolution, 1945–1960:
The Gods Bring Threads to Webs Begun

William H. Chafe

"Do you want to get killed?" he asked me.
"Hell, no!"
"Then, for God's sake, learn how to live in the south! . . . Look, you're black, black, black, see? Can't you understand that?" . . . "You act around white people as if you didn't know that they were white. And they see it."
"Oh, Christ, I can't be a slave," I said hopelessly.
"But you've got to eat. . . . When you're in front of white people *think* before you act, think before you speak; your way of doing things is alright among *our* people, but not for white people. They won't stand for it." (Richard Wright, *Black Boy*)

No black person growing up in the American south during the 1930s could avoid the pervasive reality of race. It shaped one's life, dictated one's ambitions, determined where and how one would speak, what kind of job one would hold—sometimes even whether one would survive. White people were in control. They could fire you from your job, evict you from your land, slap you for having the wrong "look" in your eye.

Sometimes their terrorism knew no bounds. In 1934 Claude Raines, a black man in Georgia, was arrested for allegedly molesting a white woman. Seized by a lynch mob, he was carried through town after town in southern Georgia and then across the border into Florida, with leaflets left in each place advertising the lynching that was about to happen. By the time the mob reached its final destination, thousands had gathered to witness the mutilation of Raines's body. No law enforcement agent acted to prevent the murder.[1] In such a context open rebellion was not an option because destruction of life and possessions was the almost certain response.

Yet the absence of mass protest did not signify passive acceptance of the status quo. If whites controlled the outer reality, they could not control the inner spirit. Throughout the years of Jim Crow, when America's laws said that blacks could not vote, share restaurant facilities, or go to school with whites, the black struggle to overcome oppression gathered strength. At times, of necessity, it took the form of playing the role of Uncle Tom in order to secure funds for a new school, a better playground, or a decent college. At other times it consisted of teaching pride in black institutions, churches, and businesses, preparing for the day when those institutions would serve as a base from which to attack the oppressor. And at still other times the struggle meant pushing back the boundaries of control and beginning to challenge segregation itself. During the late 1930s and 1940s, more and more black Americans took this third course.

Ella Baker was born and reared in Warren County, North Carolina, on a farm owned by her family since the 1870s. After graduating from Shaw University, a black school started during Reconstruction, she moved to New York City to work for the YWCA. Then, in the middle 1930s, she accepted the position of field secretary for the NAACP. The South was her territory. Traveling from town to town, she recruited blacks to join the NAACP—an act which at that time represented the equivalent of joining the Black Panthers in the late 1960s. In 1943 she went to Greensboro, North Carolina. There she so impressed Randolph Blackwell, a young high school student, that he organized an NAACP youth chapter. Blackwell subsequently initiated voter registration campaigns in Greensboro, ran for the state legislature, and helped form the Southern Christian Leadership Conference. Ella Baker, Randolph Blackwell, and the NAACP youth group that they formed together, would help reshape history in the 1950s and 1960s.[2]

Two hundred miles to the south and east, in Clarendon County, South Carolina, J. A. DeLaine pastored an A.M.E. church and taught school. ("If you set out to find the place in America . . . where life among black folk had changed least since the end of slavery," Richard Kluger wrote in 1974, "Clarendon County is where you might have come.") With a decent job and an honored position in the community, DeLaine might have been expected to act with caution. But he had a fire within him. As a youngster he had been sentenced to twenty-five lashes for pushing back a white boy who had shoved his sister off the sidewalk.

In the church he pastored—as in most black churches—he drew constant parallels between the liberation promised in Scripture and the reality of contemporary life. It was not surprising, then, that when DeLaine heard an NAACP lecturer in the summer of 1947 at a black college in Columbia, South Carolina, he decided to lead the struggle to equalize education in Clarendon County. It was, after all, an area that in 1949 spent $179 per white child in public schools and $43 per black child. Shortly thereafter, DeLaine met Thurgood Marshall, general counsel of the NAACP and a graduate of Howard University Law School, whose imagination, courage, and sheer energy were now directed toward demolishing the legal fortress of segregation. DeLaine and Marshall, too, would be heard from again.[3]

Throughout the South such acts of assertion were growing. Overt protest was never easy, but the challenge was beginning. Based on the achievements of their forefathers in a segregated world, people like Baker and Blackwell and DeLaine were launching an assault that would eventually undermine segregation itself. At a time when all too often we assume that change comes from above, it is important to remember where the civil rights movement began, who started it, and what price was paid before anyone in authority even noticed.

The new challenge grew out of the changes wrought by World War II. By causing a massive dislocation of population and forcing millions of people into new experiences, the war created a context in which many blacks—and some whites—perceived the possibility of racial activism in a new way. The vicious cycle of social control that had compelled obedience to the status quo as a price for survival was at least partially broken by the massive jolt of full-scale war. Although little was accomplished in the way of permanent progress toward equality, the changes that did occur laid the foundation for subsequent mass protest.

The war generated an accelerated migration of blacks from the South, and within the South from farm to city. Whether lured by a specific job in a munitions plant, ordered by a directive from the selective service, or simply beckoned by the hope of a better life elsewhere, hundreds of thousands of black southerners boarded trains and buses and headed north and west. When they arrived at their destination, they found living situations often less attractive than they had expected. The urban ghetto, with its overcrowded housing, hard-pressed social facilities, and oppressive discrimination, was not much better than what they had left behind. Yet there was also a difference. A northern urban political machine sought votes and offered some political recognition in return.

There was more psychological space, more opportunity to talk freely. The community was new, the imminent tyranny of small-town authority was removed, and different ground rules applied. The very act of physical mobility brought independence from the overwhelming social constraints that had been enforced in small southern communities. If the controls existed in different forms, there was at least now the possibility of a different response as well as a heightened sense of what might be done to achieve a better life.

World War II's second major impact came in the area of the economy. Some two million blacks were employed in defense plants during the war, and another two hundred thousand joined the federal civil service. Most of these jobs were at low levels. Indeed, when attempts were made to upgrade black employees, whites frequently rebelled, as when twenty thousand white workers in Mobile walked off their jobs and rioted when efforts were made to hire twelve blacks as welders in a shipyard. A wartime Fair Employment Practices Committee, established by President Roosevelt after A. Philip Randolph threatened to bring 50,000 blacks to march on Washington in protest against discrimination in defense industries, offered little in the way of substantive help because it lacked enforcement power. For the most part, blacks continued to be hired as janitors or scrubwomen, not as technicians, secretaries, or skilled craftsmen.

Nevertheless, the war had some positive impact. In 1940 the number of blacks employed in professional, white-collar, and skilled or semi-skilled jobs had been less than 20 percent. A decade later the figure had climbed to 33 percent, largely as a result of wartime changes. Black members of labor unions doubled to 1,250,000 during the war years. The end result was thus another contradiction: some upward mobility—enough to spur hope—yet pervasive discrimination as well to remind one constantly of the depths of racism to be overcome.

A third impact came in the armed forces. There, the struggle was in some ways the hardest. When blacks in Tennessee demanded that the governor appoint Negroes to the state's draft board, he responded: "This is a white man's country. . . . The Negro had nothing to do with the settling of America." The army set a quota for the number of blacks to be inducted, the navy restricted Negroes to the position of mess boys, Red Cross workers segregated blood supplies into "white" and "colored" bottles, and training camps, especially in the South, became infamous for their persecution of blacks. A Negro private at Fort Benning, Georgia, was lynched; military officials refused to act when a black army nurse was brutally beaten for defying Jim Crow seating on a Montgomery, Alabama, bus; and religious services were segregated, the sign at one base proclaiming separate worship for "Catholics, Jews, Protestants, and Negroes." But even in the armed services, some positive changes occurred: more and more blacks were trained for combat positions; some integration took place on an experimental basis; and above all, thousands upon thousands of soldiers experienced some taste of life without prejudice in places like France and Hawaii.[4]

Significantly, each of these changes exhibited a common theme: the interaction of some improvement together with daily reminders of ongoing oppression. The chemistry of the process was crucial. Simultaneous with new exposure to travel, the prospect of better jobs, and higher expectations, came the reality of daily contact with Jim Crow in the armed forces, housing, and on the job. The juxtaposition could not help but spawn anger and frustration. The possibility of some improvement generated the expectations for still more, and when those expectations were dashed, a rising tide of protest resulted.

World War II thus provided the forge within which anger and outrage, long suppressed, were shaped into new expressions of protest. Searing contradictions between the rhetoric of fighting a war against racism abroad while racism continued unabated at home galvanized anger and transformed it into political and social activism. "Our war is not against Hitler and Europe," one black columnist proclaimed, "but against the Hitlers in America." Epitomizing the ideological irony at the heart of America's war effort was the slogan among black draftees: "Here lies a black man killed fighting a yellow man for the glory of a white man."

To fight against such absurdity, blacks rushed to join protest organizations like the NAACP. Local chapters tripled in number while national membership increased 900 percent to over 500,000 people. As black newspapers took up the cry for the "double V" campaign—victory at home as well as victory abroad—their circulation increased by 40 percent. Negroes had their "own war" at home, declared the Pittsburgh *Courier*, a war "against oppression and exploitation from without and against disorganization and lack of confidence within." As if to illustrate the changes that were occurring, southern black leaders meeting in Durham, North Carolina, in October 1942 demanded complete equality for the Negro in American life "[We are] fundamentally opposed to the principle and practice of compulsory segregation in our American society," the Durham meeting declared. Ten years earlier such a statement would have been inconceivable.[5]

As the war against Hitler drew to a close, this sense of ferment and protest grew. Something had changed. Whether in northern cities or southern towns, black Americans exhibited a powerful determination to build on the energies of the war years, to secure a permanent FEPC, to abolish the poll tax, to achieve the basic right of citizenship involved in voter registration, to outlaw forever the terrorism of lynching. Over a million black soldiers had fought in a war to preserve democracy and eliminate racism. Hundreds of thousands more had achieved a glimmer of hope of what their society might become. They were not about to return quietly to the status quo of racism as usual. It was a moment of possiblity.

The veterans led the way. Sometimes even before they took off their uniforms they headed for the voter registration office at the county courthouse. In the heart of Mississippi, Medgar Evers went to cast his ballot even though whites warned that they would shoot him if he tried. In Terrell County, Georgia (long known as "Terrible Terrell"), soldiers came back intent on challenging the most oppressive structure of power in the country. In Columbia, Tennessee, black veterans made it clear that things were not going to be "business as usual" and that there would have to be a "new deal" in the jobs that blacks held, the way they were treated, the rights of manhood they insisted upon. Some places, like Winston-Salem or Greensboro or Atlanta, even witnessed the building of black political machines to choose candidates to run for city-wide office.

There were some successes. More than 18,000 blacks registered to vote in Atlanta in 1946 in response to a massive registration drive. In Winston-Salem 3,000 new voters were responsible in 1947 for choosing the first black alderman in that city. A few miles away in Greensboro, voter registration drives resulted in doubling the number of blacks on the rolls, and Randolph Blackwell, now a young veteran, helped lead a campaign against the traditional political chicanery where whites bought black votes and ignored black interests. Across the South between 1940 and 1947, the number of blacks registered to vote increased from 2 to 12 percent.

But by far the most visible response was one of terror, pure and simple. When Medgar Evers and four other veterans went to the courthouse to vote, white men with pistols drove them away. In Georgia, Eugene Talmadge won the gubernatorial nomination in a campaign where he proclaimed that "no Negro will vote in Georgia for the next four years."

Afterward, the only black man who had voted in one district was killed in his front yard by four white men. Nearby, in Walton County, whites shot and killed two other blacks; and when one of their wives recognized a member of the gang, the two women were murdered also. As Isaac Woodward got off the bus in South Carolina, still wearing his uniform, policemen blinded him with billy clubs. And in Columbia, Tennessee, where "uppity" blacks were insisting upon their rights, whites rioted in protest, seventy Negroes were arrested, and a mob broke into the jail to murder two of the prisoners. All of this occurred in the first eight months of 1946.[6]

Behind the terror lay a hundred other ways of quelling dissent. As one black story had it, whenever the registrar asked a Negro the meaning of "habeas corpus," the real message was, "habeas corpus—that means that this black man ain't going to register today." Ninety-five percent of all blacks in the South were employed by whites, the head of the white Citizens Council in Mississippi pointed out, and anyone who dared to register to vote could simply be told to "take a vacation." In Greenwood, Mississippi, a white insurance agent informed a black client that if he wished to retain his policy, he had better not register to vote. Elsewhere, as in Alabama, a black voter applicant was required to get two whites to vouch for his citizenship. The chances of doing so were summed up by a former president of the Alabama Bar Association: "No Negro is good enough and no Negro will ever be good enough to participate in making the law under which the white people in Alabama have to live." The bottom line was delivered by Senator Theodore Bilbo. Campaigning in 1946 for reelection as Mississippi's senator, he declared: "If there is a single man or woman serving [as a registrar] who can not think up questions enough to disqualify undesirables, then write Bilbo or any good lawyer and there are a hundred good questions which can be furnished. . . . But you know and I know what is the best way to keep the nigger from voting. You do it the night before the election. I don't have to tell you any more than that. Red-blooded men know what I mean." Bilbo winked and left the stage.[7]

Clearly, the commitment to protest meant nothing if those seeking their citizenship rights were not permitted to survive. The basic rights guaranteed by the Constitution—to assemble peacefully, to speak freely, to engage in political action—none of these could exist without the minimum guarantee of physical security. Yet those whites appointed and elected to enforce the law were among its most militant violators. Only if the federal government was willing to intervene, only if the Congress took steps, only if the president was willing to act could the moment of possibility become a time of achieving democracy.

The man with the most power in the federal government had a mixed record on civil rights. As a product of the Pendergrast machine in Missouri, Harry S. Truman understood the importance of paying attention to the 130,000 black voters in his constituency. Not surprisingly, his Senate record reflected these political realities. Truman supported legislation to abolish the poll tax, appropriations for the FEPC, passage of antilynching legislation, and an end to the filibuster on an anti–poll tax bill. But political astuteness did not necessarily represent personal commitment. Truman was reported to have told one southern colleague: "You know I am against this [anti-lynching bill], but if it comes to a vote, I have to vote for it. My sympathies are with you but the Negro vote in Kansas City and St. Louis is too important." On another occasion Truman held hearings on racial discrimination in the defense industry that appeared to offer sympathy and support to blacks. Yet a Truman aide told friends: "If anybody [thinks] the committee is going to help black bastards into a hundred dollar a week job, they [are] sadly mistaken." The Pittsburgh *Courier* viewed Truman's nomination as vice-president in 1944 over Henry Wallace as "an appeasement of the South," and evidently some southerners agreed. On the funeral train bringing President Roosevelt's body back to Washington, one southern senator observed: "Everything is going to be alright—the new president knows how to handle the niggers."[8]

Truman's record on the controversial FEPC issue highlighted the ambiguity of his position. In a remarkable departure from his predecessor, he intervened openly with Congress on behalf of legislation to create a permanent FEPC. To abandon the principle on which the FEPC had been built, Truman wrote the chairman of the House Rules Committee, was "unthinkable." Yet after saying this, the president appeared reluctant to do much else. "There is yet no evidence," the Pittsburgh *Courier* editorialized in September 1945, "that he has tried to use any of his great power to bring pressure on the recalcitrant Southern senators." Indeed, on the other side, Truman refused to permit the wartime FEPC to order Washington's transit system to hire black operators. The act so outraged black lawyer Charles Houston that he resigned from the FEPC, protesting the government's failure to "enforce democratic practices and protect minorities in its own capital. . . ." Such data caused one observer to wonder whether Truman's statements on behalf of civil rights were "perhaps an attempt to curry favor with liberal groups in and out of

Congress while at the same time not antagonizing those who opposed the FEPC?"[9]

Now, in the face of the brutal repression of black efforts to secure their citizenship, the president came under renewed pressure to act. All during the spring and summer of 1946, black protest groups and their white allies demanded action. "SPEAK, SPEAK, MR. PRESIDENT," pickets outside the White House demanded. Fifteen thousand people marched to the Lincoln Memorial demanding an outlawing of the Ku Klux Klan after violence in Georgia, Tennessee, and South Carolina. Eleanor Roosevelt and Channing Tobias (of the Phelps-Stokes Fund) created a National Committee for Justice in Columbia, Tennessee, and more than forty religious and civil rights organizations joined the NAACP in a National Emergency Committee against Violence. When the president met a delegation of the committee in 1946 to discuss their demands for antilynching legislation, he told the group: "My God, I had no idea it was as terrible as that. We have to do something. . . ."

The president's response was to create a Committee on Civil Rights in December 1946. The idea was introduced at the meeting with National Emergency Committee leaders by Truman's aide, David K. Niles, as though a spontaneous response to the protests of the delegation. In fact, it had already been decided upon prior to the meeting. The idea had a long history. During the racial violence of 1943, two southerners, Howard Odum and Jonathan Daniels, had suggested the creation of such a commission to FDR, only to be rebuffed because the president considered other issues more pressing. Three years later the same basic concept was revived, as a means both of satisfying black demands and of providing an authoritative sounding board for recommendations on civil rights.[10]

The committee performed its work effectively. Comprised of such distinguished individuals as Charles Wilson of General Electric, Frank Porter Graham of the University of North Carolina, Franklin Roosevelt, Jr., and Channing Tobias, it surveyed the entire spectrum of race relations in America and concluded that something was desperately wrong. "TO SECURE THESE RIGHTS," the committee's report, recommended a series of actions to correct racial inequality, including establishment of a civil rights division in the Justice Department, the creation of a permanent commission on civil rights, enactment of antilynching legislation, abolition of the poll tax, passage of laws to protect the rights of qualified voters, desegregation of the armed forces, elimination of grants-in-aid from the federal government to segregated institutions, enactment of a permament FEPC, home rule for the District of

Columbia, and support for the legal attack on segregated housing. Almost immediately, Truman endorsed the report, and the day after its release, ordered the Justice Department to intervene on behalf of plaintiffs seeking to invalidate restrictive covenants in the housing segregation case then going to the Supreme Court. As a further indication of his support, on 2 February 1948, the president submitted to Congress his message on civil rights, enthusiastically endorsing most of the major recommendations of his civil rights committee.[11]

All this took place in a sharply changing political climate. As early as 1947, Clark Clifford, Truman's leading political adviser, had concluded that the 1948 election would hinge upon winning the support of "labor and the urban minorities." Over the preceding eight years, the black population in leading northern cities had grown by almost two million. In states such as New York, New Jersey, Pennsylvania, Ohio, Michigan, and Illinois, the black vote consituted a potential balance of power; and Truman could not take this vote for granted. The more liberal wing of the New Deal coalition never fully trusted Truman, viewing him as a temporizer on social reform, a man of limited vision and stature. Henry Wallace, Roosevelt's vice-president before Truman, was now attempting to forge a new liberal coalition built around opposition to Truman's cold war policies and support for far-reaching domestic reform. As the chief spokesman for the new Progressive party, Wallace championed civil rights as one of his major issues, refusing to appear before segregated audiences, and threatening to win away from the Democratic party the black support it had become accustomed to during the previous decade.

To deflect this assault from the left, Truman pursued a two-pronged strategy. First, he depicted Wallace as a "fellow traveler" of the Communist party, naïve about Russian imperialism at best, a witting or unwitting ally at worst. Second, he depicted himself as the true heir of FDR, running on a platform fully as liberal as any domestic program yet advocated. By early 1948 Truman had announced his support for comprehensive health insurance, improved old-age benefits, and federal aid to education and housing. A strong civil rights program was pivotal to this second approach. Through such a program, Truman could prove his liberal credentials to former New Dealers, prevent the black vote from being lost to Wallace's camp, and secure the critical margin of victory in a close election. Truman even managed to join the civil rights issue to his attack on Wallace's international position, arguing that the only way to oppose the advance of Communism in the world was to show that America practiced democracy at home.[12]

Thus, for the first time in more than seventy-five years, the politics of race became critical in a presidential election. Truman himself played a dual role. After his bold civil rights message of February, the president retreated quickly. Southern governors and senators had threatened to bolt the party in protest, and white southern newspapers accused the president of "stabbing the south in the back." Hoping to appease the white South while holding on to his liberal image with blacks, Truman refrained from any action, substantive or rhetorical, on behalf of civil rights for the next five months. He even urged the democratic platform committee to stand by its ineffectual 1944 plank on "racial minorities." But that strategy would not succeed with the labor, liberal, and civil rights coalition of the Democratic party's northern wing. "To those who say the civil rights program is an infringement of state's rights," Hubert Humphrey told the Democratic convention in July, "I say this, that the time has come for the Democratic Party to get out of the shadow of state's rights and to walk forthrightly into the bright sunshine of human rights." Instead of Truman's plank, the convention endorsed a minority report, calling for the guarantee of an equal right to vote, equal employment opportunity, and equal treatment in the armed services.[13]

Not to be outdone, Truman interpreted this defeat as a victory for his own convictions, boldly announcing to the convention that he stood a hundred percent behind his civil rights program. With the most reactionary southerners already bolting to the State's Rights party candidacy of Strom Thurmond, Truman had nothing to lose. Indeed, by September, he returned to the full civil rights enthusiasm of February, becoming the first president to campaign in Harlem and trumpeting his commitment to civil rights reform. His strategy was successful. To the surprise of nearly everyone, Truman achieved victory on election day, with black support proving decisive in the states of California, Illinois, and Ohio.[14] The question was, What would that mean for those blacks still seeking their citizenship rights?

In a substantive sense the answer was clear: very little. Of all the major issues that existed in the spring of 1946—FEPC, desegregation of the armed forces, abolition of the poll tax, the right to register to vote—action occurred only in the armed forces, and then primarily for political reasons. On 26 July 1948 Truman issued two executive orders, one calling for an end to segregation in the armed forces, the other for creation of a fair employment board to eliminate discrimination in the civil service. But, Truman's timing had been dictated by a new threat from A. Philip Randolph to engage in civil disobedience and draft resistance if the armed forces remained segregated. Even then, little happened as a result of the executive order. It was not until after the Korean War that the army was integrated.

On other issues even less happened. Although Truman vigorously supported FEPC each year in policy statements, his tactics in following through were less than effective, causing some to wonder whether or not the entire process was simply a charade. When Truman had the opportunity to create a wartime FEPC by executive order during the Korean conflict, he refused to do so. Moreover, emphasis on the FEPC—by all estimates the most difficult civil rights measure to achieve—may have injured the possibility of securing legislative action on more attainable measures such as abolition of the poll tax and enactment of antilynching legislation. Senators Hubert Humphrey and Kenneth Wherry, among others, believed that less rhetoric and more action in the areas of lynching and voting could have produced results. Indeed, there seems little basis for disagreeing with historian Steven Lawson that "whether by temperament or design [Truman] often staked out a bold position and quickly retreated."[15]

Perhaps the most accurate verdict on Truman's civil rights record is to recognize him as a consummate practitioner of the "politics of gesture." He was the first president ever to address the NAACP (1947), the first president to identify civil rights as a moral issue, the first president to create a national commission to study racial injustice, and the first president to denounce racial discrimination as intolerable. These words were sufficient to outrage many southerners. Yet as the historian William Berman has observed, such southerners "failed to understand that Truman was engaged in symbolic action, with rhetoric as a substitute for a genuine legislative commitment." Thus, "a speech here and a letter there would assure him of some liberal support and gratitude for these efforts," while making unnecessary any further action.[16]

An argument could be made that Truman's position represented substantial progress. It *was* important that the president of the United States made gestures toward the rights of black Americans and helped legitimate racial justice as an issue of concern. But for those who looked from the perspective of black Americans and shared the sense of possibility that existed in the immediate postwar months, there could only be disappointment. Even the good words had come primarily in response to the political necessity of winning black votes and the international necessity of deflecting Communist propaganda. Although it was demonstrably true that southern power in Congress and the institutional barriers of the Senate filibuster made difficult the enactment of civil rights legislation, black spokesmen were correct when they said that much more could have been done, particularly in all the areas of executive action: rapid desegregation of the armed forces, using Justice Department attorneys to prosecute violators of civil rights in the South, seeking more vigorous action on antilynching and poll tax legislation. Political scientist Samuel Lubell has written that during the Truman administration the president ran as hard as he could in order to stand still. Lubell's words describe the politics of civil rights as well. Despite all the fine gestures, all the political speeches about the priority of civil rights, not very much had been done for the average black man seeking to become a full-fledged citizen.

On 8 September 1948 Isaac Nixon was warned not to cast his ballot in Wrightsville, Georgia. The army veteran disregarded the advice. He was murdered before the sun had set. A few days later another band of whites drove the president of the local NAACP branch from his home and forced him to flee to Atlanta for safety. In November an all-white jury acquitted the men accused of Nixon's murder. For these black Americans, the politics of gesture was not enough.[17]

The failure of Congress and the president to improve dramatically the citizenship status of black Americans placed an increasingly heavy burden on the judicial system as the sole source of help for civil rights advocates. From its founding in 1909, the NAACP had recognized the importance of waging legal war against the consequences of segregation and racism. One area of emphasis was voting rights. There, blacks had scored major victories in the cases of *U.S.* v. *Classic* (1942) and especially *Smith* v. *Allwright* (1944). The latter invalidated the "white primary," which excluded black voters from the only election that counted in the one-party South. Although neither Roosevelt nor Truman followed up on these victories through prosecution of violators, some major judicial battles had been won. Now, attention shifted more and more to the issue of segregation itself, initially through the demand that separate facilities in fact be made equal, and then through challenging frontally the constitutionality of Jim Crow itself. The battle was long, the courage it required enormous.

With skill and foresight, black attorneys focused initially on graduate education, the most vulnerable area of the separate but equal doctrine. No one could argue that a state provided equal law school opportunities for its black residents if Negroes were segregated in a one-room schoolhouse without adequate library resources, or sent out of state to another institution. Brilliantly, Charles Houston, the Harvard-educated NAACP counselor who would train a generation of civil rights attorneys at Howard University Law School, argued before the Supreme Court that Missouri could not train someone to practice law *in* Missouri by sending them elsewhere. In *Missouri ex rel. Gaines* (1939), the court agreed, mandating the creation of a fully equal law school for blacks in Missouri. But if that ruling was to hold, should not the same doctrine of full equality apply to high school facilities as well? And might not new definitions of equality eventually require the eradication of so many Jim Crow institutions that segregation itself would be threatened?[18]

The student of Charles Houston who would carry these questions to the Supreme Court was Thurgood Marshall, a combination preacher, community organizer, legal strategist, *bon vivant*, and political wizard. During the 1940s he traveled throughout the South, organizing teachers to fight for equal pay, parents to insist upon equal bus transportation, and lawyers to risk their practices by standing up for equality. Wherever he went he built coalitions, networks of people who would "travel the river" with him. "Everybody loved Thurgood," one NAACP staff officer said, "Marshall had the common touch." Whereas previous NAACP leaders spoke down to the people, another black observed, "Thurgood Marshall was *of* the people. He knew how to get through to them. Out in Texas or Oklahoma or down the street here in Washington at the Baptist church, he would make these rousing speeches that would have them all jumping out of their seats." Because Marshall was willing to put his own life on the line, others were willing to follow. As Herbert Hill of the NAACP observed, "He was a very courageous figure. He would travel to the court houses of the South, and folks would come from miles, some of them on muleback or horseback, to see 'the nigger lawyer' who stood up in white men's courtrooms."[19]

It was not surprising, then, that someone like J. A. DeLaine was willing to take a chance on Marshall. The black minister from Clarendon County, South Carolina, saw in the NAACP's chief counsel an ally worth suffering for. The cost was high. "Before it was over," Richard Kluger notes,

> they fired him from the schoolhouse at which he had taught devotedly for ten years. And they fired his wife and two of his sisters and a niece. And they threatened him with bodily harm. And they sued him on trumped up charges and convicted him in a kangaroo court and left him with a judgment that denied him credit from any bank. And they burned his house to the ground while the fire department stood around watching the flames consume the night. And they stoned the church at which he pastored. And fired shotguns at him out of the dark. . . . All of this . . . because he was black and brave. And because others followed when he had decided the time had come to lead.

But DeLaine and Marshall had a cause. They believed in it, and because they did, Clarendon County became one of the five cases that would eventually be called *Brown* v. *Board of Education*.[20]

The legal struggle did not go easily. In 1950 Marshall pushed the court further than ever on the issue of "separate but equal," arguing in *Sweatt* v. *Painter* and in *McLaurin* v. *Board of Regents* that equality could not be measured by dollars or physical plant alone. The reputation of the faculty, the companionship of peers, the stimulation of interchange with the best minds—all had to be considered as well. Hence, even Oklahoma's decision to accept George McLaurin as a student at the state law school "on a segregated basis" was not adequate because being required to eat in a separate alcove in the cafeteria, or sit in a roped-off area of the classroom, or be assigned a dingy segregated desk in the library could not constitute equality. Rather, Marshall insisted, such regulations created "a badge of inferiority which effects [McLaurin's] relationship, both to his fellow students and to his professors." When the Supreme Court agreed, it had gone far toward including psychological, social, and spiritual considerations in its definition of equality.

But that was not the same thing as overturning segregation, or asking the court to reverse its own precedent in the historic 1896 case *Plessy* v. *Ferguson*. The NAACP had brilliantly used the enemy's own words to erode the substance of his legal position. Now it had to take the offensive and persuade the court to arrive at a radically new legal position overturning fifty years of law. The doubts that beseiged NAACP lawyers were reflected in a memo written at the time by Associate Justice Robert Jackson of the Supreme Court:

> Since the close of the Civil War the United States has been 'hesitating between two worlds—one dead, the other powerless to be born.' War brought an old order to an end, but . . . proved unequal to founding a new one. Neither north nor south has been willing really to adopt its racial practices to its professions.

Troubled, Jackson wondered whether the Court was the proper instrument to eradicate "these fears, prides and prejudices on which segregation rests," whether the judiciary could reverse half a century of law, and chart a new course for America.[21]

Both inside the courtroom and in the judicial chambers, the battle was dramatic. Marshall cited evidence accumulated by psychologist Kenneth Clark that black children educated in segregated schools responded more positively to white dolls than to black dolls, thereby arguing that segregation helped create low self-esteem and "a badge of inferiority" in black children. His adversary, in turn, argued the irrelevance of sociological tests and the importance of upholding legal precedent. If the judges had taken a vote immediately, they would have been divided—perhaps five to four or six to three, but with no unanimity on the necessity of reversing segregation.

Then Earl Warren joined the Court. He was chosen by Dwight Eisenhower in 1953 to be the new chief justice after Fred Vinson died suddenly, and he brought to his position the leadership, compassion, sensitivity, and simplicity required to forge union out of division. A politician by training and experience, he understood the need to woo potential foes such as Justices Stanley Reed and Robert Jackson. A man of morality and vision, he understood also the importance of unanimity on behalf of principle. Hence, the decision he wrote for the Court was neither complicated nor contentious. Rather, it emphasized the simple fact that education represents a central experience in life, that what children learn in school stays with them the rest of their time on earth, and consequently that "to separate [those children] from others of similar age and qualifications solely because of their race generates a feeling of inferiority as to their status in the community that may affect their hearts and minds in a way unlikely ever to be undone." For that reason, Warren concluded, segregation was inherently unconstitutional and unequal. "Any language in *Plessy* v. *Ferguson* contrary to these findings is rejected."[22]

Fifteen years after the *Gaines* decision in Missouri, seven years after J. A. DeLaine agreed to challenge the Clarendon County School Board, and more than sixty years after Jim Crow was legally born, segregated schools were acknowledged to be an abomination. "We have won," blacks exulted. It appeared that the courts had done what politicians had refused to do.

Initially, the response to *Brown* was one of hope and optimism. Black newspapers hailed the Court's action, confident that the structure of segregation now would quickly be dismantled. Thurgood Marshall predicted the beginning of integration within six months and completion of the process within five years. Even the white South initially reacted to the *Brown* decision more with resignation than with rebellion. Only James Byrnes in South Carolina, Herman Talmadge in Georgia, and Hugh White in Mississippi indulged in the rhetoric of outraged resistance. More representative were comments that regretted the *Brown* decision, but called for calm acceptance of its consequences. Thus, Governor Francis Cherry of Arkansas declared: "Arkansas will obey the law. It always has." And "Big" Jim Folsom of Alabama stated: "When the Supreme Court speaks, that's the law." "The end of the world has not come for the South or for the nation," the Louisville *Courier Journal* editorialized. "The Supreme Court's ruling is not itself a revolution. It is rather an acceptance of a process that has been going on a long time." Cities like Louisville, Kentucky, Little Rock, Arkansas, and Greensboro, North Carolina, indicated that they were ready to begin the process of compliance.[23]

Yet the *Brown* decision by itself existed in a vacuum. It required commitment, leadership, and tangible action if it was to become more than an empty letter. As one legal scholar said at the time:

> The law is a landing force [of change]. It makes the beachhead. But the breakthrough, if it is to be significant, is broadened by forces from behind which take advantage of the opening to go the rest of the way. Where these forces are present, significant alteration of social practice is a result. Where they do not exist, the law has been unable to hold its beachhead and the legal action becomes a kind of military monument on which is only recorded, "we were here."

Despite initial positive signs, it quickly became clear that the "forces from behind" were unwilling to act. The Court itself, as one price for securing unanimity, delayed for a year its own decision on how to implement desegregation. When that decision was handed down, it called for remanding cases to the district courts, implementation procedures to begin "with all deliberate speed," but with no deadline set. In the South itself, meanwhile, those willing to act decisively in support of integration found themselves suddenly alone, without reinforcement from either economic or political leaders, or from the courts. With no tangible encouragement to proceed, they withdrew from the battle, forsaking the beachhead that had been won to defenders of the old order.[24]

No one deserved more censure for the failure to follow through than the president himself. In 1954 Dwight Eisenhower enjoyed more moral authority and political strength than any president since Franklin Roosevelt at the beginning of the New Deal. His position, in some ways, was analogous to that of Andrew Johnson at the end of the Civil War. The South had been defeated, overwhelmingly. White southerners felt resigned, helpless, waiting for cues as to how to respond. Decisive, immediate leadership in such a situation held the promise of transforming the social and political landscape.

Yet Eisenhower, like Andrew Johnson ninety years before, refused the opportunity. Had he moved forcefully into the vacuum and declared, "The Supreme Court has spoken, integration is now the law of the land. The courts' decision will be enforced by me with all the energy at my command. No resistance will be tolerated," it is likely that school districts across the South would have commenced desegregation. Their action would not have been without resistance, but there would have been no choice except compliance. Instead, Eisenhower waffled. Asked repeatedly whether he endorsed the Supreme Court's decision, he said that he would not comment on the merits of the decision. In fact, he disapproved of it vigorously, commenting to some that the appointment of Earl Warren was the biggest mistake he had ever made, and to others that "the Supreme Court decision set back progress in the South at least fifteen years."

Central to Eisenhower's posture was his conviction that the federal government had no right to intervene in affairs of local government. Although he implemented desegregation in federal installations and worked effectively to bring about integration of schools and public accommodations in the nation's capital, he did virtually nothing to support those seeking change in the southern states. After Governor Price Daniel called out the Texas Rangers to prevent the integration of a high school in Mansfield that had been ordered desegregated by a federal court, Eisenhower refused to intervene. Surely, he explained, no one would want to see a federal police force take over local police matters. When the University of Alabama expelled its first black pupil, Autherine Lucey, in direct violation of a federal district court order, the president's only response was to say, "I would certainly hope that we could avoid any interference." Even after the murder of a black seeking to register to vote in Mississippi, and dynamite explosions in Tennessee and Alabama, Eisenhower refused to speak out against violence or the widespread use of economic reprisals.

Perhaps most disturbing was the fact that those in the White House who urged a bolder response to the civil rights crisis encountered only puzzlement and indifference. When the only Negro staff member at the White House expressed concern at the president's silence in the aftermath of the lynching of fourteen-year-old Emmett Till in Mississippi, he incurred the wrath of a colleague otherwise considered to be sympathetic. Blacks had not demonstrated sufficient gratitude for all that had been done for them, the colleague said, and instead were being too "aggressive" in their demands for justice, showing an "ugliness and surliness" that was alienating white allies. Because blacks were being so "intemperate," the president had no political basis for speaking out. Ever since the presidency of Teddy Roosevelt, William E. Leuchtenburg has noted, the White House had been known as a "bully pulpit." But when Eisenhower was president, "it was an empty pulpit. It is not too much to say that a great deal of the violence as well as the fearfully slow rate of compliance after 1954 may be laid at Eisenhower's door."[25]

Even those events that might be construed as favorable to blacks suggested little positive about the administration's attitudes. When Attorney General Herbert Brownell presented a four-part civil rights bill to the Cabinet for consideration in 1956, only two of his colleagues supported him. The president, partly concerned with securing black votes in the election, endorsed creation of a permanent civil rights commission, but denied approval to a section of the bill that would sanction Justice Department intervention on behalf of desegregation. Although Brownell boldly (and inaccurately) presented the entire package as having administration backing, he was ultimately sabotaged. After Senator Richard Russell of Georgia described section three of the legislation as an effort "to bring to bear the whole might of the Federal Government . . . to force almagamation of white and Negro children in the state supported schools of the South . . . and to create another reconstruction at bayonet point," Eisenhower retreated, declaring that his only objective was to assist the right to vote. Indeed, the president said, he had read the bill that morning and found "certain phrases that I didn't completely understand." As if to settle the question, the president told a reporter that "No," he did not believe the attorney general should be empowered to bring school desegregation suits.

When an emasculated version of the civil rights bill was finally passed in 1957, southerners viewed it as a great victory for themselves. By 1959 the legislation had not added a single southern black to the voting rolls. Nor did Eisenhower's Justice Department prosecute any of the complaints of outrageous discrimination against voting in states such as Mississippi. Three years later, another act was passed to safeguard voting rights, yet this too lacked any real substance. Senator Harry Byrd, leader of "the massive resistance" forces, boasted that the bill was "in the main . . . a victory for the South," and Democrat Joseph Clark, a civil rights supporter, called the legislation "a crushing defeat." "Surely," he added, "in this battle on the Senate floor the roles of Grant and Lee at Appomattox have been reversed. . . ."[26]

Eisenhower's silence, ambiguity, and abdication of leadership encouraged segregationists to believe that nothing stood in the way of their circumventing the Supreme Court. Within a year the resignation that had prevailed after the first *Brown* decision had gradually changed into optimism about preserving the status quo, and finally into outright and systematic resistance to desegregation. Those who might have supported compliance if the president had given them no other option now found themselves competing with the rabid right for control of the political spectrum, attempting to become even more segregationist. "In this atmosphere," the historian C. Vann Woodward has observed, "where the NAACP was virtually driven underground in some states, words began to change their meanings so that the moderate became a man who dared to open his mouth, and an extremist someone who favored eventual compliance with the law, and compliance was something which was equated with treason."[27]

Resistance mushroomed in direct correlation to the growing evidence that the federal government would do nothing to counteract it. After the Supreme Court indicated in the second *Brown* decision that immediate compliance would not be necessary, state governors shifted their attention from how to comply to how to circumvent. As Eisenhower offered tacit sanction to segregationists in Texas and at the University of Alabama, state legislatures began to pass resolutions calling for massive resistance, with Virginia, Alabama, Mississippi, and Georgia claiming the right to "interpose" themselves against the federal government, and declaring the Supreme Court's decision "null, void, and of no effect." Nearly all states passed "pupil assignment laws" that transferred authority over schools to local school boards in order to avoid statewide suits by the NAACP, and then used phrases like "the general welfare" as criteria under which students could be assigned to schools, thereby eliminating race as a basis for placement even while maintaining segregation. By the spring of 1956, 101 of 128 congressmen from the former Confederate states had signed "the Southern manifesto," throwing down the gauntlet of resistance to the federal government.

The crisis at Central High School in Little Rock, Arkansas, dramatized the political forces at work. Under court order to desegregate, Little Rock school officials were prepared to comply. But Governor Orville Faubus determined to intervene. Caught in a tight reelection battle, he chose the strategy of "outniggering" his opponents, using the black school children of Little Rock as his foil. After creating a crisis by announcing that it would not be possible to maintain order in the face of integration (no such threat existed), he instructed National Guard troops to block the entry of black school children into Central High. Rallied by Faubus's words, a crowd of angry whites attacked the black children seeking admission to the school. Eisenhower refused to intervene, instead agreeing to meet with Faubus in an effort to find a compromise. Faubus gave his word that he would create no further problems, but then, unashamedly breaking his promise, the governor withdrew state troops from the high school, left the capitol, and did nothing to prevent a shrieking crowd from barring the black children.

Stunned and embarrassed, Eisenhower finally federalized the Arkansas National Guard and dispatched a thousand paratroopers to Little Rock. To have done otherwise, he recognized, would have been to "acquiesce in anarchy and the dissolution of the union." Yet his action was too little and too late. The time for the use of moral authority to prevent resistance was now past. Indeed, when Eisenhower was finally moved to act, it was because his own sense of the military code had been breached: a lieutenant (the governor) had been guilty of insubordination. The principle of integration was quite secondary. Nor was it possible, in the long run, to call the Little Rock episode a victory for desegregation. Despite a Supreme Court order, Governor Faubus closed the schools in Little Rock for the entire next year. Virginia cities did the same to prevent integration in that state. During the last three years of the Eisenhower administration, the number of school districts engaging even in token desegregation fell to 49—in stark contrast to the total of 712 during the first three years after *Brown*.[28]

Tragically, the problem was not limited to "massive resistance" states like Virginia, Alabama, and Mississippi. Indeed, the process of circumvention reached its highest form of sophistication in the more "moderate" or "progressive" states. North Carolina, for example, known for its fine universities and intellectual leaders like Frank Porter Graham, had long been viewed as "an inspiring exception to Southern racism." Yet in reality, it was simply more clever at accomplishing the task. When the *Brown* decision was first handed down, as many as seven cities across the state, including Charlotte, Winston-Salem, Raleigh, and Greensboro, indicated a readiness to comply, and local school boards met to reconsider issues such as transportation patterns and construction of new buildings in light of the *Brown* decision. For the first few months, a similar mood prevailed among state educational leaders.

But in North Carolina, as in the nation, the "forces from behind" failed to advance the beachhead established by law. Governor Luther Hodges was to North Carolina what Dwight Eisenhower was to the nation—except that instead of simply sanctioning the forces of resistance by inaction, Hodges marshalled them himself, all under the guise of the "politics of moderation." Initially, the governor simply used tactics like the 1955 Pupil Assignment Act. But as the gubernatorial election of 1956 approached, Hodges moved to a plan that would provide state money to enable any white student threatened with integration to attend a private school. The proposal would also permit any school district to close its schools if integration occurred against the wishes of the community. As Hodges presented the issue, voluntary segregation offered the only possibility of avoiding what he chose to describe as the equally untenable extremes of integration or shutting down the public school system. Although a Hodges staff member had reported that whites in North Carolina were remarkably indifferent to the issue of desegregation, the governor chose to inflame racial hostility. Unabashedly invoking the imagery of miscegenation, Hodges accused the NAACP of seeking to destroy "our interracial friendship," and of attempting the destruction of their own race by "burying it in the development of the white race." It was blacks who were responsible for the crisis, Hodges insisted. "Only the person who feels he is inferior must resort to demonstrations to prove that he is not. The person convinced of his own equality . . . of his own race respect, needs no demonstrations to bolster his convictions." By Hodges's definition, there were two extreme groups in the state—the KKK and the NAACP. Only those who followed him could achieve the "middle way."

To achieve his goals, Hodges went to the voters with his plan the same summer he was waging his own reelection campaign. To liberals he offered the assurance that his proposals did not defy the Supreme Court and only provided "safety valves" for those who wished to avoid desegregation. To conservative whites he provided the guarantee that there would be virtually no integration in North Carolina under his leadership. To blacks he offered nothing, ignoring the fact that they comprised 25 percent of the state's population. Indeed, he appeared incredulous that Negroes would dare challenge him, urging his staff to seek out blacks who had signed integration petitions in order to "ascertain their reasons" and find out "if they are in earnest." Hodges's allies in North Carolina—like Eisenhower's staff in Washington—were upset by the "intemperance . . . rudeness and complete self confidence" of those blacks who insisted on their citizenship rights.

Through tactics of "moderate" white supremacy, the initial possibilities of compliance with the *Brown* decision in North Carolina were shattered. Hodges successfully portrayed his plan as the only "enlightened" solution to the school crisis. As a consequence the real issues were totally distorted. Black citizens were viewed as the cause of the crisis, white citizens as the victims. In an ultimate irony the only people with the law on their side were defined as extremists threatening law and order.

It need not have been that way. The editor of the Winston-Salem *Journal Sentinel* concluded in 1956 that "a large number of intelligent, influential North Carolinians believe that the best way . . . is to comply." Public opinion polls showed that the vast majority of whites in the state were in the middle, between active resistance and active support for integration, and could have been led either way. But Hodges chose the

path of resistance and in the process postponed meaningful desegregation in North Carolina for more than a decade—far longer than in some
states where massive resistance was practiced. The genius of Hodges's
plan, the Shelby *Star* declared, was that it would "maintain separate
school systems," but with "a tone of moderation." Recognizing what
was really going on, one Little Rock school official wrote, "You North
Carolinians have devised one of the cleverest techniques for perpetuat-
ing segregation that we have seen."[29]

In none of this were black Americans either resigned bystanders or
passive victims. The NAACP filed suit in more than 117 cities in 1955
calling for desegregation. Thousands of black parents submitted applications for their children to attend previously all-white schools, willing
to take the risk of having their credit shut down or their jobs taken away
in order to assert their citizenship rights. In Greensboro, over a period of
eighteen months after the *Brown* decision, black parents appeared at all
but two school board meetings to demand either better black facilities or
substantive action on desegregation. Nor were these people members of
a wealthy elite. They were milkmen, barbers, maids, workers in local
stock rooms. "[White people] couldn't charge it up and say [only] the
smart niggers applied," one parent noted. All these people were willing
to withstand the threat of social ostracism and economic reprisal in
order to seek a better life for their children.[30]

But no people, however brave and resilient, could accept the bitter
disappointments of the postwar years. Every victory seemed hollow.
The words of politicians were contradicted by the inaction of government agencies. Court decisions were vitiated by legalistic manipulation.
"Nothing would be worse," Justice Felix Frankfurter had said before
Brown, "than for this court to make an abstract declaration that segregation is bad and then have it evaded by tricks."[31] Yet that is what happened. Black civil rights had been defined out of existence, with basic
guarantees of citizenship made playthings for shrewd politicians. More
than any other Americans, blacks believed in the political process, in the
sanctity of the judiciary, in the rule of law. If they were victimized by the
very processes they believed in, if those in charge would not listen to
peaceful petition within the system they themselves had established,
then it would be necessary for blacks to take action on their own terms
and to express their convictions in ways that could no longer be ignored
or misunderstood. If America was to change its ways, blacks would have
to start the process.

The decision to act began with the people. On a cold fall afternoon in

1955 in Montgomery, Rosa Parks, a black seamstress, boarded a city bus after a long day at the sewing machine. She sat in the first row of the "colored" section on the bus, but Montgomery's Jim Crow rules provided that whenever enough white people boarded a public carrier to take up all the "white" seats, blacks must move back and give up their positions until the whites were seated. As more and more whites boarded the bus that day, Mrs. Parks stared out the window. The atmosphere around her filled with tension. One black got up to give his seat, but she remained. Finally the bus driver demanded that she move. No, she said, I will stay. "I felt it was just something I had to do," she later recalled. Word of her arrest spread like wildfire through the community, and within hours, black leaders had decided the time was right to strike a blow for freedom: they would boycott the city bus system the next Monday in protest.

The city's black leaders were ready. E. D. Nixon, president of the Alabama NAACP and head of the local chapter of the Brotherhood of Sleeping Car Porters, had long been looking for a cause around which to build a mass protest. Joanne Robinson, leader of the Local Women's Political Council (parallel to the segregated League of Women Voters), was ready too. She had worked hard for the desegregation of drinking fountains and the hiring of black police in the city. The idea of a bus boycott was not a new one: earlier, when other arrests had happened under similar circumstances, there had been talk of action. But the occasion had not been right because the other defendants were not as well known or as well respected in the community. Now the time was right. Rosa Parks was one of the most revered women in Montgomery. A churchgoer, secretary of the NAACP, beloved by everyone, she was a person who could unify the community. As E. D. Nixon later recalled:

> She was decent. And she was committed. First off, nobody could point no dirt at her. You had to respect her as a lady. And second, if she said she would be at a certain place at a certain time, that's when she got there . . . so when she stood up to talk, people'd shut up and listen. And when she did something people just figured it was the right thing to do.

Because she was who she was and did what she did, Rosa Parks became the key rallying point for expressing the accumulated indignation of black Montgomery.

That night and all the next day, E. D. Nixon set in motion the groundwork for protest. More than fifty community representatives gathered at the Dexter Avenue Baptist Church to plan the bus boycott, to rally church congregations on Sunday, and to create a transportation network among Negro taxi companies to take the place of the buses. By

Monday every black in Montgomery had received a message not to ride the city buses that day. Fearful that the boycott might not succeed, yet committed as never before to action, Montgomery's black leaders rose early to watch the buses go by. As dawn turned into morning and midday, the verdict was clear: virtually no one who was black rode the bus in Montgomery that day.

The Montgomery bus boycott would last for 381 days. It provided the organizing basis for a mass movement that fought back against every legal, economic, and psychological effort to destroy it. When city leaders threatened to arrest taxi drivers for violating their chauffeur licenses, blacks created car pools instead. If whites attempted to sow seeds of division between leaders of the movement, the black community came together to affirm its support for the mass protest. And when white violence threatened to provoke black counterviolence and provide a basis for police action, the Negro community responded with discipline and devotion to the philosophy of nonviolence. No incident told better the story of what happened in Montgomery than the day when a white reporter, driving a car, stopped beside an elderly black woman walking to her work as a domestic. Asked if she wished a ride, she replied, "No, my feets is tired, but my soul is rested."[32]

The Montgomery bus boycott was important for four reasons. First, it demonstrated dramatically and conclusively that black Americans were not content with the status quo and that they would sacrifice their comfort and risk their jobs in order to stand up for their dignity. For years whites interested in appeasing their own conscience had insisted that "their black people" were happy, and that any trouble came from outside agitators. For 381 days well over 90 percent of the black citizens of Montgomery expressed with their feet, every day, their vivid rejection of that white illusion.

Second, the boycott exhibited how a movement, once begun, generates its own momentum, encouraging and enhancing its participants and creating the basis for an ever-widening belief in, and ability to achieve, social change. Ironically, the boycott did not begin with the demand that the buses be integrated. Rather, community leaders advanced only a modest three-point agenda: (a) greater courtesy toward black passengers; (b) the hiring of Negro drivers for routes predominantly black; and (c) creation of a flexible line separating the black and white sections of the bus, so that where blacks comprised the majority of passengers, they would not be forced to move when additional whites boarded the bus. Yet Montgomery's white leadership refused to respond to those demands, and as the daily sacrifice of energy created a mass sense of self-confidence and determination, the movement decided that nothing short of complete integration would satisfy its demands. Over and over again, through the next fifteen years, the same experience of working together for a common cause would generate a similar heightening of consciousness and refusal to accept anything else than full equality.

Third, the boycott produced an articulate and persuasive leader. Martin Luther King, Jr., had been in Montgomery only six months when the boycott started. Still in his mid-twenties, he was neither a radical nor an activist. Indeed, he had turned down an invitation to become head of the local NAACP because he wished to build his congregation, to finish his doctorate, and to work his way slowly into the community. But his very newness made him the ideal leader to mediate between competing factions and to speak for the forces of change. Given the burden of leadership, he rose mightily to the challenge, in the process demonstrating to America the transforming power of the message of Christian love. "There comes a time," King told more than five thousand blacks on the first night of the boycott,

> when people get tired. We are here this evening to say to those who have mistreated us so long that we are tired—tired of being segregated and humiliated, tired of being kicked about by the brutal feet of oppression. . . . For many years, we have shown amazing patience. . . . But we've come here tonight to be saved from that patience that makes us patient with anything less than freedom and justice. . . . We're impatient for justice, but we still protest with love . . . love must be our regulating ideal. . . . If you will protest courageously and yet with dignity and Christian love, in the history books that are written in future generations, historians will have to pause and say "there lived a great people—a black people—who injected new meaning and dignity into the veins of civilization." This is our challenge and our overwhelming responsibility.

As thousands listened, they reaffirmed the commitment that King had galvanized. Rosa Parks had said "no" to segregation. Now, black Americans were saying "yes" to a new philosophy of mass protest.[33]

Fourth, the Montgomery bus boycott laid the foundation for the civil rights movement for the 1960s. Thousands of people had come together. They had devised the logistical strategy to overcome the obstacles placed before them. By the time the Supreme Court ruled that Montgomery's buses must integrate, they had demonstrated beyond doubt the power of a collective body to shape a new world. Out of the bus boycott came the Southern Christian Leadership Conference, headed by Dr. King, which united black ministers throughout the South in a common determination to struggle. The church would be the central institution of the movement, and its ministers the primary spokesmen for the people.

Yet even with these accomplishments, the bus boycott did not spark a national revolt. To a large extent it was a reactive strategy that depended on the right person being arrested, under the right circumstances, with the right leadership structure in place. The genius of the boycott was also its major weakness. People could refuse to ride the bus without directly and individually placing themselves at risk. The boycott was an act of omission, not commission. Hence, thousands could use it as a means of expressing their protest without incurring the danger of immediate arrest or punishment. Ideal as a way of collective expression, it nevertheless was not a vehicle for individual assaults against the racial status quo. It did not, for example, lend itself to the goal of seeking black admittance to previously all-white schools, hotels, lunch counters, theaters, churches, or government buildings. Boycotting a restaurant from which one was already excluded was not a viable option.

Thus, a new form of expression was necessary—the sit-in—to create the primary organizing tool for the direct attack against Jim Crow. Sit-ins had been tried in Chicago in 1942, in Oklahoma City in 1958, and elsewhere. But they had not made news or caught on. Now, suddenly, all that changed. On 1 February 1960, four young black freshmen at North Carolina A&T College in Greensboro, set forth on a historic journey that would ignite a decade of civil rights protests. Walking into downtown Greensboro, they entered the local Woolworth store, purchased toothpaste and other small items, and then sat at the lunch counter and demanded equal service with white persons. "We do not serve Negroes," they were told; but instead of leaving, the students remained. The next day they returned, with twenty-three of their classmates. The day after that it was sixty-six. The next day more than one hundred. By the end of the week, a thousand students joined them in downtown Greensboro. The student phase of the civil rights revolution had begun.

The story of the Greensboro sit-in movement is a microcosm of the frustration, anger, and determination that surged through the black community in the years after the *Brown* decision. Three of the four young men who journeyed to Woolworth's that day had been raised in Greensboro, a city that prided itself on its progressivism, its enlightenment, its "good" race relations. They had come of age, intellectually and politically, in the years since the *Brown* decision. Their parents were activists; some of them belonged to the NAACP, others to churches that were in the forefront of efforts to build a stronger and better political and educational life for blacks. The young men attended school at Dudley High School, the pride of the black community, a place where teachers taught you to aspire to be the best that was in you. "We were always talking about the issues," one English teacher recalled. "We might read [a poem or a novel] as a kind of pivot," but the words of John Dunne or Thomas Hardy were always related to the inalienable right of human beings to respect, freedom, and dignity. "I had to tell youngsters," the English teacher said, "that the way you find things need not happen. . . . I don't care if they push and shove you, you must not accept [discrimination] . . . you are who you are."

The message the young men heard at school was reinforced at home and in the church. Some went to Shiloh Baptist, whose minister had led civil rights protests at Shaw University in Raleigh, and who always provided support and encouragement to activists. Some also belonged to the NAACP youth group, started by Randolph Blackwell in 1943 after Ella Baker had visited town. At the weekly meetings of the youth group, students would talk about issues such as the Montgomery bus boycott, the slow pace of school desegregation, the need to "do something" to change things. And when Martin Luther King, Jr., came to Greensboro, to deliver his sermon about Christ's message for America, things began to fall into place. Dr. King's sermon was "so strong," one demonstrator recalled, "that I could feel my heart palpitating. It brought tears to my eyes."

The situation in Greensboro provided a classic example of sophisticated American racism. Although the school board had said it would desegregate schools after the *Brown* decision, it did nothing for three years, and then admitted only six blacks to previously all-white schools in an effort to make it impossible for the NAACP to launch a class action suit against the entire state. Thereafter, nothing happened, no matter how many black parents applied for transfer of their children to previously all-white schools. Typical of the school board's approach was its response to a 1959 suit by black parents. Faced with the prospect of losing in court, the school board finally admitted four black applicants to a previously all-white school to which they had applied. Then, three months later, it transferred every single white child and every single white faculty member out of that school and replaced them with blacks. It then argued in court that the legal action of the black parents was "moot" because the students were in the school to which they had originally sought entry. As one black minister declared, "These folks were primarily interested in evading, and they weren't even embarrassed."

Elsewhere, the same duplicity prevailed. When blacks attempted to integrate the local golf course, they were arrested. Then mysteriously, the club house burned down and the golf course was closed. Black college graduates from A&T and Bennett College were told by employers that they could apply for jobs as janitors and maids, but not as sales clerks or receptionists. In all this, good manners prevailed. As one black leader said, "no one ever called me nigger here," yet the underlying structure of racism remained. Greensboro, another black leader observed, was "a nice-nasty town."

As they discussed these conditions in their dormitory room at night, the four black freshmen resolved to act. Fourteen years old when the *Brown* decision was handed down, they had grown to political consciousness in the succeeding years. They were now about to become citizens, with none of the rights of citizenship. No longer were they willing to tolerate the perpetuation of injustice that they saw all around them, particularly when the highest court in the land had condemned such practices to the junk pile of history. If whites had not been able to hear the peaceful protests and petitions offered by the older generation, perhaps they would listen to the voice of a new generation, as it recorded its vocal dissent by sitting silently at a lunch counter.

The four young men drew from each other the resolve to act. On a Sunday night at the end of January, Ezell Blair, Jr., came home and asked his parents if they would be embarrassed if he got into trouble. "Why?" his parents wondered. "Because," he said, "tomorrow we're going to do something that will shake up this town." Nervous and fearful, afraid that someone might "get chicken," the four friends shored up each other's confidence until the next afternoon. "All of us were afraid," another demonstrator recalled. "But we went and did it." The result became history. "I probably felt better that day than I had ever felt in my life," Franklin McCain noted. "I felt as though I had gained my manhood. . . ."[34]

The sit-in movement spread through the South like a flash fire. Within two months demonstrations had broken out in fifty-four cities in nine states. It was as if an entire generation was ready to act, waiting for a catalyst. Greensboro provided the spark, but young blacks throughout the South provided the tinder for the response that followed. The sit-in movement was not a radical departure from the past; rather, it grew out of a tradition of protest. But the sit-ins helped reinforce and extend that tradition, and to change the form through which old as well as young would now express their demands for dignity and equality. Building on the lessons of the older generation, the young were forging a new method for carrying on the struggle. In that sense the students represented a new stage of black insurgency, reflecting the lessons as well as the frustrations of past experiences with protest. If the courts and the politicians would not listen to traditional forms of expression, then new ones would be found. After 1960 the forms of communication between white and black would never again be the same.

It is impossible in this brief summary to do justice to the multiplicity of people and social forces involved in the movement for civil rights. Nevertheless, several important themes stand out as a basis from which to understand this critical period in our history.

First, despite dramatic changes and departures, there was remarkable continuity within the black protest movement between 1945 and 1960. The veterans who came back from World War II to demand their citizenship rights helped provide the model and inspiration for those who would carry forward the struggle during the 1950s, those who refused to ride the buses in Montgomery and who helped make the sit-in movement possible in 1960. Events like World War II or the *Brown* decision were important. They created new contexts, new possibilities. But the continuing momentum that linked these contexts to each other was the willingness of blacks to seek change, to struggle for freedom, to act for justice. It was Ella Baker in 1943 who sparked the NAACP youth group that would give birth to the sit-in movement. And it was Ella Baker in 1960 who convened the conference of student demonstrators in Raleigh, and more than any other individual, was responsible for the creation of the Student Non-Violent Coordinating Committee—perhaps the most important civil rights organization of the 1960s. It was E. D. Nixon who started the NAACP in Montgomery during the 1940s and organized the bus boycott in the 1950s. It was Medgar Evers who went to cast his vote as a returning veteran in 1946, and who led the struggle for voting rights and racial justice in Mississippi until his assassination in 1963. Such continuity was not incidental. It was inherent in the protest struggle.

Second, in ways not yet fully appreciated, this struggle grew out of, and depended upon, the strength of black institutions. The foundation for E. D. Nixon's activism was the all-black Brotherhood of Sleeping Car Porters. The NAACP meeting that inspired J. A. DeLaine to attack segregation in Clarendon County took place at Allen University, a black college. Ella Baker went to Shaw, an all-black school founded during Reconstruction, and it was at Shaw that the first meeting of SNCC took place. Black high schools generated the pride and aspiration that motivated the sit-in demonstrators, and black colleges provided the primary base of recruitment for the movement. Ironically, many of these all-black institutions, which did so much to make possible the fight against segregation, would themselves suffer as a consequence. Yet their centrality testifies to the absolute necessity in the struggle for social change of retaining a strong home base, even as one seeks integration in the wider society.

Third, the response of white political and economic leaders during these years can only be described as more revealing than they would have cared to discover. With just a few exceptions, whites in positions of power refused to support the cause of civil rights unless it was directly in their self-interest to do so. Even then, the response was more often verbal than substantive. Although Dwight Eisenhower's abdication of leadership made the rhetoric of Harry Truman seem almost courageous by comparison, Truman's own record was essentially one of routine political expediency.

Finally, the refusal of whites in power to do anything voluntarily created a constant necessity for blacks to devise new stratagems of protest. As events constantly proved, simply to demand one's rights was not enough. Even if lynching was the consequence, white officials did nothing in response. Building coalitions with white liberals also proved inadequate because once the coalitions had served their purpose, they were ignored. The law itself—even through court decisions—proved more an invitation to subtle circumvention than an instrument for securing change. It seemed that only striking at the white man's pocketbook, or creating discomfort in his life, would prompt any response. Hence, each generation of blacks, even while drawing on the traditions of the past, had to forge new tactics of protest in an unending quest for something that would work.

In the spring and summer of 1960, many hoped that this situation was finally changing. Throughout black America a spirit of idealism, hope, and confidence infused young and old alike. In white America as well, it appeared that a new seed of social activism might take root. John Kennedy spoke of carrying forward the American revolution, and eliminating social injustice. He called the governor of Alabama to ask that Martin Luther King, Jr., be released from jail, and promised to sign an executive order that would eliminate discrimination in federally financed housing.

Yet the lessons of the previous fifteen years suggested that such words were only one more moment in an ongoing drama, and that the battle between black protest and white indifference would not soon come to an end. It had been a hundred years since Frederick Douglass had said, "Power concedes nothing without a demand, it never has and it never will." Little has happened since to alter the truth of his observation.

1. For a discussion of lynching during the 1930s, see Robert L. Zangrando, "The NAACP and a Federal Anti-lynching Bill, 1934–1940," *Journal of Negro History* 50 (April, 1955): 106–17; and John B. Kirby, "The Roosevelt Administration and Blacks: An Ambivalent Legacy," in *20th Century America: Recent Interpretations*, ed. Barton Bernstein and Allan Matusow (New York, 1972). On the antilynching movement, see Jacquelyn Dowd Hall, *Revolt against Chivalry* (New York, 1978). Eleanor Roosevelt engaged in extensive correspondence about the Raines case with Walter White, executive secretary of the NAACP. See the Walter White correspondence file for 1934 in the Eleanor Roosevelt Papers, Franklin D. Roosevelt Library, Hyde Park, New York.

2. Author's interview with Ella Baker, 1977–78; author's interview with Randolph Blackwell, 1973; Eugene Walker's interview with Ella Baker, 1973; Sara Evans's interview with Randolph Blackwell, 1973. For further discussion of Ella Baker, see James Forman, *The Making of a Black Revolutionary* (New York, 1975), and the recent film on her life directed by Joanne Grant.

3. DeLaine's life is discussed extensively in Richard Kluger, *Simple Justice* (New York, 1975), pp. 3–26.

4. On the black experience during World War II, see Richard Dalfiume, "The Forgotten Negro Revolution," *Journal of American History* 55 (June 1968): 90–106; Harvard Sitkoff, "Racial Militance and Interracial Violence in the Second World War," *Journal of American History* 58 (December 1971): 661–81; and Richard Dalfiume, *Desegregation of the U.S. Armed Forces: Fighting on Two Fronts, 1939–53* (Columbia, S.C., 1969). On the FEPC see Herbert Garfinkel, *When Negroes March* (Glencoe, Ill., 1959); and Jervis Anderson, *A. Philip Randolph* (New York, 1973).

5. See Dalfiume, "The Forgotten Negro Revolution," and Sitkoff, "Racial Militance and Interracial Violence." Despite evidence of considerable change, there was also reason for skepticism. Whatever leverage blacks could mobilize at a time of national vulnerability was dwarfed by the power of white political and economic leaders to define the national agenda and control the government's response. President Roosevelt himself consistently refused to endorse black objectives. Throughout his administration he did virtually nothing to support antilynching legislation, not even permitting his attorney general to invoke the Lindbergh kidnapping statute to prosecute the mob that lynched Claude Raines in 1934. He failed to endorse abolition of the poll tax, refused to have the Justice Department join in the challenge to the white primary, and, after the Supreme Court had invalidated such techniques of disfranchisement, refused to instruct his attorney general to prosecute those who sought to enact new obstacles to voting rights. Even the FEPC represented, in retrospect, a hollow concession, lacking all enforcement power and serving primarily the purposes of exhoration and propaganda. Indeed, were it not for Eleanor Roosevelt's role behind the scenes in advocating antilynching legislation and the FEPC, there would have been virtually no one in the White House concerned about civil rights.

6. C. Vann Woodward, *The Strange Career of Jim Crow*, 3d ed. rev. (New York, 1974), pp. 140–42; Robert Donovan, *Conflict and Crisis: The Presidency of Harry Truman, 1945–1948* (New York, 1977), pp. 243–45; Steven Lawson, *Black Ballots: Voting Rights in the South, 1944–1969* (New York, 1976), pp. 100–106; William Berman, *The Politics of Civil Rights in the Truman Administration* (Columbus, Ohio, 1970), pp. 43–47; and Yollette Jones, "The Columbia Race Riot of 1946" (M.A. thesis, Duke University, 1978).

7. See Lawson, *Black Ballots*, pp. 100–102; Donovan, *Conflict and Crisis*, pp. 243–46; and Berman, *Politics of Civil Rights*, p. 4.

8. Berman, *Politics of Civil Rights*, pp. 9–28; Donovan, *Conflict and Crisis*, pp. 30–33, 172–73; and Alonzo Hamby, *Beyond the New Deal: Harry S. Truman and American Liberalism* (New York, 1973), pp. 61–65.

9. On Truman and the FEPC, see Berman, *Politics of Civil Rights*, pp. 24–28, 32–37; Hamby, *Beyond the New Deal*, pp. 46, 61–64; Donovan, *Conflict and Crisis*, pp. 31–33, 173, 230, 245; and Lewis Ruchames, *Race, Jobs, and Politics* (New York, 1958).

10. See Donovan, *Conflict and Crisis*, pp. 33, 173, 230; Berman, *Politics of Civil Rights*, pp. 5–56; and Hamby, *Beyond the New Deal*, pp. 188–90, 214–15.

11. Donovan, *Conflict and Crisis*, pp. 332–37; Berman, *Politics of Civil Rights*, pp. 56–60, 67–74; and Dalfiume, *Desegregation of the Armed Forces*, pp. 134, 145, 155–59.

12. Harvard Sitkoff, "Harry Truman and the Election of 1948: The Coming of Age of Civil Rights in American Politics," *Journal of Southern History* 37 (November 1971): 597–616; Barton J. Bernstein, "The Ambiguous Legacy: The Truman Administration and Civil Rights," in *Politics and Policies of the Truman Administration*, ed. Barton Bernstein (Chicago, 1970), pp. 269–314; Hamby, *Beyond the New Deal*, pp. 232–33, 243–44, 247, 250–51; and Berman, *Politics of Civil Rights*, pp. 79–134.

13. Berman, *Politics of Civil Rights*, pp. 79–134, esp. 107–11; Sitkoff, "Harry S. Truman and the Election of 1948"; Hamby, *Beyond the New Deal*, pp. 232–33, 247–51; and Donovan, *Conflict and Crisis*, pp. 338–56. See also Donald McCoy and Richard Reutten, *Quest and Response: Minority Rights and the Truman Administration* (Lawrence, Kans., 1973).

14. Berman, *Politics of Civil Rights*, pp. 129–35; Sitkoff, "Harry S. Truman and the Election of 1948"; and Donovan, *Conflict and Crisis*, pp. 338–39.

15. See Dalfiume, *Desegregation of the Armed Forces*; Anderson, *A. Philip Randolph*; Lawson, *Black Ballots*, pp. 78, 119–23, 137–38; Donovan, *Conflict and Crisis*, pp. 388–414; Berman, *Politics of Civil Rights*, pp. 158, 161, 168–73, 184–87, 198–99, 207–8, 238.

16. Berman, *Politics of Civil Rights*, pp. 39–42, 60–64, 187–94, 237–40; and Donovan, *Crisis and Conflict*, pp. 332–37. In a private letter Walter White wrote: "We deliberately and consciously avoided asking for a conference to hear Mr. Truman tell us that I am still for civil rights. . . . The time has come for him to do something about civil rights instead of telling us how he feels personally." The letter was written in 1951, and reflected White's growing disullusionment with the president.

17. Lawson, *Black Ballots*, pp. 131–32; Berman, *Politics of Civil Rights*, pp. 215–40.

18. For a review of court cases involving civil rights, see Kluger, *Simple Justice*; Albert P. Blaustein and Clarence Clyde Ferguson, Jr., *Desegregation and the Law* (New York, 1962).

19. Kluger, *Simple Justice*, pp. 215–39.

20. Ibid., p. 3.

21. Ibid., pp. 657–99, especially 689.

22. Ibid., pp. 700–44.

23. Ibid., pp. 710–16; Benjamin Muse, *Ten Years of Prelude: The Story of Integration since the Supreme Court's 1954 Decision* (New York, 1964); Anthony Lewis et al., *Portrait of a Decade* (New York, 1964); and Robert Crain, *The Politics of School Desegregation*, (New York, 1969).

24. Allan P. Sindler, ed., *Change in the Contemporary South* (Durham, N.C., 1965); Edgar Thompson and John C. McKinney, eds., *The South in Continuity and Change* (Durham, N.C., 1965); Kluger, *Simple Justice*, pp. 744–78; and William Chafe, *Civilities*

and *Civil Rights: Greensboro, North Carolina and the Black Struggle for Freedom* (New York, 1980), chap. 2.

25. William E. Leuchtenburg, "The White House in Black America: From Eisenhower to Carter," in *Have We Overcome? Race Relations since Brown*, ed. Michael V. Namorato, (Oxford, Miss., 1979); Charles C. Alexander, *Holding the Line: The Eisenhower Era, 1952–1961* (Bloomington, Ind., 1975), pp. 115–21, 194–200, 254; and E. Frederic Morrow, *Black Man in the White House* (New York, 1963). The experience of E. Frederic Morrow, the only Negro on the White House staff, exemplified the Eisenhower Administration's attitude on civil rights. A Republican of long standing, Morrow had been invited by Sherman Adams to join the administration shortly after the campaign ended. Then, after resigning his job at CBS, Morrow was shunted aside, his phone calls unanswered, until belatedly he was offered a position at the Commerce Department. Finally, in 1955, he moved to the White House, only to experience further frustration. On one occasion white staff members told a "nigger" story in his presence. On other occasions he was publicly embarassed, as when he promised A. Philip Randolph an appointment with the president only to have the meeting cancelled. Although Morrow provided a useful symbol for political purposes (Eisenhower took him to a World Series game in 1956), when it came to matters of policy, his voice was ignored. Loyal to the end, Morrow nevertheless could not help feeling angry when Eisenhower urged blacks to be "patient" in demanding their civil rights. "I feel ridiculous . . . trying to defend the Administration's record on civil rights," Morrow concluded.

26. James L. Sundquist, *Politics and Policy: The Eisenhower, Kennedy, and Johnson Years* (Washington, D.C., 1968), pp. 221–86; Alexander, *Holding the Line*, pp. 167–68, 194–200; J. P. Anderson, Eisenhower, Brownell, and the Congress (Kingsport, Tenn., 1964); and Morrow, *Black Man in the White House*.

27. C. Vann Woodward, *The Strange Career of Jim Crow*, p. 166.

28. Ibid., pp. 166–68; Alexander, *Holding the Line*, pp. 197–200; Morrow, *Black Man in the White House*; Sundquist, *Politics and Policy*, pp. 221–50; and Muse, *Ten Years of Prelude*.

29. Chafe, *Civilities and Civil Rights*, chaps. 1–3.

30. Kluger, *Simple Justice*, pp. 748–78; Woodward, *Strange Career*, p. 154; Muse, *Ten Years of Prelude*; author's interview with Ezell Blair, 1973; and Chafe, *Civilities and Civil Rights*, chap. 2.

31. Kluger, *Simple Justice*, p. 572.

32. Martin Luther King, Jr., *Stride toward Freedom: The Montgomery Story* (New York, 1958); Eugene Walker, "The Origins of the Southern Christian Leadership Conference" (Ph.D. diss., Duke University, 1977); and Howell Raines, *My Soul is Rested* (New York, 1978).

33. Harvard Sitkoff, *The Civil Rights Revolution* (New York, 1981); and King, *Stride toward Freedom*, pp. 61–63.

34. Chafe, *Civilities and Civil Rights*, chaps. 2–4.

American Business in the Postwar Era

Arthur M. Johnson

The decade and a half from the end of World War II to the election of John F. Kennedy as president in 1960 was one of prosperity and progress for the American economy and its business sector. Although the developing cold war with the Soviet Union overshadowed many of the developments of that period, its effect was stimulative of the domestic economy. Pent-up consumer demand from the World War II years, the availability of cheap energy, the application of government-financed wartime innovations to peacetime commercial uses, and liberal programs of foreign economic and military aid all encouraged private investment and created expanding employment opportunities. Increased productivity and the application of new tools of monetary and fiscal management helped keep the economy growing and minimized the potential for inflation and excessive swings of the business cycle. Despite the increased role of government intervention in the economy, American business enjoyed an era of market-directed growth that created an affluent society without parallel in the world. The businessman, who had been the discredited villain of the depressed 1930s and the behind-the-scenes hero of World War II, emerged again as a respected figure in American life. At the same time society's emphasis on material progress, the demands that it made on our nonrenewable natural resources, and the contrasts that it created with developing nations abroad and between the haves and have-nots at home set the stage for the troubled 1960s. But for a time American business was the dominant institution in American life.

As America faced the post–World War II era, memories of the brief depression shortly after World War I and of the Great Depression of the 1930s were still strong. But the transition from a wartime to a peacetime economy was in fact accomplished without a major economic contraction. As far as business was concerned, reconversion called first for the rapid termination of the Office of Price Administration (OPA), which had administered a program of wartime price controls and rationing since 1942. The initial effort to continue these controls into the postwar era was so weak that the legislation was vetoed by President Harry S. Truman. Although the rapid escalation of prices in the summer of 1946 led to another attempt, the resulting law was also weak, and price controls ended that November.

Wartime production peaked in early 1945, but a new uptrend began in October of that year and continued until late 1948. Encouraged by the expiration of price ceilings, prices rose rapidly. Retail distributors like Sears Roebuck expressed their confidence in an expanding postwar economy by aggressive investment. Others, like Montgomery Ward, anticipating a repeat of the experience after World War I, conserved their capital and fell behind in the race for postwar markets.

The disposition of war-built, government-financed plants and equipment affected competition in basic industries. For example, before World War II the Aluminum Company of America had been the sole domestic producer of virgin aluminum. With government support Reynolds Aluminum and Kaiser Aluminum were encouraged to produce the metal for the war effort, and both remained in the field after the end of hostilities. The wartime "Big Inch" pipelines that had moved crude oil from the Southwest to midwestern refineries and petroleum products to East Coast markets were sold for use as natural gas carriers. A large part of the government's fleet of wartime oil tankers and cargo vessels was likewise sold to private parties on favorable terms. In most instances the companies that had been operating government-financed war plants and equipment were able to acquire them at minimal cost, thus benefiting in the postwar era from public investment to meet wartime needs.[1]

Through the Defense Plant Corporation, the government had invested some $7 billion in war plants; most of them became available to their wartime operators on very favorable terms. Also, favorable "tax carry-forward" provisions of the tax laws enabled manufacturers to recover taxes paid on high wartime profits and absorb losses experienced in converting to peacetime production. Accordingly, there was an incentive to take risks in the early postwar period that otherwise would not have been present.

Wartime technological inventions, financed by the government for military purposes, provided the basis for important postwar growth industries. Radar, which had played a key role in the electronic detection of enemy aircraft and warships, had peacetime commercial applications and made significant contributions to the postwar development of commercial television. The jet military aircraft, in its early stages of development at the end of the war, came into its own during the 1950s and provided the manufacturers with indispensable experience needed for the introduction of commercial jet airliners at the end of the decade. Synthetic rubber, produced in volume during the war to replace the natural material, became standard for most postwar uses, including tires for the family motor car. Although utilization of atomic energy for commercial purposes was not encouraged until the mid-1950s, this awesome product of government-financed research and technology during the war gave the cooperating companies, universities, and their staffs valuable experience in working with radioactive materials, provided some by-products for use in medicine, and laid the basis for production of nuclear-generated electric power after the mid-1950s. Computers, which revolutionized many business operations during the latter part of the period, were developed with government encouragement and assistance to meet wartime needs.[2]

The close wartime cooperation of American business and government and the very high cost of pioneering in new areas, like atomic energy, brought about new peacetime relationships between the public and private sectors. Government became the sponsor and financier of research projects that business executed or administered. Access to government agencies and departments, as well as the more traditional lobbying efforts in Congress, became increasingly important for many firms and a growing number of industries.

Some of the scientists who participated in wartime research activities left academe after the war to found their own high-technology companies, usually in close proximity to university research centers. Such, for example, was the case with Route 128, the highway encircling Metropolitan Boston and the home of major electronics firms, which used their expertise first for defense contracts and then for commercial applications. Some universities expanded or developed research facilities to which business turned for assistance, and private consultants aided business in matters ranging from product development to problems of corporate strategy and management compensation.

These developments took place in an economy where new tools for macroeconomic management dampened swings of the business cycle.

The deep economic depression in the 1930s had resisted the many and varied approaches of the New Deal. However, new tools and concepts for managing the national economy, influenced especially by the work of the English economist John Maynard Keynes, had been developed and at least partially tested. After the war the Employment Act of 1946 expressed a national determination to use these tools to avoid a repetition of the 1930s experience. It called for an annual economic report to the nation from the president, the creation of a Council of Economic Advisers to assist him in this area, and the formation of a Joint Economic Committee of the Congress. Most important, the legislation assigned to the federal government responsibility for the maintenance of employment and economic growth consistent with continued reliance on private enterprise as the prime mover of the economy. Throughout most of the period, however, the implementation of the act was modest, and its importance was more symbolic than substantive. From the end of World War II through 1951, there were four short-lived recessions; only that of 1953–54, at the end of the Korean War, lasted more than a year.[3]

During the 1930s the federal government had put its weight behind collective bargaining, but labor strife characterized the latter part of the decade as basic American industries were organized for the first time. During the war, however, organized labor cooperated fully with management and the government in meeting wartime demands. Labor skills were upgraded as an increasing amount of production was performed on automatic machinery; tens of thousands of women entered the work force to replace the men called to the nation's military service.

A wave of strikes soon after World War II ended, however, cost organized labor the public's sympathy. After the 1946 elections Congress was controlled by Republicans for the first time in over a decade and a half, and legislation favoring business management was virtually a certainty. The Taft-Hartley Act of 1947 restored a balance to labor-management relations by its frank emphasis on the prerogatives of management, which had been largely ignored or constrained by the Wagner Act of 1935 as interpreted by the National Labor Relations Board. Taft-Hartley banned the closed shop and specified unfair union labor practices to balance the proscriptions on management contained in the Wagner Act. In addition, there was a provision for a "cooling-off" period in strikes threatening the national health or welfare. Although vetoed by President Truman and condemned by organized labor as a "slave labor act," the Taft-Hartley Act became law and survived numerous efforts to repeal it. In the succeeding decade of prosperity, there were few major strikes crippling to the economy. Militant unionism declined in favor of cooperation with business, which passed along to consumers the higher costs of labor under union contracts.[4] When a strike threatened the steel industry, President Truman seized the mills but was sharply rebuffed by the Supreme Court, which held his action to be unconstitutional.[5]

Gross hourly earnings in unionized industries were typically higher than in the nonunionized; furthermore, they climbed steadily in the postwar period. In the durable goods field, for example, gross hourly earnings rose from $1.11 in 1945 to $1.54 in 1950, and to $2.38 by 1959. In 1948 General Motors' contract with the United Automobile Workers contained an "escalation clause" that provided for wage shifts keyed to changes in the cost of living; most of the resulting pressure was predictably upward. In addition, fringe benefits, such as health insurance, became an increasingly important element in labor-management bargaining negotiations. Meanwhile, in December 1955, the American Federation of Labor and the Congress of Industrial Organizations started the process of merging after a long period of strife resulting from different concepts of labor organization and membership.

Pent-up consumer demand and deferred investment powered the economy over the post-1945 conversion back to peacetime activities. Enforced savings during the war, supplemented by liberal financial assistance to veterans, contributed to a demand for consumer items that ranged from safety pins for the booming baby population to cars and appliances, which had been unavailable since 1942. The construction industry, especially residential construction, was a key component of private investment in the early postwar period. More than 80 percent of these new homes were stand-alone, stand-apart, single-family dwellings. Movement to the suburbs became increasingly popular, contributing to and reflecting mounting problems in the cities. Many suburban communities catered to rising young executives who measured their success in terms of the price of their cars and housing, but entire new communities, like Levittown, Long Island, were mass-produced for a broader market. The demand for consumer durables continued to hold up well during the 1950s, to the point that more than 90 percent of American homes wired for electricity in 1959 had radios, televisions, refrigerators, and electric washers. However, by the latter half of the decade, services were expanding as a percentage of total consumer expenditures at the expense of durables.[6]

The rapid run-up in prices after the removal of price controls in 1946 continued until mid-1948, with an annual rate of increase in excess of 16 percent. From that time until the early 1960s, the economy was stabilized at this higher price level but at the cost of unemployment that ran from 5 percent at the end of the Korean conflict in 1953 to 7 percent at the end of the decade.

The availability of sources of cheap energy, notably petroleum, was basic to many elements of the postwar economy. Among other things, it encouraged a switch to oil burners for heating homes, which had previously depended on coal. Natural gas for both residential and industrial use became a growth industry, though federal controls on the price of interstate gas were a source of irritation to gas producers and pipeline companies after 1954. In the early 1950s the petrochemical industry began to develop rapidly, turning out petroleum-based products of great variety. The availability of man-made films, fibers, and plastics changed American life, from the packaging of the products that consumers bought, to the clothes that they wore, to the containers in which they sent the waste by-products of an affluent society to the municipal dump.[7]

From the country's earliest days, Americans had taken cheap natural resources for granted. There was little effort to conserve them since there were more for the taking just over the horizon, or so most Americans thought. The concept of waste was celebrated early in this century by economist-sociologist Thorstein Veblen, who noted the American addiction to "conspicuous consumption." Only an economy that believed itself rich beyond measure would deliberately engineer obsolescence into its products, yet that became a standard procedure in more than one American industry. There was scarcely an article used by Americans that was not available in a variety of forms, colors, and, in some cases, prices, sufficient to differentiate it from others competing for the same customer. Americans expected to live well and believed that their children would live better than they had. Accordingly they consumed natural resources of the world out of all proportion to their numbers. As a result an increasing amount of strategic resources had to be imported from overseas, underlining the country's vulnerability to developments beyond its control.[8]

The American emphasis on mobility and on cars as material symbols of success resulted in a more than doubling of the number of registered automobiles between 1945 and 1955. In the latter year alone, 8,000,000 passenger cars were produced. Auto-makers stressed size, style, power, and model obsolescence. The automobile was essential to the development of the suburbs of America's large cities, and with that development came suburban shopping centers, which could be reached only by automobile. To cope with parking problems, women drivers increasingly asked for smaller, more compact vehicles than Detroit offered. Beginning in the mid-1950s, compact foreign cars started to make significant inroads on Detroit's markets. Although the American auto-makers responded by importing small cars manufactured by their foreign subsidiaries, the German-built Volkswagen outstripped them and resisted the drop-off in auto sales at the end of the decade. Japanese imports also began to climb. By that time the Big Three (GM, Ford, and Chrysler) were experimenting with their own domestic small cars, in the belief that the earlier emphasis on large, gas-hungry, status-symbol cars was vulnerable to the public's mounting demand for low-priced transportation both in terms of original cost and operating expense. Meanwhile, recognition of the automobile as the primary mode of personal transportation was reflected in the passage of the Interstate Highway Act of 1956, which provided federal funds in a 90:10 ratio to construct superhighways across the nation.

At the start of the 1950s, there were nine firms producing cars, including the well-known Hudson, Studebaker, Packard, and Willys-Overland companies. However, the independents' days were numbered. A significant exception was Nash-Kelvinator, which merged with Hudson in 1954 to form American Motors. AMC's compact Nash Rambler proved surprisingly competitive with the products of the Big Three as the nation began to pay more attention to economical transportation. Rambler sales rose from some 100,000 in 1956 to five times that number in 1958 and 1959. On the other hand, the *de novo* effort of Kaiser-Fraser to enter the automobile market ended in failure. And even an established company like Ford, despite heavy promotion, could not induce the public to buy the Edsel car.[9]

Labor-management relations were a major concern of the postwar automobile industry. A settlement between the United Auto Workers and one of the Big Three typically set the pattern for the outcome of negotiations with the other two. In 1955 a guaranteed annual wage, insuring some 65 percent of normal compensation in the event of unemployment, was negotiated for the first time in this key industry. The very concept of a "guaranteed" annual wage reflected the high level of confidence in the performance of the private sector.

The increased interdependence between government and business, recognized during World War II and confirmed by requirements of the cold war and the Korean conflict (1950–53), led to an exchange of high-ranking personnel between the public and private sectors. Paul Hoffman of Studebaker, for example, was a key figure in administering the nation's foreign aid program of the late 1940s. The Department of Defense, created in 1947, was perceived as the ultimate big business. Symbolically, President Dwight D. Eisenhower appointed Charles E. "Engine Charley" Wilson, the head of General Motors, as his first secretary of defense. "Cost engineering" was encouraged at the operating level of the armed services, and Secretary Wilson publicly—and innocently—equated the welfare of GM with that of the nation. At lower levels retired generals and admirals regularly appeared in executive positions or on the boards of major companies doing business with the government; former government regulators and congressmen defeated at the polls found eager clients and good jobs with firms concerned about their influence or image in Washington.[10]

Graduate education for business provided a plethora of programs for those aspiring to a career in big business and, in some cases, big government or big labor. With the expansion of American firms overseas, foreign nationals appointed to major management posts were brought to the United States to be trained in the same classrooms with their American counterparts. As the 1950s wore on, leading American business schools also staffed and directed management institutes in various parts of the world. Unlike the situation that developed in the 1960s, in the 1950s a career in big business was perceived by many able young men, and even some young women, as the most rewarding way to share in shaping a business civilization and reaping its fruits.[11]

The general approbation of business was reflected in academic circles, where it had been fashionable during the depressed 1930s to condemn business and businessmen as the source of the nation's troubles. An entrepreneurial history center was established at Harvard University in 1947 and operated for a decade, probing this critical area from many different points of view. Historians like Allan Nevins, who wrote for a wider audience than most of his academic peers, complemented his 1940 study *John D. Rockefeller: The Heroic Age of American Enterprise* with a sympathetic study of Rockefeller as industrialist and philanthropist, published in 1953. The Rockefellers' major business interest, Standard Oil Company (New Jersey), itself sponsored a scholarly reevaluation of its history; other scholars found new meaning in the alleged and actual behavior of nineteenth-century business leaders like Jay Gould. Edward C. Kirkland, in the October 1960 issue of the *American Historical Review*, summed up the case for business revisionism in his article significantly entitled, "The Robber Barons Revisited."

In the light of such developments, businessmen paid increased attention to the "social responsibility" of corporate enterprise. For the most part this consisted of explicit recognition that a modern big business had multiple responsibilities—to its employees, customers, and suppliers, as well as to its stockholders. These perceptions were reflected in more-advanced companies in efforts to improve communication with various clienteles, systematic personnel development policies, and active participation in community affairs. The demands of these activities led to significant increases in public relations and personnel departments; expanded use of mushrooming academic programs for middle and senior managers; and, in some instances, the introduction of systematic long-range planning where social and technological factors assumed major importance. However, the primary emphasis of American business remained on producing profit, and most corporate activities were evaluated strictly by that yardstick. In the absence of governmental regulations on such matters as environmental pollution, the social costs of business activity were not typically included in the profit calculus.[12]

The 1950s witnessed the beginning of a new merger movement in American business. This one was different from its predecessors because of its emphasis on diversification, producing the so-called "conglomerate." Since the 1920s large, technology-based firms with major research facilities and available capital had diversified their product lines, penetrating new but related markets. Chemical companies like DuPont, electrical companies like General Electric, automobile companies like General Motors, and electronics companies like Radio Corporation of America entered new growth markets by applying their expertise to the development of new products allied to their primary output. The new conglomerate strategy was to acquire companies with entirely different product lines, thus, among other things, diminishing the possibility of antitrust action for dominance in a single market. The effectiveness of this strategy was enhanced by increased acceptance of management concepts that centralized overall corporate planning and policy-making but decentralized operating decisions.[13]

The result of these developments was increased overall concentration in American industry. In 1947 the nation's 200 largest corporations had accounted for about 30 percent of the value added by manufacturing; by 1963 they were responsible for 41 percent. Defenders of the conglomerate movement pointed out that large companies could bring to older firms that lacked comparable financial and managerial resources the means of competing more effectively. Indeed, the degree of concentration in such significant industries as electrical products, chemicals, instruments, and rubber, actually diminished during that period.[14]

Although markets and product lines figured prominently in most mergers, the opportunities for financial maneuvering were frequently of equal or greater importance. As the merger pace quickened in the 1960s, this potential became even more important. However, the weak financial underpinnings of the postwar merger movement were later revealed by the recession of 1969–70. Some of the most initially successful entrepreneurs in promoting it, like James Ling of Ling-Tempco-Vought, came tumbling down as a result.[15]

Direct investment abroad became significant for some American companies in the 1950s. In some instances the investment was to take advantage of labor costs that were substantially lower than those in the United States, as in the case of Korea and Taiwan; in other cases it was aimed at taking advantage of markets that could be served more cheaply from overseas locations than from those at home.[16] A significant amount of overseas investment was in natural resources, like petroleum and other minerals, whose cost was very substantially less than in the United States. The resulting threat to domestic producers of petroleum, for example, was such that voluntary import controls were placed on foreign oil in 1955 and mandatory controls in 1959.

As Western Europe and Japan recovered from World War II with United States financial assistance, they presented an increasing challenge to American companies in world markets, and even in some domestic ones. The Japanese, for example, had a long history of copying Western consumer items and producing cheap and inferior quality versions of them. By the end of the 1950s, however, Japan was exporting manufactured goods ranging from cameras, radios, and televisions to automobiles and ships that matched or surpassed their American counterparts in quality and undersold them in price. Ironically, many American companies in the older industries were producing with antiquated machinery while their foreign competitors were utilizing the newest equipment, much of it manufactured in the United States and financed by some of the $73 billion in foreign aid that flowed from this country between 1945 and 1959.[17]

Automation and miniaturization made possible by such electronic advances as the transistor, which appeared in 1948, helped reduce production costs and created new markets and spawned new companies. Companies like IBM in the computer field, Raytheon and Honeywell in electronics and automatic controls, and Polaroid and Xerox in the application of technology to different forms of communication, were already identified as "growth" companies.[18] The military equipment demands of the Korean War and of continuing defense expenditures afterwards were particularly significant for the new technology companies. The rapidly growing defense industry of the West Coast, especially in the Los Angeles area, attracted enterprise and investment.

Although President Eisenhower inveighed against "creeping socialism" as represented by public power projects and warned against the military-industrial complex, he could not turn the clock back. In fact, the interdependence of government and business intensified, with government adopting the structure, managerial techniques, and even financial strategies of private enterprise to accomplish specific tasks. Business executives became increasingly concerned with political and bureaucratic decisions, which established the framework in which they had to operate. Thus, although the posture of government was predominantly neutral or positive toward business during most of the postwar era to 1960, its potential to affect business decisions either directly or indirectly grew steadily.

In most respects the era from 1945 to 1960 was one of the great epochs of American business. Overall growth was steady; inflation was minimal; and society's acceptance of private enterprise was not yet clouded by disenchantment with material measures of success, poisoned by widespread fear of the military-industrial complex, or ruffled by anger at the rapid exhaustion of natural resources whose end-products polluted land, air, and water. Despite the continuing trend toward concentration in American industry, competition still commanded public allegiance as the primary regulator of the economy. But for those who would look closer, it was clear that a day of reckoning would have to come.

America was a wealthy giant in a world of have-not developing nations, and they controlled many of the natural resources on which the United States was becoming increasingly dependent. In the world of *realpolitik*, this country faced a formidable opponent in the Soviet Union, and the economic overtones, along with competition for markets from friendly nations, were unsettling. At home the very affluence that American business had created would undermine the achievement motivation of a new generation of Americans, who either took their affluence for granted or rejected it as socially and morally indefensible. These forces would come together in the 1960s to create unprecedented domestic upheaval, aggravated by an undeclared war in Vietnam and by the belated recognition that widespread social and economic inequality persisted in America and that one of the costs of reliance on private enterprise had been environmental degradation that demanded prompt remedial action. Nevertheless, faith in business, though shaken, was not destroyed. The ultimate compliment, and also the ultimate example of misunderstanding of the role of business, was the demand that it assume responsibility for solving the nation's social problems.

In important respects the launching of the Soviet Union's space-penetrating Sputnik in 1957 marked the end of a business-dominated era in this country. Under private auspices the postwar American economy, though growing, had not grown as rapidly as the U.S.S.R.'s. Although the United States had had a space program of sorts since the end of World War II, it was basically concerned with adapting German missile expertise to our defense needs. Sputnik took the American people by surprise and underlined the extent to which scientific and engineering education had been allowed to lag in this country.[19] Their revitalization under government auspices had reverberations throughout American education, extending to the social sciences and even to the humanities. But in this process, as in the space and missile race of the 1960s, the partnership between government and business, forged during World War II and continued at a reduced level through the 1950s, tilted increasingly toward government as the senior partner, making it a major source of demand and funding for private enterprise.

1. Large firms tended to dominate the prime contracts and research financed by government during the war. The Smaller War Plants Corporation in a 1946 report saw economic concentration promoted by this fact and predicted its continuation in the postwar era as a probable consequence. See U.S., 79th Cong., 2d sess. Senate Doc. 206, *Economic Concentration and World War II* (Washington, D.C., 1946). On postwar disposal of government property and its effect on economic concentration, see Walter Adams and H. M. Gray, *Monopoly in America* (New York, 1955) chaps. 5–6.

2. The story of wartime scientific research is told in James Phinney Baxter, *Scientists against Time* (Boston, 1946).

3. Origins of the 1946 statute are discussed in Stephen R. Bailey, *Congress Makes a Law: The Story behind the Employment Act of 1946* (New York, 1950). For its impact in the 1950s, see Harold G. Vatter, *The U.S. Economy in the 1950's: An Economic History* (New York, 1963).

4. Total union membership in the United States began to decline after 1957. On postwar union membership, see L. Troy, "Trade Union Membership, 1897–1962," *Review of Economics and Statistics*, February 1965, pp. 93–113. In *American Capitalism: The Concept of Countervailing Power* (Boston, 1952), John Kenneth Galbraith argued that countervailing power blocs, such as big unions versus big business, protected the public interest. Economists attacked this view as misleading, and in *The New Industrial State* (New York, 1967), Galbraith acknowledged that unions and management might team up against the public interest.

5. The Truman administration's labor policy is the subject of R. Alton Lee, *Truman and Taft-Hartley* (Lexington, Ky., 1966). See also Maeva Marcus, *Truman and the Steel Seizure Case*, Contemporary American History Series (New York, 1977).

6. Vatter, *The U.S. Economy*, pp. 104–6. The annual *Economic Report of the President* traces significant changes in the economy.

7. John Kenneth Galbraith's *The Affluent Society* (Boston, 1958) discusses the various manifestations and consequences of postwar affluence. Developments in the postwar American petroleum industry are summarized in Harold P. Williamson et al., *The American Petroleum Industry: The Age of Energy, 1899–1959* (Evanston, Ill., 1963), pp. 795–821.

8. The President's Materials Policy Commission as early as 1952 pointed out that the United States had changed from a raw materials surplus nation to a raw materials deficit nation. For the role of imports, see U.S. Department of Commerce, *Contribution of Imports to U.S. Raw Material Supplies, 1955*, World Trade Information Service, Part 3, No. 57-1 (1957).

9. Vatter, *The U.S. Economy*, pp. 158–63. Jan G. Deutsch, comp., *Selling the People's Cadillac: The Edsel and Corporate Responsibility* (New Haven, Conn., 1976).

10. In 1969 Senator William Proxmire reported that more than 2,000 retired military officers were employed by the one hundred leading defense contractors: U.S., Senate, *Congressional Record*, 91st Cong., 1st sess., 24 March 1969.

11. A portrait of "the corporation man" is painted by W. Lloyd Warner in Edward S. Mason, ed., *The Corporation in Modern Society* (Cambridge, Mass., 1961), pp. 106–21.

12. Two useful treatments of the social responsibility question are Mason's book, cited above, and Morrell Heald, *The Social Responsibilities of Business: Company and Community, 1900–1960* (Cleveland, Ohio, 1970).

13. United States Supreme Court decisions such as *United States* v. *United Shoe Machinery Corporation* (1953, 1954) modified the Court's 1920 decision in the United States Steel antitrust case, which held that size alone did not constitute an offense, to take account of practices that increased a firm's market power even though not directed against a specific rival. In 1945 Judge Learned Hand had ruled in a case involving the Aluminum Company of America that size per se could be an antitrust offense, and in 1946 the Supreme Court held that collusion could be inferred in an oligopolistic industry by parallelism of behavior.

14. W. Elliot Brownlee, *Dynamics of Ascent: A History of the American Economy* (New York, 1974), 326–27.

15. See Robert Sobel, *The Age of Giant Corporations: A Microeconomic History of American Business, 1914–1970* (Westport, Conn., 1972), pp. 205–9.

16. The creation of the European Common Market, which presented a common tariff barrier against the rest of the world, led American manufacturers to establish branch factories within that wall. After 1955 this strategy contributed to the growing unfavorable balance of payments experienced by the United States.

17. Vatter, *The U.S. Economy*, p. 17.

18. Electronics ranked 94th in terms of sales among American industries in 1939. Nurtured by wartime demands, postwar civilian demand, and continuing defense requirements, it ranked as the number-five industry in 1956. See the essays on electronics by William B. Harris in *Fortune* (1957).

19. See James R. Killian, *Sputnik, Scientists, and Eisenhower* (Cambridge, Mass., 1977).

American Workers, the Labor Movement, and the Cold War, 1945–1960

John Barnard

The cold war brought important changes to the lives of American workers and to the American labor movement. A nation whose times of war and preparation for war had been infrequent though intense interruptions of the flow of public life adjusted to permanent military preparedness. The cold war affected the kinds of jobs available to American workers and where their work was performed. The number of occupations linked to meeting the security needs of the United States increased. New jobs in the manufacture of military equipment, government agencies, the armed forces, and the development and application of scientific knowledge stemmed from the cold war. Although most of the new manufacturing and office jobs were little different in nature from those in the civilian economy, in the cases of scientific research and its application and in the armed forces some new occupations were created.

The redistribution of jobs from civilian to security purposes seems to have had only a minor effect on the number of union members. Irving Bernstein has calculated that labor unions in 1945 had a membership of 13,379,000, which was 24.8 percent of the civilian labor force. By 1960 their membership had increased to 18,607,000, which represented 26.2 percent of the civilian labor force. Since most of this growth occurred during the Korean War, the net effect of cold war conflict was to bring a few more workers, as a percentage of the labor force, into unions.[1]

The cold war was fought as much on ideological as geographical battlegrounds. It was, in a contemporary phrase, a "war for men's minds." This ideological struggle generated powerful pressures to conform to a national standard of opinion and behavior. The demand for conformity fell with great force on the leadership of organized labor. For the many labor leaders who were opposed to Communism, an affirmation of their national loyalty as defined by the government and public opinion posed no serious problem. However, other labor figures, some of them Communists or accustomed to tolerating and accepting Communist support, or others who on principle refused to accede to pressure, faced difficult choices. The results were a schism in the CIO and a realignment of power within the labor movement as a whole. The need for ideological purity was also a major force behind a movement toward a more democratic system of racial relations within the United States, including ultimately better employment opportunities for the black minority.

The beginning of the cold war marked no sharp break in the relationship between the federal government, the economy, and organized labor. During the New Deal the Roosevelt administration and Congress redefined the role of the federal government with respect to work in two significant ways: henceforth, employment would in the last analysis be a responsibility of government, and labor union growth would be encouraged. The actions of the government in World War II confirmed the New Deal's policies on jobs and unions but failed to expand its social reforms.[2] During wartime the work force increased by more than 7.5 million workers, and for unions the government enforced a "maintenance of membership" formula, a modification of the union shop, that gave them adequate security. But if World War II demonstrated the depth of the government's commitment to jobs and organized labor, it also demonstrated the limits of labor's power and role in the community. Business leadership and prestige, on the decline in the thirties, strongly revived.[3] A hostile and outspoken segment of public opinion was directed against particular unions and leaders, especially John L. Lewis. The passage of the Smith-Connally Act in 1943 showed how far Congress was prepared to go in attacking strikes that threatened the national interest in wartime.[4]

Organized labor was on the defensive when peace came. A bipartisan coalition of conservative congressmen proclaimed its intention to reduce labor's economic and political power. The passage of restrictive legislation became inevitable when the Republicans in the elections of 1946 gained control of Congress. Just a few months earlier, a Gallup poll had shown that 66 percent of the respondents favored passage of "new laws to control labor unions," whereas only 22 percent were opposed and the rest were undecided.[5] On the day the new Congress met, seventeen labor bills were introduced. Following a tortuous legislative course, Congress produced the Taft-Hartley Act, passed by decisive majorities over President Truman's veto, a major revision of the legal framework for labor-management relations. The new law sought to balance the rights of employees as established in the Wagner Act with a list of inviolable employers' rights. Employers were guaranteed an opportunity to present their views on unions to workers, and they could petition for elections to determine bargaining units. Unions were prohibited from engaging in unfair labor practices such as secondary boycotts, jurisdictional strikes, and refusal to bargain. In a complicated and largely unworkable set of provisions, the act revived the power of the executive to ask the courts for injunctions against strikes in prescribed circumstances and provided for "cooling off" periods when strikes threatened national interests. In provisions that proved partially unenforceable, the law banned the closed shop and direct political contributions by unions.

Taft-Hartley was not the "slave labor act" that union leaders denounced, yet it fulfilled some of their fears by replacing the Wagner Act's policy of facilitating labor organization nationally with a state by state autonomy that led to a regionalization of the labor movement. Under Section 14(b) of the law, state legislatures were empowered to eliminate all forms of union security including the union shop. "Right to work" campaigns, which presented the issue as one of individual liberty versus collective coercion, were launched in many states with the result that by 1954 fourteen of them, mostly in the South and the prairie and mountain West, had adopted restrictive legislation. Although the law did not directly damage strong unions, it hindered the spread of the labor movement from the industrialized into the industrializing areas of the country, freezing wage and other kinds of regional differentials.

The war had confirmed the belief that military production would put people to work. In 1937, before rearmament began, a labor economist wrote that the "one hope" for reviving business activity was a war boom. "Between prolonged depression or a war boom with the risk of war," he prophetically stated, "America will choose the latter. . . . And there will come prosperity. And along with it will come war."[6] At the outset of rearmament in 1939, unemployment was still in excess of eight million workers, about 15 percent of the work force. As military spending worked its way through the economy, jobs and prosperity returned. Industrial production rose 48 percent between 1939 and 1941, and by the fall of 1941 unemployment was negligible. By 1945 industrial production had increased another 45 percent. Not only did unemployment disappear but the work force expanded, drawing heavily on the ranks of the elderly, women, and even children. During the war years half of total production and 80 percent of durable goods production went for war purposes.[7] As the war's end approached, anticipations of the future were haunted by memories of the past. Economists of all persuasions predicted peacetime unemployment.[8] CIO economists thought that after V-E day, when the government planned sharp reductions in military spending, unemployment would rise rapidly to between two and nine million. Everyone had the "victory jitters."[9]

There was no recurrence of depression, although temporary dislocations were painful. More than 300,000 Michigan war workers, for example, lost their jobs immediately following V-J day.[10] The dammed-up purchasing power of wartime broke through to propel the economy forward. Per capita savings were at their highest level by the end of the war, aggregating more than $50 billion, and Americans, who had either gone without or made do with what they had during the depression and the war, poured into the market for durable goods, housing, and consumer items. The expenditure of these savings compensated for the steep reduction in military spending and ensured full employment. By 1949, however, consumer spending was falling off, and unemployment had risen to more than 6 percent. A period of increased military spending was begun as the cold war hit its full stride and was about to turn into a hot war in Korea. The military budget more than doubled from $14 to $34 billion from 1950 to 1951, and the share of the Gross National Product going to military expenditures went from 5 to over 10 percent. That share varied between 9 and 13 percent for the rest of the decade.[11] The growth of the economy as a whole closely paralleled changes in the level of military spending. From 1950 to 1955, dominated by the Korean War, the GNP increased at an average annual rate of 4.7 percent, but it dropped to 2.25 percent for the remainder of the decade.[12]

Increases in military spending were the result of an inextricable mixing of cold war and domestic concerns. As *Business Week* observed in April 1950, when spending was increasing:

> Pressure for more government spending is mounting. And the prospect is that Congress will give in—a little more now, then more by next year. . . . The reason is a combination of concern over tense Russian relations, and a growing fear of a rising level of unemployment here at home.[13]

Military spending showed that "the scourge of cyclical mass unemployment could be dispelled by sufficient public spending of almost any kind."[14] The effect of concentrated government expenditure was dramatically demonstrated during the Korean War. In October 1953 the unemployment rate reached its lowest point for the entire decade, 1.8

percent of the civilian labor force. Recessions in 1954 and 1958 pushed it up temporarily, in the latter instance to just over 7 percent.[15] Average unemployment for the decade of the fifties was 4.6 percent of the civilian labor force.

By 1960 the jobs of 7.5 million Americans, about one-tenth of the work force, directly depended on the military budget, and the indirect effects, extending to retail, government, and other goods and services, touched millions more. Eisenhower's secretary of defense, Charles E. Wilson, told a congressional committee in 1957 that "one of the serious things about this defense business is that so many Americans are getting a vested interest in it; properties, business, jobs, employment, votes, opportunities for promotion and advancement, bigger salaries for scientists, and all of that. It is a troublesome business."[16] Professional economists generally supported the use of military spending for keeping production and employment at high levels.[17] Only in the sixties did some begin to question its wisdom.[18]

Military spending stimulated huge investments in many industries. As the Joint Congressional Committee on Defense Production pointed out at the end of 1954,

> large expansions in basic industries have materially increased the country's capacity to produce both for war and for peace. Steel has increased from 100 million tons to 124 since 1950. Aluminum capacity has doubled in 3 years. . . . The chemical industry, committed to the largest expansion in its history, has invested approximately $5 billion since Korea.[19]

And so it went. Most industrial growth of the cold war era, and with it growth in employment, was the result of government military expenditure. A study by the Midwest Research Institute completed in 1957 concluded that "military demand has been the major and almost exclusive dynamic factor in recent years." The major growth industries of the fifties such as utilities, electrical equipment and machinery, aircraft and related products, instruments, chemicals, and rubber and plastic products, depended on government buying. According to one economist, "the growth industries of the 1950's by and large could attribute to government orders the margin between a mediocre growth performance and their striking actual record." As examples of extreme cases, about 80 percent of the business of the aircraft industry came from military agencies, and government accounted for at least two-thirds of the growth in electronics sales. The military sales of electronic firms rose about 100 percent during the last half of the decade, primarily the result of their participation in the development and manufacture of missiles.[20]

Labor leaders and presumably many rank-and-file workers recognized the tie between military expenditures and jobs. Union publications and speakers at their conventions pointed out the connection and urged support of defense-minded politicians. Articles and photographs depicting union members at work on military projects such as the Nautilus submarine, a "100 percent AFL operation," air force missiles, and aircraft frequently appeared in union periodicals.[21] When a reduction in defense budgets threatened, a meeting of the International Association of Machinists, the union most involved in aircraft production, was plunged into gloom.

> The effect of disarmament on employment and the national prosperity cast a deep shadow on the sixth IAM aircraft and guided missile conference. . . . As the 165 delegates were reminded, about one out of every three jobs in the United States is directly or indirectly dependent on defense spending.[22]

One of the most important effects of military spending and job creation was its regional distribution. The defense materials budget was spent in relatively few areas of the country, with about 70 percent of total contracts awarded in the top ten states. California led the way. By 1960 the state's manufacturers held over $6,409 million in prime defense contracts, more than the next two states, New York and Texas, combined. Almost 40 percent of all factory workers in the Los Angeles area were employed in the aircraft, missile, and electronics industries, mainly working on military equipment. In San Diego 82 percent of all manufacturing consisted of aircraft and missile production by the end of the decade. In the state as a whole, as much as 30 percent of manufacturing jobs were defense-related. In Texas employment in the transportation equipment industry, principally aircraft, grew from 21,000 in 1947 to 65,000 in 1960. Other regions that benefited in employment from military spending were central and southern New England, especially Massachusetts with its growing electronics, defense equipment, and research and development operations, and Connecticut, where aircraft engines and parts and submarines were manufactured. With many of the older New England industries, such as textiles, in decline, the threat of unemployment was offset by the growth in military production. In the Southeast, especially Georgia and Florida, production facilities and military training bases absorbed large amounts of funds. Although other considerations played some part in the shift of jobs and population into these regions, the federal defense budget was the principal one.[23]

The growth of military industries helped limit the area of collective bargaining. Serious labor disputes were rare in military industries. Government intervention in some form occurred when disputes threatened, with the result that only a limited form of collective bargaining existed in these industries.[24]

American workers by and large accepted the emergence of a cold war economy and their role in it. Jobs at good pay and often in attractive places were made available. One feature of military production employment was that a high proportion of the jobs were skilled, with important results for education, pay, and working conditions. There were more engineers, scientists, technicians, skilled craftsmen, and professional workers employed in military production than any other branch of large-scale manufacturing. The proportion of highly skilled workers increased rapidly as military equipment became more sophisticated. In 1958 the proportion of "nonproductive workers," that is, skilled and professional, in five major defense-related industries was 36 percent. By 1964 it had risen to 43 percent, compared with only 26 percent in all kinds of manufacturing, including defense-related.[25]

Aside from meeting the nation's legitimate security needs, the appeal of defense spending was that its products did not compete in the marketplace with those of established civilian manufacturers. On the contrary, as the aircraft and electronics industries demonstrated, much of the research and development cost of new and improved civilian products could be financed out of the military budget. Although some labor leaders advocated government expenditures for civilian purposes to maintain employment and purchasing power, most of the spokesmen for organized labor followed the dictates of tradition in accepting jobs for workers whatever the source and purpose.[26]

In the period of the cold war, while the shadow of atomic annihilation hung over the nation, the issue of personal security loomed large to American workers. In part, no doubt, this represented the lingering effects of the depression, but the threats and uncertainties of the postwar world contributed to a desire to create islands of stability and safety. Much of the energy of the union movement, including the unionization of mass-production industries in the thirties, had been spent in asserting the dignity of the worker and in seeking higher wages. In the postwar period emphasis shifted toward protection of the worker and his family against catastrophe. From the earliest days some unions had functioned as "friendly societies," using a portion of dues or other funds for death benefits, burial expenses, or the like. The government entered the picture during the New Deal with the contributory old age retirement benefits and the unemployment compensation provisions of the Social Security Act, and the statutory overtime pay premium of the Fair Labor Standards Act. World War II was a fruitful time for innovations in benefits. The government imposed strict controls on wages but allowed new and improved insurance, health and hospitalization benefits, vacations and holidays with pay, and higher wages for night shifts. The War Labor Board ruled that the establishment of health and insurance funds was a legitimate objective of collective bargaining, a decision resented by many companies but upheld by the courts.

A measure of the growing importance of fringe benefits as a part of total compensation can be seen in the increases in average annual supplements to wages and salaries for full-time employees. These increased from $104 in 1945 to $388 in 1960. These aggregate figures conceal significant variations that correlate in part with the extent of unionization in different industries. In manufacturing, for example, the corresponding figures for 1945 and 1960 are $129 and $543, but in services the comparable figures are $37 and $166, and in agriculture and related industries only $5 and $47.[27] By 1960 the average manufacturing establishment in the United States paid a sum equal to 21 percent of its payroll for fringe benefits, and in some other industries such as mining with 26 percent, and finance, insurance, and real estate with 23 percent, the proportion was higher. Fringe benefits were the most rapidly changing subject of bargaining. Collective bargaining contracts, once by and large confined to wages, working conditions, and union security provisions, expanded to cover disability and life insurance, supplemental unemployment, health and medical, pension, and premium pay benefits.[28]

Benefits were won both from union and nonunion firms, but most of the pioneering and the systems of benefits most favorable to workers were established in the unionized industries. By 1960 every major union had negotiated health, pension, and a variety of other kinds of welfare benefits. The large industrial unions took the lead, since they could afford the services of the specialists needed to devise, negotiate, and monitor complex benefit programs, and the risks of insurance schemes could be spread throughout their large memberships. The United Mine Workers, Steelworkers, Auto Workers, Rubber Workers, Amalgamated Clothing Workers, and Ladies' Garment Workers were among the leaders in negotiating benefit programs for their members. Disability insurance to cover temporary losses from off-the-job accidents and illnesses (with job-related disabilities covered under workmen's compensation) was available to more than half of the workers in private nonfarm industry by 1960. Basic health and surgical benefits, a major objective between 1945 and 1960, were won by more than half of the workers, with expansion to include major medical protection and dental, optical, and even psychiatric care becoming available to some in the sixties. More common than costly health and hospitalization benefits were group life insurance programs. The median benefit was about one year's earnings, although the amount varied widely. Under most plans won through collective bargaining, the employer paid the entire cost, whereas under non-negotiated plans the employee contributed although the employer usually paid the larger portion.

Pension plans supplemental to Social Security, although costly, were widely introduced, with the major breakthrough coming in the auto and steel industries in 1949. Increases in life expectancy and a trend toward earlier retirement were among the factors that gave supplemental pensions a high priority. Under collectively bargained plans it was common for employers to pay most, and often all, of the costs. By 1967 private retirement plans covered more than 25 million workers, or about half of those in private nonfarm establishments, with about 11 million covered by collectively bargained contracts. Some plans were multi-employer, that is, they could be transported by the worker if he changed jobs, but most were not.

Premium pay provisions built beyond the Fair Labor Standards Act, which required time and a half for work over forty hours per week. In many industries collective bargaining agreements provided for premium pay for work in excess of eight hours a day and for work on weekends and holidays regardless of the total worked during the week. Shift differentials granting additional pay for night work were common, and premium pay for especially hazardous jobs existed in the construction, maritime, and other industries. One of the most dramatic changes was in paid holidays and vacations. Before World War II only about one-fourth of union members were eligible for paid annual vacations, and most of those were for only one week. Major holidays were usually observed, but holiday pay for wage earners was extremely rare. By 1960 most workers covered by collective bargaining contracts were eligible for six paid holidays a year and for paid vacations, with many agreements providing for four weeks for longer-service employees.[29]

The most striking innovation in fringe benefits of the postwar era was the supplementary unemployment benefit (SUB) introduced in 1955 as a result of negotiations between the United Auto Workers and the Ford Motor Company. There were a few earlier instances of combinations of public and private unemployment insurance in England and in the United States, but the auto industry was the first to introduce the plan in a large, mass-production industry with a history of irregular employment.[30] In both the auto and steel industries, there had been an interest in a guaranteed annual wage since the thirties. With its membership subject to periodic layoffs of massive numbers owing to violent oscillations of demand and production scheduling complexities, the auto workers union had long been pursuing ways of ensuring continuous earnings. The establishment of the principle of a guaranteed wage financed by the corporations would, many in the union believed, give management an incentive to schedule production throughout the year instead of concentrating it just before and during the peak sales seasons. Although the plans that were initially established fell short of a guaranteed annual wage, they offered many of its advantages, and they were capable of improvement.

The UAW first approached General Motors with the proposal, but for tactical reasons turned to Ford following GM's rejection. Both sides intensively prepared for the negotiations, the union developing the general principles and the company concentrating, as expected, on cost projections and administrative procedures. The basic principle was to take the benefit available from the state-administered unemployment compensation insurance fund established under Social Security and add to it from a private insurance fund a sum sufficient to give an unemployed worker a total that approximated his regular wage. In the negotiations the union made important concessions on details in order to establish the principle. The plan, gained without a strike, required the company to put five cents an hour for each worker into the SUB fund. This fund could be tapped for benefits to supplement unemployment compensation up to 65 percent of take-home pay, or $25 a week, which ever was the lesser, for 26 weeks.[31] The plan proved its worth during the 1958 recession when car sales dried up and hundreds of thousands of autoworkers were laid off as more than $13 million in SUB benefits was paid out.

SUB plans expanded rapidly. As amended in the 1961 negotiations, the auto agreement provided up to 62 percent of gross pay plus $1.50 per dependent up to four, with an overall maximum of $40 per week for 52 weeks; and after 1967 a laid-off worker could receive 95 percent of take-home pay. In 1956 the steelworkers union gained 52-week coverage. By 1962 more than 2.5 million workers were covered by SUB plans, with well over half of that total in auto and steel and the bulk of the remainder in the garment trades, cement, and rubber industries. About 95 percent of SUB-plan membership was in manufacturing industries.[32] SUB plans, since they were based on a shared-risk insurance principle and were complex to administer with high overhead costs, required a large number of participants in order to reduce the costs to an acceptable level. Their applicability therefore was limited.[33] Considering all benefits, however, there was no question that much had been done in a brief time to protect millions of American workers and their families from the worst effects of both ancient and modern hazards of working life.

For most kinds of work, monetary wages more than doubled between 1945 and 1960, and real wages (that is, the monetary wage adjusted for the inflationary spurts that occurred after World War II and during the Korean War) amounted to more than a 50 percent improvement. Average annual earnings for full-time employees in all industries rose from $2,189 in 1945 to $4,707 in 1960. To this must be added average annual supplements to wages and salaries to cover the cost of fringe benefits, which rose from only $104 in 1945 to $388 in 1960. This yields a total compensation of $2,293 in 1945 and $5,095 in 1960.[34] At the bottom of the scale, the national minimum wage, which had been initially set in 1938 at 25 cents an hour and rose to 40 cents by war's end, advanced by stages to $1.15 an hour in 1961. In the same year minimum-wage coverage was extended for the first time in an important degree to include some trade and service as well as manufacturing workers. For a variety of reasons, the cold war years were generally prosperous, although pockets of poverty among particular racial, sexual, regional, and occupational groups remained.

The cold war had a major impact on the CIO's role as critic of capitalism and prophet of a new social order. The AFL, which once included many socialists within its affiliated unions, had largely shed or silenced them by the end of World War I, and the IWW had ceased to be a force.[35] The CIO, born in the turbulent depression years, might have become a voice for workers' radicalism, leading to a collectivist polity. However, the argument goes, World War II slowed the CIO's progress toward that goal, and the cold war reversed its course, converting it into another pillar of the status quo. It ceased to offer a meaningful leftist alternative, allowing a rigid cold war consensus to dominate American policy through 1960 and beyond.[36]

This analysis ignores some key facts of the Roosevelt years. Capitalism was not fatally ill, merely ailing for a season, and Roosevelt was its doctor, not the undertaker. The surge of labor was stimulated and institutionalized by government. The early organizing drives were sparked by the passage of the National Industrial Recovery Act with its defective yet encouraging statement of a collective bargaining right.[37] Although workers' victories were won through struggles in factories and streets, the most important were initiated with a keen awareness of the balance of national and state political forces. The decisive strike in the CIO's growth, the sit-down at General Motors, was planned to follow the re-election of Roosevelt and the selection of a Democratic liberal, Frank Murphy, as governor of Michigan.[38] In the Wagner Act, despite continuing employer opposition and lack of full implementation immediately after its passage, American labor gained a government-sanctioned process for the initiation of collective bargaining and the protection of union rights that was unmatched in the industrial world. In short, labor in the large industries that were being organized during the New Deal was a ward of government, and it never transcended the relationship. The depression propelled labor into a new role and gave it new power but did not provide a warrant for it to transform society. During the war labor leaders, with the conspicuous exception of John L. Lewis, drew closer to government because of the national emergency, the promise of union security, and the gigantic expenditures that produced jobs and prosperity.[39]

In the thirties, however, many workers were rebellious. Unions appeared where none had been before. Sit-down and wildcat strikes, with workers scornful of property rights and authority, broke out for a time. These undisciplined upheavals contributed to the breakthrough in industrial unionism, but they failed to lead to social transformation. The new unions took up the problems of wages, working conditions, seniority lists, and so on that unions had traditionally tackled. Most of the rank and file, including those who performed heroically during the trauma of the union's birth, expected and accepted this.[40]

Communists and close sympathizers were active in several of the CIO unions and in the national CIO organization, but they rarely acted like revolutionaries and were often on the defensive.[41] Until August 1939 they supported Roosevelt's domestic and foreign policies, returning to that position after Hitler's invasion of the Soviet Union in June 1941. During the war the Communists were superpatriots, advocating anything that might increase military production. They urged universal adoption of a piece-rate wage system and favored coercive mobilization of labor for defense jobs, positions that put them sharply at odds with most labor leaders and with millions of workers. Furthermore, despite the necessary wartime alliance with the Soviets, the differences between the two nations were accentuated by the war's antitotalitarian thrust. If the war was a battle against the principles of totalitarianism, Russia and its American defenders could not escape unscathed.[42]

Revelations of Soviet espionage operations beginning with the Gouzenko disclosures in 1946 raised tension. Some antiunion employers and their political friends quickly showed their intention to exploit the rising anti-Communist and anti-Soviet feeling to discredit labor. In 1946 the chairman of the Republican National Committee, B. Carroll Reece, said that the coming congressional elections, in which his party would score tremendous gains, offered voters a choice between "Communism and Republicanism." As proof that the Communists had absorbed the Democratic party, he noted that CIO-PAC, the CIO's political arm, was backing Democratic candidates. Richard Nixon, running for Congress, chimed in with "a vote for Nixon is a vote against the Communist-dominated PAC with its gigantic slush fund."[43] In the election only 75 of 318 CIO-PAC–endorsed candidates won, and the number of Democratic members of the House of Representatives was reduced from 242 to 188. Although many issues were involved in the election, the CIO discovered how vulnerable it was to the charge of Communist influence and how costly the result, a lesson soon reinforced by passage of the Taft-Hartley Act.

The CIO's southern organizing drive, its major postwar project, also aroused opposition. Except in some of its stronger industrial unions, such as auto and steel, the CIO had made little headway in organizing locals in the South. Differentials in wages and working conditions were the nemesis of unions, since employers would be drawn to lower costs, causing areas of union strength to lose jobs. CIO strategists believed the unionization of southern industries, particularly textiles, was crucial to the organization's future. The drive, however, was sure to encounter resistance and not only for economic reasons. The CIO challenged deeply rooted southern customs by its official commitment to desegregation. If Communists continued to play a role in the CIO, this burden would be added to those the organization had to carry. How many battles could it fight in the South and have any hope of success?[44]

The first formal action against Communists in the labor movement came from Congress in the affidavit provision of the Taft-Hartley Act. Under its terms union officers were required to file an affidavit declaring that they were not members of the Communist party or of organizations that supported it. Refusal meant the union could not participate in collective bargaining elections held by the National Labor Relations Board, a penalty that did not expel noncomplying officers but threatened the union's survival by laying it open to raids from rival organizations. The CIO took a hands-off position, leaving it to each union to decide whether to comply.[45] Many union leaders resented being singled out and subjected to a loyalty test, but nearly all eventually complied.

Challenges on constitutional grounds were not sustained by the Supreme Court, and labor's campaign to secure repeal of the entire law utterly failed.[46] By the early fifties compliance was general.

Opposition to Communists within the CIO had appeared long before the cold war began, initially as a defense against a thrust from the AFL. In undocumented testimony before the Dies Committee in 1938, John P. Frey, an AFL official, listed more than three hundred CIO leaders and organizers who, he claimed, were Communists.[47] The CIO took steps to blunt the charges. In 1939 John L. Lewis attacked Communist activity within CIO unions, telling the organization's executive board that Communist doctrines and policies would not be tolerated, and a resolution denouncing Communists and other subversives was adopted at the 1940 CIO convention.[48] Similar general condemnations were adopted by some CIO affiliates. Communists and fellow travelers within the CIO often supported these resolutions, recognizing their negligible practical effect, although the wisdom of joining in one's own denunciation was doubtful.

Potentially more serious were office-holding and membership restrictions. Lewis's mine workers' union had barred Communists from membership since 1927, and the Steel Workers kept Communists out of any official position.[49] At the UAW's 1940 convention, a "subversive elements" constitutional clause was adopted, barring from elective or appointive office in the international a member of any organization declared illegal by the United States government "through constitutional procedures."[50] In the 1941 UAW convention, the most contentious issue was the "Red Resolution," a proposal to exclude members or supporters of organizations that approved of totalitarian forms of government from offices in the international. It was adopted by an almost two-to-one vote with an amendment that specified communist, fascist, and Nazi organizations as the targets.[51] Another CIO union, the International Woodworkers of America, under the leadership of a former Wobbly, adopted a constitutional amendment barring Communists from membership.[52] Many CIO unions did not agree with a restrictive policy. In the United Electrical Workers convention of 1941, a proposal to bar Communists from office was defeated by a two-to-one margin. Nevertheless, the trend toward restrictions was well established. By 1954 a study by the Bureau of Labor Statistics showed that 59 out of 100 unions, AFL as well as CIO, with a membership of ten million, barred Communists from office in the international, and that 40 unions, with nearly six million members, barred them from membership.[53]

With the end of the war, Philip Murray, president of both the CIO and the United Steel Workers of America and a faithful organization man, occupied a key position. Although there was never any question of his personal abhorrence of communism, his deepest commitment was to maintain the strength and unity of the CIO.[54] At that time about one-fifth of the CIO's claimed six million members were in unions whose officers, whatever their formal status with regard to the party, consistently supported the Communist political position. Although no count could be made, it has generally not been claimed that more than a handful of workers were themselves Communists. Still, some locals were definitely left wing, and many unionists were pragmatically prepared to accept capable union leadership whatever its political banner as long as no great price had to be paid. Murray tried to walk a narrow line. He did not want to antagonize the dozen or so CIO unions with significant Communist elements. They were mostly small but included such substantial organizations as the United Electrical Workers, third in size in the CIO, the Mine, Mill and Smelter Workers, the National Maritime Union, the Fur and Leather Workers, and the West Coast Longshoremen's and Warehousemen's Union. Their secession could plunge the CIO into civil war, open it to incursions by the AFL, and bring about its demise. On the other hand, Murray believed he had to respond to the mounting anti-Communist tide of opinion within the CIO and the nation at large or face disaffection and attacks. At first he tried to remain neutral, but the ground shifted beneath him. Over time and with the appearance of new issues involving the Truman administration's policy of economic recovery for Europe and support for Truman's reelection in 1948, Murray moved into the anti-Communist group. In the meantime he fought a series of delaying actions in an effort to prevent an irreparable split.[55]

The first of these maneuvers occurred at the tense though outwardly harmonious CIO convention of 1946. Murray prepared the way by appointing a special six-member committee, evenly divided between the pro- and anti-Communist factions, to draft a resolution. Its members were Ben Gold, president of the Fur and Leather Workers, an avowed Communist, Abram Flaxer, president of the United Public Workers, and Michael Quill, president of the Transport Workers Union, who were, at the time, sympathizers. The anti-Communist members were Walter P. Reuther, recently elected president of the UAW, Emil Rieve of the Textile Workers, and Milton Murray of the American Newspaper Guild. "We . . . resent and reject," the statement said, "efforts of the Communist Party or other political parties and their adherents to interfere in the affairs of the CIO. This convention serves notice that we will not tolerate such interference." On the floor Murray rammed the resolution through without debate on a standing vote. So strong was his demand for its passage that only two delegates, both from the National Maritime Union, dared vote against it, and they quickly withdrew their opposition to permit a unanimous vote to be recorded. A few, however, abstained.[56]

Another issue had a more practical effect. In addition to international unions, the CIO contained hundreds of local and state industrial union councils, primarily lobbying and political organs. A large number were under left-wing control and had issued resolutions, often on national political questions, reflecting that interest. The convention ordered them to confine their statements to local and state issues and to ensure that all their positions conformed with national CIO policy. Although the councils were a minor part of the CIO, with little power in comparison with the affiliated international unions, the issuance of these guidelines showed Murray's intent to tighten the organization.[57]

In the summer of 1947, shortly after the Taft-Hartley Act was passed, Murray moved decisively away from the Communist left. At a closed session of the CIO's executive board, he launched an attack on Communists within the labor movement, saying, "If Communism is an issue in any of your unions, throw it to hell out . . . and throw its advocates out along with it. When a man accepts office . . . to render service to workers, and then delivers service to outside interests, that man is nothing but a damned traitor."[58] The statement was widely used by anti-Communist labor leaders in their campaigns. At the same time he fired Communist Len DeCaux, who had been on the CIO staff since 1936, as publicity director and editor of the *CIO News*. Lee Pressman, the CIO counsel, followed DeCaux out six months later.[59]

The 1947 CIO convention marked another stage in the isolation of the Communist-led unions. The cold war had now gone beyond trading insults. In June, Secretary of State George Marshall proposed an economic aid plan for Europe. The Soviet Union, followed by the East European countries, denounced the plan, refused to participate, and charged that the United States was preparing for the rearmament of an anti-Soviet Western bloc. The CIO's convention was dominated by foreign policy. Marshall, the first secretary of state to appear at a labor gathering, delivered a brief but strong address, asking for labor's support of the plan and warning against distortions of its intentions being spread by its enemies. The convention's foreign policy resolution was a subtle endorsement designed to allow the left wing to remain within the CIO, but little more. Although the Marshall Plan was not endorsed by name, the foreign policy of the Democratic administration was praised, and it was implied that American policy posed no threat to the independence of other nations, a position at odds with that of the Soviets and of the Communist-led American unions. In defense of the administration's economic aid proposals, Reuther argued that Truman was no more guilty of warmongering in 1947 than Roosevelt had been in 1940. The accusers, he pointed out, were the same in both instances. The CIO must, he said, "stand four-square against all forms of totalitarianism because it matters very little what kind of trademark you have on the chains that bind you."[60] No formal actions were taken at the convention against the left wing, but Murray had indicated his mounting dissatisfaction with the situation. As one observer noted, the left wing "had been granted the right to exist, but no more."[61]

Events moved quickly, propelled by the entry of Henry Wallace into the presidential campaign in December 1947. Murray and most CIO leaders resented Wallace's decision. Truman, for whom originally they had slight regard, had won labor's favor by his veto of the Taft-Hartley Act and his promise to support its repeal. As a political realist who, along with most in the CIO leadership, had long opposed a third party for practical reasons, Murray realized that Wallace's votes would be taken from Truman, thus improving the chances of Thomas Dewey, the likely Republican candidate. If Dewey was elected, there would be no chance of repealing Taft-Hartley. Furthermore, if Republicans and southern Democrats gained ground in Congress, Taft-Hartley would be entrenched and probably supplemented with even harsher measures.[62] The possibility of a sweeping antilabor reaction, comparable to that following World War I, was always a concern. The Wallace campaign threatened to sabotage labor's interests. A few union leaders who had previously been close to the Communists, such as "Red Mike" Quill of the New York Transport Workers Union, aligned themselves with Murray. "If being for Wallace will split the C.I.O.," he said, "the price is too great. I am a trade unionist first."[63]

The issue came to a head at the January 1948 meeting of the CIO executive board shortly after Wallace had announced his candidacy. The previous convention had unanimously adopted a resolution pledging "full and unstinted support" to CIO-PAC and its political endorsements. Before the meeting Murray warned all affiliated unions that this pledge was a binding obligation.[64] His strong feelings, usually kept under control, broke out in resentful attacks. "I am referred to" in left-wing publications, he cried, "as an imperialist and a God damned Wall Street war monger. . . ."[65] Reuther, whose position was vastly strengthened by his recent reelection as president of the UAW, attacked the Wallace candidacy on political grounds, pointing out that with labor's votes divided it would be impossible to elect either friendly legislators or a president. A third party supported by some unions would confuse and demoralize potential working-class voters, compounding the apathy that was the CIO's most serious problem in mobilizing a labor vote. Although Reuther favored a political realignment into liberal and conservative parties, the impetus for such a realignment should come from within the labor movement. Support of CIO-PAC endorsements, he added, had been decided upon after a full and free debate. If the affiliated unions refused to support CIO positions, including its political decisions, the ineffectual organization would ultimately perish.[66]

The board voted 33 to 11, with one abstention, to condemn the third-party movement and the Wallace candidacy. Nearly all the negative votes were cast by officers of unions that had already decided to support Wallace and would ultimately be expelled from the CIO.[67] In September, in due course, the executive board endorsed Truman, amid more charges and recriminations.[68] Clearly, the CIO leadership intended to ward off the worst evil. It was more fearful of the consequences of a Truman defeat than hopeful of positive results from his victory. Its praise of the president was restrained, but the Wallaceite Progressive party, the statement said, "offers nothing but division and defeat to really progressive Americans,"[69]

Truman's victory might have provided the occasion for resolving differences, since Wallace's poor showing discouraged his supporters and the campaign did not produce the catastrophe that Murray had feared. However, both sides were unyielding. As well as a presidential election could, the Truman victory showed that labor's rank and file preferred a place, even as a minority, within the Democratic party coalition to a separate, Communist-backed progressive party. The political weakness of the unions that had defied CIO policy was amply demonstrated. At the CIO's Portland convention, immediately after the election, neither side sought a compromise. Murray believed the Communists were prepared to wreck the CIO if necessary in pursuit of their political beliefs.[70] Their actions in the election showed, he said, that "they did not care whether Dewey was elected or the devil was elected," as long as they could defeat Truman, because of his anti-Soviet foreign policy.[71] The left wing was no more conciliatory, provoking a showdown by personal challenges to Murray. The CIO president and his defenders responded with threats such as Reuther's: "I say to the brothers, make up your minds either to get clear in the CIO or clear out of the CIO."[72] By the convention's end there was no doubt which it would be.

Over the next few months, preparations were made for the trial of the dissident unions. At the 1949 convention, the CIO constitution was amended to exclude Communists and those following Communist policy from CIO offices, including the executive board. The board was granted authority to investigate and expel by a two-thirds vote any affiliate "that consistently pursues policies and activities directed toward the achievement of the program or the purposes of the Communist Party . . . rather than the objectives and policies set forth in the constitution of the CIO."[73] The board's actions were subject to approval by the convention. "There is enough room within the CIO movement to differ about many subjects, many ideas," Murray said, "but there is no room within the CIO for Communism."[74]

The charges and evidence focused primarily on four accusations: that the union had supported the successive changes in the Communist position during the Nazi-Soviet pact and the invasion of Russia; that it had endorsed work incentive plans in World War II; that it had refused to support the Marshall Plan; and that it had supported Wallace. These charges rested on the assumption that the political objectives and influence of the CIO were among its vital interests, and therefore as legitimate and binding upon the affiliated unions as their commitment to trade unionism. Although the CIO had not always asserted this position, political uniformity had been an important consideration at times in its brief history. John L. Lewis resigned the CIO presidency in 1940 when he failed to sway the membership on a political issue. Furthermore, a strong case could be made that labor's precarious domestic situation and an honest fear of Soviet policy in Western Europe as a threat to labor's and the nation's interest compelled a united front. Division within a labor movement over politics or ideology was not unique: separate confederations of Communist and non-Communist unions existed in France, Italy, and several other countries. In France, primarily in response to the proposal of the Marshall Plan, membership in the Confédération Générale du Travail, controlled by Communists, dropped from six to three million in a few years, thanks to secessions of non-Communist unions.[75] Many unionists in both Europe and America had become convinced that political or trade union association with the Soviets or those who regularly supported Soviet policies was fatally damaging to free unions.

Following trials conducted by committees of CIO vice-presidents, eleven unions were expelled, representing about one-fifth of the CIO's membership. The committees adopted the rule that a union could be expelled if it were shown that it had publicly followed the Communist line through two or more of its changes. The decisions were approved by the executive board and by unanimous vote at the convention in November 1950.[76] Nearly all the membership of the expelled unions was concentrated in only a few of them, particularly the United Electrical Workers, the Mine, Mill and Smelter Workers, the Fur and Leather Workers, and the West Coast Longshoremen's Union.[77] Most of the rest were small, a few hardly more than paper organizations with negligible numbers. Expulsion opened the way to competition for members in which some of the locals that were raided willingly cooperated. The raiding unions included the UAW, the Steel Workers, and, from the AFL, the Machinists. To challenge the United Electrical Workers, the CIO chartered a major new affiliate, the International Union of Electrical Workers, under the former UEW president James B. Carey, which had substantial though by no means complete success in the fifties.[78]

Expulsion cleared the way for labor to support Truman's foreign policy. Recognizing that totalitarian governments were always quick to suppress free trade unions or transform them into instruments of the state, American trade unionists were committed to support antitotalitarian initiatives. Since World War II the AFL had supported the activities of anti-Communist labor leaders and organizations in Europe and South America with encouragement and backing from the American government. AFL representatives received funds from the government that they funneled into overseas union activities along with some of their own and others' money, and a few CIO officials were similarly involved.[79]

In general, CIO leaders took a more moderate approach than the AFL cold war hard line, favoring support for, and use of, the United Nations, greater American sympathy with the position of neutral nations caught between the great power blocs, and greater reliance on economic and technical aid to struggling nations instead of arms for dictators. In contrast, George Meany so abhorred any contaminating contact with Communist leaders that he refused to meet Khrushchev during the Soviet premier's visit to the United States in 1959, and he locked the door of the AFL-CIO headquarters in Washington against Anastas Mikoyan, the Soviet deputy premier, who was left outside with his nose pressed against the glass trying to catch a glimpse of the leaders of the American working class within. Delineating the differences within the AFL-CIO over Russian contacts, Reuther, the organization's vice-president, arranged and attended a dinner for labor leaders with Khrushchev but had a tumultuous and well-publicized argument with him over living conditions of workers in the United States and the Soviet Union.[80] The expulsion of the nonconforming unions from the CIO reduced the scope of political discussion and criticism within the labor movement and tied it more closely to the Democratic party. Nevertheless, in the consensus politics of the fifties, labor represented a broader range of alternatives on foreign policy than could be found within most major American institutions.

Less directly than in foreign policy or jobs, but perhaps more significant in the long run, the cold war affected some of the social and moral aspects of the lives of American workers. Although the results were not intended by those who constructed cold war policies, international rivalry helped create a climate favorable to ending racial discrimination and consequently led to improvements in the employment prospects of the largest American minority.

Previous wars, beginning with the War for Independence, had moved in that direction, although the results were always limited and often merely temporary.[81] Most recently, in World War II, the combination of a demand for labor and the antiracist ideological element in the struggle against Nazism created pressure for improving the job prospects for blacks. Although conflicts related to promotion of black employees and the opening up of previously closed occupations broke out in some war plants, black employees made significant gains. The government, corporations engaged in arms production, and labor unions in the arms industries preached interracial cooperation and appealed to all races to support the war effort. Workers in Detroit war plants were exhorted "to abandon race prejudice because it directly aided the Axis."[82] The national interest in wartime was repeatedly and directly linked with racial justice, perhaps the only combination that could persuade the majority of white Americans to yield in any significant degree to the claims of the latter. Wartime changes produced more industrial and occupational diversity and opportunity for blacks than they had ever known.[83]

Although the particulars were somewhat different, the cold war confirmed and expanded the linkage between national interest and civil rights. The claim of the Soviet Union to represent a superior kind of democracy, its criticisms of the United States for failure to implement equal rights, and the necessity of securing support among the newly independent nations of Asia and Africa with their massive colored populations forced the white American majority, in upholding the national interest, to make concessions to the black American minority.[84] As might have been expected, the concessions were often halfhearted and superficial, yet the claim to equal treatment was acknowledged to be both just and necessary and some movement did occur.

President Truman subscribed to this motivation in his advocacy of civil rights. Although not slighting the argument that blacks as American citizens had equal constitutional status and deserved equal political rights, he pointed to the need to convince the people of other nations that the United States was democratic in fact as well as in its statements of principle. In June 1947 in his first major civil rights speech, and the first in the history of the presidency, Truman said:

> The support of desperate populations of battle ravaged countries must be won for the free way of life. We must have them as allies in our continuing struggle for the peaceful solution of the world's problems. They may surrender to the false security offered so temptingly by totalitarian regimes unless we can prove the superiority of democracy. Our case for democracy should be as strong as we can make it. It should rest on practical evidence that we have been able to put our own house in order.[85]

The security and the future of the United States depended in part on establishing equal rights for all Americans.

When the presidential Civil Rights Committee reported to Truman a few months later, it noted that "our civil rights record has growing international implications."[86] The committee's proposals, which included enactment of a permanent fair employment practices law, were defended on moral, economic, and international grounds. The report frankly acknowledged that the American "civil rights record has been an issue in world politics," with "our shortcomings" constantly portrayed and analyzed. Americans, it continued, must be more "concerned with the good opinion of the peoples of the world." In the final words of the body of the report, the committee pointed out: "The United States is not so strong, the final triumph of the democratic ideal is not so inevitable, that we can ignore what the world thinks of us or our record."[87]

This motivation transformed the curtailment of racial segregation and discrimination from a matter of morality and citizenship into one of self-interest. Although it obviously did not open up jobs to blacks immediately, it gave to equal employment opportunity and civil rights questions in general a more favorable hearing within the white community than they had previously enjoyed. Truman launched, and Eisenhower continued, a desegregation of the armed forces that would eventually improve job opportunities for blacks who were in the services. Although Congress declined to create the federal fair employment practices commission that Truman's Civil Rights Committee had recommended, and President Eisenhower was opposed to a federal fair employment law, by 1961 nineteen states had adopted fair employment laws of some kind. As a cautious first step at the federal level, Eisenhower appointed a committee headed by Vice-President Richard Nixon to consider ways to curb discrimination on work done under federal contracts. In fact, the committee accomplished little although it could take credit for eliminating the ban on black bus drivers in Washington, D.C. During the Kennedy administration, under the energetic Lyndon Johnson, it became more active.[88]

In 1951, during the Korean War, the income of male Negro wage and salary earners averaged 62 percent of that of whites, the highest point yet reached, and the labor force participation rate of black males in their early twenties, another index of economic opportunity, reached a peak in 1953 at 92.3 percent.[89] Although declines in these indices and a rise in black unemployment through the rest of the fifties was a reminder of the critical importance of the aggregate level of demand for labor in determining total black employment, pressures produced by the cold war had wrought some improvement.

The union issue that loomed largest in the public mind in the postwar era was that of corruption. The CIO unions were virtually free of racketeering, gangster infiltration, and venal officials, but a few of the AFL unions had a history—in some cases a long one—of shady activities. One of the worst situations was in the New York City locals of the International Longshoremen's Association, where a fight over a corrupt administration raged in the early fifties. Under pressure from David Dubinsky of the Ladies' Garment Workers Union and others, George Meany, the AFL's new president, intervened but without much immediate success.[90]

Stronger pressure to clean up the unions and throw out the gangsters was generated by the unification of the AFL and the CIO in 1955. Reuther, formerly president of the CIO and the leading vice-president of the united organization, insisted on a determined campaign against corruption as a condition of merger. Meany, a man of strong moral perceptions, abhorred corruption and was prepared to move against it although somewhat restrained by the constitutional autonomy of the AFL's affiliates. In 1956 the authority of the Committee on Ethical Practices was enlarged and an impressive ethical code for union officials adopted. In a striking departure from tradition and a modification of the autonomy principle, the federation won the right to expel unions whose officers were corrupt.

These self-policing efforts did not avert the storm. A mounting wave of public criticism led to an extensive congressional investigation of union corruption.[91] Early in 1957 the Senate established a select committee under the chairmanship of Senator John McClellan (D., Arkansas), to "conduct an investigation and study of the extent to which criminal or other improper practices or activities are . . . engaged in the field of labor-management relations . . . to the detriment of the interests of the public, employers or employees."[92]

The McClellan committee's hearing concentrated on the Teamsters Union, the largest in the United States, and particularly on its president, Dave Beck, and some of the other officers. They were shown to have used union funds for their benefit through favorable loans and stock purchases with borrowed money. Beck, in fact, treated the union's treasury as a personal fund, buying gifts for friends, family, and self with reckless abandon. He received kickbacks from those having dealings with the Teamsters and with companies the union had under contract, carried on covert business relationships with trucking firms, and had numerous connections with gangsters and convicted felons. Sweetheart agreements in which contract concessions were made to a company in return for payments to the local officials were sometimes involved. The committee reported that many officers of the union by their corrupt activities showed "marked contempt for the welfare of the rank and file." Similar misdeeds by officials of the Baker and Confectionary Workers Union and a few other unions were also exposed.

Altogether, charges of racketeering were made against local or international officers of ten unions affiliated with the AFL. Although relatively few persons or unions were involved, the entire labor movement came under public suspicion. Strongly supported by Reuther and others, Meany engineered the removal of Beck from the executive council of the AFL-CIO and, after James R. Hoffa succeeded Beck as president, the expulsion of the Teamsters, along with two other unions. The expulsions were a brave move. None of the Teamsters' officials at that time had been convicted in court of any misdeeds although Beck had taken the Fifth Amendment before the McClellan committee more than ninety times. The Teamsters were the largest union in the country, and they had close ties with many other unions, particularly those in the building and retail service trades. All-out warfare would be very costly. But the AFL-CIO council and convention acted forcefully and rapidly, possibly with more decisiveness than many businesses or government agencies, including Congress, would have acted where one of their own was concerned. Meany believed labor had acted honorably. As the "honest plumber" later remarked when rejecting a suggestion to readmit the Teamster's to the AFL-CIO, "We would never lower our standards to match the standards of the business community or the marketplace."[94]

Politics played a part in the McClellan committee investigation. This was most clearly shown in the Republicans' attack on Walter Reuther and the UAW. Senators Barry Goldwater, Karl E. Mundt, and Carl T. Curtis insisted on an investigation of the long and bitter strike against the Kohler Company, of Sheboygan, Wisconsin.[95] Goldwater carried the ball. The tenor of his approach was indicated at a Republican dinner in Detroit in January 1958, preceding the opening of the inquiry, when he said: "Walter Reuther and the UAW-CIO are a more dangerous menace than the Sputnick or anything Soviet Russia might do to America."[96] Reuther quickly responded to this attack with the suggestion that each man choose three clergymen to judge the charge. If they found Goldwater correct, Reuther would resign as president of the UAW; if not, he said, Goldwater should resign from the Senate. For good measure, he added that Goldwater was the nation's "number one political fanatic, its number one anti-labor baiter, its number one peddler of class hatred."[97]

When Reuther appeared before the committee, its questions revolved around violence in the strike. Although he conceded that two men sent to Wisconsin by a UAW local in Detroit had assaulted nonstrikers, he denied convincingly that the union had sought to shield them or that they had acted on union instructions. They were later tried and served sentences. The Republican senators, he charged, were trying to score political points by smearing the union. "Our union has had less violence than most. . . . [But] the decison is: Reuther has got to be destroyed because his union is active in politics, and let's find some way. . . . Let's fabricate this theory of violence."[98] Eventually the UAW won the Kohler strike after the NLRB found the company guilty of unfair labor practices including refusal to bargain in good faith.

The legislative result of the McClellan committee hearings was the Landrum-Griffin Act of 1959, adopted over the strong objections of the labor movement. It included a statement of the rights of union members, guarantees of democratic procedures in unions, and protection of union funds against pirating by union officials; it also made violent actions to deprive union members of their rights a federal crime, and prohibited those convicted of certain crimes as well as members of the Communist party from serving as union officials for five years after their release from prison or after termination of party membership. From labor's point of view, a collection of additional provisions was more disturbing. The Taft-Hartley ban on secondary boycotts was broadened to cover more cases, picketing rights were limited where a rival union was recognized, and the jurisdiction of the NLRB was reduced. For the future of organized labor, this final provision was especially threatening, since it protected states with "right to work" laws from the activities of union organizers. The McClellan committee uncovered a serious problem of corruption in only a few unions, but its findings prompted the passage of harsh legislation that went well beyond the original subject of the investigation.[99]

A foreign threat perceived as a challenge to the existence of a nation is bound to have a strong influence on domestic institutions and policies. The entire American polity bent under the unprecedented strains of the cold war. No earlier generation of Americans had lived under the shadow of atomic annihilation or had to face a permanently hostile power of equal or potentially greater strength. American workers and their representative institutions were in the direct path of forces generated by the cold war. They were, however, able to maintain the position they had gained during the New Deal and World War II and even to make some progress in achieving higher standards of living and greater personal and family security. Forced to make concessions to a fearful and suspicious public in the Taft-Hartley and Landrum-Griffin acts and the expulsion of the nonconforming unions from the CIO, workers and organized labor were sufficiently strong to prevent a reaction comparable to the antilabor offensive following World War I and leading to the "lean years" of the twenties.

The cold war was a period of consolidation for American labor. Its political allies were in disarray. Without strong political organization or leadership, there was no opportunity to relive, or go much beyond, the hopeful years of the New Deal. Nevertheless, the substance of what had been won in the past was preserved, and as the most severe pressures of the cold war abated toward the end of the fifties, organized labor and American workers were still a major force in shaping their own and the nation's future.

1. Irving Bernstein, "The Growth of American Unions, 1945–1960," *Labor History* 2 (1961): 131–57; see also Albert A. Blum, "Why Unions Grow," *Labor History* 9 (1968): 39–72.

2. David Brody, "The New Deal and World War II," in John Braeman, Robert H. Bremner, and David Brody, eds., *The New Deal:* Volume One, *The National Level* (Columbus, Ohio, 1975), pp. 267–309.

3. Business, however, was not always or exclusively the beneficiary of national defense needs. Among the reasons the Ford Motor Company made concessions to the United Automobile Workers during the strike of 1941 were its need for defense orders and its reluctance to get into even more serious trouble with the federal government: Allan Nevins

and Frank E. Hill, *Ford: Decline and Rebirth, 1933–1962* (New York, 1962), p. 159; Nelson N. Lichtenstein, "Industrial Unionism under the No-Strike Pledge: A Study of the CIO during the Second World War" (Ph.D. diss., University of California, Berkeley, 1974), pp. 20–21.

4. Joel Seidman, *American Labor: From Defense to Reconversion* (Chicago, 1953), pp. 188–91; Brody, "The New Deal and World War II," p. 280.

5. David M. Oshinsky, "Labor's Cold War: The CIO and the Communists," in Robert Griffith and Athan Theoharis, eds., *The Specter: Original Essays on the Cold War and the Origins of McCarthyism* (New York, 1974), p. 126. Nevertheless, the public's general approval of unions was high and remained so. See the summaries of Gallup polls in Derek C. Bok and John T. Dunlop, *Labor and the American Community* (New York, 1970), pp. 12–15.

6. Harold J. Ruthenberg, "SWOC Confidential Outline of Business Conditions," 1 November 1937, Box A7-33, John Brophy Papers, Catholic University, Washington, D.C.; quoted in Lichtenstein, "Industrial Unionism," p. 5.

7. James L. Clayton, ed., *The Economic Impact of the Cold War* (New York, 1970), p. 16.

8. Boris Shiskin, "The Next Depression?", *American Federationist* 51 (October 1944): 3–6, 21–22.

9. See Lichtenstein, "Industrial Unionism," p. 682. For predictions of postwar depression, see Abstract of Proceedings, Conference of State Industrial Union Councils on Full Production, 18–20 June 1945, CIO National Office, Washington, D.C., p. 7; *PM*, 13 June 1945; Frank Pierson, "The Employment Act of 1946," in Colston Warne et al., *Labor in Postwar America* (Brooklyn, 1949), pp. 284–87; W. S. Woytinsky, "What Was Wrong in Forecasts of Postwar Depression?", *Journal of Political Economy* 55 (1947): 142–51.

10. Lichtenstein, "Industrial Unionism," p. 686.

11. Clayton, *Economic Impact*, p. 29.

12. Harold G. Vatter, *The U.S. Economy in the 1950's* (New York, 1963), pp. 7–8.

13. *Business Week*, 15 April 1950, p. 15.

14. Vatter, *U.S. Economy*, p. 221.

15. Ibid., p. 73.

16. U.S., Congress, House, Committee on Appropriations, Subcommittee on Department of Defense Appropriations, *Department of Defense Appropriations for 1958. Hearings*, 85th Cong., 1st sess., 1957, pt. 1, p. 74.

17. *American Economic Review* 39 (1949): 357; and 40 (1950): 191.

18. Seymour Melman, *Our Depleted Society* (New York, 1965).

19. U.S., Congress, Joint Committee on Defense Production, *Fourth Annual Report*, 84th Cong., 1st sess., House Report No. 1 (1955), p. 2; quoted in Vatter, *U.S. Economy*, p. 82.

20. Ibid., pp. 98, 164–66, 166–67.

21. Joseph C. Goulden, *Meany* (New York, 1972), pp. 227–28.

22. Bert Cochran, ed., *American Labor in Midpassage* (New York, 1959), p. 65.

23. Vatter, *U.S. Economy*, pp. 183–89; Clayton, *Economic Impact*, p. 31. For a study of military spending in two western states, see James L. Clayton, "The Impact of the Cold War on the Economies of California and Utah, 1946–1965," *Pacific Historical Review* 36 (1967): 449–73.

24. Paul Jacobs, *The State of the Unions* (New York, 1963), p. 260.

25. Clayton, *Economic Impact*, p. 56.

26. Vatter, *U.S. Economy*, p. 248; Frank Cormier and William J. Eaton, *Reuther* (Englewood Cliffs, N.J., 1970), p. 302–7.

27. U.S., Bureau of the Census, *Historical Statistics of the United States, Colonial Times to 1957* (Washington, D.C., 1960), p. 96; U.S., Bureau of the Census, *Historical Statistics of the United States, Continuation to 1962 and Revisions* (Washington, D.C., 1965), p. 16.

28. For a convenient summary see Peter Henle, "Wages: Fringe Benefits," *International Encyclopedia of the Social Sciences* 16:424–29.

29. A series of U.S. Bureau of Labor Statistics bulletins analyzes and summarizes the extent of fringe benefit provisions: see *Digest of 100 Selected Health and Insurance Plans under Collective Bargaining, Early 1958*, Bulletin No. 1236 (Washington, D.C., 1958); *Premium Pay for Night, Weekend, and Overtime Work in Major Union Contracts*, Bulletin No. 1251 (Washington, D.C., 1959); *Digest of 100 Selected Pension Plans under Collective Bargaining, Late 1964*, Bulletin No. 1435 (Washington, D.C., 1965); and *Health and Insurance Plans under Collective Bargaining: Hospital Benefits, Early 1959*, Bulletin No. 1274 (Washington, D.C., 1959). See also Raymond Munts, *Bargaining for Health: Labor Unions, Health Insurance, and Medical Care* (Madison, Wis., 1967).

30. William Haber and Merrill J. Murray, *Unemployment Insurance in the American Economy* (Homewood, Ill., 1966), pp. 464–66; Joseph M. Becker, S.J., *Guaranteed Income for the Unemployed: The Story of SUB* (Baltimore, 1968), pp. 3–49.

31. For detailed descriptions of the original auto and steel SUB plans, see U.S., Bureau of Employment Security, *Supplementary Unemployment Benefit Plans and Unemployment Insurance*, BES No. U-172 (Washington, D.C., 1957).

32. U.S., Bureau of Labor Statistics, *Major Collective Bargaining Agreements— Supplemental Unemployment Benefit Plans and Wage Employment Guarantees*, Bulletin No. 1425-3 (Washington, D.C., 1965).

33. Becker, *Guaranteed Income*, pp. 45–49.

34. U.S., Bureau of the Census, *Historical Statistics of the United States, Colonial Times to 1957*, pp. 95–96; U.S., Bureau of the Census, *Historical Statistics of the United States, Continuation to 1962 and Revisions*, p. 16.

35. For socialism in some AFL unions, see John H. M. Laslett, *Labor and the Left* (New York, 1970); and on the IWW, Melvyn Dubofsky, *We Shall Be All* (Chicago, 1969).

36. Although not in entire agreement by any means, the following works are among those reflecting this point of view: C. Wright Mills, *The New Men of Power* (New York, 1948); Daniel Bell, *The End of Ideology* (New York, 1961), p. 218; Sidney Lens, *The Crisis of American Labor* (New York, 1959); Jacobs, *The State of the Unions*, pp. 262–66; Wittner, *Cold War America*, pp. 65–66; Frank Emspak, "The Break-up of the Congress of Industrial Organizations (CIO), 1945–1950" (Ph.D. diss., University of Wisconsin, 1972); James Prickett, "Communists and the Communist Issue in the American Labor Movement, 1920–1950" (Ph.D. diss., University of California, Los Angeles, 1976); Bert Cochran, *Labor and Communism: The Conflict That Shaped American Unions* (Princeton, N.J., 1977).

37. Irving Bernstein, *Turbulent Years* (Boston, 1970), pp. 31–171.

38. Sidney Fine, *Sit-Down: The General Motors Strike of 1936–1937* (Ann Arbor, Mich., 1969).

39. Seidman, *American Labor*, p. 195.

40. The best general account is Bernstein, *Turbulent Years*; among the few studies of rank-and-file attitudes in the thirties are Ray Boryczka, "Militancy and Factionalism in the United Auto Workers Union, 1937–1941," *Maryland Historian* 8 (1977): 13–25; Peter Friedlander, *The Emergence of a UAW Local, 1936–1939: A Study in Class and Culture* (Pittsburgh, 1975); Robert H. Zieger, *Madison's Battery Workers, 1934–1952: A History of Federal Labor Union 19587* (Ithaca, N.Y., 1977); John G. Kruchko, *The Birth of a Union Local: The History of UAW Local 674, Norwood, Ohio, 1933–1940* (Ithaca, N.Y., 1972); Ronald Schatz, "Union Pioneers: The Founders of Local Unions at General Electric and Westinghouse, 1933–1937," *Journal of American History* 66 (1979): 586–602.

41. A recent study of Communist and other leftist activities in the thirties is Cochran, *Labor and Communism*, pp. 46–155.

42. See CIO, *Proceedings*, 1941, p. 146; for perceptions by some workers of the war as a crusade, see Joshua Freeman, "Delivering the Goods: Industrial Unionism during World War II," *Labor History* 19 (1978): 581–93.

43. The statement was part of a newspaper advertisement used in Nixon's campaign. His opponent, Congressman Jerry Voohis, asked CIO-PAC to withdraw its endorsement of his reelection bid: Earl Mazo, *Richard Nixon: A Political and Personal Portrait* (New York, 1959), pp. 46–47.

44. F. Ray Marshall, *Labor in the South* (Cambridge, Mass., 1967), pp. 254–69.

45. Proceedings of Executive Board, CIO, 27 June 1947, Washington, D.C., pp. 144–49; Transcript of Proceedings of Meeting of the International Executive Board, CIO, Boston, Mass., 8, 10, 17 October 1947, pp. 61–125, Labor History Archives, Wayne State University (hereinafter cited as LHA-WSU); CIO, *Proceedings*, 1947, pp. 186, 202–4.

46. *American Communications Association* v. *Douds*, 339 U.S. 382 (1950); see also David Caute, *The Great Fear* (New York, 1978), pp. 354–58. Some workers were fired from their jobs after pleading the Fifth Amendment before congressional committees: ibid., pp. 360–75. See Ralph S. Brown, *Loyalty and Security: Employment Tests in the United States* (New Haven, Conn., 1958).

47. U.S., Congress, House, Special Committee on Un-American Activities, Investigation of Un-American Propaganda Activities in the United States, *Hearings*, vol. 1, 12–23 August 1938.

48. *New York Times*, 16, 17 October 1939; CIO, *Proceedings*, 1940, pp. 24–26, 44, 218–36; Max M. Kampelman, *The Communist Party vs. the C.I.O.* (New York, 1957), p. 22.

49. Melvyn Dubofsky and Warren Van Tine, *John L. Lewis: A Biography* (New York, 1977), p. 128; Walter Galenson, *The CIO Challenge to the AFL* (Cambridge, Mass., 1960), pp. 111–12.

50. UAW, *Proceedings*, 1940, pp. 499–507; Carl Haessler, Oral History Transcript, p. 68, LHA-WSU.

51. UAW, *Proceedings*, 1941, pp. 613, 688–711, 723–24; Haessler, Oral History Transcript, p. 100, LHA-WSU; Roger Keeran, "Communists and Auto Workers: The Struggle for a Union, 1919–1941" (Ph.D. diss., University of Wisconsin, 1974), pp. 345–46; Cochran, *Labor and Communism*, pp. 192–95.

52. Cochran, *Labor and Communism*, p. 148.

53. William Paschell and Rose Theodore, "Anti-Communist Provisions in Union Constitutions," *Monthly Labor Review*, October 1954, pp. 1097–1100.

54. In May 1946 the United Steel Workers convention at Murray's insistence denounced any efforts by Communists to "infiltrate, dictate or meddle in the union's affairs": *New York Times*, 15, 16 May 1946. A recent study of the split in the CIO is Mary S. McAuliffe, *Crisis on the Left: Cold War Politics and American Liberals, 1947–1954* (Amherst, Mass., 1978), pp. 10–21, 41–47, 51–62.

55. Murray's delicate position is discussed in the *New York Times*, 9 September, 6 October, 11 November 1946.

56. CIO, *Proceedings*, 1946, pp. 111–14; Kampelman, *Communist Party vs. C.I.O.*, pp. 47–50.

57. CIO, *Proceedings*, 1946, p. 59; *New York Times*, 16–19, 23 November 1946; Kampelman, *Communist Party vs. C.I.O.*, pp. 54–57; Cochran, *Labor and Communism*, p. 267; Emspak, "The Break-up of the Congress of Industrial Organizations," pp. 92–98.

58. Kampelman, *Communist Party vs. C.I.O.*, p. 110; Cochran, *Labor and Communism*, p. 270.

59. Kampelman, *Communist Party vs. C.I.O.*, pp. 107, 146; Len DeCaux, *Labor Radical* (Boston, 1970), pp. 479–81.

60. CIO, *Proceedings*, 1947, pp. 260–62, 284–87; *New York Times*, 9, 15, 16 October 1947; *New Republic*, 27 October 1947.

61. *New Leader*, 30 October 1947.

62. For a trenchant statement of the CIO leadership's position, see "Political Action in the 1948 Campaign," CIO Executive Board Statement, 30–31 August 1948, copy in Walter P. Reuther Papers, Box 15, Folder—"CIO 1948," LHA-WSU. Even a popular song, "Have a Heart, Taft-Hartley, Have a Heart!" composed by the successful writer Jack Lawrence, failed to have an effect. A copy is in Walter P. Reuther Papers, Box 16, Folder—"CIO-Political Action Committee," LHA-WSU.

63. Kampelman, *Communist Party vs. C.I.O.*, p. 143.

64. Philip Murray to Walter P. Reuther, telegram, 8 January 1948, Walter P. Reuther Papers, Box 16, Folder—"CIO, Murray, Philip," LHA-WSU. See also *CIO News*, 12 January 1948.

65. Proceedings of the International Executive Board, CIO, 22–23 January 1948, p. 21, LHA-WSU; *CIO News*, 28 January 1948; *New York Times*, 23–24 January 1948.

66. Proceedings of the International Executive Board, CIO, 22–23 January 1948, pp. 54–76, LHA-WSU. According to John Brophy, then director of councils for the CIO, Reuther's reelection and handling of the situation in the UAW convinced Murray that the time had come "for the campaign against the Communists": John Brophy, *A Miner's Life*, ed. John O. P. Hall (Madison, Wis., 1964), p. 294.

67. Proceedings of the International Executive Board, CIO, 22–23 January 1948, p. 245, LHA-WSU.

68. Transcript of Proceedings, International Executive Board, CIO, 30–31 August and 1 September 1948, LHA-WSU, *CIO News*, 6 September 1948; *New York Times*, 31 August, 1–2 September 1948.

69. "Political Action in the 1948 Campaign," CIO Executive Board statement, 30–31 August 1948, LHA-WSU.

70. Congress of Industrial Organizations, Meetings of International Executive Board, 17, 20, 27 November 1948, Portland, Oregon, pp. 42–73, LHA-WSU.

71. CIO, *Proceedings*, 1948, p. 14.

72. Ibid., p. 171; *CIO News*, 29 November 1948; *New York Times*, 18–28 November 1948; *Daily People's World*, 24 November 1948.

73. CIO, *Proceedings*, 1949, pp. 240, 288–90.

74. Ibid., p. 327.

75. Ronald Radosh, *American Labor and United States Foreign Policy* (New York, 1969), pp. 320–21; Walter Galenson, ed., *Comparative Labor Movements* (New York, 1952), pp. 354–76 ff.

76. Proceedings of the International Executive Board of the Congress of Industrial Organizations, Washington, D.C., 14 February, 15 June, 29 August 1950, LHA-WSU. Verbatim records of the hearings are in CIO Secretary-Treasurer (James B. Carey) Papers, Boxes 108–13, LHA-WSU.

77. The UEW, in fact, seceded before it was expelled by refusing to make per capita payments to the CIO.

78. The eleven expelled unions were: American Communications Association; United Public Workers; United Office and Professional Workers; Fur and Leather Workers; Fishermen and Allied Workers; National Union of Marine Cooks and Stewards; United Farm Equipment Workers; Mine, Mill and Smelter Workers; International Longshoremen's and Warehousemen's Union; United Electrical Workers; and Food, Tobacco, Agricultural and Allied Workers. By 1968 only four (A.C.A.; Mine, Mill; Longshoremen's; and

UEW) were still in existence as separate organizations. See F. S. O'Brien, "The 'Communist-Dominated' Unions in the United States since 1950," *Labor History* 9 (1968): 184–209. For the subsequent story of the UEW by a participant, see James J. Matles and James Higgins, *Them and Us* (Boston, 1974), pp. 187–304; and Caute, *The Great Fear*, pp. 376–91.

79. Radosh, *American Labor*, pp. 431–34; Victor Reuther, *The Brothers Reuther and the Story of the UA W* (Boston, 1976), pp. 411–27.

80. Goulden, *Meany*, pp. 280–81; Cormier and Eaton, *Reuther*, pp. 363–67.

81. See John Hope Franklin, *From Slavery to Freedom* (New York, 1967), pp. 126–41, 294–96, 455–86.

82. August Meier and Elliott Rudwick, *Black Detroit and the Rise of the UA W* (New York, 1979), pp. 190, 213–15.

83. Arthur M. Rose and Herbert Hill, eds., *Employment, Race, and Poverty* (New York, 1967), p. 17.

84. For black perceptions of the new world order, see Harold R. Isaacs, *The New World of Negro Americans* (New York, 1964).

85. Truman Papers, OF 413, Harry S. Truman Library, quoted in William C. Berman, *The Politics of Civil Rights in the Truman Administration* (Columbus, Ohio, 1970), p. 63.

86. U.S., Committee on Civil Rights, *To Secure These Rights* (Washington, D.C., 1947), p. 100.

87. Ibid., pp. 147–48.

88. For an official statement of economic opportunity, see U.S., Commission on Civil Rights, *Report: Book 3, Employment* (Washington, D.C., 1961); Charles C. Alexander, *Holding the Line: The Eisenhower Era, 1952–1961* (Bloomington, Ind., 1975), p. 117.

89. Ross and Hill, eds., *Employment, Race, and Poverty*, pp. 17–19.

90. John Hutchinson, *The Imperfect Union* (New York, 1972), pp. 296–303, and Goulden, *Meany*, pp. 187–94.

91. A Gallup poll of April 1957 showed that 83% of all adults and 81% of adults in union families believed that "the labor laws should be tightened to require unions to make a full accounting of their finances": George H. Gallup, *The Gallup Poll, Public Opinion, 1935–1971, Vol. II: 1949–1958* (New York, 1972), p. 1483.

92. U.S., Congress, Senate, *Final Report of the Select Committee on Improper Activities in the Labor or Management Field*, 86th Cong., 2d sess., Report No. 1139, pt. 4, p. 868.

93. Ibid., pt. 3, p. 572.

94. Goulden, *Meany*, p. 252. On the Teamsters' investigation see Hutchinson, *The Imperfect Union*, pp. 229–70, and Robert F. Kennedy, *The Enemy Within* (New York, 1960), pp. 3–189.

95. A full account of the strike is Walter H. Uphoff, *Kohler on Strike* (Boston, 1966). Also of interest is Robert F. Kennedy, *The Enemy Within*, pp. 266–99.

96. *Detroit Times*, 21 January 1958; *Detroit News*, 22 January 1958.

97. Cormier and Eaton, *Reuther*, p. 344.

98. U.S., Congress, Senate, Select Committee on Improper Activities in the Labor or Management Field, *Hearings*, 85th Cong., 2d sess., pt. 25, p. 10197.

99. A more detailed description of some of the law's provisions is in Charles O. Gregory and Harold A. Katz, *Labor and the Law*, 3d ed. (New York, 1979), pp. 535–45.

Rural America in an Urban Age, 1945–1960

Thomas E. Williams

In 1945 the term *rural America* carried with it a quantitative dimension of population and a qualitative dimension of culture. It defined the small towns and the sparsely settled countryside as well as a culture tied to tradition revolving around agriculture. Those Americans who resided in small towns and in the surrounding areas at the end of World War II lived on the threshold of vast changes. The increased use of technology in everyday life and work that was to play such an important role in postwar America was to have a profound influence on rural America during the Truman and Eisenhower years. At the war's end many of the primary forces that were to change rural life—new forms of mass culture, an agricultural revolution, and federal farm policy—were already taking on the characteristics that would so significantly alter its nature. What was difficult to foresee in 1945 was the rapid pace of change that the next decade and a half would bring.

To some, rural America in 1945 seemed very much undisturbed by the technologically advanced, interdependent world of urban industrial America. The cover story of the 7 July 1945 issue of the *Saturday Evening Post* was "My Town," T. E. Murphy's description of small-town America in the year of Allied victories. In the article Murphy explored many of the traditional themes about rural life. He was an unabashed supporter of small-town superiority, contending that small towns exemplified the traditional American values of independence and freedom. Murphy liked the look, feel, and the physical environment of life in the American small town, and he left little doubt that he considered it superior to that in the cities. He ended with an appeal for Americans to come home to their true roots:

> Only when the major part of Americans declare their independence from the city, the machine and the treadmill of urban living can we ever again hope, as a people, to get back to the rugged but pleasant road that leads to the fulfillment of the dreams of those who founded America.[1]

A rural culture strong enough to pose a genuine alternative to urban life undoubtedly existed in the United States in the 1920s. During that decade rural America was cohesive enough and confident enough to launch a series of conflicts with the new American culture emanating from the cities. It may well have had validity in the 1930s when the depression reversed the great population flow from the countryside into the cities that had been a marked feature of American life since the late nineteenth century. The depression also set off a national search for causes of the great debacle, leading to a rediscovery of America in literature and scholarship that championed the nation's past of rural values. World War II, however, pushed rural America into the background and revived the massive migration of people into the urban areas. Murphy's contention that a rural America of genuine distinctiveness existed in 1945 was based more on nostalgia than reality, and his hope that Americans would turn back to the small town for guidance in the postwar years was to remain unfulfilled. Instead, rural America in the Truman and Eisenhower years became more and more urban-like. By 1960 it had virtually disappeared except as a statistical entity meaning a sparsely settled region.[2]

A more nearly accurate description of rural America in 1945 was presented to the readers of the same issue of the *Saturday Evening Post* in John Falter's cover illustration depicting a small town filled with people celebrating Independence Day. The obligatory school band heads the marching column of the town parade, and a serviceman waving to the crowd from an open car follows close behind. A sailor walks down the sidewalk with a girl on each arm. A policeman arrests a drunk, and a woman, who is conscious that the disturbance is drawing the attention of her young daughter, looks on disapprovingly. Across the street a small boy waving an American flag eludes the desperate grasp of his mother and is joining the band on its march. A black family enjoys the spectacle under the awning of the J. C. Moyer Building, an impressive 1895 red brick edifice that now houses the offices of the town's professional men. An extension of the crowd scene and an additional automobile representing the Red Cross dominate the background. In the upper left a train passes by the town center, and a telephone pole with its numerous connecting wires completes the scene.

Falter's small town had not rejected the machine; the automobile was featured as a prominent part of small-town life, having been interwoven into one of its basic rituals.[3] Falter's town was well integrated into the national communications and transportation network. The people in the crowd wore clothing that was not identifiable as either urban or rural; they were clearly part of a consumption community stretching far beyond the borders of their town. The building that Falter chose to place at the center of town life was not the time-honored symbol of localism, the county courthouse, but a building quartering the town lawyers and other professionals. It was these same middle-class professionals that historian Robert Wiebe has identified as the group that, beginning in the late nineteenth century, played the key role in breaking down the isolation of small-town life through their drive for professionalization and organization.[4] The Fourth of July celebrants were citizens of a national community; they were citizens of the world community as well. The local-hero serviceman leading the parade represented the town's direct contribution to World War II, and the Red Cross automobile symbolized support on the home front. Falter's small town appeared to be well integrated into the broader national and world community, and because of that his visual presentation went to the heart of rural life in the immediate postwar years.

Evidence that rural America was being absorbed into a broader national framework began appearing at the close of World War II. Home-front activities had often cut across urban-rural boundaries as both groups encountered labor shortages, witnessed women assuming new roles, listened to the war news on the radio, and took part in scrap metal drives or Red Cross campaigns.[5] A series of public opinion polls between 1945 and 1950 revealed only slight differences in rural and urban views on major issues.[6] A 1945 survey even found that urban and rural residents shared a common satisfaction with radio programming.[7] In 1951 the *New York Times* took a look at rural America through a story about a small town in Kansas. The reporter concluded:

> These people aren't isolated or isolationist. They aren't hicks. The hick-town went out with the horse-and-buggy days, and a sampling from *Who's Who in America* shows that more than half the entries were born in whistle-stop towns. These people wear the same fashions, hear the same radio programs, read the same magazines and newspaper columns as the city folk. They live here by choice. And they know what is happening in the world. They know communism for what it is.[8]

The reporter had identified one of the most important ways in which rural America was being caught up in the complex web of modern life: it had begun consuming the same goods, services, and information as urban America.

As the *Times* reporter indicated, rural America was caught up in common consumption patterns with urban America because of the penetration of modern technology into almost every geographical locality in the nation. Since the 1930s rural electrification had been a much-watched indicator of the arrival of modernity in rural America. In the United States as a whole, the proportion of homes with electricity increased from 79 percent in 1940 to 94 percent in 1950, and most of that increase was in rural homes.[9] Figures for the use of refrigeration closely followed those for electrification. In both cases they were almost universal in American homes by 1950, with the greatest increase in the previous decade in rural areas.[10] In 1960 more than two-thirds of rural American homes had access to a telephone, and more than 90 percent had radios. Rural America trailed urban America in the availability of such features of modern life as radio, electrification, refrigeration, and telephones, but the disparity was not great.[11] The countryside in the postwar years was not left out of modern technology or even seriously excluded from participation; it simply lagged slightly behind. The same was true for rural participation in the postwar period's most significant addition to America's mass-consumer society: television.

In 1950 the approximately five million television sets in use in the United States were located almost exclusively in urban homes.[12] Confinement of television to urban America continued through the Korean War when, because of the national emergency and a great backlog of station applications, the Federal Communications Commission discontinued granting new station licenses. But the end of the Korean War marked the termination of the freeze period on station licenses, and a flood of new television stations from 1954 to 1960 brought the new medium to rural America.[13] By 1960, 11.3 million rural homes had television. The once great disparity between urban and rural access to television had been reduced markedly: in 1960 82 percent of rural homes and 88 percent of urban homes had at least one television set.[14]

Television, when it came to rural America, had little rural character. There are of course solid reasons why early television was oriented to the urban resident: the original audience had been in the large urban centers and the freeze on granting of television licenses in the early 1950s locked the medium into programs that appealed to those cities. Furthermore, as a business that depended on reaching the largest audience possible, television programming was drawn to situations and themes that appealed to the much larger urban audience. Contemporary rural America, even small-town America, was seldom seen on network television except as it existed in the West of the 1870s or 1880s. The small-town family of the mass popular culture of the 1930s epitomized in movies by the Hardys of Carvel was virtually nonexistent in network television of the 1950s. The Andersons of 607 South Maple Street, Springfield, in "Father Knows Best" were the Hardys' closest counterparts; but that small-town family was vastly outnumbered by the urban apartment dwellers—the Williamses of Apartment 542 in "Make Room for Daddy," the Ricardos in Apartment 3-B in "I Love Lucy," the Kramdons and Nortons of Brooklyn in the "Honeymooners"—and the suburban families such as the Rileys of "The Life of Riley."[15] Television in the 1950s, unlike much of American culture and mass culture of preceding decades, projected urban America as the setting for the typical American family. In projecting such an image, television was accurately reflecting the true circumstances of most American families, but it also was denying rural America one of its last remaining strengths: the powerful cultural myth that "true" American values lay in the small towns and countryside.

Television was a mixed blessing for rural America in its effect on the availability of another aspect of mass culture: professional sports. In America in the Truman and Eisenhower years, professional sports meant baseball. The professional game of 1945 was made up of sixteen major league teams and a nationwide complex of minor leagues operating at various levels of play. In 1949 the minor-league component alone drew almost 42 million fans.[16] It was not necessary for a rural resident to travel to a distant metropolis to attend a professional game; organized professional baseball was available in small- and medium-sized cities throughout the country. In 1947 the Class C Mid-Atlantic league brought the professional game to such Pennsylvania cities and towns as Johnstown, New Castle, Oil City, and Uniontown; a team in Vandergrift won the league championship. By 1960 the number of minor leagues had fallen to 22, down from 58 only eleven years earlier, and attendance at minor league games had plummeted from a peak of 42 million in 1949 to fewer than 11 million.[17] The principal culprit in the decline of the minor leagues was television. Rural residents gave up their local baseball teams and came to share the teams of the major cities.[18]

As rural America was penetrated by the mass culture stemming from the cities and made privy to the great outpouring of technology and consumer goods that characterized the postwar world, it is scarcely surprising that, as sociologist Carle C. Zimmerman found in 1949, the rural personality was becoming more urban-like. Rural values were changing so as to place more emphasis on obtaining income and less on family, land, and property.[19] Tradition was losing its hold over rural America and being replaced by the more entrepreneurial and consumption-based orientation of the cities. Certainly, few Americans proved less tradition-bound than American farmers. In agriculture, as in so many other areas of rural life, the hallmark of the 1945–60 period was the rapid adoption of complex techniques and technologies. The successful postwar farmer was open to innovation and new scientific discoveries; he continued paying homage to the Jeffersonian ideal of the yeoman farmer, a useful political image, but he relied on modern business techniques and the new herbicides, insecticides, and hybrids.

Rural America's greatest industry, agriculture, the industry that had long provided the most important influence on the pace and style of rural life, underwent a sweeping series of technological and scientific changes in the years 1945–60. A biological revolution produced new hybrids and major advances in animal nutrition, sanitation, and plant and animal breeding. A chemical revolution of profound importance brought greatly increased use of fertilizer, insecticide, herbicide, and fungicide.[20] The mechanical revolution, which was complete in most of United States agriculture prior to 1945, arrived in the South in the 1950s and brought mechanization to the cotton culture. Those who survived these successive revolutions were not cast in the mold of the self-reliant, individualistic, tradition-bound American farmer. They were expert in the science of their profession, adept at managing capital and skilled at marketing techniques. In the immediate postwar years, the American farmer had to be a sound businessman because his industry became more demanding of capital than manufacturing and his fellow farmers were increasing their productivity at a faster rate than any other major sector of the economy. This was accomplished despite millions of people leaving the farms and even though acreage under cultivation declined.

One of the results of the economics of postwar agriculture was a rapid decline in the farm population. In 1945 almost 24.5 million Americans lived on farms; in 1960 that figure had fallen to 15.6 million.[21] Whereas 17.5 percent of all Americans had lived on farms at the close of World War II, only 8.7 percent did so in 1960.[22] As agriculture became increasingly difficult for small operators, many farmers sought jobs in the nonfarm sector of the economy. In the 1950s the greatest source of income for most American farmers was income from nonfarm employment.[23] In

1954 one-half of the farm operators in the United States reported some off-farm income, and in 28 percent of the cases the operator worked more than a hundred days in nonfarm employment.[24] In some cases the nature of farming was divorced from commercial crop production altogether since one of the most important trends of the 1950s was an increase in the number of residential farms. In such cases the farm became the second residence of city dwellers or perhaps a retirement retreat.[25] Thus, not only did the number of farms and farmers decrease during the 1945–60 period but the nature of the work done by farmers also changed.

The changes in agriculture and farm life resulted from government policy as well as scientific and technological progress. Agriculture enjoyed a particularly favored position in the political structure of the Truman and Eisenhower years. During those years Jeffersonian ideas about agrarian individualism, the supposed democratic propensities of farmers, and the wholesomeness of country life remained powerful parts of American culture. The farmer could, and did, mobilize sympathy and political action behind such favorable cultural symbols. In addition, there was a time lag between the decline of farmers to a statistically unimportant group and the inevitable diminution of their political power. State legislatures and thus congressional districts were weighted heavily in favor of rural areas, where farmers often wielded considerable political power. The congressional seniority system strengthened the hand of rural, particularly southern, congressmen who often saw it as their special duty to protect the interests of agriculture. With a positive public image and political representation greater than their numbers justified, American farmers used effective lobbying to exercise considerable political clout during the Truman and Eisenhower years.[26]

Interest group politics was an integral part of American agriculture in the postwar years. As the number of farmers shrank, the power of their special interest lobby increased. With the reduction in numbers came greater cohesion of opinion in various sectors of American agriculture. The most successful of the groups in the postwar era was the American Farm Bureau. It had been an important organization since the 1920s; in the postwar era its membership was much greater than any other single group, reaching 1,600,000 family memberships by 1960.[27] With its primary constituency in the Midwest and South, the Farm Bureau reflected a philosophy of support for policies that favored large farms. It generally opposed a social role for government in agriculture, preferring government intervention primarily to underwrite and support a free market in agricultural products. Postwar federal policy, particularly after the Republican triumph of 1952, reflected the desires of the Farm Bureau to a greater extent than those of any other farm group.[28]

The organization that most frequently clashed with the Farm Bureau for control over the direction of federal policy was the Farmers Union, which had 186,000 family members in 1960.[29] The Farmers Union continued a New Deal, even populist, legacy of militant defense of the family farm amid the transformation of American agriculture. The organization was based in the Great Plains and also had a following among the diminishing number of small farmers of the South. Tied closely to the Democratic party, the Farmers Union was influential during the Truman years but less so after 1952. Although it remained a respected and oft-consulted organization on federal policy throughout the 1945–60 period, the direction of federal policy was clearly that favored by the Farm Bureau.[30]

The Grange of the postwar era was less ideologically defined than either the Farmers Union or the Farm Bureau, although it most frequently supported the latter. In 1960 the Grange had 586,000 family memberships and was thus exceeded numerically among farmer organizations only by the Farm Bureau.[31] Based primarily in the Northeast, this organization represented satisfied farmers and continued to place much of its emphasis on providing social functions for its members. In the critical aspect of defining federal farm policy, the Grange played neither the leadership role of the Farm Bureau nor the adversary role of the Farmers Union.[32]

Under the primary influence of the Farm Bureau, agriculture in the postwar era did not use its political power to hold back the growing importance of specialization, complexity, and technology in rural life. Efforts to turn the political power of rural America to the purpose of shoring up the income of most farmers, who were ill-equipped to meet growing technological complexity and increased capital demands, were consistently defeated or at least poorly funded.[33] Rather than helping to preserve traditional farmers and their lifestyle, federal farm policy promoted the interests of large-scale, productive, efficient, and business-oriented farmers. In doing so, federal farm policy contributed enormously to the integration of rural America into a complex and technologically advanced national life.

Postwar federal agricultural policy was set in the Great Depression when the federal government introduced price supports for basic commodities coupled with measures to reduce production. The latter feature of New Deal policy sought to deal with the problem of overproduction that had plagued American agriculture since the early 1920s. Concerted efforts in the 1930s to reduce American farm output were largely ineffective. However, World War II generated an enormous new demand for American agricultural products and thus provided a temporary solution to America's chronic oversupply problem.

In the long run, parity was the most important feature of New Deal farm policy. Under that system, which continued into the postwar era, the federal government guaranteed a price for basic commodities— cotton, corn, wheat, and several minor crops—sufficient to provide farmers with a fair share of the national income. Initially, this fair share was defined as an income enabling farmers to enjoy a standard of living comparable to their standard in the golden age of American agriculture, the immediate pre–World War I period. The complicated parity formula varied over time, but its result was to ensure that efficient farmers had sound incomes from basic crops.[34] Furthermore, since the system worked by government guarantee of prices, the myth that the farmer was still engaged in the free market retained some surface validity; thus, farmers could avoid the negative connotations of welfare or guaranteed income.

Sheltered from low-prices by an umbrella of generous government guarantees, the large-scale and efficient farmers were able to adopt the new technology and scientific discoveries of the postwar period. Farmers were so productive in the 1950s that the federal government accumulated huge stocks of unwanted farm products. Foreign aid programs, domestic food commodity distribution to the needy, the Soil Bank program, and various schemes to stimulate foreign buying were all employed as means of disposing of or limiting America's agricultural abundance. Eisenhower's secretary of agriculture, Ezra Taft Benson, followed a policy of gradually reducing price supports and introducing more measures to reduce acreage; but commercial farmers had enough political strength to prevent any significant reduction of price supports, and their productivity was rising at such a rate that acreage reduction had little effect on total output. At the end of the Eisenhower years, the federal government held huge agricultural surpluses, and basic farm policy had not been altered.[35]

Throughout the fifteen years following World War II, the average American farm grew larger. Federal farm policies and the great capital needs of highly mechanized and scientific agriculture rewarded large operators and penalized small ones. The result was a concentration of most American agricultural production in a tiny minority of American farms. Edward Higbee has best summed up the situation using 1959 statistics:

"In other words if only 9 percent of the nation's farms were as productive as the top 3 percent there would be no need for crops from the other 91 percent. As it is, the top 3 percent produce more than the bottom 78 percent."[36]

Postwar agricultural policy did little to alleviate the plight of the poorest farmers. In 1954, 500,000 individuals classified as full-time farmers earned less than $1,200.[37] Federal farm policy, which was tied to price supports, had little effect on the income of these farmers at the bottom of the ladder because they tended to consume most of their production. Lauren Soth commented in 1957 in *Farm Trouble*: "Price support guarantees could be 'doubled' without improving the incomes of these people much."[38]

Such agricultural poverty tended to be located in specific geographic locations: the Ozarks, Appalachia, and the South in general. In 1950 average farm family income in the Ozark area of Missouri and Arkansas was $900 per year. Of the 51 areas in the United States in 1949 where median farm income was less than $1,000, 49 were in the South.[39]

The 1954 Rural Development Program, the federal government's answer to the plight of the poorest of American farmers, focused particularly on providing off-farm employment. Continued throughout the remainder of the 1950s, its funding was minuscule as part of the overall federal agricultural expenditure. In fiscal year 1961 the federal government spent $2.7 million on the development program, whereas the price support program involved a cost one thousand times as great.[40] In sum, postwar federal policy paid little heed to the plight of the bottom half-million farm families. Instead, federal agricultural efforts tended to reinforce the trends toward large farms and increased use of sophisticated technology.

The cultural and technological changes that swept through rural America in the postwar era and the capacity of those forces to produce thoroughgoing change can best be seen in the South. The South entered the postwar era as the last major region of the United States that was predominantly rural. It had been one of the centers of the great rural cultural revolt in the 1920s and was the center of the New Deal's attempts to bring modernization to rural America. More than any other region, it retained a distinctive social and cultural system that institutionalized racism and resisted outside pressures for change. When the South entered the postwar period, it was still possible for Governor Eugene Talmadge of Georgia to boast that he need not campaign in counties that had streetcars; so great was the underrepresentation of urban Georgia in state governmental institutions that streetcar counties were a waste of campaign energy.[41] Throughout the South, not just in Georgia, the rural population dominated the organs of state government. The society, culture, and governmental structure that had settled on the South in the aftermath of the Populist revolt of the 1890s appeared to be well entrenched. Nevertheless, this most rural region of America experienced a series of sweeping changes in the postwar period. The South occupied a position in rural America that was analogous to rural America's relation to the nation as a whole; it tended to lag behind the rest of rural America in economic and social indexes, but its movement was well within the same outlines: it became more urban-like and was more and more swept up in the dominant national culture.

The South's travail during the period 1945–60 can be described as one part of the assimilation of rural America into the dominant urban national culture. That change came more slowly to the South than to the rest of rural America was predictable because it was the last portion of rural America where a continued high rural population and a historical memory that gave substance to distinctiveness combined to create a society capable of resistance to modernization. In the end, however, even the South proved incapable of turning back the rapid pace of the assimilation of rural America into fuller participation in the national life.

At the close of the Eisenhower years, the foundations were firmly in place for the end of southern peculiarity. In the 1960 census the South joined the other regions of the country as predominantly urban.[42] The basic legal framework, leadership structure, and tactics that would bring an end to de jure segregation in the next few years was set. The agricultural revolution of the postwar years put an end to the economic viability of the labor-intensive plantation and sharecropping system.[43] Nor was the South any better at resisting the ubiquitous popular culture than other regions of the country. Some southern television stations practiced racism by refusing to transmit programs featuring black performers, but, by and large, the South was as thoroughly incorporated into the national network of television and its consumption patterns as other regions.[44] Most importantly, the New South creed, which was now decades old, seemed to achieve final approval throughout the region. Even as some state officials held that integration would never occur, the thrust of southern state government policy was to industrialize as rapidly as possible. In the 1950s southern governments sought industrial development with an eagerness and devotion once confined only to the preservation of white supremacy.[45] Their success was not fully apparent in 1960, but the result would be the booming and balanced economies of the following two decades. The postwar period set in motion trends of urbanization, increasing influence of mass culture, more rapid communications, and a transformation of agriculture that brought rural America fully within the national life. For the South the impact of these trends had less rapid results, but in the long run they were more thoroughgoing in their implications.

In 1960 the South had certainly not disappeared as a distinctive region. Nevertheless, the immediate postwar years had set the stage for a decade of chaos and conflict in which the old adversary of mainstream American life underwent a thorough reworking of its institutions and customs. It emerged from that decade with its segregation de facto rather than de jure; its politicians stressing efficient management rather than flamboyant personalities; and its metropolitan centers politically and culturally powerful. The changes that swept over most of rural America in the decade and a half that followed World War II triumphed in the South approximately a decade later.

Rural America did not vanish in the 1945–60 period, but it became increasingly submerged in the larger, national culture. In the 1920s rural America possessed a confidence and combativeness that led it to defend vigorously—even to attempt to export through such measures as prohibition and fundamentalism—its dominant values. The collective sense of self-worth and the willingness to assert it had clearly disappeared in the postwar era. Gone too was the 1930s national consciousness of rural life as one of the most important components of the national life. By 1960 it had become almost completely an importer of culture, particularly through the mass popular culture. At the same time rural life continued to be marked by special circumstances that new technology, however complex, could not completely wipe away: more isolation, greater distances, sparser population, and less variety. These factors, which had once created a distinct culture vying for control over the national life, operated in the postwar era more as handicaps to the rapid adoption of urban values than as creators of a valued separateness.

Peter Bogdanovich's 1971 film *The Last Picture Show* presents a perceptive critique of rural America in the period after World War II. Set in the small Texas town of Anarene in 1951, the film evokes the mood of America's declining small-town communities. It is in identifying and portraying the mood of the town that the film becomes a perceptive historical commentary. The physical decay of the town center is symptomatic of a much greater loss than mere buildings; what has been lost, and in this film is mourned, is any sense that the small town is a distinctive social institution with a set of values and ideas that are exclusive to its environment. Anarene is devoid of cultural confidence and vigor, and its best young people are leaving for the cities.

By 1960 the ineradicable features of rural American life frequently caused that segment of society to lag behind urban dwellers in some statistical categories of affluence, but it was unmistakably clear that rural and urban America were moving along a common course, a course basically charted in the cities. Rural America's energy was being consumed in trying to adapt the latest technological and scientific innovations affecting its economy and culture, and in struggling to maintain enough of the trappings of a modern consumer society to hold its young.

1. P. 15.

2. During the 1950s rural America was made up of approximately 54 million people if one includes those who lived in small towns with fewer than 2,500 inhabitants, on farms, or in dwellings in the countryside not directly related to a farm. Although the population of rural America remained stationary during the period, its percentage of the United States population dropped from 36.0% to 30.1%. The numbers are from: U.S., Bureau of the Census, *People of Rural America*, by Dale E. Hathaway, J. Allen Beegle, and W. Keith Bryant (Washington, D.C., 1968), p. 20; U.S., Bureau of the Census, *Urban and Rural Population of the United States, By States, 1960 and 1950*, 1960 Census of Population Supplementary Reports Series, No. PC(S1)-4 (1961), p. 1.

3. Even before World War II, six of ten farm families had automobiles: W. A. Anderson, "The Challenge of Tomorow's Rural Life," *Rural Sociology* 11 (March 1946): 121.

4. *The Search for Order* (New York, 1967), pp. 111–32.

5. Charles R. Hoffer, "The Impact of War on the Farm Family," *Rural Sociology* 10 (June 1945): 151–56.

6. Howard W. Beers, "Rural Urban Differences: Some Evidence from Public Opinion Polls," *Rural Sociology* 18 (March 1953): 1–11.

7. This was one of the few examples of the popular press playing upon the theme of urban-rural similarities: "Radio's Rural Ears," *Business Week*, 22 December 1945, pp. 78–80. The report cited has some excellent survey data on rural attitudes toward radio. Of special interest is a section that illustrates how radio was changing farming by disseminating market and weather information: U.S., Department of Agriculture, *Attitudes of Rural People toward Radio Service: A Nation-Wide Survey of Farm and Small-town People*, Report of Bureau of Agricultural Economics for Clear Channel Hearing, Docket No. 6741, by Committee Four, Dallas W. Smythe, Chairman (Washington, D.C., 1946), pp. 38–41.

8. Hal Borland, "Report from Whistle-stop, Kansas," *New York Times Magazine*, 7 October 1951, pp. 42–44.

9. U.S., Bureau of the Census, *U.S. Census of Housing: 1950, General Characteristics, United States Summary*, 1:xxiv.

10. Ibid.

11. U.S., Bureau of the Census, *U.S. Census of Housing: 1960, States and Small Areas, Part I: United States Summary*, 1:1–44.

12. *U.S. Census of Housing: 1950, General Characteristics, United States Summary,* 1:xxiv.

13. *U.S. Census of Housing: 1960, States and Small Areas, Part I: United States Summary,* 1:1–44.

14. Ibid.

15. The addresses are from Vincent Terrace, *The Complete Encyclopedia of Television Programs, 1947–1979* (New York, 1979), pp. 316, 461, 606.

16. Robert Obojski, *Bush League: A History of Minor League Baseball* (New York, 1975), p. 27.

17. Ibid., p. 27.

18. Among the familiar rural institutions that were rapidly disappearing was the one-room school, whose numbers fell from 75,000 in 1948 to 26,000 in 1958. See Glenn v. Fuguitt, "The City and Countryside," *Rural Sociology* 28 (September 1963): 251.

19. "The Effects of Social Change upon the Rural Personality," *Rural Sociology* 14 (December 1949): 345–52.

20. Don Paarlberg, *American Farm Policy: A Case Study of Centralized Decision Making* (New York, 1964), p. 57.

21. U.S., Bureau of the Census, *People of Rural America,* p. 21.

22. Ibid.

23. Paarlberg, *American Farm Policy,* p. 57.

24. Everett M. Rogers, *Social Change in Rural Society* (New York, 1960), p. 339.

25. Ibid., p. 338.

26. An excellent work that places the political developments of agriculture in the social context of rural America is Wayne C. Rohrer and Louis H. Douglas, *The Agrarian Transition in America: Dualism and Change* (Indianapolis, 1969).

27. Rogers, *Social Change in Rural Society,* p. 261.

28. Grant McConnell, *Private Power and American Democracy* (New York, 1966), pp. 239–40.

29. Rogers, *Social Change in Rural Society,* p. 261.

30. McConnell, *Private Power and American Democracy,* pp. 239–40.

31. Rogers, *Social Change in Rural Society,* p. 261.

32. McConnell, *Private Power and American Democracy,* p. 232.

33. Rohrer and Dougals, *Agrarian Tradition,* pp. 99–103.

34. For a concise and useful discussion of the definition of parity, see Paarlberg, *American Farm Policy,* pp. 68–74.

35. John L. Shover, *First Majority—Last Minority* (Dekalb, Ill., 1976), pp. 248–49.

36. *Farms and Farmers in an Urban Age* (New York, 1963), p. 50.

37. Lauren Soth, *Farm Trouble* (Princeton, N.J., 1957), p. 78.

38. Ibid., p. 84

39. Rogers, *Social Change in Rural Society,* p. 378.

40. Paarlberg, *American Farm Policy,* p. 120.

41. The county unit system in Georgia was so favorable to rural counties that in 1946 Talmadge captured the Democratic gubernatorial nomination, which meant election in that one-party state, even though he finished second in the popular vote and drew more than 80,000 votes fewer than his opponents: see William Anderson, *The Wild Man from Sugar Creek: The Political Career of Eugene Talmadge* (Baton Rouge, La., 1975), p. 232.

42. Combining census regions South Atlantic, East South Central, and West South Central, the South had 23.0 million urban and 24.2 million rural residents in 1950; the 1960

figures were 32.2 million urban and 22.8 million rural; U.S., Bureau of the Census, *Urban and Rural Population of the United States, by States 1960 and 1950*, p. 2.

43. Alvin L. Bertrand, "The Emerging Rural South: A Region under 'Confrontation' by Mass Society," *Rural Sociology* 31 (December 1966): 453.

44. For an interesting discussion of the mass culture and the postwar South, see John Egerton, *The Americanization of Dixie: The Southernization of America* (New York, 1974) pp. 198–207.

45. Charles P. Roland, *The Improbable Era: The South since World War II* (Lexington, Ky., 1975), pp. 12–14.

Visions of Classlessness, Quests for Dominion: American Popular Culture, 1945–1960

Roland Marchand

The constraints and sacrifices of World War II did not prepare Americans to meet the realities of the postwar era with equanimity.* Expectations ran high, despite underlying anxieties about atomic perils and the possibility of a postwar depression. Wartime discourse resonated with acclamations of equality and promises of the coming of a better, technologically wondrous life for all. The common man, idealized in nostalgic imagery, would carve out a future of unobstructed independence. Centralized controls, bureaucratic complexities, diminished autonomy for the individual—these were largely dismissed as the temporary conditions of war. Postwar popular culture reflected these expectations, expressing complacent satisfaction in the realization of some and providing vicarious compensations for the intense disappointment of others.

World War II came closer than any other twentieth-century phenomenon to enacting the drama of the melting pot in the United States, as disparate groups and values seemed to fuse into a composite national culture. Four years of war brought unprecedented national consolidation. Vast wartime migrations—to the armed forces and to war industries and boomtowns—undermined regional loyalties and broadened provincial horizons. Class barriers, and even some of the outward identifying marks of class, seemed to disappear. The nation's dramatists of

* I am indebted to the students in my fall 1979 undergraduate seminar, and to David Brody, Eckard Toy, and James Lapsley, for their criticism of ideas contained in an initial version of this essay.

popular culture, its persuaders and performers, enlisted in the task of uniting the nation behind common assumptions.

The explicitly democratic themes of wartime popular culture promoted unity. Morale-builders stressed the idea of equal sacrifices and personalized the war through such democratic figures as G. I. Joe, Rosie the Riveter, Norman Rockwell's everyman figure in the "Freedom of Speech" poster, and Rockwell's Willie Gillis (the common man as G.I.).[1] The war years also prolonged the modest redistribution of income from rich to poor that had begun during the 1930s. Although this process was to come to a standstill in the late 1940s, Americans emerged from the war confident of a snowballing trend toward economic democratization and a classless culture.[2]

Meanwhile, in what Frank Fox has characterized as "World of Tomorrow" advertising, business interests painted stirring images of the technological future. Wartime research, when applied to consumer products, would bring new power and comfort to the common man in a "thermoplastic, aerodynamic, supersonic, electronic, gadgetonic" postwar world. Popular anticipation of a precise watershed moment—when the war would end and the "future" begin—took on a millenial cast.[3] In style these wartime visions paralleled themes of the General Motors Futurama at the 1939 World's Fair. The message was one of man's technological dominion over nature, of machines as social solutions. Yet another wartime message, infused in advertising and other forms of popular culture, promised that victory would restore a cherished version of the true American way of life, based on the small town, the corner drugstore, and the close-knit family—an image aptly described as "American Pastoral."[4]

Instead, the postwar world brought bureaucratic complexity, cold war insecurity, and a shrunken sense of individual mastery. It produced a technology of atomic peril as well as material comfort. Inspired by the sweeping democratic promises of wartime ideology and a hunger for security and stability, Americans welcomed the notion of classless prosperity. Enticed by expectations of increased power and control, they reacted with dismay as they found themselves slipping into a condition of greater vulnerability and dependency. In response they embraced popular culture reveries that seemed to enhance their sense of personal dominion.

The postwar period saw the emergence of a popular culture more homogeneous than Americans had previously known, as the cold war reinforced the trend toward consolidation. This greater homogeneity

also reflected changes in demography, increasingly centralized production of popular culture images and artifacts, and more effective dissemination of popular culture by the media.

One measure of increasing homogeneity was a decline in competition
from ethnic cultures. By the time of World War II, unrestricted immigration had been cut off for a full generation. Between 1940 and 1960 the
percentage of foreign-born declined from 8.8 percent to 5.4 percent, and
the percentage of Americans with at least one parent of foreign birth fell
from 17 percent to 13.5 percent. A decline in carriers of ethnic culture
such as foreign-language newspapers, theaters, musical organizations,
and social halls reflected these demographic changes. Commercial entertainment increasingly outrivaled the attractions of ethnic folk culture and filled the new increments of leisure time. Network radio expanded its nationalizing and homogenizing influence, and radio sets in
use increased right up to the advent of an even more powerful agent of
common popular culture—television. Between 1940 and 1950 the "big
four" popular periodicals, *Life, Reader's Digest, Look*, and *Saturday
Evening Post*, increased their combined total circulation by 105 percent.
Although some groups did maintain "taste subcultures," more and more
Americans read, heard, and saw the same popular fare.[5]

Another measure of homogeneity was the decline of class and regional differences in clothing and recreation. During the late 1940s sales
of traditional work clothes fell precipitously, with the production of
men's casual pants and shirts rising almost as rapidly. More workers
wore casual clothes on the job, and off work men of different classes
seemed indistinguishable on the street. *Life* referred matter-of-factly in
1949 to blue jeans as part of a national teenage "uniform." By the 1950s
these classless, vaguely "western" progeny of democratic G.I. dungarees
had come to symbolize the triumph of denim as an equalizing casual
wear for virtually all Americans. Steady increases in the length of paid
vacations for workers had also begun to equalize the distribution of
formal leisure time. The Bureau of Labor Statistics even argued that by
1950 the earlier, distinctively "working class" patterns of spare-time activities and expenditures had almost disappeared among urban
workers.[6]

Signs of a national culture abounded. In the early 1950s, as journalist
Russell Lynes remarked, Sears, Roebuck ceased publication of regional
catalogs on the grounds that tastes in furniture had become identical
throughout the country. *Fortune* reported that tastes in food were "flat-
tening" regionally. Merchandising consultants began to talk about a
"standard middle-majority package," a laundry list of home furnishings

and other consumer goods that should be marketable to all families. One suburb looked pretty much like another; what Louise Huxtable has characterized as "Pop Architecture" dominated the landscape everywhere. Local bowling palaces, motels, and auto showrooms quickly copied the flash, glitter, and eccentric shapes of Las Vegas's "architecture of the road." Even where franchised chains did not proliferate, the designers of shopping centers and the entrepreneurs of a thousand "miracle miles" created uniform visual imagery.[7]

The leveling of styles was in many ways a leveling *down*—a fact that did not escape the champions of high culture. In their search for the culprits of cultural debasement, they excoriated first the threats to literacy, order, and good taste coming from the comic book industry, and then the affronts to high culture by the new monster, TV. No previous mass medium, not even radio, expanded its audience so explosively as television. Households with TV sets mounted from fewer than one million in 1949 to more than 46 million in 1960, at which point 90 percent of all American homes were consuming TV programming at an average rate of five hours per day. The convenience of TV and the national standards of performance it set were devastating to provincial commercial entertainment and much of ethnic culture.[8]

The 1950s would later seem a golden age of diversity and cultural quality on TV. But, fixing their gaze on Hopalong Cassidy, Milton Berle, wrestling matches, and formula westerns, contemporary critics denounced the new medium as an attack on culture and literacy. With the advance of TV, homogenized franchise operations, and organizational bureaucracy, a major debate erupted among intellectuals over the prospects and perils of mass culture. Even political concerns seemed to fade before the social menace of mass culture. Did a debased mass culture involve passivity, conformity, and a stifling of creativity in the audience and a formulaic, manipulative, whatever-will-sell attitude by the producer? Then TV seemed to its critics to have unquestionably triumphed as *the* mass culture medium.[9]

Actually, TV probably served more to nationalize and homogenize than either to uplift or degrade. Television advertising embedded slogans, brand names, and affective imagery into the national consciousness with a new intensity, creating symbols for a more uniform national language. Television also helped promote the "common language" functions of national sports spectatorship. Together with convenient air travel, TV made attractive the nationalizing of the professional sports leagues. Minor league baseball declined as did a multitude of more significant local institutions—ethnic clubs, local union meetings, local political clubs—contributing, in Martin Mayer's view, to individual feelings of anomie and powerlessness.[10]

Manufacturers of TV sets fought this negative interpretation of the social impact of TV. Their ads nostalgically depicted warm family scenes in which the connective links of the old family circle were restored in the harmony of the family semicircle plus TV. However specious the implied claims that TV would keep the kids home and the generations together, TV did serve the momentarily unifying function of making children more frequent participants in (or cospectators of) their parents' entertainment.[11]

A critical component of the popular culture that TV helped disseminate was "California Culture." Even before the war California had become the symbol of relaxed, prosperous outdoor living, linked to a "car culture." California led the nation in miles of highway and per capita ownership of cars. The supermarket and the "drive-in" flourished there. The Los Angeles area led the nation in new suburban developments, freeway construction, and experiments with outlying shopping complexes. Smog and traffic notwithstanding, the Los Angeles suburban landscape seemed the landscape of the future.[12]

The media readily promoted California culture as mobile, changing, comparatively "democratic." It had a "life-style." The ambience of that life-style was just about everything that media advertisers liked to associate with their products—an image of the new, the enjoyable, the casual. California provided models of everything from sportswear to houses, and displayed an easy contempt for environmental limits. *The Gallup Poll* reported that it ranked number one among Americans as "best state" and "ideal place to live." Los Angeles scored first among cities for best-looking women and most-desired place to live. It ranked second in climate, beauty of setting, and gaiety of night life.[13]

The imagery of California culture centered around the postwar fad in popular architecture—the California ranch house. A single-story, ground-hugging structure, it was adaptable to split-level form. Picture windows and other expanses of glass accentuated the idea of a free-flowing continuity of space and mood between indoors and outdoors. Population pressure and high costs had imposed limitations on the postwar suburban search for spaciousness. In response the ranch house nurtured illusions of open continuous space and freedom. This was particularly necessary as the sprawling ranch house (invariably pictured alone with no adjacent neighbors) was pared down to 1,200-square-foot tract dimensions.[14]

Inside, the quest for openness was linked with architectural expressions of democracy and "togetherness" (a word coined by *McCall's* in a moment of nostalgia and marketing acumen). In a servantless setting the dining room often disappeared, and the door segregating the kitchen gave way to a counter or open vista that allowed the wife to maintain contact with family and guests. A new room appeared—an amalgam of rumpus room and den. Introduced as "the room without a name," it quickly gained status as the "family room"—a casual, nurturing, and democratic gathering place for all. Naturally, the new room was where the TV was lodged, to be followed in due course by TV trays and TV dinners.[15]

By 1954 Russell Lynes pronounced the California ranch house "ubiquitous," a national symbol of the increasing unity of tastes of "the relatively poor and the relatively well-to-do," and "the standard new suburban dwelling in the suburbs of New York as of Boston, of Chicago as of . . . Los Angeles." Another commentator explained how the outdoor joys of the patio could be retained in midwestern ranch houses throughout spring and fall by the use of radiant heating coils in patio paving. Builders liked the construction efficiencies of the ranch style. Buyers saw in its casual informality, undecorated sense of impermanence, access to nature, and freedom from internal physical barriers an image of western openness and mobility.[16]

The California ranch house seemed to epitomize the postwar dream of classlessness and dominion. Everybody, presumably, was moving to the suburbs. Everyone could belong to the modern, democratic version of the "landed gentry." Limitless energy would make possible heated patios, air-conditioners, and countless appliances. A prolonged do-it-yourself craze suggested that husband as well as wife could make the suburban home a fulfilling last refuge for the exercise of competence and control. Here the common American might evade international tensions and organizational complexities and thus regain a reassuring sense of individual dominion.

The dream of suburban comfort and microcosmic control was a striking instance of upper-middle-class myopia. "Everybody" was *not* moving to the suburbs, despite impressions conveyed by Sunday supplements, TV advertisements, and popular sociology. Most housing developments were priced out of the range of those below the median income. The migration that inundated the suburbs came primarily from those among the top 40 percent in family income, especially those of the professional and technological elites who made impressive gains in income after 1945. Moreover, the most highly publicized sociological studies of suburbia focused on areas that were even more affluent than average—thus exaggerating "typical" suburban prosperity.[17] Since writers, academics, and advertising executives came from the very segment of society making the most rapid gains, they found it easy to believe everyone was riding the same wave of prosperity. The idea of a consummated classlessness struck them with the force of a revelation.

The celebration of this "classless prosperity" permeated the popular culture that other Americans of the era consumed. Russell Lynes helped popularize the new "obsolescence" of class with his essay "High-brow, Low-brow, Middle-brow" in 1949. *Life* magazine's version carried a striking two-page chart depicting the cultural tastes of Lynes's various "brows" in ten categories ranging from furniture to entertainment. Economic classes were obsolete, Lynes insisted; people now chose their pleasures and consumer goods strictly on the basis of individual taste. Sociologist William Whyte noted the "displacement of the old class criterion" by "the impulse to 'culture' and 'good taste'." Values were "coming together," he concluded, and the suburbs had become the "second great melting pot."[18]

"The distinction between economic levels in the ownership of tangibles is diminishing," the Bureau of Labor Statistics noted, thus "breaking down the barriers of community and class." Sportswriters celebrated the supposed democratization of golf: "Class lines are eliminated," they argued, "when the nation wears sports clothes." Producers of the big-money TV quiz shows nurtured popular enthusiasm for illusions of equality by creating such folk heroes as the "cop who knew Shakespeare." The sponsor of "The $64,000 Question" explained: "We're trying to show the country that the little people are really very intelligent. . . . " Winners were prototypes of the common man and woman, symbols of democratized intelligence. Advertisers now cast affluent suburban families not only as models of appropriate consumer styles but also as realistic portrayals of *average* Americans. In the 1920s and 1930s, Americans had known that they were seeing explicit models of high society "smartness" in many ads. Now they were encouraged to see the advertising models as mirrors of themselves.[19]

Such images and perceptions of classlessness eventually found expression in the language itself. The 1961 *Webster's International Dictionary* acknowledged the existence of a new word not recognized in earlier editions: *life-style.*[20] This new term, which gradually replaced the older phrase "way of life," conveyed nuances of classlessness. The phrase "way of life" had been fully compatible with a recognition of important economic class distinctions. Although people might be described as seeking to *choose* or *achieve* a certain "way of life," they could also easily be thought of as having inherited a particular way of life along with their class standing. But a "life-style" was less likely to seem class-determined or inherited. The word *style* suggested free choice, the uninhibited search for what looked and felt right. It might also connote a particular consumer-consciousness, a notion of choosing among various ensembles or "packages" of goods that represented a style consistency, i.e., that "went well together." Behind the rise of the word *lifestyle* lay the assumption that increases in real income, the equalizing qualities of new synthetic fabrics and suburban amenities, and the expansion of automobile and appliance ownership had created a totally middle-class society in which all significant differences were simply free expressions of personal tastes.

This vision reflected some real changes in American society. During the 1950s the average income of all families and individuals rose 26 percent in real dollars, and increased installment buying allowed many families to raise their living standard at an even greater rate.[21] Still, as Richard Parker has pointed out, "among those who called themselves middle class, perhaps a majority have always lacked the money to be in fact what they believe they are." It was those of high income, as ever, who consumed the bulk of popular culture products and services—whether sports event admissions, frozen foods, cars, or hi-fi components. And the gains that *were* achieved by median and marginal sectors of the society did not represent gains in relative wealth or power. In fact, those below the top 40 percent remained stationary in their proportion of national income during the 1950s, and all but the wealthiest lost in relative power. Despite the National Advertising Council's puffery about "people's capitalism," corporate assets were more narrowly held in 1960 than in 1945.[22]

Americans appreciated their new material comforts, but many no doubt sensed an erosion of independence and control as large organizations in media, government, and business overshadowed or preempted their spheres of competence and power. It fell to popular culture to exorcise these demons and provide compensating, vicarious adventures in potency and dominion.

Enter the Shmoo and Mike Hammer! Best described as a "snow-white ham with legs," the Shmoo appeared in cartoonist Al Capp's 1948 parable on the quandaries of prosperity. Lured musically into that consumer's paradise, the "Valley of the Shmoon," Capp's hero Li'l Abner recognized the Shmoo as utopia incarnate. The accommodating little creature, so eager to please that it would die of sheer happiness from one hungry look, provided for nearly all material needs. It laid eggs (in cartons) and gave milk (bottled). Broiled, it made the finest steak; roasted, it resembled pork; fried, it came out chicken. And Shmoos reproduced at a remarkable rate.[23]

A national favorite, the Shmoo recapitulated wartime promises. It offered families in Capp's Dogpatch lifelong control over the necessities of life, just as Americans had been led to dream of a technological utopia. In another sense the Shmoo, endlessly and identically reproduced, conjured up intimations of conformity, of boring and emotionless satiety. So dull was this prospect that Capp eventually had his obliging and well-merchandised progeny commit "Shmooicide." Although the spirit of the Shmoo lived on in such tangible forms as the energy consumption binge, the national credit card, and the Playboy bunny, Capp found its appropriate cartoon replacement in the Kigmy, who loved to be kicked. Americans of the era, Capp implied, sought a target for the release of aggression as keenly as they yearned for the security of the Shmoo.[24]

Mike Hammer's phenomenal success as a popular culture hero seemed to confirm that notion. First appearing in 1947 in Mickey Spillane's *I, the Jury*, detective Mike Hammer rewrote the history of American best-sellers with his escapades of vengeance. His self-righteous vigilantism breathed contempt for established institutions and authorities. He worried that prosperity would make Americans soft and weak. And he banished the specters of impotence and conformity by acting remorselessly and alone:

> . . . I killed more people tonight than I have fingers on my hands. I shot them in cold blood and enjoyed every minute of it. . . . They were Commies, Lee. They were red sons-of-bitches who should have died long ago. . . . I just walked into that room with a tommy gun and shot their guts out. They never thought that there were people like me in this country. They figured us all to be soft as horse manure. . . .[25]

For Americans beginning to suffer from a vague closed-in feeling, a restless frustration stemming from Russian threats abroad and the restraints and manipulations of large organizations at home, Mike Hammer represented recovery of a lost dominion. In postwar popular culture the defense of traditional masculinity was difficult to separate from this search for renewed dominion. John Cawelti aptly describes Spillane's "love" scenes as stripteases, many of them unconsummated sexual provocations that led ultimately to "fulfillment in violence." Contempt for women, expressed in frequent violence and sadism by Mike Hammer and in manipulative detachment by such mutant successors as James Bond and the Hugh Hefner Playboy, may have expressed fears of feminine power that went beyond insecure resentments of fancied sexual teasing. Modern society seemed to place "feminine" restraints on man's dominion. In large organizations the executive as well as the worker had to "subdue his personality to another's . . . to act like a good old-fashioned wife." One response in the popular culture was to reassert a compensating image of masculinity that conceded nothing to feminine limitations.[26]

Expressions of masculinity took a variety of forms. The Marlboro man, weathered and tattoed, evoked an aura of masculine adventure and the rugged, autonomous life. The free-spirited culture of the hot rodders canonized the car as a masculine symbol of untrammeled power, contemptuous of limits and triumphant over space and time. Men's sports and outdoor magazines surged in popularity. Professional football, built around aggressive contention for control of territory, enjoyed increasing popularity. Combining a high "courage quotient" with a metaphorical evocation of the industrial patterns of synchronization and strategic planning, professional football increased its attendance at rates far surpassing those of professional baseball.[27] In the rage for Little League baseball, fathers found ways to express and instill masculine traits. Since such sports participation was also part of socialization to adult society, it was not incongruous that Little League also taught lessons of control, teamwork, and subordination to the group. Even the Marlboro image barely disguised the subliminal message beneath its individualistic mystique: the tough, independent man, who thought for himself, exerted his masculine freedom by choosing the standardized product. The quest for a sense of dominion proved very susceptible to packaging.[28]

As if in reaction to the blurring of sexual stereotypes during the war, popular culture accentuated women's strictly "feminine" roles. With the home symbolizing the security and stability recently thwarted by war and depression, the paramount role was homemaker. Pert, streamlined housewives dominated the ads. Although married women were employed outside the home in greater numbers than ever before, the popular media romanticized domesticity and elevated it to the status of a national purpose.[29]

Less "feminine" roles for women were disparaged. "Woman driver" jokes reached a peak, and advertisements helped reassert masculine roles. Whereas automobile advertisements in the late 1920s and early 1930s had portrayed nearly as many women as men behind the wheel, those of the mid-1950s depicted far more men than women drivers. The occasional strong, independent female movie roles of the late 1930s disappeared by the 1950s. The older film seductresses who had projected poise, self-assurance, and a sense of challenge were superseded, most strikingly, by Marilyn Monroe, queen of the sexual Shmoos. Her salient qualities were availability and vulnerability. In their contribution to popular psychology, *Modern Woman: The Lost Sex,* Ferdinand Lundberg and Marynia Farnham reinforced notions of the mutual exclusiveness of feminine and masculine qualities. Women's aspirations to masculine achievement lay at the base of modern confusions and anxieties, they warned; only a return to total femininity could avert psychological disaster. In case children should fail to learn absolute gender distinctions from other forms of socialization, Cliff May's *Western Ranch Houses* described how dark wood paneling could be used to give the son's room a "strongly masculine air" and the daughter's room would be designed with "built-in femininity."[30]

The emphasis on traditional masculinity may have stemmed in part from the fear that increasing leisure would tempt Americans to become soft—perhaps to lose their competitive drive and their will to resist communism. Another part may have arisen from the loss of a sense of achievement and mastery within the workplace and from indignities experienced in lives constrained by the actions of faceless organizations. The increased collective power that had subdued nature with vast highways and massive expenditures of electrical energy did not enhance the power of individuals in their increasingly complex interactions with other people. The traditional gender of the word *mastery* in American culture had been unequivocally male. Fears of powerlessness in the midst of mass society had unsurprisingly triggered ritual efforts to reaffirm the masculine.

Americans of the postwar era also sought solace from anxieties and frustrations by turning their search for dominion inward. Both religion and popular psychology flourished in the postwar era, as did hybrids of the two.

Church membership advanced steadily during the late 1940s and early 1950s until it reached the unprecedented level of 63 percent of all Americans. Works on religion, from the Revised Standard Bible to Catherine Marshall's *A Man Called Peter,* were nonfiction best-sellers. The religious novels of Lloyd Douglas and Sholem Asch gained a comparable place in popular fiction.[31] Billy Graham, using every modern device from the card file to the television set, built upon his 1949 triumph in a Los Angeles evangelical crusade to gain a place among America's ten-most-admired men by the mid-1950s. Monsignor Fulton J. Sheen adapted his theatrical style to the new media, and in 1953 was named television's man of the year. Church construction advanced at record rates, and the appearance of drive-in churches seemed to augur the assimilation of religion to a car culture that had already produced the drive-in restaurant and the drive-in movie.[32]

In the atmosphere of a cold war against "atheistic" communism, religion tended to merge with patriotism. In the mid-1950s Congress sought to formalize the union by adding "under God" to the pledge of allegiance and establishing a prayer room in the Capitol. The physical mobility of the 1940s also enhanced the church's role as social anchor in the midst of social disruption, a place where new residents in a community might make social contacts. Theologian Will Herberg concluded that the three major faiths, Protestantism, Catholicism, and Judaism, had come to serve as a new American "triple melting pot" for third-generation immigrants as ethnic subcultures declined. But Herberg and other religious leaders also worried about the quality of the new "religious awakening." What could one make of an enthusiasm for faith in which 86 percent of all Americans declared the Bible to be the word of God, yet 53 percent could not name a single one of the four Gospels? Perhaps the answer lay in a 1957 Gallup poll in which 81 percent affirmed their expectation that "religion can answer all or most of today's problems."[33]

Postwar piety was paralleled by a surge of psychology. The prewar decades had witnessed a considerable popularization of the concepts of psychology and psychiatry, especially among the well-educated. World War II increased popular awareness of applied psychology and its contributions to personnel selection and "adjustment." Familiarity with psychological jargon—neurosis, inferiority complex, schizophrenia, maladjustment—was already widespread. But in the postwar years, psychology became a popular mania. Publishers responded to a thirst for self-analysis quizzes, how-to-do-it manuals, and psychological advice. A typical issue of *Reader's Digest* contained at least two articles of the "What's Your Personality?" and "Do You Think like a Man or a Woman?" variety.[34]

Among books and films one could almost predict that if it was "serious," it was also psychological. Even the durable western tended to become a stage setting for the playing out of psychological dramas. Advertisers threw themselves headlong into motivation research and "depth interviews" in a search for those "deep-lying habits, feelings, aversions, inner compulsions and complexes" that might inhibit the buying impulse. Artzybasheff included in his fanciful cartoon of "Improved

Design for Modern Man" for *Life* in 1951 a hole in the side of the modern woman's head labeled "Aperture for easy access to brain compartment by psycho-analyst."[35] When Lucy set up her "Psychiatric Help— 5¢" booth in Charles Schulz's popular "Peanuts" comic strip, it simply marked with mild satire a logical conclusion to the trend toward universal dissemination of popular psychology.

The craze for the psychological explanation did not reflect unequivocal acceptance of psychological techniques. True, psychologists were much in demand to provide explanations of juvenile delinquency, rock 'n' roll music, marriage problems, personal aptitudes, and college panty raids. Even the Kinsey Reports on sexual practices were accepted as useful by a majority of Americans. But the frequency with which psychology and psychoanalysis served as topics for humor attested to deep ambivalence about psychology's "contributions." Although psychology promised a kind of control, an opportunity to reshape one's personality or gain a form of dominion by understanding and manipulating others, it also awakened fears that one might be the *object* rather than the *agent* of manipulation.[36]

In *The Hidden Persuaders* (1957), Vance Packard found a large audience for his warnings about dangers embedded in motivation research and subliminal suggestion by advertisers. Americans might have been more alarmed if they had been fully aware of such new psychological "machines" and techniques as the "People Machine," Galvanic Skin Response, "Simulmatics," and "aroma mood music," to which some ad agencies were giving curious, if skeptical, attention. William Whyte, in *The Organization Man*, described the pressures toward conformity embodied in the proliferating personality tests given by business organizations. Whyte even appended a subversive chapter on "How to Cheat on Personality Tests" as his meager contribution to the preservation of personal dominion. Americans worried about "brain-washing," and 1950s science fiction movies were sometimes as concerned with loss of personal control, with invasion or infiltration by some alien force, as they were with the specter of atomic warfare. As the autonomy of the individual seemed to shrink, psychology, for all its fascination, still did not offer unequivocal assurance of gaining dominion over self.[37]

Millions of Americans, however, hopefully sought such assurance from a fusion of psychology and religion. A major element in postwar popular culture was the "cult of reassurance," promoted most effectively by the Presbyterian minister Norman Vincent Peale. An amalgam of psychology and religion, the cult gained its initial postwar impulse from Rabbi Joshua Liebman's prescriptions for the cure of inner tensions in

Peace of Mind (1946). Liebman's book topped the best-seller list in 1947 and eventually sold a million copies. Peale advanced the movement's momentum with his best-selling *A Guide to Confident Living* (1949) and then with *The Power of Positive Thinking* (1952), which dominated the nonfiction best-seller charts from 1952 to 1955, soon surpassing two million copies.[38]

Peale employed six psychiatrists and commanded radio and TV audiences in the millions. Although he had initially sought psychological knowledge for personal counseling, "Peale's deep attraction," as Donald Meyer writes, was to mass counseling. The message was simple: people's problems were individual. "Negative thinking," not technology, social forces, or institutional structures, was the cause of feelings of powerlessness and frustration. By using Peale's techniques, each follower could "become a more popular, esteemed and well-liked individual," gaining new energy and peace of mind. Through psychological self-manipulation, each could gain control over circumstances rather than submitting to them. "Positive thinking" accepted and reinforced the notion of classlessness. It proved another popular culture prescription for the nagging sense of loss of dominion.[39]

A popular culture of reassurance was not everybody's answer to powerlessness. It was true that certain consolidating tendencies—the influences of network television and the common language and repetitious visual landscapes of national advertising, pop architecture, and restaurant and motel chains—worked to reinforce the "adjustment" theme of applied psychology. And it was true also that the "packaging" craze in popular culture, from shopping centers to entertainment "worlds" like Disneyland, helped push forward the process of homogenization by offering convenience and relief from individual decision-making. In fact, the whole Disney empire, from the "disneyfication" of children's classics to TV's Mickey Mouse Club and the Davy Crockett craze, strikingly epitomized the trend toward uniformity.[40] But consolidation in popular culture did not advance undisturbed. As regional, ethnic, and visible class divergences began to fade, new fissures appeared. Some pursued the quest for dominion not through adjustment and reassurance but rather through excitement, diversity, and vicarious rebellion.

The most obvious, and to contemporaries the most shocking, new breach in society was an apparently increasing division based on age. Juvenile delinquency had appeared to rise during World War II and afterward. The striking increase in disposable income and free time among teen-agers in the late 1940s stamped adolescence as a social phenomenon rather than simply a stage in individual development. "The brute fact of today," Dr. Robert Linder warned a Los Angeles audience in 1954, "is that our youth is no longer in rebellion but in a condition of downright active and hostile mutiny." In "a profound and terrifying change," youth now acted out its "inner turmoil."[41]

Psychological analyses of juveniles, both delinquent and normal, abounded. The film industry, reacting to the loss of its mass audience to television, began to produce specialized films for minority audiences— one of which was teen-agers. Radio followed the same pattern. Advertisers soon recognized the existence of a massive teen-age market. Eugene Gilbert built a large marketing business by providing advertisers with inside information on teen-age consumers. His trick was spectacularly simple: employ teen-agers themselves to quiz other teen-agers about their wants and needs. Eventually *Life* confirmed the discovery of a teen-age market in an article entitled "A New $10 Billion Power: The U.S. Teen-age Consumer." *Life* personalized the story by featuring pictures of the loot accumulated by "the businessman's dream of the ideal teen-ager," Suzie Slattery from (where else?) California.[42]

Attempts by the media to explore the rebellious aspects of the teen-age culture created new fissures in popular culture. In the movie *Rebel without a Cause* (1955), the plot and dialogue comprise a virtual textbook of popular psychology. The police lieutenant is an amateur psychologist; the hero's mother, a castrating female. The father's multiple complexes make him a complete buffoon. The hero's friend is a self-destructive neurotic, abandoned by his parents; and the heroine's father panics at her emerging sexuality and treats her with alternating rage and condescension. *Rebel without a Cause* was a "lesson" movie for parents: be careful and understanding, or this (rebellion) could happen to you. But James Dean's portrayal of the teen-age hero, his most influential acting role, diverted attention to the style and mannerisms of the misunderstood "rebel." Youths made the movie theirs. Vicarious rebels adopted the James Dean image as an expression of contempt for the satiated and challengeless life of middle-aged suburban America.[43]

The evolution of popular music revealed even more vividly the process of disruption, the fraying of social nerves by age conflicts. Before the 1950s producers of popular music had largely ignored age differences, and the songs of adults and teen-agers were the same. As late as 1951 Gallup polls on favorite vocalists showed little variation among age groups. Far more significantly, the pollsters did not record responses for persons under 21. Yet teen-agers were already a major buying public for records, and the average age of purchasers continued to fall during the 1950s. With the rise of the 45 rpm record (cheap, unbreakable, easy to transport and change) and the transformation of radio in the early 1950s, the weight of teen-age preferences tipped the scales toward diversity in this form of popular culture.[44]

Even earlier, fragmentation had begun to appear within the popular music industry. A boycott by radio stations in the early 1940s had broken the monopoly of the "big three" record companies. Radio disc jockeys gained new power, and technological advances meant that production of quality recordings was no longer confined to a handful of studios in New York, Chicago, and Los Angeles. Independent companies, the primary producers of "race" and "hillbilly" music, gained new opportunities. Still, the resulting tremors in the industry were relatively minor. From 1946 to 1953 the six dominant recording companies—Decca, Columbia, Victor, Capitol, MGM, and Mercury—recorded all but 5 of the 163 records that sold over a million copies.[45]

Radio, in reaction to the abrupt abduction of its general audience by TV, cast about for minority tastes to satisfy. One market for subcultural programming was teen-agers. Specialized radio stations now gave them a medium of their own. Some argue that teen-age audiences created "rock 'n' roll." Others explain that TV, that powerful consolidating force in popular culture, was also, inadvertently, the cause of this vehicle of dissent and fragmentation. Both are largely correct; together these two forces set the stage for a popular culture explosion.[46]

By 1953 certain ingredients of rock 'n' roll had been fermenting for several years. Migrations out of the South had increased national familiarity with "hillbilly" and black styles in music. In the late 1940s *Billboard* magazine, the arbiter of pop music, bolstered the respectability of both styles by rechristening the "hillbilly" category as "country and western" and "race music" as "rhythm and blues." Elements of each style began to appear in pop hits. Meanwhile, with the postwar demise of the big bands, the individual singer gained prominence. Frank Sinatra epitomized the trend, winning the adulation of young "bobby-soxers" in the early 1940s and sustaining his popularity by projecting qualities of sincerity and involvement. Meanwhile, country singers Roy Acuff and then Hank Williams won huge followings with their sincere, emotional styles.[47]

Against the backdrop of a pallid, taken-for-granted prosperity and cold war perils about which youth could do little, a thirst arose among the young for forms of popular culture that would permit expressions of highly personalized emotion. Frankie Laine ("Jezebel," "Your Cheatin'

Heart," "I Believe") "sold Emotion . . . with a capital E" even more explicitly than did Sinatra. In 1951 Johnnie Ray stirred up a riotous teen-age response and set new standards for emotion and involvement in his popular hit "Cry." Ray, unlike Sinatra, was neither smooth nor controlled. He exposed an emotional vulnerability as he abandoned himself to the song's despair, "quivering, sobbing, crying and finally collapsing on the floor." Here were intimations not only of the impending rock 'n' roll performer as oracle of unconcealed emotion but also of the sensitive hero as victim.[48]

It was in 1953 that Cleveland disc jockey Alan Freed, intrigued by his discovery that white adolescents were increasingly buying "rhythm and blues" records, initiated his "Moondog's Rock and Roll Party," playing records by black singers for a largely white teen-age radio audience. *Billboard* noted Freed's success. Record companies rushed to find white performers to "cover" (copy) up-tempo, heavy beat, rhythm and blues hits. Bill Haley and His Comets made the national pop charts with "Crazy Man Crazy" in 1953. The next year Haley's cover of "Shake, Rattle and Roll" ranked in the top ten for twelve weeks, followed by an even longer run for "Rock around the Clock," the theme song from the popular film on juvenile delinquency *Blackboard Jungle*.[49]

A mystique emerged that fused elements of Marlon Brando's role in *The Wild One*, James Dean's portrayal in *Rebel without a Cause*, J. D. Salinger's Holden Caulfield in *Catcher in the Rye*, the rebels of *Blackboard Jungle*, and the driving energy and aggressive sexuality of the new heroes of rock 'n' roll into a single image. The mystique emphasized a hunger for authenticity and sensitivity. In emotional expressiveness it ranged from moody insecurity to fierce independence with nuances of sexuality, pain, and violence. Raucous, exhibitionist rock 'n' roll singers disdained the "cool" of James Dean, but both expressed a contempt for hypocrisy and conventionality and used body language to convey emotion.

In 1956 the polarizing assault by rock 'n' roll on popular music (and on American culture generally) culminated. A black original, Little Richard's strident "Long Tall Sally," outsold Pat Boone's bland cover version. With his frantic movements and raucous shouts, Little Richard, in Charlie Gillett's words, was "coarse, uncultured, and uncontrolled, in every way hard for the musical establishment to take." The lines were being drawn largely on the basis of age, although the preference of many white teen-agers for "black" music added another dimension to the rift.[50]

Critics of the new music and of the mixed-up, misunderstood hero decried the new mystique. The tough, self-pitying "sad-bad-boy" figures represented an "apotheosis of the immature." Rock 'n' roll used a "jungle strain" to provoke a "wave of adolescent riot." How could a prosperous, middle-class nation find satisfaction in such moronic lyrics and "quivering adolescents"? *Time* compared rock 'n' roll concerts to Hitler's mass meetings, and other critics denounced the new music as nauseating and degenerate, an appeal to "vulgarism and animality."[51] Could a consolidating popular culture even begin to bridge the gap suggested by such reactions?

Extreme views would remain irreconcilable. But 1955 elevated to stardom a versatile performer who brought the rock 'n' roll movement to a climax yet ultimately helped partially to reconcile rock with mainstream popular culture. Elvis Presley, the "hillbilly cat," as Greil Marcus writes, "deeply absorbed black music, and transformed it. . . ." The style of his early singles was "rockabilly"—"the only style of early rock 'n' roll that proved white boys could do it all—that they could be as strange, as exciting, as scary, and as free as the black men who were suddenly walking America's airwaves. . . ."[52] Even as Elvis moved up to RCA and national fame in 1955 and 1956 with "Heartbreak Hotel" and "You Ain't Nuthin' But a Hound Dog," he continued to evoke sexualilty, exhibitionism, and a defiance of restraint. Elvis projected emotional involvement; he encompassed the prized qualities of both toughness and vulnerability.

But Elvis not only fulfilled the image of frustrated, sensitive, rebellious hero for the new teen-age generation; he was also "hellbent on the mainstream." By the end of the 1950s, he had achieved hits with gospel songs and sentimental ballads. Eventually, one of his best-selling albums was "Blue Hawaii." His style encompassed schmaltz as well as rebellion, Las Vegas as well as Memphis.[53] Along with Pat Boone, Bobby Darin, Bobby Rydell, Paul Anka, Ricky Nelson, and a host of new teen-age crooners, and with the added influence of Dick Clark's "American Bandstand" on TV, Elvis eased rock 'n' roll's way into the mainstream. The aura of challenge and threat in rock was overshadowed by the sentimentalities of teen-age love. By 1960 the popular music industry was fragmented. The venerable and consensus-based "Your Hit Parade" had expired after a period of senility, spurred on by rock 'n' roll. More concerned with the style of performance than with the song itself, the new rock audience was bored by interpretations of hit rock numbers by "Hit Parade" regulars. But, thus far, the fissure created in American popular culture by rock 'n' roll and generational stress had proved to be a crevice rather than a chasm.[54]

Teen culture and rock 'n' roll, however, were not the only signs in the late 1950s of a possible countermarch in popular culture away from homogeneity toward segmentation. In reaction to the severe inroads of TV, movie-makers had sought specialized audiences that included intellectuals as well as teen-agers. Radio had fully adopted specialty programming. Gated, exclusive suburban developments gained in popularity. Portents of a difficult future for the great mass-circulation, general-audience magazines began to appear, as both *Life* and *Saturday Evening Post* lost advertising.[55] Despite the "whitewardly mobile" messages of middle-class black magazines like *Ebony*, inklings could be found of the eventual movement of blacks to a more protective, conserving attitude toward the distinctive qualities of their own culture. On top of everything, enclaves of "beatniks" now flaunted a life-style even more irreconcilable with mainstream popular culture than that associated with rock 'n' roll.

One prospect for popular culture at the end of the 1950s was fragmentation, with increasing specialization in production and participation. But in one significant way, the consolidating process in American popular culture continued to move ahead. The history of modern popular culture is more characteristically an aspect of the history of business than an aspect of the histories of art, literature, music, or architecture. And the business interests that determined the available choices for *most* popular culture consumers had not been verging toward fragmentation or diversity. The "popular culture establishment"—in the form of CBS, NBC, and ABC, or General Motors, Walt Disney Enterprises, MGM and *Time-Life*, or the J. Walter Thompson, Young and Rubicam, and other great advertising agencies—certainly wielded a more extensive control over the range of products and images available to the public in 1960 than in 1945. These giants, like most of the small popular culture entrepreneurs, watched the sales figures, the Nielsen ratings, and the audience surveys and produced what would sell itself or sell the sponsor's goods.

The tenor of the resulting popular culture was largely conservative and sustaining, as popular culture in any mass society is apt to be. If the problems of a society are embedded in its social structure and are insulated from change by layers of ideological tradition, popular culture is an unlikely source of remedy. It is far more likely to serve needs for diversion and transitory compensation. Tail-finned automobiles, peace-of-mind formulas, even fantasies of suburban sovereignty, pliant Playboy bunnies, or rock singers as emotional surrogates—all these promised, but did not ultimately provide, the sense of control and meaningful activity that Americans sought.

Beset by cold war fears and organizational complexities, Americans found solace in a popular culture that provided hopeful visions of an emerging classlessness and vicarious compensations for a hedged-in, manipulated feeling. Popular culture provided the fantasies, evasions, material artifacts, and vicarious experiences through which Americans tried to recapture a sense of dominion.

Appendix: What Went Up, What Went Down

A SELECTIVE STATISTICAL PORTRAIT OF
AMERICAN POPULAR CULTURE, 1945–1960

If popular culture is the description of the culture of most of the people, or at least of a great many people, statistical measures of usage and popularity should identify some of those artifacts that particularly merit discussion. The statistics in the following table suggest comparisons among noncomparable phenomena. A rough base line for comparing relative degrees of increase or decrease is suggested by items 12 and 13, the average yearly percentage of increase in gross national product and consumer price index. Because of the impressionistic intent of this compilation and the idiosyncratic selection involved, I have ignored some of the obvious problems arising from differences in years spanned by the data, occasional minor changes in methods of measurement during the years spanned, and distortions arising from comparing rates of change in artifacts already well established in the culture with those for relatively new phenomena.

A number of histories of popular culture in the 1945–60 era, some of them quite divergent in interpretation, might emerge from such suggestive statistics. I have sketched one such account. The table both corroborates some of my observations and provides a basis for other insights into the era.

Phenomenon	Period Spanned by Data	Initial Measurement	Second Measurement	Unit of Measure	Source of Data	Average Rate of Change per Year
1. Persons arrested under age 18	1946–60	38	527	Thousands of individuals	e	+ 91.9%
2. Construction contracts awarded for religious buildings	1947–60	118	789	Millions of $	b	+ 43.7%
3. Value of television advertising*	1951–60	332	1,590	Millions of $	e	+ 42.1%
4. Residential use of electrical energy	1946–60	42,919	196,269	Millions of kilowatt-hours	e	+ 25.5%
5. Potato chips produced	1947–58	155.9	424.6	Millions of lbs.	a	+ 15.7%
6. Phonograph records	1954–58	80.2	136.2	Value in millions of $	a	+ 17.5%
7. Expenditures on participant amusements (golf, bowling, skating, etc.)	1946–60	379	1,161	Millions of $	b	+ 14.7%
8. Kitchen and other household appliances	1946–60	1,900	5,000	Value in millions of constant $	b	+ 11.6%
9. Total corporate assets (per tax returns)	1946–60	454,705	1,136,668	Millions of $	e	+ 10.7%
10. Total advertising expenditures	1951–60	6,426	11,932	Value in millions of $	e	+ 9.5%
11. Miles of travel by motor vehicles	1946–60	340,880	718,485	Millions of miles	e	+ 7.9%
12. Gross National Product	1946–60	312.6	487.7	Billions of constant 1958 $	b	+ 4.0%
13. Consumer Price Index (all items)	1946–60	58.5	88.7	1967 CPI=100	e	+ 3.7%
14. Personal expenditures on spectator sports	1946–60	200	290	Millions of $	b	+ 3.2%
15. Average weekly hours of workers in manufacturing	1946–60	40.3	39.7	Weekly hours	e	– 0.1%
16. Percentage of females *not* in labor force	1946–60	69.1	62.2	% of all females	e	– 0.7%

Phenomenon	Period Spanned by Data	Initial Measurement	Second Measurement	Unit of Measure	Source of Data	Average Rate of Change per Year
17. Production of men's and boy's work shirts	1946–60	98.5	78.3	Value of production in millions of $	a	– 1.5%
18. Foreign-born as percentage of total U.S. population	1940–60	8.8	5.4	% of population	e	– 1.9%
19. Circulation of *Narod Polski* (Chicago Polish language weekly and semi-monthly—Catholic and Labor)	1940–60	120	64.4	Circulation in thousands	d	– 2.3%
20. Personal expenditures on motion picture admissions	1946–60	1,692	951	Millions of $	b	– 3.1%
21. Disapproval of women wearing shorts on the street	1951–55	69	55	% of men polled	f	– 5.1%

* Compare #10

SOURCES:

a. U.S., Bureau of the Census, *United States Census of Manufacturers*, 1958, Vol. 2, Part I.
b. U.S., Office of Business Economics, *The National Income and Product Accounts of the United States, 1929–65*.
c. U.S., Bureau of Labor Statistics, Report No. 238-5, *Survey of Consumer Expenditures*, 1960–61.
d. N. W. Ayer & Son, *N. W. Ayer & Son's Directory, Newspapers and Periodicals*, 1946 and 1960.
e. U.S., Bureau of the Census, *Historical Statistics of the United States* (Washington, D.C., 1975) 2 vols.
f. George Horace Gallup, *The Gallup Poll: Public Opinion 1935–1971*, 3 vols. (New York, 1972), Vol. 2.

1. On the democratic theme in wartime popular culture, see Richard R. Lingeman, *Don't You Know There's a War On?* (New York, 1970), pp. 174–75, 183–90, 205, 228–30, 249–51; Richard Polenberg, *War and Society* (New York, 1972), pp. 132–35; John Morton Blum, *V Was for Victory: Politics and American Culture during World War II* (New York, 1976), pp. 53–70; and Frank Fox, *Madison Avenue Goes to War* (Provo, Utah, 1975), pp. 70–80. Norman Rockwell's "Freedom of Speech" first appeared in the *Saturday Evening Post*, 20 February 1943, p. 12, and his "Rosie the Riveter" was the *Post* cover on 29 May 1943. His Willie Gillis appeared on the *Post* cover seven times between 1942 and 1946.

2. Herman Philip Miller, *Rich Man, Poor Man* (New York, 1964), pp. 34–36, 44–46; Gabriel Kolko, *Wealth and Power in America: An Analysis of Social Class and Income Distribution*, (New York, 1962), pp. 9–23; Richard Parker, "The Myth of Middle America," in Otis L. Graham, Jr., ed., *Perspectives in 20th Century America: Readings and Commentary* (New York, 1973), pp. 323–24, 328–29, 336–39.

3. Fox, *Madison Avenue*, pp. 19–22, 29–30, 39–41, 86–87, 96; *Fortune* 35 (February 1947): 91.

4. Ada Louise Huxtable, *Kicked a Building Lately?* (New York, 1976), p. 208; Norman Bel Geddes, "Futurama," in United Scenic Artists, *1940–1941 Almanac* (New York, 1941), pp. 3–4; Fox, *Madison Avenue*, pp. 74–78.

5. U.S., Bureau of the Census, *Historical Statistics of the United States* (Washington, D.C., 1975), pt. I, p. 116; Martin Mayer, *About Television* (New York, 1972), pp. 390–91, 394; Theodore Peterson, *Magazines in the Twentieth Century* (Urbana, Ill., 1964), pp. 50, 61, 449–50; Bennett M. Berger, *Looking for America: Essays on Youth, Suburbia, and Other American Obsessions* (Englewood Cliffs, N.J., 1971) p. 177; Will Herberg, *Protestant, Catholic, Jew*, rev. ed. (New York, 1960), pp. 27–39; David Riesman, "The Suburban Sadness," in William M. Dobriner, ed., *The Suburban Community* (New York, 1958), p. 378; Bill C. Malone, *Country Music, U.S.A.* (Austin, Tex., 1968), p. 185; Herbert Gans, *Popular Culture and High Culture* (New York, 1974), pp. 42, 101–2. The concept of "taste subcultures" is developed by Gans in *Popular Culture*, pp. x, 20–23, and passim.

6. U.S., Department of Commerce, Business and Defense Services Administration, *Leisure and Work Clothing: Trends and Outlook* (Washington, D.C., 1961), pp. 1–3; Michael Harrington, *The Other America: Poverty in the United States* (New York, 1962), p. 5; Russell Lynes, *A Surfeit of Honey* (New York, 1957), pp. 67–68; Francis X. Sutton, "Comments on 'Careers and Consumer Behavior'," in Lincoln Clark, ed., *Consumer Behavior*, 2 vols. (New York, 1955), 2:19; *Life*, 21 March 1949, p. 137; U.S. Bureau of Labor Statistics, *How American Buying Habits Change* (Washington, D.C., n.d. [1958]), pp. 6–7, 48, 216; Board of Governors of the Federal Reserve System, *Consumer Instalment Credit* (Washington, D.C., 1957), pt. 1, vol. 1, p. 8; Eric Larabee and Rolf Meyersohn, eds., *Mass Leisure* (Glencoe, Ill., 1958), pp. 151–52, 167; "Cone Miller: Old King Denim," *Fortune* 47 (January 1953): 89–90.

7. Russell Lynes, *The Tastemakers* (New York, 1954), p. 254; *Fortune* 45 (April 1952): 133; David Riesman and Howard Roseborough, "Careers and Consumer Behavior," in Clark, ed., *Consumer Behavior*, 2:6, 9–10; Ada Louise Huxtable, *Will They Ever Finish Bruckner Boulevard* (New York, 1970), pp. 173–74; Tom Wolfe, *The Kandy-Kolored Tangerine Flake Streamline Baby* (New York, 1963), pp. xv–xvi, 8–12; Robert Venturi, *Learning from Las Vegas* (Cambridge, Mass., 1977), passim. On the decline in regional distinctions, see also Max Lerner, *America as a Civilization*, 2 vols. (New York, 1956), 1:204–5, and Riesman, "Suburban Sadness," pp. 175–76, 185.

8. The most influential of the many exposés of comic books was Frederick Wertham's *Seduction of the Innocent* (New York, 1954). For estimates of TV usage and its effects, see Mayer, *About Television*, pp. 389–92, Peterson, *Magazines*, p. 49, and Douglas T. Miller and Marion Nowak, *The Fifties: The Way We Really Were* (New York, 1977), pp. 352–70.

9. See Dwight Macdonald, "Masscult and Midcult," in *Against the American Grain* (New York, 1956), pp. 3–75, and Bernard Rosenberg and David Manning White, eds., *Mass Culture* (New York, 1957).

10. Edward Buxton, *Promise Them Anything: The Inside Story of the Madison Avenue Power Struggle* (New York, 1972), p. 6; Mayer, *About Television*, p. 391. On advertising appropriations, see Appendix, above.

11. Mayer, *About Television*, p. 389. For examples of "family semicircle" TV ads, see *Saturday Evening Post*, 3 June 1950, p. 55; 7 April 1951, p. 72; 21 April 1951, p. 73; 15 December 1951, p. 46; *Life*, 11 September 1950, pp. 14–15; 18 September 1950, p. 143; 15 October 1951, p. 176.

12. Edward P. Eichler and Marshall Kaplan, *The Community Builders* (Berkeley, Calif., 1967), p. 27; Carey McWilliams, *California: The Great Exception* (New York, 1949), pp. 22, 219–20; Miller and Nowak, *The Fifties*, p. 143; *Fortune* 36 (September 1947): 3. The term *car culture* is taken from James J. Flink, *The Car Culture* (Cambridge, Mass., 1975).

13. Claudia B. Kidwell and Margaret C. Christman, *Suiting Everyone: The Democratization of Clothing in America* (Washington, D.C., 1974), p. 169; Reuel Denney, "The Leisure Society," *Harvard Business Review* 37 (1959): 52–53; *Life*, 12 April 1948, p. 133; Pauline Kael, *I Lost It at the Movies* (Boston, 1965), p. 5; George Horace Gallup, *The Gallup Poll: Public Opinion 1935–1971*, 3 vols. (New York, 1972), 2:1387, 1405–6, 1461–62.

14. Robert Woods Kennedy, *The House and the Art of Its Design* (New York, 1953), p. 14; Cliff May, *Western Ranch Houses* (Menlo Park, Calif., 1958), pp. 7–20, 29, 33, 67, 93. On ranch house popularity see also the Allied Chemical and Dye Corp. ad in *Saturday Evening Post*, 10 June 1950, p. 179.

15. May, *Western Ranch Houses*, pp. 93–94, 122, 161; George Nelson and Henry Wright, *Tomorrow's House* (New York, 1945), pp. 42, 76–80; *Fortune* 22 (April 1946): 165; Siegfried Giedion, *Mechanization Takes Command* (New York, 1948), pp. 617, 620–24; Lerner, *America as a Civilization*, 1:178; Lynes, *A Surfeit of Honey*, pp. 61–62, 68; John Keats, *The Crack in the Picture Window* (Boston, 1956), pp. xv–xvi, 7–8, 48, 110–11.

16. Lynes, *The Tastemakers*, p. 253; May, *Western Ranch Houses*, pp. 74–75, 80; Nelson and Wright, *Tomorrow's House*, pp. 26, 31, 34; Frederick Lewis Allen, "The Big Change in Suburbia," *Harpers' Magazine* 208 (June 1954): 26. The "California ranch school," with open, single-story, finger-plan arrangements also spread nationally: see John Burchard and Albert Bush-Brown, *The Architecture of America* (Boston, 1961), pp. 477–79.

17. See Eichler and Kaplan, *The Community Builders*, pp. xi, 106–7; Parker, "The Myth of Middle America," pp. 335–39; William H. Whyte, *The Organization Man* (New York, 1956); John R. Seeley, R. Alexander Sim, and Elizabeth W. Loosley, *Crestwood Heights* (New York, 1956); A. C. Spectorsky, *The Exurbanites* (New York, 1958); and Berger, *Looking for America*, pp. 151–84.

18. Russell Lynes, "High-Brow, Low-Brow, Middle-Brow," *Harpers' Magazine* 198 (February 1949): 19–28 and *Life*, 11 April 1949, pp. 99–101; William H. Whyte, "The Consumer in the New Suburbia," in Clark, ed., *Consumer Behavior* 1:1, 5–6.

19. BLS, *How American Buying Habits Change*, p. 195; Frederick W. Cozens and Florence Scovil Stumpf, *Sports in American Life* (Chicago, 1953), pp. 218, 222, 224; Kent Anderson, *Television Fraud* (Westport, Conn., 1978), pp. 8–10, 23, 39–40; Reuel Denney, *The Astonished Muse* (Chicago, 1957), pp. 206–7, 222; Riesman and Roseborough, "Careers," p. 9; *Fortune* 36 (November 1947): 84. The idea of the "declassing" of golf again suggests the myopia of the affluent: a 1950 Gallup poll found that 93 percent of the respondents never played either golf or tennis. It seems improbable that the remaining 7 percent contained significant representation of those of median incomes and below: Gallup, *Gallup Poll*, 2:936.

20. *Webster's Third New International Dictionary of the English Language, Unabridged*, (Springfield, Mass., 1961), p. 1307. Neither Webster's Second Edition nor the 1952 Funk and Wagnalls *New Standard Dictionary of the English Language* included *life-style* as a word.

21. U.S., Bureau of Labor Statistics, *Survey of Consumer Expenditures, 1960–61* (Washington, D.C., 1963), pp. 676, 678; BLS, *How American Buying Habits Change*, pp. 189–90, 195, 208; Lawrence Wittner, *Cold War America* (New York, 1974), p. 112.

22. Parker, "The Myth of Middle Class America," pp. 323–24, 335–39; Miller, *Rich Man, Poor Man*, pp. 34–36, 44–46; Wittner, *Cold War America*, pp. 112–13, 115; Miller and Nowak, *The Fifties*, pp. 111–12, 122. *The Life Study of Consumer Expenditures* (New York, 1957), conducted by Alfred Politz Research Inc., revealed that the top 14 percent of all families in income level bought 44 percent of all sports goods and equipment and 37 percent of all photographic equipment. Those of high income dominated the purchase of wine, liquor, and frozen foods. Another study indicated that the bottom 52 percent of all families accounted for only 20 percent of the sales of hi-fi components and kits. The lowest 31 percent accounted for only 7.5 percent of sports events admissions, whereas the top 29 percent of families accounted for 56 percent: Fabian Linden, ed., *Market Profiles of Consumer Products* (New York, 1967), p. 123. (Linden's figures are based on 1960–61 Department of Labor statistics.)

23. Capp's sequences on the Shmoo can be found in most major daily newspapers beginning 27 August 1948. "Instant analysis" of the Shmoo appeared in *Life*, 20 September 1948, p. 46, and 20 December 1948, p. 22. A provisional estimate of its awesome merchandising power appeared in *Newsweek*, 5 September 1949, pp. 49–50. The Shmoo also shared the cover of *Time* with Li'l Abner and Daisy Mae on 6 November 1950. Capp offered a reflective view in the *New Yorker*, 23 October 1963, pp. 39–40. See also Arthur Asa Berger, *Li'l Abner: A Study in American Satire* (New York, 1960), pp. 115–19.

25. Mickey Spillane, *One Lonely Night* (New York, 1951), pp. 153–54; John Cawelti, "The Spillane Phenomenon," *Journal of Popular Culture* 3 (1969): 9.

26. Cawelti, "The Spillane Phenomenon," pp. 11, 13, 22; Miller and Nowak, *The Fifties*, pp. 167–68.

27. Bruce Lohof, "The Higher Meaning of Marlboro Cigarettes," *Journal of Popular Culture* 3 (1969): 442–44, 446, 448–49; Edward M. Gottschall and Arthur Hawkins, eds., *Advertising Directions: Trends in Visual Advertising* (New York, 1959), p. 207; Wolfe, *Kandy-Kolored Baby*, pp. 33, 88, 100–101; Cynthia Golomb Dettelbach, *In the Driver's Seat* (Westport, Conn., 1976), p. 109; Peterson, *Magazines*, pp. 310, 368; Denney, *The Astonished Muse*, pp. 111, 118–20; Robert Lipsyte, *Sportsworld: An American Dreamland* (New York, 1975), p. x; Michael R. Real, *Mass-Mediated Culture* (Englewood Cliffs, N.J., 1977), pp. 103–7; Gallup, *Gallup Poll*, 2:988.

28. Cozens and Stumpf, *Sports*, p. 229; Jack W. Berryman, "From the Cradle to the Playing Field: America's Emphasis on Highly Organized Competitive Sports for Preadolescent Boys," *Journal of Sport History* 2 (1975): 116, 119–20, 125; Gottschall and Hawkins, *Advertising Directions*, p. 198. Another major impetus behind organized boys' sports was the growing threat of juvenile delinquency: see Berryman, "From the Cradle," p. 124.

29. *Historical Statistics*, 1:133; William H. Chafe, *The American Woman: Her Changing Social, Economic, and Political Roles, 1920–1970* (New York, 1972), pp. 190–95, 218–20; Riesman "Suburban Sadness," p. 384; Lynes, *A Surfeit of Honey*, p. 51; "A Man's Place Is in the Home," *McCalls*, 81 (May 1954): 29–34; Betty Friedan, *The Feminine Mystique* (New York, 1963), passim. On the legacies of World War II in reinforcing sex role stereotypes, see also Lisle A. Rose, *The Long Shadow: Reflections on the Second World War Era* (Westport, Conn., 1978), p. 115.

30. Miller and Nowak, *The Fifties*, p. 167; Kael, *Movies*, pp. 36–37; Marjorie Rosen, *Popcorn Venus: Women, Movies, and the American Dream* (New York, 1973), pp. 159, 183, 245–48, 271–75; Roger Manvell, *Love Goddesses of the Movies* (New York, 1975), pp. 110, 115; Ferdinand Lundberg and Marynia F. Farnham, *Modern Woman: The Lost Sex* (New York, 1947), pp. 23, 355–70, 381–86; May, *Western Ranch Houses*, p. 158. The estimate on automobile advertising is based on a survey of full-page advertisements in *Life* for the months of October 1951, May 1952, April 1953, and November 1955.

31. Sidney E. Ahlstrom, *A Religious History of the American People* (New Haven, Conn., 1972), pp. 950–54; Alice Payne Hackett and James Henry Burke, *80 Years of Best Sellers, 1895–1975* (New York, 1977), pp. 144–58; Miller and Nowak, *The Fifties*, pp. 85–86.

32. William Gerald McLoughlin, *Billy Graham: Revivalist in a Secular Age* (New York, 1960), pp. 45–52; 147–73; Real, *Mass-Mediated Culture*, pp. 155, 162–68, 176–80; Gallup, *Gallup Poll*, 2:1386, 1462, 1535; "Great Preachers," *Life*, 6 April 1953, p. 132. On church construction see Appendix, above, and U.S., Department of Commerce, Office of Business Economics, *The National Income and Product Accounts of the United States, 1929–1965* (Washington, D.C., 1966), pp. 80–81.

33. Herberg, *Protestant, Catholic, Jew*, pp. 2, 27–41, 59, 78–84; Miller and Nowak, *The Fifties*, p. 89; Gallup, *Gallup Poll*, 2:1482.

34. Donald Seymer Napoli, "The Architects of Adjustment: The Practice and Professionalization of American Psychology, 1920–1945" (Ph.D. diss., University of California, Davis, 1975), pp. 181–214, 284–88; "Psychology—What It Means in Modern Life," *Life*, 7 January 1957, pp. 68–82, and succeeding issues. Between 1947 and 1957 the major shifts in nonfiction content in *Reader's Digest* and *Saturday Evening Post* were toward the categories of "personal affairs" and "physical, mental, or spiritual health": see Jerome Ellison and Franklin, T. Gosser, "Non-fiction Magazine Articles: A Content Analysis Study," *Journalism Quarterly* 36 (1959): 30, 34. On *Reader's Digest* see, for example, the issues of January 1947, August 1948, March 1950, October 1950, and November 1955.

35. Garth S. Jowett, "The Concept of History in American Produced Films: An Analysis of the Films Made in the Period 1950–1961," *Journal of Popular Culture* 3 (1970): 807, 811; Horace Newcomb, *TV: The Most Popular Art* (New York, 1974), pp. 71–78; Justus George Frederick, *Introduction to Motivation Research* (New York, 1957), pp. 20, 29, 85–87; Pierre Martineau, *Motivation in Advertising* (New York, 1957), pp. 27–39; *Life*, 12 March 1951, p. 21.

36. *Life*, 26 May 1952, pp. 28–31; Gallup, *Gallup Poll*, 2:1162.

37. Vance Packard, *The Hidden Persuaders*, (New York, 1957) pp. 38–45, 57–83; "A Presentation of Young and Rubicam, 1961," and "Young and Rubicam 2nd International Research Conference, 1958," typescripts, Young and Rubicam archives, New York City. Whyte, *The Organization Man*, pp. 171–201, 405–10; Susan Sontag, "The Imagination of Disaster," in *Against Interpretation* (New York, 1961), pp. 220–23.

38. Miller and Nowak, *The Fifties*, pp. 86, 94; Donald B. Meyer, *The Positive Thinkers* (New York, 1965), pp. 274–75; 327–30; Hackett and Burke, *80 Years of Best Sellers*, pp. 142–56. The term *cult of reassurance* is taken from Miller and Nowak.

39. Meyer, *The Positive Thinkers*, pp. 259–67; "Great Preachers," *Life*, 6 April 1953, p. 129; Miller and Nowak, *The Fifties*, pp. 95–96; Norman Vincent Peale, *The Power of Positive Thinking* (New York, 1952), pp. viii–ix, 16–17, 201, 232, and passim.

40. Richard Schickel, *The Disney Version* (New York, 1968), pp. 18–29, 295–96, 316–22, 350–54; Real, *Mass-Mediated Culture*, pp. 47–48, 75–86.

41. Dwight Macdonald, "A Caste, A Culture, A Market," *New Yorker*, 22, 29 November 1958, pp. 62–65, 74; Gallup, *Gallup Poll*, 1:571, 597, and 2:801, 995, 1354.

42. Harrison Salisbury, *A Shook-up Generation* (New York, 1958), and Benjamin Fine, *1,000,000 Delinquents* (New York, 1957). On the youth market see Macdonald, "A Caste," pp. 57–58, 74, 88–89; *Life*, 31 August 1959, pp. 78–84; and Wolfe, *Kandy-Kolored Baby*, pp. 76–79.

43. "Delirium over Dead Star," *Life*, 24 September 1956, pp. 75–80; Kael, *Movies*, pp. 46, 55–57; Robert Brustein, "America's New Culture Hero: Feelings without Words," *Commentary* 25 (1958): 128; Charlie Gillett, *The Sound of the City* (New York, 1970), pp. 18–19.

44. Miller and Nowak, *The Fifties*, p. 293; Gallup, *Gallup Poll*, 2:954, 957; Paul M.

Hirsch, "Sociological Approaches to the Pop Music Phenomenon," *American Behavioral Scientist* 14 (1971): 377; Carl Belz, *The Story of Rock* (New York, 1969), pp. 53–56.

45. Ian Whitcomb, *After the Ball: Pop Music from Rag to Rock* (New York, 1972), pp. 206–17; Gillett, *The Sound of the City*, p. 7; Hirsch, "Sociological Approaches," p. 382; Belz, *The Story of Rock*, p. 20.

46. Paul M. Hirsch, "Processing Fads and Fashions: An Organization-Set Analysis of Cultural Industry Systems," *American Journal of Sociology* 77 (1972): 641; Hirsch, "Sociological Approaches," pp. 380–81; Gillett, *The Sound of the City*, p. 18; Whitcomb, *After the Ball*, pp. 216–17.

47. Gillett, *The Sound of the City*, pp. 5, 7, 9, 135–36, 163; Whitcomb, *After the Ball*, pp. 197–203, 213–15; Malone, *Country Music, U.S.A.*, pp. 192–93, 202, 206, 216, 236.

48. Whitcomb, *After the Ball*, p. 204; Gillett, *The Sound of the City*, pp. 5–6; Miller and Nowak, *The Fifties*, p. 295.

49. Gillett, *The Sound of the City*, pp. 1, 15–17; Whitcomb, *After the Ball*, pp. 223–26; David Ewen, *All the Years of American Popular Music* (Englewood Cliffs, N.J., 1977), p. 554.

50. Gillett, *The Sound of the City*, pp. 33, 47, 49, 238; Belz, *The Story of Rock*, pp. 25–28; Miller and Nowak, *The Fifties*, pp. 298–99.

51. Brustein, "America's New Culture Hero," pp. 125, 128; Belz, *The Story of Rock*, pp. 56–69; Gerald Weales, "MOVIES: The Crazy-Mixed-up Kids Take Over," *Reporter*, 13 December 1956, pp. 40–41; Kael, *Movies*, pp. 45–46; John Sharnik, "The War of the Generations," *House and Garden* 110 (1956): 40; *Time*, 18 June 1956, p. 54; *Newsweek*, 23 April 1956, p. 32; 18 June 1956, p. 42; *America*, 23 June 1956, pp. 294–95; Thomas B. Morgan, "Teen-Age Heroes: Mirrors of Muddled Youth," *Esquire* 53 (March 1960): 65, 67, 71.

52. Greil Marcus, *Mystery Train: Images of America in Rock 'n' Roll Music* (New York, 1976), pp. 148, 162, 165, 177–82.

53. Ibid., pp. 142, 156, 157, 182, 185–86, 198.

54. Ibid., pp. 198–99; Whitcomb, *After the Ball*, pp. 236–38; Belz, *The Story of Rock*, pp. 102–6; Gillett, *The Sound of the City*, pp. 48–50, 54, 66, 122, 195, 239–40; Morgan, "Teen-Age Heroes," pp. 67, 71; Ewen, *All the Years*, pp. 295–96, 512, 564–67.

55. Norman L. Friedman, "American Movies and American Culture, 1946–1970," *Journal of Popular Culture* 3 (1970): 819–21; David Cort, "Face-Lifting the Giants," *Nation*, 25 November 1961, pp. 424–25; Peterson, *Magazines*, pp. 111–12, 401.

PART TWO

Public Problems and Public Policy

Poverty and Welfare in America, 1945–1960

James T. Patterson

When Americans "rediscovered" poverty in the early 1960s, social scientists were appalled to realize how little they knew about it. The economist Kenneth Boulding lamented that knowledge of poverty was "scanty"; the statistician Herman Miller complained that it was "deplorable." Daniel Bell recalled, "When the poverty issue arose, nobody was really prepared, nobody had any data, nobody knew what to do."[1]

Social scientists bemoaned not only the shortage of data on poverty but also the paucity of serious studies that might assist policy-makers in the field of welfare. Most graduates of schools of social work, one critic grumbled, "hardly knew how to go about posing and executing a researchable problem." A sociologist complained later, "During the 1940's, the 1950's, and the first few years of the 1960's, the topic of poverty was virtually nonexistent in the sociological literature." Two students of welfare concluded in 1963, "It is not known for certain how many [on relief] have the basic external and internal resources to become self-sufficient in a short time with just a little temporary aid, how many when provided with a number of external socio-cultural and economic resources can make a go of it, or how many, regardless of assistance, will find it difficult to move into the mainstream."[2]

This imperfect understanding of poverty reflected a benign neglect of scattered information gathered on the subject during the 1940s and 1950s. If these years had been as prosperous as many contemporaries believed, this neglect would not have mattered much. But by the late 1950s, critics perceived that a host of social problems remained, leaving in their wake a poverty population of nearly 40 million people, and a group of "near poor" who numbered perhaps 15 million more. These 55 million comprised about a fourth of the population. Most of them received little help from a jerry-built welfare system that was less generous and comprehensive than those of Western Europe and that struck liberals as uniquely mean-spirited.[3]

Any effort to understand this benign neglect of poverty and welfare inevitably concerns itself with several related questions. What were the dimensions of American poverty during those years? How well did the welfare system operate? Why was poverty neglected? And what was the impact on policy of attitudes toward the poor? Tentative answers to such questions can offer insights into larger concerns, for as R. H. Tawney once observed, "There is no touchstone, except the treatment of childhood, which reveals the true character of social philosophy more clearly than the spirit in which it regards the misfortunes of those of its members who fall by the way."[4]

Experts who later tried to measure the dimensions of American poverty in the 1940s and 1950s agreed on some broad trends. The most striking of these trends was progress, rooted in economic growth, in the percentage of Americans with incomes above "poverty lines." One careful study by Herman Miller employed contemporary definitions of minimum subsistence—life deemed compatible with "decency and health" —and found that the percentage of families in poverty had risen from about 40 percent in 1929 to 48 percent in 1935–36, and then fell steadily—to 33 percent in 1940, 27 percent in 1950, and 21 percent in 1960. This was 39 million people in 1960, compared with 61 million in 1935–36, 44 million in 1940, and 41 million in 1950. James Tobin, one of President John F. Kennedy's Council of Economic Advisers, reported even more striking gains:

Percentage of Families with Annual Incomes Below $3,000 (1965 dollars)

1896	67%	1950	30%
1918	63%	1960	20%
1935–36	51%	1965	17%

Although other definitions of poverty arrive at slightly different figures, all authorities perceive considerable progress in the diminution of absolute poverty between 1938 and 1941, steady gains against poverty during World War II, continuing, though much less spectacular, advances from 1946 to 1956, and sluggish improvement from 1957 to 1960.[5] The key to the progress was not welfare—that was relatively insignificant—but economic growth.

These American poor of the 1940s and 1950s were staggeringly well off by world standards. The per capita income of Harlem ranked with the top five nations in the world. Blacks in Mississippi—among the poorest groups in the nation—had a median income in 1959 of $944, compared with a median for Puerto Ricans of $819; Puerto Rico then ranked in the top fourth of the world's nations in per capita income. In Harlan County, Kentucky, one of the country's poorest, two-thirds of the homes in 1960 were "substandard," and one-fourth lacked running water. Yet, 67 percent had TV, 42 percent had telephones, and 59 percent had a car.[6]

Most writers agree also that this progress in the 1940s and 1950s in the United States was part of a continuing secular trend that was to drop the incidence of absolute poverty, according to official definitions, to between 12 and 15 percent in the 1970s. All these gains, moreover, reflected contemporary standards of what people thought should be a subsistence level of living. In the postwar years these standards rose considerably, so people under the poverty line as defined in 1960 lived much better than had poor people in the past. If the relatively generous lines used in 1960 are applied to measure poverty in earlier periods, the gains become striking. Use of a family poverty line of $3,800 (in 1960 dollars) results statistically in proportions of poor families of 70 percent in 1929, 70 percent in 1935–36, 53 percent in 1941, 34 percent in 1950, and 22 percent in 1960. This kind of reckoning admittedly ignores contemporary standards and expectations, but it reveals the great improvement in the standards of living enjoyed by poor and nonpoor alike since 1930.

Scholars agree also on the major changes and continuities in the composition of the poor during these years. Far and away the most significant change stemmed from the technological revolution affecting agriculture. In 1943 the mechanical cotton picker began its domineering history. It reduced the number of man-hours necessary to produce a bale of cotton from 160 to 25 and displaced perhaps 2.3 million family farm workers. Economic growth in the area absorbed only a fourth of these people. Many of the rest left the South, which experienced a net loss from interregional migration of 2.2 million in the 1940s and 1.4 million in the 1950s.

Most of these migrants settled in cities, which became the main locus of poverty. By 1960 some 55 percent of the poor lived in the city, 30 percent in small towns, only 15 percent on farms—as opposed to about 50 percent who had done some farming in the mid-1930s. This northernization and urbanization of poverty was a historic shift. By the mid-1960s it helped make poverty visible again, and facilitated community organization and political pressure from the poor.

The main dimensions of poverty were otherwise fairly stable during the 1940s and 1950s. The incidence among small farmers was higher than among any other single occupational group, and twice that of non-farmers. In 1963, 43 percent of America's 3.1 million farm families lived in poverty, compared with 17 percent of the nation's 44 million nonfarm families. This was almost 5 million farm people, or one-seventh of the total poverty population. About half of these poor farm families lived in the South, which (as always in American history) had the highest incidence of poverty. Indeed, 45 percent of poor families lived in the South. In Alabama and Mississippi 50 percent of these families earned less than $2,000 per year. About three-fourths of them were white in 1960—a larger percentage than in 1940, before the mass migration of blacks to the city.[7]

Statistics reveal continuity in the composition of other groups especially susceptible to poverty—the aged, nonwhites, and members of broken families. In 1962 nearly 50 percent of aged families earned incomes less than the poverty line (set by the Council of Economic Advisers at $3,000 for a family of four). So did 43 percent of nonwhite families and 47 percent of those that were female-headed. These percentages contrasted sharply with those measuring the poverty of families headed by persons aged 25 to 64 (13 percent), by whites (16 percent), and by males (15 percent). More alarming, these groups seemed more prone to poverty, relative to other groups, as time passed. In 1962, 33 percent of poor families in America were headed by people over 65, 22 percent by nonwhites, and 25 percent by females, compared with percentages of 20, 18, and 16 respectively in 1947. This poverty among the aged and broken families with children represented an important statistic often overlooked by opponents of welfare: more than one-third of people in all poor families, or 11 million people in 1963, were children, and almost half the poor were not in the labor market. Nearly 60 percent were younger than 18 or older than 65. For these very young and very old Americans (and for the disabled and nearly 3 million female heads of families with children under 6), public transfer payments were usually vital.[8]

These figures did not mean that poverty was restricted only to specially disadvantaged groups. Some 40 percent of poor families in 1963 were headed by able-bodied males aged 25 to 54. These were the working poor, 78 percent of them white. As ever, millions of poor family heads were white workingmen whose jobs paid so little that they could not rise above the line of poverty.

Still, it was a fact that the proportion of the poor who were in specially disadvantaged families rose in the 1940s and 1950s. That happened because economic growth nudged many of the white working poor over the poverty line. The increased proportion of the disadvantaged groups, and their concentration in accessible urban areas, helped expose poverty as a problem in 1960. So it was that Michael Harrington could claim at the time to discover a "new" hard-core poor made up of old people, female-headed households, and minority groups.[9]

In other ways writers attempting to describe poverty in the 1940s and 1950s tended to disagree, often hotly. They argued, first, over what defined a decent, healthful life, and therefore over poverty lines. Experts, indeed, distinguished between poverty lines facilitating "minimum subsistence," "minimum adequacy," and "minimum comfort." One application of these three definitions resulted in percentages of poor households of 11 percent, 26 percent, and 40 percent respectively for 1960.[10]

Attempting to still some of the debate, in the early 1960s the Social Security Administration adopted one system for measuring poverty. The SSA accepted the Department of Agriculture's "economy" food budget, and then multiplied it by three to get a minimum subsistence for families. Rounding figures off, the Council of Economic Advisers in 1962 set a poverty line of $3,000 for families of four and $1,500 for single individuals. It was a line that experts admitted was low—about $8.40 per day for a family of four—50 percent lower in fact than the "modest but adequate" budget used by the Bureau of Labor Statistics for a city worker's family. For this and other reasons, debate over the location of the line continued.

Debate mounted especially over the utility of any absolute measure of poverty. Critics of these measures observed that millions of "nonpoor" Americans lived, as the expert Mollie Orshansky put it in 1966, "with privation as their daily portion." Many of these—she numbered them then at 16 million in 1964, in addition to 34 million "poor"—slipped in and out of poverty. Living in a mass media age, they could not help but be aware of the growing gap that separated them from the middle classes. Experts who focused on this gap began by 1965 to insist that absolute poverty was but a small part of the broader problem of income maldistribution and relative deprivation.[11]

Experts hardly possessed the data even in the 1960s to settle another key question about poverty in the 1940s and 1950s: What percentage of poor people, however defined, were long-term and what percentage were borderline types who slipped in and out? Some analyses of this question used samples from the population on public assistance—an atypical minority of the poor—or measured the percentage of poor people in one year who climbed above the poverty line in the next. But in the 1960s experts did not complete comprehensive studies of poverty populations over extended periods of time, or always ask hard questions of their data. Thus, early studies suggested that approximately 40 percent of parents who got relief under the Aid to Families of Dependent Children (AFDC) program in 1960 had themselves been children in welfare families.[12] A common conclusion from this widely cited finding was that 40 percent of welfare families were multigeneration, "multi-problem" families—a "hard-core" poor living in an intransigent "culture of poverty." Yet, when it is remembered that at least 35 percent of Americans received relief at some time in the 1930s, this statistic tells little. As the historian Stephan Thernstrom observed in 1965, "Those who are convinced that poverty is increasingly being meted out in life sentences have yet to do the homework to substantiate the claim."[13]

These disputes among experts since 1960 seem technical, even arcane. But they are relevant to any historical account of American poverty between 1945 and 1960, if only because they reveal the limited amounts of solid information available to that generation of welfare reformers. The disputes also expose another difficulty: historians concerned with postwar poverty must deal with what one expert has aptly called "cross-sectional snapshots" instead of "longitudinal motion pictures" of American destitution.[14]

What was the role of welfare policies in this diminution of American poverty in the 1940s and 1950s?

The answer depends again on the frame of reference. By contrast to 1930, before the dawning of the modern welfare state, public policies in 1960 were staggeringly broad in coverage and generous in benefits. The number of people receiving benefits from the Old Age, Survivors, and Disability Insurance program (OASDI) increased from 1.3 million in 1945 to 14.8 million in 1960. The number receiving aid from AFDC—by 1960 the most important welfare program—increased from 701,000 to 3 million during the same period. Average monthly payments per family from AFDC increased from $33 to $124 between 1940 and 1962, a hike of 77 percent in real purchasing power. Total social welfare expenditures, including social insurance and public assistance (but excluding education and veterans benefits), were 1.8 percent of national income in 1944–45, and 7 percent (the same level as in the depression year of 1935) by 1959–60. They represented in 1960 more than 40 percent of the total income of the poor.[15]

Two social programs provided most of this aid between 1940 and

1960: old age and survivors insurance and public assistance, or "welfare." Public assistance was either "categorical" or "general." Categorical aid, funded by federal-state matching grants, went to four needy groups by 1960: the blind, the aged, the permanently and totally disabled, and families with dependent children. General assistance, from state and local funds, went to needy people not otherwise covered.

But neither social insurance nor welfare was comprehensive or generous enough to satisfy reformers in the 1940s and 1950s. Social Security, which paid a retired worker $69.60 a month in 1960, was insufficient in itself to remove people from poverty. Financed by regressive taxes on employee salaries and employee payrolls, it drained off potential purchasing power. It supported many nonpoor as well as poor; about half of America's aged poor families got no coverage under Social Security in 1960.[16]

Reformers were especially alarmed at what they considered the inadequacy of welfare. Only a fifth to a sixth of the country's poor families in the 1950s got either categorical or general assistance. This was between 2.7 percent and 4 percent of the population between 1945 and 1960. Money spent for public welfare regularly represented less than 1 percent of the Gross National Product. Those who did receive aid were not to be envied. Of households on AFDC, 28 percent in 1960 lacked flush toilets and hot water, and 17 percent did without running water at all. Some 50 percent of these households relied entirely on AFDC payments, which averaged $30 per recipient and $115 per family per month in 1960. What they got depended on where they lived, for levels of aid varied widely. The same weaknesses characterized state-local general assistance. In 1959 twenty-three states provided no general assistance to poor families in which there lived a supposedly employable adult.[17]

The condition in 1960 of AFDC families in New York City, which set its subsistence level budget at the unusually high level of $2,660 per year for a family of four, suggests the conditions under which welfare recipients had to live if they expected welfare workers to certify them as in need. Such families were permitted to rent a small five-room flat. The living room might have two chairs, a mattress and springs on legs to serve as a couch, a drop-leaf table for eating, and two straight chairs. Linoleum, not rugs, was expected to cover the floors. There could be one or two lamps, but electricity was to be used carefully. The family could have a refrigerator and electric iron, and play the radio an hour a day— there was no provision for using TV. The weekly food budget allowed for stewing lamb, beef liver or heart, fillet of haddock, or perhaps a boned veal roast. No allocation existed for frozen foods, tobacco, beer, or telephone calls. The clothing allowance provided for protection against the weather, but left no room for impulse buying or fashion, and barely coped with the problem of wear. A woman's coat was to last for five years. Breakage (say, of light bulbs) or spillage (of flour) meant that the family did without. This budget provided no "frills"—haircuts more than once a month, home permanents more than once a year, drugs other than aspirin, candy or ice cream for the children, movies, coffee for visitors.

New York's standard of $2,660 offered more in real dollars than budgets used there in the mid-1930s. It was high compared with the average standard nationally of $2,150 per year in 1960, and well above the $1,600 defined as subsistence in the five least-generous states. Families with outside income managed on it. But (as almost everywhere) the standard was below the $3,000 poverty line, and far below the $5,464 that the Bureau of Labor Statistics considered the "minimum comfort" standard for a family of four in 1960. Moreover, these standards were goals that social workers thought should be reached, not sums paid by public authorities in practice. Most states could not or would not pay public clients the amount that their social agencies set for subsistence.[18]

Reformers complained also that American welfare policies were less generous and comprehensive than were those of Western Europe. Experts cautiously agreed that the percentage of America's net national income spent on social insurance plus public assistance—about 7 percent in 1960—suffered by comparison with percentages during the 1950s of 12 to 20 percent in Belgium, Austria, France, and West Germany. Although the level of American spending for these items was close to that in Canada, Sweden, and the United Kingdom, it lagged well behind the performance of these nations, too, when public health care is defined as a social welfare item.[19]

Advocates of improved social services in the United States lamented especially the spirit under which aid was given. In Western Europe administrators tended to try to maximize coverage and minimize the stigma of accepting public aid; by contrast, American relief administrators sought to cut expenses and exclude from the rolls all people considered able to care for themselves. As one expert complained, "The general public does not know what you are talking about when you talk about professional competence and the need for better skills [in welfare administration]. *A good administrator* is one who can keep chisellers off the rolls—public welfare is as simple as that to them."[20]

This spirit pervaded the AFDC program, where states developed in the 1940s and 1950s a range of regulations designed to evade federal guidelines. Many states denied aid to families with "employable mothers," dawdled in servicing applications, established lengthy residence requirements (usually a year or more), and intimidated prospective applicants—sometimes by stationing police outside relief offices. Irritated officials in the Bureau of Public Assistance issued endless regulations to force states to comply with federal guidelines: by the 1960s its Handbook of Public Assistance Administration was more than five inches thick. But this effort resulted mainly in heaps of paper work for caseworkers. In the absence of pressure from the poor themselves, who were ill-organized in the 1940s and 1950s, the bureau lacked the means and the will to engage in debilitating skirmishes with cost-conscious politicians in the states and localities.[21]

States proved particularly adept at denying AFDC to children whose absent fathers were suspected of being able to provide support or of being in the vicinity. This concern of states, minor in the early 1940s, intensified with the increase in broken families—and therefore in the case load—in the late 1940s and 1950s. Alarmists began to fear that AFDC, originally intended to take care of "deserving" widows with children, was becoming a haven for "immoral" (increasingly black) "welfare mothers." As early as 1950 Congress passed an amendment mandating local welfare agencies to notify law enforcement officers whenever aid was granted to children whose father had deserted the family. States and towns, meanwhile, dispatched agents on "midnight raids" to welfare homes in order to catch men in the house. States relied especially on "suitable home" regulations aimed at denying aid to "undeserving" mothers. All such regulations required caseworkers to pry into the private lives of recipients. Arkansas cut off help to mothers engaged in a "nonstable, nonlegal union"; Oregon, to mothers who housed "Roger the lodgers"; Michigan, to families with "male boarders"; Texas, to "pseudo–common law marriages." To receive aid, some mothers had to sign affidavits like this one:

I . . . do hereby promise and agree that until such time as the following agreement is rescinded, I will not have any male callers coming to my home nor meeting me elsewhere under improper conditions.

I also agree to raise my children to the best of my ability and will not knowingly contribute or be a contributing factor to their being shamed by my conduct. I understand that should I violate this agreement, the children will be taken from me. . . . [22]

When federal officials looked about for allies in their quest for better welfare, they found very few. In the 1930s they had been able to count on some activist social workers, but the return of better times in the 1940s seemed to sap the reformist spirit in the profession. The majority of well-trained workers went into private charity employment, where they got better pay and the chance to apply their courses in psychiatrically oriented casework. These courses stressed rehabilitation of individuals and of families, not reform of public welfare. Conferences of social workers regularly featured sessions on such subjects as "Working with the Child in His Own Home," "The Hard to Reach Multiple Problem Families," "Managing a Case Load," and "Opportunities for Professional Social Work Training."[23] Sessions on "public welfare" were less numerous, for many social workers continued to believe that public assistance, as one worker explained, was "an albatross around the neck of social service." The dirty work of public welfare often fell by default to elected, nonprofessional town and county officials, whose goal was to control costs.[24]

Those social work professionals and bureaucrats who did concern themselves with public welfare began mobilizing lobbies in the mid- and late 1950s. Among the most important of these was the Committee on Social Issues and Policies of the National Social Welfare Assembly (which was itself a holding company for a variety of social work organizations). The leaders of this effort focused their efforts on HEW, where many of them worked or had close contacts. In the early 1960s, dealing with an administration sympathetic to new approaches to public welfare, they lobbied successfully for welfare legislation. In the 1950s, however, they had to settle for modest changes in social security. They had to contend also with complacency among many of their colleagues in social work. These believed that economic progress was wiping out social injustice, leaving only individual problems. The director of the American Public Welfare Administration explained in 1957, "We expect the volume of public assistance cases to decrease in the future. As this happens, hopefully public welfare workers can begin to realize one of their major objectives, namely the opportunity to focus more attention on the preventive and rehabilitation aspects of their work."[25]

Advocates of improved aid found equally little support from popular magazines in the 1940s and 1950s. Those few articles written on poverty tended to carry scare headlines and to fret about the cost of welfare. One headline read, "When It Pays to Play Pauper." Another proclaimed, "The Hillbillies Invade Chicago." A third, entitled "I Say Relief Is Ruining Families," publicized the views of a New York City domestic relations court judge who intoned, "The relief setsup is sapping the will to work . . . encouraging cynicism, petty chiselling and bare-faced immorality." Another article, entitled "Welfare: Has It Become a Scandal?," complained that "relief without rehabilitation has spawned a vicious circle in welfare, so that now a second generation of reliefers is maturing on welfare rolls." It cited as a "typical case" a 40-year-old man with 4 children and 29 grandchildren, all illegitimate. "The girls take their pregnancies as a matter of course. The home is like Grand Central Terminal. Members vanish and stay away five days at a time. All the girls should have been put in homes. . . . It's a vicious circle." And another, "Detroit Cracks Down on Welfare Chiselers," was certain that "relief clients have thought this whole thing out carefully, weighing the advantages of being on relief against working for a living," and choosing welfare. "When perfectly executed, this consists of a person going off the aid-to-dependent children rolls upon reaching his twenty-first birthday, immediately establishing himself upon the relief rolls, and remaining there forever, if possible."[26]

Readers of such pieces were probably less hardhearted than the authors. Although public opinion on the subjects of poverty and welfare in the 1940s and 1950s is impossible to quantify, studies of polls suggest ambivalent feelings among middle-class Americans. When asked about "welfare" or "relief," people took the conservative line that public assistance was wasteful and demoralizing. But when asked if the government should help those in "need," they responded affirmatively. Polls revealed also that a majority of Americans supported a broadening of social security, which was widely (though inaccurately) perceived as a strictly insurance proposition.

Still, advocates of more generous welfare were probably correct in concluding that most middle-class Americans distinguished between social security—a necessity—and public welfare—a wasteful handout. Congress, reflecting this distinction, contented itself with taking the simple way out: liberalizing social insurance, and otherwise maintaining a policy of benign neglect. It refused to mandate a national minimum of payments to force states to pay benefits up to their inadequate definitions of need, or to involve the federal government in general assistance. In so doing, Congress reflected what was almost surely the dominant coolness among the middle classes toward welfare.[27]

Congress reflected also a historically powerful aspiration of American reformers in the field: that poverty could ultimately be prevented. This goal emphasized "rehabilitation" of people, not income maintenance. In employing such approaches in the 1950s, Congress discussed a variety of policies, including vocational rehabilitation, youth conservation work, and manpower training. Unsure of how to proceed (and anxious to save funds), it placed ever greater emphasis on upgrading the training of social workers—an upgrading that the social work professionals were happy to promote. In 1956 it passed an amendment to the Social Security Act authorizing federal matching money to those states that provided services—in addition to cash assistance—to relief clients. This "services" approach became the Bible of HEW Secretary Abraham Ribicoff in 1961, and resulted in the much-heralded Public Welfare amendments of 1962. These expanded the federal authorization for services, on the assumption that trained, professional caseworkers could rehabilitate the poor.[28] President Kennedy hailed these amendments as "the most far-reaching revision of our public welfare program since it was enacted in 1935 . . . a turning point in this nation's efforts to cope realistically and helpfully with these pressing problems."[29]

This renewed stress on prevention had deep roots in the history of Western approaches to poverty. As in the past it was nourished by the ethic of self-reliance that characterized American attitudes toward welfare. But Congress, despite the authorization of money for services, did not actually appropriate any before 1964. Moreover, no one satisfactorily explained how rehabilitation through services could do much for the needy in the short run, or address broad economic inequalities. Few people explored such questions at the time. Prevention and rehabilitation appealed to many liberals, who wanted the government to do something; to social work professionals, who saw in them a chance to upgrade their field of expertise; to bureaucrats in the Social Security Administration; and to conservatives, who wanted to cut the cost of cash assistance and cause dependency to wither away. The inadequacy of this approach had to be shown before still another, different orthodoxy—provision of economic opportunity—prevailed in the mid-1960s. But that is another story.

Many explanations of the arrested state of American public welfare in the 1940s and 1950s have tended to stress impersonal forces. These explanations include a psychological interpretation emphasizing the need of all societies to define poor people, among others, as deviants or scapegoats; an economic interpretation focusing on the desire of elites to force poor people off welfare into low-paying work; and a social interpretation arguing that many approaches to welfare—almshouses in the early nineteenth century, Charity Organization Societies in the 1880s and 1890s, psychiatric casework in the 1920s and 1950s—were efforts at "social control" of potentially disorderly elements in American life.[30] Other grand theories emphasize the racism of America, the distinctive power of the work ethic and related attitudes, and the peculiarly American faith in political decentralization. Together, these forces tended to abandon the poor to cost-conscious local elites.[31]

Although these interpretations are useful, no single grand theory accounts for middle-class opinions, which lent elites the crucial support they needed between 1940 and 1960.[32] A better way of exploring such attitudes is to see them in the context of the times. The dominant attitudes of most middle-class Americans in the 1940s and 1950s grew naturally from recent experiences and memories. Paramount among these experiences was the Great Depression of the 1930s. The hard times of the thirties hit a country in which charity workers had long distinguished between the "deserving" and "undeserving" poor. Although the depression shook this set of ideas, it did not destroy them. Even those who had been forced to accept welfare in the depression years tended to blame themselves, not the system, and to look down on those who could not find work in 1940. Americans carried into the 1940s and 1950s the notion of an undeserving poor and the related idea that prolonged welfare promoted dependency.[33]

It followed that the government ought to prevent dependency, and thereby reduce the costly burdens of welfare. Experts believed that prevention could be built into the system. Many state plans for unemployment insurance assumed that individual employers—faced with heavier taxation if they laid people off—could help prevent joblessness.[34] Similar thinking underlay New Deal relief, which was to be temporary. "It goes without saying," said Harry Hopkins, "that the plan which helps to make further relief unnecessary is the best and cheapest form of relief." Like most Americans, Hopkins thought that the government ought to prevent dependency, not provide long-run income maintenance.[35]

These emphases on the deserving poor and on prevention coexisted with other perceptions of poverty that were strengthened in the 1930s. People were certain, first, that the problem was not so much poverty as unemployment. Unemployment, in turn, was cyclical and temporary. Give the men shovels for digging and the women (not too many) needles for sewing, but do not rely on the dole or concentrate on training people. With time the problem of unemployment—THE problem—would "wither away." Such a view, of course, made it easy to ignore the predepression poor, whose plight stemmed from low income, not unemployment.

Domestic changes during World War II appeared to undermine some of these popular attitudes and to promote the idea of a welfare state. The war enhanced the political power of organized labor, which by then included some unskilled and low-wage workers; it promoted the spread among economists of Keynesian notions concerning the role of fiscal policy in promoting growth; and it led Congress to approve generous veterans benefits affecting nearly one-half of the population. The war expanded the federal bureaucracy—even in the field of social welfare—and it accelerated the nationalization of politics. Perhaps the most significant long-run outcome of the war was unprecedented prosperity. In such a society poverty was obviously an un-American anomaly, and leisure a goal as cherished as hard work had been in the heyday of industrial growth. This affluence ultimately prompted great expectations among the poor as well as the nonpoor, and irresistible pressures on government to provide the good life. By the 1960s reformers were ready to believe that poverty could and must be abolished.

These developments, however, were the long-run legacies of the war. In the short run it strengthened conservative popular attitudes toward public aid. In this sense the American experience was distinctive. Most Western European countries suffered appalling loss of life and property during the war. Their experience generated a sense of sacrifice and of common cause that immediately intensified demands for social service. England, France, Denmark, Norway, and the Low Countries embarked on major expansions of social insurance programs in the 1940s and 1950s.[36] No such developments occurred in the United States, where only veterans—not the poor—were perceived to have sacrificed much. War instead enhanced the power of corporate groups, the military, and the conservative coalition in Congress, which scuttled New Deal relief agencies. Until the mid-1960s, when the long-range socioeconomic forces became compelling, conservative middle-class attitudes toward poverty and welfare dominated the scene.

The prosperity engendered by war, moreover, gradually promoted among contemporaries an optimistic—indeed, fatuous—sense of national well-being. Complacent writers thought that the nation had shed its ethnic, racial, and class divisions. Even observers uncomfortable with what they perceived as the conformity and "other-directedness" of American life at the time, conceded that the old conflicts had subsided. And the cold war accentuated this stress on unity and classlessness. Social scientists, indeed, labored diligently to contrast the class cleavage and rigidity of Soviety society with the mobility and opportunity available in America. As one sociologist put it for *Life*, "The saving grace of the American social system is that our social positions are not fixed artificially, as they are in the so-called "classless' society of Russia."[37]

Writers easily identified the source of America's fortunate condition in the 1940s and 1950s. That source was economic growth. By the mid-

1950s, younger Americans who had not lived as adults during the 1930s began to take prosperity and growth for granted. Economists, too, grew increasingly confident. By the 1950s many had been converted to Keynesian notions about the positive role of fiscal policy in promoting prosperity. These Keynesians were not complacent. They were nonetheless optimistic. Like many Americans in the 1940s and 1950s, they rejoiced in the blessings of technical and financial aid that the Marshall Plan and Point 4 seemed to be bringing to poor people abroad. There, and at home, economic growth seemed to be the single greatest force guaranteeing the ultimate withering away of poverty.[38]

This notion of "withering away" remained a dominant motif of thinking about poverty in the 1940s and early 1950s. It helped explain why even the reformers in the Social Security Administration paid little attention to the Bureau of Public Assistance, their ugly and unwanted stepchild. A program for the poor, these experts continued to believe, was politically a poor program. The main goal should be to broaden the contributory social security programs. These would provide insurance, at no extra cost to taxpayers, against disability and old age. Meanwhile, economic growth would curb unemployment. And poverty would wither away.[39]

Given the power of such optimistic attitudes in the 1940s and 1950s, it was not surprising that other perspectives toward poverty struggled in vain for a hearing. Of these, three offered overlapping insights that, if heeded, might have enhanced public understanding. These may be called the cultural, liberal, and structuralist views.

The cultural perspective on poverty was the very antithesis of older views that there was a sodden "culture of poverty." It argued instead that various groups and social classes possessed distinctive, even admirable, cultural traditions that sustained them in crisis times. One who emphasized this view was the sociologist William F. Whyte, whose work influenced many academics in the 1940s. Whyte labored especially to demolish the notion that "social disorganization" afflicted the slums. Not so, he argued. Groups that seemed disorganized and deviant in fact held to recognizable and useful values.

Other writers echoed this focus on the distinctive cultural patterns of groups in American society. One was E. Wight Bakke, a discerning researcher whose studies of jobless Americans in the 1930s revealed that working-class people cherished sturdy traditions. Bakke, like Whyte, did not romanticize these, but he thought them functional. Endowed with such values, which differed subtly from those of the middle classes, the unemployed managed to cope fairly well even after prolonged periods out of work.[40]

The studies of W. Lloyd Warner and his many followers also challenged indirectly the thesis that the lower classes lived in "social disorganization." Applying techniques of cultural anthropology to small and middle-sized communities, Warner and others emphasized the persistence of social classes in American life. Members of the different classes had different values: the poor were not would-be middle-class people in tattered clothing and ramshackle homes. Warner stressed that the values of lower-class people were functional, not deviant. As an associate put it in 1951, "Behavior which middle-class teachers, clinicians, and psychiatrists often regard as 'delinquent' or 'hostile' or 'unmotivated' in slum children is usually a perfectly realistic, adaptive, and—in slum life—socially acceptable response to reality.[41]

Cultural anthropologists like Warner came under attack from some sociologists, who denounced both the community study approach and what they said was an unsystematic reliance on interviews. Cultural anthropologists, these critics complained, concentrated on the values and life-styles of people. This focus encouraged the notion that class—and poverty—was cultural instead of economic. Critics added that Warner defined social class according to the prestige and status that people enjoyed in the eyes of others, and slighted more important matters involving income, wealth, and economic power. The true tests of class were economic, not cultural.[42]

Although incisive, these critics were not so audible in the 1940s and 1950s as those who simply denied the importance of social class. These writers were so sure of the ultimate homogenization of American society that they slighted ethnic and regional traditions and forgot that many lower-class people do not have, or gladly adopt, middle-class values. Working in an age of supposed consensus, these observers assumed the success of the melting pot and left the impression that there was such a thing as a culturally undifferentiated poor. Against this prevailing view, potentially useful arguments that stressed the persistence of class and cultural divisions made little headway in the 1940s and 1950s.

A second insightful approach to poverty in the 1940s, the liberal view, came especially from the handful of social scientists, social workers, and bureaucrats who had been closely associated with New Deal welfare programs in the 1930s. Many of these people were familiar with statistical studies of unemployment and relief done by the Works Progress Administration, the National Resources Planning Board (NRPB), and other federal agencies in the 1930s. Unlike most Americans who thought the economic revival of 1940–42 would solve the problem of destitution, they insisted that social insurance and welfare must remain important elements of public policy.

No group was more persuaded of this continuing need than the NRPB. After substantial study it produced in December 1941 a report that resembled the much more widely publicized Beveridge Report in England in 1942. The NRPB observed frankly that "even in so-called 'good' times a disturbingly large proportion of the population has a precarious existence as a result of inadequate or no private income." The Great Depression, it argued, was "different in degree . . . and in kind" from previous depressions, in that unemployment had lasted longer, effectively severing many older workers—increasing as a percentage of total population—from the job market.

The NRPB stressed also the existence of the large and growing number of families headed by unemployables—not only the aged but the sick, the disabled, and women with dependent children. Calculating conservatively, it foresaw a more or less permanent "public aid burden" of at least 3.25 million households. This was about 14 million people, or one-eighth of the population. To address this need, the government had to take from localities the burden of general assistance, to require states to liberalize residency and eligibility standards, to increase federal contributions for various forms of categorical assistance, and to change the matching grant formulas for categorical aid so as to reflect regional needs and the fiscal capacity of the states.

Although the NRPB actually underestimated the extent of need, its report was in every way a far-seeing document. It called in effect for a federally supported floor under income. President Roosevelt dallied with the report, waiting sixteen months before forwarding it to Congress, but he ultimately reflected the NRPB's point of view in his "Economic Bill of Rights" of January 1944. All citizens, he said, deserved useful and remunerative jobs; income to provide sufficient food, clothing, and recreation; decent lodgings; medical care; protection against the hazards of old age, sickness, accident, and unemployment; and a good education.[43]

Another group of government-employed professionals was reaching equally liberal conclusions at about the same time. This was the leadership of the Social Security Board. In the mid-1930s it had stressed that the Social Security program, based on employer and employee contributions, must be a strictly business-like insurance operation. The government, far from dispensing welfare, was to be a piggy bank, storing contributions and paying them back with interest at age 65. By 1938, however, an advisory council appointed to help the Social Security Board liberalize social insurance was beginning to discard this piggy bank concept and to favor, for example, support of the disabled at levels that would approximate the wages they earned in their best-paid years. Such a program, of course, would mean giving many disabled workers far more than they had contributed to the system. Private insurance executives, recognizing this lapse from the prevailing orthodoxy, opposed it. But the Social Security Board adopted the principle in 1941, and lobbied for it in Congress throughout the 1940s.

This deviation from insurance principles appears unexciting in retrospect. But the change in perspective reflected a movement toward merging social security and welfare, and was so recognized by the planners who adopted it. As one participant put it, "We went through not just a political but sort of an intellectual and religious reformation. We began to come out with a perspective that none of us had when we first began doing these things. Between 1939 and 1942 we were changed persons."[44]

This liberal outlook slowly found a place in public policy. As early as 1939, Congress placed widows and survivors of covered workers under the old age insurance system, henceforth called Old Age and Survivors Insurance (OASI). Congress tied the old age benefit not to lifetime contributions but to average earnings over a shorter covered period. The result was to establish minimum benefits related to need as well as to contributions—a departure in practice from the supposedly sacrosanct actuarial principles of social insurance. At the same time Congress increased the federal contribution to aid to dependent children from one-third to one-half. By 1964 it had increased the federal share to this and the other categorical assistance programs nine more times, so that Washington was providing nearly 60 percent of all money for public assistance—compared with 41 percent in 1945.

Other amendments, especially in the 1950s, quietly added previously uncovered workers to the OASI system, and began to increase welfare benefits. In 1950 Congress rectified its original neglect of mothers of dependent children by offering them a "caretaker" grant. It set up a matching grant program for a new category, the permanently and totally disabled. In 1956 it added disability insurance to social security, and in 1958 it adopted a partial sliding scale for assistance grants that resulted in more-generous federal contributions to states with low per capita income. Amendments to the Social Security Act in 1960 set up a matching grant program (Kerr-Mills) to provide medical care for the indigent aged. These and other changes did not supply the money or involve the federal control that most reformers wanted. Still, these advances, especially in coverage under social insurance, broadened existing programs. In this sense the liberal approach gathered strength in the 1940s and 1950s.[45]

A structuralist approach represented a third useful line of thinking about poverty and welfare in the 1940s and 1950s. It resembled the liberal view in that it assumed the long-term need for extensive public welfare. Most of its practitioners were Keynesian liberals or democratic socialists. The structuralists concentrated more sharply, however, than did other liberals on what they perceived as the pronounced stratification of capitalist society. More than other liberals, they worried about inequality, and they called for great increases in public assistance as well as for major initiatives to counter low wages and underemployment. The most visible structuralists were not social workers or government bureaucrats who looked for ways of improving the situation of individuals, but social scientists and radical critics who took a broad and reformist view of the functional relationship between inequality and the social system.

Among them was the sociologist Robert Merton, whose classic article on anomie in 1938 stressed that lower-class Americans began with mainstream values, only to be set back by structural barriers blocking their economic opportunity. This approach greatly influenced later structuralist writings. Another was Gunnar Myrdal, the Swedish social scientist whose *American Dilemma* (1944) stressed the barriers to economic opportunity confronted by American Negroes. Myrdal emphasized that poverty was a "vicious cycle" that created a deprived "underclass." An optimist, he believed that public policy could break the vicious cycle at any of several points. Smash the structural barriers and the underclass could rise above itself.[46]

This structuralist approach had little impact on public policy in the 1940s. The debate in 1946 over the Employment Act was virtually silent on structural unemployment. Within a few years, however, the situation began to change slightly. Senator Paul Douglas of Illinois championed the cause of aid to depressed areas.[47] At the same time a congressional subcommittee headed by Senator John Sparkman of Alabama investigated "low income families." Using a poverty line of $2,000, the subcommittee found that 25 percent of families were poor in 1948 and 22 percent in 1955. It highlighted demographic trends such as the aging of the population and the rise in broken families and documented the high incidence of poverty among such groups. It emphasized also the prevalence of low-wage work. Staff reports of the committee stressed the concentration of income in the hands of a small percentage of families. These reports showed that millions of working families who were non-poor in one year were poor in the next. Low income was clearly a problem that plagued far more families than a one-year snapshot of poverty could expose.

The Sparkman committee's concern with "low income" was a significant step toward a no-nonsense, quantitative definition of poverty. It was resolutely economic in emphasis; it eschewed crude and subjective stereotypes; it linked poverty to the flaws in the marketplace; it placed the poor within the context of what the committee perceived as a maldistributed income structure; above all it suggested the desirability of policies placing a floor under income.[48] If Congress as a whole had heeded the committee—which it did not—it would have found itself forced to deal with a range of public policies promoting not only Keynesian fiscal measures and post-Keynesian growth economics but also much-expanded social services. Advocates of guaranteed minimum income in the 1960s and 1970s ultimately adopted the logic of this approach.

In 1958 John Kenneth Galbraith published *The Affluent Society*, the liveliest summary of structuralist thinking to that time. Repeating Myrdal and others, Galbraith reminded readers that the country confronted a vicious cycle of poverty. This cycle involved insular poverty (depressed areas), as well as case poverty affecting families without employable breadwinners. Galbraith went so far as to call attention to the inequality in American society and therefore to question purely absolute definitions of poverty. "People are poverty-stricken," he wrote, "when their income, even if adequate for survival, falls radically behind that of the community." This perspective took him beyond those Keynesians who hoped that counter-cyclical fiscal policy would promote economic progress. It led him to demand great increases in social services that would reduce the gap between the rich and the poor. In a hesitant way Galbraith anticipated the concern with egalitarianism that was to become a pronounced feature of social thought in the late 1960s and 1970s.

Many reviewers noticed that Galbraith did not carry his arguments about poverty very far. His poverty line for families was $1,000 per year, a cutoff that placed only 8 percent of the population in poverty. Activists complained that the line should have been at least as high as $2,000, at which point poverty might have measured 25 percent. Other critics thought he should have stressed even more the inequality in American society, instead of talking about the "affluence" and materialism of the middle classes.[49]

Galbraith's structuralism was nonetheless ahead of the times. Even then few people considered poverty and unemployment to be permanent problems, or wanted to believe that the economy was structurally unsound. This continuing optimism ensured that structuralist thinking had little impact on policy in the 1950s. One of President Kennedy's antipoverty warriors later regretted this: "I don't think any of us were using the term 'a structural approach'. . . . We were not talking about changing the nature of the organization of the society. . . . That's probably the Achilles heel of what we were attempting to do, in that we did not have a more solid structural framework for what we were about."[50]

Social problems of the late 1950s finally challenged the optimists who held to the withering away hypothesis. In particular the recession of 1958–59 made people doubt the automatic character of economic growth. Worse, these problems increased the burdens of public assistance. Between 1953 and 1961 the number of families receiving aid under the AFDC program increased from 543,000 to 921,000. In the face of such persistent need for public aid, a gradual though very slow reconsideration of poverty and lower-class life developed in the mid- and late 1950s.

This reconsideration, however, pursued familiar lines of thought. Leading social thinkers continued to emphasize that levels of prestige and status, not deep-seated economic inequality, stratified American society. They largely ignored blacks, whose frustrations were shortly to explode. A prominent sociologist, Robert Nisbet, concluded in 1959 that the United States was a consensual, largely egalitarian society. "As far as the bulk of Western society is concerned," he said, "and especially in the United States, the conception of class is largely obsolete."[51]

Those sociologists who did try to describe the poor entered a swamp. One observer correctly complained in 1965, "Until recent time insight into the 'lower lower class' has moved little beyond the broad sweeping descriptions provided by students of stratification over twenty-five years ago."[52] A common denominator of such academic discussion of the lower classes in the 1940s and 1950s was the idea that poor people belonged to "multiproblem families" that were "hard to reach" and psychologically "troubled." This view virtually ignored the problem of low income and studiously avoided talking about poverty. One critic observed acidly that this semantic mystification would soon result in designating poor people as "exceptional families."[53]

A similar perspective emphasized that the poor were present-minded—unable to "defer gratification." This view, an old one in American thought, gained strength from the growing vogue among social scientists at the time for psychological explanations. In the same vein writers purported to show that the poor were apathetic, lacking in self-confidence, ill-informed, socially disorganized, and sexually immoral—in short, denizens of a different, deviant culture.[54] This perspective did not usually portray poor people as potentially violent or dangerous; that stereotype became common again only in the 1960s. But the focus on apathy and present-mindedness was no less stereotypical and stigmatizing. Distorting the work of Whyte and others, this approach did not attempt to define or to understand the cultural traditions of different kinds of poor people. It settled rather for an old-fashioned, psychologically reassuring conclusion that there was a culture of poverty.

Ironically, it was a socialist of sorts, Michael Harrington, who unintentionally popularized some of these notions. Harrington was a structuralist. But like all activists, he wanted to dramatize his cause. He argued, therefore, that poverty was not only a "vicious cycle" but a "separate culture, another nation, with its own way of life. The poor are least capable of taking advantage of new opportunities, first to be struck down by social crisis."[55] His argument showed how easy it was for structuralists to employ very old and potentially stigmatizing notions about the poor.

Such talk about a "culture of poverty" unintentionally obscured structural flaws in the economy, but that was, of course, one reason why it enjoyed some appeal. Those who wanted to believe the worst of the poor, or to spend as little money as possible on welfare, could be comforted by the thought that the poor, after all, were to blame for their plight. It was natural for such middle-class observers to conclude that there were only two logical responses to poverty. One was to do nothing—after all, something as deep-rooted as a culture is not easily changed. The other was to try over time to eradicate that culture by changing people instead of the system. Even those who were aware of structural problems sought ways to make poor people into productive citizens who would no longer be a drain on the public treasury.

Senator Sparkman, while investigating low-income families, illustrated how liberal and structuralist premises could be bent to such purposes. The goal, he said in 1955, was to find ways "to help the low-income groups to help themselves." HEW Secretary Marion Folsom concurred. "I believe strongly, he said, "that all our policies and programs should have one emphasis: prevention and elimination of need rather than the mere relief of need after it develops." For Folsom and other experts, the goal was not abolition of poverty but prevention of dependency. In the 1950s, as throughout American history to that time, prevention was the basic alternative to costly welfare.[56] Significant changes in emphasis, first to expansion of "opportunity," then to income maintenance, awaited the much different era of the 1960s.

1. For Boulding see Herman P. Miller, ed., *Poverty, American Style* (Belmont, Calif., 1968), p. 49; for Miller, "Changes in the Number and Composition of the Poor," in Margaret S. Gordon, ed., *Poverty in America* (Berkeley, Calif., 1965), p. 81; for Bell, "Relevant Aspects of the Social Scene and Social Policy," in Eveline Burns, ed., *Children's Allowances and the Economic Welfare of Children* (New York, 1968), pp. 163–71. Similar judgments are expressed by Robert J. Lampman, the economist whose studies of income distribution provided a data base for the war on poverty, in "Ends and Means in the War against Poverty," in Leo Fishman, ed., *Poverty amid Affluence* (New Haven, Conn., 1966), pp. 18–42; Herbert Gans, "Culture and Class in the Study of Poverty," in Daniel Moynihan, ed., *On Understanding Poverty: Perspectives from the Social Sciences* (New York, 1968), pp. 201–28; and by Henry J. Aaron in his authoritative *Politics and the Professors: The Great Society in Perspective* (Washington, D.C., 1978), p. 17.

2. Gilbert Y. Steiner, *Social Insecurity: The Politics of Welfare* (Chicago, 1966), p. 190; Frederick Hayes, in "Poverty and Urban Policy: Conference Transcript of 1973 Group Discussion of the Kennedy Administration Urban Poverty Programs and Policies," 2 vols., John F. Kennedy Library, p. 67; Jack K. Roach and Janet K. Roach, eds., *Poverty* (London, 1972), p. 9; M. Elaine Burgess and Daniel O. Price, *An American Dependency Challenge* (Chicago, 1963), pp. 156–57. Also Elizabeth Wickenden to Alvin Schorr, 11 June 1959, National Social Welfare Assembly Papers, Box 61, Social Welfare History Archives, University of Minnesota (SWHA). She wrote, "Social work does not attract or produce many individuals who are gifted at the objective analysis and clear exposition of the social implications of the programs that determine and support the ultimate tasks of social work."

3. Important comparative perspectives are Henry J. Aaron, "Social Security: International Comparisons," in Otto Eckstein, ed., *Studies in the Economics of Income Maintenance* (Washington, D.C., 1967); Hugh Heclo, "Income Maintenance Patterns," in Arnold J. Heidenheimer, Hugh Heclo, and Carolyn Teich Adams, *Comparative Public Policy: The Politics of Social Choice in Europe and America* (New York, 1975), pp. 187–226; Gaston Rimlinger, *Welfare Policy and Industrialization in Europe, America, and Russia* (New York, 1971); Morris Janowitz, *Social Control of the Welfare State* (Chicago, 1976); and especially Harold Wilensky, *The Welfare State and Equality: Structural and Ideological Roots of Public Expenditures* (Berkeley, Calif., 1975). See also Jacqueline R. Kasun, "United States Poverty in World Perspective," *Current History* 64 (June 1973): 247 ff.; Martin Rein and Hugh Heclo, "What Welfare Crisis? A Comparison among the United States, Britain, and Sweden," *Public Interest* 33 (Fall 1973): 61–83; and Sidney E. Zimbalist, "Recent British and American Poverty Trends: Conceptual and Policy Contrasts," *Social Service Review* 51 (September 1977): 419–33.

4. *Religion and the Rise of Capitalism* (New York, 1926), p. 268.

5. Miller, "Changes," pp. 81–101. The following pages depend heavily on this article; on Miller, *Rich Man Poor Man* (New York, 1964), pp. 56–83; on Miller, "The Dimensions of Poverty," in Ben B. Seligman, ed., *Poverty as a Public Issue* (New York, 1965), pp. 20–51; on James N. Morgan et al., *Income and Welfare in the United States* (New York, 1962); on Oscar Ornati, *Poverty amid Affluence* (New York, 1966), esp. chap. 3; and on Council of Economic Advisers, "Problem of Poverty in America," *Economic Report of the President*

(Washington, D.C., 1964), pp. 55–83. Other relevant sources include Christopher Green, *Negative Taxes and the Poverty Problem* (Washington, D.C., 1967); Peter Townsend, "The Meaning of Poverty," *British Journal of Sociology* 13 (September 1962): 210–27; and Diana Karter Appelbaum, "The Level of the Poverty Line: A Historical Survey," *Social Service Review* 51 (September 1977): 514–23. All statistics used here concern the number who remained poor after public transfer payments. For Tobin see "It Can Be Done," *New Republic*, 3 June 1967, pp. 14–18.

6. Wilson C. McWilliams, "Poverty: Public Enemy Number One," *Saturday Review*, 10 December 1966, pp. 48 ff.; Miller, *Rich Man*, pp. 57–58.

7. J. Wayne Flynt, *Dixie's Forgotten People: The South's Poor Whites* (Bloomington, Ind., 1979), pp. 96–97; Miller, "Changes," pp. 81–101; Larry Long, *Interregional Migration of the Poor: Some Recent Changes*, Current Population Report, Census Bureau (November 1978).

8. *Low Income Families and Economic Stability: Materials on the Problem of Low Income Families*, Sen. Doc. 231, 81st Cong., 2d Sess., 1950; and *Report* of the Subcommittee on Low Income Families of the Joint Committee on the Economic Report, Sen. Doc. 146, 81st Cong., 1st Sess., March 1950. For 1963, figures used are those developed by the Council of Economic Advisers and pulled together conveniently in Mollie Orshansky, "Counting the Poor: Another Look at the Poverty Profile," *Social Security Bulletin* 28 (January 1965): 3–29. Orshansky's figures are widely used. Unless otherwise noted, figures deal with poverty in families, and do not include poverty of individuals not in families. Orshansky also reported statistics on poverty based on the Social Security Administration's so-called economy budget. These differ slightly from those used here.

9. *The Other America: Poverty in the United States* (New York, 1962).

10. Ornati, *Poverty*, p. 158.

11. For official methods see Orshansky, "Counting the Poor"; and Orshansky, "Who Was Poor in 1966?", in Burns, ed., *Children's Allowances*, pp. 19–57; for debates over measures see Orshansky, "Recounting the Poor—A Five Year Review," *Social Security Bulletin* (29 April 1966): 2–19; Orshansky, "How Poverty Is Measured," *Monthly Labor Review* 92 (February 1969): 37–41; Morton Paglin, "The Measurement and Trend of Inequality: A Basic Revision," *American Economic Review* 65 (September 1975): 598–609; Mayer N. Zald, "Demographics, Politics, and the Future of the Welfare State," *Social Service Review* 51 (March 1977): 110–24. See especially John B. Williamson and Kathryn M. Hyer, "The Measurement and Meaning of Poverty," *Social Problems* 22 (June 1975): 652–62; Joseph A. Kershaw, *Government against Poverty* (Washington, D.C., 1970), chap. 1; and Robert D. Plotnick and Felicity Skidmore, *Progress against Poverty: A Review of the 1964–1974 Decade* (New York, 1975), pp. 30–40.

12. M. Elaine Burgess, "Poverty and Dependency: Some Selected Characteristics," *Journal of Social Issues* 21 (January 1965): 79–97. See also *Characteristics of the Low Income Population*, pp. 1–5, 43–50; Morgan, *Income and Welfare*, pp. 216–17; and Robert H. Mugge, "Aid to Families with Dependent Children: Initial Findings of the 1961 Report on the Characteristics of AFDC Recipients," *Social Security Bulletin* 26 (March 1963): 3–15.

13. "Is There Really a New Poor?", *Dissent* 15 (January–February 1968): 59–64.

14. Aaron, *Politics and Professors*, p. 17.

15. Figures from U.S., Bureau of the Census, *Statistical History of the United States, Colonial Times to the Present* (Washington, D.C., 1976), pp. 340–41, 346–49, 356–57. See also Council of Economic Advisers, "Problems of Poverty," p. 68. Survivors insurance was not added to social security until 1939, aid to mothers of dependent children in 1950, disability insurance in 1956. In addition, the number receiving old age assistance ranged between 2 and 2.8 million between 1945 and 1960, and the number getting unemployment insurance between 1 and 1.5 million. Another 430,000 to 1.1 million got state-local general

assistance in those years. Private spending against poverty was around $3 billion in 1960, compared with $49 billion in public funds. See Ornati, *Poverty*, pp. 100, 105.

16. For a characteristic liberal critique, see Eveline Burns, *Social Security and Public Policy* (New York, 1956). Charles I. Schottland, *The Social Security Program in the United States* (New York, 1963), is factual. Martha Derthick, *Policymaking for Social Security* (Washington, D.C., 1979), is authoritative and absorbing.

17. Morgan, *Income and Welfare*, p. 216; Burgess and Price, *American Dependency Challenge*, pp. xii, 182; Winifred Bell, *Aid to Dependent Children* (New York, 1965), p. 204.

18. Ornati, *Poverty*, pp. 21–22; Charles Lebeaux, "Life on A.D.C.: Budgets of Despair," in Louis Ferman et al., *Poverty in America* (Ann Arbor, Mich., 1965), pp. 401–11; Mary Wright, "Public Assistance in the Appalachian South," *Journal of Marriage and the Family* 26 (November 1964): 406–9.

19. Margaret S. Gordon, *The Economics of Welfare Policies* (New York, 1963), chap. 2; Harold Wilensky, "The Problems and Prospects of the Welfare State," in Wilensky and C. N. Lebeaux, *Industrial Society and Social Welfare* (New York, 1965), pp. 157–59; Ida Merriam, "Social Welfare in the United States, 1934–54," *Social Security Bulletin* 18 (October 1955): 3–14; Kathleen Woodroofe, "The Making of the Welfare State in England: A Summary of Its Origin and Development," *Journal of Social History* 1 (Summer 1968): 303–24. Such studies did not ordinarily compare extents of need. The assumption— supported by the high percentages of poor people in America—was that need in the United States was as great as it was in Western Europe.

20. Martha Derthick, *The Influence of Federal Grants: Public Assistance in Massachusetts* (Cambridge, Mass., 1970), pp. 79–80.

21. Derthick, *Influence*, pp. 23, 87–89, 269; Ellen J. Perkins, "AFDC in Review, 1936–62," *Welfare in Review* 1 (November 1963): 1–16; U.S., Bureau of Public Assistance, *Families Receiving Aid to Dependent Children, Oct., 1942*, Part I, *Race, Size, and Composition of Families and Reasons for Dependency*, Report No. 7 (Washington, D.C., 1945); U.S., HEW, Bureau of Public Assistance, *Characteristics of State Public Assistance Plans under the Social Security Act*, Report No. 50 (Washington, D.C., 1962).

22. Bell, *Aid*, pp. 47–48, 77–87; Joel F. Handler and Ellen Jane Hollingsworth, "The Administration of Social Services and the Structure of Dependency: The Views of AFDC Recipients," *Social Service Review* 43 (December 1969): 406–20. It is worth noting that the effect of AFDC's denial of aid to families in which an unemployed parent lived in the home probably contributed only slightly to separations: see Heather L. Ross and Isabel V. Sawhill, *Time of Transition: The Growth of Families Headed by Women* (Washington, D.C., 1975), p. 177.

23. Titles from regional conference of American Public Welfare Assn. (APWA), Charleston, S.C., 25 September 1957, in Box 2, APWA Papers, SWHA.

24. Quote from editorial in *Social Work*, 1962, cited in Steiner, *Social Insecurity*, p. 188. See also Derthick, *Influence*, p. 135; Ernest Greenwood, "Social Science and Social Work: A Theory of Their Relationship," *Social Service Review* 29 (March 1955): 20–33; Roy Lubove, "The Welfare Industry: Social Work and the Life of the Poor," *Nation*, 23 May 1966, pp. 609–11; Charles O'Reilly, "Sociological Concepts and Social Work Theory," *American Catholic Historical Review* 21 (Fall 1960): 194–200; and especially Clarke A. Chambers, "Social Service and Social Reform: A Historical Essay," *Social Service Review* 37 (March 1963): 76–90; and Elizabeth Wickenden, "Social Security and Voluntary Social Welfare," *Industrial and Labor Relations Review* 14 (October 1960): 94–106.

25. Loula Dunn, speech, 4 March 1957, APWA Papers, Box 2, SWHA. For the work of the Committee on Social Issues and Policies, see National Assn. of Social Workers Papers, Box 45, SWHA. These files, and those in boxes 1–5 of the APWA, reveal the network of activists who intensified efforts for welfare reform after 1957. Important

among them were Elizabeth Wickenden, the chief Washington lobbyist, and Cohen, then teaching at the University of Michigan, and shortly to return to HEW in the Kennedy administration. Their efforts spearheaded the public welfare amendments of 1962.

26. Jacob Panken, "I Say Relief Is Ruining Families," *Saturday Evening Post*, 30 September 1950, pp. 25 ff.; Fletcher Knebel, "Welfare: Has It Become a Scandal?", *Look*, 7 November 1961, pp. 31–33 ff.; Rufus Jarman, "Detroit Cracks Down on Welfare Chiselers," *Saturday Evening Post*, 10 December 1949, pp. 19 ff. See also "Slums: An Encroaching Menace," *Life*, 11 April 1955, pp. 125–34; Raymond Moley, "Vanishing Proletariat," *Newsweek*, 19 January 1959, p. 92; Albert N. Votaw, "The Hillbillies Invade Chicago," *Harper's Magazine* 216 (February 1958): 64–67; Charles Stevenson, "When It Pays to Play Pauper," *Nation's Business* 38 (September 1950): 29 ff.

27. Sources attempting to quantify and to discriminate among attitudes are Michael E. Schiltz, *Public Attitudes toward Social Security, 1935–1965* (Washington, D.C., 1970); Gilbert Y. Steiner, *The State of Welfare* (New York, 1971); Joe R. Feagin, *Subordinating the Poor: Welfare and American Beliefs* (Englewood Cliffs, N.J., 1975); and Leonard Goodwin, *Do the Poor Want to Work? A Social-Psychological Study of Work Orientations* (Washington, D.C., 1972). Important articles include Zavada D. Blum and Peter H. Rossi, "Social Class Research and Images of the Poor: A Bibliographic View," in Moynihan, ed., *On Understanding Poverty*, pp. 343–97; David J. Kallen and Dorothy Miller, "Public Attitudes toward Welfare," *Social Work* 16 (July 1971): 83–90; John B. Williamson, "Beliefs about the Motivation of the Poor and Attitudes toward Poverty Policy," *Social Problems* 21 (June 1974): 635–48; and Williamson, "The Stigma of Public Dependency: A Comparison of Alternative Forms of Public Aid to the Poor," ibid., 22 (December 1974): 213–23. Also Gallup polls of 11 August 1961, and 15 December 1964.

28. Berkowitz, "American Disability System"; Burgess and Price, *American Dependency Challenge*, p. 186; Derthick, *Influence*, pp. 131–32; Charles E. Gilbert, "Policy-Making in Public Welfare: The 1962 Amendments," *Political Science Quarterly* 81 (June 1966): 196–224; Steiner, *Social Insecurity*, pp. 36–39; President's Office Files, Box 79, Kennedy Library.

29. *New York Times*, 27 July 1962.

30. **Psychological:** William Ryan, *Blaming the Victim*, rev. ed. (New York, 1976); Kai Erikson, *Wayward Puritans: A Study in the Sociology of Deviance* (New York, 1966); John P. Sisk, "The Specter of the Poor: Psychological Defenses in the War against Poverty," *Commonweal*, 25 June 1965, pp. 439 ff.; David Matza, "The Disreputable Poor," in Reinhard Bendix and Seymour Martin Lipset, eds., *Class, Status, and Power: Social Stratification in Comparative Perspective*, 2d ed. (New York, 1966), pp. 289–302; Lee Rainwater, "Neutralizing the Disinherited: Some Psychological Aspects of Understanding the Poor," in Vernon Allen, ed., *Psychological Factors in Poverty* (Chicago, 1970), pp. 9–28. **Economic:** Frances Fox Piven and Richard A. Cloward, *Regulating the Poor: The Functions of Public Welfare* (New York, 1971); Richard A. Cloward and Richard M. Elman, "Poverty, Injustice, and the Welfare State," *Nation*, 28 February 1966, pp. 230–35, and 7 March 1966, pp. 264–68; Marvin E. Gettleman, "Charity and Social Classes in the United States, 1874–1900," *American Journal of Economics and Sociology* 22 (April 1963): 313–30, and (July 1963): 417–26; James Weinstein, "Big Business and the Origins of Workmen's Compensation," *Labor History* 8 (Spring 1967): 156–74. **Social:** David Rothman, *The Discovery of the Asylum: Social Order and Disorder in the New Republic* (Boston, 1971): Roy Lubove, "Economic Security and Social Conflict in America," *Journal of Social History* 1 (Fall 1967): 61–87, and 1 (Summer 1968): 325–50; Kenneth Kusmer, "The Functions of Organized Charity in the Progressive Era: Chicago as a Case Study," *Journal of American History* 60 (December 1973): 657–78; Nathan I. Huggins, *Protestants against Poverty: Boston's Charities, 1870–1900* (Westport, Conn., 1971); Eric H. Monkkonen, *The Dangerous Class: Crime and Poverty in Columbus, Ohio, 1860–1885* (Cambridge, Mass., 1975).

31. **Racial:** Kenneth B. Clark, *Dark Ghetto: Dilemmas of Social Power* (New York, 1965). **Ethnic:** Gunnar Myrdal, *Beyond the Welfare State: Economic Planning and Its International Implications* (New Haven, Conn., 1960), pp. 53–55, 97–101; Nathan Glazer, "A Sociologist's View of Poverty," in Gordon, ed., *Poverty in America*, pp. 12–26. **Exceptionalist:** Oscar Handlin, "Poverty from the Civil War to World War II," in Fishman, ed., *Poverty amid Affluence*, pp. 3–17; R. Richard Wohl, "The 'Country Boy' Myth and Its Place in American Urban Culture: The 19th Century Contribution," *Perspectives in American History* 3 (1969): 77–158. **Ideological:** Daniel Rodgers, *The Work Ethic in Industrial America, 1850–1920* (Chicago, 1978). **Political:** Derthick, *Policymaking for Social Security*; Wilensky, *The Welfare State and Equality*, pp. 52, 70–73, 102–6; Wilbur Cohen, "Government Policy and the Poor: Past, Present, and Future," *Journal of Social Issues* 26 (March 1970): 1–10.

32. Relevant criticisms of such views are Gerald Grob, "Reflections on the History of Social Policy in America," *Reviews in American History* 7 (September 1979): 293–306; Eugene Durman, "Have the Poor Been Regulated? Toward a Multivariate Understanding of Welfare Growth," *Social Service Review* 47 (September 1973): 339–59; and William A. Muraskin, "The Social Control Theory in American History: A Critique," *Journal of Social History* 9 (Summer 1976): 559–68. Comparative views expose some flaws of single interpretations. See note 3, above, especially Aaron, Wilensky, and Heclo. Also T. H. Marshall, "The Welfare State: A Sociological Interpretation," *Archives Européenes de Sociologie* 2 (1961): 281–300.

33. John Garraty, *Unemployment in History: Economic Thought and Public Policy* (New York, 1978).

34. Daniel Nelson, *Unemployment Insurance: The American Experience, 1915–1935* (Madison, Wis., 1969); Roy Lubove, *Struggle for Social Security, 1900–1935* (Cambridge, Mass., 1968).

35. Hopkins, *Spending to Save* (Seattle, 1972), p. 142.

36. T. H. Marshall, *Class, Citizenship, and Social Development* (Garden City, N.Y., 1964), pp. 267–68, 293; J. F. Sleeman, *The Welfare State: Its Aims, Benefits, and Costs* (London, 1973), pp. 41–43.

37. "A Sociologist Looks at an American Community," *Life*, 9 September 1949, pp. 108–18.

38. A useful look at economic writing of the time is Gordon, *The Economics of Welfare Policies*, esp. pp. 46–50, 117–19.

39. Derthick, *Policymaking*, pp. 160, 216; Gilbert Y. Steiner, "Reform Follows Reality: The Growth of Welfare," *Public Interest* 36 (Winter 1974): 47–65.

40. Whyte, *Street Corner Society: The Social Structure of an Italian Slum* (Chicago, 1943); Bakke, *Unemployed Worker*. Regionalism, especially as explored by sociologists such as Howard Odum, was also sensitive to cultural and subcultural forces: see Mildred Mell, "Poor Whites of the South," *Social Forces* 17 (December 1938): 153–67; Odum, "The Way of the South," *Social Forces* 23 (March 1945): 258–68. The work of Robert Coles in the 1960s has stressed the importance of culture; for a sample see "Poor Don't Want to Be Middle Class," *New York Times Magazine*, (19 December 1965), pp. 7ff. See also Warner and P. S. Lunt, *The Social Life of a Modern Community* (New Haven, Conn., 1941).

41. Allison Davis, "Ability and Survival," *Survey* 87 (February 1951): 60–63. See also Davis and Robert J. Havighurst, "Social Class and Color Differences in Child Rearing"; and Davis, "The Motivation of the Underprivileged Worker," in W. F. Whyte, ed., *Individualism and Society* (New York, 1946); Warner, "Social Anthropology and the Modern Community," *American Journal of Sociology* 46 (May 1941): 785–96.

42. Ruth Rosner Kornhauser, "The Warner Approach to Social Stratification," in Bendix and Lipset, eds., *Class, Status, and Power*, pp. 224–55; C. Wright Mills, "The

Professional Ideology of Social Pathologists," *American Journal of Sociology* 49 (September 1943): 165–80; Harold W. Pfautz and Otis Dudley Duncan, "A Critical Evaluation of Warner's Work in Community Stratification," *American Sociological Review* 15 (April 1950): 205–16; Dennis Wrong, "The Failure of American Sociology," *Commentary* 28 (November 1959): 375–80.

43. NRPB, *Security, Work, and Relief Policies* (Washington, D.C., 1942), pp. 24, 42, 130–33, 446–47, 518; Howard, *WPA*, passim; Joanna C. Colcord, *Cash Relief* (New York, 1936); F. Stuart Chapin and Stuart A. Queen, *Research Memorandum on Social Work in the Depression* (New York, 1937); WPA, *Urban Workers on Relief* (Washington, D.C., 1936); Barry D. Karl, *Charles E. Merriam and the Study of Politics* (Chicago, 1974), pp. 276–77. See also "American Assn. for Social Workers Platform on the Public Social Activities," May 1944, NASW Papers, Folder 238, SWHA; and Social Security Board, "An Expanded Social Security Program," 29 September 1941, OF 1710, Box 3, Franklin D. Roosevelt Library. For FDR's speech see Samuel Rosenman, comp., *Public Papers and Addresses of Franklin D. Roosevelt*, vol. 12 (N.Y., 1950), pp. 40–41.

44. Edward D. Berkowitz, "The American Disability System in Historical Perspective," in Berkowitz, ed., *Disability Politics and Government Programs* (New York, 1979), pp. 16–74. Quotation by I. S. Falk is on p. 34.

45. Eveline Burns, *Social Security and Public Policy* (New York, 1956); Daniel S. Sanders, *The Impact of Reform Movements on Social Policy Change: The Case of Social Insurance* (Fair Lawn, N.J., 1973); Charles Schottland, *The Social Security Program in the United States* (New York, 1963).

46. Merton, "Social Structure and Anomie," in Merton, *Social Theory and Social Structure*, rev. enl. ed. (Glencoe, Ill., 1957), pp. 131–60; Myrdal, *American Dilemma: The Negro Problem and Modern Democracy* (New York, 1944). See also Robert Heilbroner, "Who Are the American Poor?", *Harper's Magazine* 200 (June 1950: 27 ff.

47. James L. Sundquist, *Politics and Polity: The Eisenhower, Kennedy, and Johnson Administrations* (Washington, D.C., 1968), pp. 57–110; Ornati, *Poverty amid Affluence*, pp. 82–84.

48. See note 8, above. Also Joint Committee on the Economic Report, Subcommittee on Low Income Families, *Characteristics of the Low Income Population and Related Federal Programs*, 84th Cong., 1st Sess., 1955.

49. Galbraith Papers, Box 123, Kennedy Library, conveniently collect reviews of the book. See especially the exchange of letters between Galbraith and the economist Leon Keyserling (Box 38).

50. Sanford Kravitz, "Policy and Urban Policy," Kennedy Library, pp. 56–57.

51. Nisbet, "The Decline and Fall of Social Class," *Pacific Historical Review* 2 (Spring 1959): 11–17. See also Walter R. Goldschmidt, "Social Class in America: A Critical Review," *American Anthropologist* 52 (October–December 1950): 483–98; and Gerhard Lenski, "American Social Classes: Statistical Strata or Social Groups?", *American Journal of Sociology* 58 (September 1952): 139–44.

52. Burgess, "Poverty and Dependency," p. 80. A useful book is Milton Gordon, *Social Class in Modern Sociology* (New York, 1958).

53. Matza, "Disreputable Poor."

54. For example, the much-reprinted article, Genevieve Knupfer, "Portrait of an Underdog," *Public Opinion Quarterly* 9 (Spring 1947): 103–14. Subtler arguments that stress the particular values of lower-class people are Herbert H. Hyman, "The Value Systems of Different Classes: A Social-Psychological Contribution to the Analysis of Stratification," in Bendix and Lipset, eds., *Class, Status, and Power*, pp. 426–41; and Walter B. Miller, "Lower Class Culture as a Generating Milieu of Gang Delinquency," *Journal of Social Issues* 14 (1958): 5–19. An evaluation of such arguments is in Ellen Ryerson, *The Best-Laid Plans: America's Juvenile Court Experiment* (New York, 1978), pp. 126–28.

55. Harrington, "Our 50 Million Poor: Forgotten Men in the Affluent Society," *Commentary* 28 (July 1959): 22. Talk of a "culture of poverty" dominated debate in the early 1960s: see Oscar Lewis, *La Vida: A Puerto Rican Family in the Culture of Poverty—San Juan and New York* (New York, 1965), pp. xli–lii. Later criticisms of that concept include Hylan Lewis, "Culture of Poverty? What Does It Matter?", in Eleanor Leacock, ed., *Culture of Poverty* (New York, 1971), pp. 345–63; and Charles Valentine, *Culture and Poverty: Critique and Counterproposals* (Chicago, 1968). Balanced views are Lee Rainwater, "The Lower Class Culture and Poverty-War Strategy," in Moynihan, ed., *On Understanding Poverty*, pp. 229–59; Hyman Rodman, "The Lower Class Value Stretch," *Social Forces* 42 (December 1963): 205–15; and especially Elliot Liebow, *Tally's Corner: A Study of Negro Streetcorner Men* (Boston, 1967).

56. *Low Income Families*, U.S. Senate, Hearings, November 1955, pp. 2, 9, 709. Also Folsom, "Cut the Roots of Poverty," *Business Week*, (24 December 1955), pp. 60–64. See also Roswell Perkins, "New Challenges in Public Welfare," 15 October 1956, APWA Papers, Box 1, SWHA. ("In these enlightened, relatively prosperous times, we should be concerned with the *prevention* of dependency rather than just palliative measures—however worthy—after dependency has occurred.")

Education: Schools as Crucible in Cold War America

Ronald Lora

Few Americans knew in 1945 and 1946 that they were about to enter the most confusing and demanding years in the history of American education. To the informed, however, World War II had revealed weaknesses in the nation's schools that would prove intolerable in a protracted cultural and military conflict. Positive developments, too, would compel a fundamental reorientation of purpose and method: the United States was reaffirming its democratic commitment to educate all the nation's young people; student enrollment was increasing enormously; and parents continued to utilize the schools as a means of propelling their children up the ladder of success. The cold war exacerbated existing problems and added others, particularly those involving defense needs and the relationship between educational institutions and the federal government. The purpose of this paper is to discuss the impact of the cold war on American education, with primary emphasis on the secondary schools.[1]

The American public school system is a striking social invention. Never before had a nation employed an educational system to provide its children a more equal chance in life. But differing ideologies can quickly convert a free public school system into a battleground over objectives. Since the earliest days of the Republic, American education not only taught the basics of reading, writing, and arithmetic but also attempted to Americanize millions of immigrants, inculcate the ideals of democracy and equality, create national unity, and facilitate the adjustment of a rural population to industrial and urban life. Early in this century it was widely believed that public education could improve the efficiency of industrial society by creating a disciplined labor force and by channeling students into needed roles. Schools advanced the ideology of private enterprise and served as guardians of health and morals. Long before the ill-fated life-adjustment movement, schools were to develop vocational and homemaking skills, solve boy and girl problems, and provide recreation and entertainment. By the late 1940s growing numbers of parents and educators feared that since societal needs had changed, the schools no longer were providing children with the requisite skills and attitudes for either individual or national well-being. Critics said that education had become flabby, soft, attuned to life-adjustment rather than life-enhancement. Many generations of Americans had assumed that when individual welfare was pursued, the social order itself was enhanced. The cold war, and especially the Soviet success with Sputnik, diminished somewhat the concern for individual goals and brought to the fore the claims of the nation. Defense needs coalesced with the pursuit of excellence to restructure American education, a process that began in earnest in the 1950s and took more than a decade to consolidate.

It should be emphasized for historical perspective that the cold war was the third grave crisis to hit American education in less than twenty years. The first, the long depression of the 1930s, had wreaked havoc on the nation's schools: it proved impossible for local communities to provide adequate staffing and classrooms; many teachers received irregular payments; the quality of instruction declined as vacancies sometimes were filled by accepting the lowest bidder. Throughout the decade expenditures per pupil were lower than they had been in 1929, for the mechanisms facilitating adjustment to financial exigencies did not exist.[2] Inequalities were ubiquitous, existing in expenditures per pupil; expenditures on equipment, instructional materials, and health and welfare services; teacher's salaries; the length of the school year; the percentage of pupils per age grouping in high school; and the value of school property. Variations on each of these items existed not only between states but within states, and were particularly marked in rural areas.[3]

World War II marked the second crisis for education. Its enormous impact on educational practices and on attitudes regarding appropriate relationships between education and the state was signalized by the many ways in which the schools served national needs from 1941 through 1945.[4] Depending on location, facilities, and defense needs, schools offered summer programs, provided round-the-clock use of vocational school equipment to train men and women for wartime production, and retrained workers dislocated in the conversion of industrial plants to defense production. School programs emphasized health and physical fitness, and safety from war hazards. The Red Cross and civil defense groups utilized school facilities; war workers and servicemen in need of temporary housing sometimes did likewise. Operating out of school buildings, the federal government registered millions of men for Selective Service, sold $2 billion worth of war bonds and stamps, and distributed 415,000,000 ration books. School savings plans enlisted the participation of 25,000,000 students. Thus, for five years the public schools operated on a war footing, providing the nation with nearly every service that could be imagined.[5]

The war also revealed serious deficiencies. As late as 1945–46, 50 percent of elementary and secondary school teachers received less than $2,000 per year, 16 percent less than $1,200 per year. Consequently, teacher shortages were the most immediate consequence of war as more than 350,000 teachers left their profession forever—some to enter the services, most to work in wartime factories. Not only were insufficient numbers educated in mathematics, science, English, and history, but conceptual frameworks were years out of date, particularly in math and science. Millions of young men, moreover, were rejected for military service. The Selective Service revealed to a surprised public the sobering statistics: 676,000 men rejected for mental or educational deficiencies, a substantial minority of whom had completed less than five years of school, and 350,000 registrants for the draft who could not sign their names. Tens of thousands had to be taught basic literary skills after induction into the armed services. Table 1 details the reasons for the rejection of 4,458,000 eighteen- to thirty-seven-year-olds by the end of 1944.[6]

Under these circumstances, the normal functioning of educational

TABLE 1

PRINCIPAL CAUSES FOR REJECTION	NUMBER			PERCENTAGE		
	Total	White	Negro	Total	White	Negro
Manifestly disqualifying defects	469,300	405,800	63,500	10.5	11.3	7.3
Mental diseases	759,600	671,000	88,600	17.1	18.7	10.2
Mental deficiency	620,100	340,700	279,400	13.9	9.5	32.1
Physical defects	2,542,000	2,116,600	425,400	57.9	59.0	48.9
Nonmedical	67,000	53,900	13,100	1.5	1.5	1.5

institutions was impossible. For the second time in a quarter-century, Americans were asked to accommodate even their most prized institutions to the demands of war mobilization. Attitudes forged in the grueling experience of total war proved difficult to eradicate and continued into the postwar period with scarcely a hitch. They well may have expressed themselves in policy formation regardless of the specific Soviet threat that emerged. To believe otherwise is to deny the powerful legacy of war in our recent history and to ignore the important ways in which it has shaped social policy.

At V-J Day educators believed that America faced an auspicious moment in the history of democracy. The armies of fascism had been routed, and the longing for freedom and independence stirred the souls of people everywhere. Although darkening clouds of other authoritarian systems loomed on the horizon, political and educational leaders occasionally spoke as if an "American century" were at hand. The institutions of free public education, moreover, would contribute significantly to this new and better world.

This roseate vision soon collapsed in crisis. As the cold war grew in intensity and anxiety over the use of atomic weapons deepened, the world seemed ever less amenable to American ambitions: the two superpowers could not agree on the shape of the postwar world; the Soviet Union subjected Eastern Europe to military control, exploded an A-bomb in 1949 and an H-bomb four years later; populous China turned Communist. Spies had infiltrated American defense installations and the State Department, or so Americans read in the newspapers. When North Korean troops entered South Korea in June 1950, Americans surmised that the invasion prefigured Soviet and Communist expansion elsewhere in the world. Seven years later, with the launching of Sputnik, the event most immediately responsible for the revamping of American education, new fears arose, especially among conservative groups, that the United States was actually losing the cold war.

Center-stage among American anxieties was Communism, more particularly the Soviet Union. The swift revival of traditional American hostility to Soviet Communism gave a decidedly negative tone to the postwar debate on education. How far could the educational system be used to solve noneducational problems and still retain its educational integrity? As one educator put it, is an educational system that tries to solve the problem of unemployment, or acts as an aid to agriculture, or as "a basic resource of national defense, something different from what it has been in the past?" Are the values and purposes of "a basic resource of national defense" similar to those of an educational system that does not serve as such?[7] Everywhere there emerged charges of Communist party subversion and questions about teacher loyalty. In a world that witnessed genocide, slave labor camps, the terrors of *Gleichschaltung*, and the subversions of fifth columnists, it is understandable that loyalty should have concerned Americans. But old beliefs and past associations, however innocent and long-repudiated, could, when pursued to unreasonable lengths of inquiry, endanger lives. It was just, and obligatory, for civil libertarians to insist that the search for domestic subversives operate on the basis of evidence. One tragedy of the new age of suspicion was that self-anointed keepers of the nation's ideological health so often had no evidence, or had evidence of a very specious sort.

For teachers the baptism of fire awaited 1948 when it became clear how vulnerable they were to the social and political forces shaping (and distorting) postwar society.[8] Community-centered, the public schools depended on local taxes and were controlled by elected boards, making them extraordinarily sensitive to organized pressures. Not surprisingly, voter sentiments reflected the structure of the tax base and the economic conditions of the community. Superimposed on local problems were national and international issues. Groups made tense by expansive communism, military alliances, and racial integration could do little about the president, Congress, and the Supreme Court, the state legislature and judicial system, but they could vent effectively their frustrations on the schools. Bringing a deeply emotional bias, at once frenetic and poignant, to the questions of curriculum and educational policies, they made the schools centers of intense political debate and conflict.

Among the signs that troubled times lay ahead for education was a pamphlet published by the House Committee on Un-American Activities (HCUA), "100 Things You Should Know about Communism and Education." Chaired by J. Parnell Thomas (N.J.) and energized by such red-baiting members as Karl E. Mundt (S.D.) and Richard M. Nixon (Calif.), the HCUA distributed hundreds of thousands of this pamphlet that linked national politics to subversives in the schools and included scurrilous propaganda simplicities like the following:

Q. What is Communism?
A. A conspiracy to conquer and rule the world by any means.
Q. Is it aimed at me?
A. Right between your eyes.
Q. What do the Communists want?
   a. To rule your mind and your body from the cradle to the grave.
   b. Power; Communists all have a craze for power.

Q. How can I tell a Communist?

A. A Communist will criticize the President of the United States of America, but not Stalin.

Q. Are there many Communist fronts and fellow travelers in the United States school system?

A. There are, and they are a deadly danger.

Q. What's biting these people, anyhow?

A. Here is at least one part of the answer given by John Hanna, a professor of Columbia University. "The girls' schools and women's colleges contain some of the most loyal disciples of Russia." "Teachers there are often frustrated females. They have gone through bitter struggles to attain their positions." "A political dogma based on hatred expresses their personal attitudes."

Q. You mean there are actually Communist schools in this country?

A. Yes.

Q. Do many of our teachers play the Communist game?

A. The files of our Committee show that the Communists have always found the teaching group the easiest touch of all the professional classes.[9]

Thousands of copies were distributed to schools, a few of which used it as a sociology text. Such activities made the HCUA the first symbol of a new American witch hunt,[10] soon termed McCarthyism.

Professors were among the first to face the cold war inquisition. A significant test of academic freedom began in March 1948 at the University of Washington, where six tenured members of the faculty were charged with past or present membership in the Communist party. After a short but exceedingly rancorous struggle that featured savage denunciation and the browbeating of professors, three of the accused were dismissed and three suspended. The issue debated was not whether they were Communists (several admitted as much), but whether they could be objective teachers. Yet dismissal and suspension came not because of their teaching records, which were good, but because they were judged heretics by an administration intolerant of their economic philosophies.[11] From the University of Washington, the testing of academic freedom spread to Oregon State College, the Massachusetts Institute of Technology, Evansville College, the University of Kansas City, Rutgers University, and elsewhere.[12] No complete count exists of teachers and professors who lost their jobs through dismissal, suspension, refusal to take loyalty oaths, or resignation following harrassment, but the number runs well into the thousands. The California Senate Un-American Activities Committee announced in March 1953 that, in the previous ten months alone, more than a hundred California teachers and professors were dismissed or had resigned because of alleged Communist activities.[13]

Meanwhile, the proximate event that caused public school administrators and teachers to shudder was the firing (forced resignation) of Dr. Willard E. Goslin, superintendent of schools in Pasadena, California. A leading advocate of progressive education, Goslin had a national reputation, having been elected president of the American Association of School Administrators in 1948, the year he arrived in Pasadena. The immediate issue of a tax proposal facing the new superintendent was soon eclipsed by others of greater political consequence, including the purpose of school expenditures, alleged Communist party infiltration of the schools, and the candidacy of two socialists in the school board election. When it became widely known in the community that Goslin had invited William Heard Kilpatrick, of Columbia Teachers College, to a teacher-training workshop, opponents mounted a campaign against progressive education, arguing that it was part of a plan to bring collectivism to America. Additionally, desegregation formed a controversial part of the superintendent's plans for the Pasadena school system. With these emotional issues muddying the currents of discussion, few could have been surprised in 1950 when Pasadenians defeated the tax measure and called for Goslin's dismissal.

Dissatisfied with general news accounts of the episode, the investigative reporter David Hulburd began asking questions. In early 1951 he published *This Happened in Pasadena*, which demonstrated the intense involvement of Allen Zoll's National Council for American Education, an outside organization concerned with alleged Communist infiltration of the schools. Zoll's organization supplied Goslin's opponents with pamphlets linking progressivism with crime, juvenile delinquency, and Communism. That kind of misinformation and unsupported allegation intensified emotions, spread suspicion, and, in the end, set neighbor against neighbor.[14]

The intervention of organized, right-wing national groups in local matters represented a spreading phenomenon of cold war America. The most common assertions of rightist groups were that the schools harbored either Communists or Communist sympathizers, that they cost too much money, and that they failed to teach the three Rs properly. Two leading organizations were the Friends of the Public Schools of America and the aforementioned National Council for American Education (NCAE). Allen Zoll, who served the NCAE as executive vice-president, was a Fascist propagandist and head of American Patriots, an organization the U.S. attorney general named as subversive. The NCAE published a monthly bulletin, *Educational Guardian*, and a "Red-ucator" series that purported to reveal Communist party influences at numerous universities. Among the more famous NCAE pamphlets were "How Red Are the Schools?", "The Commies Are after Your Kids," and "Progressive Education Increases Juvenile Delinquency."[15]

Other influential groups included the American Education Association, Church League of America, Conference of American Small Business Organizations Committee on Education (sponsor of *Educational Reviewer*, a right-wing review of textbooks edited by Lucille Cardin Crain), and Employers Association of Chicago, publishers of "How Red Is the Little Red School House?" The Committee for Constitutional Government, opposed to welfare statism, collectivism, and Marxism in America, distributed thousands of copies of right-wing books such as John T. Flynn's *The Roosevelt Myth* (1948) and *The Road Ahead: America's Creeping Revolution* (1949) and cooperated with dozens of smaller organizations to warn Americans of spreading socialism. The National Economic Council, a nationalist-isolationist group headed by Merwin K. Hart and similar to the Committee for Constitutional Government, opposed immigration, public housing, TVA, the UN, civil rights measures, federal aid to education, and, like every group, Communist influence in the schools. Groups effective in assorted local campaigns were the Daughters of the American Revolution, the Sons of the American Revolution, the Anti-Communist League of America, Defenders of American Education, and the American Coalition of Patriotic Societies.

The rightist groups leading the bitter assault on the nation's schools also worked tenaciously to pass state loyalty oath statutes for teachers. Oath statutes passed during the 1920s and 1930s were reaffirmed after World War II, with laggard states adding new ones. By 1953 thirty-two states had passed loyalty oath legislation. Counting states not singling out teachers, the number rises to thirty-six, or 75 percent of the states. (Most statutes enacted after 1947, however, referred specifically to teachers.) In addition, twenty-six states expressly prohibited subversives from teaching.[16] The belief that teachers were peculiarly vulnerable to the blandishments of radicals was one of the many unfounded suppositions of McCarthyism.

Criticism of teacher loyalty and the curriculum spread to textbooks and supplementary reading materials. All over the land, boards of education, citizen groups, and Parent-Teacher Associations examined reading materials for indications of political and moral waywardness. In one case (frequently ridiculed, later), *Robin Hood* was removed from Indiana school libraries on the conjecture that the story supported Communist party doctrine. In Los Angeles rightist pressure groups, supported by the Hearst press, succeeded in forcing the removal of UNESCO materials from the classrooms. D. H. Lawrence's *Studies in Classic American Literature* proved unacceptable reading for Houston high-schoolers; suspension awaited two teachers who read passages to students.

The battle of the books that rocked Scarsdale, New York, betokened the irrational character of the subversive reading phenomenon. Scarsdale was not a community likely to succumb to communist ideas. Extremely wealthy and heavily Republican, it was the home of numerous front-rank Manhattan executives. One Manhattan banker, long interested in Communist party front organizations, discovered in the school library ten books by Howard Fast and one by Anna Louise Strong, still favorites of leftist readers. That discovery, together with subsequent demands for the removal of various volumes, including novels, biographies, and texts, soon entangled the entire community of 14,500 people. School board meetings were further enlivened when the Reverend William C. Kernan joined the crusade to cleanse the libraries. Communism, he declared, was the antithesis of Christianity, and he saw it on the rise in the heavily conservative community. To one questioner who had asked what lay behind the house-cleaning crusade, he answered: "What's behind this is to keep Communism out of the Scarsdale school system. It's already there and you don't know Communism when you see it."[17] After the teachers themselves fell under suspicion of disloyalty, Scarsdale became a community on fire, fueled by petition and counterpetition, and embittered by gratuitous charges and countercharges.

Eventually, Scarsdale concluded that whatever the political and social preferences of the authors, exposure to books was a better risk than censorship. But it stood as a warning to other communities, such as Port Washington, New York; Denver, Colorado; Eugene, Oregon; Englewood, New Jersey; Richland, Washington; Houston, Texas; Little Rock, Arkansas; and Lafayette, Indiana—many of which concluded otherwise. These cities were but a few of the communities that stood out in the nationwide anxiety over Communist infiltration of the schools and the textbook industry. Here again, nationwide organizations played an important role. Lucille Cardin Crain, secretary of the Conference of American Small Business Organizations Committee on Education, drew attention in her newsletter, *Educational Reviewer*, to books that undermined the free enterprise system or failed to criticize the Soviet economy and government. With Allen Zoll and hundreds of other active guardians of the American verities, she contributed to the dark shadow of suspicion and distrust that characterized McCarthyism.

The numerous national groups, to be sure, reflected various concerns.

Some proclaimed economic freedom to be their goal; others, political liberty. Still others defended exclusive versions of Americanism. Yet, when reading the enormous literature, it is clear that variations were a matter of degree only; that though indeed fearful of Communist subversion, the guardians of rectitude manipulated those fears to justify fierce attacks on social and economic experiments of which they disapproved, such as the New Deal, Wagner Act, TVA, UN, Social Security, and the progressive income tax.[18] The literature reveals the hatred with which the Right viewed Franklin D. Roosevelt and the New Deal, a hatred by groups apprehensive of fundamental social change and willing to use the loyalty issue not only against subversives, who were seldom found, but against proponents of progressive education, liberals, welfare statists, intellectuals, and strikers.[19] The genuine poignance of the situation, when it was that, may move us to empathy; but the confusion, anger, oppressive tactics, and willingness to tamper with the schools revealed an appalling readiness to sacrifice children's education to adult anxieties.

Not all the forces affecting education were ideological, however. Other powerful pressures for educational reform existed quite independent of cold war matters. The public realized that the postwar baby boom necessitated new school construction and the hiring of more teachers, but it was unprepared for the spiraling numbers that ensued. Total school enrollment, virtually unchanged for twenty years, in the 1950s expanded by 13 million pupils (table 2). Much of this increase came at the lower levels. Enrollment in kindergarten and grades one through eight, stable in the 1940s, jumped by more than 10 million in the 1950s. The twentieth century provided no precedent for such growth, a veritable explosion that meant heavier financial burdens for states and local communities. After tripling in the 1940s, state revenues for public schools increased by another 166 percent in the following decade. Local revenues doubled in the 1940s, then in the 1950s nearly tripled (table 3). Expenditures per pupil enrolled in public schools leaped 370 percent from $92 in 1940 to $433 two decades later (table 2).

Enrollment growth in higher education outstripped even that in the public schools, rising from 1.5 million in 1940 to 2.6 million in 1950 and to more than 3.2 million in 1960 (table 4). Measured as a percentage of population, ages 18–21, higher education enrollment rose from 15.6 percent (1940) to 36.6 percent (1960). Expenditures burgeoned from $758 million in 1946 to $6.6 billion in 1960, a hefty 773 percent increase (table 4). The explosive growth of higher education during the late 1940s was largely attributable to government policies, especially the G.I. Bill

TABLE 2

ELEMENTARY AND SECONDARY SCHOOLS
ENROLLMENT, ATTENDANCE, AND EXPENDITURES, 1870–1960[20]

School Years Ending	Total Enrollment (Public and Nonpublic Schools)	Enrollment in Public Schools			Enrollment in Nonpublic Schools	Public School Attendance		Expenditures	
		Total	Kindergarten and Grades 1–8	Grades 9–12 and Post-graduates		Average Length of School Term (Days)	Average Number of Days Attended per Enrolled Pupil	Total Expenditures in the Educational System (millions of Dollars)	Expenditure per pupil Enrolled in Public Schools (Dollars)
1870	....	6,871,522	7,481,355 (1871)	80,227 (1871)	....	132.2	78.4	....	9
1900	16,854,832	15,503,110	14,983,859	519,251	1,351,722	144.3	99.0	....	14
1910	19,372,289	17,813,852	16,898,791	915,061	1,558,437	157.5	113.0	480	24
1920	23,277,797	21,578,316	19,377,927	2,200,389	1,699,481	161.9	121.2	1,036	48
1930	28,329,059	25,678,015	21,278,593	4,399,422	2,651,044	172.7	143.0	2,604	90
1940	28,044,589	25,433,542	18,832,098	6,601,444	2,611,047	175.0	151.7	2,594	92
1950	28,491,566	25,111,427	19,386,806	5,724,621	3,380,139	177.9	157.9	6,673	232
1960	41,762,000	36,087,000	27,602,000	8,485,000	5,675,000	178	160.2	18,105	433

TABLE 3

PUBLIC ELEMENTARY AND SECONDARY SCHOOLS: REVENUE
BY SOURCE OF FUNDS, 1920–1960[21]
(Dollar amounts in millions)

SCHOOL YEAR ENDING	TOTAL REVENUE	FEDERAL		STATE		INTERMEDIATE AND LOCAL SOURCES	
		Amount	Percentage	Amount	Percentage	Amount	Percentage
1920	$ 970	$ 2	0.2	$ 160	16.5	$ 808	83.3
1930	2,089	7	0.4	354	16.9	1,727	82.7
1940	2,261	40	1.8	684	30.3	1,536	68.0
1950	5,437	156	2.9	2,166	39.8	3,116	57.3
1960	14,747	652	4.4	5,768	39.1	8,327	56.5

TABLE 4

HIGHER EDUCATION:
EXPENDITURES, ENROLLMENT, AND GRADUATES
1920–1960[22]
(Dollar amounts in millions)

SCHOOL YEAR ENDING	TOTAL EXPENDITURES, CAPITAL OUTLAY, AND INTEREST			ENROLLMENT	HIGHER EDUCATION ENROLLMENT AS PERCENTAGE OF POPULATION, Age 18–21	GRADUATES
	Total	Public	Private			
1920	$ 267	$ 116	$ 151	597,880	8.1	48,622
1930	632	289	343	1,100,737	12.4	122,484
1940	758	392	367	1,494,203	15.6	186,500
1950	2,662	1,430	1,233	2,659,021	27.2	432,058
1960	6,616	3,753	2,864	3,236,000	36.6	392,440

of Rights (officially known as the Servicemen's Readjustment Act of 1944). Enacted by Congress without a dissenting vote and signed by President Roosevelt just two weeks after the Normandy invasion, the act reflected national concern over the welfare of veterans. Sponsors feared that returning GIs, having already sacrificed a normal civilian life, in addition would have to face unemployment. College-bound veterans, therefore, were offered subsistence allowances and payments of tuition fees and school supplies. The response far surpassed expectations. In the 1949–50 academic year, for example, higher education enrolled 2,659,000 students, of whom veterans numbered 853,000, or nearly one-third of the total enrollment. Overall, approximately 7,800,000 veterans went to school under the G.I. Bill at a cost to the government of $14.5 billion. Inasmuch as the education provisions were part of a larger program that included medical benefits, home and business loans, and help in securing employment, the wartime act did not signal a special commitment to the principle of federal aid for all deserving college students.[23] As an investment in democracy and jobs, as well as education, the G.I. Bill was one of the wisest wartime decisions of the U.S. government.[24] Yet it was a harbinger of later federal-collegiate relations in that higher education passively accepted a momentous program that the federal government had determined was in the national interest.

The foregoing transformations helped generate a national debate over teacher shortages, school construction (which during hostilities had slowed to a virtual standstill), districting, and racial segregation.[25] The questions were as numerous as they were difficult. What kind of education was appropriate for masses of students? What constituted quality in mid-twentieth-century America? Now that a commitment to educate all had been made, could all potential students be reached? What about problem students? Gifted students? Should students be taught to resist communism or merely enabled to understand it, thereby betting that free choices would strengthen national loyalties? How should subject areas, having grown complex, be taught? It is little wonder that education became a major battleground in postwar America. The cold war created none of these problems but exacerbated all of them by providing an environment of anxiety coupled with a sense of national urgency that otherwise would have been absent.

With the education question becoming a central problem of cold war America, educational organizations were forced to respond. The largest and most influential of the organizations, the National Education Association (NEA), took its stand in June 1949 when its Educational Policies Commission (chaired by John Norton of Columbia Teachers College and including such luminaries as James B. Conant and Dwight D. Eisenhower) published a remarkable fifty-four-page pamphlet entitled "American Education and International Tensions." The pamphlet revealed the thinking of leading educators on communism, the cold war, and the relationship of education to both. The educators drew attention to major paradoxes of the cold war: the world was split asunder at the very time that science and technology had made the "world seem small and compact"; amid talk of peace went furious preparations for war. These formed the major realities around which educational policy must evolve, perhaps for the remainder of the century.[26]

Despite its brevity the report sought balance. The major sources of fear were to be found in the new weaponry that threatened not only soldiers but entire populations, surging population growth, and world-wide economic dislocations. Vast, inequitable disparities of resources would in all probability "keep the world in a state of cold war for years to come." On the other hand, the educators saw reason for hope. Acknowledging that nationalism, at its worst fanatical, irresponsible, and arrogant, would continue, they argued that it represented "the most massive achievement to date in widening the areas of law and unity." There was no inherent need to fear the dissolution of old empires and emergence of new nations as long as the developing nations avoided entanglement in great power rivalries. Technology could be a healing instrument for removing ancient causes of misery. Trade, transportation, and new developments in communications technology together with the vast network of international machinery ranging from the United Nations to the Organization of American States were strong forces of interdependence uniting men and nations. Although the future would be shaped by the decisions of governments, "the prospect is that the present pattern of East-West tensions will continue indefinitely without armed conflict." On the educational matter most on the public mind—loyalty and subversion in the schools—little was said. The report's most significant recommendation was firm, however, and stated twice: "Members of the Communist Party of the United States should not be employed as teachers."[27]

Approval was swift. President Truman endorsed the report the day after U.S. Commissioner of Education Earl McGrath presented it to him. A month later the eighty-seventh annual convention of the NEA, amid a tumultuous session in Boston, overwhelmingly endorsed the report. There was little doubt that the NEA, never in its history a conspicuous champion of academic freedom, had made a peace offering to the anti-Communist critics of public education.[28]

Two-and-a-half years later, the Educational Policies Commission and the American Council on Education, with funding from the Carnegie Corporation, published a second pamphlet, "Education and National Security," describing the nature of American international obligations and suggesting ways in which education at all levels could contribute to the national effort. It spoke of great stresses on American society during the recent hazardous years: political confusion and division, the expensive armaments program, failures in public and private morals, and increasing "sensuality and materialism." Worse, "America faces the problem of treason in a degree and manner unknown to our past experience and shocking to the assumptions by which we live." Because it appeared shortly after the outbreak of the Korean War, the report reflected a greater sense of urgency than its predecessor. It envisaged a limitless war of words in which the United States should attempt to outstrip the propaganda techniques of the Communists: although not yet communicating the right ideas, "our film industry, our radio systems, the producers of image and idea in comic books and popular literature and magazines and newspapers have great inherent capacity." During the critical years in national security, it was incumbent on educators to see that schools serve as an instrument of national policy. It was necessary, particularly at the elementary and secondary levels, to establish good citizenship education programs. The schools must educate for moral and spiritual values, teach democracy, and increase devotion to public welfare. In particular, the schools would make "efficient producers" of the young, whom the fashioners of educational policy called a "resource" to be used by the government for national purposes.[29]

Unlike its predecessor, "Education and National Security" accented the pivotal role of colleges and universities, whose students would serve as the "scouts, mapmakers, and guides" for the complex technological world being born. It cited with approval an earlier study by the American Council on Education that offered the federal government the use of campus physical plants, suggested ways to use manpower efficiently, and volunteered assistance in community civil defense programs.[30] Though committee members disguised the extent to which their program would curtail individual freedom in curriculum selection, they did acknowledge that certain traditional rights enjoyed in academe must yield to the developing coordination of educational policies and military service. Colleges and universities were now obliged to lift "each student to his highest capacity to contribute to the nation's strength," meaning that they must train more students in medicine, the sciences, psychology, statistics, and—to execute President Truman's Point Four Program—agronomy, animal husbandry, geology, and the various branches of engineering, particularly chemical, industrial, marine, mining, and sanitary. Nor was this all. They would contribute to the national defense by educating a major portion of the officer corps and by producing a young population that was unflinchingly anticommunist.[31]

By the time of the Korean War, then, cold war tensions had enabled educators to include education in the canon of national security and to fashion it into a vital arm of the welfare-warfare state. The traditional focus of the schools on personal goals, even when related to industrial needs, shifted perceptibly to national goals. It should be remembered, too, that this new orientation was demanded in the first instance not by the political elite but by leading educators sensitive to public opinion and attuned to the interests of the modern security-minded state. The enthusiastic public reception of their reports reassured them and encouraged their belief that further public displays of anticommunism would redound to the well-being of academic institutions. To teachers and other workers in education, it seemed that their leaders were playing a directing role in the cold war.[32]

Although the American Council on Education and the powerful National Education Association expressed the prevailing viewpoint, individual educators disagreed that the first priority of education was to enhance national security. Although very much concerned about the health of the state, they stressed instead intellectual training and curricular reform. Their central criticism was of progressive education, a subject of endless confusion and controversy. Debated in literally countless speeches and essays in the first decade of the cold war, this philosophy had developed in opposition to educational methods dominant in late nineteenth-century America. As people moved into cities and factories, industrial methods and values heavily influenced the contemporary emphasis on drill, memorization, discipline, order, and moral didacticism. If modern industrial society required a literate public and skilled workers, then the education system would provide them. Although too much can be made of the fact, the regimentation required in the nation's factories and assembly lines sanctioned and hardened an already existing regimentation in the schools.

Hoping to replace an educational philosophy so narrowly conceived, progressive educators encouraged children to develop according to their talents and along lines enabling them to adjust not only to factory routine but to all manner of life situations; hence, the "child-centered" school. Following the lead of John Dewey and Francis W. Parker,[33] educators and school administrators in the 1920s took up the new philosophy and schooled themselves in personality formation, the psychology of learning, the physical and mental health of children, and creative expression in the arts. Individual projects, exhibits, and field trips became the vehicles of such interests. As the twenties gave way to the thirties, economic breakdown evoked serious questions about the efficacy of the social-economic order of the United States and caused heartache and practical problems for education. Educators turned en masse to a more liberal progressivism that stressed the social responsibilities of the schools and emphasized the need for planning a new social order. Many teachers without necessarily intending to came to accept an activist role for the state.

The social orientation of the progressive educators was short-lived, however. As the economy slowly recovered and war clouds gathered over Europe, progressive educators veiled or even relinquished their recently found social views in the interest of preserving the democratic way of life. The new emphases were political democracy, intergroup relations, intercultural education, and later, winning the war. Suffering psychological fatigue and a loss of cohesion, liberal progressivism dwindled in national influence and interest.[34]

Following World War II, however, progressive education experienced a final burst of energy through the life-adjustment movement. This alternative to intellectual education originated in the Vocational Education Division of the United States Office of Education, which in 1944 began a study of educational needs in the years ahead. At the final conference of the study, in May and June 1945, participants demanding a more realistic education for secondary school youth passed the following resolution:

> It is the belief of this conference that, with the aid of this report in final form, the vocational school of a community will be able better to prepare 20 percent of the youth of secondary-school age for entrance upon desirable skilled occupations; and that the high school will continue to prepare another 20 percent for entrance to college. We do not believe that the remaining 60 percent of our youth of secondary school age will receive the life-adjustment training they need and to which they are entitled as American citizens— unless and until the administrators of public education with the assistance of the vocational education leaders formulate a similar program for this group.

A subsequent rewording of the resolution made clear that the educators meant to serve "an increasing number of youth for whom college preparation or training for skilled occupations is neither feasible nor appropriate."[35] The trend to new courses in homemaking, health, commercial English, and auto mechanics that had emerged during the interwar years now reached new heights. Athletic programs proliferated. As schools came to teach everything the local community demanded, traditional fare such as history, grammar, and foreign languages suffered.

Although the movement for life-adjustment education had its origins in the U.S. Office of Education, other groups and commissions provided support. For example, in 1944 the Educational Policies Commission, appointed by the NEA and the American Association of School Administrators, published a lengthy volume entitled *Education for All American Youth.* The word *All* was underlined, and readers immediately discovered why, for the report accentuated the diversity of students attending school. Differences existed in intelligence and aptitude, occupational interests and outlooks, availability of educational facilities, types of communities, social and economic status, parental attitudes and cultural backgrounds, personal and avocational interests, and finally, mental health, emotional stability, and physical well-being.[36] No single mode of education could adequately respond to the flourishing of American cultural pluralism.

Chapter four of the report, written from the vantage point of a future historian surveying recent educational progress, celebrated the expansion of services, particularly in vocational education: advanced schools had expanded the "restricted" vocational offering of yesterday—"metal trades, machine shop, auto mechanics, electrical trades, some of the building trades, business education, retail selling, and homemaking"— and now offered training in such fields as "air conditioning, refrigeration, airplane construction, air transportation, housing construction, radio and television, and the manufacture of synthetic products." Nothing was said about the intellectual disciplines. Perhaps the anti-intellectual educational climate of the times is best revealed by the fact that the Educational Policies Commission of the NEA worried not that intellectual education might suffer but rather that "civic competence and personal development" had been slighted.[37]

The final chapter, entitled "The History That Must Be Written," discussed federal aid to education, state education associations, education officials, and the collection of information on occupational trends. Although curriculum warranted just one paragraph, the overall thrust was clear. School curricula had focused too heavily on college preparatory courses. In the new era the claims of the majority not bound for college would direct curricular planning. "*What affects the happiness and welfare of the young people of our community is of direct and vital concern to our staff.*" That meant that the schools must concern themselves with the total, generally nonintellectual, experiences of the community. If the student had a poor home life, the school would countervail with social activities. If his health was poor, the school would undertake corrective measures. If the recreational life of the community was "mean and tawdry," the school would provide better programs and facilities.[38] Thus was born the school as welfare institution; its primary function would not be intellectual growth.

The commission's report, published by two of the nation's most prestigious educational associations and expressing the views of prominent educators,[39] reflected opinion forged in the experience of war. It enjoyed nationwide distribution, particularly among teachers and educational administrators, running through eight printings until May 1952, when a revised edition appeared.[40] By that time James B. Conant had become chairman, but little else had changed. The revised edition did not recommend substantial changes in the educational principles and school practices advocated in the original volume.

It was this version of progressive education that came under scorching criticism in the postwar reappraisal of public education. Books, articles, and pamphlets proliferated, as did reprints of government study groups and commissions. Hollis Caswell, then dean of Columbia Teachers College, remarked that never since the days of Horace Mann had such a widespread discussion of basic educational issues taken place. Denying the "plot theory" of extremists who detected socialist prejudices everywhere, he acknowledged that reform energies were strong, but that for the first time in two generations they were not of the progressive variety.[41] In the first place, the new reformers criticized the lack of qualitative standards. Having rigidly eschewed a dual school system—one for the socially privileged and another for those who were not—educators had eliminated traditional requirements and unnecessarily lowered standards in an attempt to meet the putative needs of students who themselves were unable to define needs. The second line of criticism dealt with teaching methods, stressing that the schools should cease efforts to produce educated students through a slavish devotion to interests and to beget democrats by observing meetings of the town council. Rather, they should transmit the rudiments of civilization and prepare the mind to reason.

This critique originated in three groups: academicians who opposed the power of professional educationists; intellectuals who had philosophical objections to the instrumentalist thrust of progressive education;[42] and popular writers who merged these themes with criticism that the schools were too collectivist. Early statements came in 1949 from Bernard Iddings Bell (*Crisis in Education*) and Mortimer Smith (*And Madly Teach*), both arguing that American schools needed to stress basic subject matter, hard work, and greater discipline in order to return education to its historic role as moral and intellectual leader.[43]

The restoration of the intellectual eminence of schooling soon found other advocates. The banner year was 1953, when four important books appeared, all critical of progressive education: Arthur Bestor's *Educational Wastelands*, Robert Hutchins's *The Conflict in Education*, Paul Woodring's *Let's Talk Sense about Our Schools*, and Albert Lynd's *Quackery in the Public Schools*. The following year brought Mortimer Smith's *The Diminished Mind* and Randall Jarrell's brilliant satire, *Pictures from an Institution*.[44] No volume on education during the first decade of the cold war generated more discussion than Bestor's *Educa-*

tional Wastelands. To the analyses of earlier critics, the Illinois professor of history added historical perspective, up-to-date data, and a more sophisticated defense of the thesis that all students could profit from immersion in the basic academic disciplines. His *bête noire* was life-adjustment education and its perpetrators—education professors, school administrators, and government education officials. This "interlocking public school directorate" (held up to savage review) monopolized both the preparation of teachers and the process by which state laws supported the distended educational curriculums and requirements. The central purpose of education, the "deliberate cultivation of the ability to think," could be restored only by successfully challenging the directorate for the control of schooling and by providing sound training in the fundamental ways of thinking represented by history, science, mathematics, language, art, and other intellectual disciplines.[45]

With like-minded critics of progressive education, including Mortimer Smith and James Koerner, Bestor in 1956 helped establish the Council for Basic Education, with headquarters in Washington, D.C. It defended the view that schools must concentrate on developing intellectual skills in order to better transmit the intellectual and moral heritage of civilization. The council's statement of purpose read in part: "It insists that only by the maintenance of high academic standards can the ideal of democratic education be realized—the ideal of offering to all the children of all the people of the United States not merely an opportunity to attend school, but the privilege of receiving there the soundest education that is offered any place in the world." Financed by foundation grants and membership dues, the council published the *CBE Bulletin* and supported research and publications that strengthened basic education.[46]

Although Bestor, like Bell and Smith earlier, was interested mainly in the intellectual renewal of education, he nevertheless revealed his sensitivity to cold war realities when he suggested that a literate population was necessary and vital to the health of the nation. This assertion was developed by Vice-Admiral Hyman G. Rickover, who in dogged prose related the curricular reforms Bestor had in mind directly to the needs of national security. In a series of addresses beginning in 1956, the father of the *Nautilus* and the nuclear navy boldly charged that American educational institutions were endangering the security of the country, most notably by undervaluing intellectual competence, ignoring the creative expert, and stressing know-how subjects instead of solid learning and fundamental principles. Like Bestor, Smith, Lynd, and the Council on Basic Education, he scorned the "piddling problems" of life-adjustment education. Courses in the use of the camera, telephone, consumer credit, and the techniques of being well-liked were worse than worthless, for they minimized the "vexing problem of mental inequalities," and in so doing, failed to develop potentialities and to produce professionals.[47]

Rickover had the engineer's distaste for inefficiency and waste wherever they were found—the waste of good farmland, forests, oil, clean rivers and lakes, and bright minds, "our most valuable national asset." Because "the man of the future on whom we shall depend more and more is the technical expert," the schools must replace shallow socialization courses with those that nurture intellect. *"The only acceptable coin which buys an education is hard intellectual effort."* He told Edward R. Murrow that education is "even more important than atomic power in the Navy, for if our people are not properly educated in accordance with the terrific requirements of this rapidly spiraling scientific and industrial civilization, we are bound to go down. The Russians apparently have recognized this." To obtain the needed number of scientists, engineers, mathematicians, and foreign language experts, Rickover proposed money incentives for competent teachers and graduates in those areas, ability grouping, accelerated high schools, an extension of the school year from 180 to 210 days, and, like a growing number of other critics, an end to the power of professional educators.[48]

Rickover shared with earlier critics a concern about anti-intellectualism in America but differed from them in openly insisting upon what one historian of education has called "the sorting machine" function of public education: government utilization of the schools to channel students into areas of training where their talents would best serve the interests of society and the state.[49] He differed also in the urgency with which he emphasized that the United States must never run second to the Soviet Union. "Russian engineering and scientific development constitute a threat to our military power. . . . There can be no second place in a contest with Russia and there will be no second chance if we lose." Thus, it was Russian scientific and technological progress that prompted Rickover to criticize American education. His somber message was that "the future belongs to the best-educated nation"; his foremost objective was to make it ours.[50] Despite Rickover's cold arrogance, growing numbers deemed his message appropriate as the 1950s wore on, especially as it held out the promise of victory in the long cold war struggle. When Sputnik finally pierced the thick armor of American pretensions to superiority, Rickover looked very much like a prophet whose time had come.

Less elitist in educational philosophy than Rickover, but in agreement that the nation needed more mathematicians, scientists, and engineers, James B. Conant in early 1959 capped a decade of stormy educational criticism with a constructive report on the comprehensive high school. Funded by the Carnegie Corporation, this widely influential, national study of 103 high schools and 4 school systems began a month before Sputnik, after a half-year of planning. Convinced that university professors had been unduly harsh on American public education, Conant defended the concept of the comprehensive high school, arguing that it could be made satisfactory "without any radical changes in the basic pattern."[51]

Conant's message was blunt: the number one need of many states was to eliminate the small high school with its sharply limited program. Unless a school had a graduating class of at least a hundred students, it could not offer the diversified curriculum necessary to fulfill individual and national needs. By that criterion 17,000, or approximately 80 percent, of the nation's senior high schools were too small. Millions of students had no opportunity to study physics, a modern foreign language, or trigonometry. For example, only 12,000 of the 21,000 high schools offered a physics course, and some of those were of substandard quality. The high cost of educational facilities and adequate instruction meant that little would be achieved in the absence of school district reorganization and consolidation. Larger schools would also facilitate more efficient utilization of the inadequate numbers of competent teachers.[52]

To enhance the intellectual foundation of the curriculum, the former president of Harvard University recommended that all pupils complete four years of English, three or four years of social studies (including two years of history), one senior course in American politics or government, one year of mathematics, and at least one year of science. For academically talented pupils, estimated at 15 percent of the student population and in whom Conant became increasingly interested as the study progressed, minimum standards were more rigorous: four years of mathematics, four years of English, four years of one foreign language, three years of social studies, and three years of science.[53] Wary of inflexible teaching programs that branded individuals for life, Conant called for ability grouping by subject matter, the possible undemocratic aspects of which would be countered by daily homeroom periods involving all students in the rudiments of representative government. Thus did Conant, seeking intellectual quality, reach back to the Committee of Ten report (1894) and attempt to effect its basic program in a period of mass education. The modern high school would challenge the best students with advanced work without segregating them into special schools.

Uppermost in the mind of the former high commissioner to West

Germany was the cultural and military conflict with the Soviet Union. Fearing that American citizens were slow to understand the implications of nuclear weapons and Soviet imperialism for education, he warned frequently of a possible Soviet world conquest. Taken together, his educational writings, extending over many years, constitute a powerful statement of why a democratic industrial and military power must mobilize its educational institutions to serve foreign policy objectives. Concerned with the effective utilization of all student talents, Conant was especially bothered about "the loss to the nation" suffered when bright students avoided programs of solid study. For their own sake and for the "sake of the nation," the better students could be expected to do their homework.[54]

Unlike most prophets, whose warnings of distant and calamitous events go unfulfilled, critics of education seemed vindicated when on 4 October 1957 the Soviet Union thrust into orbit a man-made satellite. Most press accounts of Sputnik emphasized the miraculous scientific and technological advances of the Soviets and extolled the impressive educational system that lay behind them. American education, however, suffered a renewed barrage of criticism.[55] It was a rare article that did not relate education to national goals; indeed, education and science, together with military weaponry, now constituted three of the main battlegrounds of the cold war. The first wave of suggestions ranged from curriculum reform to a complete overhaul of American university education, increased spending on schools, federal aid to education, improved incentives for teachers and graduate students, and scholarships for talented students. Cultural criticism often emerged in the exhortation that the United States begin honoring its intellectuals and through ways unspecified revise its faltering spiritual heritage.[56] Even I. F. Stone, not one to panic on East-West issues, wrote shortly after the Soviets orbited Sputnik II (3 November 1957) that the United States must revolutionize its educational system "if our national pride is to be saved." But he added that the U.S.S.R. had an enormous weakness with its lack of individual freedom and political democracy, and that the outlook for the United States need not be bleak if it avoided an arms race and encouraged freedom at home.[57]

The most popular post-Sputnik assault on education appeared in March and April 1958 when *Life* published a five-part series of picture essays entitled "Crisis in Education."[58] *Life* depicted a crisis of overcrowded buildings, overworked and "grossly underpaid" teachers, confusion over what the schools should teach, a bewildering proliferation of elective courses, ill-advised attempts by the schools to be all things to all people, and, most appalling, a startling deterioration of educational standards. Millions of readers learned that Alexei, a sixteen-year-old Soviet student, studied several hours each day, excelled in science, and was well-read both in Russian and English literature. Chess, concerts, and piano practice claimed his leisure time. A tenth-year student, he would enter the university the following year to study physics. Stephen, his American counterpart from Chicago, already in his eleventh year, would have to wait two years for college, yet upon entry would be no further advanced than Alexei. His school day was not taxing. After walking to school with his girl friend, he went to typing class and continued through a schedule that, however respectable, he did not take seriously. Underworked and lacking discipline, Stephen disregarded assignments and devoted most of his time and nearly all his considerable energies to extracurricular activities.

Life's conclusion followed closely the views of the basic educationists: the United States was falling behind the Soviets, whose Spartan system was producing many students "better equipped than ours to cope with the technicalities of the Space Age." The editors agreed with the judgment of novelist and education critic Sloan Wilson: "It is hard to deny that America's schools, which were supposed to reflect one of history's noblest dreams and to cultivate the nation's youthful minds, have degenerated into a system for coddling and entertaining the mediocre." The way out was to remove "the debris left by 40 years of the progressive educationists," insist on a stiff academic curriculum for the college-bound, require plenty of science and mathematics, eliminate trivial courses, throttle the power of teachers colleges, and shore up the quality of teaching.[59]

The launching of Sputnik virtually ended the belief that the Soviets had merely stolen the A-bomb and the H-bomb and the jet airplane, and brought to decision-time the major reassessment of education that had begun a decade earlier. Eight months after the Russian launching, Congress passed the National Defense Education Act (NDEA); President Eisenhower signed it on 2 September 1958. The act had three salient features. First, it was primarily a defense bill. Section 101 of the General Provisions declared that "the defense of this Nation depends upon the mastery of modern techniques developed from complex scientific principles"; and later, national security interests require that "the Federal Government give assistance to education for programs which are important to our defense." Accordingly, the act was specifically designed to "correct as rapidly as possible the existing imbalances in our educational programs which have led to an insufficient proportion of our population educated in science, mathematics, and modern foreign languages and trained in technology." It provided grants to states for the acquisition of laboratory equipment and for the improvement of instruction in science, mathematics, and foreign languages. Generous graduate fellowships awaited qualified students working in those areas.[60]

Second, government funds were to be withheld from potential beneficiaries who refused to sign a loyalty oath and file an affidavit with the Commissioner of Education. Section 1001 (f) read:

> No part of any funds appropriated or otherwise made available for expenditure under authority of this Act shall be used to make payments or loans to any individual unless such individual (1) has executed and filed with the Commissioner an affidavit that he does not believe in, and is not a member of and does not support any organization that believes in or teaches the overthrow of the United States Government by force or violence or by any illegal or unconstitutional methods, and (2) has taken and subscribed to an oath or affirmation in the following form: "I do solemnly swear (or affirm) that I will bear true faith and allegiance to the United States of America and will support and defend the Constitution and laws of the United States against all its enemies, foreign and domestic."[61]

Third, the NDEA was enacted by the government without significant advice from the schools and universities. During the first fifteen years of the cold war, in fact, little reciprocity existed between the federal government and educational institutions. Washington provided for its own needs; educational institutions served as passive fulfillers of those needs. In retrospect, it should not surprise us that each specialized act tied the schools ever closer to the federal government and contributed to the steady nationalization of the universities. Politicians had come to understand that in a complex, technical world, the institutions of learning could be converted into guarantors of the national security. By helping to convert a difference in technological priorities into a crisis of national defense, Sputnik had forced the federal government to respond. Perhaps Robert Maynard Hutchins put it best in remarking that the NDEA was passed because of the technical achievements of the Soviet Union and by "assimilating education to the Cold War and calling an education bill a defense bill."[62]

Excepting defense-related activities, the federal government's role in education was comparatively small.[63] Three obstacles stood in the way of a long-term, general federal aid program for education. The religious issue predominated during the Truman presidency as Catholic groups provided powerful opposition to all bills that did not include aid to parochial schools. During the Eisenhower presidency, notably after the *Brown* v. *Board of Education of Topeka* decision, race became a decisive factor as southern Democrats, fearful of the broader social implications of federal aid, aligned with conservative Republicans to defeat all federal aid bills. The Eisenhower administration stood as a third obstacle to federal aid. Although Eisenhower in 1955 proposed a limited school-construction program, his heart was not in it. Three years later he withdrew his support.[64]

The cold war produced results, however, in the form of specialized educational acts. By establishing the National Science Foundation (NSF), Congress in 1950 fulfilled the dream of Vannevar Bush, director of the Office of Scientific Research and Development during World War II, who in the last months of the war called for just such an institution, arguing that basic scientific research had become a requisite component of national security and economic well-being. Charged with the task of strengthening science by initiating and supporting basic research in the mathematical, physical, biological, and engineering sciences, the NSF developed summer institutes for science and mathematics teachers and established a system of undergraduate and graduate fellowships.[65] Later, with additional funding provided under the NDEA, it effectively promoted curricular reform. The NSF was a straw in the wind, for it reflected emerging federal interest in science when identified with national security and brought higher education into close contact with the federal government and monies.

"Impacted Areas" legislation also cleared both houses in 1950 and became law when President Truman signed Public Law 815 and Public Law 874. The first provided school construction grants, and the second, school operating monies in areas where the presence of government personnel significantly increased school enrollment (primarily because of the expansion of defense activities following the outbreak of the Korean War) and where federal land purchases created a smaller tax base. After eight years $1.5 billion in federal funds, together with $350 million in local funds, permitted the construction of 42,562 classrooms serving an estimated 1,232,665 pupils. By the end of the 1950s, Congress had appropriated $618,170,000 to cover operating costs.[66]

At the close of fiscal year 1959, the U.S. government operated approximately 440 educational programs costing $3.8 billion, a majority of which was spent for defense-related activities. Among the programs were military academies, primary and secondary schools abroad for the children of military and civilian personnel, in-service training of government employees, schools for Indian children, the National School

Lunch Program, and of course the Impacted Areas programs and those of the NSF and the NDEA. At the decade's end the federal government sponsored 155 junior division units of the U.S. Army's Reserve Officers Training Corps and the National Defense Cadet Corps in 338 schools.[67] In the vast majority of these programs, the goal of the federal government was not to promote education; rather, the government responded to needs for trained personnel and acted in disjoined circumstances to meet emergencies and social or national crises. Without the political and military challenges posed by the Soviet Union, it is difficult to imagine that much of the aforementioned legislation would have been introduced, much less passed.

The reluctance of Congress to shoulder responsibility for the nation's schools was reflected in the proportionate sources of school revenues. The data demonstrate that though federal expenditures for education were increasing in the postwar years, the conspicuous reality was that local and state sources accounted for more than 95 percent of public school revenues (table 3). Partisans demanding a larger role for the federal government were on strong ground, for federal policies such as the G.I. Bill and student deferments made heavy demands on existing physical plants and faculty. Second, a momentous shift in taxing patterns had occurred: in 1900 approximately half of all tax revenues derived from local sources, but by the end of World War II approximately 85 percent were collected by the federal government.[68] This dramatic shift severely curtailed resources normally available to states and localities at the very time requests for funding multiplied. Third, the rising Gross National Product covered the cost of increased federal expenditures without appreciably altering the percentage of budgetary allocations to education. And fourth, appeals for increased federal aid to education could be made on the sound philosophical ground that because an enlightened citizenry is so essential to a democratic society, the federal government in the interest of self-preservation had a duty to support education.

Although passage of a comprehensive federal education program would await Lyndon Johnson's Great Society, widespread intellectual criticism combined with the pressures of the cold war to produce sweeping substantive and methodological innovations, concentrated first at the high school level, but spreading quickly to the elementary and higher educational levels. The conceptual apparatus in physics, biology, and even mathematics long had been outdated, partly because so little contact existed between teachers in the schools and scientists working on the frontiers of their disciplines. It was crucial to the reform movement that experts move to the forefront of curriculum revision. When they did, scientists and popularizers alike wrote of a "new" mathematics, a "new" physics, a "new" biology. New texts appeared, and with them new readings, educational materials, visual aids, laboratory experimentation, and testing programs. The twin essentials of the new curriculum were thought and discovery; hence, the stress on unifying concepts and on understanding those concepts within given structures of knowledge. As the steering committee of the Biological Sciences Curriculum Study put it:

> The writers seek to teach science as a way of thinking—as a method of seeking answers. To do this, they stress underlying concepts and understandings. Student work is centered in the laboratory, where real problems are explored; open-ended experiments and other materials are used as the media for conveying an understanding of science. Through emphasis on basic concepts in many varied ways, the student is given practice in drawing generalizations, in seeking relationships and in finding his own answers.[69]

The reform movement had its greatest success in mathematics and in the physical sciences, which in recent decades had experienced explosive increases in knowledge. Funds from the NDEA provided more-sophisticated science equipment for high schools. Science curricula became better coordinated, more unified, and more sequential. First of the programs was the Physical Science Study Committee (PSSC), initiated by physicist Jerrold Zacharias of the Massachusetts Institute of Technology and supported by distinguished and politically influential scientists, including Vannevar Bush, the person most responsible for the establishment of the NSF. The new physics course for the high school was laboratory-centered, emphasizing the basic structure of physics and the need to understand rather than memorize concepts. In addition to a text covering the concepts of time, space, matter, motion, the behavior of light, the kinematics of waves, culminating in quantum theory, the PSSC developed a complete program of laboratory experiments, films, tests, and a teacher's guide. The program began on a limited basis in 1957–58, with the first full-year physics course offered in 1960. By 1963–64, 40 to 45 percent of all high school students in physics courses were participating in the program. Ample funds helped account for its early success. As in other programs of curricular revision in science, the NSF (the recipient of vastly increased appropriations in 1958) provided the financial support, which for the PSSC amounted to $6,000,000 by 1961.[70]

Although curriculum reform in mathematics had been under way on an ad hoc basis for a decade, the School Mathematics Study Group (SMSG) produced the most sophisticated and widely used of the several new programs. Sponsored by the American Mathematics Society, the group first convened four months after Sputnik. Again, the NSF underwrote the project, paying out nearly $6,000,000 in the first five years. Written by professional mathematicians and mathematics educators, the new texts, prepared for each grade from kindergarten through high school, emphasized understanding the structure and basic properties of mathematics, and led students through progressively more difficult levels of abstraction. For example, in laying the primary basis for the new mathematics, the text for grade four introduced set theory as a means of learning arithmetical and algebraic concepts. Elementary school children then studied simple geometry. Points, lines, and plane figures were introduced. At the high school level, subject compartmentalization gave way to a fusion of algebra, geometry, and trigonometry in order to better illuminate the unity and overall structure of mathematics.[71] By the senior year, students were ready not only for polynomial, logarithmic, and trigonometric functions, but matrix algebra and systems of linear equations.[72]

The PSSC and the SMSG were the two foremost programs in the new curriculum dating to the late 1950s, but sophisticated programs were also introduced in the life sciences and in chemistry, the most prominent being the Biological Sciences Curriculum Study, organized in 1959 and chaired by Bentley Glass; the Chemical Bond Approach Project; the Chemical Education Materials Study; and various elementary school science curriculums. These too were expensive: with the Biological Sciences Curriculum Study $6,500,000 in its first four years.[73]

The teaching of English and modern foreign languages underwent serious reevaluation in the late 1950s and the 1960s, but neither enjoyed the coordination (and for English, the funding) common to similar efforts in the natural sciences. The debate in English derived its impetus from dissatisfaction with the English curriculum, from contemporary demands for increased rigor in basic subject matter, and, to a lesser extent, from the developing science of linguistics. The major point that emerged was that English consisted of no more than three subjects: language, literature, and composition. Studies of how they interacted and grew through time and use begot a new field of research. Fundamental change was slow in coming. Not until 1962 would a federally sponsored program in English appear. Project English, sponsored by the Cooperative Research Program of the United States Office of Education, enlisted the help of leading universities to develop new curriculum programs that were sequential and cumulative from elementary through graduate school. Together they established university curriculum study centers, and arranged conferences and seminars to encourage research in the teaching of English.[74]

Foreign language studies fared better, in large part because of funding provided under the terms of the NDEA. The Modern Language Association had for several years worked hard to improve language instruction, but its inclusion in the NDEA reflected the nation's increasing responsibilities in world affairs and the conviction that foreign language expertise would enable the United States to compete more effectively with the Soviets in the developing world. Time had not yet dimmed memories of the shortage of competent translators during World War II. Section 603 of the NDEA authorized the appropriation of $8,000,000 per year to establish centers for the teaching of modern foreign languages and to pay stipends to individuals taking advanced training in a modern foreign language. Section 611 authorized $7,250,000 for each of four years to operate institutes at colleges and universities offering advanced training in new teaching methods and instructional materials. The response was immediate and productive. The number of elementary students studying foreign languages increased tenfold in a decade; secondary school enrollment more than doubled. Instead of emphasizing reading and grammar, teachers employed new methods to develop oral competence in the early stages. Beginning language study in the third or fourth grade reflected conceptual advances in the nature of language and the learning process that were popularized in books such as Jerome Bruner's *The Process of Education* and Martin Mayer's *The Schools.*[75]

Despite ample discussion in the social sciences, significant curriculum revisions on the order of those gracing science and mathematics were not forthcoming. Experimental projects were organized in geography and anthropology, but significant revision in those and other areas did not occur until the 1960s.[76] Curricular reform in history consisted mainly of demands to include it in the curriculum. For example, in 1942 only 18 percent of colleges and universities required students to take American history. By the 1949–50 school year, 34 percent did. Thirty-nine states in 1948 required students to study American history before graduating from high school, and all but two states required instruction in the Constitution of the United States. The requirements were intended to enable students to resist alien ideologies and to restore a basis not only for citizenship training but for moral and spiritual training that many supposed had been neglected in the school curriculum.[77] Unfortunately, substantive changes were meager. World history courses continued to give far too little attention to the non-Western world, despite the rising importance of Asian, African, and South American countries. Rare indeed was the teacher who, however respectful of "the facts," also taught history as a way of learning.

For the American school system, the years following World War II were difficult in the extreme. States and local communities found it impossible to keep up with exploding student enrollments and physical plant needs, let alone repair the damage brought about by fifteen years of neglect. Except when its interests were clearly at stake, Washington refused to increase its financial assistance to a level commensurate with its growing portion of public revenues. The knowledge explosion complicated matters by requiring fundamental revision of the methods by which intellectual advance is attained. Most serious of all was the repressive climate of McCarthyism. Although some may wish to believe otherwise, the issues of teacher loyalty and Communist party influence in the schools set many a community ablaze, a disheartening number of teachers found a cowering posture expedient, if not becoming, and books were removed from shelves and reading lists. The loyalty oaths of the day stand as mute testimony to events one would rather forget but dare not.

Yet out of the maze and discord, significant results emerged. However inadequate in amount, classrooms were built and teachers' salaries improved. The reappraisal of education, whether substantive or political in nature, laid the foundation for the curricular changes that followed. These reforms moved away from life-adjustment aims and were designed to bring intellectual content and intellectual excitement to the academic curriculum.

Of the various factors causally significant in effecting curriculum change, the cold war was the preeminent catalyst. It gained for educational critics an audience they would otherwise not have enjoyed, and it provided the political dynamic for change. This was particularly true after Sputnik. So frequently do we see references to the first Soviet satellite that a danger exists of not taking it seriously. But Sputnik eliminated many psychological and political blocks to curriculum reform and to federal aid. With the National Science Foundation and the National Defense Education Act, the federal government accredited the instrumentalist views of Vannevar Bush, Admiral Rickover, and others that national survival depended on the mobilization of university science and technology. That the social sciences and the humanities were not similarly exalted was a major failure, but that failure accurately reflected both the priorities and the fears of cold war America.

1. Aside from permitting greater depth at one level, the focus on the secondary schools reflects the postwar debate on education: public school criticism was aimed more at secondary than at elementary education. When Sputnik provoked an outcry over the declining quality of schooling in America, the public again had the secondary schools most in mind. Moreover, significant curriculum reform appeared first at the secondary level. Focusing as it does on the cold war and its impact on the nation's schools, this paper will not attempt to discuss the educational implications of *Brown* v. *Board of Education of Topeka*.

2. David L. Marden, "The Cold War and American Education," 2 vols. (Ph.D. diss., University of Kansas, 1975) 1:13–14; Educational Policies Commission of the National Education Association, *Research Memorandum on Education in the Depression* (New York, 1937), pp. 87–105. Because the defects of the nation's schools were so numerous, President Roosevelt's Advisory Committee on Education argued that federal aid was necessary: *The Federal Government and Education* (Washington, D.C., 1938), p. 1. With other matters pressing for attention, Roosevelt refused to endorse the conclusions of his advisory committee, saying that he was willing to assist only those states unable to meet their own educational needs.

3. Numerous documents revealing the impact of the Great Depression on schools and teachers are brought together in Robert H. Bremner et al., eds., *Children and Youth in America: A Documentary History*, 3 vols. (Cambridge, Mass., 1971–74), 3:1579–1610. It is estimated that salaries of teachers were reduced in nearly all rural schools and in 80 to 90 percent of all city school systems (pp. 1580–81). Also see I. L. Kandel, *The Impact of the War upon American Education* (Chapel Hill, N.C., 1948), pp. 66–67.

4. The Educational Policies Commission of the NEA published a series of reports that discussed the functions of education in a democracy and ways to meet the challenge posed by totalitarian ideologies: *The Unique Function of Education in American Democracy* (1937); *The Structure and Administration of Education in American Democracy* (1938); *The Purposes of Education in American Democracy* (1938); *Education and Economic Well-Being in American Democracy* (1940); and *The Education of Free Men in American Democracy* (1941) (all published in Washington, D.C.). Two relevant studies published by the John Dewey Society for the Study of Education and Culture are Harold B. Alberty and Boyd H. Bode, eds., *Educational Freedom and Democracy* (New York, 1938); and George E. Axtelle and William W. Wattenberg, eds., *Teachers for Democracy* (New York, 1940).

5. Data from several planning commissions and reports on the work of the schools in wartime are brought together in Kandel, *The Impact of the War*, pp. 26–38. Roy Woods, "Effect of World War II on American Education," *American School Board Journal* 134 (June 1957): 35–36, includes data on enrollments, teacher salaries, and school revenue and expenditures during the 1940s. Colleges and universities also yielded willingly to government requests for permission to conduct research and training programs on their premises as they mobilized for the defense effort, adding war-oriented courses, year-round classes, and three-year programs. See Hollis P. Allen, *The Federal Government and Education* (New York, 1950), p. 108. Henry C. Herge et al., *Wartime College Training Programs of the Armed Services* (Washington, D.C., 1948), tells the story of higher education preparing for war. For a prewar discussion of the tasks awaiting higher education, and for an example of the enthusiasm with which college and university administrators called for participation in the war effort, see American Council on Education, Studies, *Organizing Higher Education for National Defense* (Washington, D.C., 1941). A more sober analysis, concerned with the social impact of the war, is the report of Committee A, American Association of University Professors, Edward C. Kirkland, "Academic Freedom and Tenure," *Bulletin of the American Association of University Professors* 30 (February 1944): 13–28.

6. Kandel, *The Impact of the War*, pp. 41–43. Total rejections are approximately 8 percent higher when the period is extended to July 1945: see Bremner et al., eds., *Children and Youth in America*, 3:114.

7. Harold W. Stoke, "Education as National Policy," in Department of Higher Education, *Current Issues in Higher Education* (1950), pp. 11–16.

8. Several reports of the American Association of University Professors remarked on the declining number of cases during and immediately after the war involving violations of academic freedom. The annual report for 1948 began to tell a different story, however. Edward C. Kirkland, "Annual Report of Committee A on Academic Freedom and Tenure," *AAUP Bulletin* 31 (Spring 1945): 5–17; Kirkland, "Annual Report of Committee A," *AAUP Bulletin* 32 (Spring 1946): 5–17; George Pope Shannon, "Report of Committee A," *AAUP Bulletin* 34 (Spring 1948): 110–33; and William T. Laprade, "Report of Committee A," *AAUP Bulletin* 35 (Spring 1949): 49–65.

9. U.S., Congress, House, Committee on Un-American Activities, *100 Things You Should Know about Communism and Education*, 81st Cong., 1st sess., 1949.

10. Carey McWilliams draws a useful distinction between witch-hunting and the milder form of scapegoating in *Witch Hunt: The Revival of Heresy* (Boston, 1950). Scapegoating is a universal and largely "individual phenomenon" arriving out of "mild frustration," whereas "witch hunting is a product of collective madness" occurring in the wake of social dislocations: "wars, disasters, plagues, famines, and revolutions." Scapegoating is perennial; witch-hunts appear only in time of stress (pp. 246–47).

11. The literature on the Washington cases is extensive, but see *Communism and Academic Freedom: The Record of the Tenure Cases at the University of Washington* (Seattle, Wash., 1949); McWilliams, *Witch Hunt*, pp. 139–232; T. V. Smith, "Democratic Compromise and the Higher Learning at Seattle," *School and Society* 69 (26 February 1949): 137–41; Raymond B. Allen, "Communists Should Not Teach in American Colleges," *Educational Forum* 13 (May 1949): 433–40. For a symposium, including statements by the three dismissed professors, see "Communism and Academic Freedom," *American Scholar* 18 (Summer 1949): 323–54. Also see Vern Countryman, "The Canwell Committee," in *The States and Subversion*, ed. Walter Gellhorn (Ithaca, N.Y., 1952), pp. 282–357. Walter Gellhorn, a professor of law at Columbia University who studied closely the subversive phenomenon in states and municipalities, concluded that "the influence of American Communists seems on the whole to be at low ebb, rather than ever mounting as the state legislatures formally declare," and that "the statutes and the investigations considered in this volume were intended to strike at enemies of freedom. In many instances, however, they hit others instead—educators, public employees, political minorities, and even religious groups" (ibid., pp. 362–91).

12. Dixon Wecter, "Commissars of Loyalty," *Saturday Review of Literature*, 13 May 1950, pp. 8–10, 52–53; "Academic Freedom and Tenure—Evansville College," *AAUP Bulletin* 35 (Spring 1949): 74–111; Walter Goodman, *The Committee: The Extraordinary Career of the House Committee on Un-American Activities* (New York, 1968), pp. 315–16. Contemporary assessments of the loyalty question and academic freedom are John L. Childs, "Liberty in America: Communists and the Right to Teach," *Nation*, 26 February 1949, pp. 230–31; Ernest O. Melby, "Education and the Defense of America," *Saturday Review of Literature*, 9 September 1950, pp. 9–10, 47–49; Sidney Hook, "Academic Confusions," *Journal of Higher Education* 20 (November 1949): 422–25; Hook, "The Danger of Authoritarian Attitudes in Teaching Today," *School and Society* 73 (20 January 1951): 33–39; Hook, "Can We Trust Our Teachers?", *Saturday Review of Literature*, 18 April 1953, pp. 11–12, 45–47; Alan Barth, "The Loyalty of Free Men," *AAUP Bulletin* 37 (Spring 1951): 5–16; Lyle Owen, "Communism and Our Colleges," *AAUP Bulletin* 36 (Autumn 1950): 437–46: Benjamin F. Wright, "Should Teachers Testify?", *Saturday Review of Literature*, 36 26 September 1953, pp. 22–23.

13. *New York Times*, 10 March 1953.

14. David Hulburd, *This Happened in Pasadena* (New York, 1951); James B. Conant, "The Superintendent Was the Target," *New York Times Book Review*, 29 April 1951, pp. 1, 27; James B. Boyle, "Pasadena, Calif." *Saturday Review of Literature*, 8 September 1951, pp. 7–8. Agreeing with Hulburd that a small group of vocal critics was responsible

for Goslin's dismissal was the National Commission for the Defense of Democracy through Education: *The Pasadena Story* (Washington, D.C., 1951). For a view of the Pasadena case from the Right, see Mary L. Allen, *Education or Indoctrination* (Caldwell, Idaho, 1956).

15. Ernest O. Melby, *American Education under Fire: The Story of the "Phoney Three-R Fight"* (New York, 1951), pp. 7–17; Robert A. Skaife, "Groups Affecting Education," in National Education Association, Association for Supervision and Curriculum Development, *Forces Affecting American Education* (Washington, D.C., 1953), pp. 43–86; Frederick Woltman, "Zoll, Hate Monger, Promotes New Racket," *New York World-Telegram*, 25 August 1948. Other sources discussing the ideology and activities of right-wing groups are Mary Anne Raywid, *The Ax-Grinders: Critics of Our Public Schools* (New York, 1962); Donald Janson and Bernard Eismann, *The Far Right* (New York, 1963); Daniel Bell, ed., *The Radical Right* (Garden City, N.Y., 1964); and Arnold Forster and Benjamin R. Epstein, *Danger on the Right: The Attitudes, Personnel, and Influence of the Radical Right and Extreme Conservatives* (New York, 1964).

16. Marden, "The Cold War and American Education," p. 86. Appendix A of Gellhorn, *The States and Subversion*, describes state statutes (including teacher's oath statutes) concerned with subversive activities. The National Education Association, the American Federation of Teachers, and scores of college and university presidents agreed that Communists should not be permitted to teach anywhere in the United States. A small minority, including John Dewey, Robert Maynard Hutchins, Alexander Meiklejohn, and I. L. Kandel, dissented, arguing that the free play of the mind should be protected.

17. Quoted in Robert Shaplen, "Scarsdale's Battle of the Books," *Commentary* 10 (December 1950): 538.

18. Examples of this kind of criticism in the postwar years can be found in any number of the journals *Human Events, American Mercury,* and *Freeman.*

19. Particularly artless examples of the literature linking progressive education with liberalism and communism are Kitty Jones and Robert Olivier, *Progressive Education Is REDucation* (Boston, 1956): and Allen, *Education or Indoctrination.*

20. Data for table 2 are drawn from the following sources: U.S., Bureau of the Census, *Historical Statistics of the United States, Colonial Times to 1957* (Washington, D.C., 1960); U.S., Bureau of the Census, *Statistical Abstract of the United States* (Washington, D.C.), years 1944–45, 1963, and 1972; and U.S., Bureau of the Census, *Long Term Economic Growth, 1860–1965: A Statistical Compendium,* Es4-No. 1 (1966). (Because data were derived from a variety of sources, certain figures will not tally perfectly; for example, total expenditures and expenditures per pupil.)

21. Data are drawn from U.S., Bureau of the Census, *Historical Statistics of the United States,* and *Statistical Abstract of the United States* (1963).

22. Source: U.S., Office of Education, *Biennial Survey of Education in the United States, 1954–56,* chap. 1, "Statistical Summary of Education: 1955–56" (Washington, D.C., 1960); U.S., Bureau of the Census, *Long Term Economic Growth; Statistical Abstract of the United States* (1963).

23. *Biennial Survey of Education in the United States, 1948–50,* chap. 1, p. 37; John R. Emens, "Education Begets Education: The G.I. Bill Twenty Years Later," *American Education* 1 (September 1965): 11–12; Director of War Mobilization, *The Veteran and Higher Education* (Washington, D.C., 1946), pp. 30–32.

24. Cf. President Truman's Commission on Higher Education, calling for increased expenditures and a program of federal aid: "Higher education is an investment, not a cost. It is an investment in free men. It is an investment in social welfare, better living standards, better health, and less crime. It is an investment in higher production, increased income, and greater efficiency in agriculture, industry, and government. It is an investment in a bulwark against garbled information, half-truths, and untruths; against ignorance and intolerance. It is an investment in human talent, better human relationships, democracy, and peace": A Report of the President's Commission on Higher Education, *Higher Educa-*

tion for American Democracy, 6 vols. (Washington, D.C., 1947), 5:26, 28. Concerned that the institutions of higher education might fall short in meeting the needs of thousands of returning veterans, Truman established the presidential commission in the summer of 1946, requesting that it "reexamine our system of higher education in terms of its objectives, methods, and facilities; and in light of the social role it has to play.": vol. 1, *Establishing the Goals*, "Letter of Appointment of Commission Members." Two critiques disagreeing with the commission's work are Robert M. Hutchins, "Double Trouble: Are More Studies, More Facilities, More Money the Key for Better Education?", *Saturday Review of Literature*, 17 July 1948, pp. 7–8, 30–31; and Robert Lynd, "Who Calls the Tune?", *Journal of Higher Education* 19 (April 1948): 163–74. A defense from a member of the commission can be found in T. R. McConnell, "A Reply to the Critics," *Journal of Educational Sociology* 22 (April 1949): 533–51.

25. On the sorry state of the public schools after World War II, see Benjamin Fine, *Our Children Are Cheated: The Crisis in American Education* (New York, 1947). Fine, making a survey for the *New York Times*, discovered school systems that had broken down, buildings in disrepair, inadequacies in curricula, and low teacher morale. In 1946–47 he found 123,492 teachers on substandard licenses, compared with 2,300 in 1940–41. Less than half of the nation's teachers had completed college (pp. 23–25).

26. NEA, Educational Policies Commission, *American Education and International Tensions* (Washington, D.C., 1949), pp. 1–2.

27. Ibid., pp. 14, 3, 18, 6, 4, 39, 53.

28. Benjamin Fine, "NEA Leaders in Bitter Session Back Plan to Ban Red Teachers," *New York Times*, 6 July 1949.

29. NEA, Educational Policies Commission, and the American Council on Education, *Education and National Security* (Washington, D.C., 1951), pp. 2, 11, 20.

30. Ibid., pp. 31–32; Francis J. Brown, ed., *Higher Education in the National Service* (Washington, D.C., 1950).

31. *Education and National Security*, pp. 45, 37–38.

32. James B. Conant, for example, was a member of both educational groups that published *Education and National Security* and was currently serving as chairman of the Educational Policies Commission of the NEA. For a critical assessment of his influence on the developing relationship between educational institutions and the modern security-minded state, see Thomas Grissom, "Education and the Cold War: The Role of James B. Conant," in Clarence Karier, Paul C. Violas, and Joel Spring, eds., *Roots of Crisis: American Education in the Twentieth Century* (Chicago, 1973), pp. 177–97. Grissom argues that the cold war was the "*justification* of our nation's behavior, not the cause of it," and that in Conant's writings "one discovers an ideology born of a pervasive insecurity, one that proposes the reform of certain internal and temporary evils *and*, at the same time, insures against the disruptive influence of *any* alien ideology by identifying in the American nation-state the source and defender of all that is valuable. Conant sought to integrate and unify America's institutions—public and private—its critical and supportive ideas, and its national objectives, both realized and unachieved, into a political philosophy that could describe enemies and prescribe responses. That is the importance of his work prior to 1951" (p. 196).

33. For an excellent discussion of the educational views of Parker (now nearly forgotten except in education circles), see Merle Curti, *The Social Ideas of American Educators* [With New Chapter on the Last Twenty-Five Years] (Paterson, N.J., 1959), pp. 374–95.

34. Lawrence A. Cremin, *The Transformation of the School: Progressivism in American Education, 1876–1957* (New York, 1961), remains the finest history of the progressive education movement. John L. Childs's *Education and Morals* (New York, 1950) and *American Pragmatism and Education* (New York, 1956) provide an articulate defense of progressive education. A superb critique is Boyd H. Bode, *Progressive Education at the Crossroads* (New York, 1938).

35. U.S., Federal Security Agency, Office of Education, *Life Adjustment for Every Youth* (Washington, D.C., 1951), pp. 16, 19.

36. NEA, Educational Policies Commission, *Education for All American Youth* (Washington, D.C., 1944), pp. 11–17.

37. Ibid., pp. 191, 190.

38. Ibid., pp. 406–7.

39. Among the twenty members of the EPC were former U.S. Commissioners of Education J. W. Studebaker and George F. Zook, James B. Conant, and Willard Givens. William G. Carr served as EPC secretary.

40. NEA, Educational Policies Commission, *Education for All American Youth: A Further Look* (Washington, D.C., 1952).

41. Hollis L. Caswell, "The Great Reappraisal of Public Education," *Teachers College Record* 54 (1952–53): 12–22.

42. Barbara Barksdale Clowse, "Education as an Instrument of National Security: The Cold War Campaign to 'Beat the Russians' from Sputnik to the National Defense Education Act of 1958" (Ph.D. diss., University of North Carolina, Chapel Hill, 1977): 67.

43. Bernard Iddings Bell, *Crisis in Education: A Challenge to American Complacency* (New York, 1949): Mortimer Smith, *And Madly Teach: A Layman Looks at Public School Education* (Chicago, 1949).

44. Other notable books would soon appear, including Paul Woodring, *A Fourth of a Nation* (New York, 1957); and Russell Kirk, *Academic Freedom* (Chicago, 1955). Several of Kirk's essays of the 1950s on progressive education appear in his volume *Decadence and Renewal in the Higher Learning* (South Bend, Ind., 1978).

45. Arthur E. Bestor, *Educational Wastelands: The Retreat from Learning in Our Public Schools* (Urbana, Ill., 1953), pp. 102, 14, 18, 3–7. Also see Bestor, " 'Life-Adjustment' Education: A Critique," *AAUP Bulletin* 38 (September 1952): 413–41; and "Future Direction of American Education," *Phi Delta Kappan* 35 (June 1954): 373–78, 384. Two critical professional reviews of *Educational Wastelands* are Harold C. Hand, "A Scholar's Documentation," *Educational Theory* 4 (January 1954): 27–48, 53; and R. Will Burnet, "Mr. Bestor in the Land of the Philistines," *Progressive Education* 31 (January 1954): 65–85.

46. James D. Koerner, ed., *The Case for Basic Education: A Program of Aims for Public Schools* (Boston, 1959), p. v.

47. Hyman G. Rickover, *Education and Freedom* (New York, 1959), pp. 15–38, 136–39.

48. Ibid., pp. 129, 19, 150, 6, 115–28.

49. Joel Spring, *The Sorting Machine: National Educational Policy since 1945* (New York, 1976). In his excellent study Spring examines the role educators and educational institutions played in helping the nation to meet its manpower needs.

50. Rickover, *Education and Freedom*, pp. 50, 52, 38.

51. James B. Conant, *The American High School Today: A First Report to Interested Citizens* (New York, 1959), p. 96. Appendix B lists the schools visited.

52. Ibid., pp. 37–38, 80–81; Conant, *The Child, the Parent, and the State* (Cambridge, Mass., 1960), p. 38.

53. Conant, *The American High School Today*, pp. 47, 57, ("As I discussed with teachers and guidance officers the work of the more able students, I became more and more interested in programs of the academically talented" [p. 20]). By 1961 Conant, fearing the social dynamite building in urban ghettos, had shifted his attention to the disadvantaged: *Slums and Suburbs: A Commentary on Schools in Metropolitan Areas* (New York, 1961).

54. Conant, *The Child, the Parent, and the State*, p. 72; *The American High School Today*, pp. 59–60.

55. *New York Times*, three articles: "Blow to U.S. Seen," 6 October 1957; "Senators Attack Missile Fund Cut," 6 October 1957; and "Soviet Gains in Science," 13 October 1957. For a sampling of the first response of educators, aware that education had a crucial role to play in the cold war, see the following in the *New York Times*: "Educators Upset by Soviet Stroke," 11 October 1957; "Satellite Called Spur to Education," 12 October 1957; "Educators Urge High School Shift," 31 October 1957; and "Educators Urge Wakened Nation," 9 November 1947. Books such as John Francis Latimer, *What's Happened to Our High Schools?* (Washington, D.C., 1958), reflected with a sense of urgency the belief that Americans had failed in their educational responsibilities.

56. The following essays represent early attempts of educators to ascertain the import of Sputnik for American education: Thomas N. Bonner, "Sputniks and the Educational Crisis in America," *Journal of Higher Education* 29 (April 1958): 177–84, 232; Earl J. McGrath, "Sputnik and American Education," *Teachers College Record* 59 (April 1958): 379–95; Chester S. Williams, "Teacher Education in America as Challenged by the Soviet Education Effort," *Teachers College Journal* 30 (May 1959): 112–16; Edgar Collins Bain, "Russian Lesson for Americans," *National Parent-Teacher* 53 (June 1959): 24–25; Gerald H. Read, "Sputnik, Kaputnik, and American Education," *Educational Forum* 24 (January 1960): 165–72; Mark Graubard, "Soviet Technology, American Education, and our Post-War Hysteria," *Science Education* 44 (December 1960): 331–45; and Francis Magyar, "In the Shadow of the Sputniks," *Education* 81 (January 1961): 293–96.

57. I. F. Stone, *I. F. Stone's Weekly*, 11 November 1957, p. 1.

58. *Life*, 24 and 31 March 1958; 7, 14, and 21 April 1958.

59. Ibid., 21 April 1958, p. 34; 24 March 1958, p. 37; 31 March 1958, p. 32.

60. National Defense Education Act of 1958. *United States Code*, 1964, Title 20, 2 September 1958, P.L. 85-864, 72 Stat. 1581.

61. Ibid., p. 1602.

62. Quoted in Clowse, "Education as an Instrument of National Security," p. iii. The point can not be made too strongly that the NDEA was primarily a defense bill. Erwin D. Canham, chairman of the National Manpower Council, wrote in 1960 that it "probably would not have become law had the word 'Defense' been lacking in the title.": Foreword to Henry David, ed., *Education and Manpower* (New York, 1960). Senator Lister Hill of Alabama had for years tried to steer an aid-to-education program through Congress, always unsuccessfully. Sputnik provided the catalyst he needed. As he observed when preparing the bill, his colleagues "would not dare vote against both national defense and education when joined in the same bill.": quoted in James L. Sundquist, *Politics and Policy: The Eisenhower, Kennedy, and Johnson Years* (Washington, D.C., 1968) p. 176.

63. Two excellent historical studies in this connection are Gordon Canfield Lee, *The Struggle for Federal Aid—First Phase: A History of the Attempts to Obtain Federal Aid for the Common Schools, 1870–1890* (New York, 1949); and Frank J. Munger and Richard F. Fenno, Jr., *National Politics and Federal Aid to Education*, The Economics and Politics of Public Education 3 (Syracuse, N.Y., 1962).

64. Munger and Fenno, *National Politics and Federal Aid to Education*, pp. 14–15; George A. Kizer, "Federal Aid to Education, 1945–1963," *History of Education Quarterly* 10 (Spring 1970): 84–102.

65. U.S., Congress, House, Committee on Education and Labor, *Federal Educational Policies, Programs, and Proposals*, 90th Cong., 2d sess., 1968, H. Doc. 398, p. 33; Homer D. Babbidge, Jr., and Robert M. Rosenzweig, *The Federal Interest in Higher Education* (New York, 1962), pp. 35–38. Vannevar Bush's views on science and public policy are discussed in his end-of-the-war report, *Science, The Endless Frontier: A Report to the President* (Washington, D.C., 1945).

66. *Federal Educational Policies, Programs, and Proposals*, pp. 22–23; Elaine Exton, "Federal Activities in Education," *American School Board Journal* 141 (September 1960): 42.

260 | *Reshaping America*

67. Exton, "Federal Activities in Washington," pp. 36–37, 42, 44.

68. Carl B. Franzen, "Public Schools and the Federal Government," *School Executive* 72 (July 1953): 19. The U.S. Department of Commerce reported in 1958 that the federal government collected approximately 65 percent of the tax dollar and paid for approximately 4 percent of the nation's education bill: cited in Sidney W. Tiedt, *The Role of the Federal Government in Education* (New York, 1966), p. 36.

69. "About BSCS Biology," *BSCS Newsletter* 17 (March 1963): 7.

70. Jerrold R. Zacharias and Stephen White, "The Requirements for Major Curriculum Revision," in *New Curricula*, ed. Robert W. Heath (New York, 1964), pp. 68–81; John Goodlad, *School Curriculum Reform* (New York, 1964), pp. 23–25; Paul E. Marsh and Ross A. Gortner, *Federal Aid to Science Education: Two Programs*, The Economics and Politics of Public Education 6 (Syracuse, N.Y., 1963), pp. 30–38.

71. Max Beberman, "An Emerging Program of Secondary School Mathematics," and William Wooton, "The History and Status of the School Mathematics Study Group," in Heath, *New Curricula*, pp. 9–34, 35–53. For a full description of the origin and activities of the SMSG, see Wooton, *SMSG: The Making of a Curriculum* (New Haven, Conn., 1965).

72. For example, see School Mathematics Study Group, *Mathematics for High School: Introduction to Matrix Algebra*, rev. ed. (New Haven, Conn., 1960). This experimental edition presents the theory of matrices and vectors, introducing terms like *group, ring,* and *field* as unifying concepts. The SMSG also prepared films to improve the skills of elementary-school teachers. Interested lay students of the revolutionary developments in mathematics taking place during the 1950s will find useful Irving Adler, *The New Mathematics* (New York, 1960).

73. J. A. Campbell, "Chem Study: An Approach to Chemistry Based on Experiments," and Bentley Glass, "Renascent Biology: A Report on the AIBS Biological Sciences Curriculum Study," in Heath, *New Curricula*, pp. 82–93, 94–119; Goodlad, *School Curriculum Reform*, pp. 25–34; Matthew B. Miles, ed., *Innovation in Education* (New York, 1964). John Goodlad, "Curriculum Reform Sorts Out Basic Concepts," *Nation's Schools* 73 (March 1964): 68–70, is a critical analysis of the strengths and shortcomings of new curriculum developments.

74. Francis A. J. Ianni and Lois S. Josephs, "The Curriculum Research and Development Program of the U.S. Office of Education: Project English, Project Social Studies, and Beyond," and Edwin H. Sauer, "New Approaches to College Preparatory English," in Heath, *New Curricula*, pp. 161–212, 213–30; Edwin H. Sauer, *English in the Secondary School* (New York, 1961).

75. James Bruner, *The Process of Education* (Cambridge, Mass., 1960); Martin Mayer, *The Schools* (New York, 1961); *The Scholars Look at the Schools* (Washington, D.C., 1962), pp. 13–15; Glen Heathers et al., "Innovations in Instruction," *National Elementary Principal* 43 (September 1963): 8–62; Harold G. Shane et al., "Elementary Education," *NEA Journal* 51 (September 1962): 41–51.

76. Goodlad, *School Curriculum Reform*, pp. 42–46.

77. Marden, "The Cold War and American Education," 1:175–76. The postwar concern that schools were ignoring moral and spiritul values resulted in solid contributions such as John L. Childs, *Education and Morals: An Experimentalist Philosophy of Education* (New York, 1950), but also in hackneyed generalizations such as those offered in Educational Policies Commission, *Moral and Spiritual Values in the Public Schools* (Washington, D.C., 1951).

Cities, Suburbs, and Government Policy

Mark I. Gelfand

Viewed against the backdrop of the American urban experience, the significance of the 1945–60 period lies less in the character of community changes that occurred than in the velocity of those changes. In terms of form and structure, these fifteen years produced little that was unique, but by transmuting a well-defined trend into fact, the era produced a new America, one that both fulfilled and mocked the country's promise.

The rate of change assumed such importance in this period because of the previous decade-and-a-half of lost opportunities. The Great Depression and World War II, whatever their effect on other aspects of American life, represented breaks with the previous patterns of physical and social development in the nation's metropolitan areas. The usual social trends and personal expectations no longer applied; whether out of work in the 1930s or on the war-plant assembly lines in the early 1940s, Americans felt they had little control over their lives. Much of the hectic pace of the post-1945 years can be ascribed to the widespread desire to get back to life as it was before 1929, and, to a remarkable extent, people succeeded.

Government programs contributed to this rush to fill the vacuum created by deprivation and sacrifice. For more than half a century, public authority had been gearing up to aid directly large segments of the population. Local government's service role had long enjoyed legitimacy, but it was not until the New Deal that the federal government acquired a similar place. World War II expanded Washington's influence, if only temporarily, and with the cold war on, the federal government remained active. Because of interest-group politics, these public programs reinforced the nearly universal desire to make up for lost time.

Still, although the New Deal thrust the federal government into a new economic role, it was as a supporting player, rather than protagonist. The 1930s witnessed a broadening of federal regulatory power and welfare responsibility, but generally the government continued to defer to the market. Free enterprise was not so much to be supervised by federal bureaucrats as to be made more profitable by the national government's spending and tax policies.

The federal government also lacked middle vision. Officials saw the big picture—the economy as a whole—and its prominent component parts—business, labor, agriculture—but not how these elements were related below the macroeconomic level. Neither by political orientation nor bureaucratic structure was the federal government ready to promote sound living patterns. Because community development was of secondary, or even tertiary, concern in national politics, metropolitan expansion after 1945 took off without federal recognition, even as it was being propelled by federal action. With the states content to maintain a hands-off attitude, with the localities unable to contain the pressures around them, and with the federal government fueling the fires of growth, community-building in the postwar period differed from earlier eras only in speed and detail. As before, private decision-making and individual self-interest largely determined the outcome.

GOVERNMENT PROGRAMS AND HOME OWNERSHIP

For centuries people flocked to the cities, lured by the economic and cultural opportunities they offered. But if the search for success and recreation drew people into cities, the predominant urban structure was not the factory or the store, the theater or the museum, but the residential unit. People not only worked and had fun in the city, they also lived there and accordingly built houses of all descriptions. By themselves these houses would have attracted few people to the cities, and, indeed, for many urban families poor housing was the worst feature of city life. Particularly in the post–World War II years, the inability of American cities to provide the housing their residents wanted would drive millions beyond the city boundaries. Housing, in fact, became the prime factor in the population upheaval in the nation's metropolitan areas.

In a society that believed in free enterprise and popular government, the owning of property was blessed both economically and politically. Only by owning property could one enjoy profit, rent, and interest—the holy trinity of capitalism. Politically, property ownership was champi-

oned as both giving to the individual certain safeguards against tyranni-
cal government and making him a more responsible member of the body
politic. As long as the United States was agrarian, these virtues were
protected by the widespread availability of farmland; but as the country
turned to industry and millions were hired by large corporations, the
urban home replaced the freehold farm as the symbol of individualism.
If one could no longer operate his own business, then owning his home
would give him a stake in the American system.[1]

By the middle of the twentieth century, most Americans wanted to
own their home—for both rational and irrational reasons.[2] In an image-
conscious consumer society, owning one's home conferred immediate
prestige as a visible symbol of upward mobility. After World War II,
messages from every podium, pulpit, and medium of mass communication promised blue-collar workers automatic entry into the middle class
with purchase of their own home.[3] Status aside, there were also practical
reasons for owning one's home. Families with more children required
additional indoor space; as they grew older, more outdoor space. Usually, such space could be obtained only by buying a house.[4]

The Great Depression and World War II had reinforced these feelings. A decade of economic stagnation had denied millions membership
in the middle class; although wartime prosperity gave financial success,
the curbs on nonessential goods had prevented people from showing off
their wealth. Once the war was over, Americans rushed to satisfy their
long-denied wants and to impress their neighbors; consumers, their savings accounts bulging, could seriously consider getting their own home.
Further, the nation's birthrate, which had reached an all-time low of 20
births per 1,000 population in the mid-1930s, climbed sharply: from
1950 through 1960 it stood at 24 births per 1,000. This "baby boom"
brought a new demand for dwellings to house families with three to five
children; for middle-class families such accommodations were to be
found only in the sales market.[5]

For reasons philosophical, psychological, and practical, many city
residents were thus prepared to buy homes after 1945. Such sentiments
had existed before 1930, but inadequate reservoirs of credit, steep initial
costs of purchasing, and high interest rates on mortgages had prevented
fulfillment. The federal government had moved, first under Herbert
Hoover and then under Franklin D. Roosevelt, to lower these barriers.
With the return of prosperity after 1945, then, thanks to the opening of
new lending channels and the provision of federal home mortgage guarantees, owning a home became possible for many more American
families.

Although this depression-spawned governmental intervention into the housing market drew social legitimacy by encouraging home owner-ship, its primary goals were economic. The building material and con-struction industries accounted for about 15 percent of the Gross Na-tional Product, and the construction trades accounted for about 5 percent of the labor force. Residential construction had been in a slump even before the 1929 stock market crash, and the subsequent deteriora-tion of economic conditions had almost dried up new housing starts. Renewed home-building was one way of reversing the economic slide. Because the chosen instruments of recovery—greater availability of credit and mortgage insurance—did not involve direct federal financing or threaten government ownership, they enjoyed wide backing. Business would be aided, jobs created, and consumers able to get better housing. For the first time the nation had housing programs, but they were iso-lated links in the chain of economic policy.[6]

Basic economic concepts also had their effect on the housing pro-grams. The Federal Housing Administration (FHA), the agency in charge of mortgage insurance, was under statutory instructions to fol-low conventional business wisdom in issuing loan guarantees. Accord-ingly, it backed sales rather than rentals on the argument that individu-ally owned homes are better credit risks than rental units because a homeowner is purportedly a better guardian of property than an inves-tor, who might skimp on maintenance. Similarly, the FHA believed its money was safer in sales housing because, whereas the supply of single-family homes is closely tied to demand, rental housing is usually pro-duced in advance of a demand that might not materialize. Furthermore, the law required the FHA to exercise much greater continuing regula-tion over the rental projects the agency assisted than it did in the case of homes put up for sale. For this reason both the FHA and builders pre-ferred the sales housing market.[7]

Home ownership in the postwar period received a boost from another federal agency, the Veterans Administration (VA). Because it permitted veterans to buy a house on easy credit terms with, and this was very important, little or no down-payment, the VA housing program was "probably as effective an instrument for narrowing the market for new, family-sized rental units as was ever devised." Families actually found it cheaper to buy under the VA program than to rent and, for probably the first and only time in American history, apartment-renters had higher average incomes than home-buyers.[8]

The outstanding characteristic of the housing picture in the second half of the 1940s was the critical shortage of dwellings. New housing construction had virtually ceased during the war, extending to nearly two decades the drought in residential building. Compounding the supply problem was the massive demand brought on by a doubling of the rate of household formation. Marriages and children long deferred now proliferated, and there were not enough houses and apartments to absorb them. Estimates of the housing shortage in 1946–47 ranged from three to six million units.[9]

Almost every city had its own housing horror stories. In New York a newly wed couple moved into the display window of a department store for two days, and the publicity brought them the offer of an apartment. In Chicago 250 streetcars were put on sale as potential homes. An ad in an Omaha newspaper read: "Big Ice Box, 7 by 17 feet, could be fixed up to live in." In San Francisco respectable, solid citizens were living in cars parked on city streets, using the restrooms in the public library, and cooking over wood fires in the park.[10]

Direct federal efforts to deal with the housing shortage did little. After first lifting controls on building material allocations in October 1945 to spur residential construction, President Truman reimposed them in December when it became obvious that builders had no intention of putting up homes in the medium price range. Before the winter of 1946 was over, a Veterans' Emergency Housing Program had been unveiled by the White House; using federal regulation, loans, and subsidies as tools, it set a goal of 2.7 million new homes within two years. But because of bureaucratic infighting, lack of organization within the building industry, labor strife, and a conservative attack on big government, the program resulted in very few homes and great loss of public support. When the president removed virtually all price controls following the Republican sweep in the 1946 congressional elections, he, in effect, canceled the Veterans' Emergency Housing Program. The federal government was henceforth content to resume a passive sustaining role.[11]

HOME-BUILDING AND SUBURBIA

With long-held beliefs and new government programs combining to assure that the answer to the housing shortage would be the construction of single-family, owner-occupied homes, the next question was where these dwellings would be built. Because speed was the prime concern, this matter was settled largely by default. Siting would be determined by the ease with which the land could be readied; it was just common sense that vacant land was more desirable than land already occupied. This vacant land might be inside or outside the city, but for a variety of reasons, suburban areas gained the most.

Although the situation varied from area to area, many central cities no longer had much open land. Particularly in the older cities of the Northeast and the Midwest, a century or more of large population inflow had given most parts of the municipality a built-up appearance. Although many lots were still not improved and there was actually considerable room left for construction, this filling-in process satisfied neither the economic nor psychological temper of the times. Few central-city sites lent themselves to the mass-production techniques recently introduced to the housing field, and, ironically, the very existence in place of such utilities as sewers, gas lines, and roadways rendered city neighborhoods less attractive to builders experimenting with new construction methods. Rather than conform to existing street layouts and strict housing codes, the new home-builders sought freedom on the cheaper, unregulated land in the suburbs.[12]

If postwar home-builders liked suburbia because of its opportunities, home mortgage-granting institutions liked its security. Urban real estate was a volatile investment, profitable but risky. Zoning offered some protection against changing land uses, but practically none against neighborhood decay and population movement. From the finance officers' viewpoint, the central city suffered from old age and diverse residency, which in combination created a climate of great uncertainty. In postwar America the central cities were seen as heading rapidly out of middle age toward decrepit dependency. Furthermore, blighted neighborhoods signified not merely physical deterioration; they also demonstrated the melting pot mistake. That racial and ethnic groups did not mix well was assumed by the financial community, itself a preserve of long-established families. To them, cities were inherently unstable because they tried to do what could not be done—bring various peoples together harmoniously. Such mixing, it was believed, had but two consequences: the decline of both the human race and property values.[13] Given the chance, bankers would do for their business what they had already done for themselves in private life—leave the city.

The suburbs, accordingly, grew; by 1910, the year of the first Decennial Census to define "metropolitan district," 25 percent of the population of such districts were living outside central city limits. Twenty years later, with the automobile widely accepted, it was 35 percent.[14] The 1920s were the first decade that the rate of suburban growth exceeded city growth. With its happy combination of city and country life, the suburb was considered a natural and positive development in residential patterns.[15]

The early 1900s also witnessed the political encirclement of the central cities. Much of the population gain registered by the big cities in the nineteenth century came by simply moving the city limits outward. After about 1910 this wave of annexation subsided nearly everywhere, marking the flowering of suburban political strength. Cities were no longer bordered by nondescript settlements that could be amalgamated without difficulty; the upper-middle-class suburb of the early twentieth century was strongly anti-urban. Their residents were affluent, articulate, and aroused, and exerted considerable political influence unrelated to their actual numbers. The split between central city and suburb was one of many fault lines in predepression America.[16]

The depression and subsequent war affected the pace of metropolitan development, but not its direction. Suburban growth fell off in the 1930s, but city growth rates dropped even more. Both experienced population growth as mobilization revived industries but, for logistic and security reasons, the federal government had war plants placed outside the central cities. This set the stage for even more rapid dispersal of population and jobs to the suburbs after the war.[17]

In 1945, by every major indicator, America's suburban destiny seemed assured. Fifteen years of induced social solidarity had not weakened the American preference for privacy; indeed, the twin crises of depression and war had given it even greater appeal. As one young soldier-turned-urban analyst later recalled, the consuming desire of veterans was to rediscover conditions of intimacy. Starting one's own family and finding one's own home became primary objectives.[18] The strength of these feelings was reflected in the experience of William Levitt, head of one of the large suburban home-construction firms:

> We started to sell in March 1949. We advertised that beginning the next Monday we would accept deposits. Wednesday night they began camping out. It was bitterly cold; we set up a canteen. One of the women on the line was pregnant; we had to take her to the hospital to have her baby. That Monday night we closed, from seven-thirty to eleven o'clock, fourteen hundred contracts.[19]

Federal home-financing policies also favored the suburbs. The FHA was no more a charitable institution than the local bank; each was motivated by the drive to maximize profits.[20] If the FHA hesitated to guarantee mortgages on central-city housing, it was precisely because private lenders had already expressed doubts about the safety of such investments.[21] In the absence of a directive from Congress to take risks, the FHA did what all bureaucracies do: it followed the flow of the market. The push to the suburbs seemed, and probably was, inevitable; the FHA merely facilitated the process.[22]

For the federal authorities to reverse, or even to slow, the suburban migration would have required a tremendous act of will. The constitutional question of national power with respect to housing remained unsettled. "Doubt as to how far federal legislation may reach out still acts as a restraining influence," observed housing expert Charles Abrams in 1946. "It compels the shaping of a gradual policy in a field that does not lend itself to graduality."[23] Political realities further limited government intervention. The scope of social engineering that "a plan for national urban land development" (Abrams's phrase) would have entailed was totally unfeasible. It required a consensus on ends and means that did not exist; the liberal state was still under challenge at the ballot box, and the concept of federal allocation of resources had been decisively rejected by Congress in 1943 when it abolished the National Resources Planning Board.[24] Government was surely more active in the postwar years than it had been before 1930, but this activity remained confined, both as to range and depth. The FHA was helping to build houses, not communities. Where the houses were put was far less important than that they were built and the government investment secure. The public wanted the government to assist them in finding places to live; they did not expect it—indeed, did not want it—to tell them how to live.[25] Suburbia was essentially the handiwork of the economic and social marketplace; government merely confirmed its triumph.

OUT OF THE MARKET: PUBLIC HOUSING

The federal government's public housing program in the postwar period was a dismal experience, and it demonstrated why politicians preferred to keep out of social policy-making. Few domestic issues consumed as much of Congress's time as this effort to aid the poor, and none gave government officials so much heartache. Only one group really gained from the venture—investors in the tax-exempt, federally guaranteed bonds issued by local authorities.[26] The intended beneficiaries, slum dwellers, were either not reached at all or supplied with a defective product.

If most federal welfare programs were well disguised or indirect, public housing was up front and exposed. Unlike the bulk of federal spending that assisted producer groups, public housing removed a part of the consuming population from the private housing market. This interference with the mechanism of supply and demand earned the hostility of realtors, home-builders, and mortgage bankers. Almost from the start of public housing in 1938, these groups sought to replace it with a system of aid to private business. During World War II the program's opponents succeeded in virtually shutting it down, but when peace came, public housing's friends resumed the battle at home.

The political strength of public housing came not from a broad popular base but from the intensity of its few supporters. Among them only labor unions possessed real clout at election time; the other public housing lobbyists, local officials and socially conscious members of the middle and upper classes, were more adept at gaining publicity than in delivering votes. Since the expected recipients of this largesse were thought to be in the big cities, there was little incentive for congressmen from smaller communities to identify themselves with such a "socialistic" program. Only the unexpected results of the 1948 elections, combined with the active leadership of President Truman, gave public housing a boost in 1949, but even then it cleared the last legislative hurdle in the House of Representatives by the narrowest of margins, 209–204.[27]

This victory turned out to be more symbolic than substantive. War once again, this time in Korea, provided the program's enemies with a pretext for reducing funds. Moreover, the change of administration in 1953 deprived public housing of an executive branch willing to lobby on its behalf; the middle-of-the-road temper of the decade's political culture was generally inhospitable to programs that aided the lower classes. The result was that Congress, which in 1949 had authorized the construction of 810,000 units over six years, cut back at almost every session, so that only 322,000 new starts were actually funded from 1949 to 1960. Thus, while the suburban-oriented FHA was gaining additional lending authority from the legislature, public housing was being starved.

Public housing's poor standing in ideologically conscious and budget-minded Washington was not surprising; more unexpected was its poor reception in the cities and among those it was supposed to help. Part of the problem at the local level was the federal government's tough spending restrictions. Because of congressional instructions that public housing not compete with the private sector, bureaucrats ruthlessly cut expenses; doors would not be provided for closets, elevators would not stop at every floor, cinder blocks would be left exposed in corridors. Individually, none was significant, but the overall effect of hundreds of economies like these was to deny public housing those little comforts that make a rental apartment a home. Nor were adequate maintenance services supplied to keep the buildings in good repair. Federal regulations excluding families with incomes over specified levels also contributed to the deterioration. Those able to improve their economic position had little incentive to keep up their apartments; many that stayed lacked the experience or tools to care for their surroundings. Many eligible families turned public housing down because of the low character of the projects' residents and the institutional quality of the projects' environment.[28]

But if penny-pinching detracted from its appeal, it was the social implications of public housing that rendered it downright unpopular. The mixing of income groups in residential neighborhoods had been a common feature of American cities for decades; it was the result of the complex interactions of shifting land uses, new modes of transportation, and economic mobility that accompanied urban growth. The well-to-do did not enjoy intermingling, but they could live with it, at least for a while; furthermore, the same impersonal market forces that had created the unhappy arrangement could also undo it. Public housing, however, was something else. The housing shortage that prompted private homebuilders to seek out vacant land in the suburbs also led municipal public housing agencies to favor undeveloped land within the city and for the same reasons of expediency, adaptability to new designs, and ready availability. Most was to be found in middle-class neighborhoods that vehemently resisted having public housing put into their midst; it was sure to overtax local services, change the character of the neighborhood, and lower property values. The only way this menace could be stopped was in the political arena. Experienced at battling on this terrain, the middle class had little trouble in pushing public housing and the poor back into the slums.

Giving added dimension to this middle-class hostility was race. The distaste prosperous Americans felt for socialization across class lines was minor compared with the abhorrence with which white Americans of all classes regarded racial integration. In northern cities operators of the private housing market were as effective as any law might have been in keeping blacks within the ghettos. Their population growth required constant enlargement of these ghettos, but the pressures were generally relieved by realtors in an orderly way that allowed whites to find new preserves; the race riots in Detroit and other cities during World War II demonstrated the delicate nature of the neighborhood transition process. Continuing postwar black migration to northern cities exacerbated the problem. In this tense atmosphere public housing resembled a bull in a china shop; because so many of the families eligible for public housing were black, any project in white areas was almost certain to breach the racial barricades. Accordingly, such neighborhoods mobilized politically and ensured that where public housing could not be blocked altogether, it was sited in the ghettos.[29] Eventually, tens of thousands of federally authorized public housing units went unclaimed by localities, and some high-rise projects were later torn down as public nuisances.

By any standard public housing was a misfit. It challenged, rather than reinforced, the icons of status, privatism, and security. No one really believed in it—not its federal or local administrators, its proponents, or its clientele. Yet it survived. Staying alive was testimonial more to bureaucratic inertia than to any public sense of social obligation. Allowing public housing to continue an existence maintained the fiction that the poor were being helped. Public housing sharpened racial divisions, and, to an extent never seen before, the suburbs became a refuge for whites fleeing blacks.[30] Thus did market take its revenge on the welfare state.

CHALLENGING THE MARKETPLACE: URBAN RENEWAL

As the federal government's mortgage insurance programs buttressed decisions being made by the private sector, and as public housing sought to supplement free enterprise, so did urban renewal attempt to modify marketplace conditions. By giving central-city real estate an economic attractiveness it did not have on its own, Title I of the Housing Act of 1949 tried to conserve the nation's investment in urban buildings and utilities. Not only did this recycling effort run counter to the American urban experience, it was also out of step with postwar America.

When the proposals for urban renewal had begun taking shape in the late 1930s and early 1940s, the emphasis was on planning. The depression had tarnished the image of the exploitive model of development; with the opportunities for future growth apparently limited, greater control of resources was required. The goal was to make cities both more efficient and more humane; they would be restructured to meet the demands of advanced technology, and there would be special attention to housing for the lower classes. It was also envisioned that this community-rebuilding program would show little respect for local political boundaries; rehabilitation of the central city depended upon regulating development in the outskirts.[31]

By the time the urban renewal measure passed Congress in 1949, both the rationale for, and the design of, the program had been undermined. The postwar boom had reinvigorated faith in capitalism; government would be allowed to play only a secondary role in influencing urban growth. Planning was to be carried out in the narrowest of fashions, on a building-by-building basis, rather than in relation to the city as a whole. Controlled metropolitan development also went by the boards as the housing shortage was relieved by mass-produced housing in the suburbs. Subdivision developers' profits and consumer satisfaction could not, and would not, wait for public authorities to get their affairs in order. Urban renewal had to operate in a more turbulent world than its liberal sponsors had foreseen and with fewer tools than they had believed necessary.

Cooperation between government and private enterprise of the scope that urban renewal entailed had not been seen in America since the heyday of canal and railroad building. Plenty of mistakes were committed, and much waste accompanied those earlier projects; but the social benefits and private gains were so huge as to mask the errors and corruption. Urban renewal, however, had the same problems without the offsetting advantages; operating in advance of the marketplace was easier than functioning in the midst of one.

Management and money were at the heart of its difficulties. Title I required the agreement of three partners: the federal government, the local government, and the private developer.[32] Only the latter two could initiate projects, but authority for final approval rested at the national level. Cranking up this cumbersome administrative machinery would have been easier if all the participants had believed in it, but only local government truly wanted it to succeed. Private developers, who could see the suburbs siphoning off the central city's middle-class population, demanded greater rewards for risking their money in urban renewal. Federal bureaucrats also doubted the program's viability, and were under pressure to protect the government's money; they gave proposed projects long, hard scrutiny before granting approval. Only the local politicians had much to lose if urban renewal failed. Further decline of the inner core would hurt property assessments, lead to a deterioration in city services, and accelerate the movement to the suburbs. Those elected officials smart enough to grasp Title I's promise and adept enough to act as brokers between the developers and Washington gained political power and delayed their community's day of financial reckoning.

Urban renewal also faced psychological obstacles. Although cities had been growing, people had been leaving the urban cores for decades; they were not mentally prepared, in the absence of some great crisis, to reverse their negative impressions of urban life. "Frustrated city planners," observed *Fortune* magazine in 1946, "can take comfort in the fact that nearly two-thirds of the people now in cities of over 100,000 would rather live almost anywhere else."[33] Large-scale projects impressive enough to catch the imagination might hold some prospective emigrants and even lure back some earlier evacuees, but there was never enough money to have much effect. New shopping malls or civic centers would still be surrounded by old, decrepit neighborhoods. The Republicans' attempt after 1954 to put the emphasis on rehabilitation as a way of making the funds go further may have been the right approach in the long run, but in the 1950s it made no sense as long as the suburbs remained a less-expensive alternative. It was difficult to get excited about fixing up a sixty-year-old brownstone when a new house with open space could be purchased with ease.

Besides trying unsuccessfully to turn the metropolitan marketplace around, urban renewal also obscured the social ills of the metropolis. Title I focused on the physical structure of the central city and its tax base. By strengthening these foundations, it was believed the cities could be revived. If massive sums of urban renewal money had indeed been supplied, to implement what the 1960s would call a "Marshall Plan for the cities," perhaps the anticipated benefits would have been realized. The cities might have become so comfortable and pleasant that the middle class would have stayed. But the promise was not backed up by cash. New downtown complexes were built, but the schools declined, municipal services shrank, and jobs continued to flow to the suburbs. Government might have deluded itself and part of the citizenry into thinking that the cities were being saved, but the white middle class was getting out, leaving the city to the poor and the blacks. On an individual basis most people could grasp urban renewal's failure, but on the administrative and political level, few were prepared for the social unrest of the 1960s.[34]

RIDING TO MARKET:
PUBLIC TRANSIT AND THE PRIVATE AUTOMOBILE

Urban life and form have always been heavily shaped by the prevailing modes of transportation. First as trading centers and then as manufacturing locales, cities were concerned about accessibility, both externally and internally. The advent of rail vehicles in the nineteenth century not only enabled cities to trade on a national scale but also permitted their population to expand outward. With the coming of streetcars, people no longer had to live close to where they worked, and commuting became common in the American metropolis. By the close of the 1920s, another technological innovation challenged the streetcar's primacy: the automobile. Soon after 1945 the automobile was victorious.

Many of public transit's postwar woes arose from its own weaknesses. Organized during the flush times of municipal corruption at the turn of the century, most transit companies were so heavily mortgaged that any operating profits were swallowed up by interest costs. This shaky financial base was not compensated for by wise management. Transit operators assumed that they had a captive market, and instead of trying, in the 1920s, to adapt their product to meet the changing needs of customers, they cut service and raised fares whenever revenues declined. This all but assured further reductions in patronage, and the cycle was repeated.

The popular image of public transit as a private business further damaged its competitive position. Following the Progressive era's crusade against municipal graft, transit companies often were required to pay high local taxes and were subjected to control by regulatory commissions that sometimes refused to permit higher fares in inflationary periods. A little-noticed provision of the Public Utility Holding Company Act of 1935 may have also undermined the well-being of public transit. By forcing many power companies to divest themselves of their transit subsidiaries, the act denied some transit firms needed financial support and executive talent. Because of its bad reputation and because it was taken for granted by the 1940s, public transit received virtually no support from any level of government.[35]

In contrast, the automobile had been a pampered child. If Americans had put up with public transit for lack of choice, they loved the car because it gave them privacy and greater control of their daily life. And Americans were willing to pay for this freedom through user taxes. Almost from the start, road-building was considered a public necessity that benefited the entire community. The enthusiasm with which localities improved streets in the 1920s meant serious trouble for public transit in that decade; depression and war gave transit operators a respite, but once peace and prosperity returned, transit's fall was rapid. Transit patronage in 1955 was but one-half of its wartime high, while automobile passenger miles doubled over the decade.[36]

After the war all levels of government tried to meet the public's demand for roads. Hundreds of millions of dollars were spent annually by public agencies on highways, but it never seemed enough. As John Kenneth Galbraith noted in 1958: " . . . Use of privately produced vehicles has, on occasion, got far out of line with the supply of the related public services. The result has been hideous road congestion, an annual massacre of impressive proportions and chronic colitis in the cities."[37] Yet even though federal highway policy has often been singled out as a major factor in the exodus from the city by making the suburbs more accessible, as in the case of the home mortgage guarantees, government actions seem to have reinforced, not mandated, decisions made in the private market. In the face of political pressures, the national government had little choice but to go along with consumers, who were spending billions for automobiles.[38]

Legislative approval of the 41,000-mile, $37 billion Interstate Highway System in 1956 revealed both the strength of those pressures and the lack of clear governmental policy. The highway lobby brought together automobile and tire manufacturers, oil companies, construction firms, and motorist groups; and when they could agree on a financing mechanism, legislative and executive approval was assured. Less settled was the question of where the roads were to be built: were they to come into central cities or bypass them? To the extent that the matter was discussed, which was minimal, legislators revealed little understanding of how this program might affect metropolitan areas. Just as the government wanted homes built but did not particularly care where, so the government wanted roads, without regard to their social and economic consequences. The 1956 act came too late to influence community-building in the immediate postwar period, but it helped extend the suburban trend into the 1960s and beyond.[39]

LOOKING TO WASHINGTON

The postwar metropolitan migrations created pressures for wider federal aid for community development. Whether localities were gaining or losing population, their internal resources proved inadequate to cope with the resulting needs. New suburban areas experienced growth pains as expansion outran local government's ability to furnish such essential services as schools and sewers. Central cities, on the other hand, had their infrastructures in place, but discovered them increasingly expensive to maintain as the character of their populace changed. Limited success in raising revenues and even less success at regional cooperation left but one practical option: national assistance.

Both central cities and suburbs underwent alterations in order to maintain local autonomy. Realizing that modern manufacturing techniques and the automobile had shifted the industrial advantage to the periphery, central cities began emphasizing the service sector as employer. New office buildings added to the tax rolls and provided white-collar jobs, but because many of these workers were commuting from the suburbs, the gains were only marginal. Nothing municipal government could do, it seemed, touched the deeper problem of getting jobs—and homes—for the unskilled.[40] The suburbs, furthermore, discriminated in deciding which industries could move in. They kept out businesses that employed poorly educated people at low wages, or that polluted the environment. Such screening preserved neighborhood insularity, but it retarded broadening of the tax base.

Because they owed their fashionableness to exclusivity, postwar suburbs, although demographically different from their early twentieth-century antecedents, continued to oppose political amalgamation with the central cities. Indeed, the new members of the middle class were often more provincial than their upper-crust neighbors. The latter, because of their family traditions and financial strength, persisted in trying to direct the city even after they left it; by mid-century they favored bringing the core and periphery together under a federative arrangement. Not so with the more recent arrivals. The city was in their past and they wanted it kept that way. They saw no need to link up with the declining central city.[41] If they could not make it alone, they would turn not to their neighbors for help but to the federal government.

Throughout the 1950s the entire concept of federal assistance was gaining legitimacy. Ideologically the nation may have remained devoted to free enterprise, but in practice it found comfort in the New Deal's welfare state. Millions were enjoying Social Security, veterans were benefiting from the G.I. Bill, and government contracts were providing hundreds of thousands of jobs. Older communities were already getting help under the public housing and urban renewal programs, and it was not difficult to argue that those grants be expanded so that similar assistance for schools, water, sanitation, and recreation would be extended to the suburbs. Here was a solution on which both the cities and suburbs could agree: let Uncle Sam foot the bill for the population explosion.[42] It was a strange partnership, but one based on a common understanding. Federal money would only paste over the central city–suburban cleavage, not heal it, and each recipient was to use the funds to improve its position with respect to its neighbors. The larger federal grants demanded by the late 1950s went to serve the same sort of parochial goals that government programs had usually aided.

POLITICS IN THE METROPOLITAN AGE

The migrations of the 1940s and 1950s that sent local officials to Washington for federal assistance also left their mark on the nation's politics. The exodus of the white middle class to the suburbs and the influx of poor blacks to the northern cities somewhat affected party coalitions but did not radically alter the balance of power between the two major parties. They also put new pressures on the party system at both the local and national levels.

In the central cities there appeared an efficiency movement reminiscent of the Progressive era. But unlike that effort, which had been obsessed with the corruption and waste of the machine bosses, the postwar reform took aim at the physical obsolescence of the old core cities. If the cities were to survive, they would have to be rebuilt almost from the ground up. A new generation of political leaders appeared, shaped by their corporate and World War II organizational experiences. Streamlining municipal government to make it more decisive and responsive, and seeking out business cooperation, became the hallmarks of big-city politics. Although the Democrats kept control of most of the nation's city halls, they were often allied with Republican-led chambers of commerce. Improvements in the central business district, not the promise of patronage, made the difference at elections. These new coalitions and programs did not demolish completely the traditional political apparatus, but the neighborhood focus of political campaigning steadily gave way to media-based appeals that stressed candidate rather than party.[43]

Simultaneously, partisan identification assumed less importance in the suburbs. The old, upper-class enclaves had always had a refined Republican air about them, but the ideal was consensual, public-spirited politics. It was this model that the burgeoning postwar suburbs sought to emulate. Physically removed from the inner-city working-class neighborhoods that instilled party loyalty, usually Democratic, the middle-class migrants did not adopt the Republican label so much as they did a position of independence. Having come to the suburbs for private autonomy, the newcomers joined, not a party, but less formal and temporary groupings that took stands on issues. Local politics revolved around schools, zoning, and related aspects of community life; in this context the usual party tag had little meaning.[44]

These trends in metropolitan politics created both problems and opportunities for presidential hopefuls. With many blacks moving to northern cities and voting there, Democratic candidates were caught between demands to promote racial equality and continuing loyalties to the rural South and northern ethnic neighborhoods. Out in the suburbs potential Democratic torchbearers could promise federal aid, but still had to assure that such assistance entailed neither higher federal taxes nor further federal intervention in local affairs. Meanwhile, the loosening of party ties that accompanied the move from inner city to suburb provided the Republicans with potential support from the upwardly mobile middle class, but designing a program that would attract these independents required as much juggling as was demanded of the Democrats. To remain steadfast to the G.O.P. commitment to reduce federal spending without rejecting suburban pleas for help called for a heavy reliance on private enterprise. Greater private investment was also part of the Republican solution for central-city ills, but here the G.O.P.'s effort was something less than wholehearted; the big cities had been Democratic for so long that Republicans had all but written them off.

The presidential contest of 1960 pitted two suburban-born candidates against one another. Although identified with Irish Boston, John F. Kennedy had actually spent his childhood in such affluent suburbs as Brookline, Massachusetts, and Bronxville, New York. As the Democratic nominee, Kennedy pledged a program of aid that overwhelming numbers of central-city whites and blacks, and a good share of the suburban middle class as well, could support. In contrast, Richard Nixon, whose ill-defined roots were in the amorphous lower-middle-class suburbs of Los Angeles, could not decide how to approach the issues posed by metropolitanization; he carried the suburbs, but not by enough to offset the majority Kennedy rolled up in the central cities.[45] The geographical and racial polarization that Nixon would exploit eight years later was not completely in place in 1960.

TOWARD "TWO SOCIETIES"[46]

By 1960 the nation was well on the road to social polarization. Prosperity, advances in technology, private investment decisions, and government action had conspired to speed the decline of the central city and the rise of the suburbs, keeping the poor—particularly the black poor—in the city while encouraging the white middle class to move to the suburbs. There had been no conscious decision to create this divided society; rather the "invisible hand" of the marketplace had woven the independent judgments of countless producers, consumers, bureaucrats, and politicians into a fabric that highlighted the contrasts in American life. Privatism, spiced by heavy doses of prejudice, was given a free hand and a free ride in affluent postwar America. A more socially conscious era would feel its effects.

1. Stephan Thernstrom, *Poverty and Progress: Social Mobility in a Nineteenth Century City* (Cambridge, Mass., 1964), pp. 116–17; Sam Bass Warner, Jr., *Streetcar Suburbs: The Process of Growth in Boston, 1870–1900* (Cambridge, Mass., 1962), pp. 8, 15.

2. William L. Slayton and Richard Dewey, "Urban Redevelopment and the Urbanite," in *The Future of Cities and Urban Redevelopment*, ed. Coleman Woodbury (Chicago, 1953), pp. 322–29; Nelson N. Foote et al., *Housing Choices and Housing Constraints* (New York, 1960), pp. 187–90.

3. John P. Dean, *Homeownership: Is It Sound?* (New York, 1945); Charles Abrams, *The Future of Housing* (New York, 1946), pp. 36–54. Both Dean and Abrams criticized the propaganda blitz on behalf of home ownership.

4. Peter H. Rossi, *Why Families Move: A Study in the Social Psychology of Urban Residential Mobility* (Glencoe, Ill., 1955), pp. 177–80; Foote, *Housing Choices*, pp. 190–96; Herbert J. Gans, *The Levittowners* (New York, 1967), pp. 31–42; cf. Howard P. Chudacoff, *Mobile Americans: Residential and Social Mobility in Omaha, 1880–1920* (New York, 1972), pp. 158–59.

5. Marion Clawson and Peter Hall, *Planning and Urban Growth: An Anglo-American Comparison* (Baltimore, 1973), pp. 88–89; John Morton Blum, *V Was for Victory* (New York, 1976), pp. 103–5.

6. The most-detailed account of the early federal involvement in housing is William L. C. Wheaton, "The Evolution of Federal Housing Programs" (Ph.D. diss., University of Chicago, 1953).

7. Louis Winnick, *Rental Housing: Opportunities for Private Investment* (New York, 1958), p. 77. The FHA's one major effort during the postwar period to spur rental housing, the Section 608 program, was both successful in building new units and short-lived. Because 608 allowed developers to make huge profits with practically no investment, the program became enmeshed in scandal and was eliminated by Congress. Despite the FHA's withdrawal from the field, rental housing construction started to boom in the late 1950s; because of new population and employment patterns, such housing was in high demand: Robert Schafer, *The Suburbanization of Multifamily Housing* (Lexington, Mass., 1974).

8. Winnick, *Rental Housing*, pp. 74–76.

9. Clawson and Hall, *Planning and Urban Growth*, pp. 88–89.

10. Joseph C. Goulden, *The Best Years, 1945–1950* (New York, 1976), p. 133; Richard O. Davies, *Housing Reform during the Truman Administration* (Columbia, Mo., 1966), p. 41.

11. Barton J. Bernstein, "Reluctance and Resistance: Wilson Wyatt and Veterans' Housing in the Truman Administration," *Register of the Kentucky Historical Society* 65 (1967): 47–66.

12. Barry Checkoway, "Large Builders, Federal Housing Programs, and Postwar Suburbanization," *International Journal of Urban and Regional Research* 4 (1980): 21–44.

13. Calvin Bradford, "Financing Home Ownership: The Federal Role in Neighborhood Decline," *Urban Affairs Quarterly* 14 (1978–79): 320–23.

14. The 1930 figure is for the same cities that had achieved "metropolitan district" status in 1910; if all the cities that were centers of metropolitan districts in 1930 are included, the figure is lower.

15. Gregory H. Singleton, "The Genesis of Suburbia: A Complex of Historical Trends," in *The Urbanization of the Suburbs*, ed. Louis H. Masotti and Jeffrey K. Hadden (Beverly Hills, Calif., 1973), pp. 29–50; Kenneth T. Jackson, "Urban Decentralization in the Nineteenth Century: A Statistical Inquiry," in *The New Urban History*, ed. Leo F. Schnore (Princeton, N.J., 1975), pp. 110–42; Joel Schwartz, "Evolution of the Suburbs," in *Suburbia: The American Dream and Dilemma*, ed. Philip C. Dolce (Garden City, N.Y., 1976), pp. 1–36; Edwin C. Mills, "Urban Density Functions," *Urban Studies* 7 (February 1970): 5–20; Blaine A. Brownell, *The Urban Ethos in the South, 1920–1930* (Baton Rouge, La., 1975), pp. 65–69.

16. Kenneth T. Jackson, "Metropolitan Government versus Political Autonomy: Politics on the Crabgrass Frontier," in *Cities in American History*, ed. Kenneth T. Jackson and Stanley K. Schultz (New York, 1972), pp. 448–55; Jon C. Teaford, *City and Suburb: The Political Fragmentation of Metropolitan America, 1850–1970* (Baltimore, 1979), pp. 5–63, 76–104.

17. John F. Kain, "The Distribution and Movement of Jobs and Industry," in *The Metropolitan Enigma*, ed. James Q. Wilson (Garden City, N.Y., 1970), pp. 5–12; Philip J. Funigiello, *The Challenge to Urban Liberalism: Federal-City Relations during World War II* (Knoxville, Tenn., 1978), pp. 10–11.

18. Robert Wood, "Suburban Politics and Policies: Retrospect and Prospect," *Publius* 5 (Winter 1975): 46.

19. Quoted in Martin Mayer, *The Builders* (New York, 1978), p. 308.

20. One urban analyst has observed that the FHA was "the most successful single business ever launched." Because the FHA was so prudent in its loan guarantees and charged customers for its services, it actually made contributions to the federal treasury: George Sternlieb, "Housing, Urban Development, and Rehabilitation," *South Atlantic Urban Studies* 1 (1977): 42.

21. Bradford, "Financing Home Ownership," p. 324.

22. Gail D. Shelp and Ursula A. Guerrieri, "The Role of Federal Housing Programs in the Community Development Process," in U.S., Department of Housing and Urban De-

velopment, *Housing in the Seventies: Working Papers* (Washington, D.C., 1976), pp. 1583–84. In an unpublished paper Kenneth T. Jackson compiled an impressive set of figures demonstrating how the FHA's loan policies fostered abandonment of large parts of the central cities, but he concluded that "the Federal Housing Administration was not the *sine qua non* in the mushrooming of the suburbs": "The Spatial Dimensions of Social Control: Race, Ethnicity, and Government Housing Policy in the United States, 1918–1968," p. 59. See also Jackson, "Race, Ethnicity, and Real Estate Appraisal: The Home Owners Loan Corporation and the Federal Housing Administration," *Journal of Urban History* 6 (1980): 419–52.

23. Abrams, *Future of Housing*, p. 201.

24. See Otis L. Graham, Jr., *Toward a Planned Society* (New York, 1976), pp. 52–58, 79–98.

25. This attitude was not confined to the average citizen; see the reminiscences of Nathaniel S. Keith, a former federal official and longtime advocate of federal housing aid: *Politics and the Housing Crisis since 1930* (New York, 1973).

26. The federal government paid the principal and interest on the long-term bonds localities issued to construct public housing projects; this subsidy allowed municipalities to charge rents within the means of low-income families.

27. The political history of public housing in the postwar era is chronicled in Leonard Freedman, *Public Housing: The Politics of Poverty* (New York, 1969).

28. Peter Marris, "A Report on Urban Renewal in the United States," in *The Urban Condition*, ed. Leonard Duhl (New York, 1963), pp. 120–21; Chester Hartman, "The Limitations of Public Housing," *Journal of the American Institute of Planners* 29 (November 1963): 284.

29. The classic case study of the problems presented by site selection is Martin Meyerson and Edward C. Banfield, *Politics, Planning, and the Public Interest: The Case of Public Housing in Chicago* (New York, 1955).

30. Without question the FHA contributed to this division. Before 1950 the agency actively fostered residential segregation in the suburbs by encouraging the use of racially restrictive covenants; from 1950 until 1962 it took no positive steps in the development of open occupancy and integrated housing. Because of public housing's total reliance upon local initiative, suburbs were under no compulsion to put up public housing, and virtually none did. Because of racial and income discrimination, blacks were bottled up in the central cities.

31. For the legislative background to Title I of the Housing Act of 1949, see Funigiello, *Challenge to Urban Liberalism*, pp. 217–45; and Mark I. Gelfand, *A Nation of Cities: The Federal Government and Urban America, 1933–1965* (New York, 1975), pp. 105–56.

32. Urban renewal had the federal government put up two-thirds of the cost of "writing down" (i.e., the difference between the high prices local redevelopment agencies paid for blighted real estate and the lower prices at which they resold these parcels to private builders) the land values, which was believed necessary to make the properties attractive for redevelopment; the local government supplied the other one-third. With the exception of government office buildings, it was expected that private investors would finance the new construction on these sites.

33. "The Fortune Survey," *Fortune* 33 (April 1946): 275.

34. The literature on urban renewal is voluminous; James Q. Wilson, ed., *Urban Renewal: The Record and the Controversy* (Cambridge, Mass., 1967), remains the best starting place.

35. George M. Smerk, *Urban Mass Transportation: A Dozen Years of Federal Policy* (Bloomington, Ind., 1974), pp. 12–13, 137; Stanley Mallach, "The Origins of the Decline of Urban Mass Transportation in the United States, 1890–1930," *Urbanism Past and Present*, no. 8 (Summer 1979), pp. 1–17. Also see Mark Foster, "City Planners and Urban

Transportation: The American Response, 1900–1940" *Journal of Urban History* 5 (May 1979): 365–96.

36. Paul Barrett, "Public Policy and Private Choice: Mass Transit and the Automobile in Chicago between the Wars," *Business History Review* 49 (Winter 1975): 473–97; David Owen Wise and Marguerite Duprie, "The Choice of the Automobile for Urban Passenger Transportation in Baltimore in the 1920s," *South Atlantic Urban Studies* 2 (1978): 153–79; Alan Altshuler, *The Urban Transportation System: Politics and Policy Innovation* (Cambridge, Mass., 1979), pp. 22–23.

37. John Kenneth Galbraith, *The Affluent Society* (Boston, 1958), p. 255.

38. Mark H. Rose, *Interstate: Express Highway Politics, 1941–1956* (Lawrence, Kans., 1979).

39. Gary T. Schwartz, "Urban Freeways and the Interstate System," *Southern California Law Review* 49 (March 1976): 466–513.

40. See Hal Burton, *The City Fights Back* (New York, 1954); Kain, "Distribution and Movement of Jobs and Industry," pp. 12–31.

41. Teaford, *City and Suburb*, pp. 175–80. In the central cities opposition to metropolitan government was most intense in the black ghettos, which feared a diminution of black voting power by suburban amalgamation.

42. "Cities Ask for More," *Economist* 194 (January 1, 1960): 36; *Proceedings of the First Urban County Congress* (Washington, D.C., n.d. [1959]).

43. Seymour Freedgood, "New Strength in City Hall," in The Editors of Fortune, *The Exploding Metropolis* (Garden City, N.Y., 1957), pp. 81–96; Robert H. Salisbury, "Urban Politics: The New Convergence of Power," *Journal of Politics* 26 (November 1964): 775–97.

44. Robert C. Wood, *Suburbia: Its People and Their Politics* (Boston, 1959), pp. 153–225; Frederic M. Wirt et al., *On the City's Rim: Politics and Policy in Suburbia* (Lexington, Mass., 1972), pp. 145–74. The "conversion" theory, which argued that Democrats became Republicans when they moved from the central city to the suburbs, a popular concept in the 1950s (Fred I. Greenstein and Raymond H. Wolfinger, "The Suburbs and Shifting Party Loyalties," *Public Opinion Quarterly* 22 [Winter 1958–59]: 473–82), is effectively refuted in Wirt, *On the City's Rim*, pp. 81–100.)

45. Frederick M. Wirt, "The Political Sociology of American Suburbia: A Reinterpretation," *Journal of Politics* 27 (August 1965): 647–66.

46. For use of this phrase, see U.S., National Advisory Commission on Civil Disorders, *Report* (Washington, D.C., 1968), p. 1.

Cops and Crooks: The War at Home

Eugene J. Watts

America emerged from World War II eager to continue the march of progress that only momentarily had been sidetracked by the great conflict. This sense seemed especially strong among law-enforcement officials and others involved in the movement to reform the urban police. After 1945 most plans designed to make the police more efficient and professional moved from blueprint to implementation. The successes of police reform, however, appeared in the public mind only to keep pace with a mounting crime problem that rapidly reached crisis proportions. By the dawn of the sixties, in almost prophetic fashion, public perception would be matched by a skyrocketing increase in crime that clearly revealed the limits of police effectiveness. During that troubled decade Americans would search for new solutions to the crime problem and also would grapple with several unforeseen consequences of police reform. Yet, in the atmosphere of the immediate postwar period, the pessimism that today permeates the administration of criminal justice would have seemed foreign. It was a time to put our crime-fighting forces in shape and to win the war on crime.

World War II, like other military conflicts, temporarily reduced the number of conventional crimes, but had deleterious effects on law enforcement. The urban police were forced to allocate a large share of their resources to those things—national security investigations, civilian defense measures, prostitution, juvenile delinquency, and racial unrest—that threatened the war effort and domestic unity but were not previously a major part of their mission. Police adoption of new technology, especially the radio and the automobile, was severely retarded by the armed services' demands for such equipment. Military service and wartime prosperity also drained off qualified applicants and officers already in the ranks. Thus, from 1940 to 1945, the numbers of police and their ratio to the population steadily declined. Many departments relaxed age requirements and postponed plans to raise other recruitment standards simply to fill vacancies. As inflation eroded the favorable position of police salaries compared with other occupations, police unionism underwent a revival that thoroughly alarmed administrators.[1]

Thus, the war appeared to turn back the clock on the movement to reform the urban police that had gathered steam during the 1930s, but it proved to be a brief hiatus. The period from 1945 to 1960 witnessed more profound changes in the urban police than in any comparable period since their inception in the mid-nineteenth century. Several institutions and individuals were instrumental in promoting these changes. The FBI's high standards of recruitment and training, utilization of science and technology, insistence on honest and accurate record-keeping, and adherence to a tough "law and order" approach to crime served as a model for police reform. Through its Police Training School, renamed the National Academy in 1945, the FBI indoctrinated hundreds of local police officers. A new generation of reform-minded administrators dominated the influential International Association of Chiefs of Police (IACP). The proceedings of the IACP's annual meetings, published as *Police Yearbook*, tirelessly recited the litany of reform. The *Municipal Year Book* of the International City Management Association performed a similar function, although the title of its section, "Police Administration," anticipated a significant alteration in the reform message after the war.

The bond between police administrators and academic advisers had remained strong during the war, even though several prominent police consultants momentarily turned their attention to the military effort. The growth of public administration as a specialty within political science was particularly important. At the close of the conflict, practitioners, particularly those affiliated with the Institute for Public Administration in New York, resumed propagation of their message of managerial efficiency in police surveys. Other academics, including an emerging cadre of criminologists within the discipline of sociology, transmitted their views in such publications as the *Journal of Criminal Law and Criminology* as well as in specialized studies of crime prevention, traffic engineering, patrol allocation, community relations, and so on, commissioned by individual departments.

Experts on policing from within and without the law-enforcement community preached the gospel of professionalism, which promised to transform police work into a full-time career, free from political manipulation, with a commitment to abstract ideals of public service and an organized body of scientific knowledge. As initially enunciated by August Vollmer, the most prominent prewar reformer, later refined by Bruce Smith, and popularized by O. W. Wilson, professionalism had several tenets. Personnel reform, however, was paramount before the war. Vollmer and like-minded reformers underlined the need to recruit higher-caliber officers, to provide them with better training, and to guarantee them higher salaries, better fringe benefits, and adequate retirement plans.[2]

Although the premier postwar reformers, Bruce Smith and O. W. Wilson, continued to advocate these measures, they were much less confident than Vollmer about attaining the true professional ideal in which characteristics of personnel are more important than those of the organization. Instead, they emphasized a sweeping internal reorganization and acceptance of advances in technology to achieve more effective control over the day-to-day activities of officers. Centralization of authority, continuity in administration, simplification of chain of command, functional organization, bureaucratic regularity, independence from political interference, specialization, and improved communications and mobility became the watchwords.[3]

Smith, working for the Institute for Public Administration, presented this view in surveys of municipal and state police agencies and, most clearly, in the 1949 revision of his monumental *Police Systems in the United States* (1940). Governmental Research Institutes allied with the Institute for Public Administration carried Smith's message to cities across the land. Even more influential was O. W. Wilson, a protégé of Vollmer, police chief in Wichita from 1928 to 1939, and professor of police administration (in 1950 dean of the nation's first School of Criminology) at the University of California, Berkeley, from 1939 to 1960. Wilson wrote several important studies of policing and compiled the section on police administration in the *Municipal Year Book* for 1936 to 1943 and again from 1952 to 1960. His most significant work, *Police Administration* (1950), which combined the views of Vollmer and Smith with the scientific management approach of F. W. Taylor, became the bible of professionalism. By the time of Smith's death in 1954, Wilson was the acknowledged prophet of police reform. Following the guidance of police reformers, as well as the internal logic of large organizations, police departments in the postwar period evolved from simple, decentralized, loosely controlled territorial organizations to complex, highly specialized, functionally arranged bureaucracies.[4]

The recipe for reform after the war continued to include stricter entrance tests, higher qualifications, and improved training for recruits. The *Journal of Criminal Law and Criminology* reported an "upward trend in the quality of police personnel" in 1945, citing scores made by applicants in many departments on a newly developed intelligence examination, the Army Alpha Test. Most big-city police forces adopted this and other intelligence tests in the late 1940s, and several raised the passing score in the next decade. In consultation with psychologists, police supervisors developed police aptitude tests that further routinized police selection, lessened political patronage, and enshrined their conservative attitudes into regulations. Although the rate of innovation differed by departments, virtually all police forces streamlined their screening process, adopted medical examinations and physical requirements modeled on those of the armed services, and utilized more thorough character investigations. A handful of departments, including those in Los Angeles, Philadelphia, and Pasadena, experimented with psychiatric examinations. Most of these changes, however, appeared to be designed to eliminate the obviously unfit rather than to secure superior personnel.[5]

Police departments finally implemented long-standing requests of reformers to revise the qualifications of candidates for the force. Most important were age limits of twenty-one to thirty, a high school education or its equivalent, and the end of local residence requirements. In 1946 the California State Peace Officers' Association (composed of the state's chiefs of police) endorsed these suggestions, and police forces in California generally led the way in adopting them. In addition, police departments everywhere overwhelmingly selected recruits with military experience, a practice more in tune with a renewed emphasis on a military model for policing than with the momentary postwar sentiment to reward returning heroes.[6]

Recruitment of younger men, argued reformers, provided a better return on the investment in training, promoted the development of long-term careers, fostered rank-and-file acceptance of military training and discipline, and eliminated "failures" in other occupations from consideration. World War II marked a temporary interruption in the perceptible trend toward selection of younger recruits that accelerated after the conflict. Several departments instituted "cadet" programs in the 1950s to attract recent high-school graduates not yet old enough to enter commissioned ranks, and by 1960 most police forces largely recruited men in their early twenties.[7]

Efforts to eliminate residence requirements met with more limited success. The potential to curtail political patronage provided the impetus for, and resistance against, this alteration in several cities, such as Chicago, where as late as 1945 one thousand police positions were parceled out to ward committeemen. Reformers also pointed out that statewide or even national recruitment would provide a larger pool of applicants and thus permit departments to upgrade other standards without encountering difficulties in filling vacancies. The Dallas police had dropped its residence rule during the severe manpower shortage engendered by the war, and many forces began to reduce their requirement in the late 1940s for the same reason. Rank-and-file desires to move to the suburbs, however, provided the major reason for the complete elimination of the rule among several big-city police forces during the 1950s, and only a handful of these, including Los Angeles, Saint Louis, San Francisco, and Oakland, actually conducted recruitment drives outside their cities.[8]

Most large urban police forces and many medium-sized departments instituted some education requirement by the late 1940s. By 1960 most mandated at least a high-school diploma or its equivalent. The increase in high-school education among the general population made these changes feasible. Although several big-city departments stated a preference for college-trained personnel, only a few were able to attract significant numbers of such recruits. The Los Angeles Police Department was exceptional, for more than one-third of its 4,500 officers in the late 1950s had attended or were attending college. Many took advantage of the specialized police training programs pioneered at several California schools, notably Berkeley, San Jose State, and Fresno State. By the mid-1950s twenty-two colleges and universities offered such programs, and several institutions outside California, including Michigan State University and Washington State University, enjoyed national reputations. From 1950 to 1959 these schools produced more than 1,800 BAs and 50 MAs in law enforcement or "criminalistics."[9]

Stricter tests and higher standards eliminated the overwhelming majority of police candidates by the late 1950s. From 1956 to 1961 success rates for applicants decreased from 30 percent to 22 percent nationally, and many big-city police forces rejected 90 percent or more of their candidates. Black applicants appeared as the major casualties of reform in many cities, and their complaints presaged a major reaction to the professionalization of the police in the following decade. Most police forces mandated stricter requirements for women than men, and even those severely strapped to fill vacancies refused to hire females except in juvenile divisions. Police experiments with female traffic officers in the early 1940s clearly were wartime expedients that were quickly discarded at the close of hostilities.[10]

In addition to high elimination rates for applicants, several factors contributed to acute police recruitment problems at the end of the 1950s. Beginning in the 1930s, more officers had made police work their lifetime career (and fewer were dropped for political reasons) and thus reached retirement age by 1960. Moreover, most police forces had increased in size in the postwar period. Despite a tremendous growth in population from 1945 to 1960, the ratio of police per 1,000 people increased in all cities over 10,000 from 1.58 to 1.72, and in the largest cities from 2.11 to 2.78. Police departments also began to reduce the forty-eight-hour work week in 1945. The forty-hour movement gathered steam in 1948 and became the popular mode by 1960. This change alone required departments to increase their force by approximately 17 percent simply to maintain the same number of man-hours.[11]

The low prestige and relative decline in salaries of the police during the 1940s and 1950s limited options in recruitment. Although the police ranking on the North-Hatt occupational prestige scale rose eight points from 1947 to 1963, police officers still ranked only forty-seventh out of ninety occupations in the latter year. Many departments introduced substantially better fringe benefits—including free uniforms and equipment and life and health insurance—and won repeated pay raises for their members after 1945. The median entrance salary for patrolmen in all cities over 10,000 stood at $2,100 in 1945. Fifteen years later, recruits in cities under 25,000 received $4,030 and their counterparts in the largest cities garnered $4,800. As a 1954 study by New York City's Patrolmen's Benevolent Association revealed, however, other occupational groups fared even better. In 1960 police earned more than automobile mechanics, carpenters, and social workers, but less than electricians, plumbers, and teachers. Police supervisor salaries were higher, but four of five officers never rose above the rank of patrolman. As a consequence of relatively poor pay, a large number of police officers moonlighted, in most cases contrary to department rules.[12]

Gains in salaries and benefits were at least partly the result of rank-and-file unionization attempts. In the late 1930s the American Federation of State, County, and Municipal Employees (AFSCME) revived police organization efforts that had been dormant since the disastrous

Boston police strike in 1919. By 1944 AFSCME claimed 5,000 police members in thirty-six police locals and in twenty-eight other municipal public employee locals. In addition, the Fraternal Order of Police (FOP), a national rank-and-file association whose local units sometimes sought to represent their members on issues of salaries and grievances, had 169 chapters linking 1,072 cities over 10,000 population. The IACP in 1944 published a major policy statement against unions, collective bargaining, the dues checkoff, and use of the strike (which all police unions and associations disavowed), calling police unions a threat to professionalism and impartial police service.[13]

Individual departments mounted an all-out assault against police unions, although many became increasingly tolerant of other employee associations. After the Teamsters, AFSCME, and FOP tried to organize the Detroit police in 1944, the department high command agreed to the nonaffiliated Detroit Police Officer's Association as an acceptable way to regulate rank-and-file militance. Similarly, the New York Police Department firmly resisted an organization attempt by the Transport Workers Union in 1951, but gradually granted more influence to the Patrolmen's Benevolent Association. These nonunion police associations, at least, were not linked to other labor groups and thus did not pose a threat to impartial police service in the event of strikes. Open harassment by police and city government officials destroyed nascent police unions immediately after the war in many other cities, including Atlanta, Chicago, and Los Angeles. When these tactics failed, administrators turned to the courts. The key decisions involved police unions in Jackson, Mississippi, and in Saint Louis, in which the courts upheld the right of officials to fire officers for union activity. Many cities, however, granted pay raises and improvements in working conditions to an aroused rank and file.[14]

These actions severely curtailed police unionization. An IACP survey in 1947 of 77 cities over 100,000 population revealed that only ten had police unions. The AFSCME, which still claimed fifty-five locals, mostly in medium-sized and smaller communities, expanded its efforts in the early 1950s. The number of AFSCME locals rose to sixty-one in 1951 and to sixty-five in 1959. Many of these unions, however, were transitory. Of fifty-five cities with police unions at the end of World War II, only eleven continued to exist in 1957. An announcement by Jimmy Hoffa in 1958 that the Teamsters Union would attempt to organize the nation's police, beginning with the New York Police Department, dealt a severe blow to the movement. Reaction was so swift and severe that Hoffa almost immediately withdrew his proposal. Police administrators reiterated their tough position, and a Gallup poll revealed that 55 percent of the public opposed police unions and only 27 percent supported them. Despite this climate the decade of the 1960s witnessed the successful resurgence of police unionism, based on rank-and-file reaction to reform and to police administrators' policy toward black protest groups as much as on the desire for traditional labor union goals.[15]

Improvements in training from 1945 to 1960 were even more impressive than changes in recruitment. By the late 1940s virtually every big-city police force had its own training school. Many, such as those in Saint Louis and Atlanta, were modeled on the FBI's National Academy. Most police forces extended the length of the training period and enriched their curriculum with human relations and criminology courses, but only a few departments presented good in-service training for men already in the ranks. Several states, notably California, Kansas, Michigan, New Jersey, and Washington, inaugurated state-operated police training schools. In 1959 California, Missouri, and New York mandated establishment of statewide minimum training standards.[16]

Even departments with modern police academies relied on several special institutions for advanced training, particularly for would-be instructors in their own schools. Most important was the National Academy, which from 1935 to 1960 trained 2,563 officers, including 29 percent of the executive heads of all agencies still in service in 1959. The technical excellence of the National Academy evoked universal praise, but some critics complained that the FBI paid too much attention to the mainstays of traditional police curriculum—marksmanship, defensive tactics, and disarming methods. In contrast, human relations courses designed by social scientists were a major focus of the Southern Police Institute at the University of Louisville, which opened in 1951. Initially limited to southern police administrators, the institute quickly expanded to embrace police officers from around the country. By 1960 it had graduated almost 500 officers from its long-term course and over 300 from midwinter seminars. The Northwestern University Traffic Institute, the Yale Bureau of Highway Safety, the University of Southern California's Delinquency Control Institute, and the University of Chicago's Institute for Municipal Administration offered more specialized training. By 1955 the Northwestern Traffic Institute and several regional traffic centers designated by the IACP were certifying nearly 1,300 law-enforcement officials annually.[17]

The emergence of these institutes reflected the growing specialization in police work. Detective divisions generally had divided into specialized squads—homicide, vice, and so on—before the 1940s, but the simple police organization in which the great majority of officers worked on patrol evolved into a much more complex structure after World War II. Greater attention to traffic regulation was only one example of this specialization, albeit the most onerous, for police departments faced staggering problems with traffic control in the postwar era. Reserve or auxiliary units, personnel divisions, training staffs, special communications and record-keeping sections, and crime prevention units were the wave of the 1940s. Internal affairs bureaus designed to monitor activities of police officers, intelligence squads developed to keep tabs on organized crime, and canine corps imported from England to control crowds, detect narcotics, and deter physical attack or flight by hoodlums, became the fashion of the fifties.[18]

Specialization was a hotly debated topic throughout the 1950s. Opponents argued that it provided a poor background for future supervisors and created rivalries within the department. More important, it led to a lower proportion of officers assigned to patrol, the mainstay of police work. Proponents, led by O. W. Wilson, insisted that efficiency and effectiveness depended upon it, pointing to planning and research divisions as their favorite example. Appearing in the early 1950s, first in Oakland and then in Los Angeles, these divisions quickly spread to other large urban departments. They epitomized the new professionalism, for they relied heavily on technology, fostered relations with outside consultants, and provided a systematic basis to policing. Research and planning divisions assisted commanders with personnel management, including the creation of efficiency ratings and written promotion examinations. By analyzing the percentage of calls answered in a reasonable time and the number of people served per officer and per dollar, they aided administrators in quantitative analysis of police performance. In several cities these divisions reorganized beats and reallocated patrol manpower on the basis of behavioral patterns such as the incidence of crime rather than on arbitrary rules, thus lessening the importance of local experience and political considerations. From the perspective of patrol officers, however, such "professionalism" seemed to change their vocation from a skilled trade in which they exercised considerable judgment to one resembling a combination of assembly-line work and bookkeeping.[19]

Increased specialization led to a sizable increase in staff and other positions in the department, as many "modern" forces felt it was imperative to hire criminalists, engineers, social workers, lawyers, public relations experts, and, particularly, statisticians. In 1958 *Police* magazine began a section entitled "Statistics for Police Efficiency" to keep abreast of the application of statistical methods as a management tool and technique to cope with crime. This tendency dramatically increased the number of civilian employees on police forces, especially since police veterans successfully fought lateral entry at high-commissioned rank for outside experts. One of the reformers' major concerns—untangling the chain of command—therefore became more pressing in the postwar period. The solution, paradoxically, was the creation of several additional senior commanders of functional units, such as patrol or detectives, who alone reported to the chief. Under older, territorial arrangements, each district commander controlled all activities in his area and had been directly responsible to the chief.[20]

Reformers also successfully recommended elimination of many district stations, thereby helping to sever the close connection between ward leaders and police captains in many cities. By the early 1950s, moreover, most police forces were under control of a single administrator rather than a commission or civilian board. Indeed, reform won its greatest successes in the managerial revolution based on the corporate model and in the partial disjunction between politics and the police, failing only to guarantee the tenure of police chiefs for good behavior. Although William Parker in Los Angeles, Herbert Jenkins in Atlanta, and Jeremiah O'Connell in Saint Louis served long terms, very few other administrators at the end of the 1950s held their positions more than three or four years before being removed by a change in city administration.[21]

An enthusiastic acceptance of science and technology, another component of professionalism, encouraged specialization and bureaucratization. The American police exhibited the same fascination with gadgets and wonder drugs as the general public, who feasted on a diet of fact and fiction regarding the successes of the forensic sciences. By the 1940s a host of experts in ballistics identification, serology, toxicology, and other areas applied their talents to crime-solving. Entrepreneurs eager to market their various wares advertised speedy improvements in police performance through journals and at the IACP national convention. Throughout the late 1950s *Police* carried such articles as "The Striagraph: A New Police Science Instrument" and "Criminal Detective Devices Employing Photography." Not to be outdone, the more scholarly *Journal of Criminal Law and Criminology* added *Police Science* to its title and presented such articles as "The Helicopter—New York Police on Patrol" and "Introduction of Infra-Red Surveillance Devices in Police Services."[22]

Police laboratories increased in number and sophistication in the postwar period. The array of microscopes, spectograph equipment, and X-ray diffraction cameras produced better testimony on physical evidence and strengthened the police claim to professionalism. Police readily employed the polygraph to verify claims of suspects and, in a few departments, to aid in recruit selection and disciplinary proceedings. In 1959 the Academy for Scientific Interrogation held its tenth annual seminar in praise of the polygraph. Police used the moving picture camera and elaborate sound recording equipment to record criminal acts and statements of offenders, and utilized punch cards, mechanical tabulating devices, and microfilm in criminal identification as well as personnel administration. The slogan "Better living through chemistry" appealed to the police: by the late 1950s the drug Nalline, which produced reactions in users of opium derivatives, was widely used to keep probationers and parolees "clean" and to rid communities of narcotics addicts.[23]

Some of these innovations may not have provided enough return to justify their considerable expense, but the wholesale utilization of the radio and automobile had a profound effect on policing. The number of police forces using the radio had increased from 4 to 2,000 during the 1930s, underlining the issue of gross duplication of services within large urban areas that would later lead to proposals for metropolitan police forces. Not until the postwar period were two-way radios, which ended the isolation and independence of patrol officers, widely introduced into police work. By the mid-1950s several police forces employed radio transmissions and telephone lines to transmit photographs, fingerprints, and sundry documents, as well as compact radios concealed in the pockets of officers. More important, the police assumed a reactive rather than active style of patrol as an increasingly demanding public used the telephone to call complaints to a central headquarters, which then dispatched officers to the scene. The resultant enhancement of social service and order-maintenance roles at the expense of law enforcement activities was bitterly resented by the rank and file, who preferred "real" police work rather than dangerous domestic disputes and often frivolous complaints.[24]

Widespread adoption of automobiles after the war gave the police the mobility to respond quickly to such calls as well as the capability to catch criminals in cars. Automobiles afforded officers protection from weather and fatigue, greater speed and ability to travel longer distances, increased facility to move prisoners and medical emergency cases, and, in combination with the radio, better safety. Automobiles also isolated officers from routine encounters with ordinary citizens in friendly situations, increasingly restricting police-public interaction to problematic contacts. Every issue of the *Municipal Year Book* in the postwar period documented the increase in motorized patrol. Although 78 percent of all police forces still employed foot patrol on a limited basis in 1960, the venerable beat patrolman, with his intimate knowledge of his territory and many of its inhabitants, was rapidly appearing to become a relic of less-troubled times. So, too, was the motorcycle officer, for automobiles could be used for traffic regulation in all seasons and in all kinds of weather. To their chagrin, regular patrol officers also became charged with apprehending traffic violators, and many of their brethren in traffic units specialized in accident investigation and use of newly developed portable radar instruments.[25]

O. W. Wilson's enthusiastic championing of the one-man patrol car earned him the especial enmity of the rank and file. Officers complained about difficulties in driving and observing their environment at the same time. Even with the radio, safety remained a problem in situations that demanded immediate action or when backup cars were also busy. These objections increasingly were outweighed by an appreciation for the one-man car's greater economy—the department could cover a greater area with fewer men. From 1945 to 1960 the percentage of all cities over 10,000 population using one-man cars exclusively rose from 18 to 26, and the percentage employing them together with two-man cars increased from 34 to 64. The big-city police were slower than smaller communities to accept one-man patrol, especially on the busy night watch, but by the mid-1950s their reluctance began to recede. The proportion of the largest cities using only two-man cars declined from 62 percent after the war to 20 percent in the early 1960s.[26]

Most of the new technological developments of the 1940s and 1950s were designed to fulfill a fourth tenet of police professionalism—an emphasis on aggressive crime-fighting. In the closing days of World War II, law-enforcement officials began to plan postwar crime prevention programs. They publicly worried about a tremendous increase in crime similar to that following World War I, and in 1945 their prophecy appeared to be fulfilled. The FBI's *Uniform Crime Reports* recorded the highest increase in crimes—12.4 percent—since the advent of the national reporting system in 1930. Reporting on the figures, *Newsweek* commented that the "boomtime spirit had hit the nation's criminals no less than other parts of the population."[27]

Crime, the more spectacular the better, was as newsworthy from 1945 to 1960 as it had ever been. The classic psychotic outburst occurred in 1949 when quiet, brooding Howard Unruh, a twenty-eight-year-old former artilleryman and devout Bible reader who lived with his mother in East Camden, New York, shot and killed thirteen neighbors for their "derogatory remarks." That same year also witnessed the biggest cash holdup of all time, when eight men stole $1,219,000 from the Boston garage of Brinks, Inc. The prize for postwar teenage violence went in 1953 to Fred Eugene McManus, an eighteen-year-old Marine who killed a college student for his car, picked up his younger sweetheart, and left a trail of four more dead before his capture in Iowa. The brutal kidnap-murder of six-year-old Bobby Greenlease in Kansas City, Missouri, was probably the most shocking crime of the era. Carl Austin Hall and Bonnie Brown briefly enjoyed the largest ransom ever paid— $600,000—but died in Missouri's gas chamber in December 1953. The nation's newspapers, television, and radio had no shortage of material to startle, scare, and outrage the American audience.[28]

Alarmed observers also pointed out that much crime went unreported and that police record-keeping procedures often underestimated the known amount of crime. Most Americans, however, believed that crime statistics at least accurately indicated trends in criminal behavior, and that the pattern was inexorably upward. In fact, the long-term trend in crime in the United States had been declining steadily since the late nineteenth century, with world wars producing in their aftermath only slight, short-run rises in the downward curve. The choice of 1945 as a benchmark, which appeared appropriate to most analysts, therefore led to an impression that was at best misleading.[29]

The postwar increase in crime, moreover, was to some extent an artifact of other developments, particularly the professionalization of the big-city police. The much greater magnitude of reported crime in the nation's largest cities throughout the era was partly the result of major urban police forces' adherence to higher standards of law enforcement and improvements in record-keeping. After prodding by the FBI, several cities, including Saint Louis, Philadelphia, Chicago, and New York, reported whopping increases in crime after revising their records systems. The FBI had refused to publish the crime statistics of the New York police in 1950 because they were so obviously doctored; in the next year reported robberies rose 400 percent and reported burglaries climbed 1,300 percent in New York. The FBI also helped many other local law-enforcement agencies improve their recording and reporting systems. As a result, crimes that previously went unrecorded began to be included in the national figures.[30]

Uniform Crime Reports, however, contributed to serious misunderstandings on the part of the press and public. Reliance upon census year population figures exaggerated crime rates (numbers of crimes per

100,000 population) in intercensus years. Furthermore, the Part One, "major crime," category of the *Uniform Crime Reports* actually comprised for the most part petty larcenies, culpable traffic fatalities, and teen-age "joyriding." Thus, the public received a distorted view of the magnitude of "serious" crime and especially the juvenile contribution to it. Recognizing these problems, in 1958 the FBI instituted important changes in the *Uniform Crime Reports*, utilizing annual estimates of population and eliminating larcenies under fifty dollars, manslaughter by negligence, joyriding, and statutory rape from the "major crime" category, which was renamed Index Crimes. Still, critics correctly concluded that the United States had the least reliable crime data of all Western societies.[31]

The FBI considered Index Crimes sufficiently serious and likely to be reported by citizens and recorded by police to furnish an indicator of the actual amount of crime—an untested, somewhat doubtful, but widely accepted assumption. Based on Index Crimes, the FBI reported in 1959 that serious crime had increased 69 percent since 1950 and 128 percent since 1940, outracing population growth by a ratio of four to one. Analysis of the components of the index reveals a less-alarming picture. Crimes against persons remained remarkably stable from 1940 to 1960, and the trend in homicide and non-negligent manslaughter was clearly downward. Only in the largest cities did significant increases in aggravated assault and forcible rape occur, and the latter figures dropped sharply after removal of statutory cases from the accounting. Not until the early 1960s did these four crimes begin a skyrocketing ascent to all-time-high rates in the mid-1970s. In contrast, serious crimes against property started to climb earlier. Burglary and auto theft began to increase in large and smaller cities after World War II, and larceny figures started to rise ten years later.[32]

Many experts attributed the reported increase in crime in large part to the rising proportion of youth in the population, and some pointed with trepidation to future police problems that would result from the 1940s' baby boom. Great concern over juvenile delinquency surfaced as early as 1940, when J. Edgar Hoover laid the blame "at the doorstep of the American Home." Hoover's statement reflected a national obsession with juvenile crime that continued throughout the war. This obsession led O. W. Wilson and others to resurrect the long-standing belief among police reformers that suppression of juvenile delinquency was the most effective means of long-range crime prevention. More and more police departments created specialized crime prevention units intended to "give adolescents a square deal instead of threatening them, clubbing them, and branding them as 'bums, liars, and punks. . . .' "[33]

The popular police text *Techniques of Law Enforcement in the Treatment of Juveniles* (1944) summarized reform thinking. In addition to handling all young offenders, specialized police juvenile bureaus served as a liaison between the police and other community agencies such as child-guidance clinics and schools. More important, these divisions endeavored to discover and eradicate potential sources of delinquency through aggressive patrol. Policewomen were assigned a particularly important role in these crime prevention units, and, unlike male officers, often were expected to have some college training and experience in social work. By 1953 more than three hundred police forces had special juvenile divisions, double the number reported in a 1940 IACP survey; and the IACP exhorted departments without such units to create them if for no other reason than "keeping abreast of the times." In addition, many police forces provided recreational activities for youths, especially in Police Athletic Leagues, and included special courses on juvenile problems in their training programs.[34]

Despite this development police interest in juvenile delinquency momentarily abated after the war, as arrests and court cases for youths dropped dramatically. In 1949 the *Municipal Year Book* announced that the "exaggerated" public attention to "the Juvenile Problem" had subsided to a "reasonable level." A 30 percent increase in juvenile arrests from 1948 to 1952 changed police opinion, and in 1953 some experts estimated that the police handled more than a million juveniles annually. Only one-quarter of these encounters reached juvenile court; the remainder were discharged by officers in "street corner courts." From 1948 to 1960 juvenile arrests and court cases more than doubled while the population of young people increased by less than one-half. The arrests of juveniles rose six times as fast as those for older persons, and by 1958 nearly half of all people arrested were under the age of eighteen.[35]

These startling figures were partly the result of improved record-keeping and the creation of specialized juvenile bureaus. Arrest statistics for juveniles reported in the *Uniform Crime Reports* referred to total number of arrests rather than number of offenses. Since juveniles acted in groups far more than adults and, when arrested, were more likely to implicate accomplices, official figures overstated the known amount of juvenile crime. Proliferation of police crime prevention units in which specially trained officers more actively sought out actual and potential delinquents also led to an increase in the number of young people brought into the criminal justice system. Juvenile crime tended to be highest in large cities with professional police forces.[36]

Not all the increase in juvenile crime resulted from better reporting practices or increased police activity. By 1959 the fifteen-to-nineteen age group accounted for most robberies, burglaries, larcenies, auto thefts, stolen property, and weapons offenses. Moreover, "self-report" surveys among various cross-sections of American youth initiated by sociologists in 1946 revealed that many youths who never officially entered the criminal justice system had nonetheless repeatedly committed offenses. Awareness of this situation raised serious alarm among a public already convinced that the gyrations of Elvis Presley signified a tilt toward youthful degeneration. Movies like *Blackboard Jungle, Rebel without a Cause,* and *The Wild Ones* further dramatized a dangerous drift toward delinquency. Public apprehension swiftly led to official action.[37]

Psychological explanations and prescriptions for delinquency were prevalent in the 1940s and 1950s. Psychologists and psychiatrists filled key positions in the juvenile justice system, focusing attention upon early identification programs for individual children and emphasizing specialized treatment for youths brought into the criminal justice network. The National Mental Health Act in 1946, which required the Public Health Service to sponsor and conduct research on delinquency, was a particular boon to psychologists.[38]

By the mid-1950s a new group of specialists within sociology, called criminologists, began to supplant psychologists in the fight against delinquency. As criminologists studied the social pathology of the urban slum, the "delinquent subculture," and the structure of juvenile gangs, the environment reemerged as the center of concern. Academics now advocated altering the environment rather than removing the juvenile from it. The gradual shift in emphasis to the social setting was evident in 1953, when a special Senate subcommittee held widely publicized hearings on juvenile delinquency and the U.S. Children's Bureau and the IACP conducted a joint conference to facilitate a police-community crusade against youthful crime. The proposals of sociologists were more susceptible to government action than the individualized medical approach of psychologists, and criminologists eventually had an enormous impact on public policy, manifested by the creation of the President's Committee on Juvenile Delinquency and Youth Crime and the passage by Congress of the Juvenile Delinquency and Youth Offenses Control Act in 1961.[39]

A second, less serious but even more sensational, crime scare surfaced in the postwar period. Organized crime became a prominent feature of

American folklore, as the mythic "mob" and "Mafia" captured the imagination of national politicians, pundits, and the public, if not that of the police. Organized crime was a reality, in the sense that individuals engaged in illicit activities in order to make a profit. This was particularly obvious in gambling, a growth industry in the years following World War II. But the concept of a monolithic national crime syndicate, composed solely of Italian-Americans whose principal method of operation was bloodshed, was more fanciful than real.[40]

Many factors contributed to the popularization of the myth, including a deep strain of nativism and a willingness to believe in alien conspiracies. Throughout the 1940s and 1950s, the mass media reinforced public susceptibility to such notions. Readers who bought copies of *Murder, Inc.* and television viewers who watched "The Untouchables" were entertained if not enlightened. Gangsters appeared as urban cowboys, attired in silk suits and surrounded by all the trappings of the consumer society while still adhering to a frontier code of decisiveness, physical action, and loyalty to friends and family. Mobsters also evoked a Horatio Alger image. Indeed, Columbia University sociologist Daniel Bell referred to organized crime in the early 1950s as "one of the queer ladders of social mobility in American life." Bell, however, pointed out that no real evidence existed for a nationwide syndicate and that the notion of a Mafia grossly distorted and exaggerated organized illegal enterprises.[41]

Congress contributed to the popular concern and misconceptions regarding organized crime. Senator Estes Kefauver, of Tennessee, seeking to enhance his national popularity, secured the chairmanship of a special Senate subcommittee in 1950 to investigate "the manner in which the facilities of interstate commerce are made a vehicle of organized crime." The Kefauver committee held hearings in most of the nation's large cities, focusing primarily on operations of racing-news wire services. When the hearings moved to New York in March 1951, they were televised, thus bringing millions of viewers into contact with hoodlums and other characters. Television interest centered on Frank Costello, purported head of an organized crime family. Although the Kefauver committee failed to prove the existence of a nationwide syndicate that dominated bookmaking, it embraced the Mafia theory previously expounded by Harry Anslinger, head of the Federal Bureau of Narcotics. Ironically, by the early 1950s Anslinger deemphasized this notion, citing instead a Communist party conspiracy behind the drug trade in order to win congressional support for the repressive Boggs Act of 1951, which included mandatory prison terms for offenders, and the even more punitive Narcotics Control Act of 1956, which called for an increase in mandatory minimum prison sentences and, in some cases, the death penalty.[42]

The Kefauver committee added little new information on organized crime, but for the first time assembled in one place evidence on illegal business activities collected by local law-enforcement agencies, which denied knowledge of any nationwide syndicate. The committee also uncovered a pattern of corruption among local politicians, police, and gamblers and vice entrepreneurs that shocked the nation. In scores of cities grand jury investigations, legislative inquiries, and other revelations led to ousters of chiefs and other high-ranking law-enforcement officials. The American Bar Association commissioned a study by Earle W. Garrett on police corruption because "at no time in history has public criticism of police service been as severe and as widespread as it is today." This was an exaggeration, and several police forces, especially in Berkeley, Cincinnati, Dallas, Detroit, Kansas City, Los Angeles, Milwaukee, and Saint Louis, had national reputations for honest, efficient, and progressive departments. Others, however, were notorious for corruption and inefficiency, especially those in New York and Chicago.[43]

The New York Police Department suffered the most spectacular scandal of the 1950s. Harry Gross, a Brooklyn bookie, testified before the Kefauver committee that he had paid one million dollars annually to about one thousand officers of all ranks. The disclosure eventually led to the dismissal of forty-five officers, the hurried resignations of many others, and the disciplining of nearly two hundred more. Captain Daniel Gilbert, of the Chicago Police Department, dubbed "the richest cop in the world," admitted before the Kefauver committee that he had amassed $360,000 in stock market speculations and bets placed at an illegal gambling operation in the heart of the city. At the end of the 1950s, Chicago also endured the Summerdale scandal, which involved wholesale bribery and extortion by police officers. Mayor Richard Daley ordered a large-scale shake-up of the force and persuaded O. W. Wilson to become police chief in 1961.[44]

Sensational scandals, generally of police connivance in commercialized vice, also rocked the police forces of Atlantic City, Cleveland, Miami, New Orleans, Oakland, Pittsburgh, and Tulsa during the 1950s. These exposés revealed a widespread cover-up among cops personally untainted by corruption and an almost neurotic belief among police that they were a persecuted minority and scapegoats for public ills. Police chiefs in New York and Chicago insisted that their departments were clean even in the face of convincing evidence of large-scale corruption. Police benevolent and fraternal associations exhibited the greatest sensitivity to public criticism. The Police Benevolent Association in New York referred to Bruce Smith's thoughtful survey as a "malicious smear." Strict adherence to the theory of the solitary "rotten apple," when congressional and local investigations were uncovering scandals by the bushel, did not reassure an apprehensive public.[45]

The Kefauver committee left a path of political ruin in its wake, making it, and Kefauver in particular, highly unpopular with many Democratic leaders on Capitol Hill. Congress rejected most of the committee's recommendations, including creation of a Federal Crime Commission to continue investigations and to suggest appropriate legislation. Critics of this proposal, such as Raymond Moley, considered it an unrealistic and unnecessary infringement on local law enforcement. Moley wrote a series of articles for *Newsweek* which argued that federal legislation could not solve problems of gambling and local corruption. Instead, Moley advocated an increase in the number of state and municipal crime commissions that had been spawned by the Kefauver investigations. By 1953 a dozen large-city commissions formed the National Association of Citizens' Crime Commissions, which, although never very successful, supported several local investigations throughout the 1950s.[46]

Interest in organized crime shifted from gambling to labor union racketeering about the time of Marlon Brando's 1956 performance in *On the Waterfront*. As early as 1953, subcommittees in both houses of Congress investigated fraud in union welfare funds, and the chairman of the Senate subcommittee, John L. McClellan, of Arkansas, predicted additional investigations. In 1955, when Democrats took control of the Senate, McClellan became chairman of the Senate Permanent Subcommittee on Investigations and began a study of improprieties in clothing procurement by the armed forces. Under McClellan and chief counsel Robert F. Kennedy, the subcommittee found "East Coast gangsters" involved in some unions. In 1957 the Senate Select Committee on Improper Activities in the Labor or Management Field, with McClellan as chair and Kennedy as chief counsel, began its celebrated hearings. Employing the largest staff ever assembled on Capitol Hill, more than 100 people, the McClellan committee called 1,525 sworn witnesses (343 of whom took the Fifth Amendment) in more than 500 open hearing sessions conducted over a two-and-one-half-year period.[47]

Among the first order of business for the committee was an investigation of a highly publicized 1957 meeting in Apalachin, New York, of seventy-five underworld figures, including Vito Genovese, Joe Bonanno, Carlo Gambino, and others. Their specific ties with each other, however, remained a mystery until the revelations of Joseph Valachi in

1963 fixed attention on a criminal society he called "La Cosa Nostra." Initially, however, the McClellan committee concluded on very weak evidence that the 1957 meeting had occurred for some nefarious purpose largely because it lacked any other explanation. Robert Kennedy underlined the ominous fact that twenty-two of the participants were engaged in labor activities or labor-management relations.[48]

Aside from this investigation, the McClellan committee directly analyzed the structure and leadership of labor unions. The committee conducted especially extensive examinations of the Teamsters, eventually compiling a list of 107 union officials with various underworld connections. As a result the AFL-CIO expelled the Teamsters in 1957. The committee spent more time with Jimmy Hoffa—in eighteen interviews—than any other person. Hoffa was indicted in 1960 for using the mails to defraud the Teamsters in the Sun Valley Florida land-development project. The investigations also toppled from command several other prominent union leaders, including Dave Beck of the Teamsters, James Cross of the Bakers (also expelled from the AFL-CIO), and William Maloney from the Operating Engineers, as well as a large number of lesser officials. Throughout the hearings committee members and Robert Kennedy acted on the belief that corruption resulted from evil leaders. The proper response, Kennedy argued in his book *The Enemy Within* (1960), was government action to protect the powerless rank and file. Indeed, the principal legislative outcome of the McClellan committee hearings was the passage in 1959 of the Landrum-Griffin Act (Labor-Management Reporting and Disclosure Act), which was designed primarily to ensure democratic conditions within unions and to guarantee honest reporting on virtually all union activities, especially those involving the collection and expenditure of funds.[49]

Independent of congressional investigations, the Department of Justice attempted to wage war on organized crime during the 1950s. J. Edgar Hoover, who was deeply suspicious of other divisions of the Justice Department, used his considerable influence in Congress to sabotage the Organized Crime and Racketeering unit created in 1954. The FBI chief was momentarily overruled in 1958, when eighteen federal attorneys formed the Special Group on Organized Crime. Hoover quickly found an influential ally, however, after the special task force became embroiled in arguments with the McClellan committee staff. After Hoover called one investigation in New York a "fishing expedition," Robert Kennedy publicly lambasted the Justice Department for incompetence. Ironically, the Justice Department effort expanded enormously in 1961 when Kennedy became attorney general.[50]

Despite all the publicity generated by congressional and Justice Department investigations, the attack on organized crime during the 1950s was feeble. The FBI, which was best equipped to undertake the task, did virtually nothing, as Hoover insisted that national crime syndicates did not exist and that centralization of efforts against organized crime in the national government threatened the primacy of local law enforcement. Under intense pressure in 1957, Hoover created the Top Hoodlum Program modeled on the FBI's most successful publicity device, the Ten Most Wanted List, started in 1950. He later established the Special Investigative Division to monitor activities of underworld figures, mainly through wire-tapping, the FBI's favorite information-gathering technique.[51]

An all-out effort against organized crime would have drained resources from other FBI activities. Although Hoover always disclaimed any priorities for the bureau, he had one overriding obsession throughout the postwar period. Television's popular "I Led Three Lives" program, which dramatized the counterespionage exploits of Herbert Philbrick, more accurately indicated the interests and activities of the FBI than the later broadcast featuring Ephraim Zimbalist, Jr. Hoover's virulent anti-Communism was well publicized throughout the 1940s and 1950s in numerous speeches, essays, articles, and a book, *Masters of Deceit* (1958), published under his name but actually written by Fern Stukenbroeker. Hoover was not a learned man, and one tale whispered at FBI headquarters was that not only had Hoover not written the book, he had not even read it.[52]

Hoover had become the hero of the American Civil Liberties Union in 1924 when he had helped discontinue the FBI's investigations of domestic radical political organizations; but at President Roosevelt's direction, he had resumed this practice in the late 1930s. The FBI had major jurisdiction over counterintelligence and counterespionage cases during the war, and so successfully infiltrated the Communist party of the United States of America that all major meetings were attended or recorded by FBI agents during the conflict. The FBI became a kind of ideological security force after the advent of the "attorney general's list" and Truman's Federal Employee Loyalty Program, developing its own Security Index of persons to be detained under the Emergency Detention Act of 1950. The FBI received most of the eleven million dollars appropriated by Congress for loyalty programs, and by 1953 had analyzed more than four million sets of fingerprints and loyalty forms and investigated more than 20,000 federal employees. Loyalty investigations created the most havoc in the State Department, from which 425 people were dismissed from 1947 to 1953 without much regard for due process.[53]

President Eisenhower's Federal Employee Security Program, initiated in 1953, led to an even broader interpretation of what constituted a security risk for government employment, and Hoover eagerly seized upon it to widen his net of investigations. A memorandum from Attorney General Herbert Brownell in the next year gave the FBI even greater latitude in the use of wire-tapping than it previously had exercised. Throughout the 1950s, therefore, the FBI formed a solid anti-red block along with the House Committee on Un-American Activities. This preoccupation contributed to mistrust between the FBI and many local police forces, who felt that the bureau focused too much on such activities and other "cheap" victories, leaving more difficult areas of crime to them.[54]

Although police departments in several larger cities during the 1950s maintained small, specialized antisubversive squads as well as intelligence units to investigate organized crime, urban police concentrated upon other forms of crime-fighting. Indeed, many police administrators argued forcefully that the police should eliminate many other services unrelated to law enforcement because they drained manpower and funds from the primary mission of waging "war on crime." The foremost spokesman for this position during the 1950s was Chief William Parker, of the Los Angeles Police Department, which many reformers, including O. W. Wilson, judged the nation's most professional police force. Parker argued that the police formed a "thin blue line" between civilization and savagery, and he perfected the aggressive preventive patrol in which officers collared, questioned, and searched large numbers of "suspicious" persons on the street. The popular "Dragnet" television show, in which Detective Joe Friday endlessly searched for "just the facts," symbolized the Los Angeles police as relentlessly efficient crime-fighters.[55]

Police and public alike seemed to appreciate this image, but it deflected attention from the facts that most police duties still involved noncriminal matters and, more important, that neither the police nor the FBI could do much to actually prevent crime. They enjoyed some success, however, in apprehending criminals. Clearance rates—crimes "solved" by arrests—remained high for offenses against persons throughout the period from 1945 to 1960, ranging from about 90 percent for murder to 72 percent for rape, but were consistently lower for crimes against property, ranging from about two-fifths of robbery cases to less than one-fourth for larcenies. Since many persons arrested by the police were quickly released because of insufficient evidence or later were dismissed by the courts for the same reason, the percentage of those arrested who were later found guilty was markedly lower than the clearance rate. Statistics at the end of the 1950s showed an improvement only in homicides, rising from 62 percent to 68 percent during the period, and declining, but only slightly and unevenly, in all other cases to figures of 70 percent for larcenies, 67 percent for burglaries, 63 percent for robberies, 62 percent for auto thefts, 52 percent for rapes, and 41 percent for aggravated assaults. The *Municipal Year Book* in 1960 suggested that "restrictions that have been imposed on the police by appellate decisions" may have explained this embarrassing decline, although in practice the police were little affected by "liberal" court rulings before the 1960s.[56]

Despite the professionalization of the police, crime continued to climb during the 1950s and would begin to soar in the next decade. Moreover, police professionalism had unintended, unanticipated, and unwelcome consequences. Attacked by police consultants as inferior in background and training, branded by national and local investigations as corrupt, caught in a downward spiral of salaries relative to other workers, denied rights of union organization, enraged by the introduction of one-man cars and voluminous paperwork, and forced to succumb to more efficient supervision, the rank and file drew the strings of their historic "blue curtain" ever tighter. In his 1950 dissertation sociologist William Westley first spotlighted a police subculture that increasingly seemed paranoid, secretive, isolated, and defensive. As a result of its strong internal orientation, the police increasingly became removed from effective political supervision and control. Most citizens agreed with reformers that severance of the close connection between the police and partisan politics, especially the patronage system, was highly desirable, but during the 1960s some Americans would begin to question the extent to which the police should be independent of external supervision. One measure of the triumph of professionalism is that the major battles over this issue, centering around civilian review boards, were won by the police.[57]

Police officials also recognized that reform, especially the independence and isolation of the police that it fostered, contributed to a loss of the very public understanding and cooperation that was essential for fighting crime and for securing substantial increases in the police budget. Gradual replacement of foot patrol officers with motorized patrol, and the disappearance of the fixed beat altogether in a few cities, for example, removed police from close contact with the citizenry. What was needed, argued many police administrators and consultants, was development of public relations programs. Indeed, one reformer wrote in 1949, "Policing, in striving to raise itself to the level of a profession, will succeed in doing so in direct proportion to the amount of public relations work that it conducts." The Public Relations Committee of the IACP reported in 1955 on ten points that "may be used as a guide in perfecting a stronger [public-relations] program," including the important mission of explaining the inability of the police to stop the increase in crime. The committee assured the convention that "public understanding replaces misunderstanding when citizens know the limited budget, shortage of personnel, geographical area patrolled, and other problems of the department." This was disingenuous, since from 1945 to 1960 police budgets had skyrocketed from $268,099,000 to $854,118,000, or from $4.17 to $14.42 per capita, as the number of officers had soared, geographical areas generally remained constant, and police had successfully eliminated several time-consuming chores. Throughout the 1950s police departments held community symposia and "open houses," and most major police forces printed glossy, professional-looking annual reports filled with photographs and self-justifying statements aimed at city officials, newspapers, and business and citizen organizations. Public relations efforts had some effect. The portrayal of the police in the media changed from bumbling lower-middle-class ethnics (mainly Irish) to purposeful and efficient middle-class Americans, at least in part because of lobbying by the IACP, especially by its Radio and Television Committee formed in the mid-1950s.[58]

Professionalism also meant playing by the rules rather than relying upon the discretion of individual officers, and few citizens punished for routine traffic violations or minor infractions of the law appreciated this aspect of reform. As one commentator noted in 1949, the "public is prone to look upon them [officers] as members of a machine rather than protector servants of the people." Uniform application of the law by highly centralized police departments, moreover, diminished police toleration of activities that were considered inappropriate by the majority of citizens (and thus defined as illegal) but that were regarded as legitimate or at least as harmless in various areas of the city. The resultant crackdown on such practices as crap-shooting in alleys contributed to friction between certain groups and the police. Adoption of aggressive crime prevention programs such as "stop-and-frisk" tactics further alienated and embittered members of minority groups who were singled out because of their group's identification with high crime rates. Many blacks complained that they were caught in a vicious circle. Since the climbing crime rate occurred almost entirely within the black community, police became particularly attentive to black citizens, with the result that the black arrest and crime rate continued to spiral and the police became even more aggressive. To combat black frustration, a separate subset of public relations, generally called "police-community relations," grew in the postwar period.[59]

The immediate cause of this program was a series of urban disorders in the early 1940s that reached a peak with the Detroit and Harlem race riots and the Los Angeles "zoot suit" riot between Mexican-Americans and whites in 1943. The police-community relations movement that emerged after the riots brought together a few reform-minded police administrators, race relations specialists, and some elected officials, especially in California. Among police chiefs Joseph Kluchesky of Milwaukee was the leading figure. He lectured to the IACP convention in 1945, served as a consultant to several big-city police forces, and authored a training manual used by other police departments. Harvard psychologist Gordon W. Allport and University of Chicago sociologist Joseph Lohman reached an even wider audience of academics and police, and Lohman's *The Police and Minority Groups* (1947) became perhaps the leading manual on the subject. The strongest police-community relations program surfaced in California with the full support of Governor Earl Warren and the California Peace Officers' Association.[60]

All these materials and programs emphasized the professional ideal of impartial police service to counter individual prejudice of officers. The techniques for handling urban disorders were based on the experience of the 1940s, in which white mobs often were encouraged by lack of determined police action. Thus, the police planned an early, vigorous show of force, including the speedy arrest of agitators, to quickly end such riots. During the 1960s the police would be forced to change these contingency plans, for they proved counter-productive in dispersing black mobs who viewed the police as a principal target. Finally, police departments were urged to establish formal contacts with black community leaders and to hire additional black police officers. During the 1950s the big-city police sent representatives to biracial commissions and created storefront centers in the black community to signify their greater attentiveness to black concerns. They were not, however, willing to halt their aggressive war on crime that often offended black citizens, and the success of reform made them more immune from political pressure that might have ameliorated this approach or at least forced stronger disciplinary actions against police who violated the professional code.[61]

Most police forces also remained reluctant to hire large numbers of black officers. Gunnar Myrdal's *An American Dilemma* (1944) had noted the paucity of black police in the United States, particularly in the South. This situation improved noticeably by the late 1940s, and the trend continued throughout the 1950s. Still, by 1960 blacks formed only 3.5 percent of the nation's police. Because of their dramatic increase in the urban population and resultant political strength, blacks doubtless would have made much greater gains under the more highly politicized arrangements that existed before World War II. Also, the reformers' insistence on stricter entrance examinations and qualifications appeared to have a more adverse affect on black than on white candidates.[62]

Despite the police-community relations movement, therefore, by 1960 the stage was set for a serious confrontation between the police and the black community. The staggering crime increase that would begin in the early 1960s occurred mainly in the black community, to be met by the tough "law-and-order" approach of professionalized, highly mobile police forces largely resistent to political pressure. Thus, as the police approached fulfillment of goals defined before 1945, they confronted a new set of problems that would soon explode into a national crisis. Efforts to solve that crisis would lead to a reexamination of, and even reaction to, reform on the part of both blacks and white liberals on the one hand and rank-and-file police on the other. But in 1960, although the storm clouds gathered, most knowledgeable observers agreed that law-enforcement agencies had progressed a long way since World War II, and a few wistful souls felt they would one day win the war on crime.

1. Documentation for the above developments can be found in the section "Police Administration," in the *Municipal Year Book*, published annually in Chicago by the International City Management Association, for the years 1941 to 1946. Authors for this section were O. W. Wilson from 1936 to 1943 and from 1952 to 1960, Theodore E. Hall in 1944, and J. D. Holstrom from 1945 to 1951. Since this source appears frequently throughout this article, I shall simply cite *MYB*, the year of publication, and appropriate pages. For this note the sources are *MYB* (1941), 437–39; *MYB* (1942), 475; *MYB* (1944), 420–21; *MYB* (1945), 472; *MYB* (1946), 402.

2. Three excellent examinations of police reform now exist, and the author's debt to them is acknowledged here rather than repeatedly throughout the essay: Robert M. Fogelson, *Big-City Police* (Cambridge, Mass., 1977); James F. Richardson, *Urban Police in the United States* (Port Washington, N.Y., 1974); and Samuel Walker, *A Critical History of Police Reform* (Lexington, Mass., 1977).

3. Bruce Smith, "The Great Years of American Police Development," *Journal of Criminal Law and Criminology* 34 (1943–44): 127–34; *MYB* (1942), 473–74; Gene Carte,

"Technology vs. Personnel: Notes on the History of Professional Police Reform," *Journal of Police Science and Administration* 4 (1976): 285–97.

4. Bruce Smith, *Police Systems in the United States* (1949); E. J. Watts, "Bruce Smith," *Dictionary of American Biography, Supplement Five* (New York, 1977), pp. 638–39. O. W. Wilson's *Police Administration* (New York, 1950) outsold every other text in McGraw-Hill's College Division by 1972. William J. Bopp, *O. W.: O. W. Wilson and the Search for a Police Profession* (Port Washington, N.Y., 1977), p. 76. These changes applied basically to big-city police. For trends in other locales, see John M. Gleason, "Policing the Smaller Cities," pp. 14–21; Edward J. Hickey, "Trends in Rural Police Protection," pp. 22–30, and Earle W. Garrett, "Special Purpose Police Forces," pp. 31–38, all in *Annals of the Academy of Political and Social Science* (January 1954), hereafter cited as *Annals* (1954).

5. "Upward Trend in the Quality of Police Personnel," *Journal of Criminal Law and Criminology* 36 (1945–46): 105; Philip H. DuBois and Robert I. Watson, "The Selection of Patrolmen," *Journal of Applied Psychology* 34 (April 1950): 90–95; *MYB* (1946), 404–5; *MYB* (1954), 427.

6. These recommendations were reiterated in Richard L. Holcomb, *Selection of Police Officers* (Iowa City, Iowa, 1946). George H. Brereton, "California Studies Mandatory Minimum Police Personnel Standards," *Police* 2 (1957–58): 25–28. General trends in recruitment are discussed in E. J. Watts, "St. Louis Police Recruits in the Twentieth Century," *Criminology* 19 (1981): 77–113.

7. Robert S. Seares, "The Police Cadet," *Annals* (1954), pp. 107–12.

8. Albert Deutsch, "Cut-Rate Cops Are a Bad Bargain," *Collier's*, 16 October 1953, p. 74; *MYB* (1949), 387; A. C. Germann, "Hurdles to Professional Police Competence," *Police* 2 (1957–58): 51–53; "In-residence Requirement Continues to Lose Ground," *Police* 3 (September-October 1958): 71–72.

9. *MYB* (1946), 405–6; Albert Deutsch, "Modern Science Is the Cop's Best Weapon," *Collier's*, 1 October 1954, pp. 31–33; Robert H. Gault, "Instruction in Police Science," *Journal of Criminal Law and Criminology* 36 (1945–46): 151–52; "College Enrollment of Police Officers Increases," *Police* 1 (May-June 1957): 64; A. J. Bandstatter, "University Level Training for the Police Services," *Police* 3 (January-February 1959): 28–31; *MYB* (1960), 392.

10. President's Commission on Law Enforcement and Administration of Justice, *Challenge of Crime in a Free Society* (New York, 1967), p. 98; *MYB* (1949), 388; Felicia Shpritzer, "A Case for the Promotion of Policewomen in the City of New York," *Journal of Criminal Law, Criminology, and Police Science* 50 (1959–60): 415–19; Samuel Walker, "The Rise and Fall of the Policewomen's Movement, 1905–1975," in Joseph M. Hawes, ed., *Law and Order in American History* (Port Washington, N.Y., 1979), pp. 101–11.

11. *MYB* (1936), 84; *MYB* (1946), 405–17; *MYB* (1960), 394–97; *MYB* (1951), 402; *MYB* (1952), 415–17; U.S., Federal Bureau of Investigation, *Uniform Crime Reports* (1959), p. 18, hereafter cited as *UCR*.

12. Arthur Niederhoffer, *Behind the Shield: The Police in Urban Society* (Garden City, N.Y., 1967), p. 21; *MYB* (1945), 422; *MYB* (1946), 408–17; *MYB* (1951), 401; *MYB* (1958), 406; *MYB* (1960), 394–97; Bruce Smith, "The Policeman's Hire," *Annals* (1954), pp. 119–26; James D. Nicol, "The Economic Plight of the Policeman," *Journal of Criminal Law, Criminology, and Police Science* 45 (1954–55): 240.

13. Clayton W. Hall and Bruce Vanderporten, "Unionization, Monopoly Power, and Police Salaries," *Industrial Relations* 16 (1977): 94–100; John H. Burpo, *The Police Labor Movement* (Springfield, Ill., 1971), pp. 3–19; 67–70; Margaret Levi, *Bureaucratic Insurgency* (Lexington, Mass., 1977); Allan Z. Gammage and Stanley L. Sachs, *Police Unions* (Springfield, Ill., 1972), pp. 35–57; "Police Organizations," *Business Week*, 5 August 1944, pp. 96–98; IACP, *Police Unions* (Washington, D.C., 1944, rev. ed. 1958).

14. "Cops and Unions," *Newsweek*, 3 July 1944; *MYB* (1945), 424; James W. Ashley, "Police Fraternity Contrary to Public Policy," *Journal of Criminal Law and Criminology*, 38 (1947–48): 440–41; *MYB* (1948), 383–84.

15. *MYB* (1947), 373; *MYB* (1949), 388; *MYB* (1951), 402; Carl E. Heustis, "Police Unions," *Journal of Criminal Law, Criminology, and Police Science* 48 (1957–58): 643–46; Edmund P. Murray, "Should the Police Unionize?", *Nation*, 13 June 1959, pp. 530–33; Don L. Kooken and Loren D. Ayres, "Police Unions and Public Safety," *Annals* (1954), pp. 152–58; Robert Sheehan, "Lest We Forget," *Police* 4 (September-October 1960): 14–18.

16. *MYB* (1946), 405; *MYB* (1956), 402; Raymond E. Clift, "Police Training," *Annals* (1954), pp. 113–18; Earle W. Garrett, "The Police and Organized Crime," in Morris Ploscowe, ed., *Organized Crime and Law Enforcement* (New York, 1952), p. 188; John Chisholm, "Police Training," *Police Yearbook* (1954), pp. 146–54; George H. Brereton, "Law Enforcement—A Profession," *Police* 1 (May-June 1957): 12–19; "California Legislates Minimum Police Qualifications and Training Standards," *Police* 4 (November-December 1959): 83; Bernard C. Brannon, "A Proposed Uniform Law Enforcement Examination Act," *Police* 4 (November-December 1959): 71–73; *MYB* (1960), 391–92.

17. *UCR* (1959), p. 28; Deutsch, "Modern Science," pp. 31–33; Sam Stavisky, "Police Students of the FBI," *Coronet* 35 (March 1954): 73–77; David A. McCandless, "Southern Police Institute at the University of Louisville," *Journal of Criminal Law and Criminology* 42 (1951–52): 105–11, and "The Southern Police Institute," *Police* 2 (1957–58): 18–25; Donald E. J. MacNamara, "Police Training in Prevention of Crime and Delinquency," *Journal of Criminal Law and Criminology* 42 (1951–52): 262–69; Franklin M. Kreml, "Report of the IACP Traffic Division," *Police Yearbook* (1955), pp. 285–306.

18. Cyrille Leblanc, "President's Address," *Police Yearbook* (1954), pp. 1–3; Russel E. McClure, "Traffic—A Problem," *Police* 1 (July-August 1957): 62; Franklin M. Kreml, "The Specialized Traffic Division," *Annals* (1954), pp. 63–72; Jacob A. Jessup, "A Study of the Use of Police Reserves or Auxiliaries," *Police* 4 (January-February 1960): 26–29; *MYB* (1950), 402; *MYB* (1952), 413; *MYB* (1956), 401; *MYB* (1958), 405.

19. Raymond E. Clift, "Specialization in Police Work," *Journal of Criminal Law and Criminology* 42 (1951–52): 131; O. W. Wilson, "Progress in Police Administration," *Journal of Criminal Law and Criminology* 42 (1951–52): 141–54; George Mingle, "Police Personnel Evaluation and Development," *Journal of Criminal Law and Criminology* 36 (1945–46): 277–89; *MYB* (1954), 420; *MYB* (1956), 400.

20. *MYB* (1958), 405; O. W. Wilson, *Police Administration*, pp. 4–10; John I. Griffin, "Effective Statistical Presentation for Police Administrators," *Journal of Criminal Law, Criminology, and Police Science* 48 (1957–58): 262–67, and "Statistical Methods as a Management Tool for Police Administrators," *Police* 2 (May-June 1958): 61–63.

21. Walter A. Lunden, "Mobility of Chiefs of Police," *Journal of Criminal Law, Criminology, and Police Science* 49 (1958–59): 178–83; Deutsch, "Cut-Rate Cops," p. 76.

22. Ralph F. Turner, "Organization and Standardization of Police Science Techniques," *Journal of Criminal Law and Criminology* 39 (1945–46): 675–80; Wilson, "Progress in Police Administration," pp. 141–54; John E. Davis, "The Striagraph," *Police* 1 (November-December 1956): 26–29; and Harris B. Tuttle, "Criminal Detection Devices Employing Photography," *Police* 2 (January-February 1957): 7–11; Hans Arnet, "Introduction of Infra-Red Surveillance Devices," and Walter E. Klotzback, "The Helicopter—New York Police on Patrol," *Journal of Criminal Law, Criminology, and Police Science* 48 (1957–58): 112, 547.

23. Richard L. Demmerle, "New York City Police Laboratory," *Journal of Criminal Law and Criminology* 39 (1948–49): 126; Deutsch, "Modern Science," pp. 31–33; Paul L. Kirk, "Progress in Criminal Investigations," *Annals* (1954), pp. 54–62; Fred W. Nicol, "Polygraphy as a Profession," *Police* 4 (September-October 1959): 61–63; "Academy for Scientific Interrogation Holds 10th Annual Convention," *Police* 3 (January-February

1959): 68; *MYB* (1957), 393; Jerome H. Skolnick, *Justice without Trial* (New York, 1966), pp. 152–53.

24. *MYB* (1938), 98–99; Joseph A. Poli, "The Development and Present Trend in Police Radio Communications," *Journal of Criminal Law and Criminology* 33 (1942–43): 193–97; Virgil W. Peterson, "Issues and Problems in Metropolitan Area Police Services," *Journal of Criminal Law, Criminology, and Police Science* 48 (1957–58): 127–48; Wilson, "Progress in Police Administration," pp. 141–54; *MYB* (1955), 405; John A. Lyddy, "Report of the Communications Committee," *Police Yearbook* (1954), pp. 61–66; Roy C. Neibuhr, "The Use of Telephonic Recording Equipment in Police Reporting," *Police* 3 (September-October 1958): 18–20; Albert J. Reiss, *The Police and the Public* (New Haven, Conn., 1971).

25. *MYB* (1955), 404; *MYB* (1960), 394–97; *MYB* (1954), 426; "Importance of Foot Patrol in the Large Cities," *American City*, May 1950, p. 17; "Foot Patrolmen," *Journal of Criminal Law and Criminology* 31 (1940–41): 86–87; Stanley R. Schrotel, "Changing Patrol Methods," pp. 46–53, and Wilber S. Smith, "Widening the Traffic Enforcement Front," *Annals* (1954), pp. 73–77; *MYB* (1957), 391.

26. *MYB* (1946), 408–17; *MYB* (1952), 413; *MYB* (1955), 404; *MYB* (1956), 400; *MYB* (1958), 405; *MYB* (1960), 394–97; *Challenge of Crime in a Free Society*, p. 117. Richard J. Runyan and Samuel Ostertag wrote a series of eleven articles on the one-man car for *Police* in 1958; see, for example, "The One-Man Patrol Car," *Police* 2 (July-August 1958): 7–8.

27. *MYB* (1944), 475; *UCR* (1945), p. 73; *Newsweek*, 1 April 1946, p. 24. For a brief description of the *Uniform Crime Reports*, see V. A. Leonard, "Crime Reporting as a Police Management Tool," *Annals* (1954), pp. 127–34.

28. *Newsweek*, 8 February 1954, pp. 50–53; Mark Fishman, "Crime Waves as Ideology," *Social Problems* 25 (1978): 531–43.

29. *Challenge of Crime in a Free Society*, p. 21; Theodore N. Ferdinand, "The Criminal Patterns of Boston since 1849," *American Journal of Sociology*, July 1967, pp. 84–99; Ted Robert Gurr, *Rogues, Rebels, and Reformers* (Beverly Hills, Calif., 1976), pp. 35–66.

30. Deutsch, "Cut-Rate Cops," p. 75; Harold E. Pepinsky, "The Growth of Crime in the U.S.," *Annals* (1976), p. 27; *Challenge of Crime in a Free Society*, pp.2 5–27; *MYB* (1957), 392–93.

31. Thorston Sellin, "Crime in the U.S.," *Life* 9 September 1957, p. 48; *UCR*, *Special Report* (1958), pp. 21, 68; *UCR* (1959), pp. 22–30; *MYB* (1959), 405–7; Charles E. Silberman, *Criminal Violence, Criminal Justice* (New York, 1978), pp. 447–55.

32. *UCR* (1959), pp. 4–5. Trends from 1945 to 1960 were analyzed by the author, using the annual data in the *Uniform Crime Reports*.

33. J. Edgar Hoover, "Problems of Law Enforcement," *Police Yearbook* (1940), p. 12; *MYB* (1944), 420–21; *MYB* (1946), 406; *UCR* (1946), pp. 122–23; John R. Ellington, "New Police Methods with Children," *American City*, January 1949, p. 91; Michael Gaffey, "Report on the Committee on Crime Prevention," *Police Yearbook* (1955), pp. 113–20. Some analysts continue to blame the large youth population for the crime increase that began in the 1960s: see James Q. Wilson, *Thinking about Crime* (New York, 1975), pp. 15–22.

34. U.S., National Advisory Police Committee in Social Protection, *Techniques of Law Enforcement in the Treatment of Juveniles and the Prevention of Juvenile Delinquency* (Washington, D.C., 1944); Albert Deutsch, "There Are Bad Boys and Bad Girls," *Collier's*, 23 July 1954, pp. 48–52; *MYB* (1948), 382; James B. Nolan, "Police and Youth," *Journal of Criminal Law and Criminology* 43 (1952–53): 339–45; Jacob Chwast, "Police Methods for Handling Delinquent Youth," *Journal of Criminal Law, Criminology, and Police Science* 45 (1954–55): 255–58; Beverly Ober, "Report on Crime Prevention," *Police Yearbook* (1954), pp. 98–103; Jane E. Rinck, "Supervising the Juvenile Delinquent," *Annals* (1954), pp. 78–86.

35. *MYB* (1949), 388; *MYB* (1950), 401; Deutsch, "There Are Bad Boys," pp. 48–52; *UCR* (1959), pp. 16–17.

36. In 1958 the FBI eliminated twenty cities from the tabulation of juvenile arrest statistics because their reported change of 20 percent in juvenile arrests from the previous year obviously reflected alterations in reporting rather than in juvenile crime: *UCR* (1958), p. 11. Lawrence W. Sherman, "The Sociology and the Social Reform of the American Police: 1950–1973," *Journal of Police Science and Administration* 2 (1974): 256.

37. *MYB* (1959), 409; *UCR* (1959), p. 16; Harold Pepinsky, *Crime Control Strategies* (New York, 1980), pp. 197–244; *Newsweek*, 8 February 1954, pp. 50–53.

38. Bonnie Bondavalli, "The Relationship between Delinquency Theory and Juvenile Law and Policy: An Historical Summary," Newberry Library Papers in Family and Community History (Chicago, 1979).

39. Deutsch, "There Are Bad Boys," pp. 48–52; Robert H. Bremner, et al., eds., *Children and Youth in America: A Documentary History*, vol. 3, parts 5–7 (Cambridge, Mass., 1974), pp. 1003–4.

40. E. J. Allen, "La Mafia and Omerta: Doctrine of the Underworld," *Police Yearbook* (1955), pp. 152–65; Humbert Nelli, *The Business of Crime* (New York, 1976); Dwight C. Smith, *The Mafia Mystique* (New York, 1975); Mark H. Haller, "Bootleggers and American Gambling, 1920–1950," in Commission on the Review of National Policy toward Gambling, *Gambling in America*, appendix 1 (Washington, D.C., 1976).

41. Alan A. Block, "History and the Study of Organized Crime," *Urban Life*, January 1978, p. 455–74; B. B. Turkus and S. Feder, *Murder, Inc.* (New York, 1951); A. G. Anderson, *The Business of Organized Crime: A Cosa Nostra Family* (Stanford, Calif., 1979), pp. 1–16; F. D. Homer, *Guns and Garlic* (New York, 1974), pp. 30–45; Daniel Bell, "Crime as an American Way of Life: A Queer Ladder of Social Mobility," in *The End of Ideology* (New York, 1960), pp. 127–71.

42. William Howard Moore, *The Kefauver Committee and the Politics of Crime, 1950–1952* (Columbia, Mo., 1971); Joseph B. Gorman, *Kefauver: A Political Biography* (New York, 1971), pp. 80–90; David F. Musto, *The American Disease: Origins of Narcotics Control* (New Haven, Conn., 1973), pp. 210–12; George P. Monaghan, "The Narcotics Problem," *Police Yearbook* (1954), pp. 113–22; B. T. Mitchell, "Narcotics Law Enforcement," *Police Yearbook* (1955), pp. 142–47.

43. Joseph L. Nellis, "Legal Aspects of the Kefauver Investigation," *Journal of Criminal Law and Criminology* 42 (1951–52): 163–70; V. A. Leonard, "Crusade against Crime," *Journal of Criminal Law and Criminology* 43 (1952–53): 80.

44. Albert Deutsch, "The Plight of the Honest Cop," *Collier's*, 18 September 1953, pp. 23–27; Bopp, *O. W.*, pp. 84–87; Cyril D. Robinson, "The Mayor and the Police: The Political Role of the Police in Society," in George Mosse, ed., *Police Forces in History* (Beverly Hills, Calif., 1975), p. 301.

45. Albert Deutsch, "It's Tough, Very Tough, to Buck the System," *Collier's*, 2 October 1953, pp. 84–89; and "Vice Squad," *Collier's*, 28 May 1954, pp. 66–70; Herbert Brean, "A Really Good Police Force," *Life*, 16 September 1957, pp. 71–73.

46. Gorman, *Kefauver*, pp. 83–85; Raymond Moley, "After Kefauver—What?" *Newsweek*, 16 April 1951, p. 112; "A Big Laugh on the Law," *Life*, 1 October 1951, p. 19–23; *MYB* (1952), 409; *MYB* (1953), 409; *MYB* (1954), 425.

47. John Hutchison, *The Imperfect Union: A History of Corruption in American Trade Unions* (New York, 1970), pp. 151–69; Robert F. Kennedy, *The Enemy Within* (New York, 1960), pp. 160–61.

48. *Challenge of Crime in a Free Society*, pp. 191–97; Kennedy, *The Enemy Within*, p. 228.

49. Hutchinson, *The Imperfect Union*, pp. 170–268, 357–66; Kennedy, *The Enemy Within*, pp. 110, 137, 302–4.

50. Sanford J. Ungar, *FBI* (Boston, 1975), pp. 177–80; *Challenge of Crime in a Free Society*, p. 196; Ronald W. May, "Organized Crime and Disorganized Cops," *New Republic*, 27 June 1959.

51. George Mingle, "Report of the Committee on Federal, State, and Local Cooperation," *Police Yearbook* (1955), pp. 79–83; *Challenge of Crime in a Free Society*, p. 204; Patrick V. Murphy, *Commissioner* (New York, 1977), p. 96; Ungar, *FBI*, pp. 387–93, 428–45.

52. J. Edgar Hoover, *Masters of Deceit* (New York, 1958); Ungar, *FBI*, pp. 272–73.

53. Ungar, *FBI*, pp. 85–127; Michael Belknap, *Cold War Political Justice* (Westport, Conn., 1977); Athan Theoharis, *Spying on Americans* (Philadelphia, 1978); *MYB* (1942), 473; *MYB* (1951), 400.

54. Ungar, *FBI*, pp. 125–33, 430–31; Murphy, *Commissioner*, pp. 82–99. On the other hand, the FBI continued to cement alliances with local police through the National Academy, *Uniform Crime Reports*, Fingerprint Identification Division, and Crime Laboratory. Rolf T. Harbo, "The FBI and the Police," *Police Yearbook* (1955), pp. 99–103; Hugh Clegg, "Police Cooperation," *Police Yearbook* (1954), pp. 20–24; J. E. Hoover, "The Basis of Sound Law Enforcement," *Annals* (1954), pp. 39–45. Many police also supported the anti-Communist crusade: see Leblanc, "President's Address," pp. 1–3.

55. Deutsch, "Cut-Rate Cops," pp. 72–78; William H. Parker, "The Police Challenge in Our Great Cities," *Annals* (1954), pp. 5–13. Police, particularly Chief J. D. Holstrom, of the Berkeley Police Department, did play a pronounced role in civil defense preparations, providing a reason to maintain throughout the postwar period auxiliary forces created during World War II: V. A. Leonard, "Police Advisor for Civil Defense Planning," *Journal of Criminal Law and Criminology* 39 (1948–49): 657; *MYB* (1950), 400; *MYB* (1951), 399–401; *MYB* (1952), 410; "Civil Defense: Plans and Uncertainties," *Newsweek*, 18 December 1950, p. 19; V. A. Leonard, "Television for Police," *Journal of Criminal Law and Criminology* 43 (1952–53): 789; Charles W. Woodson, "Report of the IACP Advisor Committee on Civil Defense," *Police Yearbook* (1954), pp. 29–33; Arthur E. Kimberling, "Police Planning and Activities in Civil Defense," *Police Yearbook* (1955), pp. 24–32.

56. James Q. Wilson, *Varieties of Police Behavior* (New York, 1973); Reiss, *The Police and the Public*. Trends were analyzed by the author using annual data in the *Uniform Crime Reports*. *MYB* (1960), 390; "Power of the Police," *New Republic*, 7 April 1958, pp. 3–4.

57. David R. Johnson, "Police Reform and the Blue Curtain in Historical Perspective," paper delivered to Second Annual Conference on Public History, Pittsburgh, April 1980; William A. Westley, *Violence and the Police* (Cambridge, Mass., 1970).

58. Raymond E. Clift, "Police, Press, and Public Relations," *Journal of Criminal Law and Criminology* 39 (1948–49): 667–74; Lou Smyth, "Report of the Public Relations Committee," *Police Yearbook* (1955), pp. 186–91; *MYB* (1946), 408–17; *MYB* (1960), 394–97; George F. Morris, "Open House—The Gateway to Improved Public Relations," *Police* 1 (May-June 1957): 20–22; Paul H. Ashenhust, "Police and Public Attitude," *Police* 3 (September-October 1958): 30–33; Fogelson, *Big-City Police*, pp. 235–37.

59. Ervis W. Lester, "Some Aspects of Police Problems," *Journal of Criminal Law and Criminology* 40 (1949–50): 796–809; G. Douglas Gourley, "Police Public Relations," *Annals* (1954), pp. 135–42. Before World War II the most heated conflict between police and civilians occurred in labor disputes, but this confrontation became much less noticeable in the postwar period. *MYB* (1946), 403; *MYB* (1947), 372; *MYB* (1948), 382; *MYB* (1950), 401; Elliot M. Rudwick, "Police Work and the Negro," *Journal of Criminal Law, Criminology, and Police Science* 50 (1959–60): 596–99; Division of Police, Louisville, Kentucky, *Principles of Police Work with Minority Groups* (Louisville, 1950); Silberman, *Criminal Violence, Criminal Justice*, pp. 117–65.

60. Joseph Kluchesky, *Police Action in Minority Problems* (New York, 1946); Joseph D. Lohman, *The Police and Minority Groups* (Chicago, 1947); Samuel Walker, "The Ori-

gins of the American Police-Community Relations Movement: The 1940s," *Criminal Justice History* (1980), pp. 225–46.

61. Walker, "Origins of the American Police-Community Relations Movement," pp. 225–46.

62. Gunnar Myrdal, *An American Dilemma*, 2 vols. (New York, 1964), 2:542–45; Elliot Rudwick, *The Unequal Badge: Negro Policemen in the South* (Atlanta, 1962); W. M. Kephart, "The Integration of Negroes into the Urban Police Force," *Journal of Criminal Law, Criminology, and Police Science* 45 (1954–55): 325–33; *MYB* (1949), 388; *MYB* (1950), 402; E. J. Watts, "Black and Blue: Afro-American Police Officers in Twentieth-Century St. Louis," *Journal of Urban History* 7 (February 1981): 131–68.

The Government-Science Complex

Kenneth M. Jones

The relationship between the United States government and the American scientific community was drastically altered during World War II and the cold war. Before 1940 the government paid little attention to science, and most scientists were wary of what they regarded as political involvement. During World War II, however, the American scientific community was mobilized by the federal government in an enormously effective manner. Since penicillin, sulfa drugs, and the atomic bomb all seemed to be the fruit of this new relationship, most Americans were convinced that a continuation was essential. This consensus was reflected in the rapidly rising level of expenditures for science. In 1940 only 0.8 percent of the federal budget was allocated for scientific research and development. The figure had doubled by the end of the war, and rose spectacularly thereafter. By 1960, 10.1 percent of the federal budget was spent on research and development.[1] As the government's investment in research increased, so did its role in the nation's overall scientific development. Before the war, industry had provided 68 percent of all money spent on science in the United States, whereas the government contributed only 20 percent. By the end of the war, the division was almost even—and by 1960 the prewar proportions had been reversed.[2]

This rapid expansion of federal support meant that government decisions played a significant role in shaping the direction of American scientific research. Despite the change the government did not develop a systematic policy designed to maximize science's ability to address a broad range of national needs. Instead, science was supported through a decentralized structure that was dominated by national security concerns. This situation resulted from three major factors: the cold war, popular conceptions of the requirements of scientific advance, and the response of the American scientific community.

Even before the atomic destruction of Hiroshima and Nagasaki, science's wartime achievements inspired proposals for continued government support in peacetime. Vannevar Bush, director of the Office of Scientific Research and Development, agreed, but did not want his centrally controlled, narrowly focused wartime agency to serve as the model. To guarantee consideration of an alternative approach, Bush prompted President Franklin D. Roosevelt in November 1944 to request from him an analysis of the nation's postwar scientific needs. By July 1945 Bush had responded with a plan that gave scientists access to the public purse with minimal government control.[3]

Immediately after the release of *Science, the Endless Frontier*—as Bush's report was entitled—Senator Warren Magnuson (D., Washington) introduced legislation to implement Bush's vision. Magnuson proposed the creation of a "national science foundation" to support scientists outside the government in basic research, provide fellowships, and "develop and promote" a national science policy. Magnuson's organizational structure guaranteed that scientists, rather than political appointees, would determine the policies of the agency.[4] The Bush-Magnuson conception of the proper postwar relationship between science and government was immediately challenged by Senator Harley Kilgore (D., West Virginia), who proposed a foundation broader in scope and less independent of public control. Kilgore envisioned a foundation that would coordinate all federal scientific activities and fund both basic and applied research in "fields of recognized public interest."[5] Although there was little discussion of the rival proposals, the concept of a national science foundation received substantial public support in late July 1945.[6]

The use of the first atomic bombs in August 1945 sharply increased public awareness of science. Instead of serving man, scientific research seemed to have propelled the world into a new era. "Science now rules the roost and our lives," *Business Week* noted. "We went to bed Aug. 5 in George Washington's time; we woke up on Aug. 6 the first citizens of a truly modern world."[7] Americans were not only awed by the destructive power of the atomic bomb, but expected great benefits from cheap nuclear power. Otherwise sober commentators predicted the early development of atomic-powered cars, and speculated that atomic energy would become so cheap that it would be like "free air" at the service station.[8]

The military significance of the new force alone would have been sufficient to necessitate government action, but eight of nine Americans also believed that federal controls were necessary to develop its peaceful benefits.[9] As President Truman told the nation, atomic energy required "drastic" government action because it was "too revolutionary to consider in the framework of old ideas."[10] The release of atomic energy thus guaranteed that the government would accept new responsibility for at least one area of science after the war.

The debate over the precise nature of this new responsibility began on 3 October 1945, when the May-Johnson bill was introduced in Congress.[11] Although this measure gave control to a civilian atomic energy commission, it reflected the army's experience in the wartime Manhattan Project. Most significantly, it stressed development of atomic energy's military uses and emphasized the need for strict security with regard to the "secret" of the bomb. Many scientists who had worked on the Manhattan Project were appalled by what they regarded as a continuation of wartime attitudes and an attempt to protect a secret that no longer existed. They insisted that the nation's future security—and mankind's survival—would be better served by efforts to achieve international control of atomic energy. These scientists and laymen who shared their views supported the proposal of Senator Brien McMahon (D., Connecticut), which largely excluded the armed forces, emphasized the peaceful potential of atomic energy, called for international control, and sought to promote scientific freedom rather than strict secrecy.[12] McMahon's bill received the support of President Truman, and appeared to be headed for passage until February 1946, when the revelation of a wartime Russian espionage ring in Canada and increasing distrust of the Soviet Union caused the balance to swing back toward a more restrictive approach.[13]

In the resulting Atomic Energy Act of 1946, the Atomic Energy Commission's sweeping powers were to be exercised by civilians, but the "paramount objective" of the commission was described as "assuring the common defense and security."[14] The act emphasized secrecy, restricting the dissemination of information, requiring an FBI investigation of scientists, and providing rigorous penalties for violation of security regulations.

While the government was accepting responsibility for the control of atomic energy, proposals for the creation of a national science foundation languished. Although the most immediate reason was continued disagreement between supporters of the Bush and Kilgore approaches, popular attitudes and the response of the American scientific community were also important. Since many laymen regarded science as synonymous with atomic energy, the need for "another" scientific agency beyond the Atomic Energy Commission (AEC) did not seem imperative. The proposed foundation also failed to generate enthusiasm because the need for extensive basic research did not correspond with the lay public's perception of the requirements for scientific achievement. These views had been shaped largely by news accounts of the Manhattan Project, which implied that any specific goal could be realized simply with adequate organization and massive funding. The scientists' efforts to correct these misconceptions were hampered by their involvement in the battle over atomic energy legislation. Since most scientists regarded control of the new force as their highest priority, they were unwilling to risk their unanimity of public support by simultaneously battling for a particular science foundation bill. All these factors together prevented the strong push that might have overcome the Bush-Kilgore division.[15]

Failure to establish a national science foundation immediately after the war facilitated the emergence of a pluralistic structure, as the federal investment in science was funneled through a variety of agencies, each made intelligible to the public by identification with a particular end. The most prominent of these agencies was the AEC, which gradually expanded its mandate to include the granting of fellowships and the support of some basic research that otherwise would have been funded by a national science foundation. The AEC's budget grew accordingly, rising from $84 million in its first full year (1948) to $121.1 million in 1950.[16] This growth was aided by the commission's identification with national defense, and by the dedicated support of its congressional overseers on the Joint Committee on Atomic Energy.

In a similar manner the proposed foundation's responsibility for medical research was largely assumed by the Public Health Service's National Institutes of Health (NIH). The NIH grew rapidly in the late 1940s by adding a series of specific disease-oriented branches, such as the National Heart Institute and National Arthritis and Metabolic Diseases Institute. Congress was much more willing to support such specific agencies than it was to fund general medical or biological research. As one congressman later explained, "Nobody ever heard of a person dying from microbiology."[17] The NIH's success in selling its work to Congress was reflected in a 600 percent increase in the agency's total appropriations between 1947 and 1950.[18]

The proposed foundation's principal function—support of basic reseach—was assumed by the Office of Naval Research (ONR) of the Department of the Navy. This agency was created by Congress in August 1946 on the assumption that it would pursue scientific solutions to specific military problems. The administrators of the ONR did not, however, make military relevance their primary criteria for the distribution of funds, but instead sponsored projects of interest to scientists. This somewhat clandestine support for basic research filled the gap left by the absence of a national science foundation, but depended on the ONR's ability to defend such investments against those who demanded an emphasis on more immediate navy problems.[19] In addition to the ONR, each of the service branches increased its research budget. As a result, by 1947 the armed forces spent thirty-eight times as much money on research and development as in 1937.[20]

Proliferation of functionally defined science agencies caused some members of the Truman administration to seek other routes to the broad perspective and coordination that had been regarded as part of the proposed foundation's duties. This led first to the creation of the President's Scientific Research Board in 1946, and then to the Interdepartmental Committee on Scientific Research and Development in 1947. The latter was to "achieve balance among the several scientific activities of the Government, and the closing of gaps in the present programs."[21] These organizations were largely ineffective, however, because they lacked prestige and could not allocate funds.[22]

By the time the National Science Foundation (NSF) was created in May 1950, it was clear that it would be "only another pillar in the edifice of government science, rather than the capstone of the whole structure."[23] Control of the more popular areas of scientific research had already been established. For example, the new agency was expressly forbidden to engage in military or atomic energy research without the consent of the secretary of defense or the AEC. The foundation did retain a Division of Medical Research, but since the NIH had already created separate Cancer and Heart institutes, the new agency was effectively prevented from appealing to Congress for research funds in those popular areas. The NSF also lacked real authority to coordinate federal scientific efforts, as the 1950 act authorized it only to "encourage the pursuit of a national policy."[24]

The actual functions of the NSF were essentially two: support of basic research, and the distribution of science scholarships. Even in these areas it did not play a central role, but rather supplemented the programs already established by the ONR and the AEC. The low status and limited appeal of such an agency was soon revealed in its struggle for appropriations. In 1945 Vannevar Bush had recommended a "modest beginning" of $33.5 million for the first year, but he expected the mature foundation to have a budget of $122.5 million annually. President Truman's recommendation for fiscal year 1952 (the first full year of the foundation's existence) was $14 million; Congress appropriated only $3.5 million.[25] What had been envisioned as the nation's paramount scientific agency thus began its life with a weak mandate and an even weaker access to the public purse.

In the years immediately after World War II, federal aid to science was thus channeled through a pluralistic system of goal-oriented agencies. The specific objectives of the proliferating agencies were more easily understood by most laymen, and the approach conformed with the apparent requirements of scientific advance as revealed in the Manhattan Project Applied research and development received priority, while the role of basic research was seldom acknowledged. This structure meant that in the midst of the cold war federally funded science would be overwhelmingly devoted to immediate national security needs.

Although a unified scientific program did not emerge after World War II, American scientists achieved a significant role as advisers to government officials. The military sought help on new weapons and beginning in 1948 sponsored "Summer Studies," where scientists devoted their expertise to the analysis of specific technical and strategic problems. Of all roles played by scientists, their most significant post was the General Advisory Committee (GAC) of the Atomic Energy Commission. The ability of GAC members to influence policy, however, was tenuous. As advisers rather than representatives of an independent political entity, their authority rested on the willingness of laymen to listen. The limits of the committee's powers became obvious in 1949.

On 23 September 1949 President Truman informed the American people that the Soviet Union had exploded a nuclear device; the American monopoly on the atomic bomb had ended much sooner than conventional wisdom had predicted.[26] Immediately after the Soviet atomic bomb was revealed, AEC member Lewis Strauss called for a major effort to create a much larger hydrogen, or "super," bomb. He insisted that such a "quantum jump" in the nation's destructive capacities would be the most effective response to the Soviet achievements.[27] His enthusiasm was shared by a group of scientists, including Edward Teller and Ernest Lawrence. Teller had worked on the possibility of a hydrogen bomb during the war, and had subsequently served as a consultant to those who were continuing studies in that area. The net result had not been very encouraging. As physicist Herbert York later noted, "Despite several years of thinking by some very bright people, no one then knew how to make a 'super.' "[28] Although the project faced potentially insurmountable technical barriers, Strauss and the scientists were able to generate substantial support for an immediate, massive effort comparable to the Manhattan Project.

Reacting to this pressure, the AEC requested the GAC to make recommendations on the appropriate response to the Soviet achievement— including the possibility of a crash program to develop the hydrogen bomb. The GAC's report, delivered on 30 October 1949, urged increased production of fissionable material, development of tactical atomic weapons, and testing of the boosting principle that would improve the efficiency of a fission (atomic) explosion. The committee, however, marshalled several arguments against a massive effort to achieve the hydrogen bomb. On a more technical level, they argued that a high-priority effort was unwise because fundamental theoretical studies related to the hydrogen bomb were insufficiently advanced. There was, therefore, no assurance that even a concerted attack on the problem would be successful. Until more basic research and tests had been completed, a crash program might actually weaken the nation by diverting key materials and manpower from the atomic bomb program. The GAC also argued against the hydrogen bomb on moral grounds. Warning that the destructive power of the "super" made it a "weapon of genocide," the scientists urged that the United States publicly renounce it. "In determining not to proceed to develop the super bomb," a majority of the GAC argued, "we see a unique opportunity of providing by example some limitations on the totality of war and thus of limiting the fear and arousing the hopes of mankind." If the Soviets failed to exercise similar self-restraint, GAC Chairman J. Robert Oppenheimer reminded the commission, the nation's atomic weapons would provide for "adequate reprisal."[29]

The GAC's report was accepted by the commission on a three-to-two vote. Strauss led the minority, while AEC Chairman David Lilienthal emerged as the leading defender of the GAC position. President Truman, however, disregarded both the AEC's recommendation and the views of what had been the government's most prestigious scientific body. On 31 January 1950 the president announced that he was directing the AEC to "continue its work on all forms of atomic weapons, including the so-called hydrogen or superbomb." Six weeks later Truman ordered that the program be shifted from the somewhat ambiguous "continue" to an all-out effort.[30] The decision received overwhelming public support.[31]

The president was inclined toward the hydrogen bomb for both personal and political reasons, but his decision was influenced by other factors as well. Most important was the division within the scientific community. With eminent scientists on both sides of the issue, President Truman was free to choose the politically more congenial advice offered by Edward Teller. Those who argued against the bomb were thought to prove the political naïveté of most scientists. Typically, Joint Committee on Atomic Energy (JCAE) Chairman Brien McMahon dismissed the GAC's arguments against the hydrogen bomb "as simply an emotional reaction to a difficult situation."[32] This attitude precluded a rational discussion of whether emphasis on the hydrogen bomb or expanding production of atomic weapons would best ensure national security.

The decision to follow Teller rather than the GAC was also encouraged by lay assumptions about the requirements of scientific advance. Truman, members of the JCAE, and other laymen who insisted on pursuing the hydrogen bomb ignored the GAC's emphasis on the need for more basic research. They were able to do so because Teller's views corresponded with their assumption that government direction and money would produce results. Fortunately, a year after the crash program had been initiated, Teller and mathematician Stanislaw Ulam made the critical theoretical breakthrough.[33] By June 1951 this concept had led to a new design that, in the words of J. Robert Oppenheimer, was "technically so sweet that you could not argue."[34] The United States exploded the first fusion bomb on 1 November 1952 and tested a deliverable hydrogen bomb in the spring of 1954. Although the program was successful, the process did nothing to encourage lay understanding of the importance of basic research. Americans would continue to assume that the requisite scientific rabbits could be pulled out of the hat anytime the federal government chose to apply sufficient money and organization.

Following the hydrogen bomb decision, scientists and scientific administrators who were not fully committed to the pursuit of more and bigger weapons lost influence rapidly. Lilienthal resigned in February 1950, and was replaced as AEC chairman by Strauss's ally Gordon Dean. Dean appointed several more pliable scientists to replace those who were leaving the GAC in 1950, and generally made it clear that he expected the committee to be more cooperative in the future.[35] These changes were not sufficient, however, to convince the JCAE that the AEC could be trusted to pursue the military applications of atomic energy with sufficient zeal. The JCAE made clear its intention to exercise greater oversight in June 1951, when the members voted to end their longstanding refusal to accept top secret data on production rates and the weapons stockpile from the AEC. The JCAE also pressured the AEC to launch an all-out effort to at least double the nation's nuclear stockpile. After a substantial budget increase in January 1952, the AEC largely followed the JCAE's recommendation.[36]

The AEC's declining influence was also apparent in the decision to create a second weapons laboratory to supplement the work done at Los Alamos. The impetus for a second laboratory was provided by Edward Teller, who insisted it was essential for the rapid development of hydrogen bombs. The AEC rejected Teller's request in December 1951 on the grounds that it would divide the nation's efforts, but Teller used personal contacts to reach Thomas Finletter, the secretary of the air force. In April 1952, at Finletter's urging, the National Security Council authorized the creation of the second weapons laboratory at Livermore.[37]

The process of narrowing the range of scientific advice and focusing the nation's scientific efforts on weapons continued during the Eisenhower administration. After the Republican victory in 1952, Gordon Dean resigned, which allowed the new president to appoint Lewis Strauss chairman of the AEC. During the next five years, Strauss used his position as head of the nation's paramount scientific agency—and his good personal relations with the president—to function as Eisenhower's scientific adviser.[38] Like Teller, Strauss believed that the nation's scientific resources should be devoted to improving our ability to inflict massive destruction on the Soviet Union through the use of large nuclear weapons. He also possessed a strong concern for secrecy and an intense distrust of the Soviets. As a result, he effectively blocked proposals for neutral observers at American nuclear tests and weakened Eisenhower's 1953 Atoms for Peace proposal.[39] Strauss's approach, which linked science almost exclusively with the development of offensive military power, was well received because it coincided with the needs of the Eisenhower administration and other politically powerful groups.

The Strauss-Teller hegemony was also furthered by the general absence of dissent from within the scientific community. This was partly because the outbreak of the Korean conflict and the continued cold war had overcome most scientists' resistance to secrecy and weapons research.[40] More important, however, those who disagreed with Teller on how best to use science to achieve national security were frequently reluctant to speak out, particularly after Strauss and Teller played key roles in the Eisenhower administration's decision to withdraw J. Robert Oppenheimer's security clearance in 1954.

Although Strauss and Teller were largely able to fill the vacuum created by the demise of the GAC, the Science Advisory Committee of the Office of Defense Mobilization (SAC/ODM) constituted an alternative and potential rival. The primary impetus for the SAC/ODM came from the Bureau of the Budget. Worried by what he saw as uncoordinated federal investment in science and the "adequacy of long-term coverage," Budget Director F. J. Lawton ordered William T. Golden to study the government's scientific organization.[41] In December 1950 Golden recommended the appointment of a full-time scientific adviser to the president and the creation of a president's science advisory committee. The scientific adviser was to stay informed of all research programs of military significance conducted by the government, and "be available to give the president independent and comprehensive advice on scientific matters inside and outside the government."[42]

President Truman approved Golden's recommendations, but before they were implemented, two changes occurred that substantially altered the final result. First, the office of scientific adviser was downgraded to simply chairman of the science advisory committee. This was done at the insistence of Dr. Oliver Buckley, who agreed to assume the post only if it did not require aggressive leadership. The ability of the scientists to influence policy was further decreased by a second change that placed the science advisory committee under the jurisdiction of the director of the Office of Defense Mobilization. Although the committee retained the right to make recommendations directly to the president if its members saw fit, the new apparatus ensured that the agency would have limited impact.[43]

The creation of SAC/ODM was officially announced by President Truman on 20 April 1951. Chairman Buckley was joined by ten other scientists from government service, universities, and industry. Buckley's cautious approach was immediately apparent in his admonition to his colleagues that their function was to "work with and through existing agencies; avoid fanfare and minimize public appearances."[44] Very little was accomplished by May 1952, when Buckley was replaced by California Institute of Technology President Lee A. DuBridge. Although DuBridge tried to provide more aggressive leadership, members of the SAC/ODM were so dispirited by the fall of 1952 that they met to decide whether they should recommend discontinuance of their role. They decided not to disband, but pleaded that they be allowed to report directly to the president or at least to the National Security Council.[45] Their suggestion was rejected, and the SAC/ODM continued in relative obscurity throughout the first year of the Eisenhower administration.[46]

Finally, in March 1954, the committee was given its first major opportunity to advise the president. When Eisenhower challenged the scientists to find ways to reduce the danger of surprise attack on the United States, the SAC/ODM organized the Technical Capabilities Panel under Massachusetts Institute of Technology President James Killian.[47] Its report, presented to the National Security Council on 14 February 1955, criticized the administration's massive-retaliation doctrine and offered recommendations in five major areas. The scientists on the panel urged the National Security Council to give the intercontinental ballistic missile program the highest priority, investigate defenses against Soviet missiles, improve technological capacities for limited warfare, unify Department of Defense communications systems, and develop the U-2 high-altitude reconnaissance aircraft.[48]

These recommendations met with varying success, even though the president endorsed all but those in the area of limited war. Like limited warfare, the missile defense program found few friends within the government and was generally ignored. The intercontinental ballistic missile program was dramatically accelerated, but with separate efforts in each service rather than the unified approach favored by the panel. Interservice rivalries were also responsible for blocking the integration of defense communications until the end of the Eisenhower administration. Only the development of the U-2 went ahead smoothly, and that was largely because the president transferred responsibility to the Central Intelligence Agency rather than leaving the program in the Defense Department.[49]

The Technological Capabilities Panel's influence was limited because it did not have ongoing access to the president and was unable to aid in the implementation of the policies that he did accept.[50] Furthermore, the group was unable to overcome Eisenhower's reliance on Strauss. When the president suggested that the panel continue its efforts with a study of a moratorium on nuclear tests, Strauss objected, and Eisenhower retracted the offer.[51] Finally, the panel's efforts were limited to a relatively narrow area, and therefore it could not address the larger questions of how science could best serve the nation.

The organization that—theoretically—could have provided that advice was the NSF. Although watered down, the foundation had come into existence in 1950 with some authority to oversee federal science policy. That charge was, however, more than offset by the agency's small budget and the attitude of its first director, Alan T. Waterman, who insisted that his agency should stay clear of any supervisory or coordinating role that would offend stronger agencies.[52] This restricted view was not shared, however, by officials in the Bureau of the Budget. They were determined that the NSF should play a substantial role in their efforts to supervise rapidly growing federal expenditures for science. Accordingly, in May 1952, Budget staffer William Carey pressured Waterman to begin a program of evaluation and coordination. Waterman's response, according to Carey, was to "duck out of sight under the table."[53]

With the advent of a new administration in 1953, Carey resumed his efforts, suggesting that President Eisenhower issue an executive order enhancing the foundation's coordinating power. Carey's proposed executive order also strengthened the NSF by asserting that it was the "primary agency for the support of basic scientific research."[54] Waterman reluctantly acquiesced, but AEC Chairman Strauss and others vehemently attacked NSF "encroachment."[55] The final document, Executive Order 10521, was not what Carey had intended. It reiterated, but did not substantially increase, the foundation's ability to oversee the nation's scientific investment, and made it clear that other agencies would provide funds for the most popular areas of basic research.[56]

The Budget Bureau eventually gave up on the NSF as a mechanism for the overall coordination of federal science policy. In the spring of 1956, Budget Director Rowland Hughes wrote the president, "I think it is very doubtful if anything like the type of supervision that I believe you had in mind can be effected through that group."[57] Despite the best efforts of the Budget Bureau, the foundation thus failed to emerge as a significant factor in the formation of federal science policy. The consequences of the foundation's weaknesses and the other developments in the government-science relationship were amply clear by the mid-1950s.

A decade after World War II, the government-science complex fully reflected the impact of the cold war and the lay direction of science. Convinced that federal investment in science was good, Congress appropriated more and more funds for research. In fiscal year 1946 federal research and development expenditures were $918 million, or 1.5 percent of the total federal budget. By fiscal year 1956 the figures were $3,446 million, or 5.2 percent. This money was not distributed by a central authority or according to an overall assessment of the nation's long-term scientific needs. Instead, thirty-eight separate agencies sought funds for their own particular projects.[58] Since their success depended upon congressional support, these agencies tended to promote goal-oriented research that had an immediate and obvious bearing on national concerns.

The NIH, with its popular and easily identifiable targets, was one of

TABLE 1

FEDERAL EXPENDITURES FOR RESEARCH AND DEVELOPMENT BY AGENCY
AS A PERCENTAGE OF THE TOTAL
(Dollars in millions)[61]

Agency	FY 1940	FY 1948	FY 1953	FY 1958	FY 1961
Agriculture Department	38.6%	5.3%	1.4%	2.5%	1.5%
	($28.4)	($40.7)	($55)	($126)	($143)
Atomic Energy Commission	...	11%	10.6%	16.1%	9.3%
	...	($84)	($393)	($804)	($850)
Defense Department	35.9%	70.1%	82%	73.4%	72.5%
	($26.4)	($534.2)	($3025)	($3664)	($6574)
National Aeronautics and Space Administration*	2.9%	3.9%	2.1%	1.7%	8.5%
	($2.2)	($29.8)	($79)	($89)	($777)
National Institutes of Health	0.9%	2.2%	1%	3.2%	4.1%
	($0.7)	($16.9)	($37.5)	($160.2)	($375.4)
National Science Foundation	...	...	0.05%	0.6%	0.9%
	...	...	($2)	($33)	($84)
Other	21.3%	7.4%	2.5%	2.2%	2.8%
	($15.7)	($56.4)	($95.5)	($113.8)	($255.6)
Total federal expenditure for research and development	($73.4)	($762)	($3687)	($4990)	($9059)

* National Advisory Committee for Aeronautics prior to 1958

the more successful participants in this situation. Public enthusiasm for medical research was spurred by rapid progress after World War II. Cortisone brought relief from crippling arthritis, and antibiotics such as streptomycin controlled over forty previously fatal diseases. When Dr. Jonas Salk's vaccine curtailed polio in 1955, public praise grew even louder.[59] Although the NIH did not play a major role in these developments, it benefited from the general hope that organized medical research would yield similar triumphs in other areas. With congressmen frequently suggesting new diseases to attack, the agency inaugurated or expanded research on arthritis, cancer, diabetes, heart disease, mental health, and tooth decay. These programs were so politically popular that Congress routinely raised the NIH budget above the amount requested by the administration. By 1960 the agency spent approximately ten times as much on research as it had in 1950.[60]

The NIH budget grew rapidly, but the clear relationship between science and national defense guaranteed that the military would dominate the competition for federal research funds. As table 1 indicates, in fiscal year 1940 the armed forces controlled a smaller percentage of the federal government's research and development funds than did the Department of Agriculture. During World War II, however, the military's share escalated sharply, reaching more than 80 percent of the total. Although overall military budgets were reduced and the army's wartime responsibility for atomic energy was transferred to the new Atomic Energy Commission, the Department of Defense still controlled 70.1 percent of government's investment in research in 1948.[62] After a slight drop before the Korean War, that percentage rose even higher in the 1950s. Other agencies also funded scientific projects devoted to military ends. A Budget Bureau analysis of fiscal year 1953 classified all the National Advisory Committee for Aeronautics' budget and 75 percent of the AEC's expenditures as military-related.[63] If these amounts were added to the Department of Defense share for that year, the total devoted to military purposes was 92.1 percent.

Given the cold war and lay assumptions, it was inevitable that most of the nation's scientific resources would be devoted to national defense and that occasional boondoggles like the Aircraft Nuclear Propulsion Project would occur.[64] These were, however, decisions that could be reversed if and when the climate of opinion changed. The structure of federal support for science also affected the nation's research effort in more subtle ways that were less easily rectified. This was particularly true in the provision of funds for basic research and in the allocation of monies among the various sciences.

One of Vannevar Bush's original arguments for federal support of science after World War II was that only the government could afford to fund essential basic research. Universities and private institutions could no longer supply the large sums necessary, and industry was reluctant to invest in work that did not have clear commercial potential. Although Bush did not specify what percentage of the federal research budget should be devoted to basic research, he insisted that substantial amounts were needed. In 1947 presidential adviser John Steelman urged a quadrupling of funds, explaining that "the support of basic research is the most important single element in the entire National Science Program."[65] If his suggestions had been followed, the percentage of federal research and development money allocated to basic research would have risen from approximately 8 percent in 1947 to between 17 and 20 percent a decade later.

During the mid-1950s the federal government's investment in basic research fell far below these expectations. For fiscal year 1954 the NSF estimated that only 6 percent of the total federal outlay for scientific activities went to basic research. Between fiscal year 1954 and fiscal year 1958, the situation did not improve. While the overall federal investment in science grew 1.7 times faster than the total federal budget, funds allocated to basic research increased by a factor of 1.3. The dollar amount thus increased, but the percentage of federal investment in basic research fell to slightly more than 3 percent of the total.[66] Furthermore, more than 70 percent of the federal funds for basic research were distributed through defense-related agencies that were especially tempted to cut long-range basic research in favor of applied projects that promised a more immediate return.[67]

Federal support for basic research lagged in part because of the public's lack of understanding of its role in the scientific process. Believing that any scientific goal could be achieved within a short period of time if adequate resources were committed, Americans apparently did not see the value in a continuing program of basic research.[68] Moreover, basic research could have little hope for success in a situation where various scientific agencies competed for appropriations by promising to fulfill the specific needs of laymen.

A further indicator of the imbalance in federal support for research was the excessive concentration on certain areas of science. In fiscal years 1953–54, 90 percent of the federal government's total investment in research and development was in the physical sciences, with only 7 to 8 percent going to the life sciences and the remainder for statistical collection in the social sciences. Even within the physical sciences, there were serious imbalances, with the more glamorous physics getting nearly twice as much as chemistry.[69]

By the mid-1950s the government-science relationship was characterized by a pluralistic structure that poured out substantial sums of money in response to various political stimuli. National security concerns were dominant, broad areas of science were inadequately supported, and there was little overall coordination of the federal investment. The existing structure and weakness of the science advisory process made it unlikely that the situation would be rectified. Still, Americans assumed that the federal government's science policy had played a major role in creating what was believed to be unquestioned scientific supremacy.

On 4 October 1957 the Soviet Union orbited Sputnik, the first manmade satellite. This achievement, combined with the success of the even larger Sputnik II on 3 November, shattered the nation's technological complacency. The most alarming assessment came from Edward Teller, who warned a television audience that the United States had lost "a battle more important and greater than Pearl Harbor."[70] Most Americans did not share Teller's apocalyptic view, but they were shocked and anxious that the nation recover its lost prestige. G. Mennen Williams, the Democratic governor of Michigan, put his concerns into doggerel:

> Oh Little Sputnik, flying high
> With made-in-Moscow beep,
> You tell the world it's a Commie sky,
> And Uncle Sam's asleep.
> You say on fairway and on rough,
> The Kremlin knows it all,
> We hope our golfer knows enough
> To get us on the ball.[71]

The shock of Sputnik and the attendant political uproar led to widespread efforts to improve the nation's ability to compete in the scientific sphere. Both Congress and the executive searched for immediate ways to narrow the Soviet lead, and for structures that would provide long-term solutions. The major consequences included an upgrading of scientific advice within the White House, creation of the National Aeronautics and Space Administration, reorganization of research within the Defense Department, and passage of the National Defense Education Act. Although these efforts altered the existing government-science relationship, many of the old assumptions and problems remained.

The Eisenhower administration's immediate response to Sputnik was to downplay the Soviet achievement and reassure Americans about the nation's security. On 9 October 1957 the president began by stressing that Sputnik did not indicate Soviet superiority in ballistic missile delivery capabilities. The United States, he explained, had chosen to separate its military missile and satellite programs, with the latter being developed more slowly as a purely scientific endeavor. Without such separation military security would have prevented the American satellite from becoming "a gift to the scientific community of the entire world."[72] A continuation of the existing program, according to Eisenhower, would facilitate international cooperation and avoid the expense of competition in a nonessential area.

Instead of beginning a major new satellite program, Eisenhower altered the scientific advisory process within the White House. Eleven days after Sputnik, the president met with the SAC/ODM for a conference that had been scheduled before the Soviet achievement. The earlier agenda was quickly discarded as the meeting turned into a general discussion of how to improve American science. Isador Rabi proposed establishing a scientific adviser to the president, and Eisenhower quickly seized on the idea.[73] The president's receptiveness to this suggestion was due in part to Sputnik, but also must be attributed to his growing sense of unease with the one-sidedness of the Strauss/Teller advice.[74] On 7 November the president announced that he had appointed James Killian to the new position of special assistant to the president for science and technology. The special assistant was to be aided by an expanded and upgraded SAC/ODM—renamed the President's Science Advisory Committee.[75]

Although Eisenhower was content with these changes, some Americans desired a more direct and dramatic response to Sputnik. *Newsweek* found a consensus for "some kind of new emphasis, a speed-up, perhaps even another Manhattan Project."[76] While the White House delayed, Senate Democratic Majority Leader Lyndon Johnson responded to the public mood by having his Senate Preparedness Investigating Subcommittee hold a series of hearings "to determine what steps can be taken to strengthen our position and restore the leadership we should have in technology."[77] Johnson did not attack the president directly, but when the subcommittee's final report was issued in January 1958, it contained repeated references to the nation's "complacency" and demanded immediate action in a number of areas.[78] Meanwhile, the administration's approach—and the nation's confidence—suffered another setback in December when the Vanguard rocket carrying the first American satellite exploded on the launch pad. After "Flopnik" and the subcommittee's report, congressmen of both parties scrambled to introduce measures for a major American program to meet the Soviet challenge.[79]

By early 1958 President Eisenhower apparently recognized the inevitability of some sort of expanded satellite program to counter the Soviet achievement. At the president's request Killian and other administration officials began to search for a solution that would meet the public clamor while avoiding excessive expenditures. Their recommendations, presented to the president on 5 March 1958, called for the creation of a "National Aeronautics and Space Administration (NASA)" to direct civilian space programs. The new agency would absorb the National Advisory Committee for Aeronautics, thus saving money and providing NASA with an immediate structure. Although the line between military and civilian efforts was left imprecise, the implication was that the military would be restricted to missiles and the new agency would control all satellites.[80] After approval by the president, a bill embodying the report's recommendations was introduced in Congress on 14 April 1958.

The administration's bill passed the House with relatively few changes, but in the Johnson-led Senate, it was a different story. Before approving the measure, the Senate substantially altered it by enhancing the military's authority to develop its own satellite programs and altering NASA's organizational structure so that the agency would be more responsive to lay concerns. A new space council, composed of high-ranking government officials, would define the nation's goals in space and instruct the director accordingly.[82] No progress was made on reconciling the House and Senate bills until a private meeting was held between Senator Johnson and the president on 7 July. Although Johnson conceded that NASA's director would be under immediate presidential control, he got Eisenhower to accept the space council and the other major Senate changes.[83] Both houses then passed what was essentially the Senate version, and the bill was signed into law on 29 July 1958.[84]

The administration also attempted to rationalize scientific research within the Department of Defense. Prior to the Soviet success, military missile programs had been fragmented and frequently overlapped. The interservice rivalries that had created this situation naturally intensified after Sputnik, as each branch tried to prove that its program should have priority. The three services lobbied heavily, bringing congressional and public pressure to bear wherever possible. The administration was not in a strong position to resist; the Soviet achievement had increased concerns about the nation's missile capabilities, and no one wanted to cancel a program that might in some eventuality prove helpful. The pre-Sputnik chaos was therefore perpetuated during the last two months of 1957 as the secretary of defense authorized the further development of three sets of overlapping missile programs.[85] The result, according to one participant, was:

> We spent about twice as much money and we employed about twice as many people on these development programs as we should have. Furthermore, from the point of view of military security such excesses were harmful because they caused us to stretch our resources thinner than was really necessary.[86]

In order to provide more effective supervision in the future, the secretary of defense created the Advance Research Projects Agency (ARPA) in February 1958, with the aim of ending the chaos in the military missile program. This largely temporary effort was expanded and given greater legitimacy when Congress accepted the administration's Defense Reorganization Act in the fall of 1958. Included in that act was Killian's proposal for a director of defense research and engineering, who would occupy a position in the hierarchy equivalent to the service secretaries. The director would supervise ARPA and control all military research.[87]

In addition to prompting new organizational structures for science,

Sputnik opened the way for expanded federal support of basic research and science education. Encouraged by his new scientific advisers, Eisenhower stressed the necessity of enhancing the nation's long-term scientific capabilities:

> In the face of Soviet challenges, the security and continued well-being of the United States depend, as never before, on the extension of scientific knowledge. Our technological progress requires a higher level of support for basic research. . . . It also demands a growing supply of highly trained manpower—scientists, engineers, teachers, and technicians.[88]

To meet these needs, the president urged government agencies to increase their expenditures for basic research, and specifically asked Congress to double the NSF's research appropriations. Furthermore, he requested a fivefold increase in the foundation's budget for fellowships and science education.[89]

The president also recommended that the nation's scientific resources be strengthened through a "temporary" program of federal aid to education, asking for a four-year program of approximately $146 million per year for college scholarships and matching grants to states for the improvement of science education.[90] Although conservatives protested that Sputnik was allowing the "socialists" to sneak the federal camel into the tent of local control, congressional liberals joyously reshaped Eisenhower's proposal into the National Defense Education Act of 1958.[91] By the time they were finished, the price of the program had doubled, and the more elitist scholarship provision had been transformed into loans based on need. Eisenhower signed the bill on 2 September 1958.[92]

The post-Sputnik changes enhanced federal support of science, but some earlier difficulties remained. The National Defense Education Act improved the quality of science education in the United States, and marked the beginning of a large, continuing federal involvement in education. The nation's long-term scientific wealth was also increased by larger appropriations for the NSF. Following the president's recommendations, Congress gave that agency $134 million in fiscal year 1959 —an increase of 269 percent over the preceding year.[93] The legislators proved more parsimonious in succeeding years, but the foundation's budget gradually edged upward. These increases, plus greater expenditures by other agencies, caused the percentage of the total federal research and development budget devoted to basic research to rise to 9 percent by fiscal year 1961. Although this was a great improvement over the 3 percent before Sputnik, much of this money continued to be controlled by agencies with relatively narrow scientific interests. The Defense Department, the AEC, and NASA still provided 64.2 percent of the total spent on basic research. The NIH's parent—the Department of Health, Education, and Welfare—supplied another 16.6 percent, whereas the NSF controlled only 9.3 percent.[94]

The nation derived mixed benefits from the new missile and satellite programs. The Defense Reorganization Act—especially the creation of the office of director research and engineering—began to bring order to the multiplicity of military research projects. That control, however, was achieved with difficulty and suffered frequent lapses. For example, it took almost two years and presidential intervention to terminate the Army Ballistic Missile Agency, even though that unit was building a missile which was completely outside the army's assigned role.[95] More significantly, since the NASA Act had not clearly limited military space activities, the military services continued to initiate new programs. The director of defense research and engineering blocked some of the more bizarre efforts, but the language of the NASA Act made it difficult to keep the Defense Department from developing its own satellite program.[96]

The creation of NASA as a civilian agency prevented space exploration from being inextricably linked with national security. The space agency, however, perpetuated other facets of the cold war government-science relationship. Above all, it reflected and reinforced the Manhattan Project idea that science could fulfill lay requirements if another agency was created, organization provided, and the requisite funds poured in. Like the AEC after World War II, NASA became the nation's paramount scientific agency in the popular imagination and prospered accordingly.

The most significant post-Sputnik change was the improvement of the scientific advisory process within the White House. The special assistant and the President's Science Advisory Committee (PSAC) provided the institutional structure for more sustained and diverse advice. The special assistant attended the meetings of various high-level policy-making groups (including the National Security Council), and reported directly to the president on all matters pertaining to science. The two men who served successively as Eisenhower's special assistants—Killian and George Kistiakowsky—were relatively effective in this role because of good personal relations with the president. The upgraded and revived PSAC expanded the range of expertise immediately available and tried to ensure that the president would receive somewhat more diverse scientific advice.[97]

The new structure for providing scientific advice in the White House had substantial impact on the nuclear test-ban issue. For a variety of reasons in 1957, President Eisenhower became concerned about deescalating the nuclear arms race. He was encouraged in this by a PSAC report that indicated that it was theoretically possible to monitor violations of a nuclear test ban treaty with some degree of accuracy. Eisenhower's subsequent efforts to work out an acceptable treaty with the Soviets met with intense opposition from Edward Teller, Lewis Strauss, and others.[98] When those who had been the paramount purveyors of scientific advice prior to 1957 suggested ways the Soviets might evade effective monitoring, Eisenhower's new advisers found technical solutions to the objections and sustained the president's commitment. Unfortunately, Kistiakowsky's most promising proposal for monitoring test-ban violations was a victim of the 1960 U-2 incident.[99]

In addition to advising the president directly on issues such as the test ban, Killian and Kistiakowsky saw their primary responsibility as bringing some order to the nation's enormous investment in military and space research. They could claim a major victory for rationality with the transfer of the Army Ballistic Missile Agency to NASA, but problems remained. As Kistiakowsky ruefully acknowledged, the government was still supporting twenty-two separate space vehicle programs in 1959, and the story was much the same in nonspace areas of military research.[100]

Eisenhower's scientific advisers had somewhat greater success in controlling NASA. Since Killian and Kistiakowsky wanted the space program to fit into a balanced national scientific effort, they insisted that NASA goals be shaped by scientific objectives. This attitude reflected the president's views, but was in direct conflict with those of many congressmen and "empire builders" at NASA. According to Kistiakowsky, the agency's leaders lacked legitimate scientific goals, but were very willing to exploit the cold war atmosphere so that they could build "expensive equipment" and "feed the many hungry NASA mouths."[101] Kistiakowsky's views did not win him many friends at the space agency, but his arguments often gave the Budget Bureau sufficient ammunition to trim NASA proposals. Most significantly, Eisenhower's scientific advisers accepted NASA plans for manned space flight, but adamantly opposed competition with the Soviets in manned space exploration. Kistiakowsky insisted that such an effort could be justified only as "a political rather than a scientific enterprise."[102] His analysis was confirmed in 1961, when President John F. Kennedy committed the nation to what would ultimately be a $30 billion lunar landing program. Kennedy acted—without consulting his scientific adviser—to shore up American prestige.

Although the major areas of federal scientific endeavor—the military and space—received the most attention, some time was also devoted to the broader problems of federal science policy. Both the special assistants and the PSAC pushed to increase the funds supplied for basic research through the NSF. Without these efforts it is doubtful that the foundation's budget would have increased as it did during the late 1950s.[103] Kistiakowsky also occasionally expressed outrage at the relative distribution of research funds within the government. An investigation of Defense Department budgets caused him to become "indignant on discovering that the cost of exclusively paper studies in industrial establishments on 'Strategic Defense of Cis-Lunar Space' and similar topics amounted to more dollars than all the funds available to the NSF for the support of research in chemistry."[104] Despite such outbursts he generally insisted that the setting of research priorities was outside the scope of his office.

The special assistants also attempted to promote the coordination of all scientific activities conducted by the federal government. The main vehicle for this was the Federal Council for Science and Technology, which was composed of representatives of each of the agencies with substantial research programs. Expectations were high when Eisenhower created the council in March 1959. Unfortunately, the entrenched power of the various agencies was too great for a coordinating body to overcome, even with the support of the president's scientific adviser. The council's attempt to gather a five-year projection of research priorities from the various agencies foundered as the NIH, the Department of Defense, the AEC, and the Commerce Department all refused to cooperate.[105] Each agency was intent on preserving its own independence and its ability to tap funds through its congressional connections.

The special assistants and the PSAC provided the president with a broader spectrum of scientific advice on a sustained basis. Still, the impact of the new structure was understandably limited by the ongoing cold war, the absence of political pressure for a more balanced approach, and the entrenched status of various scientific agencies. In short, the new advisers were unable to transform federal support for science into a federal science policy.

By the end of 1960, the government was spending 10.1 percent of the federal budget on scientific research and development—approximately ten times the proportion invested twenty years earlier. The rate of increase had been especially sharp in the late 1950s, and would continue to rise during the first half of the next decade, reaching 15.6 percent by

1965.[106] Although overall spending for science had increased in a relatively steady manner, scientists had experienced substantial ups and downs in their relationship with political power. After 1957 they were once again in a position to offer advice on issues involving science.

Although federal spending was generous and scientists resided in high places, the nation did not adopt a coherent science policy. Earlier developments had created a welter of scientific agencies that no presidential adviser could coordinate or control, and each sought to maintain itself by forging alliances with congressional committees and special interest groups. The most successful, of course, were those that could relate their scientific efforts to the cold war. By 1960 these agencies—the Department of Defense, the AEC, and NASA—accounted for 90 percent of the total federal expenditures for science.[107] The NIH was also highly successful, downplaying basic research in the life sciences in favor of specific disease-related institutes. The result was some duplication, an imbalance between various areas of science, and relative neglect of basic research. Without a balanced science policy that acknowledged the need for basic research in diverse fields, the nation was poorly prepared to turn its scientific resources to new areas as the intensity of the cold war waned.

1. National Academy of Sciences, *Basic Research and National Goals* (Washington, D.C., 1965), p. 316.

2. Vannevar Bush, *Science, the Endless Frontier* (Washington, D.C., 1945), p. 86; U.S., Department of Commerce, *Long Term Economic Data* (Washington, D.C., 1966), pp. 198–99; National Science Foundation, *Science Indicators, 1974* (Washington, D.C., 1975), p. 173.

3. Bush, *Science, the Endless Frontier*, pp. 1–40. For a discussion of the origins of Bush's report, see Daniel Kevles, "The National Science Foundation," *Isis* 68 (March 1977): 5.

4. S. 1285, introduced 19 July 1945, 79th Cong., 1st sess.

5. U.S., Congress, *Congressional Record*, 79th Cong., 1st sess., 1945, p. A5384; S. 1297, introduced 23 July 1945, 79th Cong., 1st sess.

6. See editorials collected in Truman Papers, OF 53, Pamphlet File, Harry S. Truman Library.

7. "Atomic Bomb," *Business Week*, 18 August 1945, p. 119.

8. *New York Times*, 8 August 1945; Donald Geddes, ed., *The Atomic Age Opens* (New York, 1945), p. 184. A full discussion is in Kenneth Jones, "Science, Scientists, and Americans" (Ph.D. diss., Cornell University, 1975), pp. 44–78.

9. National Opinion Research Center poll, September 1945, National Opinion Research Center Library, Chicago.

10. *Public Papers of the Presidents: Harry S. Truman, 1945* (Washington, D.C., 1951), p. 365.

11. S. 1463, 79th Cong., 1st Sess.

12. S. 1717, introduced 20 December 1945, 79th Cong., 1st sess.

13. *New York Times*, 3 February 1946; Jones, "Science, Scientists, and Americans," pp. 190–91.

14. U.S., Congress, *Congressional Record*, 79th Cong., 2d sess., p. 9470; Jones, "Science, Scientists, and Americans," pp. 193–262.

15. Jones, "Science, Scientists, and Americans," pp. 273–75, 306–10.

16. National Science Foundation, *Annual Report* (Washington, D.C., 1952), p. 77.

17. Natalie Spingarn, *Heartbeat* (Washington, D.C., 1976), p. 24; Stephen Strickland, *Politics, Science, and Dread Disease* (Cambridge, Mass., 1972), pp. 48–53, 76–87.

18. National Institutes of Health, *Almanac, 1980* (Washington, D.C., 1980), p. 135.

19. "The Evolution of the Office of Naval Research," *Physics Today* 14 (August 1961): 35; Jones, "Science, Scientists, and Americans," pp. 359–63.

20. $495 million versus $13 million. Research and development budgets for civilian agencies went from $38 million to $85 million during the same period: Funds for Research and Development, 1937 Compared to 1947, "Research and Development Budget," President's Scientific Research Board Files, Truman Library.

21. John Steelman, *Science and Public Policy* (Washington, D.C., 1947), p. 66.

22. Milton Lomask, *A Minor Miracle* (Washington, D.C., 1976), p. 94.

23. Carroll Pursell, "Science and Government Agencies," in David Van Tassel and Michael Hall, eds., *Science and Society in the United States* (Homewood, Ill., 1966), p. 244.

24. Jones, "Science, Scientists, and Americans," pp. 366–68.

25. Bush, *Science, the Endless Frontier*, p. 33; Library of Congress, Science Policy Research Division, *The National Science Foundation: A Review of Its First 15 Years* (Washington, D.C., 1965), p. 32.

26. In 1945 most scientists associated with the Manhattan Project had estimated that the Soviet Union would be able to develop an atomic bomb within five years. Many Americans, however, had chosen to believe Defense Department predictions of fifteen years or more: Jones, "Science, Scientists, and Americans," pp. 117, 396.

27. Lewis Strauss, *Men and Decisions* (Garden City, N.Y., 1962), p. 217; Richard Hewlett and Francis Duncan, *Atomic Shield, 1947–1952* (University Park, Pa., 1969), p. 373.

28. Herbert York, *The Advisors* (San Francisco, 1976), p. 45.

29. GAC Report, reprinted in York, *The Advisors*, pp. 150–59.

30. York, *The Advisors*, p. 70.

31. A poll taken in February 1950 found that 77 percent approved of the decision to develop the hydrogen bomb even though the wording of the question discouraged a positive response: *Public Opinion Quarterly* 14 (Summer 1950): 372.

32. Hewlett and Duncan, *Atomic Shield*, p. 402; Jones, "Science, Scientists, and Americans," pp. 388–95.

33. York, *The Advisors*, pp. 76–81; Hewlett and Duncan, *Atomic Shield*, p. 440.

34. U.S. Atomic Energy Commission, *In the Matter of J. Robert Oppenheimer: Transcript of Hearing* (Cambridge, Mass., 1970), p. 251.

35. Hewlett and Duncan, *Atomic Shield*, pp. 486–87.

36. Ibid., pp. 548–78.

37. Ibid., p. 583.

38. The extent to which Strauss dominated the scientific advice received by Eisenhower can be seen in his relative access to the president. Prior to the reorientation that occurred

after Sputnik in 1957, Strauss met with Eisenhower 104 times. In contrast NSF Director Alan Waterman and National Academy of Sciences President Detlev Bronk each gained access to the president only seven times. Lee DuBridge did not see the president while he was chairman of SAC/ODM. His successor, Isidor Rabi, had four meetings: Daily Appointments, Eisenhower Records as President, Dwight D. Eisenhower Library.

39. Thomas Murray to Eisenhower, 4 January 1954, and Strauss draft of Eisenhower reply, 11 January 1954, Eisenhower Papers, AF, Box 4, Eisenhower Library; John Lear, "Ike and the Peaceful Atom," *Reporter*, 12 January 1956, p. 11.

40. L. N. Ridenour, "Science and the Federal Government," *Bulletin of Atomic Scientists* 7 (February 1951): 35–37; H. D. Smyth, "The Stockpiling and Rationing of Scientific Manpower," *Bulletin of Atomic Scientists* 7 (February 1951): 38–42.

41. James Killian, *Sputnik, Scientists, and Eisenhower* (Cambridge, Mass., 1977), p. 62.

42. William Golden to Truman, 18 December 1950, Truman Papers, OF 3000-D, Truman Library.

43. Detlev Bronk, "Science Advice in the White House," *Science* 186 (11 October 1974): 118; James Katz, *Presidential Politics and Science Policy* (New York, 1978), p. 22.

44. Bronk, "Science Advice," p. 119.

45. Ibid., p. 120; Lee DuBridge to John Steelman, 11 November 1952, Truman Papers, OF 3000-D, Truman Library.

46. The first Office of Defense Mobilization summary of activities did not even mention the Science Advisory Committee: Report of President, 1 October 1953, Eisenhower Papers, AF, Box 15, Eisenhower Library.

47. Killian, *Sputnik, Scientists, and Eisenhower*, pp. 68–69.

48. Ibid., pp. 70–81.

49. Ibid., p. 82; George Kistiakowsky, *A Scientist at the White House* (Cambridge, Mass., 1976), p. 120.

50. SAC/ODM unsuccessfully recommended an upgrading of its status to resolve these difficulties: Arthur Flemming to Lee DuBridge, 5 July 1955, Eisenhower Papers, OF, Box 906, Eisenhower Library; DuBridge to Flemming, 13 February 1956; WHO Papers, Project Clean-Up, Box 32, Eisenhower Library.

51. Memo of Conference with President, 25 March 1955, Eisenhower Papers, AF, Box 15, Eisenhower Library.

52. Lomask, *A Minor Miracle*, p. 96; Daniel Greenberg, *The Politics of Pure Science* (New York, 1971), p. 144.

53. Quoted in Lomask, *A Minor Miracle*, p. 91.

54. Draft Executive Order, 9 July 1953, WHO Papers, Project Clean-Up, Box 32, Eisenhower Library.

55. Lomask, *A Minor Miracle*, p. 102.

56. Executive Order No. 10521, 17 March 1954, Eisenhower Papers, OF, Box 224, Eisenhower Library.

57. Memo for President, 30 March 1956, Eisenhower Papers, OF, Box 743, Eisenhower Library.

58. James Clayton, *The Economic Impact of the Cold War* (New York, 1970), p. 133; National Science Foundation, *Organization of the Federal Government for Scientific Activities* (Washington, D.C., 1956), p. 19.

59. "Arthritis," *Life*, 6 June 1949, p. 107; "15 Useful Antibiotics Discovered," *Science Digest* 37 (February 1955): 51; "A Hero's Great Discovery Is Put to Work," *Life*, 2 May 1955, p. 105.

60. From $27,694 to $280,628: National Institutes of Health, *Almanac, 1980*, p. 144.

61. Comparisons between years may be misleading since criteria for inclusion changed: National Science Foundation, *Annual Report* (Washington, D.C., 1952), p. 77; National Institutes of Health, *Almanac, 1980*, pp. 135, 144; Preliminary Report on Government Sponsored Research, 25 June 1957, WHO Papers, Cabinet Secretariat, Box 17, Eisenhower Library; Richard Barber, *The Politics of Research* (New York, 1966), p. 37; National Science Foundation, *Science Indicators, 1974*, p. 188.

62. The Office of Naval Research distributed approximately 4 percent of the Defense Department's total research and development budget for basic research frequently unrelated to national security concerns. If this sum was subtracted, the military proportion of the total would decline to approximately 68 percent.

63. Preliminary Report on Government Sponsored Research, 25 June 1957, WHO Papers, Cabinet Secretariat, Box 17, Eisenhower Library.

64. W. Henry Lambright, *Shooting Down the Nuclear Plane* (Indianapolis, 1967), pp. 1–26.

65. Bush, *Science, the Endless Frontier*, p. 22; Steelman, *Science and Public Policy*, pp. 6, 12, 28, 31. During the mid-1970s approximately 15 percent of the total federal research and development budget went to basic research: National Science Foundation, *Science Indicators, 1974*, p. 188.

66. National Science Foundation, *Basic Research: A National Resource* (Washington, D.C., 1957), p. 44; Basic Research, 30 July 1957, WHO Papers, Cabinet Secretariat, Box 17, Eisenhower Library; U.S., Bureau of the Census, Historical Statistics (Washington, D.C., 1975), p. 1116.

67. Memo for Mr. Gray, 19 July 1957, Eisenhower Papers, OF, Box 674, Eisenhower Library; Alan Waterman to Andrew Goodpaster, 26 September 1957, WHO Papers, Staff Research Group, Box 15, Eisenhower Library.

68. In 1955 several articles appeared that emphasized the need for more basic research, but they provoked little public response. See, for example, Eric Hodgins, "The Strange State of American Research," *Fortune* 51 (April 1955): 112; Thomas Grainger, "The Emergency in Basic Science," *Saturday Review*, 16 July 1955, p. 11.

69. National Science Foundation, *Annual Report* (Washington, D.C., 1953), p. 3. These figures include substantial amounts for expensive development programs, but the trend is also apparent when only basic research is considered. In fiscal year 1954, 79 percent of federal funds for basic research went to the physical sciences: National Science Foundation, *Basic Research*, pp. 34–35, 44.

70. Quoted in Killian, *Sputnik, Scientists, and Eisenhower*, p. 8. For a full collection of editorial comment, see mounted clippings in Senate Papers of Lyndon Johnson, Space, Boxes 1–2, Lyndon B. Johnson Library.

71. Quoted in Killian, *Sputnik, Scientists, and Eisenhower*, p. 8.

72. *Public Papers of the President: Dwight D. Eisenhower, 1957* (Washington, D.C., 1958), pp. 720–35; Dwight D. Eisenhower, *The White House Years: Waging Peace* (Garden City, N.Y., 1965), p. 209.

73. Memo of Conference with the President, 15 October 1957, Eisenhower Papers, Staff Notes, DDE Diary Series, Box 18, Eisenhower Library.

74. Killian, *Sputnik, Scientists, and Eisenhower*, p. 225; Eisenhower to Lewis Strauss, 30 August 1956, Eisenhower Papers, AF, Box 4, Eisenhower Library.

75. Killian, *Sputnik, Scientists, and Eisenhower*, pp. 20–28.

76. *Newsweek*, 28 October 1957, p. 31. Even some Eisenhower advisers took this view: see note by Andrew Goodpaster, n.d., WHO Papers, Office of the Staff Secretary, Subject Series/White House Subseries, Box 4, Eisenhower Library.

77. Quoted in Rowland Evans and Robert Novak, *Lyndon B. Johnson: The Exercise of Power* (New York, 1966), p. 206.

78. Preparedness Subcommittee Report, n.d., Senate Papers of Lyndon Johnson, Box 355, Johnson Library.

79. Twenty-nine bills were introduced by April 1958.

80. Enid Schoettle, "The Establishment of NASA," in Sanford Lakoff, ed., *Knowledge and Power* (New York, 1966), pp. 232–40; Memo of Conference with the President, 5 March 1958, Eisenhower Papers, Staff Notes, DDE Diary Series, Box 19, Eisenhower Library; Memo for the President, 5 March 1958, Papers of President's Science Advisory Committee, Box 4, Eisenhower Library.

81. U.S., Congress, H.R. 12575, 85th Cong., 2nd Sess., 1958.

82. Schoettle, "The Establishment of NASA," pp. 257–58; Main Problems in the Senate Bill, n.d., Eisenhower Papers, OF, Box 937, Eisenhower Library.

83. Memo for Record, 7 July 1958, Eisenhower Papers, Staff Memos, DDE Diary Series, Box 21, Eisenhower Library.

84. U.S., Congress, *Congressional Record*, 85th Cong., 2d Sess., 1958, p. 13978.

85. Memo of Conference with the President, 6 February 1958, Eisenhower Papers, Staff Notes, DDE Diary Series, Box 18, Eisenhower Library; Schoettle, "The Establishment of NASA," pp. 191–94.

86. Herbert York, *Race to Oblivion* (New York, 1970), p. 103.

87. Killian, *Sputnik, Scientists, and Eisenhower*, p. 235; York, *Race to Oblivion*, p. 118.

88. *Public Papers of the Presidents: Dwight D. Eisenhower, 1958* (Washington, D.C., 1959), p. 46.

89. Ibid., p. 48.

90. Ibid., pp. 47–49.

91. U.S., Congress, *Congressional Record*, 85th Cong., 2d sess., 1958, p. 16583; Paul Douglas, *In the Fullness of Time* (New York, 1971), p. 418.

92. U.S., Congress, H.R. 13247, *Congressional Record*, 85th Cong., 2d sess., 1958, p. 19078.

93. $49 million in 1958: Katz, *Presidential Politics and Science Policy*, p. 84.

94. National Science Foundation, *Science Indicators, 1974*, pp. 188–89.

95. York, *Race to Oblivion*, p. 139; Kistiakowsky, *A Scientist at the White House*, pp. 99–100, 125.

96. York, *Race to Oblivion*, pp. 127–28, 133; Killian, Notes of Matters Discussed with President, 15 July 1959, Eisenhower Papers, Staff Notes, DDE Diary Series, Box 27, Eisenhower Library.

97. To prevent dominance by the special assistant, PSAC elected its own chairman and reported directly to the president when it differed with the special assistant: Eisenhower to James Killian, 7 December 1957; Terms of Reference for Special Assistant; Terms of Reference for PSAC; all in Eisenhower Papers, CF, Box 61, Eisenhower Library.

98. Kistiakowsky, *A Scientist at the White House*, pp. 5–6; Memo of Conference with President, 17 April 1958, Eisenhower Papers, Staff Notes, DDE Diary Series, Box 19, Eisenhower Library.

99. Kistiakowsky, *A Scientist at the White House*, pp. 210, 222, 288.

100. Ibid., pp. 57, 110, 153.

101. Ibid., p. 110, 182.

102. Ibid., pp. 409, 172; Killian, *Sputnik, Scientists, and Eisenhower*, pp. 142–44.

103. Killian, *Sputnik, Scientists, and Eisenhower*, p. 184; Kistiakowsky, *A Scientist at the White House*, pp. 101, 189.

104. Kistiakowsky, *A Scientist at the White House*, pp. 141, 249.

105. Ibid., pp. 64, 176, 205, 278; Kistiakowsky to Eisenhower, 19 May 1960, WHO Papers, Office of Special Assistant for Science and Technology, Box 12, Eisenhower Library; Killian, *Sputnik, Scientists, and Eisenhower*, pp. 185–86.

106. National Science Foundation, *Basic Research*, p. 316.

107. Barber, *The Politics of Research*, p. 37.

The Presidency Triumphant:
Congressional-Executive Relations, 1945–1960

Gary W. Reichard

The American presidency was in robust condition at the end of World War II.* The need for government intervention into the economic affairs of the nation during the Great Depression, followed by the demands of all-out war, strengthened the executive branch and, perhaps more importantly, legitimized expansion of its powers. The war in particular led to the creation of a gigantic bureaucracy with direct connections to the White House. In these developments Congress was often a mere spectator, though occasionally it gave the process active assistance. Passage of the first and second War Powers acts (1941 and 1942), for example, gave the president substantial freedom of action to enlarge and reshape the government "for the duration," though Congress technically retained the right to review or terminate the powers granted. Franklin D. Roosevelt, occupying the White House for the twelve years spanning the depression and World War II, made the most of the opportunities presented him, and the public generally approved.

By the time the war ended, some Americans expressed reservations about the power shift. The specter of totalitarianism produced a fear of unrestrained government and unlimited executive power. Among scholars there developed a school of thought which maintained that the Constitution intended and imposed checks on arbitrary power; neo-constitutionalists like Edward S. Corwin, Charles A. McIlwain,

* The author wishes to thank the Graduate School and the College of Humanities of the Ohio State University, and the Harry S. Truman Library Institute, for grants in aid to support much of the research for this essay.

William Y. Elliott, and Carl J. Friedrich called for renewed emphasis on the separation and balancing of powers.[1] What they feared most was a blurring of constitutional lines of authority. As Corwin wrote in the 1945 edition of his influential text *The President: Office and Powers*, "The principle of the separation of powers as a barrier preventing the fusion of presidential and congressional power is today pretty shaky if it is not altogether defunct."[2]

These concerns were reflected in public opinion. In April 1945, when Harry S. Truman succeeded Roosevelt, a national poll showed that 65 percent of Americans thought Congress should enjoy increased importance and power in the future; only 16 percent disagreed. On the other hand, the ambiguity of the public mind was evident when people were asked a few months later whether Truman should press Congress more forcefully to carry out his recommendations: 52 percent agreed, and only 21 percent said no.[3] Restiveness also appeared within Congress, as it had during the waning days of the New Deal. With the war over a strong movement emerged in support of reforming Congress to allow that body, as Congressman Jerry Voorhis put it, "to maintain its position as a truly co-equal branch of government in full control of national legislation."[4]

Partisan motives typically influenced these theoretical considerations. Although Voorhis was a Democrat, it was the Republicans— frustrated after long years of Democratic presidential activism—who pressed most energetically for a greater congressional role. It was logical that members of the G.O.P., opposed to the activist policies espoused by Democratic New Dealers and internationalists, took up constitutional arguments in behalf of the separation of powers. Yet the stridency and partisan tone of their arguments in the immediate post–World War II era undermined their effectiveness, making them sound self-serving and narrowly political.

Other factors also weakened the impact of neo-constitutionalist arguments. One of them was the inability of Congress to win the people's affection. Marked by dispersion of power and internal discord, that body often appeared to be the "bickering branch."[5] The ambivalent public responses to pollsters' questions concerning Truman and Congress surely reflected such a popular perception in 1945. By way of contrast, whatever misgivings Americans may have had concerning the powers of the presidency, they seemed to regard the office as a source of stability and predictability, especially in threatening times. As the only representative of all the people, the president was seen as standing alone for the national interest.[6]

All in all, the outlook for the congressional-executive balance after the war was mixed. In the circumstances the most likely development seemed to be a new coordination, or collaboration, between the branches. Congressional historian George Galloway put the case for "collaborationism" succinctly, asserting that "the doctrine of the separation of powers and the system of checks and balances have become a serious handicap" and that the Framers had never intended "that Congress and the Executive should live as suspicious rivals in separate worlds." By 1947 even the neo-constitutionalist Corwin was recommending "a better organization of the relationship of President and Congress," rather than a straight rollback of presidential powers. This view also had proponents in high public places. "There must be an intimate relationship between the President and Congress," wrote Senator (soon to be Vice-President) Alben Barkley in 1948, "if our Government is to function according to our desires. . . ."[7]

The collaboration that prevailed in the postwar period did not produce the steadying balance expected by its advocates. President Truman, insecure about his personal position but reverential toward the presidency as an institution, battled fiercely for the prerogatives of the office even while claiming to seek a true partnership with Congress.[8] His successor, Dwight D. Eisenhower, affected even greater deference toward the legislative branch, but further expanded presidential authority. Briefly, Congress launched an offensive of its own, but in the end the president emerged on top.

When Truman became president, Congress was in the mood to assert itself but in a poor position to do so. As one perceptive observer remarked, the legislative branch needed first to modernize its machinery, especially its committee structures and procedures, before it could regain its rightful influence. The Legislative Reorganization Act of 1946 aimed to achieve this goal by expanding congressional oversight of executive agencies and their activities and improving the legislature's access to information. Senator Robert LaFollette, Jr., a chief sponsor of the bill, originally included a provision for a joint legislative-executive council to close the "gap between the executive and legislative arms of the Government," which he felt had developed over the years.[9] That provision did not pass, but the act streamlined the committee structure in both houses and established committees that corresponded to agencies and jurisdictions in the executive branch, thus permitting more effective communication. Committees were also given full-fledged professional staffs and were formally charged with exercising "watchfulness" over agencies in the executive branch. In addition, all Senate committees and four in the House received subpoena powers.[10] The assertive spirit behind the Reorganization Act also inspired the Administrative Procedure Act of 1946, which set statutory safeguards and guidelines for procedures in the bureaucracy.[11] These innovations helped Congress, but represented no panacea; the bureaucracy's capacity to expand in size and complexity easily outstripped the ability of Congress to control it, and a number of the committees became more captive than captor of the agencies whose activities they monitored.

Partisan motives were often intertwined with institutional objectives as Congress tried to counter growing presidential power in the immediate postwar period. In March 1947, for example, it passed on to the states a constitutional amendment limiting the president to two terms. The measure enjoyed broad popular support, but it was also true that the Republican party had pressed for such an amendment in its 1940 and 1944 platforms. The Republican-controlled House Judiciary Committee held only one day of hearings on it before sending it to the floor, and debate thereafter centered mainly on the record of Franklin Roosevelt. G.O.P. legislators voted unanimously in favor of the proposal, which was ratified as the Twenty-second Amendment in February 1951.[12]

The most effective device employed by Congress to check executive power after World War II was the legislative veto. Although varying in detail, legislative vetoes usually required that specified executive plans for action be submitted to Congress before becoming operative, with Congress retaining the right to disapprove the proposed action. Disapproval could be by concurrent or simple resolution (neither of which required presidential signature) or even, if stipulated in the law, by action of a standing congressional committee.[13] Such procedures, though not strictly constitutional, could be effective. Corwin summed up the case for the legislative veto in 1947, writing that the line between inevitable delegation of authority by Congress and outright abdication of its powers could only be maintained "by rendering the delegated powers recoverable without the consent of the delegate; and for this purpose the concurrent resolution seems to be an available mechanism, and the only one."[14]

Congress clearly intended the legislative veto to be more than a theoretical power, disallowing twelve of Truman's forty-one proposed administrative reorganization plans between 1949 and 1953 and extending the device to foreign policy measures too. Beginning with the Greek-Turkish aid package in 1947, legislation affecting foreign aid, defense, trade, and stockpiling of strategic materials regularly included provisions for congressional disapproval. Between 1951 and 1960 every annual foreign aid act included such a stipulation, as did the amendments to the Atomic Energy Act adopted in 1958. Presidents Truman and Eisenhower questioned the constitutionality of the legislative veto, and from time to time each penned vigorous veto messages protesting "encroachment" into executive functions. But political expediency triumphed over constitutional niceties; when needing particular legislation, each signed measures including legislative veto provisions.[15]

One of the most important ways in which Congress tried to increase its authority after 1945 was through investigation of executive branch activities—a function supposedly made easier by its revised committee structure. Both the number and scope of congressional investigations increased in the period after World War II, generated by partisan antagonism toward Truman and zealous bipartisan concern about internal security. A measure of the increase in investigatory activity was the rising budget for such probes. In 1940 the Senate had spent only $170,267 for inquiries. This figure ballooned in the 1950s: the Eighty-third Congress (1953–54) spent more than $5 million on investigations, the Eighty-sixth (1959–60) more than $11 million.[16]

By his defensive and often acerbic responses to congressional inquiries, President Truman worsened matters. His offhand comment about "red herrings" at the time of the Alger Hiss case, for example, predictably made Congress more intent on pursuing its anti-Communist investigations. On the other hand, Truman devised some useful means of warding off what he viewed as excessively zealous congressional oversight activities. The practice of classifying documents, greatly expanded after World War II, was particularly effective. The words *confidential, secret,* and *top secret* stamped on executive documents served to keep them from a curious legislative branch. Truman went well beyond Roosevelt's practice of classifying only military documents; in 1951 he issued an executive order empowering all agencies to classify documents when necessary in the interest of "national security."[17]

In response to congressional probes, Truman repeatedly invoked the right to executive secrecy, beginning in 1946 with an inquiry concerning the conduct of government cryptanalysts before the attack at Pearl Harbor. In defense of his actions, Truman later insisted that the president's right to keep materials secret "has been recognized since the beginnings of our Government. . . . No President has ever complied with an order of the Legislative Branch directing the Executive Branch to produce confidential documents, the disclosure of which was considered by the President to be contrary to the public interest." In 1950 he issued an executive order protecting "military secrets" from congressional scrutiny; a second order a year later extended the veil of secrecy over nonmilitary agencies as well, authorizing any executive body to classify information if "necessary" for national security. This precedent was later taken up by Eisenhower, who in 1953 reasserted the president's right to classify materials. Although Eisenhower changed the criterion from "national security" to the supposedly narrower grounds of "national defense," he neither introduced checks on those doing the classifying nor provided any scheme for ultimate declassification of sensitive materials.[18]

Both Truman and Eisenhower employed executive privilege—a term coined during the Eisenhower years—to block congressional investigations. The Truman administration's most sweeping assertions of the right to conceal information after the fact came in the hearings conducted by the combined Senate Armed Services and Foreign Relations committees after the dismissal of General MacArthur from his Korean command in the spring of 1951. A sharp exchange on the issue of concealment of information occurred when General Omar Bradley refused to divulge the nature of the advice he had given Truman while a member of the Joint Chiefs of Staff. Although Republicans on the joint committee strenuously objected to Bradley's action, Democrat Richard Russell, chairman of the panel, ruled he had the right to withhold the information. After three days of heated partisan dispute over the constitutional question involved, the committee sustained Russell's ruling, significantly advancing the cause of executive privilege. Certain Republicans on the committee suggested that Truman himself should testify, but the president refused. Even Senator Taft, who wanted Truman to comply, confessed that the Senate could not compel him to do so.[19]

Even after leaving the White House, Truman maintained his right to withhold information. In November 1953, as a private citizen, he refused to honor a subpoena to appear before the House Committee on Un-American Activities. "In spite of my personal willingness to cooperate with your committee," he responded to the committee, "I feel constrained by my duty to the people of the United States to decline to comply with the subpoena." After presenting a mini-treatise on the precedents for his refusal, the former president asserted, "If the doctrine of separation of powers and the independence of the Presidency is to have any validity at all, it must be equally applicable to a President after his term of office has expired. . . ."[20]

This sort of resistance to congressional investigations, strongly reinforced by the later actions of Eisenhower, helped neutralize the impact of such probes, despite the momentary political damage done to the Truman administration by Senator Joseph McCarthy's activities. It was clear by the time Harry Truman left office that Congress faced a very difficult task in attempting to increase its powers with respect to the executive branch.

The Korean War proved to be an especially dramatic period in the history of congressional-executive relations. Truman's handling of the nation's military response and his use of emergency powers at home stimulated a fierce attack on the presidency. During the years 1950 to 1953, Congress seriously challenged the president's powers as commander-in-chief, supported imposing limits on his emergency powers, and attempted to alter permanently the executive's treaty-making power. In the end, however, these efforts failed. The legislative offensive, based in large part on the Republicans' partisan objections to Truman and his policies, resulted only in the elimination of Truman himself from the political picture. By mid-1953, with Eisenhower occupying the White House and the Korean conflict ended, the road-was clear for executive power to grow once again.

Events of 1950–51 revived old suspicions in Congress about unilateral presidential actions in foreign affairs. Through early 1950 attacks by congressional Republicans on the administration's Asia policy centered on substantive matters. American entry into the Korean War altered the situation. Partisan motives remained important, but Truman's failure to ask Congress to authorize American military action left him vulnerable to criticism on purely constitutional grounds. Opposition rhetoric swiftly shifted in that direction.

The constitutional issue surfaced almost immediately after American troops were dispatched to Korea in late June of 1950. Both Truman and Secretary of State Dean Acheson rebuffed questions from Republican senators about the basis for American involvement by assuring them that all U.S. action was "pursuant to" a United Nations resolution, even though evidence suggested that Truman's decision predated U.N. action. When Republican Senate Leader Kenneth Wherry pressed the president on the need to consult formally with Congress, the most he could get from Truman was the statement, "If there is any necessity for Congressional action, I will come to you. But I hope we can get these bandits in Korea suppressed without that."[21]

In retrospect Truman erred in not requesting formal support from Congress. At least in the summer of 1950, Republicans would certainly have supported a resolution authorizing military action. Yet, apparently influenced by Acheson, the president gave no serious thought to drafting, or even requesting, a joint resolution.[22] As the tide of war turned against the United States in late summer, Republicans in Congress vented their outrage on the constitutional issue. Senator Taft was typical, writing privately that "if the President could send troops to defend the Republic of Korea against outside aggression, he could send troops to any nation in the world. . . . I do not believe there is any such constitutional authority." Republicans raised the constitutional issue repeatedly—and with some success—in the 1950 elections. After the G.O.P. scored important gains in those elections, one journalist suggested that Truman appoint a new secretary of state and begin regular consultations with prominent senators-elect, and a Republican congressman advised the president to name General Eisenhower (not yet publicly identified with the G.O.P.) as "deputy president" to direct the mobilization effort.[23] Congressional Republicans also attacked executive secrecy in diplomatic exchanges, proposing in early December a resolution to require President Truman to reveal the contents of his private talks with British Prime Minister Attlee that were then occurring; in the middle of the same month, the Senate Republican Conference adopted a resolution calling for the dismissal of the secretary of state.

The congressional offensive intensified in 1951 as a result of the so-called Great Debate and the controversy surrounding Truman's firing of General Douglas MacArthur from command of the troops in Korea. The Great Debate, touched off by Truman's announced plans to send four American divisions to Europe as a part of a NATO defense force, produced several congressional proposals to tie the chief executive's hands in sending troops abroad. One resolution, offered by Republican Congressman Frederic Coudert, of New York, banned the use of future appropriations for sending American troops overseas unless Congress specifically approved such action. Another, proposed by Senator Kenneth Wherry (Nebraska), stated that no American troops could be sent to Europe "pending determination by Congress of a policy on that matter." After three months of intense dispute, the issue was put to rest but not resolved. The Senate passed two resolutions, one approving the sending of troops and the other requiring the president to consult before committing any additional forces. Neither resolution had statutory force, but it was significant that a number of Democrats supported the measure requiring further consultation. The rift was clearly more than partisan.[24]

Truman's dismissal of MacArthur in April 1951 exacerbated criticisms of presidential high-handedness. In this instance, however, congressional Democrats did not join Republicans in protesting the president's actions, and after more than three months of hearings, the matter subsided. The fact that the war had stabilized in the meantime helped as much as anything to quiet Truman's critics. On reflection most Americans seemed willing to accept that the president had the right to fire a general, even if they disagreed with this particular action.

The issue of emergency presidential powers also roused sharp controversy during the Korean War. Congress had questioned the proper extent of such powers both before and immediately after World War II, and the two branches had clashed openly over extension of the Office of Price Administration in 1946 (Congress won, and the OPA was abolished). In the course of that conflict, Senator Taft had placed the issue in its strictly constitutional context, charging that Truman had "assumed to write a law for Congress [to continue OPA], although the Constitution of the United States gives the Congress power to state the conditions on which price controls shall be continued."[25]

Truman's expansive concept of his emergency powers was obvious. Although he had unsuccessfully vetoed the Taft-Hartley Act in 1947, he several times used injunction powers granted by the law. Occasionally he tried to go considerably further, claiming the right to seize control of operations in key industries when they were threatened with work stoppages. In 1949 when Truman, relying on the opinion of his attorney general, Tom Clark, asserted that he had "inherent" authority to do anything necessary to protect the general welfare against looming strikes in the steel and coal industries, a large group in Congress was indignant. Speaking as usual for many of his colleagues, Taft pointed out that the injunction powers included in the Taft-Hartley Act ruled out executive seizure of any industry. Truman remained unconvinced— as later events would demonstrate. The question, concluded columnist Arthur Krock in 1949, was "in a disputed area of the laws."[26]

Truman's insistence on the presidency's "inherent" powers caused him to ask for only limited mobilization authority during the Korean War. The crisis atmosphere in September 1950 led Congress to cooperate; the Defense Production Act granted Truman all he wished and more. When the president declared a state of national emergency in December, he invoked a series of sweeping price and wage controls and established centralized machinery to deal with industrial priorities and allocation of raw materials—all without serious objection from Congress. By the spring of 1951, however, political backlash had set in. Congress rebuffed Truman's efforts to get stronger anti-inflationary powers added to the 1950 act, and he had to accept a weak bill.

The sharpest clash over emergency powers came in April 1952, when Truman seized the steel industry to avert a possible steelworkers' strike. Disdaining both the authority bestowed on him by the Taft-Hartley Act and a second possible statutory authorization for seizure, Section 18 of the Selective Service Act of 1948, he based his take-over on his "inherent powers" as commander-in-chief. Before both the District Court and the Supreme Court, the administration pressed the "inherent powers" argument, quoting Justice Holmes's dictum that "a page of history is worth a volume of logic." When District Judge David Pine objected that this rationale sounded like a resort to pure expediency, an administration spokesman had the bad judgment to reply that the court might call it that "but we say it is expediency backed by power." This ill-considered line of defense not only failed to persuade Judge Pine, who issued an injunction against the president's action, but alienated many of Truman's supporters in Congress.[27] When the Supreme Court upheld the District Court's ruling, Truman was forced to give in, to the delight of his critics. The strike itself was settled in late July.

The steel seizure decision did not settle conclusively the issue of what "inherent" powers a president has because so many of the high court's justices filed opinions. Justice Black's opinion was to prove most useful as a precedent. He argued that presidential powers had to come from *either* legislation or the Constitution, and President Truman's seizure of the mills was based on neither. The continuing uncertainty concerning lines of executive and congressional authority was underscored, however, by the widely cited opinion of Justice Jackson, who contended that there existed a "zone of twilight" where the two branches held, in effect, concurrent power; in this case, Jackson said, Congress had already spoken, through the Taft-Hartley Act, but the president had chosen to act in defiance of that law and his action was therefore unjustifiable.[28]

Although the judiciary ultimately settled the issue, some observers saw the crisis as a conflict between the president and Congress. Despairing of the likelihood of a Court-imposed solution in April 1952, Republican Senator Everett Dirksen of Illinois asserted that if the president were to be blocked, "it must be done in that branch of the Government which James Monroe characterized as the very core and center of the Government of the United States, namely, the Congress." Writing after the crisis was ended, Edward Corwin took the same view. "The moral from all this is plain," he wrote in 1953, "namely, that escape must be sought from 'presidential autocracy' by resort not to the judicial power, but to the legislative power—in other words, by resort to timely action by Congress. . . . " Yet Congress accomplished little along these lines after the steel crisis passed. By 1960 serious observers noted "a growing tendency" for Congress to want to share with the president powers to terminate "emergency" situations, but such provisions were limited in their application. In fact, various presidential emergency powers—including those dating from the Korean War—remained on the books into the seventies, their existence unchallenged by the legislative branch.[29]

Congressional critics of growing presidential power were heartened by the Court's action in the steel case, and in its immediate aftermath they pushed hard for the most significant limitation of executive power attempted in the cold war years: the Bricker amendment. For a time enactment of this measure to circumscribe the president's treaty-making power appeared likely. But the years 1952–53, while the amendment was under discussion, can be seen in retrospect as the high point of congressional efforts to erode the powers of the presidency. Collapse of the amendment cause in early 1954 signaled the resumption of growth in executive power.

The Bricker amendment aimed to ensure that all executive agreements with other nations, like all treaties, would come before Congress for approval, and to prevent treaties from becoming operative as "domestic law" unless Congress specifically approved. First introduced by Senator John W. Bricker (Ohio) in 1951, the measure was part of the Republican attack on Truman's handling of foreign policy and the Korean War, but it also represented a wider assault on the powers of the presidential office. This was certainly Bricker's intent. "The constitutional power of Congress to determine American foreign policy is at stake," he had warned the Senate during the Great Debate. "It is our duty to preserve that power against presidential encroachment."[30] Shortly thereafter, he introduced the amendment.

Bricker and his supporters had identified a genuine issue. By announcing policies first and then seeking legislative endorsement, Truman had co-opted Republicans into "bipartisan" support of broad-ranging foreign policy programs and secured a relatively free hand in conducting American foreign policy. By the 1950s the Senate's "advise and consent" function had shrunk to little more than its having a say as to whether a proposed treaty would be ratified. Foreign policy was increasingly being conducted by resort to executive agreements—

completely outside the realm of congressional oversight. For this reason Congress required in 1950 that all executive agreements, as well as treaties, be compiled and published, but that was poor insurance that all such agreements would be discovered, let alone controlled, by Congress.[31]

The Bricker amendment made no significant progress in Congress during the last months of the Truman administration, as Democratic leaders succeeded in bottling it up in committee. With the Republicans in control after the 1952 elections, the outlook changed; Bricker had sixty-three cosponsors when he reintroduced the measure in January 1953, enough to guarantee passage in the Senate (a two-thirds vote was required). But amendment backers soon received a surprise. Despite Bricker's assurances that he had no intention of "hamstringing the President in the conduct of the Nation's foreign policy," and notwithstanding the Republican platform's support for the amendment in 1952, President Eisenhower made known his opposition to it. Throughout 1953, as the administration negotiated with Bricker to make the wording of the proposed amendment more innocuous, both sides began to lose patience. In January 1954 Eisenhower exploded at a high-level strategy conference that the amendment was a "stupid, blind violation of [the] Constitution by stupid, blind isolationists." Wisely, he was more discreet in public; in working to win congressional support for his view, the president avoided stressing the constitutional issue, emphasizing instead the need to retain maneuvering room in foreign policy because of the Soviet threat.[32]

In February 1954, after a flurry of last-minute negotiations and floor amendments, a revised version of the Bricker amendment was defeated in the Senate by a single vote. Bricker reintroduced it in slightly altered form in 1955 and again in 1957, but Eisenhower remained opposed, and the amendment never again had a real chance of passage. Its defeat marked the beginning of a successful presidential offensive that, by the end of the decade, left the executive branch indisputably in control of foreign policy-making.

Eisenhower's tactics in repelling the pro–Bricker amendment forces were consistent with his general approach to questions touching on the balance of power between Congress and the presidency. Always outwardly deferential, he fiercely resisted legislative intrusions when he felt them inappropriate—particularly in matters of foreign policy and national security. Yet in fighting off congressional interference, he avoided confrontational rhetoric, stressing instead the need for unity in the face of cold war dangers. He also tried to avoid unnecessary day-to-day tensions with Congress. Bricker's own willingness to support Eisenhower after defeat of his amendment testified to the success of Eisenhower's tactics. "Naturally, I was disappointed when the President opposed my proposed constitutional amendment," the Ohio Senator wrote a diehard supporter of the measure in 1956. "However, . . . the President's treaty-making policy has conformed very closely to the objectives sought to be established in the amendment. President Eisenhower, unlike his two immediate predecessors . . . , has not abused the power. . . . "[33] Indeed, Eisenhower's tactics and personality—and not least, the fact that he was a Republican—helped disarm critics of presidential power, so many of whom were Republicans themselves. Yet defenders of congressional prerogative should have been concerned about the tide of events in the fifties.

One area of activity in which the executive branch clearly established dominance in the 1950s was legislative planning. Here the Truman administration had laid a sound foundation, instituting new machinery for legislative clearance that rapidly evolved into a tool for formulating legislation. Under Truman the Bureau of the Budget took over the coordination of all agency proposals and established regular contact with both majority and minority members on most major congressional committees, involving the executive branch in the early stages of the bill-drafting process. After election in his own right in 1948, Truman was especially aggressive in this respect, insisting that the bureau work up draft legislation to put his campaign promises into action.[34]

Thereafter, the executive branch provided most major policy initiatives. President Eisenhower did not present a detailed program in 1953, but beginning the next year he issued annual comprehensive packages, specific in detail and well defined in substance.[35] By 1960 the volume of administration-sponsored bills had escalated dramatically. At the same time, the evolution of a formal congressional liaison network in the White House, itself a reflection of the expanded legislative role of the executive branch, gave the president another powerful new tool to influence Congress. Eisenhower paid close personal attention to liaison, and his administration saw the creation of the first publicly acknowledged congressional liaison staff in the White House; although it did not grow beyond five before 1960, the precedent was set for a more elaborate operation to develop. However much Eisenhower may have preferred in theory to defer to Congress, he wholeheartedly accepted his expanding role. "After all," he remarked during his second term, "the Constitution puts the President square into the legislative business."[36]

President Eisenhower also carried forward Truman's practice of asserting authority by vigorous use of the veto. The volume of presidential vetoes from 1945 to 1960 was high: 250 by Truman, 181 by Eisenhower. Especially noteworthy was Eisenhower's frequent use of the pocket veto, which because it takes effect after congressional adjournment cannot be overridden and must be countered by passage of a new bill. In his last budget messages, Eisenhower even called for institution of an item veto, which would have strengthened his hand in shaping legislative results, but Congress would not go that far.[37]

In giving great emphasis (and a new name) to the executive branch's right to maintain secrecy, the Eisenhower administration further enhanced the powers of the presidency. When Attorney General William P. Rogers invented the term *executive privilege* in 1958, it had— according to Arthur M. Schlesinger, Jr.—"the advantage of sounding like a very old term." Certainly Eisenhower had resorted to the practice many times by then, beginning in early 1953 with the so-called Bohlen case. When the Senate demanded to see secret FBI files concerning Charles E. Bohlen, Eisenhower's choice for ambassador to the Soviet Union, the president insisted that the materials be seen only by Senators Taft and John Sparkman. Assaults on the executive branch by Senator Joseph McCarthy and his followers in 1953 and 1954 only firmed the administration's resolve to resist pressures for disclosure of information. In May 1954 Eisenhower issued a sweeping policy statement concerning the privilege attaching to information from the executive branch. Addressing his comments to Secretary of Defense Charles E. Wilson, he ordered all members of the executive to withhold materials related to deliberative processes within the administration. An accompanying memorandum from Attorney General Herbert Brownell asserted, without citing any specific cases, that the courts had "uniformly held that the President and the heads of departments have an uncontrolled discretion to withhold . . . information and papers in the public interest." Between 1955 and 1960 the Eisenhower administration refused information to Congress on the basis of executive privilege more than forty times.[38]

In the face of Eisenhower's determination, attempts by Congress to limit executive privilege were ineffective. The president's position was well stated in his rebuff of an effort by Congress in 1959 to require regular information on decisions affecting the foreign aid program. "I have signed the bill," he wrote,

> . . . on the express premise that the three amendments relating to disclosure are not intended to alter and cannot alter the recognized Constitutional duty

and power of the Executive with respect to disclosure of information, documents, and other materials. Indeed, any other construction of these amendments would raise grave Constitutional questions under the Separation of Powers Doctrine.[39]

The growing autonomy of the executive branch in the 1950s was reflected in the free reign given by Congress to the Central Intelligence Agency (CIA). From its inception in 1947, the CIA had been shielded from congressional scrutiny. When it became more of a "cloak-and-dagger" operation and assumed greater importance in American foreign policy-making during the Eisenhower years, however, there was reason to question the agency's immunity to oversight. Once again, congressional efforts got nowhere. Eisenhower and Secretary of State Dulles successfully opposed a bipartisan proposal by Senators William Knowland and Lyndon Johnson in 1955 to set up a "Cold War Strategy Board," which, in Eisenhower's view, threatened "to put Congress into doing the Executive's business."[40] A more serious challenge came a year later, in the form of Senator Mike Mansfield's bill to establish a joint congressional committee on central intelligence. Mansfield presented the case for his bill in the starkest constitutional terms, predicting that without it "as time passes the Congress will become less of an equal branch under our Constitutional system." Wayne Morse, backing Mansfield, was even more outspoken, charging that the administration was intentionally keeping the people uninformed on foreign policy. "What is happening today, in connection with the trend toward government by secrecy in America," said Morse, "is that Congress has been standing by and has not been insisting upon exercising its power to check the executive branch of the Government in many fields including foreign policy." Morse may have been right, but Congress did not choose to exercise power in this instance either. Mansfield's bill (S. Con. Res. 2) went down to defeat, 59-27.[41] Thereafter, the CIA went unchecked. Eisenhower had won an important victory in terms of the congressional-executive balance. "In no way perhaps," concluded Arthur Schlesinger in *The Imperial Presidency*, "did the old Whig more effectively deprive the Congress of a voice in foreign policy than by confiding so much power to an agency so securely out of congressional reach. . . ."[42]

Eisenhower's most significant innovation expanding presidential autonomy was the "area resolution," which provided congressional authorization for unspecified future executive actions in specific parts of the world. The Formosa Resolution of 1955 and the Middle East Resolution of 1957, both drafted with firm guidance from the White House, were the first instances of this new device. The genius of the area resolution was that one could see in it what one wanted, a fact that suited Eisenhower's purposes admirably, as it would those of later presidents. Contemporary observers, including many members of Congress, tended to view the resolutions as evidence of Eisenhower's belief that he had to ask Congress specifically for any powers not clearly granted to the president in the Constitution; yet it is clear that Eisenhower saw the area resolution as a way to avert later congressional criticism if events should go awry.

President Eisenhower's tactics in seeking the Formosa Resolution (authorization of future presidential action in the area of Formosa, as necessary, to counter Communist aggression) helped disarm, or at least confuse, Congress. Although he briefed congressional leaders before presenting his request in a special message in late January 1955, he did not seek their collective advice ahead of time. Rather, he acted as Truman so often had, preparing an "essential" foreign policy request and then presenting it to Congress. Moreover, aware of the ambiguous constitutional issue involved, Eisenhower delivered his request in most conciliatory terms. In his special message he noted that he might already possess the powers in question, but promised that "the authority *that may be accorded by Congress* would be used only in situations which are recognizable as part of, or definite preliminaries to, an attack against the main positions of Formosa and the Pescadores" (italics added).[43] Secretary of State Dulles was equally deferential in the executive hearings of the Senate Foreign Relations and Armed Services committees, telling the members:

> There is at least doubt as to whether or not the President could, without Congressional authorization, take the kind of action which I am talking about. The area of authority as between the President and the Congress in these areas is admittedly a shady one.
> . . . The legal position I think needs to be clarified so that there can be no doubt about it. Even if there was no doubt whatever about the legal position, even if it was perfectly clear that the President did have this authority, I believe it would be indispensable that the Congress should indicate its concurrence in it as a matter of policy. . . . [44]

Both Eisenhower's and Dulles's language showed awareness that the executive probably did not need a grant of authority such as the Formosa Resolution, yet the lesson of Truman's problems over Korea was on their minds. To co-opt Congress early could avert later criticism, at least on the constitutional issue. They also worked hard to avoid raising unnecessary partisan antagonisms. Dulles urged Republican congressional leaders not to "needle" Democrats by emphasizing the contrast between Eisenhower's "constitutional" procedure in this instance and Truman's earlier unilateral actions, and Eisenhower played down the significance of the resolution. He rejected a suggestion from G.O.P. forces that he personally deliver a statement clarifying to Congress why a resolution was needed, holding that such an action on his part would "indicate a policy, purpose [and] possible action that is greater than we intend. . . . " The request for a resolution, he believed, should be kept as routine as possible, so as not to arouse Democratic suspicions.[45]

Congress responded largely as Eisenhower hoped. Only a small number of Senate Democrats opposed the resolution as a dangerous "blank check" (the most eloquent critic, Senator Morse, held that Congress was "being asked in effect to underwrite by our approval not only all the words of the resolution, but all the meanings of the resolution to be found between the lines. . . . ") By contrast, most members of Congress, regardless of party, shared the belief that the resolution was innocuous because unnecessary. Republican Congressman Walter Judd of Minnesota even feared that it "might be construed as setting a precedent limiting the power the President has under the Constitution." To most, it was reassuring that Eisenhower had asked for their consent. As G.O.P. Representative Timothy Sheehan (Illinois) put it, "President Eisenhower has certainly shown consideration of Congress and his deep adherence to the principles of constitutional government. . . . " Added Massachusetts Republican Congressman Laurence Curtis, "This is democracy at its best."[46] In the end Congress endorsed the Formosa Resolution with only three dissenting votes in each house. Such cooperation made an interesting counterpoint to the congressional hostility greeting Truman's deployment of forces to Europe four years earlier.

In late 1956, in the wake of a dangerous crisis over Egyptian nationalization of the Suez Canal and the threat of a wider conflict in the Middle East, the Eisenhower administration resolved to repeat the strategic coup it had scored with the Formosa Resolution. In early December the president authorized the State Department to draw up an area resolution for the Middle East for submission to the new Congress, scheduled to assemble in January 1957.[47] Unlike the earlier Formosa Resolution, the new proposal included advance authorization for the president to grant unspecified amounts of economic aid to Middle Eastern governments, in addition to permitting use of American armed forces in the area.

By 1957, however, congressional critics were more outspoken than in 1955. The potential costliness of the economic "blank check" in the

Middle East Resolution bothered some fiscal conservatives, but the basic constitutional issue surrounding the president's power to commit troops abroad produced greater concern. Democrats, frustrated by Eisenhower's triumphant reelection in 1956 and aware of the need to build a foreign policy record of their own for 1960, were especially critical. "I would support a naked statement that we will come into the Middle East with all of our military might to aid any country that is attacked by the Communists," said Democrat Richard Russell of Georgia, speaking for many of his party colleagues. "But I do not propose to vote for any statement of national policy giving practically unlimited military and economic authority to the President in this case." Senator J. William Fulbright, an important Democratic spokesman on foreign policy matters, asserted that the resolution was unnecessary and dangerous. Fulbright rejected the claim that Eisenhower already had the powers being requested, an interpretation generally accepted at the time the Formosa Resolution was adopted. Rather, he argued, the president possessed "what is called among legal circles 'the emergency power of the President.' That is a procedure that he has followed in many cases, which requires him to come to the Congress for affirmance after he has acted in pursuance of emergency power." The senator concluded, "It would not, in my opinion, be a proper discharge of our duty as Senators to give him a blank check ahead of time and say, 'Whatever you do is all right.' "[48]

But if opponents of the Middle East Resolution were more suspicious and vociferous than they had been in the case of the Formosa Resolution, their opposition proved ineffective. Administration tactics, as implemented by Secretary of State Dulles, again produced success. In closed hearings on the proposal, Dulles undermined critics by downplaying the novelty of the provisions for economic aid and accepting the right of Congress to share authority to terminate the resolution. The sharing of authority to terminate, he told the Senate Foreign Relations and Armed Services committees, was "a matter which would be fully discussable with the President"; such a provision was included in the resolution as adopted. Most effective of all was the secretary's invoking of Eisenhower's personal prestige and credibility as a leader of the free world in the cold war, an image carefully nurtured by the president in his dealings with Congress since 1953. It was up to Congress, Dulles stated, "to decide whether or not they wish to respond, whether they prefer to take the responsibility of saying they know more about the conduct of foreign affairs than the President does. That is their right and privilege to do."[49]

Ultimately the administration accepted an important (though not decisive) change in wording, substituting for congressional "authorization" of military force a general declaration that the United States stood "prepared to use armed forces" if the situation warranted. The battle basically won, Eisenhower and Dulles chose to follow the advice of Senate Majority Leader Lyndon Johnson, "to treat this as a victory. . . . "[50] In a real sense it was. By securing a second area resolution in the space of two years, Eisenhower had institutionalized the practice of co-opting Congress in future, unspecified military actions. The importance of this, of course, would be apparent to all in the 1960s after passage of the Tonkin Gulf Resolution.

The growing frustration of congressional Democrats in the late 1950s led them, as it had led the Republicans almost a decade earlier, to try to increase their influence over foreign policy. Plans for an offensive against the executive branch were laid right after the presidential election of 1956 as Adlai Stevenson, the defeated Democratic candidate, wrote to John Sparkman, a member of the Senate Foreign Relations Committee, asking for action. "I really don't believe Eisenhower would have been too hard to beat if he had been chopped up a little beforehand," wrote Stevenson. "I want so much to talk with you about mounting a more effective opposition this time. I suspect it will be up to you and Fulbright and a few others on the Foreign Relations Committee to keep picking at them and make them answer some questions." Meetings between the committee Democrats, Stevenson, and other interested party strategists occurred over the next several months. The Soviets' surprise launching of Sputnik in late 1957 intensified the Democrats' commitment to conduct a full-scale examination of foreign policy by Congress. With Fulbright taking the lead, in August 1958 the Foreign Relations Committee authorized $300,000 for a broad reexamination of U.S. policy.[51]

In conducting this review, which dragged on until June 1960, committee Democrats expressed varying opinions concerning their authority. Fulbright acknowledged that the president had the unarguable right to exercise daily leadership in foreign affairs, writing in 1958 that, "without intelligent and forceful leadership from the executive department the Senate cannot really initiate or administer effectively any policy." Yet once the review was under way, he offered a less-guarded view, observing that it was "difficult . . . for a legislative committee to direct policy, but we will give it a try." Fulbright's committee colleague Wayne Morse more forcefully emphasized the right of Congress to take on the executive. With some passion Morse remarked in committee that "we do have a responsibility under our system as a major committee of the

Senate to keep ourselves informed along the lines of this broad policy. . . . As a legislative committee, we have an independent duty here to make our own findings of fact and to appraise how our foreign policy is going, because we are the legislative check on that policy. . . . " The Democratic Advisory Council, a policy-making arm of the party's national committee, also got into the act, issuing a statement outlining the institutional matter at stake in the Foreign Relations Committee review:

> No one questions the Constitutional authority of the President to command the armed forces of the United States and to conduct negotiations with foreign nations. . . . But there is much more to formulating and carrying out foreign policy than ordering troop movements and negotiating with foreign nations. There is the vast responsibility of determining our national purposes and of providing the capacity and means for attaining them. Here the Legislative Branch has its own Constitutional tasks both in devising policy and in wisely exercising the power to grant legal authority for its execution. . . . [52]

Although it produced fifteen detailed reports between August 1959 and June 1960, the Democrat-led Foreign Relations Committee succeeded no better in increasing congressional influence over foreign policy than had Republican critics earlier in the decade. Their failure did not stop Eisenhower from complaining to Henry Luce about what he believed were unfair constraints on his authority. "Except for my first two years in office," the president wrote in 1960,

> I have had to deal with a Congress controlled by the opposition and whose partisan antagonism to the Executive Branch has often been blatantly displayed. The hope of doing something constructive for the nation, in spite of this kind of opposition, has required the use of methods calculated to attract cooperation, even though a natural impulse would have been to lash out at partisan charges and publicity-seeking demagogues.[53]

Eisenhower was correct in believing partisan resentments lay behind much of the congressional assertiveness he saw; that had been true in the Truman years as well. But he ignored the very real reasons that led legislators to attack the executive branch once again: his success with "methods calculated to attract cooperation" had strengthened the presidential hand to an unprecedented degree. By 1960, no amount of partisan criticism from Congress could alter that fact.

Despite many indications after World War II that the congressional-executive balance would shift in favor of the legislative branch, during the next decade and a half the reverse occurred. Building on its strong position at the end of the war, the presidency emerged after the Truman and Eisenhower years an even more powerful institution. By 1960 the "cult of the presidency" flourished as never before, as the chief executive engaged regularly in legislative planning and systematic liaison efforts with Congress and enjoyed nearly unchecked control of foreign policy. There were many reasons for this outcome—some institutional, some political, others related to personality. It was clear that the sheer size and unmanageability of the executive bureaucracy played an important part in developments; vastly expanded during depression and war, the executive branch proved too large for Congress to supervise or even monitor effectively. Also, the intermingling of partisan and institutional motives in congressional attempts to weaken the presidency undermined the credibility and force of those efforts. Republicans like Robert A. Taft who led the initial attacks on presidential authority in the Truman years were caught in obvious inconsistency when they argued for checks on presidential activism in foreign policy while enthusiastically supporting enlargement of executive power against organized labor (the Taft-Hartley Act). Having employed the rhetoric and tactics of fervent anti-communism in their drive to circumscribe President Truman's powers, moreover, G.O.P. legislators later found it impossible to deny President Eisenhower the Formosa and Middle East resolutions when he employed similar rhetoric and tactics in making his requests. By the same token, Democrats who had defended Truman against the Republicans' constitutionalist offensives in the early fifties were unconvincing when they decried the dangers of excessive presidential power near the end of Eisenhower's second term. Finally, the sharply divergent personalities of Harry S. Truman and Dwight D. Eisenhower served to shield the growing power of the presidential office—Truman because in some ways he struck observers as personally limited and thus less a threat, Eisenhower because he succeeded in appearing to be thoroughly deferential to Congress.

The vast accretion of presidential power that occurred between 1945 and 1960 produced no effective opposition, or even loud complaint. Perhaps it should be noted, however, that the cumulative impact of World War II and the cold war on American institutions was largely irreversible; the task of continuous vigilance in world affairs seemingly required a permanently enlarged, more autonomous presidency than ever before, a fact which even zealous defenders of congressional prerogatives could not ignore. At the end of the Eisenhower era, Congress remained largely quiescent; the public continued to revere the office of president as it did the incumbent; and neo-constitutionalism had gone out of fashion among scholars, journalists, and other commentators. Leading students of American government such as Clinton Rossiter, James MacGregor Burns, and Arthur M. Schlesinger, Jr., all extolled the virtues (and necessity) of an expanded presidency. Typical, if somewhat florid in language, was the description of the presidency offered by Theodore White in 1960:

The President of the United States is more than an emblem. He is at once High Priest of our secular democracy and the Magistrate of its power. So vast is the nature of his power and so complicated its mechanics that he cannot, constitutionally, be brought to a table of negotiation and pinned down in detail. . . . Nor can he be offended personally without suffering offense for all Americans. If the President chooses to bargain with foreign powers he can most wisely bargain through deputies. . . . About the President there must always be an air of remoteness and distance to make majestic American power.[54]

It could not have been predicted in 1945 that such views of the presidential office would hold sway unchallenged a decade and a half later. Nor would it prove easy to reverse the trend after 1960; it took the twin reverberations of the Vietnam War and Watergate to produce any real reaction against the "imperial presidency" at all. Even then the movement was incomplete. At the start of the 1980s, there is strong evidence to suggest that the reaction against the executive branch will be short-lived, a temporary interruption in the development of the presidential government so dramatically advanced in the fifteen years after World War II.

1. Herman Belz, "Changing Conceptions of Constitutionalism in the Era of World War II and the Cold War," *Journal of American History* 59 (1972–73): 641, 645, 652.

2. Corwin, *The President: Office and Powers; History and Analysis of Practice and Opinion*, 3d ed. rev. (New York, 1948), p. 149. See also Francis G. Wilson, "Public Policy in Constitutional Reform," *Review of Politics* 7 (1945): 58–73.

3. Hadley Cantril, ed., *Public Opinion, 1935–1946* (Princeton, N.J., 1951), p. 888; James MacGregor Burns, *Presidential Government: The Crucible of Leadership* (Boston, 1965), pp. 103–4.

4. Voorhis, "Congress and the Future," *Review of Politics* 7 (1945): 138; also 131, 132.

5. Thomas E. Cronin, "A Resurgent Congress and the Imperial Presidency," *Political Science Quarterly* 95 (1980): 236.

6. James MacGregor Burns, "President and Congress: A Crucial Test," *New York Times Magazine*, 4 January 1953, p. 36. The consistency of public support for the presidency is evident in presidential approval ratings as recorded by national polls. Between April 1945 and early 1969, the Gallup poll asked the "presidential approval" question about 300 times; favorable responses ranged from less than 30 percent to over 85 percent, but the average was a sizeable 58 percent: John E. Mueller, "Presidential Popularity from Truman to Johnson," *American Political Science Review* 64 (1970): 18–19.

7. George B. Galloway, *Congress at the Crossroads* (New York, 1946), pp. 205, 211; Edward S. Corwin, *Total War and the Constitution* (New York, 1947), p. 180; Barkley, "President and, Not versus, Congress," *New York Times Magazine*, 20 June 1948, p. 14.

8. Truman's reverence for the presidency has been documented by his close associates. "He had an interesting faculty," noted aide George Elsey years later, " . . . of detaching himself from the Presidency itself. He had a tremendous veneration and respect for the institution of the Presidency. He demanded at all times respect for the President of the United States. He didn't demand any respect at all for Harry S. Truman . . . ": George Elsey Oral History, Harry S. Truman Library, p. 33.

9. Henry F. Pringle, "Can Congress Save Itself?", *Saturday Evening Post*, 6 October 1945, p. 28; U.S., Congress, *Congressional Record*, 79th Cong., 2d sess., 1946, 92, pt. 5, pp. 6345, 6365, 6370.

10. Some had wanted the act to go further, requiring committees to undertake "surveillance" of related agencies: see ibid., p. 6446. The act is described in Ernest S. Griffith, *Congress: Its Contemporary Role*, 2d ed. rev. (New York, 1956), pp. 44–45, 61, 62, 71, 94; Joseph P. Harris, *Congressional Control of Administration* (Washington, D.C., 1964), p. 263.

11. Louis Fisher, *The Constitution between Friends: Congress, the President, and the Law* (New York, 1978), pp. 134, 136.

12. Susan M. Hartmann, *Truman and the Eightieth Congress* (Columbia, Mo., 1971), p. 31; Donald G. Morgan, *Congress and the Constitution: A Study of Responsibility* (Cambridge, Mass., 1966), pp. 227–28, 232, 236–37, 239, 240. Popular attitudes toward the amendment after ratification continued to be ambivalent. Polls showed steadily increasing support for it, but in 1960 nearly 60 percent of those questioned indicated they would readily support President Eisenhower for a third term if he were eligible to run: Burns, *Presidential Government*, p. 104; Roberta S. Sigel and David J. Butler, "The Public and the No Third Term Tradition: Inquiry into Attitudes toward Power," *Midwest Journal of Political Science* 8 (1964): 41, 52, 54.

13. Harris, *Congressional Control*, p. 204; Richard M. Pious, *The American Presidency* (New York, 1979), p. 224; J. Malcolm Smith and Cornelius P. Cotter, *Powers of the President during Crises* (Washington, D.C., 1960), pp. 102–3.

14. The concurrent resolution had precedent in Congress as early as 1843, and its use for purposes of vetoing an executive action dated from the 1939 Executive Reorganization Act. See Doyle W. Buckwalter, "The Congressional Concurrent Resolution: A Search for Foreign Policy Influence," *Midwest Journal of Political Science* 14 (1970): 437–40; Harris, *Congressional Control*, pp. 204–5; Fisher, *Constitution between Friends*, pp. 99–101.

15. Smith and Cotter, *Powers of the President*, p. 105; Harris, *Congressional Control*, pp. 206, 209, 211, 223–24, 238–39; Buckwalter, "The Congressional Concurrent Resolution," pp. 441, 444–45; Fisher, *Constitution between Friends*, pp. 107–8.

16. Harris, *Congressional Control*, pp. 249–50, 261, 263–65.

17. William F. Mullen, *Presidential Power and Politics* (New York, 1976), pp. 80–82; Arthur M. Schlesinger, Jr., *The Imperial Presidency* (Boston, 1973), p. 340.

18. Adam C. Breckenridge, *The Executive Privilege: Presidential Control over Information* (Lincoln, Neb., 1974), pp. 57–58; Harris, *Congressional Control*, pp. 267–68; Harry S. Truman to Sen. Millard Tydings, 3 April 1950, in *Public Papers of the Presidents: Harry S. Truman, 1950* (Washington, D.C., 1965), p. 241; Schlesinger, *Imperial Presidency*, pp. 340, 349.

19. Morgan, *Congress and the Constitution*, pp. 17–19; Robert A. Taft to Alexander Wiley, 22 May 1951, Alexander Wiley Papers, Box 30, Wisconsin State Historical Society.

20. Truman to Rep. Harold H. Velde, Chairman, House Committee on Un-American Activities, 12 November 1953, *New York Times*, 13 November 1953, p. 14.

21. Minutes of Congressional Leadership Meeting, 27 June 1950, and Minutes of Meeting of Cabinet, Congressional Leaders, Military and Defense Officials, 30 June 1950, George M. Elsey Papers, Box 71, Truman Library.

22. Memorandum, George Elsey to Beverly Smith, 16 July 1951, Elsey Papers, Box 71,

Truman Library; David B. Truman, *The Congressional Party: A Case Study* (New York, 1959), pp. 35–36; Ronald J. Caridi, *The Korean War and American Politics: The Republican Party as a Case Study* (Philadelphia, 1968), pp. 33–34, 37.

23. Taft to Col. Robert McCormick, 25 July 1950, Robert A. Taft Papers, Box 822, Library of Congress; Raymond Moley, "The Constitutional Crisis," *Newsweek*, 11 December 1950, p. 100; "The Elections and Asia," *Life*, 20 November 1950, p. 38; Rep. Jacob Javits to Truman, 11 December 1950, Truman Papers, OF 408, Truman Library.

24. *Congressional Quarterly Almanac* 7 (1951): 222, 226, 229–30; *Washington Post*, 3 April 1951.

25. See Corwin, *President: Office and Powers* (1940 ed.), pp. 165, 189–90, 194; Corwin, *Total War and the Constitution*, p. 65; Louis W. Koenig, *The Presidency and the Crisis: Powers of the Office from the Invasion of Poland to Pearl Harbor* (New York, 1944), pp. 1–2. On the OPA fight see Cornelius P. Cotter and J. Malcolm Smith, "Administrative Accountability to Congress: The Concurrent Resolution," *Western Political Quarterly* 9 (1956): 964; Smith and Cotter, *Powers of the President*, pp. 19, 101; Robert J. Donovan, *Conflict and Crisis: The Presidency of Harry S. Truman, 1945–1948* (New York, 1977), pp. 198–99, 235–36; Hamby, *Beyond the New Deal: Harry S. Truman and American Liberalism* (New York, 1973), pp. 79–80; James T. Patterson, *Mr. Republican: A Biography of Robert A. Taft* (Boston, 1972), pp. 308–12; radio speech by Robert A. Taft, 1 July 1946, Taft Papers, Box 757, LC.

26. Clark had advised Truman in 1948, in connection with a threatened rail strike, that a 1916 statute gave him the necessary authority to seize the railroads, but even without that law "a strong argument could be made that the President in time of peace has emergency authority to preserve the functioning of the national economy." Clark urged Truman to seek specific congressional approval anyway, however, to "remove any possible doubt as to the validity of the seizure . . . ": Clark to Truman, n.d., Clark Clifford Papers, Box 10, Truman Library. See Arthur Krock, "Strikes Revive Issues of President's Powers," *New York Times*, 30 October 1949.

27. Maeva Marcus, *Truman and the Steel Seizure Case: The Limits of Presidential Power* (New York, 1977), pp. 75–78, 124–25, 158; Smith and Cotter, *Powers of the President*, pp. 134–36.

28. Smith and Cotter, *Powers of the President*, pp. 135, 137–38; Marcus, *Truman and the Steel Seizure Case*, pp. 197, 199–201, 209–10, 216.

29. U.S., Congress. *Congressional Record*, 82d Cong., 2d sess., 1952, 98, pt. 3, p. 4151; Corwin, "The Steel Seizure Case: A Judicial Brick without Straw," in Richard Loss, ed., *Presidential Power and the Constitution: Essays by Edward S. Corwin* (Ithaca, N.Y., 1976), p. 137; Smith and Cotter, *Powers of the President*, pp. 24–25, 144–45; Mullen, *Presidential Power and Politics*, pp. 94–95.

30. U.S., Congress, *Congressional Record*, 82d Cong., 1st sess., 1951, 97, pt. 2, pp. 2863, 2864.

31. Thomas G. Paterson, "Presidential Foreign Policy, Public Opinion, and Congress: The Truman Years," *Diplomatic History* 3 (1979): 14; Breckenridge, *Executive Privilege*, p. 133.

32. Bricker to John Foster Dulles and Bricker to Herbert Brownell, 7 January 1953, John W. Bricker Papers, Box 91, Ohio Historical Society; James A. Hagerty diary entry, 14 January 1954, Hagerty Diaries, Eisenhower Library. For a summary of the Bricker amendment controversy, see Gary W. Reichard, "Eisenhower and the Bricker Amendment," *Prologue: The Journal of the National Archives* 6 (1974): 88–99.

33. Bricker to Carl R. Turner, 27 July 1956, Bricker Papers, Box 123, Ohio Historical Society.

34. Memorandum, Richard E. Neustadt to Elmer N. Staats, 22 November 1948, Richard E. Neustadt Papers, Box 1, Truman Library.

35. Richard E. Neustadt, "Presidency and Legislation: Planning the President's Program," *American Political Science Review* 49 (1955): 981; Stephen J. Wayne, *The Legislative Presidency* (New York, 1978), pp. 78, 105; Mullen, *Presidential Power and Politics*, p. 57.

36. Mullen, *Presidential Power and Politics*, pp. 38–39, 61–63, 78–79; Abraham Holtzman, *Legislative Liaison: Executive Leadership in Congress* (Chicago, 1970), p. 16; Gary W. Reichard, *The Reaffirmation of Republicanism: Eisenhower and the Eighty-third Congress* (Knoxville, Tenn., 1975), pp. 218–25. Eisenhower quotation in Clinton Rossiter, *The American Presidency* (New York, 1960), p. 110.

37. Pious, *The American Presidency*, pp. 204, 205, 208; U.S., Senate, Secretary, *Presidential Vetoes, 1789–1976* (Washington, D.C., 1978), p. 349.

38. Mullen, *Presidential Power and Politics*, pp. 89–90; Schlesinger, *Imperial Presidency*, pp. 156–59. See Eisenhower to Wilson, 17 May 1954, and Brownell memorandum, 2 March 1954, in *Public Papers of the Presidents: Dwight D. Eisenhower, 1954* (Washington, D.C., 1960), pp. 483–85.

39. Statement of 24 July 1959: *Public Papers of the Presidents: . . . 1959*, p. 549.

40. See memoranda of telephone conversation, John Foster Dulles and Eisenhower, 24 May 1955, Ann C. Whitman Diaries, Whitman Files, Box 5, Eisenhower Library, and John Foster Dulles Papers, Box 10, Eisenhower Library.

41. S. Con. Res. 2 originally had thirty-two cosponsors, including thirteen Republicans, and was recommended for adoption by the Senate Rules Committee. For Mansfield and Morse remarks, see U.S., Congress, *Congressional Record*, 84th Cong., 2d sess., 1956, 102, pt. 5: 5923–24, 5926.

42. *Imperial Presidency*, p. 175.

43. James Robinson, *Congress and Foreign Policy-Making: A Study in Legislative Influence and Initiative*, rev. ed. (Homewood, Ill., 1967), pp. 54–55; *Public Papers of the Presidents: . . . 1955*, p. 209.

44. U.S., Senate, Committees on Armed Services and Foreign Relations, *Hearings on Resolution Authorizing the President to Employ the Armed Forces of the United States for Protecting the Security of Formosa, the Pescadores and Related Positions and Territories of that Area. Executive Session*, 2 vols., 84th Cong., 1st sess., 1955, 1:46, 47, RG 46, Records of the United States Senate, Committee on Foreign Relations, National Archives.

45. Memorandum of telephone conversations, Eisenhower-Dulles (25 January 1955) and Sen. William F. Knowland-Eisenhower (21 January 1955), Dwight D. Eisenhower Papers, 1953–1961, Box 5, Eisenhower Library.

46. U.S., Congress, *Congressional Record*, 84th Cong., 1st sess., 1955, 101, pt. 1, pp. 667, 672, 677, 682, 738. See also arguments of Senators Herbert Lehman and Hubert Humphrey, ibid., pp. 826, 926, 929, 986.

47. Memorandum on Eisenhower-Dulles telephone conversation, 8 December 1956, Dulles Papers, Box 11, Eisenhower Library.

48. *Congressional Quarterly Weekly Reports*, 15 (11 January 1957): 41; U.S., Senate, Committees on Armed Services and Foreign Relations, *Hearings on S.J. Res. 19, Authority for Economic and Military Cooperation with Nations in the Middle East. Exeuctive Session*, 85th Cong., 1st sess., 1957, pp. 1133–34, RG 46, Records of the U.S. Senate, Committee on Foreign Relations.

49. Ibid., pp. 9, 10, 16, 57.

50. Memorandum of Dulles-Johnson telephone conversation, 5 March 1957, Dulles Papers, Box 6, Eisenhower Library.

51. Stevenson to Sparkman, 11 November 1956, Adlai E. Stevenson Papers, Box 479, Princeton University Library; memorandum, Carl Marcy to Senator Theodore F. Green,

6 January 1958, RG 46, Records of U.S. Senate, Committee on Foreign Relations; *Congressional Quarterly Weekly Reports*, 16 (8 August 1958): 1026.

52. Fulbright to James P. Warburg, 10 June 1958 and 9 February 1959, James P. Warburg Papers, Box 16, John F. Kennedy Library; Robinson, *Congress and Foreign Policy-Making*, pp. 185–86; U.S., Senate, Committee on Foreign Relations, *Hearings on Proposal for a Broad Study of Foreign Policy, Executive Session*, 85th Cong., 2d sess., 1958, pp. 21–22, 28; Democratic Advisory Council press release, 7 December 1958, Stevenson Papers, Box 745.

53. Eisenhower to Luce, 8 August 1960, Eisenhower Papers, 1953–1961, Box 33, Eisenhower Library.

54. Theodore H. White, "Perspective 1960," *Saturday Review*, 2 July 1960, p. 7.

Reflections on Politics, Policy, and Ideology

Bernard Sternsher

Since historical forces seldom synchronize with presidential terms, or decades, or decades-and-a-half, historians struggle with stubborn problems of periodization. In terms of party-systems analysis, which treats enduring patterns in voter behavior, the period 1945–60 becomes intelligible only within the framework of the New Deal party system that saw the Democratic party hold normal majority status from 1936 to 1964. As one moves beyond examination of voter-behavior studies to discussion of broader political topics, one finds that the main themes in American foreign policy, political economy, and ideology from 1945 to 1960 show the persistence of the New Deal party system during the Truman-Eisenhower years.

Since 1960 research in historical voting behavior has revealed party systems, or striking stability over extended periods in percentages of the vote obtained by the major parties. The idea of party systems is tied in with the concept of normal majority status: short-term factors being equal, the presidential candidate of the party enjoying normal, or long-term, majority status can expect to receive 53–54 percent of the two-party vote. This status comprises quantitative and qualitative elements. The quantitative component is entailed in the expectation of a majority of the vote. The qualitative ingredient is party identification or party loyalty—voters' tendency to vote according to party preferences. During the third party, or Civil War, system, 1860–93, there was a competitive situation: neither party enjoyed normal majority status. Under the fourth party, or Industrial, system, 1894–1932, the Republican party enjoyed normal majority status. In the era of the fifth party, or New Deal, system, 1936–64, the Democrats enjoyed normal majority status as the result of a realignment of the electorate in the 1930s. Since 1964 there has emerged a two-tier system: neither party has enjoyed normal majority status at the presidential level, while the Democrats have continued to dominate at the subpresidential level[1] (until 1980, when the Republicans gained control of the Senate and received 50 percent of all votes cast for House candidates). The period 1945–60 thus falls between two transformations of the electorate—one in the 1930s and one in the 1960s and 1970s—and within the span of the New Deal party system.

Just as the Republicans' normal majority status from 1894 to 1932 was not overturned by Wilson's election in 1912, the result of a major-party bolt, so the Democrats' normal majority status from 1936 to 1964 was not eliminated by Eisenhower's victories. Many persons who voted for Eisenhower in 1952 and 1956 continued to think of themselves as Democrats. This assertion is supported by the percentages for party identification: the Democrats led 53 to 36 in 1936, a differential of 17 percentage points, and 42 to 18 in 1974, a differential of 24 percentage points, with this differential ranging from 15 to 27 in presidential election years from 1940 to 1972. Eisenhower, moreover, ran ahead of his party, and the Democratic percentage of the vote in House elections actually showed a modest secular rise during his presidency, from 51 percent in 1952 to 56 percent in 1960.[2]

One can also characterize the years 1945–60 in electoral terms by considering the typology of elections that party-systems analysts have developed. A "critical" or "realigning" election is one in which a competitive system ends with the acquisition of normal majority status by a party, as in 1894, or one in which normal majority status passes from one party to another, as in 1936. Students of the New Deal realignment have long debated whether the critical election occurred in 1928, 1932, or 1936. Elsewhere I have argued that the election of 1936 exhibited both the quantitative and qualitative characteristics of a critical election: Roosevelt received 62.4 percent of the two-party vote *and* enjoyed, for the first time, the support of the loyal, enduring Roosevelt coalition of partisan identifiers.[3] In any event, the formation of the Roosevelt coalition at the presidential level by 1936 is generally agreed upon. It was composed of city dwellers, workers, ethnics, Catholics, Jews, blacks, intellectuals who favored increased governmental activity, and the Solid South (an individual voter, of course, could fall into more than one of these categories).

The elections of 1940, 1944, and 1948 were "maintaining" elections in which the basic partisan commitments resulting from the New Deal re-alignment guided the vote. Eisenhower's triumphs in 1952 and 1956 were "deviating" elections: "The outcome was different from that which would be predicted on the basis of party affiliation, but the implication was that once the short-term force that dominated these elections—the personal appeal of Eisenhower—faded, the system would return to normal." The election of 1960 was a "reinstating" election. With the popular Eisenhower on the sidelines, one would have expected the normal majority status of the Democratic party to reassert itself so that the Democratic candidate would receive 53 to 54 percent of the two-party vote. Kennedy fell short of this percentage because he suffered a net loss among voters supporting or opposing him on the grounds of his religion. To put it another way, a Protestant Democrat probably would have won by the expected margin in an election that was essentially devoid of policy-issue content.[4]

Two additional approaches that political scientists use are helpful in characterizing the years 1945–60: analysis of the groups composing party coalitions and of voter traits. The authors of *The Changing American Voter* (1976) consider partisan identification, 1952–72, for eleven groups: White Protestant Southerners, White Native Southerners, High Status Native White Southerners, Low Status Native White Southerners, Northern White Protestants, Higher Status Northern White Protestants, Lower Status Northern White Protestants, Northern Blacks, Southern Blacks, Jews, and Catholics. The point that is most relevant to our concern emerges when one divides their data into two periods: 1952–60 and 1960–72. The major changes in partisan identification occurred in the 1960s, mainly among younger voters.[5]

The most important analysis for our purposes is concerned with voter traits. *The American Voter* (1960) found voters of the 1950s only modestly involved in politics, unsophisticated in their view of political matters, inconsistent across a broad range of issues (thereby reducing "the ability we would have to predict a person's position on one issue from his position [liberal or conservative] on another"), strongly committed on a long-term basis to one of the major parties, and relatively satisfied with the political system. All of this changed in the 1960s. New issues, more interest, a rise in the level of conceptualization, and increased issue consistency were accompanied by declining partisanship and growing independence, ticket-splitting, and alienation from parties. The next step was issue voting. Voters, of course, cannot vote issue positions unless they are given a choice—which is what Goldwater gave them in 1964. Nor are issue voting and party voting necessarily incompatible. They were, in fact, harmonious in the 1930s, but issue voting in the 1960s militated against party voting because the new issues of that decade cut across the parties, especially the Democratic party, which was associated with both the old economic liberalism and the new social-cultural liberalism and evoked contradictory responses within both the upper and lower socioeconomic status groups.[6]

Examining issue consistency and issue voting, the authors of *The Changing American Voter* apply correlation analysis to answers— obtained in 1939, 1956–60, and 1964–72—to questions regarding five issues: social welfare, welfare for blacks, size of government, racial integration in schools, and the cold war. In the 1930s there was substantial issue coherence but only with respect to "the core issues of the New Deal—government control and regulation of the economy and government commitment to welfare." In the Eisenhower years there was a low level of consistency in all areas and virtually no issue voting. After 1964 there was moderate to high issue consistency across all issue areas and issue voting on multiple issues. During the Eisenhower years the New Deal issues had lost their salience (or entry into the daily life of individuals), but they had not been replaced by new issues that might affect older voters' partisanship or impede new voters' assumption of their parents' partisan commitments.[7]

In the Eisenhower years the most important issues tended to be foreign-policy issues. Although these issues unified Americans around the president, but not his party, the traditional economic issues tended to reinforce party ties. The issues of Korea, Communism, and Corruption, denoted in the Republicans' 1952 campaign formula, "K_1C_2," were short-lived. Eisenhower's victory, writes V. O. Key, Jr., "seems to have been at the bottom a victory that rested on a transient majority which could exist no longer than the issues around which it was built. On the great and continuing economic questions of domestic policy, a popular majority remained hostile to the Republican position—as it saw that position."[8] In the 1960s the waning of older issues, the emergence of new salient issues, and a new generation of voters combined to loosen the grip of party commitments. In sum, with respect to issue consistency and issue voting, the Eisenhower years represented a low point between two higher points. Given this nadir and the persistence of the partisan ties formed in the 1930s, the authors of *The American Voter* might have entitled their study *The American Voter in an Age of Inertia*.

Voters in the cold war era were still largely the children of the New Deal realignment, with one outstanding exception: early defectors among white southern Democrats. The demise of the Solid South is one of the most written-about subjects in the field of voter behavior. In the 1930s the South was more supportive of New Deal programs, with the exception of legislation helpful to trade unions, than any other section, but 1944 was the last time the South would be conclusively Democratic in presidential voting—69 percent. In 1948 Truman received 52 percent of the southern popular vote. The Democratic percentage was slightly lower in the next four elections and then plunged to about 35 percent in 1968 and 29 percent in 1972. In 1976 southerner Jimmy Carter won 54 percent of the vote in the South but only 45 percent of southern white Protestants' ballots. These Democratic losses have not been accompanied by commensurate Republican gains in identifiers because Democratic defectors have moved mostly to Independence. From 1936 to 1974 Democratic identifiers fell from 78 to 50 percent of the southern electorate; Republican identifiers increased from 13 to 16 percent; Independents rose from 8 to 33 percent. Republicans can nevertheless produce victories "with a fair degree of regularity," although their gains in local electoral contests have been more modest than in state and national elections.[9]

Voters in general in the cold war era lived in a period of relative calm in American politics. The one potentially divisive issue, domestic Communism, faded away during Eisenhower's first term, and in four years the issue and ideological content of politics were substantially reduced. This reduction was evident in several measurements of voter behavior. From 1940 to 1960 the middle class grew in numbers, but the possibility that this development might cause class division was not realized. With growing affluence and the entry of many Americans into the middle class, some observers advanced a "conversion" thesis: attainment of middle-class status meant a shift to Republicanism. But survey data show that the Democratic party did not suffer with the growth of the middle class. In 1944 the general public voted 51 percent for Democratic congressional candidates, the professional-managerial stratum 32 percent; in 1956 the corresponding figures were 51 percent and 47 percent. And the same pattern held in partisan identification. There was also a sizable decline in status polarization between the middle and working classes, apparent in a decrease in the differential between these two groups over policy issues. The percentage-point differential in their respective attitudes toward unions, government regulation of business, and social welfare programs fell from 30–40 in the years 1936 to 1948 to almost zero by the late 1950s.[10]

Analyses of voter behavior in presidential elections in the cold war era also indicated lessening divergence between Protestants and Catholics and between high and low socioeconomic status (SES) groups. In the years 1940–60 non-southern white Protestants voted about one-third Democratic, and non-southern white Catholics about two-thirds Democratic. Percentage point differentials in Democratic presidential voting, however, show that the two groups were closest in the Eisenhower years. Catholics voted 31 percentage points more Democratic than Protestants in 1940, 30 in 1944, 24 in 1948, 22 in 1952, 17 in 1956, and 40 in 1960, with the division waning again after 1960. The Eisenhower years also saw a decline in differentials in pro-Democratic presidential voting between low and high SES whites outside the South. The low SES group voted 33 percentage points more Democratic than the high SES group in 1936, 33 in 1940, 24 in 1944, 38 in 1948, 20 in 1952, 12 in 1956, and 25 in 1960. Everett Carll Ladd, Jr., and Charles D. Hadley believe that if similar data were available for the years before 1936, "it is likely that the uniqueness of the Roosevelt-Truman elections would have been even more dramatically evident." The period 1936–48 represents the high-water mark of class saliency in voter behavior. Given declining salience of issues generally, it is unlikely that any president could have kept alive the degree of class differences in the presidential voting of 1936–48 in the 1950s. Certainly Eisenhower made no such attempt. He did not package issues in such a way as to offer voters a clear choice. On the contrary, he presented "a political image above the issues," and his "leadership style was such as to mute whatever issues did exist."[11]

The reference here to relative political calmness is not intended to connote acceptance of the designation of the 1950s in general as America's "placid" decade. Herbert S. Parmet, in his important study of the Eisenhower presidency, declares, "It was not, as some have maintained, a 'placid' decade. No years that contained McCarthy and McCarthyism, a war in Korea, constant fear of other conflicts and atomic annihilation, and spreading racial violence could be so described." Expressing a similar view, Lynn Waldeland states that the decade was "not only the age of the grandfatherly Eisenhower but that of the communist-hunting McCarthy, the age of Sputnik and brinkmanship, the Cold War and bomb shelters, James Dean and Elvis Presley, Charles Starkweather and other rebels without causes, and, over it all, the ominous sight of a mushroom-shaped cloud." Waldeland also specifies the insights of novelist Wright Morris and the favorable response to J. D. Salinger's defeatism as indicative of the discontent that would become evident to all in the 1960s. Anthony O. Edmonds sees the decade as "fraught with anxiety, discontent, and even rebellion against established norms" in at least three areas: popular music, the civil rights movement, and the

"beat" generation's culture and literature reveal "something quite different from the conformity and apathy generally ascribed to the period."[12]
How, then, can one reconcile anxiety, discontent, and rebellion with conformity and apathy or placidity? The answer lies in distinguishing between ideological conformity and behavioral conformity, between the majority and minorities, and between outer appearances and inner personal realities. Unsettling factors associated with the cold war resulted in a rallying around the American Way that was transmuted into considerable ideological conformity on the part of the majority. How this development related to behavioral conformity—*The Organization Man* and the "other directed" Americans[13]—scholars have by no means ascertained with any precision. It is also appropriate to note that the dissenters or nonconformists—admirers of Elvis Presley and James Dean and other heroes of the rebellious lifestyle, devotees of rock-and-roll music, civil rights activists, the "beats" and readers of beat literature, Salinger's stories, and Morris's novels—were minorities within minorities, youthful or black. Finally, ideological and behavioral conformity and the placidity associated with them may have concealed as much as they revealed. Joseph F. Trimmer sees them as products of internal psycho-emotional needs deriving from a threatening external world. The 1950s were marked by "the desire on the part of many Americans to find tranquility at any price. The trauma of world and national events produced a kind of 'future shock,' a desire to retreat from the world of crisis, conflict, and public commitment to a world of security, stability and noninvolvement." Americans engaged in this withdrawal, Trimmer asserts, not as individuals but as conformists: "Instead of arguing for creative tension between individual and community, the philosophy of the decade seemed to suggest the necessary acceptance of a bad world where adjustment to the system provided at least for the solace of security."[14]

Whether Trimmer is correct in his linkage of outer conformity to inner uncertainty remains for historians to determine, as does the relationship in the 1950s between Americans' psycho-emotional state and their political behavior. Of particular interest here is that the data cited above showing shrinking differentials between Catholics and Protestants and between middle and lower and upper and lower SES groups in partisan voting and in positions on policy issues indicate Eisenhower's numbing effect on the electorate.

Political scientists' depiction of the electorate having been considered, it seems opportune to delineate at least three major historical themes that, like the New Deal party system, transcended the years 1945–60 and provided a context for voter inertia in the 1950s: the bipartisan policy of containment, 1947–65; a widespread desire for retention without expansion of the New Deal, 1936–64; and consensus on the American Way, free enterprise and democracy, and its promotion through the New Economics or the Keynesian trade-off between unemployment and inflation, 1955–65.

There were some strains in the Grand Alliance during World War II, and this tension persisted after the Allied victory. By the winter of 1946, Washington accepted the containment view: the United States "should devote itself to preventing the expansion of Communism, awaiting the day when a new, less dogmatic, and more tractable generation had risen to power in Russia." The containment view became containment policy in Iran in December 1946 and in Greece and Turkey with the pronouncement of the Truman Doctrine three months later. Under Truman and Eisenhower the United States committed itself to defend—in addition to Europe and South Korea—Japan, Formosa, South Vietnam, most independent states in Southeast Asia, Middle Eastern states on the southern border of the Soviet Union, and, under the Eisenhower Doctrine, all Middle Eastern nations. The landing of American troops in Lebanon in July 1958 and American support of United Nations intervention in the Congo in July 1960 demonstrated that the American government was determined to prevent the spread of Communism in all parts of the world. There were limits—the United States accepted a compromise in Laos and refrained from dispatching troops against Castro in Cuba—but they were few, as was evident in the risking of nuclear war in the Cuban missile crisis, the stern warning to Peking when the Chinese crossed the Indian border in 1962, the sending of Marines to Santo Domingo in 1965, and the deployment, beginning in early 1965, of 500,000 troops to Vietnam.[15]

The New Left, or Open Door, interpretation attributes the globalization of containment to the needs of the American capitalist economy for overseas markets, raw materials, and investment opportunities. This thesis, however, does not explain the nation's involvement in Vietnam, one of the very largest overseas commitments of men and resources in American history. There were no resources in Vietnam that "could tempt an ITT or Exxon, in the pursuit of exploitative profit, to lean on Congress or propagandize the American public to start the war or to continue it," and Lyndon Johnson's economic advisers informed him at the time that the surge of 1965 in defense spending imperiled the steady progress then being made toward full employment with reasonable price stability. More persuasive is the view of Ernest R. May, who relates the universalism of American views and policies to "the spirit of uplift, the mood of the secular missionary, the *mission civilisatrice.*" In the first phase of containment, the United States opposed the Soviet Union's imperial expansion over adjacent nations, but a second stage soon developed "when it became the American aim to resist the spread of an alien ideology." This objective arose from "a vision, with deep historical roots, of a world in which all men would enjoy political, economic, and social institutions similar to those in the United States." The Russians, for their part, followed a parallel path marked by ever widening commitments combined with ideological zeal and the desire to remake the world in their own image.[16]

The theme of containment is illustrated by certain aspects of the Truman and Eisenhower presidencies. Truman's pronouncement of the Truman Doctrine in March 1947 ended two years of indecisiveness in which he struggled to get on top of his job while his approval rating in Gallup polls declined—to 32 percent in October 1946—and the Republicans captured control of both houses of Congress in November 1946. His proclamation also initiated the age of containment, as toughness became the hallmark of his cold war diplomacy. The Berlin blockade crisis resulted in a decision by Thomas E. Dewey, in July 1948, to refrain from criticizing Truman's foreign policy. Meanwhile, Truman benefited in the election from his careful handling of the blockade—"a tough policy that stopped short of war." The long-run consequence of Dewey's removal of foreign policy from the campaign, and of bipartisanship, Robert A. Divine laments, was the silencing for two decades of significant dissent on foreign policy.[17]

Divine means dissent that generated substantial popular support. Truman's foreign policy met with dissent from individuals on the right like Senator Robert A. Taft and on the left like Senator Glen H. Taylor, Senator Claude Pepper, and Henry A. Wallace; the latter's supporters accounted for 2.4 percent of the total popular vote in the presidential election of 1948. A recent study of public opinion concludes that the American people did not clamor for the tough policy Truman laid down in March 1947. On the other hand, another inquiry holds that Soviet behavior, anti-Soviet images in the press, and private organizations' anti-Communist campaigns by themselves generated anti-Communist attitudes among Americans, and that presidential rhetoric struck a responsive chord. Still another investigation, correlating public opinion polls with measurements of international tensions, shows that those who expected a major war within fifty years increased from 59 percent in early 1944 to 80 percent in early 1946, that those who expected a major war within twenty-five years increased from 29 percent in early 1944 to 68 percent in early 1946 (registering 59, 63, 66, and 64 percent in polls conducted through late 1946—*before* the Truman Doctrine address).[18] At any rate, the American people did not object to Truman's foreign-policy stance, and they approved of Eisenhower's pursuit of the containment policy without involving the nation in armed conflict.

Nor did politicians provide substantial dissent from the containment policy after Eisenhower became president. The Democrats, striving to establish their anti-Communist credentials, abdicated the scrutinizing parliamentary role of the loyal opposition, while Eisenhower, as Gary W. Reichard's roll-call analysis of the Eighty-third Congress (1953–54) shows, transformed his party in the field of foreign policy. The high degree of Republican support he enjoyed in this area represented a watershed within the GOP since many of his supporters had previously held nationalist or noncommital views.[19]

Stopping short of war, Eisenhower enjoyed wide room for maneuver, leaving "a Cuban invasion force and four hundred advisors in Vietnam for his successor to deploy . . . [while] the CIA's department of dirty tricks helped rearrange the governments of Iran, Guatemala, Egypt, and Laos." He also "encircled the Soviet Union and China with a network of air bases, sponsored geographical pacts designed to 'contain' communism, urged the 'liberation' of Eastern Europe, and endorsed the strategy of nuclear 'massive retaliation.' " But it should be noted, as Fred I. Greenstein has pointed out, that Secretary of State John Foster Dulles was assigned "the 'get tough' side of foreign policy enunciation, thus placating the fervently anti-Communist wing of the Republican Party. Meanwhile, amiable Ike made gestures toward peace and international humanitarianism—for example Atoms for Peace, Open Skies, and Summitry at Geneva." As John Lewis Gaddis observes, the Eisenhower-Dulles strategy, misleadingly labeled "massive retaliation," was much more subtle than a blunt threat to obliterate Moscow or Peking. Its main objective was deterrence, to be attained by rendering the enemy uncertain as to the United States response, which might be conventional, nuclear, economic, diplomatic, or none at all. As to the Atoms for Peace and Open Skies proposals, Thomas F. Soapes concludes that they were much more than gestures; they were aspects of a definite strategy of attaining, through small steps, gradual mitigation of the nuclear arms race and reduction of "tensions, fears, and suspicions that, in the minds of many, justified that arms race." This strategy was flawed but not a failure as the superpowers "began to move, however slowly, away from nuclear confrontation and toward negotiation."[20]

During the years 1950–52 one finds general agreement that opposition to Communism abroad and at home was the nation's first item of business, and that Truman, whose leadership was the Republicans' main target, was not effective in dealing with either Russians or subversives. The stage was set for McCarthyism, actually part of a broader loyalty hysteria that created an atmosphere fostering Republican success at the polls. In 1950 the GOP gained 28 seats in the House and 5 in the Senate. In 1952 Truman's approval rating plunged to 26 percent while the Republicans devised their campaign slogan of "Korea, Communism, and Corruption." This formula covered three of the four leading issues (the other was inflation) identified by respondents in a Roper poll of August 1952 as the most important for the next administration to deal with. Another August poll showed that a solid majority of voters believed the Republican party was more likely to be effective in dealing with the issues judged most important. None of the four leading issues Roper's respondents specified (or, for that matter, none of the six additional issues they mentioned) involved repudiation of containment or of the welfare state. A majority of the electorate wanted them placed under new management. As Key puts it, "All the questions the voter faced in 1952 were bundled up in the question whether he approved of . . . Mr. Truman."[21]

A second longer-run theme or development that antedated Truman's administration and postdated Eisenhower's was the majority's preference for retention without expansion of the New Deal. Within two years of Roosevelt's overwhelming triumph at the polls in 1936, William E. Leuchtenburg notes, the president sustained a series of defeats that precluded a new era of reform. After passage of the Fair Labor Standards Act (wages-and-hours law) in June 1938, there was a "politics of dead center . . . [in which] almost no innovative domestic legislation was adopted for the next quarter of a century"—until the enactment of Lyndon Johnson's Great Society legislation in 1964–65—with liberals lacking the leverage in Congress to overcome a bipartisan conservative coalition that had emerged in the fall of 1937. Thus the years 1945–60 fell within an era between agendas, which was satisfactory to the majority of voters. Middle-of-the-road government, Leuchtenburg states, was in harmony with the becalmed spirit of the fifties.[22]

The theme of retention without expansion of the New Deal does not exactly coincide chronologically with the era between agendas. In one of the earliest election polls ever taken, a Roper poll of October 1936 concerning attitudes toward Roosevelt's reelection, 33 percent of the respondents judged his reelection essential for the good of the country, and 26 percent felt "he may have made mistakes, but no one else can do as much good." The cross-tabulation of the answers to a second question by the answers respondents gave to the first question revealed that 5 percent of the 33 percent who considered Roosevelt's reelection essential also thought that he would become more radical in a second term, 8 percent thought he would become more liberal, 17 percent thought he would become more conservative, and 59 percent thought he would "remain as has been." The corresponding percentages for the 26 percent (first question) who judged Roosevelt the best man despite mistakes were almost identical. According to Elmo Roper, these polls show that "people in general did not expect him [FDR] to lead the nation very much farther to the left, nor did they want him to." In giving Roosevelt a second term, the people were "expressing preference for, if not precisely more of the same, as much as they had been getting, or possibly a little less." Key concurs: "By 1936 the innovative period of the New Deal had pretty well run its course, and in that year the voters responded with a resounding ratification of the new thrust of governmental policy."[23] Other observers of American politics see the theme of retention without expansion of the New Deal persisting beyond 1936.[24]

The theme of retention without expansion of the New Deal can be illustrated by reference to aspects of the Truman and Eisenhower presidencies. In the campaign of 1948, Truman adopted an effective negative tactic. Taft-Hartley, for example, was "probably more valuable to the President as a law, passed over his veto, than as a bill which had died in Congress or had been weakened through compromise." Truman flayed the Eightieth Congress, whose efforts to emasculate the New Deal he had restrained. "Under the circumstances," writes one of his harshest critics, "no president could have done more." Although the Republican threat to the New Deal in 1947–48 may have been for the most part rhetorical rather than actual, that Truman perceived it as ominous is apparent in his use of executive reorganization to protect certain New Deal measures from reactionary efforts at repeal. After his triumph over Dewey, Truman presented to the Congress a long list of proposals concerning domestic policy (the Fair Deal), but many of them were not accomplished. Truman's greatest achievement in domestic affairs may have been the preservation of the New Deal.[25]

As president, Eisenhower, in word and deed, was definitely not a Republican New Dealer. He wanted, as he later wrote, to make it clear that "we would not simply be a continuation of the New Deal and the Fair Deal, either in purpose or execution." This intention, however, was not readily apparent in Eisenhower's 1952 campaign as he played the artful dodger on domestic issues. Dean Albertson finds the crusade campaign vague about dissolving the New Deal welfare program, and a Roper poll of December 1952 registered this imprecision. The respondents were more uncertain about what Eisenhower would do with the New Deal than they were about his probable course of action with respect to seven of eight other matters. Therefore, it cannot be argued persuasively that Eisenhower was elected to dismantle the New Deal. The mandate for the Republicans in 1952 was essentially negative; the voters did not want Korea, Communism, and Corruption.[26]

Reichard shows that in each of three areas of domestic policy—fiscal and economic policy, welfare policy, and power and resources development policy—at least 80 percent of the Republicans in each house took the president's position at least 60 percent of the time. This substantial support was due to Republican legislators' loyalty to the administration, Eisenhower's leadership—personal diplomacy, meetings and liaison with Republican Congressmen, the use of patronage, selective campaigning, and compromise—and, above all, ideological agreement: Eisenhower's domestic programs diverged little from what most Republicans in Congress would approve of as public policy. Eisenhower's announced "Middle Way" and Arthur Larson's "New Republicanism" were less reality than rhetoric. That there was no transformation of the Republican party in domestic policy cannot be ascribed to Eisenhower's failure as a leader. He did not want to effect such a transformation. To be sure, Eisenhower's continuation of limited public housing, Social Security, and other such programs and his commitment to full use of federal strength if depression threatened "did in a general way represent the official entry of the Republican party into the New Deal 'political orbit.' " But Social Security and TVA, for example, were accepted as accomplished facts. Twentieth-century political and economic realities made inevitable acquiescence by conservatives to some aspects of the New Deal. That acquiescence was more submission than assent, as was made evident by Eisenhower's limited countercyclical response to the relatively severe recession of 1957–58 and by the relative decline in federal welfare-type expenditures, other than Social Security, as a percentage of national income: 5.3 percent in calendar 1952 and 4.3 percent in fiscal 1960. "Where the classical budgetary principles impinged on the welfare state, they were deliberately or inadvertently inimical to it."[27]

Just as Eisenhower was not elected to dismantle the New Deal, the Democrats' gains in the elections of 1954, when they won control of both houses, did not signify a resolute rejection of his program; and his personal status, if not enhanced, remained intact. True, his approval rating in the Gallup poll had fallen from 70 in August 1954 to 57 after the elections in November, but it rose to 69 in January 1955, 71 in March, and 79 in August before dropping slightly to 75 in December.[28]

A third relevant theme that was only partly contained within the period 1945–60 was the consensus characterizing the years 1955–64. The term *consensus* has been applied to both intellectuals and Americans in general in a considerable body of literature. In regard to intellectuals, whole volumes have been devoted to consensus historiography, sociology, and political thought. In a social and cultural history of the fifties, Douglas T. Miller and Marion Nowak devote a chapter to "Intellectuals: The Conservative Contraction." Intellectuals in government, business, and the universities were obsessed by the effort to comprehend, and account for, America's virtues. Since the main problems in American society had been solved by the New Deal, there was no need, intellectuals held, for ideology. Major innovations in society were unnecessary, and such minor changes as were called for could be effected through bargaining among politicians representing "competing yet not incompatible power groups or interest blocs (business, labor, farmers, military, and so forth)" with their elite leaderships. Scholars who criticized American society were usually apologetic, and most intellectuals shunned causes. The prevailing intellectual climate was "profoundly conservative. Proclaiming an end to ideology, intellectuals held dogmatically to an ideological pluralism, capitalism, anti-communism, and elitism."[29]

An important aspect of consensus had to do with economics and political economy. Describing "The Ideology of the Liberal Consensus" in *America in Our Time* (1976), Godfrey Hodgson writes of the period from the mid-fifties to the mid-sixties: "Whether you look at the writings of intellectuals or at the positions taken by practical politicians or at the data on public opinion, it is impossible not to be struck by the degree to which the majority of Americans in those years accepted the same system of assumptions." The assumptions on which consensus was built amounted to an intellectual system, which Hodgson boils down to these maxims:

1. The American free-enterprise system is democratic, creates abundance, and has a revolutionary potential for social justice.

2. Economic growth renders social conflict over resources between classes obsolete.

3. American society is in the process of abolishing social class.

4. Like industrial problems, social problems can be solved through programs designed by government enlightened by social science.

5. The main threat to this beneficent system comes from communism.

6. It is the duty and destiny of the United States to bring the good tidings of the free enterprise system to the rest of the world.

This broad consensus "fragmented," Hodgson believes, after 1965, and dissolved altogether by 1968.[30]

Underlying the liberal consensus was the confidence of the New Economics, culminating in the sixties in economists' assertions of their ability to "fine tune" the economy. This self-assurance can be viewed as marking the last phase of a theme going back to 1938. In the spring of that year, Roosevelt, after a protracted period of indecision, resumed deficit spending to combat the recession that had begun in the fall of 1937. This decision foreshadowed policy in the post–World War II era: except during the Korean War and the years 1971–73, when President Nixon adopted a four-phase wage-and-price-control plan, for forty years both Democratic and Republican administrations formulated economic policies within the framework of the Keynesian trade-off between unemployment and inflation. Only in the seventies did the effectiveness of the Keynesian formula come under serious scrutiny.[31]

As Eisenhower regretfully and permanently lost the opportunity to work with a Congress controlled by his own party, the nation entered the first part of the consensus era. Eric F. Goldman's phrase the "Eisenhower Equilibrium" denotes Americans' assumption that both Russia as a great power and the New Deal were here to stay. In international affairs the United States continued to follow the path suggested by the concepts of containment and coexistence. In economic affairs Eisenhower showed greater concern with inflation than unemployment, incurring three recessions (1953–54, 1957–58, and 1960–61) and an annual average rate of economic growth of just 2.9 percent. Real Gross National Product increased at an annual average rate of 4.7 percent from 1950 to 1955 and 2.25 percent from 1955 to 1959.[32]

Despite economic difficulties and the Democrats' retention of control of both the House and the Senate in 1956, Eisenhower's popularity remained high. Some historians nevertheless designate the years 1958–60 as a distinct, nonconsensual period, and others discern in the last three years of Eisenhower's presidency a feeling among Americans of drift, of lack of national purpose. Ronald Steel, for example, credits Eisenhower with rescuing the nation from deep, immobilizing division and restoring it to sanity, "but what was relaxation for four years turned into paralysis when stretched into eight." Historians often cite Kennedy's victory in

1960, after his campaign stressing the need to get America moving again, as confirmation of Americans' concern over national drift.[33]

The years 1958–60 may nonetheless be treated as part of the consensual period. Although some publicists lamented want of a sense of national purpose in 1960, most Americans seemed satisfied with the centrist politics of the past generation. Politicians had recognized this contentment in 1956. The Democratic presidential candidate, Adlai E. Stevenson, boasted of his party's conservatism and, with the exception of his mild opposition to continued bomb testing, the positions he took on most issues were similar to Eisenhower's. In 1960 both major parties chose presidential candidates who had been associated with the prudent politics of the 1950s.[34]

Meanwhile, although in 1956 Eisenhower had become the first president since Zachary Taylor to be elected without his party carrying at least one house of Congress, it is generally assumed that if there had been no Twenty-second Amendment and he had chosen to run, he would have won again. As it turned out, Kennedy's triumph by 0.2 percent of the vote, accompanied by a Republican gain of twenty-one seats in the House and the loss of only three in the Senate, was not a mandate to get America moving again. Nor did this outcome reflect an electorate equally divided between movers and nonmovers, for none of the studies of voter behavior in 1960 cites the quest for national purpose as a causal factor.[35] The consensus era had a few more years to run.

Eisenhower's effect on the electorate, as noted above, was that of a cooling agent, and it is widely held by historians, including those who liked Ike for one term but not for two, that in 1953 the nation needed a Prestone President. Thus Parmet affirms, "To label him a great or good or even a weak President misses the point. He was merely necessary." This fulfillment of Americans' need, William L. O'Neill states, was "no small thing." Under Eisenhower's "benign guidance the feverish witch-hunts and polemics of the McCarthy era gave way to something like business as usual . . . if the country cannot have progress, at least it deserves stability, as under Eisenhower. After 1965 there was precious little of either."[36]

The coincidence of Eisenhower's feat and the abiding dominance of the New Deal party system suggests several facts about the period 1945–60. The source of the persistence of the 1930s alignment was, through the election of 1948, ideological disagreement over the New Deal. The continuation after the ideologically climactic Truman-Dewey contest of widespread support for, or acceptance of, containment, the welfare state, and the New Economics, and the inertial perpetuation of Democratic prevalence in partisan identification and in voting below the presidential level together indicate that the considerable discontent and discord in American life and politics during Truman's second term and the decline of dissatisfaction and division in the Eisenhower era can be attributed to clashes not over ideology and policy but over governmental management or, more precisely, the identity of the managers, especially the president.

One can thus submit that the fate of a policy can depend, at least in part, on who proposes or sponsors it. Irwin Ross conjectures that Dewey would not have changed the direction of American foreign policy and might have secured passage of more liberal domestic legislation than Truman did because he could be more persuasive with Republicans in Congress. Ross states with certainty that the McCarthy crusade, which Truman's loyalty program failed to prevent, would not have developed if Dewey had been elected. In addition, it is a commonplace that the settlement Eisenhower obtained in Korea would have been unacceptable coming from Truman.[37]

One can only speculate as to whether and to what extent Dewey, if he had been so inclined, could have overcome the general lack of interest in expanding the New Deal. It is clear that Truman's proposals to enlarge the New Deal did not elicit majority approval, but Eisenhower's policy of retention without extension did. That being the case, it is tempting to conclude that Truman, in proposing the Fair Deal, defied the limitations imposed by the times and suffered politically, and Eisenhower, in shunning the Fair Deal, accepted these limitations and prospered politically. But such a judgment would fly in the face of data cited above. The very loss of salience of the New Deal issues that accounted for the absence of popular clamor for more welfare statism meant that Truman's recommendation of the Fair Deal generated indifference rather than hostility. It may have been that his offering the Fair Deal was more or less inevitable given his consistent espousal of the urban liberalism of the presidential Democratic party, as well as his perception of a real Republican threat to dismantle the New Deal. One can also argue that a byproduct of his efforts for post–New Deal programs was to put the New Deal out of the realm of political debate. But these exertions do not appear to be the reason for the decline of Truman's public standing.

Truman's identity entailed a legacy from Roosevelt, an inheritance embracing the politics of dead center and the accumulation of frustrations, aggravated by Truman's victory in 1948, that inevitably developed in the Republican party, especially its right wing, when the Democrats won five successive presidential elections, the last four over "me-too" candidates, and in Congress after years of strong executive leadership in depression and war. Further frustration arose among Americans with the Korean War. Above all, it was probably McCarthyism as "a movement of revenge" (to borrow Alonzo L. Hamby's phrase) with anti-Rooseveltian roots that created an atmosphere which prevented a rational response to Truman's proposals and policies. Consequently, the identity of the manager and all that it symbolized both hampered his performance and rendered it irrelevant to public assessments of his presidency. In other words, Truman found himself in a situation in which it would have been virtually impossible for him to win substantial public approval regardless of his traits and capabilities and no matter what he did or tried to do.[38]

Truman's disadvantage was Eisenhower's opportunity, but one cannot assume that any Republican president would inevitably have exploited this favorable circumstance the way Eisenhower did. His achievement, no small thing, was not the accomplishment of an innocent or inactive leader. Political scientists' inquiries and public-opinion polls suggest that too much can be made of the grandfatherly Eisenhower either as attractive candidate or presidential performer. Although his appeal transcended social boundaries, it did not lie in charisma but in the impression he conveyed to voters of integrity, sincerity, and competence. Eisenhower sustained this impression through his style of executive leadership, creating conditions conducive to placidity, especially seven-and-one-half years of peace. He "avoided the potential erosion of support," Greenstein writes, "that even a national icon would have experienced if his performance in office had seemed disastrous to the general public." Greenstein holds that Eisenhower's skills were underestimated because, as an aspect of his skills, he wanted them to be. "There can be little question," Arthur M. Schlesinger, Jr., stated in 1979, "that Eisenhower was a much abler man than his critics, this writer included, supposed in the 1950's." Without meaning to imply that consideration of the presidency is a shortcut to full understanding of a given period, and eschewing the ranking of presidents, one can gain through contemplation of the Truman and Eisenhower administrations some sense of Americans' yearning after 1948 for relief from disquiet.[39]

1. Walter Dean Burnham, "Party Systems and the Political Process," in William Nisbet Chambers and Burnham, eds., *The American Party Systems: Stages of Political Development* (New York, 1967), pp. 289–304; Philip Converse et al., "Stability and Change in

1960: A Reinstating Election," *American Political Science Review* 55 (1961): 274; Converse, "The Concept of a Normal Vote," in Angus Campbell et al., *Elections and the Political Order* (New York, 1966), pp. 9–39; Bernard Sternsher, "The Emergence of the New Deal Party System: A Problem in Historical Analysis of Voter Behavior," *Journal of Interdisciplinary History* 6 (1975): 143–44; Paul Kleppner, "From Ethnoreligious Conflict to 'Social Harmony': Coalitional and Party Transformation in the 1890's," in Seymour Martin Lipset, ed., *Emerging Coalitions in American Politics* (San Francisco, 1978), pp. 43–46; Jerome M. Clubb, "Party Coalitions in the Early Twentieth Century," in Lipset, ed., *Emerging Coalitions*, pp. 61–79; Everett Carll Ladd, Jr., with Charles D. Hadley, *Transformations of the American Party System: Political Coalitions from the New Deal to the 1970's*, 2d ed. (New York, 1978), pp. 31–128; Everett Carll Ladd, Jr., "The Shifting Party Coalitions, 1972–1976," in Lipset, ed., *Emerging Coalitions*, pp. 81–102.

2. Norman H. Nie, Sidney Verba, and John R. Petrocik, *The Changing American Voter* (Cambridge, Mass., 1976), p. 30, fig. 5.1, p. 83; Ladd and Hadley, *Transformations*, p. 125; fig. 2.7, p. 127.

3. Sternsher, "The Emergence of the New Deal Party System," pp. 128–30, 143–44.

4. Nie et al., *The Changing American Voter*, pp. 40, 213; Converse et al., "Stability," p. 280; Gerald Pomper, "Classification of Presidential Elections," *Journal of Politics* 29 (1967): 555; Walter Dean Burnham, *Critical Elections and the Mainsprings of American Politics* (New York, 1970), pp. 118–19, 126–27, 142–43. On elections typology see also Angus Campbell, "A Classification of Presidential Elections," in Campbell et al., *Elections and the Political Order*, pp. 63–77; V. O. Key, Jr.'s seminal "A Theory of Critical Elections," *Journal of Politics* 17 (1955): 3–18; and Nancy Zingale's formulation of four types of electoral change, "Third Party Alignments in a Two Party System: The Case of Minnesota," in Joel H. Silbey, Allan G. Bogue, and William H. Flanigan, eds., *The History of American Electoral Behavior* (Princeton, N.J., 1978), pp. 109–11.

5. Nie et al., *The Changing American Voter*, pp. 217–32.

6. Angus Campbell et al., *The American Voter* (New York, 1960), passim; Nie et al., *The Changing American Voter*, pp. 23, 98, 151, 159, 163, 165–73, 193, 281–82, 291; Ladd and Hadley, *Transformations*, pp. 383–84. James L. Sundquist, *Dynamics of the Party System: Alignment and Realignment of the Political Parties in the United States* (Washington, D.C., 1973), p. 297, distinguishes between an issue that cuts across both parties and a coincident issue or one that coincides with the existing lines of party cleavage, with most Democrats on one side of the issue and most Republicans on the other. Sundquist actually discusses two kinds of cross-cutting issues: (1) an issue on which both parties are internally divided (there are many pros and many antis in each party) and (2) an issue on which both parties are in agreement (there are mostly pros in both parties or mostly antis in both parties). In his analysis (ibid., pp. 277, 297), the New Deal was a cross-cutting issue of the first type before it became, with electoral realignment, a coincident issue. An example of the second type of cross-cutting issue is Communism in the 1950s, concerning which both parties were on the same side.

7. Nie et al., *The Changing American Voter*, pp. 46, 185, 187–89, 191–93.

8. Ibid., pp. 98–99, 104; Campbell et al., *The American Voter*, p. 551; V. O. Key, Jr., *The Responsible Electorate: Rationality in Presidential Voting, 1936–1960* (New York, 1968), p. 71.

9. Ladd and Hadley, *Transformations*, pp. 130–32, 135–36, 138–40, 144, 150, 280–81, fig. 3.2, p. 145; Paul T. David, *Party Strength in the United States, 1872–1970* (Charlottesville, Va., 1972), pp. 42, 45.

10. Ladd and Hadley, *Transformations*, pp. 91, 94–100, 105–10.

11. Ibid., pp. 74, 111–20, fig. 1.2, p. 73; Nie et al., *The Changing American Voter*, pp. 97, 151. The figures on low-high SES differentials are compatible with the conclusions concerning the relationship between class and party as agents of cleavage and consensus in the polity in Heinz Eulau, *Class and Party in the Eisenhower Years: Class Roles and*

Perspectives in the 1952 and 1956 Elections (New York, 1962), pp. 140–44. Angus Campbell, Gerald Gurin, and Warren E. Miller, *The Voter Decides* (Westport, Conn., 1954), analyze cleavage and consensus within individual voters in 1952 with respect to congruence or incongruence of orientations toward parties, issues, and candidates.

12. The phrase is from Joseph Satin, ed., *The 1950's: America's "Placid" Decade* (Boston, 1960); Herbert S. Parmet, *Eisenhower and the American Crusades* (New York, 1972), p. 577; Lynne Waldeland, "The Deep Sleep: The Fifties in the Novels of Wright Morris," in *Silhouettes on the Shade: Images from the 50s Reexamined* (Muncie, Ind., 1973), pp. 29–43; Anthony O. Edmonds, "America in the 1950s: The Roots of Our Discontent," in *Silhouettes*, p. 4.

13. See William H. Whyte, *The Organization Man* (New York, 1956); David Riesman, *The Lonely Crowd: A Study of the Changing American Character* (New Haven, Conn., 1950).

14. Joseph F. Trimmer, "The Byron of Fairmont: James Dean as Cult Hero," in *Silhouettes*, pp. 47–48.

15. Ernest R. May, "The Cold War," in C. Vann Woodward, ed., *The Comparative Approach to American History* (New York, 1968), pp. 333–39. On the globalization of containment, see Ronald Steel, *Pax Americana* (New York, 1967); Richard J. Barnet, *Intervention and Revolution* (New York, 1968); and Stephen Ambrose, *Rise to Globalism: American Foreign Policy since 1938* (Baltimore, 1971).

16. Paul A. Samuelson, "Economic Postmortem," *Newsweek*, 5 February 1973, p. 78; May, "The Cold War," pp. 339–44. The prophet of the Open Door view is William Appleman Williams; see his *The Tragedy of American Diplomacy* (Cleveland, 1959). See also Harry Magdoff, *The Age of Imperialism* (New York, 1969). Like May, John Lewis Gaddis, "Strategies of Containment," *Newsletter, Society for Historians of American Foreign Relations*, 11 (June 1980): 5, describes a shift in policy that reflected "a difference in the perception of threat. Where [George F.] Kennan [who is identified with the containment policy in its first phase, 1947–49] had seen it strictly in terms of the Soviet Union, NSC-68 [National Security Council document 68, 7 April 1950] shifted the focus of concern to the international communist movement as a whole." On the American sense of mission in studies of the cold war, see Arthur A. Ekirch, Jr., *Ideas, Ideals, and American Diplomacy* (New York, 1966); and Ernest Lefever, *Ethics and United States Foreign Policy* (New York, 1957). Ambrose, *Rise to Globalism*, stresses both economic aggressiveness and anti-Communism, as well as racism, as basic sources of American foreign policy.

17. Daniel Yergin, "Harry Truman—Revived and Revised," *New York Times Magazine*, 24 October 1976, pp. 83–84; William E. Leuchtenburg, "The Pattern of Modern American National Politics," in Stephen E. Ambrose, ed., *Institutions in Modern America: Innovation in Structure and Process* (Baltimore, 1967), pp. 57–58; Thomas G. Paterson, *On Every Front: The Making of the Cold War* (New York, 1979), chap. 5, "Toughness: The Tactics of Truman's Diplomacy," pp. 92–112; Robert A. Divine, "The Cold War and the Election of 1948," *Journal of American History* 59 (1972): 106–7, 109–10.

18. George H. Quester, "Origins of the Cold War: Some Clues from Public Opinion," *Political Science Quarterly* 93 (1978–79): 656–60; Dale Sorenson, "The Language of a Cold Warrior: A Content Analysis of Harry Truman's Public Statements," *Social Science History* 3 (1979): 171–86; John E. Mueller, "Public Expectations of War during the Cold War," *American Journal of Political Science* 23 (1979): fig. 1, p. 304. On dissenters see Thomas G. Paterson, ed., *Cold War Critics: Alternatives to American Foreign Policy in the Truman Years* (New York, 1971); Ronald Radosh, *Prophets on the Right: Profiles on Conservative Critics of American Globalism* (New York, 1975); and Justus D. Doenecke, *Not to the Swift: The Old Isolationists in the Cold War Era* (Lewisburg, Pa., 1979), which deals with the period 1943–54. Among the few scholarly publications in the 1950s concerned with the assumption of obligations beyond the nation's capacity to respond were Edwin O. Reischauer, *Wanted: An Asian Policy* (New York, 1955); and Norman A.

Graebner, *The New Isolationism* (New York, 1956). In the late 1960s and 1970s, a number of studies stressed American overcommitment: see, for example, Adam B. Ulam, *The Rivals: America and Russia since World War II* (New York, 1971).

19. Gary W. Reichard, *The Reaffirmation of Republicanism: Eisenhower and the Eighty-Third Congress* (Knoxville, Tenn., 1975), pp. 87–88, 95.

20. Stephen J. Whitfield, "The 1950's: The Era of No Hard Feelings," *South Atlantic Quarterly* 74 (1975): 296; Stanley Karnow, "I'm like Ike," *New Republic*, 28 October 1972, p. 17; Fred I. Greenstein, "Eisenhower as an Activist President: A Look at New Evidence," *Political Science Quarterly* 94 (1979): 582; Gaddis, "Strategies of Containment," p. 6; Thomas F. Soapes, "A Cold Warrior Seeks Peace: Eisenhower's Strategy for Nuclear Disarmament," *Diplomatic History* 4 (1980): 69–71.

21. Daniel Yergin, "Harry Truman," p. 40; Elmo Roper, *You and Your Leaders: Their Actions and Your Reactions, 1936–1956* (New York, 1957), pp. 249–54; Dean Albertson, ed., *Eisenhower as President* (New York, 1963), p. xvii; Key, *The Responsible Electorate*, p. 74.

22. Leuchtenburg, "The Pattern," pp. 55–56; 62; Robert Booth Fowler, *Believing Skeptics: American Political Intellectuals, 1945–1964* (Westport, Conn., 1978), p. 50. Studies of the conservative coalition are cited in Bernard Sternsher, *Consensus, Conflict, and American Historians* (Bloomington, Ind., 1975), p. 396 n. James T. Patterson, "American Politics: The Bursts of Reform, 1930s to 1970s," in Patternson, ed., *Paths to the Present: Interpretive Essays on American History since 1930 (Minneapolis, 1975), pp. 57*–101, and Otis L. Graham, Jr., ed., *The New Deal: The Critical Issues* (Boston, 1971), pp. 174–78, discuss obstacles that have limited the number and extent of spurts of reform legislation.

23. Roper, *You and Your Leaders*, pp. 28–29; Key, *The Responsible Electorate*, p. 33.

24. See John M. Allswang, *The New Deal and American Politics: A Study in Political Change* (New York, 1978), p. 127; John W. Jeffries, *Testing the Roosevelt Coalition: Connecticut Society and Politics in the Era of World War II* (Knoxville, Tenn., 1979), pp. 144, 243; Key, *The Responsible Electorate*, pp. 77–78. Irwin Ross, *The Loneliest Campaign: The Truman Victory of 1948* (New York, 1968), p. 243, states that Truman enjoyed considerable popularity among farmers in the Midwest because of fears that the Republicans would put an end to the New Deal agricultural program.

25. Robert Griffith, "Truman and the Historians: The Reconstruction of Post-war American History," *Wisconsin Magazine of History* 59 (1975): 36; Harvard Sitkoff, "Years of the Locust: Interpretations of Truman's Presidency since 1965," in Richard S. Kirkendall, ed., *The Truman Period as a Research Field: A Reappraisal, 1974* (Columbia, Mo., 1975), pp. 90–91; Athan Theoharis, "The Truman Presidency: Trial and Error," *Wisconsin Magazine of History* 55 (1971): 53; Susan M. Hartmann, *Truman and the 80th Congress* (Columbia, Mo., 1971), pp. 213–14; William E. Pemberton, *Bureaucratic Politics: Executive Reorganization during the Truman Administration* (Columbia, Mo., 1979), passim; Yergin, "Harry Truman," p. 91.

26. Reichard, *The Reaffirmation of Republicanism*, pp. 6, 10, 233; Albertson, ed., *Eisenhower as President*, p. xiii. Roper, *You and Your Leaders*, pp. 259–61.

27. Reichard, *The Reaffirmation of Republicanism*, pp. 146, 175–76, 193, 196, 218–27, 229, 234–35, 237; Harold G. Vatter, *The U.S. Economy in the 1950's: An Economic History* (New York, 1963), pp. 138, 142–43. Roper, *You and Your Leaders*, p. 247, presents a poll of August 1952 in which 87 percent of the respondents judged Social Security and 68 percent designated TVA a "Good Thing." Eisenhower's traditional Republicanism is evident in Edward L. Dale, Jr., *Conservatives in Power: A Study in Frustration* (Garden City, N.Y., 1960), by an economic journalist.

28. Reichard, *The Reaffirmation of Republicanism*, p. 216; Roper, *You and Your Leaders*, pp. 267, 270.

29. Sternsher, *Consensus, Conflict, and American Historians*; Job L. Dittberner, *The*

End of Ideology and American Social Thought, 1930–1960 (Ann Arbor, Mich., 1979); Fowler, *Believing Skeptics*; Douglas T. Miller and Marion Nowak, *The Fifties: The Way We Really Were* (Garden City, N.Y., 1977), pp. 221, 224–25, 236–37, 241. On consensus regarding the "broker state," see Otis L. Graham, Jr., *Toward a Planned Society: From Roosevelt to Nixon* (New York, 1976), pp. 96–97. Jeffrey Hart, "The 1950's," *National Review* 32 (1980): 290, 292–94, denies that there was stagnation in literature, literary criticism, poetry, art, and theology but discerns stifling manners and morals, especially sexual attitudes. Miller and Nowak, *The Fifties*, pp. 375–92, find novels of the decade outside the "main culture" in emphasizing alienation and abdication and describe "mock-Victorian" attitudes toward the sexes (ibid., pp. 146–81). Charles C. Alexander, *Holding the Line: The Eisenhower Era* (Bloomington, Ind., 1975), pp. 101–58, is excellent on social and cultural history. Granville Hicks, "Liberalism in the Fifties," *American Scholar* 25 (Summer 1956): 283–96, in defending liberal intellectuals who have become responsible and moderate, offers a paean to the virtues of American society that conveys an impression of a certain complacency about its defects. Bernard Sternsher, "Liberalism in the Fifties: The Travail of Redefinition," *Antioch Review* 22 (1962): 315–31, discusses the attempt of some liberals to move beyond the New Deal by shifting from "quantitative" to "qualitative" liberalism. See also Martin K. Doudna, *Concerned about the Planet: The Reporter Magazine and American Liberalism, 1949–1968* (Westport, Conn., 1977). Alonzo L. Hamby, *American Liberalism: From the New Deal to the New Politics* (St. Louis, 1975), and Alfred Eckes, *American Conservatism: From Hoover to Nixon* (St. Louis, 1973), taken together, reveal greater differences in rhetoric than in policy.

30. Whitfield, "The 1950's," p. 339; Godfrey Hodgson, *America in Our Time* (New York, 1978), pp. 68, 76, 272–73, 353, 466.

31. Thomas Balogh, "Is Keynes Dead?," *New Republic*, 7 June 1980, pp. 15–16, states that the postwar period of Keynesian predominance was an unmatched triumph but ended, in 1971, in failure that "resulted either in the fight against rising prices causing unemployment beyond what was politically acceptable, or in measures to mitigate unemployment bringing intolerable price explosions." See also John A. Garraty, *Unemployment in History: Economic Thought and Public Policy* (New York, 1978), chap. 12, "The End of the Golden Age," pp. 233–50.

32. Eric F. Goldman, *The Crucial Decade—and After: America, 1945–1960* (New York, 1961), p. 292; Vatter, *The U.S. Economy*, pp. 7–8. Paul A. Samuelson, who advocates using a variety of counter-cyclical measures, thinks Eisenhower's policies "were not without their toll": "Britain: Don't Expect a Miracle," *Newsweek*, 28 May 1979, p. 76. Milton Friedman, who insists on maintaining a fixed rate of growth of the money supply while eschewing manipulation of public spending, taxes, and interest rates, feels the nation was fortunate to have for eight years a president who defied the prevailing spirit of the time to curb the creeping inflation of the early 1950s even at the cost of recessions and Nixon's defeat in 1960. This was lucky, in Friedman's view, because inflationary antirecession measures lead only to greater recessions later on: "To Jimmy [Carter] from James [Callaghan]," *Newsweek*, 6 December 1976, p. 87. On Eisenhower's economic policies see also John A. Garraty, *Unemployment in History*, pp. 239, 241; and Saul Engelbourg, "The Council of Economic Advisers and the Recession of 1953–1954," *Business History Review* 54 (1980): 192–214.

33. Peter D'Arcy Jones, *The USA: A History of Its People and Society since 1865*, 2 vols. (Homewood, Ill, 1976), 2:712–17; Miller and Nowak, *The Fifties*, pp. 15–18; Ronald Steel, "Mr. Clean," in Steel, *Imperialists and Other Heroes: A Chronicle of the American Empire* (New York, 1971), p. 331. Goldman, *The Crucial Decade*, pp. 343–44, cites some favorable comments on Eisenhower's first term and some harsh judgments on his second. Richard H. Rovere, "Eisenhower Revisited—A Political Genius? A Brilliant Man?", *New York Times Magazine*, 7 February 1971, p. 14 ff., considers the second term "anticlimax almost all the way." See also Jim F. Heath, *Decade of Dissillusionment: The Kennedy-Johnson Years* (Bloomington, Ind., 1975), p. 11; and John W. Jeffries, "The 'Quest for National Purpose' of 1960," *American Quarterly* 30 (Fall 1978): 469–70.

34. Goldman, *The Crucial Decade*, pp. 305, 342; Leuchtenberg, "The Pattern," p. 63; Miller and Nowak, *The Fifties*, p. 223; William L. O'Neill, *Coming Apart: An Informal History of America in the 1960's* (New York, 1971), p. 13.

35. Key, *The Responsible Electorate*, table 5.15, p. 140, indicates that voters who supported Eisenhower in 1956 but intended to vote for Kennedy in 1960 approved of Eisenhower's performance as president by two to one. Converse et al., "Stability," pp. 269–80, and Key, *The Responsible Electorate*, pp. 107–48.

36. Walter Johnson, *1600 Pennsylvania Avenue: Presidents and the People, 1929–1959* (Boston, 1960), p. 317; Parmet, *Eisenhower*, p. 578; O'Neill, *Coming Apart*, p. 7. Alexander, *Holding the Line*, pp. 292–93, expresses a judgment similar to O'Neill's.

37. Ross, *The Loneliest Campaign*, pp. 250–51; Alexander, *Holding the Line*, p. 47.

38. James V. Compton, *Anti-Communism in American Life since the Second World War* (St. Louis, 1973), p. 3; Alonzo L. Hamby, "The Clash of Perspectives and the Need for New Syntheses," in Kirkendall, ed., *The Truman Period as a Research Field*, p. 135. Robert J. Williams, "Harry S. Truman and the American Presidency," *Journal of American Studies* 13 (1979): 406, maintains that limitations on liberal reform are neglected by liberals whose criticism of Truman proceeds from "an exaggerated notion of presidential power [and] ignores Roosevelt's own legislative deadlock" and by radical critics who adduce "no evidence . . . to suggest that a more far-reaching program could have had any prospect of legislative success." I am indebted to Alonzo Hamby for his criticism of my treatment of Truman in an earlier version of this paper.

39. Philip E. Converse and Georges Dupeux, "DeGaulle and Eisenhower: The Public Image of the Victorious General," in Campbell et al., *Elections and the Political Order*, p. 344; James C. Davies, "Charisma in the 1952 Campaign," *American Political Science Review* 58 (1954): 1083–1102; Roper, *You and Your Leaders*, p. 273; Greenstein, "Eisenhower as Activist," pp. 576–77, 579, 584, 586–87, 590, 592, 594–95, 597–98; Arthur M. Schlesinger, Jr., "The Eisenhower Presidency: A Reassessment," *Look*, 14 May 1979, p. 42.

Notes on the Contributors

JOHN BARNARD, professor of history at Oakland University is the author of *From Evangelicalism to Progressivism at Oberlin College, 1866–1917* and a coeditor of *Children and Youth in America: A Documentary History.*

ROBERT H. BREMNER is professor emeritus of history at Ohio State University and author of *The Public Good: Philanthropy and Welfare in the Civil War Era* and a coeditor of *Children and Youth in America: A Documentary History.*

WILLIAM H. CHAFE, professor of history at Duke University, has written *The American Woman: Her Changing Social, Economic, and Political Role, 1920–1970* and *Civilities and Civil Rights: Greensboro, North Carolina, and the Black Struggle for Freedom.*

MARK I. GELFAND is associate professor of history at Boston College and author of *A Nation of Cities: The Federal Government and Urban America, 1933–1965.*

ARTHUR M. JOHNSON, who holds the Bird Professorship in History at the University of Maine at Orono, is the author of *Petroleum Pipelines and Public Policy, 1906–1959* and *Winthrop W. Aldrich: Lawyer, Banker, Diplomat.* He has recently completed a history of the Sun Oil Company in the post–World War II period.

KENNETH M. JONES is assistant professor of history at Saint John's University, Collegeville, Minnesota.

RONALD G. LORA, professor of history at the University of Toledo, is author of *Conservative Minds in America* and editor of *America in the Sixties.*

ROLAND MARCHAND, who is associate professor of history at the University of California, Davis, has written *The American Peace Movement and Social Reform, 1898–1918.*

JAMES T. PATTERSON, teaches history at Brown University and is the author of *Congressional Conservatism and the New Deal: The Growth of the Conservative Coalition in Congress, 1933–1939* and *Mr. Republican: A Biography of Robert A. Taft.* He has recently completed a study of poverty and welfare in twentieth-century America.

GARY W. REICHARD, associate professor of history at Ohio State University, has written *The Reaffirmation of Republicanism: Eisenhower and the Eighty-third Congress* and is coauthor of *America: Changing Times.*

LEILA J. RUPP, who teaches history at Ohio State University, has written *Mobilizing Women for War: German and American Propaganda, 1939–1945* and is coeditor of *Nazi Ideology Before 1933: A Documentation.* She is currently working on a study of American feminism since World War II.

BERNARD STERNSHER is University Professor of History at Bowling Green State University and is the author of *Rexford Tugwell and the New Deal* and *Consensus, Conflict, and American Historians.*

EUGENE J. WATTS, associate professor of history at Ohio State University, is author of *The Social Bases of City Politics, Atlanta, 1865–1903,* and is currently working on a study of the Saint Louis police force.

THOMAS E. WILLIAMS is assistant professor of history at Emory University.

Index

Abrams, Charles, 268
Academic freedom, 227–32
Acheson, Dean, 349, 350
Ackley, Fannie, 51–52
Administrative Procedure Act (1946), 346
Adolescence, 176–81
Advance Research Projects Agency (ARPA), 332
Advertising, 35, 39, 164, 165, 167, 172, 175, 177
Agriculture and agricultural policy, 152–56; and parity, 155; and price supports, 155–56
Aid to Dependent Children (ADC) and Aid to Families of Dependent Children (AFDC), 22–25, 198–201, 210, 213
Aid to the Blind, 25–26
Aldrich, C. Andrews, and Mary M.: *Babies Are Human Beings: An Interpretation of Growth* (1938), 12
Allender, Nina, 53, 54
Allport, Gordon, 307
Aluminum industry, 102
Alva Belmont House, 54
American Academy of Pediatrics, 18–19
American Association of University Women, 44, 50, 57
American Council on Education, 236–37, 238
American Farm Bureau Federation, 153–54

American Federation of Labor (AFL), 120, 125, 134, 137, 138
American Federation of Labor-Congress of Industrial Organizations (AFL-CIO), 50, 105, 134, 138, 139, 302
American Federation of State, County, and Municipal Employees (AFSCME), 288–89
American Journal of Public Health, 18
American Voter, The (1960), 371, 372
Anslinger, Harry, 299
Antifeminist backlash, 39, 40, 42–43, 48, 49, 57
Area resolutions, 357–61, 363. *See also* Formosa Resolution, Middle East Resolution
Atomic energy, 103; atomic bomb, 316; Manhattan Project, 317, 318, 320, 321, 334; hydrogen bomb, 320–23; Atoms-for-peace, 323; test-ban, 335. *See also* Atomic Energy Act
Atomic Energy Act (1946), 317; amendments to (1958), 347
Atomic Energy Commission (AEC), 318, 319, 320–23, 326, 328, 333, 334, 336, 337
Automobiles, 106–7, 273–74, 275

Baker, Ella, 68, 69, 94, 96
Bakke, E. Wight, 207
Barkley, Alben, 345
Barney, Nora Stanton, 48–49